A HISTORY OF PERSIA

A HISTORY OF PERSIA

Percy Sykes

VOLUME ONE

with a new introduction by
Antony Wynn

LONDON AND NEW YORK

First published 1915 by Macmillan & Co. Ltd.

This edition reprints the 1969 third edition published by
Routledge

This edition published 2004
by Routledge
2 Park Square, Milton Park, Abingdon, Oxon, OX14 4RN

Simultaneously published in the USA and Canada
by Routledge
711 Third Avenue, New York, NY 10017

Routledge is an imprint of the Taylor & Francis Group

First issued in paperback 2011

Copyright © 1915 by Sir Percy Sykes
Introduction copyright © 2004 by Antony Wynn

Typeset in Times by Keystroke, Jacaranda Lodge, Wolverhampton

All rights reserved. No part of this book may be reprinted or reproduced or utilised in any form or by any electronic, mechanical, or other means, now known or hereafter invented, including photocopying and recording, or in any information storage or retrieval system, without permission in writing from the publishers.

British Library Cataloguing in Publication Data
A catalogue record for this book is available from the British Library

Library of Congress Cataloging in Publication Data
A catalog record for this book has been requested.

ISBN 0-415-32678-8 (Set)
ISBN10: 0-415-32679-6 (hbk)
ISBN10: 0-415-67998-2 (pbk)

ISBN13: 978-0-415-32679-7 (hbk)
ISBN13: 978-0-415-67998-5 (pbk)

Publisher's Note
The Publisher has gone to great lengths to ensure the quality of this reprint but points out that some imperfections in the original book may be apparent

INTRODUCTION

SIR PERCY SYKES AND THE HISTORY OF PERSIA

Antony Wynn

Born in 1867, Sir Percy Sykes had a conventional start to life. His family were industrialist bleachers who had settled into prosperous squiredom in Cheshire and his father was an army chaplain who had served in the Crimea and was later a chaplain to Queen Victoria. It was natural that, after school at Rugby, Sykes should go to Sandhurst to train as an army officer and then join a cavalry regiment serving in India. That was the end of the conventional part of his career, for in India he spent his leaves exploring the Himalayas and was soon seconded to Army Intelligence, who in 1893 sent him to Persia.

At that time the British were concerned that Russia might attempt an invasion of India. The shortest route ran through Afghanistan, but arrangements had been made with the Afghan government to ensure that the Russians would meet with effective resistance. Persia, with its weak, corrupt and bankrupt government, was in no position to offer such resistance and offered a soft route for invasion, were the Russians to embark on such a course. Little was known about the region that bordered India and Sykes was sent to explore it.

After Sykes had undertaken a number of expeditions in the provinces of Kerman and Baluchistan, it was decided in 1894 to establish a permanent British presence in a new consulate at Kerman, from which he could establish a network of informants covering the eastern frontier of Persia. With a short break for the Boer War, Sykes was based there until 1905. He explored and surveyed every corner of his territory – much of it in very rough country – but, more importantly, he established good relations with all the leading local figures. Having arrived with the

INTRODUCTION

mindset of an archetypal imperialist, he soon fell under the spell of Persian good manners and absorbed himself in Persian culture, religion and history.

Kerman is still the most relaxed and easy-going of all the Persian cities. Here Sykes met the Ne'matullahi Sufis and the Sheikhis, the most liberal and enlightened of the Persian Muslims, whose refreshing company he enjoyed. He learned Persian and even studied the Quran. He was fascinated by the local people and their affairs and became almost a gossip. He was also an avid reader of the Classics and, in his journeys of exploration, he traced the routes taken by Alexander the Great and Marco Polo, collecting archaeological items and recording inscriptions on the monuments that he found as he went. He wrote down everything that he found and made very detailed maps of the country, recording where water and fodder could be found for passing military forces, be they British or Russian. For all of this in 1902 the Royal Geographical Society awarded him their Gold Medal.

At this time, Persia was caught between Russia to the north and British India to the south-east, while the Royal Navy controlled the Persian Gulf. Persia was powerless and her only strength lay in being able to play each power against the other in an auction of personal favours by the Shah and his ministers. It has long been fashionable to belittle Curzon's exaggeration of the Russian threat of southward expansion, but it is often forgotten that in Sykes's time Russia had made the north of Persia a Russian colony in all but name. Russian consuls were established in all the towns of any size in the north and they even collected taxes for the Russian government. The local Persian governors were mere puppets and could do nothing about it. Russia was regarded as malevolently omnipotent until 1905, when the Japanese destroyed the Russian fleet at the battle of Tsushima. This showed the Persians that the Russians were no longer invincible and inspired the modernisers in their efforts to form a constitution and institute reforms.

It was against this background that Sykes took up his new post as consul-general at Mashhad. Having spent his years in the southern wildernesses, he was now in an important metropolis, a great city of pilgrimage, where the immensely wealthy shrine of the Imam Reza owned much of the local wealth and where the clerics were far more powerful than the government officials. By now he was thoroughly imbued with Persian culture and had acquired an extensive and detailed knowledge of the most important personages of the land. He was, untypically of his compatriots at the Legation in Tehran, sympathetic to the Persians and he treated all of them, of whatever background, with an unfailing respect, which they duly reciprocated.

INTRODUCTION

The Persians looked to the British to support them against Russia and Sykes's personal prestige rode high on this wave of patriotic feeling for two years until 1907, when the British and the Russians divided Persia into two zones of influence, where each power undertook not to interfere with the interests of the other. The Persian Constitutionalists regarded this as an act of betrayal by the British, and were not satisfied by statements that Persia's independence would be assured. The Russian consul-general at Mashhad, flying in the face of the treaty with England, did all he could to cause disturbances that would justify his bringing in large numbers of troops from Ashgabad into Khorasan. Sykes's success in calming the various opposing factions in the face of Russian agitation was instrumental in frustrating Russian designs.

After his tour of duty at Mashhad Sykes was sent to relieve George Macartney, the British consulate-general at Kashgar. While he was there he set about writing this History. The style is ponderous and Victorian, not at all the sort of history that is considered useful today. It is almost a pastiche of a list of 'kings and queens', but at the time there was nothing else on the subject, in English or in Persian, other than Sir John Malcolm's history, written one hundred years earlier. However, considering the circumstances in which it was written, far from any libraries or academics that he could consult, and bearing in mind that Sykes was not a university man, this work of a Victorian soldier-scholar must still be seen as a classic.

The later editions come to life in their final chapters, for in them Sykes tells the story of his own involvement with Persia. His many critics found his account of the South Persian Rifles to be not only self-centred, but also self-serving. It gives the impression that Sykes ran the whole show on his own and it gives little credit to Consul Gough or to his own long-suffering subordinate officers. Moberly's Official History, written much later, is a more balanced account.

It is now fashionable to scorn histories such as this one, but it is worth bearing in mind that its appearance was welcomed in Persia itself and it was translated into Persian. Every country needs a chronicle, and this is what this book is. Sykes gave copies of the History as wedding presents to his offspring, children and grandchildren. Not all of them were grateful, but we should acknowledge the effort that he made to make Persia better understood.

Plate 1: Brigadier-General Sir Percy Sykes, KCIE, CB, CMG
(*Photograph courtesy of Mr Mark Sinclair, grandson of Sir Percy Sykes*)

Abdul Hussein Mirza Farman Farma

> We scrutinize the dates
> Of long-past human things,
> The bounds of effaced states,
> The lines of deceased kings;
> We search out dead men's words, and works of dead men's hands.
>
> MATTHEW ARNOLD'S *Empedocles on Etna*.

BAS-RELIEF OF CYRUS THE GREAT.

(From Perrot and Chipiez's *History of Art in Ancient Egypt*. Chapman & Hall, Ltd.)

A
HISTORY OF PERSIA

BY

BRIGADIER-GENERAL SIR PERCY SYKES
K.C.I.E., C.B., C.M.G.

GOLD MEDALLIST OF THE ROYAL GEOGRAPHICAL SOCIETY
JOINT-AUTHOR OF 'THROUGH DESERTS AND OASES OF CENTRAL ASIA'
AND 'THE GLORY OF THE SHIA WORLD'

ACHAEMENIAN GOLD PATERA.
(From British Museum.)

WITH MAPS AND ILLUSTRATIONS

IN TWO VOLUMES—VOL. I

THIRD EDITION
WITH SUPPLEMENTARY ESSAYS

LONDON
ROUTLEDGE

Dedication

THIS EDITION IS DEDICATED TO THE BRITISH AND INDIAN OFFICERS, NON-COMMISSIONED OFFICERS AND MEN WHO SERVED WITH ME IN SOUTH PERSIA DURING THE GREAT WAR. THROUGH THEIR VALOUR, RESOURCEFULNESS, AND CHEERFUL ENDURANCE A GRAVE PERIL WAS AVERTED AND A DIFFICULT TASK WAS SUCCESSFULLY ACCOMPLISHED.

FROM A COPPER LANTERN.

PREFACE TO THE THIRD EDITION

DURING the last decade Persia has changed, perhaps more than in any period of her eventful history. Mainly owing to the personality of Shah Riza, the founder of the Pahlavi dynasty, a strong national spirit has been awakened, the authority of the Government has been successfully asserted throughout the length and breadth of the land, the finances have been placed on a sounder footing, a gold standard has been adopted, and communications by air, by railway and by motor car are changing the outlook of this conservative nation and are making for progress. Nor have the changes in foreign policy been less momentous. Persia has shaken herself free from the hated Capitulations, just a century after they were imposed on her by Russia, and she now makes treaties with European powers on equal terms.

These and many other questions are dealt with in the present edition. By taking advantage of a new process it has proved possible to reproduce the last edition at a considerably lower price after necessary corrections had been made in the text, while the number of maps and illustrations has been curtailed. New material, which includes the great discoveries at Ur, and the successful quest of Aornos, has been embodied in Preliminary Essays, while the second volume concludes with a Final Essay. The most important works that have been consulted are referred to in the essays, and where necessary, references to the new material have been made in the text.

My thanks are due to the Secretary of State for War, who has granted me access to documents in the Historical Section of the War Office bearing on the campaigns in Persia. Mr. Leonard Woolley has, very kindly, checked the brief account I have given of his excavations, while Sir Percy Cox and Mr. E. M. Eldrid have helped me with valuable suggestions in the Final Essay. To conclude, I hope that the third edition of this work may be of some service to the people of Persia, among whom I spent the happiest years of my life, while if it helps Europeans and Americans to realize the profound influence of Persia on our art and civilization down the ages, I shall be richly rewarded.

P. M. S.

FROM AN ENAMELLED BOX.

PREFACE TO THE SECOND EDITION

DURING the six years that have elapsed since the first edition of this work was published, much has happened in Persia. Her historical soil has re-echoed, time and again, to the tramp of British, Russian, and Turkish troops, and, to some extent, she has suffered the lot of an invaded country. On the other hand, the Russians saved the capital and perhaps the very existence of Persia by defeating the Turks; and the overthrow of the Kashgais and other raiding tribes in the South restored some measure of security in that part of the country. Moreover, the belligerents greatly improved the communications, and the large sums of money spent by Great Britain and, in a lesser degree, by Russia and Germany may, to some extent, be reckoned as a set-off to the serious loss of life, stock, and crops in the Western Provinces. The stirring events of the Great War are now recorded, and this history is thereby brought up to date. But the new chapters constitute only one part of the work. The other has been to revise the entire text of the first edition in the light of subsequent exploration and study; the criticisms of reviewers have also been carefully considered. In this task I have been helped by my friends.

Dr. G. E. Pilgrim, who has travelled in Persia and Mesopotamia, has allowed me, in the section referring to geology, to make use of his discoveries. Mr. H. R. Hall, who recently excavated in Mesopotamia, has also given me the benefit of his discoveries and knowledge; Messrs. G. F. Hill and A. G. Ellis have examined the periods in which they rank as leading authorities ; Sir Louis Dane and Messrs. F. H. Brown and E. M. Eldrid have read the new chapters, and Mr. E. Edwards has helped me in more than one period. Indeed, every effort has been made to ensure that the second edition shall be better than the first.

As to maps, I am again using that of the Royal Geographical Society. It may interest my readers to mention that this map, which was sent to the prison camp at Kastamuni, Asia Minor, in the cover of my history, enabled a party of British officers to escape. Moreover, I have been permitted, through the courtesy of the Geographical Section of the War Office, to use a recent map " Persia and Afghanistan," which also includes Russian and Chinese Turkestan and shows the recently constructed railways. I have also been allowed to reproduce a plan of the neighbourhood of Shiraz. Finally, a new sketch-map of Arabia, which includes the results of recent exploration, has been specially prepared for this work.

In conclusion, the severance of my long connexion with Persia enables me to express my opinions freely and to place all the facts of a difficult and complicated problem before my European and Persian readers.

P. M. S.

PART OF A PERSIAN HUNTING SCENE.
(From a Polychrome Terra-cotta Vase in the Hermitage Museum.)

PREFACE TO THE FIRST EDITION

JUST a century has elapsed since the publication of Sir John Malcolm's *History of Persia*. In this long period the mystery of the cuneiform inscriptions has been solved, Susa has yielded up its secrets, and in many other directions a notable advance has been effected. Each important discovery has been embodied in some work of special value, but no book has been written dealing with Persia as a whole and embodying the rich fruits of this modern research.

After much hesitation I have attempted to fill what is undoubtedly a serious gap; for Persia has exercised considerable influence, extending over many centuries, on India and Central Asia, on Greece, on the Roman Empire, and consequently on Europe.

My primary aim has been to furnish fellow-officials serving in Persia and adjoining countries, and students, whether European or Persian, with a work which is, as far as possible, self-contained and complete. With this object I have focussed what is known of the ancient empires in their relations with Elam, Media, and Persia; and I have dealt somewhat more fully than would otherwise have been necessary with such subjects as the rise of Macedonia.

Having enjoyed the great advantage of twenty-one years' residence and travel in Persia, I am able to present certain facts more vividly than would have been possible without the special knowledge thus gained. I also claim to have acquired to some extent the Persian point of view.

My thanks are due to the Government of India and to the India Office for much help, including a recently published map of Persia. Dr. F. W. Thomas placed the resources of the library of the India Office at my disposal even in Persia, and but for this I could not have carried out my plan; Mr. A. G. Ellis has also constantly given me valuable advice. Messrs. E. Edwards, L. W. King, H. B. Walters, and J. Allan, of the British Museum, have helped me in the periods and subjects on which they are authorities; while Mr. J. B. Capper has assisted me in seeing the book through the press. The chapters dealing with Nadir Shah have been read by Sir Mortimer Durand, who has made a special study of this period. I am indebted to many friends for illustrations, which Mr. Emery Walker has taken great pains to reproduce.

In my two former books I have described the unexplored parts of Persia, and have portrayed the customs and manners of the friendly race among whom I have spent the best years of my life. In the present work I realize an ambition of many years' standing, and I hope that the result may be considered to be useful by the Government I serve, as well as by my fellow-countrymen who create public opinion, which can have no safe and enduring basis in the absence of historical knowledge. If it is also used occasionally by students of Greek and Roman history, who may desire to learn something of the Persian point of view; and if, finally, it helps Persians to realize more fully the splendour of their own history, my efforts, involving many years of study, will not have been in vain.

P. M. S.

A SPHINX.
(Achaemenian Gold Medallion from British Museum.)

CONTENTS

PRELIMINARY ESSAY xxix

CHAPTER I

CONFIGURATION AND CLIMATE 1

The Situation of Persia—Boundaries and Provinces—Meaning of Iran and of Persia—The Formation of the Iranian Plateau—The Resemblance of Persia to Spain—The Aridity of Central Asia—The Climate of Persia—The Rainfall—Cold and Heat—Wind—The Climate of Ancient Persia—Population—The Mountains of the Iranian Plateau—The Northern Ranges—The Southern Ranges.

CHAPTER II

DESERTS, RIVERS, FLORA, FAUNA, AND MINERALS . . . 18

The Lut, the Desert of Persia—Rivers—The Oxus—Lakes—The Persian Gulf—The Caspian Sea—Communications—Flora—Fauna—Minerals.

CHAPTER III

THE GEOGRAPHY OF ELAM AND BABYLONIA 36

Early Civilization—Elam, the Home of the Earliest Civilization of Persia—Physical Changes in Elam and Babylonia since the Dawn of History—The Rivers of Babylonia and Elam—The Euphrates—The Tigris—The Kerkha—The Ab-i-Diz—The Karun—The Expedition of Sennacherib—The Voyage of Nearchus—The Rivers of Babylonia and Elam at the Present Day—The Boundaries of Elam—Its Cities, Ancient and Modern—The Natural Fertility of Elam—The Boundaries of Babylonia—Meaning of Sumer and Akkad—Chaldea and Babylonia—Description of Babylonia—Climate, Flora, and Fauna.

CHAPTER IV

ELAM AND SUSA, THE CAPITAL 49

Recent Study of Origins—The Meaning of Elam—Negrito Aborigines—The Legend of Memnon—The Various Tribes of Elam—Anzan or Anshan—The Ancient Language—The Religion—Susa, the Ancient Capital—Excavations by Loftus—The Dieulafoy and de Morgan Missions—The Four Quarters of Susa—The Prehistoric Period—The Archaic Period—Elam in the Legend of Gilgames.

CHAPTER V

ELAM, SUMER, AND AKKAD AT THE DAWN OF HISTORY . . 61

Sumerians and Semites—The Legend of Oannes—The Sumerian Language—Religion—The Earliest Sumerian Settlements—Eannatum, King of Lagash, before 3000 B.C.—Victories of Eannatum over the Elamites—The earliest-known Letter and Elam—Elam and the Kish Dynasty, 2900–2800 B.C.—The Empire of Akkad, 2800 B.C.—The Campaign of Sargon against Elam—The Stele of Naram-Sin—The Kingdom of Guti—Gudea, *Patesi* of Lagash, 2500 B.C.—The Rise of the Third Dynasty of Ur—The Administration of Elam by Dungi—The Overthrow of the Third Dynasty of Ur—The Sack of Erech by Kudur-Nankhundi, *circa* 2280 B.C.—The Dynasty of Isin or Nisin, *circa* 2339–2115 B.C.—The Influence of Sumerian Civilization.

CHAPTER VI

ELAM AND BABYLON 73

The Rise of Babylon—A Retrospect—The Difficulty of connecting Early Elamite Dynasties with those of Sumer—The one certain Synchronism between Elam and Babylonia—The Elamite Conquest and its Results—Chedorlaomer, King of Elam—The Decay of the Elamite Empire—The First Dynasty of Babylon, 2225–1926 B.C.—The Laws of Hammurabi—The Second Dynasty of the Sea-land, *circa* 2068–1710 B.C.—Contemporary Elamite Dynasties—The Kassite Dynasty of Babylon, *circa* 1925–1185 B.C.—The Position of Elam—Shutruk-Nakhunta, King of Elam, *circa* 1190 B.C.—The Pashe Dynasty of Babylon, *circa* 1184–1053 B.C.—The Sea-land and Bazi Dynasties, *circa* 1052–1032 B.C.—The Chaldaeans, *circa* 970–732 B.C.

CHAPTER VII

THE ASSYRIAN EMPIRE AND THE DOWNFALL OF ELAM . . 82

The Rise of Assyria—The Old Empire—The Aramaean Immigration—The Middle Assyrian Kingdom, *circa* 900–745 B.C The New Assyrian Kingdom, 745–606 B.C.—Sargon II., 722–705 B The First Battle

CONTENTS

between Assyria and Elam—Sennacherib, 705-682 B.C.—His Campaigns against Elam—The Capture and Sack of Babylon, 689 B.C.—Esarhaddon, 681-669 B.C., and his Relations with Elam—The Conquest of Egypt, 670 B.C.—Assurbanipal, 669-626 B.C.—The First Campaign against Elam—The Battle of Tulliz, 659 B.C.?—The Revolution at Susa—The Triumph of Assyria—The Rebellion of Babylon—The Second Campaign against Elam, 651 B.C.—The Capture of Babylon, 648 B.C.—The Third Campaign against Elam—The Capture and Sack of Susa, *circa* 647 B.C.—The Statue of Nana restored to Erech—The Disappearance of Elam.

CHAPTER VIII

THE ARYANS OF PERSIA—THEIR ORIGIN AND TRADITIONS . . 95

The Contrast between the Plains and the Uplands of Persia—The Uplands dominated by the Aryans—The Aryan Question—The Cradle-land of the Aryans—The Tradition of the Aryans of Persia—The Arrival of the Aryans in Persia—The Dates of the Migration—The Medes and the Ancient Inhabitants—Aryan Myths.

CHAPTER IX

THE RELIGION OF THE MEDES AND PERSIANS 102

The Common Religion of the Aryans of Persia and of India—Indo-Iranian Legends, Yama or Jamshid—Zoroaster, the Prophet of Iran—Gushtasp, the First Royal Convert—The Date of Zoroaster's Birth and Death—The Avesta—Ormuzd, the Supreme God—Ahriman, the Spirit of Evil—The Three Principles of Zoroastrianism—Turanian Influences on Zoroastrianism—The Magi—The Doctrine of the Resurrection—The Iranian Paradise—The Influence of Zoroastrianism on Judaism—Summary.

CHAPTER X

THE RISE OF MEDIA AND THE FALL OF ASSYRIA . . . 115

A Description of Media—The Nisaean Horses—The Expedition of Tiglath-pileser I., *circa* 1100 B.C.—The Expeditions of Shalmaneser, 844 B.C.—The Invasion of Adad-nirari III., 810 B.C.—The Campaigns of Tiglath-Pileser IV., 744 B.C.—Israel carried Captive into Media by Sargon II., 722 B.C.—Esarhaddon's Expeditions, *circa* 674 B.C.—The Tradition of the Medes—Deïokes, the Founder of the Royal Dynasty—Ecbatana, the Capital—The Language of the Medes—Sennacherib and the Medes—The Expansion of Media—The Conquest of the Persians by the Medes—The Later Years of Assurbanipal—The First Attack by the Medes—The Accession of Cyaxares—The First Siege of Nineveh—The Scythian Invasion—The Second Siege of Nineveh—The Fall of Nineveh, *circa* 606 B.C.—The Verdict of History on Assyria.

CHAPTER XI

MEDIA, BABYLONIA, AND LYDIA 126

The State of the Ancient World after the Fall of Nineveh—The Position of Media—The New Kingdom of Babylonia—The Campaign of Necho II.—The Victory of Nebuchadnezzar over Necho II., 604 B.C.—The "Hanging Gardens" of Babylon—The Campaigns of Cyaxares—The Empire of Lydia—The Mermnad Dynasty—The Invention of Coinage—The War between Media and Lydia—The Battle of the Eclipse, 585 B.C.—The Death of Cyaxares, 584 B.C.—Astyages, the Last King of Media—The Luxury of the Median Court—The Defeat of Astyages by Cyrus the Great—The Later Kings of the New Babylonian Kingdom.

CHAPTER XII

THE HEROIC AGE OF PERSIA 133

The Legendary Nature of Early Persian History—The Pishdadian Dynasty—Jamshid and Zohak—Feridun and Kawa—The Three Sons of Feridun—Sam, Zal, and Rudabah—Rustam the Champion—The Keianian Dynasty—Kei Kaus, to some extent, identified with Cyaxares—Sohrab and Rustam—Siawush and Kei Khusru—Kei Khusru not Cyrus the Great—Lohrasp and Gushtasp—Isfandiar—Bahman or Ardeshir Dirazdast—The End of the Heroic Period.

CHAPTER XIII

THE RISE OF PERSIA 139

The Early Organization of the Persians—The Rise of Cyrus the Great according to Herodotus—The Tragedy of Harpagus—Fresh Light on Persian History—Achaemenes, the Founder of the Royal Family—The Double Line of Achaemenian Monarchs—The Defeat of Astyages by Cyrus—Cyrus, King of Anshan, becomes King of Persia—Croesus of Lydia—The Perso-Lydian Campaign—The Capture of Sardes, 546 B.C.—The Fate of Croesus—The Geographical Position of Hellas—Recent Progress in Knowledge of Greek History—The Aryan Invasion of Greece—The Greek Colonies in Asia Minor—Their Conquest by the Persians—The Eastern Campaigns of Cyrus—The Surrender of Babylon, 538 B.C.—The Traditional Account—The Latter Years of Cyrus—The Repatriation of the Jews—The Death of Cyrus, 529 B.C.—His Character.

CHAPTER XIV

THE PERSIAN EMPIRE AT ITS ZENITH 156

The Accession of Cambyses, 529 B.C.—The Death of Bardiya, 526 B.C.—The Egyptian Campaign—The Battle of Pelusium, 525 B.C.—The Suicide of Cambyses, 521 B.C.—Gaumata, the Pseudo-Smerdis of the Greeks—The Slaying of Gaumata, 521 B.C.—The Accession of Darius, 521 B.C.—The Eight Rebellions—Darius the Administrator—The

CONTENTS

Satrapies—The Royal Road—The Expansion of the Empire—The Object of the Scythian Campaign—The Course of the Campaign, *circa* 512 B.C.—The Annexation of Thrace and the Submission of Macedonia—The Indian Campaign, 512 B.C.—Summary.

CHAPTER XV

THE ANCIENT PERSIANS—THEIR CUSTOMS, LANGUAGE, AND ARCHITECTURE . 170

The Virility of the Persians—Customs—Laws—The Position of Women—The King and his Court—The Language of the Ancient Persians—The Trilingual Inscriptions at Behistun—The Ruins of Pasargadae—The Palaces of Persepolis—The Rock-Tombs—Enamelled Brick-work, etc.—The Achaemenian Goldsmiths' Work—The Bronze Implements of Khinaman—Summary.

CHAPTER XVI

PERSIA AND HELLAS DURING THE REIGN OF DARIUS . . . 186

The Issues at Stake—The Greek Subjects of Persia—The Intercourse between Hellas and Asia Minor—The Position in Greece—The Ionic Revolt, 499-494 B.C.—The Battle of Lade and the Fall of Miletus, 494 B.C.—The Campaign of Mardonius in Thrace, 493 B.C.—The Punitive Expedition against Athens and Eretria, 490 B.C.—The Destruction of Eretria—The Battle of Marathon, 490 B.C.—The Rebellion in Egypt, 486 B.C.—The Death of Darius, 485 B.C.—His Character.

CHAPTER XVII

THE REPULSE OF PERSIA BY HELLAS 195

The Accession of Xerxes, 485 B.C.—The Rebellion in Egypt crushed, 484 B.C.—The Revolt of Babylon, 483 B.C.—The Composition and Numbers of the Great Expedition—The Military Position in Greece—The March of the Great Army—The Defence of Thermopylae, 480 B.C.—The Naval Engagements off Artemisium—The Advance of the Persian Army and the Capture of Athens—The Battle of Salamis, 480 B.C.—The Retreat of Xerxes—The Carthaginian Invasion of Sicily, 480 B.C.—The Campaign of Mardonius—The Battle of Plataea, 479 B.C.—The Battle of Mycale, 479 B.C.—The Capture of Sestos, 478 B.C.—The Final Results.

CHAPTER XVIII

THE PERSIAN EMPIRE AFTER THE REPULSE FROM HELLAS . . 212

Xerxes after the Retreat from Hellas—The Greek Raids on Asia Minor and the Battle of the Eurymedon, 466 B.C.—The Assassination of Xerxes, 466 B.C.—His Character—The Accession of Artaxerxes I., 465 B.C.—The Rebellion of Hystaspes, 462 B.C.—The Revolt of Egypt, 460-454 B.C.—The Peace of Callias, *circa* 449 B.C.—Spain and England compared with Persia and Athens—The Rebellion of Megabyzus—A Period of Anarchy, 425 B.C.—The Reign of Darius Nothus, 424-404 B.C.—Tissaphernes and the Alliance with Sparta, 412 B.C.—The Story of Terituchmes.

CHAPTER XIX

THE DECLINE OF THE PERSIAN EMPIRE 220

Cyrus the Younger—His Relations with Sparta—The Accession of Artaxerxes Mnemon, 404 B.C.—The March of Cyrus on Babylon—The Battle of Cunaxa, 401 B.C.—The Retreat of the Ten Thousand—Persia and Hellas after Cunaxa—The Peace of Antalcidas, 387 B.C.—The Egyptian Campaigns—The Expedition against the Cadusians—The Latter Days of Artaxerxes Mnemon—The Accession of Artaxerxes III., 358 B.C.—The Capture of Sidon and the Reconquest of Egypt, 342 B.C.—The Murder of Artaxerxes III., 338 B.C.—The Accession of Darius Codomannus, 336 B.C.

CHAPTER XX

THE RISE OF MACEDONIA UNDER PHILIP AND ALEXANDER . . 234

The Geography of Macedonia—The People—The Early History—Philip the Organizer, 359–336 B.C.—The Battle of Chaeronea, 338 B.C.—The Election of Philip as Captain-General of Hellas, 337 B.C.—Olympias—The Assassination of Philip, 336 B.C.—The Extraordinary Fame of Alexander the Great—The Alexander Romances—His Youth and Accession—His Recognition by Hellas—The Destruction of Thebes, 335 B.C.

CHAPTER XXI

THE BATTLES OF THE GRANICUS AND OF ISSUS . . . 244

The Situation before the Great Expedition—The Start of the Expedition, 334 B.C.—The Battle of the Granicus, 334 B.C.—The Surrender of Sardes, 334 B.C.—The Campaign in Caria, Lycia, Pamphylia, Pisidia, and Phrygia—The Death of Memnon, 333 B.C.—The Battle of Issus, November 333 B.C.—The Siege of Tyre and its Capture, 332 B.C.—The Annexation of Egypt, 332–331 B.C.

CHAPTER XXII

THE CAREER OF ALEXANDER THE GREAT TO THE DEATH OF DARIUS CODOMANNUS 255

The Battle of Arbela, 331 B.C.—The Capture of Babylon and Susa—The Occupation of Persepolis and Pasargadae—The Capture of Ecbatana, 330 B.C.—The Pursuit and Death of Darius Codomannus, 330 B.C.

CHAPTER XXIII

THE LIMIT OF CONQUEST 264

The Conquest of Hyrcania, Parthia, and Areia—The Annexation of Sistan and the March up the Helmand—The Crossing of the Hindu Kush and the Annexation of Bactria, 328 B.C.—The Capture of Bessus—

CONTENTS

The Advance to the Jaxartes or Sir Daria—The First Macedonian Disaster—The Capture of the Sogdian Rock—The Invasion of India, 327 B.C.—Nysa, a Colony founded by Dionysus—The Passage of the Indus—The Battle with Porus, 326 B.C.—The Limit of Conquest.

CHAPTER XXIV

THE DEATH OF ALEXANDER THE GREAT—HIS ACHIEVEMENTS AND CHARACTER 275

The Voyage to the Indian Ocean—The March from the Indus to Susa, 325 B.C.—The Voyage to Babylon—The Death of Alexander the Great, 323 B.C.—An Analysis of Hellenism—A Comparison between the Hellenized and the British Empire—The Fruits of Hellenism—The Achievements and Character of Alexander the Great.

CHAPTER XXV

THE WARS OF THE "SUCCESSORS" 284

The Problem of the Succession—The Death of Perdiccas, 321 B.C.—The Rise of Seleucus—The Fight for Power—Antigonus and Eumenes—The Supremacy of Antigonus on the Death of Eumenes, 316 B.C.—The Destruction of the Family of Alexander the Great—The Battle of Gaza, 312 B.C.—The Reoccupation of Babylon by Seleucus, 312 B.C.—The Raid of Demetrius on Babylon, 311 B.C.—The Making of the Empire of Seleucus, 311–302 B.C.—Antigonus and Ptolemy—The Battle of Ipsus, 301 B.C.—The Career of Demetrius Poliorcetes after Ipsus—His Accession to the Throne of Macedonia—His Captivity and Death—The Defeat and Death of Lysimachus, 281 B.C.—The Assassination of Seleucus Nicator, 281 B.C.

CHAPTER XXVI

THE SELEUCID EMPIRE TO THE RISE OF PARTHIA . . . 295

The Accession of Antiochus Soter, 281 B.C.—The Invasion of the Gauls and the Death of Ptolemy Keraunus, 280 B.C.—The Defeat of the Gauls by Antiochus I.—The Divisions of the Empire of Alexander after the Invasion of the Gauls—The Death of Antiochus Soter, 262 B.C.—Antiochus Theos, 262–246 B.C.—The Revolt of Bactria, 256 B.C., and of Parthia, 250 B.C.—The Third Syrian War and the Invasion of Syria and Persia, 245 B.C.—The Battle of Ancyra, *circa* 235 B.C.—The Campaign of Seleucus II. against Parthia—Attalus of Pergamus and Antiochus Hierax—Seleucus III., 226–223 B.C.—The Close of a Great Period—Iran under Macedonian Rule—The Greek Cities in the Persian Empire.

CHAPTER XXVII

THE RISE OF PARTHIA AND THE APPEARANCE OF ROME IN ASIA . 305

Parthia Proper—The Authorities for Parthian History—The Arsacid Dynasty—The Birth-Year of the Arsacid Dynasty, 249–248 B.C.—The

Career of Arsaces I., 249-247 B.C.—Hecatompylus, the Capital—The Conquest of Hyrcania under Arsaces II., 247-214 B.C.—Arsaces II. and Seleucus II.—Dara, the New Capital of Parthia—The Early Career of Antiochus the Great, 223-213 B.C.—Arsaces III. and Antiochus the Great, 209 B.C.—The March of Antiochus through Bactria, the Panjab, and Kerman, 208-204 B.C.—Early Relations between Hellas and Rome—The First Macedonian War, 215-205 B.C.—The Spoliation of Egypt by Philip V. and Antiochus the Great—The Second Macedonian War, 200-197 B.C.—Antiochus the Great and Rome, 200-191 B.C.—The Battle of Magnesia, 190 B.C.—The Peace of Apamea, 188 B.C.—Parthia until the Reign of Mithradates I., 209-170 B.C.—Bactria, 205-170 B.C.—Summary.

CHAPTER XXVIII

The Expansion of Parthia and the Downfall of the House of Seleucus 324

The House of Seleucus, 188-175 B.C.—The Succession of Antiochus Epiphanes, 175 B.C.—The Battle of Pydna, 168 B.C.—The Evacuation of Egypt by Antiochus, 168 B.C.—The Eastern Campaigns of Antiochus and his Death, 165-164 B.C.—Antiochus Epiphanes and the Jews—Demetrius the Saviour, 162-150 B.C.—The Conquests of Mithradates I. of Parthia, 170-138 B.C.—The House of Seleucus, 150-140 B.C.—Mithradates I. and Demetrius II.—The Death of Mithradates I., 138 B.C.—Antiochus VII. Sidetes, 138-129 B.C.—Antiochus Sidetes and Phraates II., 130-129 B.C.—The Downfall of the House of Seleucus—Its Place in History.

CHAPTER XXIX

Parthia, Rome, and Pontus 333

The Nomadic Peril—The Victories of the Nomads over the Parthians—Mithradates II. of Parthia, 124-88 B.C.—Parthia and Armenia—The Expansion of Rome, 190-129 B.C.—The Making of the Empire of Mithradates VI. of Pontus, 120-90 B.C.—The First Intercourse between Parthia and Rome, 92 B.C.—The Earliest Intercourse of China with Parthia, 120-88 B.C.—An Obscure Period of Parthian History, 88-66 B.C.—Mithradates VI. and Rome, 89-66 B.C.—The Career of Pompey in the East, 67-63 B.C.—Pompey and Phraates III. of Parthia—The Suicide of Mithradates VI., 63 B.C.—The Results of Pompey's Campaigns.

CHAPTER XXX

Parthia and Rome—The First Trial of Strength . . 346

The Internal Affairs of Parthia, 57-55 B.C.—The Appointment of Crassus to Syria, 55 B.C.—The Projected Invasion of Parthia, 53 B.C.—The Plan of Campaign of Orodes—Parthian and Roman Troops compared—The Battle of Carrhae, 53 B.C.—The Parthian Invasion of Syria, 51-50 B.C.

CONTENTS

CHAPTER XXXI

ROME AND PARTHIA—THE SECOND TRIAL OF STRENGTH . . 354

The Civil War between Caesar and Pompey, 49–48 B.C.—Caesar and the Near East, 47 B.C.—The Early Career of Mark Antony—The Parthian Invasion under Pacorus and Labienus, 40–39 B.C.—The Peace of Brundisium, 40 B.C.—The Victories of Ventidius, 39 B.C.—The Defeat and Death of Pacorus, 38 B.C.—The Death of Orodes, *circa* 37 B.C.—The Expedition of Antony against Parthia, 36 B.C.—His Campaigns in Armenia, 34–33 B.C.—Phraates IV. and Tiridates, 33–30 B.C.—The Restoration of the Roman Standards, 20 B.C.—The End of the Second Trial of Strength.

CHAPTER XXXII

THE ORGANIZATION, RELIGION, AND ARCHITECTURE OF THE PARTHIANS 364

The Organization of the Parthians—The Position of the Monarch—The Army—The Court—The Position of Women—The Life of the Parthians—Their Dress—Laws and Customs—Religion—Literature—Architecture and Art—Coinage.

CHAPTER XXXIII

THE STRUGGLE FOR ARMENIA 373

The Armenian Question—The Murder of Phraates IV., 2 B.C., and the Treaty with Rome, A.D. 1—Phraataces, Vonones, and Artabanus III.—Rome, Parthia, and Armenia, A.D. 18–35—The Vicissitudes of Artabanus III., A.D. 36–37—The Peace with Rome, A.D. 37—Vardanes and Gotarzes, A.D. 40–51—The Struggle for Armenia—Volagases and Nero, A.D. 55–63—The Investiture of Tiridates by Nero, A.D. 66—An Obscure Period of Parthian History, A.D. 66–108.

CHAPTER XXXIV

THE DECLINE AND FALL OF PARTHIA 380

The Roman Empire at its Zenith—Trajan and Armenia, A.D. 114–115—The Conquest of Mesopotamia and of Babylon, A.D. 115–116—The Retreat of Trajan, A.D. 116—The Evacuation of Armenia and Mesopotamia by Hadrian, A.D. 117—The Inroad of the Alani, A.D. 133—The Invasion of Syria by Volagases III., A.D. 161—The Campaigns of Avidius Cassius, A.D. 163–165—The Eastern Campaigns of Severus, A.D. 194–197—Artabanus and Volagases, the last Kings of Parthia, A.D. 209–226—The Treachery of Caracallus, A.D. 216—The last Battle between Rome and Parthia, A.D. 217—The Downfall of Parthia, A.D. 226—The Intercourse of China with Persia, A.D. 25–220—The Cult of Mithras in Europe—Summary.

CHAPTER XXXV

THE RISE OF THE SASANIAN DYNASTY 391

The Origin of the Sasanian Dynasty—The Coming of Ardeshir—Ardeshir and Ardawan—The Battle of Hormuz, A.D. 226—The Eastern Campaigns of Ardeshir—Ardeshir and Severus Alexander, A.D. 229–232—The Conquest of Armenia by Ardeshir—Ardeshir, the Reviver of the Good Religion—His Achievements and Character.

CHAPTER XXXVI

SHAPUR I., THE CAPTOR OF VALERIAN 399

The Succession of Shapur I., A.D. 240—The Revolt of Armenia and of Hatra, A.D. 240—The First Campaign against Rome, A.D. 241–244—The Second Campaign : the First Phase, A.D. 258–260—The Capture of Valerian, A.D. 260—The Second Phase of the Campaign, A.D. 260—Shapur and Odenathus of Palmyra, A.D. 260–263—Zenobia—The Public Works of Shapur—The Manichaeans—The Death of Shapur I., A.D. 271—Hormisdas and Bahram I., A.D. 271–275—The Early Campaigns of Bahram II., A.D. 275–282—The Campaign of Carus, A.D. 283—The Seizure of Armenia by Tiridates, A.D. 286—The Campaigns of Narses against Rome, A.D. 296–297—The Defeat of Narses and the Cession of Five Provinces to Rome, A.D. 297.

CHAPTER XXXVII

SHAPUR THE GREAT 411

The Birth of Shapur II., A.D. 309—His Minority and Early Campaigns, A.D. 309–337—The First War with Rome, A.D. 337–350—The Great Persecution of the Christians—The Eastern Campaigns of Shapur, A.D. 350–357—The Treaty between Armenia and Rome, *circa* A.D. 352—The Second War with Rome to the Death of Constantius, A.D. 359–361—The Expedition of Julian, A.D. 363—His Retreat and Death, A.D. 363—The Restoration of the Five Provinces and of Nisibis to Shapur, A.D. 363—The Policy of Persia and Rome in Armenia and Iberia—The Conclusion of Peace between Rome and Persia, A.D. 376—The Death of Shapur, A.D. 379.

CHAPTER XXXVIII

THE STRUGGLE WITH THE WHITE HUNS . . . 427

Ardeshir II., A.D. 379–383, and Shapur III., A.D. 383–388—The Partition of Armenia, A.D. 384—Bahram IV., A.D. 388–399—Yezdigird the Wicked, A.D. 399–420—His Policy towards the Christians—The Curious Legend of his Death—The Contested Succession of Bahram Gur, A.D. 420—His Campaign against Rome, A.D. 420–421—The Peace with

CONTENTS

Rome, A.D. 422—The Declaration of the Independence of the Eastern Church, A.D. 424—Persian Armenia reduced to a Satrapy, A.D. 428—The Coming of the White Huns—The Campaigns of Bahram Gur against the White Huns—Bahram Gur, the Mighty Hunter—His Achievements and Character—Yezdigird II., his Campaigns against Rome and the White Huns—His Persecutions in Armenia and Mesopotamia—The Usurpation of Hormisdas, A.D. 457, and his Overthrow by Firuz, A.D. 459—The First Campaigns of Firuz against the White Huns—The Revolt of Armenia, A.D. 481–483—The Defeat of Firuz by the White Huns and his Death, A.D. 483—Persia tributary to the White Huns, A.D. 483–485—The Agreement with Armenia—Controversies on Doctrine among the Christians in Persia.

CHAPTER XXXIX

THE CRUSHING OF THE WHITE HUNS 441

The Accession of Kobad, A.D. 487—His Campaigns against the Khazars—The Rise of Mazdak—The Deposition of Kobad and his Imprisonment, A.D. 498–501—His Second Reign, A.D. 501–531—His First War with Rome, A.D. 503–505—The Final Campaign against the White Huns, A.D. 503–513—The Massacre of the Mazdakites, A.D. 523—The Rebellion in Iberia—The Second War with Rome, A.D. 524–531—The Importance of the Reign of Kobad—The Connexion between China and Persia under the Sasanian Dynasty.

CHAPTER XL

NOSHIRWAN THE JUST 449

The Disputed Succession of Noshirwan, A.D. 531—The Execution of Mazdak and the Massacre of his Followers—Peace concluded with Rome, A.D. 533—Roman Successes in Africa and Italy, A.D. 533–539—The Capture and Sack of Antioch by Noshirwan, A.D. 540—The Campaigns in Lazica, A.D. 540–557—The Second Peace with Rome, A.D. 562—The Coming of the Turks—The Subjugation of the White Huns—The Campaign against the Khazars—The Arabian Campaign, *circa* A.D. 576—The Campaign with the Turks—The Third War with Rome, A.D. 572–579—The Christian Community under Noshirwan—The Character and Achievements of Noshirwan—Buzurgmihr.

CHAPTER XLI

ORGANIZATION, LANGUAGE, AND ARCHITECTURE UNDER THE SASANIAN DYNASTY 461

The Administration of the Sasanian Empire—The Land Tax—Improvements in Irrigation and Communications—The Army—The Monarch and his Court—The Pahlavi Language—Pahlavi Rock Inscriptions—Pahlavi Literature—The Models of the Sasanian Architects—The Main Features of Sasanian Architecture—The Firuzabad Palace—The *Tak-i-Kisra*—The Palace of Khusru at Kasr-i-Shirin—The Palace at Mashita—The Bas-Reliefs at *Naksh-i-Rustam*—The Hunting Scenes of Khusru Parviz—The Work of the Sasanian Silversmiths—The Statue of Shapur I.—An Impression of Sasanian Architecture and Art—Alleged Byzantine Influences.

CHAPTER XLII

KHUSRU PARVIZ AND HERACLIUS 476

The Continuation of the Roman War by Hormisdas IV.—The Invasion and Defeat of the Turks, *circa* A.D. 588—The Campaign in Lazica, A.D. 589—The Revolt of Bahram Chubin and the Assassination of Hormisdas—The Accession of Khusru Parviz, A.D. 590—His Defeat and Flight to Mesopotamia—His Restoration by a Roman Army, A.D. 591—The Outbreak of War with Rome, A.D. 603—The Battle of Zu-Kar, *circa* A.D. 610—The Accession of Heraclius, A.D. 610—The Sack of Antioch and the Capture of Jerusalem by the Persians—The Fall of Chalcedon, A.D. 617—The Desperate Condition of the Roman Empire—The Famous Campaigns of Heraclius, A.D. 622–627—The Victory over Shahr-Baraz, A.D. 622—The Flight of the Great King, A.D. 623—The Surprise of the Army of Shahr-Baraz, A.D. 624—The Defeat of Shahr-Baraz on the Saras, A.D. 625—The Siege of Constantinople and the Defeat of Shahin, A.D. 626—The Sack of Dastagird and the Flight of Khusru Parviz, A.D. 627—The Deposition and Death of Khusru Parviz, A.D. 628—His Character—The Progress of Christianity under the later Sasanian Monarchs.

CHAPTER XLIII

THE OVERTHROW OF THE PERSIAN EMPIRE BY THE ARABS . . 488

The Accession of Kobad II. and the Peace with Rome, A.D. 628—The Massacre of his Brothers and his Death, A.D. 629—The Usurpation of Shahr-Baraz and his Death, A.D. 629—A Period of Anarchy, A.D. 629-634—The Accession of Yezdigird III., A.D. 634—The Campaign of Khalid against the Western Provinces of the Persian Empire, A.H. 12–13 (633–634)—The Campaigns of Mothanna, A.H. 13–14 (634–635)—The Organization of a Great Army for the Persian War, A.H. 14 (635)—The Embassy to Yezdigird, A.H. 14 (635)—The Battle of Cadesia, A.H. 14 (636)—The Capture of Madain, A.H. 16 (637)—The Battle of Jalola, A.H. 16 (637)—The Annexation of Mesopotamia and the Capture of Obolla, A.H. 16 (637)—The Foundation of Basra and of Kufa, A.H. 17 (638)—The Failure of the Expedition from Bahrein—The Conquest of Khuzistan and the Capture of Shuster, A.H. 19 (640)—The Battle of Nahavand, A.H. 21 (642)—The Annexation of the Provinces of Persia—The Death of Yezdigird III., A.H. 31 (652).

CHAPTER XLIV

THE CAREER OF MOHAMED AT MECCA 503

A Description of Arabia—The Importance of Mecca—The Ancient Religion of the Arabs—The Kaaba—The Ancestors of the Prophet Mohamed—The Political Situation in Arabia before and after the Birth of the Prophet—The Childhood, Youth, and Early Manhood of Mohamed—The Divine Commission conveyed by Gabriel—The Assumption of the Prophetical Office, A.D. 613-614—The Temporary Emigration to Abyssinia, A.D. 615.

CHAPTER XLV

THE FLIGHT TO MEDINA AND THE ESTABLISHMENT OF ISLAM . . 514

The *Hijra*, or "Emigration" to Medina, A.D. 622—The Erection of the First Mosque at Medina—The Breach with the Jews—The Battle of Badr, A.H. 2 (623), and the Expulsion of the Beni Kainucas—The Battle of Ohod, A.H. 3 (625), and the Expulsion of the Beni Nazir—The Siege of Medina and the Massacre of the Beni Koreitza, A.H. 5 (627)—The Truce of Hodeibia, A.H. 6 (628)—The Embassies sent by Mohamed, A.H. 7 (628)—The Conquest of Khaybar, A.H. 7 (628)—The "Fulfilled Pilgrimage," A.H. 7 (629)—The Battle of Muta, A.H. 8 (629)—The Capture of Mecca, A.H. 8 (630)—The Last Campaign of Mohamed, A.H. 9 (630)—The Final Orders of the Prophet—The "Farewell Pilgrimage," A.H. 10 (630)—The Death of Mohamed, A.H. 11 (632)—His Character—The Koran.

CHAPTER XLVI

ISLAM UNDER THE FIRST FOUR CALIPHS 525

The Period of the Caliphate, A.D. 632-1258—The Genealogical Table of the Kureish—The Election of Abu Bekr—The Rebellions, A.H. 11 (632)—The Battle on the Yermuk, A.H. 13 (634)—The Death of Abu Bekr and the Accession of Omar, A.H. 13 (634)—The Capture of Damascus, A.H. 14 (635)—The Capture of Antioch and the Capitulation of Jerusalem, A.H. 15 (636)—The Conquest of Egypt, A.H. 19-20 (640-641)—The Assassination of Omar, A.H. 23 (644)—The Accession of Othman, A.H. 24 (644)—The Expansion of Islam to the West, A.H. 25-31 (646-652)—The Campaigns in Persia, A.H. 31 (652)—The Murder of Othman, A.H. 35 (656)—The Election of Ali, A.H. 35 (656)—Muavia, the Governor of Syria—The Proclamation of War against Muavia by Ali, A.H. 35 (656)—The Battle of the Camel, A.H. 36 (656)—The Battle of Siffin, A.H. 37 (657)—The Arbitration, A.H. 37 (658)—The Kharijites—The Last Years of Ali's Caliphate—His Assassination, A.H. 40 (661)—His Character—The Position of Persia.

CHAPTER XLVII

THE TRAGEDY OF KERBELA 538

The Accession of Hasan and his Abdication, A.H. 40 (661)—The Death-bed Warning of Muavia to Yezid, A.H. 61 (680)—The Invitation to Husayn from the Inhabitants of Kufa—The March on Kufa—The Tragedy—The Journey to Damascus and the Return to Medina—The Passion Plays—The Historical Basis of the Shia Sect—Its Religious Basis and Doctrines.

CHAPTER XLVIII

PERSIA A PROVINCE OF THE OMAYYAD CALIPHATE . . . 545

The Omayyad Dynasty—The Position of Muavia strengthened by the Adherence of Ziad—Moslem Progress in the East—The Achievements and Failures of Muavia—Yezid declared Heir-Apparent, A.H. 56 (676), and his Succession in A.H. 61 (680)—The Rebellion of Ibn Zobayr, A.H. 61 (680)—The Bokhara Campaign—The Campaign of the Northern Beduin against the Southern Beduin, A.H. 46–65 (666–685)—The Divisions in the Caliphate, A.H. 61–73 (680–692)—The Massacre of the Enemies of Husayn, A.H. 66 (685)—The Azrakites—The Rebellion of Ibn-al-Ashath, A.H. 80 (699)—The Rebellion of Musa ibn Khazim—Death and Character of Abdul Malik—The Campaigns in Central Asia, A.H. 86–96 (705–714)—The Advance to the Indus, A.H. 89–96 (707–714)—The Achievements of Welid, A.H. 89–96 (705–714)—The Campaigns of Yezid in Gurgan and Tabaristan, A.H. 98 (716)—The Second Attempt on Constantinople, A.H. 99 (717)—Khorasan under the Caliphate of Omar II., A.H. 99–101 (717–720)—The Reign of Yezid II., A.H. 101–105 (720–724)—The Abbasid Propaganda—The Rebellion of Zayd, A.H. 122 (740)—The Caliphate of Hisham, A.H. 105–125 (724–743), and the Battle of Tours, A.D. 732—Welid II. and Yezid III., A.H. 125–126 (743–744)—The Rebellion of Abdulla, Ibn Muavia, A.H. 126–129 (744–747)—The Raising of the Black Standard in Khorasan, A.H. 129 (747)—The Battle of the Great Zab, A.H. 132 (750)—The Condition of Persia under the Omayyad Dynasty.

CHAPTER XLIX

PERSIAN ASCENDANCY IN THE EARLY ABBASID PERIOD . . . 558

The End of Moslem Unity—The Accession of Abul Abbas, A.H. 132 (749)—The Massacre of the Omayyads—The Reign of Abul Abbas and his Death, A.H. 136 (754)—Abu Jafar, Mansur, A.H. 136–158 (754–775)—The Execution of Abu Muslim, A.H. 137 (754)—The Rebellions in Persia, A.H. 138 (756), and A.H. 141–143 (758–760)—The Ravandis, A.H. 141 (758)—The Rebellion of the Descendants of Hasan, A.H. 144 (761)—The Foundation of Baghdad, A.H. 145 (762)—The Rising at Herat, A.H. 150 (767)—Persian Influence under Mansur—Mehdi, A.H. 158–169 (775–785)—The Veiled Prophet of Khorasan, A.H. 158–161 (774–777)—Hadi, A.H. 169–170 (785–786).

THE SELEUCID ELEPHANT.

ILLUSTRATIONS

	FACE PAGE
Bas-Relief of Cyrus the Great	*Frontispiece*
Kuh-i-Taftan	16
Elamite (?) God and Prisoners	46
The Stele of Naram-Sin	66
The Last Arrow of Teumman	90
The Tomb of Cyrus the Great	154
Darius and the Rebel Leaders	162
Bas-Relief and Inscription in the Palace of Xerxes	180
Bronze Axe-heads, etc., from Khinaman	184
Achaemenian Gold Jug in the British Museum	228
Alexander charging Darius Codomannus at the Battle of Issus	250
Shapur the First and Valerian	400
Silver Dish of Bahram Gur	434
The Arch of Chosroes, Ctesiphon	496
The Angel Gabriel appearing to Mohamed	512

MAP

Vol. I

Babylonia, showing the sites of Ancient Cities . . *At end*

COIN OF NASIR-U-DIN SHAH.

FROM LUSTRED POTTERY.

VOLUME I

PRELIMINARY ESSAY

(To be read with Chapters V. and VI.)

The Flood.—During the decade which has elapsed since the publication of the second edition of this history, Leonard Woolley has made discoveries at Ur which undoubtedly mark an epoch. "A few years ago," to quote the great archaeologist, "the Flood, even if not dismissed as a legendary fiction, seemed something too remote and vague to be admitted into history."[1] To-day all this is changed and although its exact date cannot be fixed, we know whereabouts it came in the sequence of ancient history which eight years of strenuous but fruitful effort have revealed to the world.

The discovery was made by digging a pit 75 feet wide and 48 feet deep on a site which denudation had worn down to the period of 3200 B.C. Eight successive layers of buildings were discovered with floors of rammed clay, which had preserved specimens of different types of pottery, some of which was new to the finders. In the upper levels the potter's wheel was used, but, in the lower, the ware was made by hand. The buildings were all of good quality, with different kinds of bricks, some being made of cement, the earliest known use of that material. The stone figure of a wild boar, the most ancient piece of sculpture which Ur has yielded, was found at a depth of 28 feet, and its antiquity must be prodigious.

A stratum of clear sand, measuring 11 feet, the work of the Flood, was discovered at 40 feet, and below it an irregular

---

[1] For Mr. Woolley's most recent discoveries I am indebted to his lectures and to his kind assistance. I have also consulted his work *The Sumerians*; the *History and Monuments of Ur*, by C. J. Gadd; and the contributions of Professors Langdon and Campbell Thompson to the *Cambridge Ancient History*.

stratum which showed signs of continuous occupation by the pre-Flood population. These men were not savages. They lived not only in reed huts but also in brick houses with wooden doors set in sockets of imported stone. They used weapons and tools of copper, but polished stone axes were also found. They spun thread, wove cloth, and manufactured pottery of good quality. In the graves the corpse was laid extended on its back with the feet together. Clay figurines, representing females with inhuman heads, and vessels of painted clay were placed by the dead. To conclude this brief account, the men who inhabited the site after the Flood were of the same stock as those who lived before it, using the same pottery. But they were a poorer and a decadent race. Then follows a complete change of culture and we find the relics of a different race from that which knew the Flood. The newcomers were presumably the Sumerians.

The Cradle-land of the Sumerians.—One problem of great importance, in which distinct progress has been made, is that of the Sumerians. Who were they ? Where was their cradle-land ? And when did they reach Babylonia ?

The Sumerians, a dark-haired race—the "black-heads" of the texts—were of Indo-European stock. Their original home was mountainous, this being indicated by the fact that their gods are represented as standing upon mountains. It was also a land of forests, as the architecture of their earliest buildings, based on a tradition of timber construction, clearly proves. A verse in Genesis is also to the point : " And it came to pass as they journeyed from the east, that they found a plain in the land of Shinar ; and they dwelt there."[1] This undoubtedly refers to the Sumerians, Shinar being Sumer, and again serves as an indication. Nor is this all. Quite recently the world was astonished by the discovery in the Indus Valley of remains of a very early civilization, which closely resembled that of Sumer. In the rectangular stamp seals bearing identical inscriptions, in buildings, and in terra-cotta figures, there is clear proof that the two civilizations sprang from a common stock, and it is evident that their cradle-land was somewhere in the mountains of Eastern Persia, in Afghanistan, or in Baluchistan.

In Chapter V.[2] reference is made to the legend of Oannes,

---

[1] Genesis, xi. 2.
[2] All references, unless otherwise stated, refer to this History.

who led a race of beneficent monsters from the Persian Gulf, and introduced agriculture, the art of writing, and working in metals. Here again we have an indication that the Sumerians, representing a higher civilization, reached Babylonia by sea and, conquering the inhabitants of the marshes, founded towns, for the Sumerians were emphatically town-dwellers. This is the era of great archaeological discoveries, and we may hope that, within the next decade, the port from which these conquerors set out on their great adventure may be identified. Were I asked where to start the quest, I should suggest Harmuza, the port at which Nearchus beached his fleet on the Minab River, before marching inland to report its safety to Alexander the Great. To-day neighbouring Bandar Abbas is the natural outlet for trade from Herat, from Meshed, and from the intervening centres.

The Sumerian problem is somewhat complicated by the discovery, referred to on page 50, of a fine painted pottery, which is as ancient as the earliest graves at Ur. It is older than the earliest Elamite ware and therefore constitutes a powerful argument against the Sumerians being of Elamite origin, a theory which at one time appeared to be plausible in view of the text quoted above, the mountainous nature of Elam and its forests. Similar pottery has been discovered at Carchemish and elsewhere, which proves that the pottery cannot be Sumerian. Campbell Thompson favours a proto-Elamite population which was driven out by the Sumerians, whereas Woolley, who considers that the land only became fit for human occupation when man had reached the chalcolithic age, is inclined to favour an Akkadian Babylonia which was conquered by the Sumerian invaders.

Very Ancient Dynasties.—Recent discoveries prove that the Sumerians had a much longer connection with Babylonia than was previously suspected. About 2000 B.C., after the downfall of the Third Dynasty of Ur, the scribes drew up records of the previous dynasties and of their achievements. Most of these chronicles have perished, but, fortunately for us, the lists of their kings have survived. In these lists, ten kings are shown who reigned before the Flood. The length of their reigns is apparently fantastic, but perhaps we do not understand the system of reckoning that is used. The same remark, albeit to a lesser degree, applies to the lists of the first two dynasties that ruled after the Flood, preceding the First Dynasty of Ur. Until recently none of the names given could be identified, but the discovery of monuments of the First Dynasty proves its historical character. We are therefore justified in accepting the records of the scribes who mention not only kings but also cities as existing before the Flood, notably Eridu.

The Ancient Cemetery at Ur.—Among the most important discoveries at Ur was that of a cemetery, in which the earlier graves may be dated at about 3500 B.C., while the latest may come down to 3100 B.C., the date of the foundation of the First Dynasty of Ur, which ruled until 2930 B.C. The royal graves consisted of buildings constructed at the bottom of shafts and the great architectural surprise was the discovery that the Sumerians used not only the column but also the arch, the vault, and the dome, thousands of years before they were known in Europe.

Another surprise was the discovery that royal burials were accompanied by human sacrifice on a large scale. In the grave of Queen Shub-ad, the ladies of the Court were killed and laid in two parallel rows, and two corpses were found, one lying at the head and the other at the foot of the bier. In no text is there any reference to these awful funeral rites, which may be explained by the deification of the early monarchs, and this fact alone proves the great antiquity of these tombs. The offerings in these graves included gold and silver bowls for libations, cups, daggers with golden blades, beads of gold and *lapis lazuli*, and an amazing gold helmet. Below the royal tombs were found graves of a much earlier type, in which pictograph seal-impressions were discovered with a linear design. These seal-impressions, which are of great antiquity, are adorned with a linear design similar to those discovered a generation ago by the De Morgan Mission at Susa, and thus prove the connexion between the two countries. To sum up, "in 3500 B.C. Sumerian art stood at a level seldom reached in the ancient world, and it must have had behind it centuries of growth and experience."[1]

In the land of Sumer neither minerals nor stone were found. Consequently one of the problems to be solved is the source whence the raw materials for these skilled craftsmen were derived. The copper has recently been proved by analysis to have come from mines in Oman, a fact of great importance ; and

[1] Woolley, *Op. cit.* p. 45.

PRELIMINARY ESSAY

diorite was brought from Magan, which may have been a port in the same country. As to the *lapis lazuli*, Woolley considers that it came from Badakshan.[1]

The above facts tend to prove the existence of an extensive foreign trade, eastwards with Elam and Central Asia, and southwards down the Persian Gulf. Westwards, too, about the time of the First Dynasty in Egypt, mace-heads and other objects of Sumerian manufacture reached the valley of the Nile. Viewed from another point of view, Sumer perforce exported her wares to pay for her raw materials. We are therefore fully justified in believing that, in the fourth millennium B.C., there were trade-routes radiating in every direction from Sumer, and that merchants travelled by land or sea with some measure of security.

The Sumerian Army.—Few sayings are truer than that civilization advances on a powder-cart. In the case of the Sumerians, who founded their empire among brave and warlike races, superiority in the science and organisation of war was essential. Thanks again to Leonard Woolley, we now know something of the military organisation and of the weapons used by the Sumerians in the middle of the fourth millennium B.C. Our information is mainly based on a "standard," a mosaic of shell and *lapis lazuli* that was discovered in a royal grave at Ur, as also were the weapons. The "standard" is arranged in three rows. In the bottom row are chariots, drawn by four asses. In each chariot there was a driver and a warrior armed with "light throwing-spears carried in a quiver attached to the car," and with thrusting spears. In the middle row, the infantry advance in close order. They wear conical copper helmets and long cloaks, and their weapon is a thrusting spear. This phalanx is preceded by skirmishers, armed with axes, swords, or spears. In the top row, the King, armed with an adze and a specially heavy spear, is represented as the victor, receiving the prisoners. Among the weapons found in these early tombs were arrow-heads of more than one type and fragments of bows. It has hitherto been believed that archery was not practised by the Sumerians until the reign of Dungi,[2] but here we have the proof that it was known in the middle of the fourth millennium B.C. and probably very much earlier. Coming down the centuries, on the "Stele of the Vultures," referred to on page 66,

---
[1] *Vide* p. 33, footnote 2.
[2] *Vide* Chapter V. p. 69.

Eannatum leads a compact phalanx of spearmen, whereas in the "Stele of Naram-Sin," the bow, the spear, the javelin, and the battle-axe are all in use.

In early times the entire population would, if required, serve in the army, but under Sargon and Hammurabi there was a standing nucleus of guards, supported by what may be termed the territorial force. In view of the campaigns undertaken for the purpose of foreign conquest, this arrangement was inevitable, but it involved national decay. So also did the ruthlessness of the victors, who massacred their prisoners and destroyed the cities which they captured. It is obvious that these barbarous methods of waging war between cities, inhabited by people of the same race, led to the final downfall and disappearance of the Sumerians.

The Period of Civil Wars.—The First Dynasty of Ur ruled for rather less than two centuries. It was succeeded by ten dynasties about which we know very little. Generally speaking, the period was one of chronic disorder, of which the Elamites took advantage both to raid and to conquer. Although there were Sumerian dynasties in this dark period, among them the Second Dynasty of Ur, the Semites gradually gained the upper hand, Kish, Opis, and Mari becoming the capital in turn. In the imperfect lists it is clear that there is overlapping, while, to add to the confusion, the name of Fannatum of Lagash,[1] who certainly ruled over a united Sumer, does not appear.

The Dynasty of Akkad.—On page 67 a reference is made to Elam and the Kish Dynasty which, in view of recent discoveries, is not entirely accurate. The prosperous dynasty of Lagash was overthrown by Lugal-zaggisi, who founded a short-lived Sumerian empire with Erech as his capital, Lagash having been treated with customary ruthlessness by the victor. But the Sumerian, after a successful reign of twenty-five years, was defeated and captured by Sargon, the founder of the dynasty of Akkad, whose capital, Agade, is believed to be represented by the ruins of the mound ed-Der, situated a few miles to the south-west of Baghdad.

Sargon was succeeded by his son Rimush (not Urumush as I have given it), and then by Manishtu, both of whom were erroneously considered to be Kings of Kish, although there is no doubt as to the successful campaigns which they waged. But Naram-Sin, the "conqueror of nine armies," was the

[1] *Vide* p. 65.

greatest of Sargon's sons, whose bas-relief can still be seen in the mountains of Kurdistan, thus proving the wide range of his conquests.

The Guti.—The glory of Akkad faded, and there was a short-lived dynasty at Erech, but Sumer and Akkad alike, as also Elam, were overwhelmed by the Guti. Under these barbarians, " business documents and works of art are alike lacking." Yet, as the years passed, the city-states recovered some measure of independence, Gudea of Lagash, for instance, ruling under Guti overlords, but undoubtedly living to see Sumer freed from their tyranny.

The Third Dynasty of Ur.—Sumerian reaction under Ur-Nammu, a *Patesi* of Ur, created another empire of Sumer and Akkad, Ur once again becoming the capital. To this, the Third Dynasty, which ruled from about 2278 to 2150 B.C., we owe the great Ziggurat tower, the temple of Nana, the royal palace, and other buildings. Nor was their activity less in digging great canals, one of which connected Ur with the Persian Gulf, thereby enabling vessels to unload at the quays of the city. Generally speaking, the prosperity of the country, alike from agriculture and from commerce, reached its zenith, and the standard of life was higher than at any subsequent period in its history. Against this must be set the fact that arts and crafts were in a decadent state. To quote Woolley : " Only architecture and sculpture in the round equal or outstrip the effort of a younger civilization." The overthrow of this prosperous empire was sudden. The Amorites under Ishbi-Irra of Mari, invaded Akkad, and the Elamites crossed the Tigris. In the words of the chronicler, " Ur was smitten with weapons," and the glory of Sumer as an independent nation departed for ever.

Isin, Larsa, and Elam.—On page 71 some details are given about the states of Isin and Larsa, which it is now possible to amplify. Ishbi-Irra founded a dynasty at Isin, which ruled for five generations. But, practically at the same time, a rival state was founded at Larsa, situated at the head of the marshes of the lower Euphrates and only distant seventy miles from Isin. This curious state of affairs can best be explained by the fact that Elam, which had not directly annexed any Sumerian territory after the overthrow of the empire of Ur, although its last King " went in fetters to Elam and wept and fell," was protecting Larsa.

The Amorite dynasty was permeated with Sumerian culture, as is proved by the transfer of its capital to Isin, where it set to work to rebuild the cities of Sumer that had suffered in the invasion. As was inevitable, hostilities broke out between the two rival states, in which Isin was, at first, victorious. But the scene changes, and we find Warad-Sin, an Elamite, enthroned at Larsa, which was reduced to the state of a vassal kingdom by his father, Kudur-Mabug, King of Western Elam. A few years later, under Rim-Sin, Isin was taken, with the result that the whole of Sumer and part of Akkad was ruled by the Elamite monarch.

During this period the Western Semites had been growing in power and had founded a dynasty at Babylon. Hammurabi, the great figure of the age, ascended the throne just after Rim-Sin's capture of Isin, which state had been allied to Babylon. For some years Hammurabi did not feel himself strong enough to take up the challenge. When he did so, he seized Isin and and then waited twenty-five years. By this time Rim-Sin was very old and Hammurabi drove the Elamites back to their own country, and thereby made himself supreme ruler of Sumer and Akkad.

The Greatness of Sumer.—In summing up the claims of Sumer to immortality, Woolley points out that the prehistoric civilization of Egypt and that of Sumer have nothing in common. He then goes on to state that, between prehistoric Egypt and the First Dynasty of Egypt, there were changes, amounting to a new culture, which were due to foreign influence. In its early stages we have mace-heads of stone, cylinder-seals and stone vases of Sumerian manufacture, and, in view of the recently proved greater antiquity of the civilization of the lower Euphrates, there is no question that Egypt was deeply indebted to Sumer. To go farther, our fathers were taught that we owed to Hellas all our arts and our entire civilization, and it is only in the present generation that it has been acknowledged that the Greeks learned from Crete, from Lydia, from Persia, and from Egypt. But, behind all these great centres of civilization was Sumer, the great Mother of Arts and Civilization.

(*To be read with Chapter X.*)

A recently discovered clay tablet has shed new light of great importance on the downfall of Assyria. It is written by a Babylonian scribe to recount the chief events that occurred during the tenth to the seventeenth years of the reign of Nabopolassar, or B.C. 616-609.

From this record we learn that Nineveh fell in 612, but that a body of the garrison broke through the besiegers' lines and set up a new King at Harran, where he maintained his position for a short time, with ever increasing difficulty. Probably the end came with the defeat, at Carchemish in 605, of Necho, who had evidently marched to his assistance.

(To be read with Vol. I., p. 270.)

The important discovery made by Sir Aurel Stein in 1926 of the site of Aornos,[1] the scene of perhaps the most splendid feat of arms of Alexander the Great, affords a good opportunity for reconsidering the whole question of the campaign in India, on which so much fresh light has been shed.

The main body marched from the neighbourhood of Kabul, by a route that lay to the north of the Khyber Pass, to the Lower Swat Valley, with instructions to prepare the passage of the Indus, which was, it is now believed, crossed a few miles above Attock. Alexander led a picked force into the mountains to the north in pursuance of his policy of leaving no possible enemy unsubdued on his flanks. He marched up the fertile and populous Kunar Valley, and, traversing the range to the east, invaded the land of the Assakenoi, who inhabited the Swat Valley. This Aryan people, although strong enough to raise an army which included elephants, feared to meet Alexander in the field and decided instead to defend their fortified cities. Stein, who was the first European explorer to tread in the footsteps of mighty Iskandar in this area, identifies the cities, and, using the lucid account of Arrian, takes us to Massaga, Bazira, and Ora. The capture of the last-named stronghold concluded the campaign in the Swat Valley, the dispirited Assakenoi fleeing eastwards into the Indus Valley, where they occupied the natural fortress of Aornos. Alexander thereupon marched south and rejoined his main body in the Indus.

The reason that prompted the "Lord of the Two Horns" to undertake what was, in effect, a new expedition against Aornos was surely due to the desire to accomplish a great feat

[1] *On Alexander's Track to the Indus*, by Sir Aurel Stein.

of arms, rather than owing to any military necessity. Under Stein's guidance we are led to the famous stronghold on a great precipitous mountain, situated in a bend of the Oxus, and now termed Pirsar. Not only did Stein discover this stronghold, but, with Arrian as his guide, he traces the difficult operations, which included filling up a ravine with earth and timber, and finally in the present Una Peak he discovers the origin of Aornos.

(To be read with Chapter XLI.)

During the course of his journey across Eastern Persia in 1915, Sir Aurel Stein visited the Kuh-i-Khoja, the Sacred Hill of Sistan.[1] There, thanks to his remarkable flair and knowledge, he discovered the first pre-Moslem mural paintings found in Persia, and dating from Sasanian times. The most striking of these was a portrait of Rustam, the mighty champion, seated, "holding a curved mace painted in red with yellow ornaments. The head of the mace was in the form of an ox-head, this corresponding with the famous *gurz* of Rustam. In a position of worship stands a three-headed figure, which in treatment is similar to figures discovered in Chinese Turkestan."

Among other wall paintings was "a robed figure, standing and nearly life-size, which in pose and dress distinctly had the typical appearance of a Bodhisattra, as made familiar by Central Asian Buddhist sculptures and frescoes."

The importance of these discoveries is considerable, as proving the wide range of Buddhist art, and it is possible that these paintings were executed to the order of Sakae rulers, who gave its name to Sakistan, the modern Sistan.[2]

While dealing with the question of the fresh light that has been shed on Sasanian art by Sir Aurel Stein, a passing reference must be made to the important part played by the Sarmatians, an Iranian tribe which settled in the steppes of South Russia.[3] In the fourth century A.D., apparently in alliance with the Goths, they invaded the Crimea; they also pressed hard on the Danubian frontier of the Roman Empire. As a result of this connexion, the Sarmatians taught the Germanic tribe cloisonné, with the garnet as the stone chiefly employed, and this art

---

[1] *Innermost Asia*, by Sir Aurel Stein (Clarendon Press, 1928), ch. xxviii. p. 915.
[2] I. 433.
[3] Vide *Iranians and Greeks in South Russia*, by M. Rostovtzeff (Clarendon Press, 1922).

spread all over the Roman Empire to France and to England. In the latter country the art was confined to Kent, and "exhibits an interesting and original development characteristic of the rich civilization which flourished there from the fourth to the sixth century." So widespread was Persian art in the Sasanian period.

DARIUS HUNTING LIONS.
(Agate Cylinder Seal in British Museum.)

CHAPTER I

CONFIGURATION AND CLIMATE

There is a certain tawny nudity of the South, bare sunburnt plains, coloured like a lion, and hills clothed only in the blue transparent air.—R. L. STEVENSON.

A lamp gives no light in the Sun :
And a lofty minaret looks mean on the slopes of Alvand.
The *Gulistan* of Sadi.

The Situation of Persia.—Between the valleys of the Indus on the east and of the Tigris on the west rises what is generally termed the Iranian plateau. Persia fills the western and larger portion of this elevated tract, the eastern portion being occupied by Afghanistan and Baluchistan. These countries are surrounded on all sides by gigantic ranges, which are highest on the west and north, and the interior is divided into two chief basins. That on the west, which includes about three-fifths of Persia and is subdivided into many smaller basins, joins the eastern, the basin of Sistan, not very far from the province of that name. This latter area is chiefly drained by the classical Etymander, now termed the Helmand, and by minor rivers most of which, in flood time at any rate, discharge into the *hamun* or lake of Sistan.

In altitude the plateau exceeds 5000 feet at Kerman, 5000 at Shiraz, and 3000 in the region of the great northern cities of Teheran and Meshed, while Tabriz, in the extreme north-west, exceeds 4000. Of the central cities, Isfahan exceeds 5000 feet, and Yezd 4000. These figures are of interest, for they bring out the contrast between the inhabited part of the plateau and the great desert which occupies the heart of the country and lies considerably lower, although rising almost everywhere above 2000 feet.

Boundaries and Provinces.—In describing the boundaries of Persia I propose also to refer to its chief provinces, which almost all lie away from the centre and within reach of the frontiers.

The eastern province of Khorasan is bounded on the north by a series of ranges which rise in stern beauty above the steppes of Turkestan. Some years ago I visited the extraordinary natural fortress of Kalat-i-Nadiri [1] and climbed its northern wall, which is one of the mountains in this range. From the crest I looked across the yellow plain, stretching northwards in level monotony, and was struck by its immensity; for I realized that it extended as far as the tundra and the distant Arctic Ocean, with no intervening mountains. This range does not form the Persian boundary throughout, but, under the names of Kopet Dagh and Little Balkans, runs off in a north-westerly direction to the Caspian Sea. A little farther west, just within the limits of Iran, lie the rich valleys of the Atrek and Gurgan. In its lower reaches the Atrek forms the Russo-Persian boundary until it discharges into the Caspian Sea.

The district of Kuchan, which lies on both banks of the upper Atrek, is the richest in Khorasan and, like Bujnurd lower down the valley, is inhabited by Kurdish tribes which were transplanted from the Turkish frontier by Shah Abbas to act as "Wardens of the Marches." The valley of the Gurgan is also naturally rich, with an abundant rainfall and fertile lands ; but at present most of the country is inhabited by only a few thousand families of nomadic or semi-nomadic Turkoman belonging to the Yamut and Goklan tribes.

The Gurgan district was the classical Hyrcania, and the Vehrkano of the Avesta, and was famous for its fertility Strabo wrote : "It is said that in Hyrcania each vine produces seven gallons of wine and each fig-tree ninety bushels of fruit. That the grains of wheat which fall from the husk on to the earth, spring up the following year ; that bee-hives are in the trees, and the leaves flow with honey." [2]

In the central section of the northern frontier the rich

---

[1] *Vide Journal R.G.S.*, December 1906.
[2] Strabo, ii. 1. 14 (translation by Hamilton and Falconer).

maritime provinces of Mazanderan and Gilan lie between the great Elburz range and the Caspian Sea, and present a complete contrast to upland Persia by reason of their heavy rainfall and mild climate and the dense forests these produce. To the west of Gilan, Persia again marches with Russia, the boundary, since the treaty of Turkomanchai,[1] running from the frontier port of Astara almost due north until it strikes the River Aras, which in its upper reaches divides the two countries. At the north-west corner is the superb mountain mass of Ararat, the Hebrew form of Urartu, where the three empires of Russia, Turkey, and Persia meet.

The north-west province of Iran is Azerbaijan, with its chief centre, Tabriz, the largest city in Persia, situated at a point where roads from the distant Bosphorus and from Trebizond meet others from the Caucasus and the valley of the Tigris. Here the great trunk route into Persia and Central Asia is entered. The rainfall is more abundant than in the districts lying to the east, and the province is very fertile. As these pages will show, it has always played an important part in Persian history.

On the west Persia is bounded by the valleys of the Tigris and Euphrates. On this flank parallel, serrated mountains, in range after range, known to the ancients as the Zagros, divide the Iranian plateau from the plains. These rise gently, and not sheer to their full height, as do the mountains of the Armenian plateau when approached from the south. The classical empires of Media and of Persia came into existence in these bracing uplands, which are comparatively well-watered and fertile so far as the hill country is concerned ; though the interior districts of Kum, Kashan, and Isfahan are arid and almost rainless.

To the west of the southern section of this barrier is the rich valley of the Karun, now the province of Arabistan, which, under the name of Elam, was the first portion of Persia to be civilized, centuries before the Aryans appeared on the scene. To the south the plateau containing the provinces of Fars and Kerman looks down upon a narrow, low-lying strip of country bordering the Persian Gulf, termed the *Garmsir* or " Hot Country " ; and here again intercourse has been made exceptionally difficult by nature, with the

---

[1] *Vide* Chapter LXXVI.

result that Persians, who are no engineers, have ever been averse from the sea.[1]

The province of Fars is much drier, and consequently less fertile in the east than in the west, and the interior district of Yezd is more or less a sandy desert. The province of Kerman, too, is saved only by the height of its ranges from hopeless aridity. In Kerman, and still more in Persian Baluchistan, which marches with British Baluchistan, there are large semi-desert areas apart from the barren Lut.

In Persian Baluchistan, where the ranges, which invariably run parallel to the coast, trend more east and west, communication with the sea is equally difficult; and north of this outlying province is Sistan, the delta of the Helmand, with a solitary hill, Kuh-i-Khwaja, on which Sir Aurel Stein discovered ruins and frescoes of the first Buddhist sanctuary ever traced on Persian soil.[2] Farther north, again, a desert divides Persia from Afghanistan until the Hari Rud is struck at the point where it makes its great bend from west to due north. Known in its lower reaches as the Tejen, this river divides the two countries until, at Zulfikar Pass, the kingdom of the Amir ends and two boundary pillars—which I saw, from the Persian side of the river, shining in the sun—mark the spot where, some thirty-five years ago, the Russo-Afghan Boundary Commission began its labours. The Tejen continues to form the boundary of Persia as far as Sarakhs, which is situated at the north-east corner of Iran, and only a few miles from grim Kalat-i-Nadiri, where our survey started.

To summarize, upland Persia is strongly protected by titanic natural ramparts along her northern frontier, except where the Tejen breaks through into the sands of Turkestan. Along the western frontier the ramparts are still more serrated, and the only natural route—a difficult one—passes through Kasr-i-Shirin, Kermanshah, and Hamadan. Farther south, the modern province of Arabistan, lying in the rich valley of the Karun, has never been fully and permanently absorbed by Persia, owing to the difficult ranges which cut it off from the province of Fars. The coast districts along the Persian Gulf, too, have always been separated from the uplands and,

---

[1] To give a single example, Abdur Razzak, mentioned in Chapter LX., wrote: "As soon as I caught the smell of the vessel, and all the terrors of the sea presented themselves to me, I fell into so deep a swoon that for three days respiration alone indicated that life remained within me."—*India in the Fifteenth Century* (Hakluyt Society).

[2] "Third Journey of Exploration in Central Asia" in *Journal R.G.S.*, Aug. and Sept. 1916.

like Arabistan, inhabited by a non-Aryan people : and even to-day few Persians can keep their health if forced to reside at the ports on the Persian Gulf. Persian Baluchistan is a distant province of torrid deserts, where the authority of the Shah is weak. On the east, in the southern section, the deserts of British Baluchistan are as hopelessly arid and as great an obstacle to intercourse as can be imagined. But where the boundary marches with North-West Afghanistan, the routes are wide and easy. This accounts for the fact that until comparatively recently Afghanistan was a Persian province. The last campaign in which a Persian sovereign took part in person was the attempt to recover Herat in 1838. To-day, however, although Persia welcomes Afghans, who are the chief owners of camel transport, no Persian or other foreigner can enter the kingdom of the Amir without running risk, and Afghanistan can now claim the doubtful title of being the last Hermit Kingdom in Asia.

Meaning of Iran and of Persia.—Persians call their country Iran and themselves Irani, a word which is the Airiya of the Avesta and signifies the "land of the Aryans" or "Illustrious." Thus the modern meaning of Iran is restricted when used in a political sense to apply to modern Persia only ; and the geographical use of the term Iranian plateau to include part of Baluchistan and also Afghanistan is, strictly speaking, more correct. The term " Persia," employed by Europeans and most other foreigners, is derived from the classical Persis. This latter word signified the province of Parsa, now Fars, which gave birth to the ruling dynasty of the Achaemenians, and in consequence had its meaning extended so as to include the entire country and also its people. Even to-day the province of Fars is held to be the most typically Persian province in the empire. The word *farsi* is employed by the Persians to describe their own language, although, when applied to an individual, it is restricted to an inhabitant of the province of Fars. It should be added that the Parsis of India are so called from being followers of the old Persian religion. Parsi is the Persian word, and Farsi its Arabic form which has been generally adopted, there being no *p* in the Arabic language. The term Farsistan, which some European writers affect, is incorrect.

The Formation of the Iranian Plateau.—Much work still remains to be done on the geology of Persia, many portions of it having never been visited by a geologist. At the same time it is possible to give in outline an account of the origin and history of the Iranian plateau, which would appear to be sufficient for our purpose.

During the latter part of the Cretaceous period most of Persia was under the sea. An important exception was a strip of country, which ran across what are now the straits of Hormuz, in continuation of the mountain chain of Oman and the peninsula of Musandam, and extended in a broad belt, at first northward through portions of the provinces of Fars and Kerman, and then north-westward between Kerman and Niriz, through the Isfahan province into Azerbaijan and the Caucasus. The tract to the eastward of this old land area was elevated into dry land early in the Eocene period, and, except near the coast, has never since been submerged.

The region which lay to the south-west of the old land surface continued to be open sea throughout the Eocene and most of the Oligocene periods. In the Miocene period movements of the sea floor separated portions of the Persian water area from the main body of the ocean, converting much of it into inland seas and lakes, which by their evaporation produced the great beds of salt and rock-gypsum that characterize this part of Persia. The land of Iran was, at this period, still cut off from land communication with Europe, and it was not until the very end of the Miocene period that much of the country occupied by these large bodies of water was elevated. The establishment of a land connexion between the two continents coincides with the migration of the Asiatic land-fauna to Europe, where its fossil remains have been found in abundance in Upper Miocene and Pliocene deposits.

No doubt the elevation of the Iranian plateau proceeded throughout the Pliocene period, but by far the most intense uplift seems to have occurred at the close of the Pliocene. Numerous lakes, many of them of great size, existed on the Persian plateau during the Pleistocene as they probably had in Pliocene times, and the country was covered by forests and meadows supported by a humid climate, probably even more so than that of the Caspian provinces to-day. The gradual drying up of these lakes is a phenomenon which is still in operation at the present day. We must include amongst the lake areas that region which is now occupied by the plains of Mesopotamia and the Persian Gulf. Much of this may even have been a large inland sea, but, in any case, there is distinct evidence that the old land stretching across the Straits of Hormuz was not finally submerged until after the Pleistocene period, since the traces of buried valleys beneath the sea in the neighbourhood of Musandam are still apparent, and lake deposits of recent age are to be seen in Mesopotamia as well as in some of the islands of the Persian Gulf.

During a portion of the Pleistocene period the Persian plateau, in common with Europe and Central Asia, may have experienced the rigours of the glacial epoch, and may have been buried beneath glaciers, and have been uninhabitable for long periods, which may be reckoned in millennia.[1] After these cataclysms what was left in Persia ? Vast lakes of salt water occupying what is now the great desert ; lofty, bare ranges covered by receding glaciers ; the sea penetrating into the continent, and volcanoes such as Ararat, Demavand, Sahand, and Taftan vomiting out destruction and death. The Iranian plateau was indeed at this period a land of death.

But on its western side the action of the numerous rivers began. By these soil was brought down and gradually formed a land, which was not only inhabitable, but was destined in the course of the ages—owing partly, at any rate, to its natural advantages—to be the home of what was among the earliest civilizations of the world.

The Resemblance of Persia to Spain.—In many ways Persia resembles Spain to a remarkable degree. The traveller from the north no sooner quits France than he rises through the Pyrenees on to a plateau of an average height of between two and three thousand feet, where the jagged ranges are aptly termed Sierras or " Saws," and where the country is generally bare and treeless. Traversing this great plateau for some four hundred miles, he crosses the " hot country " of Andalusia, which corresponds to the low-lying coast district of Persia, before the sea is reached. Again to the north, as if to complete the analogy, the provinces bordering on the Biscayan Sea differ from the Spain of the plateau as the Caspian provinces do from the rest of Persia. Moreover, although Persians are termed the French of the East, it would

---

[1] I am much indebted for the above information to Dr. G. E. Pilgrim of the Geological Survey of India, who is publishing the results of his discoveries in South Persia and Mesopotamia.

be more apt to compare them with the Spaniards, whose customs and whole manner of life are akin to the Persian.

The Aridity of Central Asia.—Central Asia, of which Persia forms a part, is mainly composed of deserts, and although the variations in elevation are stupendous, ranging from the Caspian Sea and the basin of Turfan, which lie below sea-level, to the Pamirs and Tibet, where the traveller is seldom below 10,000 feet, yet everywhere, except in the actual ranges, aridity is the marked feature common to all countries alike, whether Turkestan, Persia, Afghanistan, Tibet, or Baluchistan. This aridity, which is due to the scanty rainfall, results in rivers of such weak volume that they fail to reach the sea. From this cause the whole enormous area, stretching for some three thousand miles from east to west, is composed of basins, none of which have any outlets. Again, owing to the scanty rainfall, there are immense desiccated areas, and the whole region may be described as consisting partly of desert pure and simple, and partly of desert tempered by oases. In other words, we are dealing with a vast area in which cultivated districts capable of sustaining population are rare and far apart. To put it another way, if the desert tracts could be removed, the cultivable districts would together make up a very small country. I lay considerable stress on this fact ; for dwellers in Europe, where almost the whole of the land is valuable owing mainly to abundant rainfall, can with difficulty realize the utterly different conditions which prevail in Central Asia.[1]

The Climate of Persia.—The marked feature therefore of Persia and of Central Asia generally is aridity.

The Rainfall.—The amount of rainfall on the plateau is now observed, mainly at the offices of the Indo-European Telegraph Department, and, thanks to the courtesy of Mr. Gilbert Walker, Director-General of Observatories in India, I am able to give the following table, which is based on observations taken for a period of ten years :

Jask	4.17	inches annual rainfall.
Bushire . . .	11.07	,, ,,
Isfahan . . .	4.74	,, ,,
Teheran . . .	9.30	,, ,,
Meshed . . .	9.37	,, ,,

---

[1] This question has been dealt with in a remarkable book termed *The Pulse of Asia*, written by Ellsworth Huntington. His main thesis of a progressive desiccation in Central Asia has by no means gained universal acceptance, but no writer on the subject can neglect his works.

In view of the latitude and the power of the sun, the amount of rainfall here shown compares most unfavourably with the 39.5 inches of the British Isles and their cloudy skies, or the 27.65 inches of the Delhi District.

Persia, both in its situation and its physical conformation, is unfortunate so far as rainfall is concerned, since the high ranges intercept the greater portion of the moisture-laden clouds, which discharge very freely in the Caspian provinces, but rarely cross the Elburz. Nothing is more striking than to stand on this gigantic rampart with luxuriant forest-clad slopes on its northern face and an absolutely naked prospect to the south when once the crest is reached. Fortunately such moisture as there is (snow in terms of water being included in the table given above) falls mainly during the winter and spring, when the " treasures of the snow . . . reserved against the time of trouble."[1] can be stored in the mountains to replenish springs, on which the irrigation of the country depends. Indeed, but for the high ranges the whole of the plateau would be a desert ; and, conversely, the size of the cities and the destiny of the population depend on the height and width of the range from which the water-supply is drawn. In a huge country like Persia it is obvious that the amount of rainfall must vary. Central, South-Eastern, and Eastern Persia are less favoured than other parts. In Khorasan, for example, in a good year 65 per cent of the grain crops are *daima* or rain-fed, whereas in South-East Persia all crops have to be kept alive by irrigation, and there are practically no rain-fed crops at all.

It has already been pointed out that in the Caspian provinces the conditions are entirely unlike those which prevail elsewhere. Instead of a treeless, arid country, there is jungle too dense to traverse. The rainfall exceeds 50 inches, and moisture is everywhere so abundant that the climate is generally fatal to Persians of the plateau. These in turn entirely fail to appreciate the natural wealth of the three Caspian provinces of Astrabad, Mazanderan, and Gilan.

Cold and Heat.—Persia is a land of extremes in climate : yet the atmosphere is one of the most invigorating and delightful imaginable. In winter the thermometer occasionally sinks below zero in the plains and frequently in the mountains ; but, if the weather be fine, the cold is seldom

[1] Job xxxviii. 23.

trying, and it is delightful to spend whole days in the open throughout the winter. Yet the waves of cold can be intense, and every winter men and animals are frozen to death when caught in a blizzard far from shelter. In the uplands snow lies occasionally for four or five months, preventing all agricultural operations, and causing heavy loss to live stock. Considered, however, as a whole, the Persian winter is as near perfection as can be imagined, and if the traveller sometimes has to walk the entire stage because it is too cold to ride, he experiences in return such a sense of vigour and vitality as is rarely felt in less dry and less bracing climates.

Let us now take the opposite extreme and seek an example of a torrid climate. In this respect Arabistan bears the palm with its capital Shuster (more correctly Shushtar), perhaps the hottest place on earth. I shall never forget my experience there in the month of June 1896, with the thermometer registering the shade temperature with monotonous regularity at 129°, and the withering heat-waves reflected off the low rocks, which also kept off any cooling breeze from the north. The Persian Gulf, too, is perhaps the hottest body of sea in the world, and I recollect feeling the Red Sea comparatively cool after experiencing the heat of "The Gulf." On the plateau the conditions are quite different; for, as a rule, the heat during the day is not trying and the nights are invariably cool. In fact at Meshed the highest recorded night temperature during 1912 was 74°, and the highest day temperature 102°, in the same year. Outside, however, in the open country the heat, and still more the glare, are very trying, and caravans usually travel by night. The proximity of mountains makes it easy almost everywhere to seek a hill retreat during the hottest months; and at Teheran, at Meshed, at Kerman, and indeed at most places on the plateau, there are cool resorts within a few hours' ride, and these amenities make the summer months delightful.

Wind.—The winds of Persia blow with remarkable uniformity either from the north-west or from the south-east. The reason for this is the situation of the Atlantic Ocean and Mediterranean and Black Seas in the one direction, and of the Indian Ocean[1] in the other. The bearing of the

---

[1] I have to thank Mr. Gilbert Walker for the following valuable note: "From October to April the southernmost storms from the Atlantic travel over Italy, the eastern Mediterranean, and Syria; and a large proportion—I believe at least 60 per cent—pass on into Mesopotamia, Persia, Afghanistan, or Baluchistan and the plains of India."

axes of the mountain ranges, too, lies mainly in the same direction. As the powerful sun beats on the treeless plains it produces a stratum of heated air, and this, as it rises, draws a current of colder air mainly from the north-west. The prevalent wind in the autumn and winter is north-westerly, and in the spring and summer south-easterly. The close juxtaposition of high ranges with low-lying tracts and the absence of trees all make for windiness. There are, indeed, various unfortunate districts where there blows an almost perpetual gale. In the case of a valley in the province of Kerman which runs down somewhat abruptly from 8000 feet to 3000 feet, this characteristic is recorded in the following lines :

> They asked the wind, " Where is thy home ? "
> It replied, " My poor home is in Tahrud : but occasionally I tour round Abarik and Sarvistan."

But it is in Sistan that the wind displays its fullest strength. There blows the famous " Wind of one hundred and twenty days," with a maximum velocity of seventy-two miles an hour. This summer gale is known in the Herat valley as the " Wind of Herat," and probably originates in the Pamirs. It then follows down the Perso-Afghan frontier, and its power ceases a few stages south of Sistan. Its maximum velocity is attained at Lash-Juwein in Afghan Sistan, and one can only feel sorry for the unfortunate inhabitants. To give some idea of what gales are in Sistan, Sir Henry McMahon reported one in March 1905, which blew at the rate of one hundred and twenty miles an hour.[1] It is possible that this wind suggested the invention of windmills, which were known in Persia before the Arab conquest, and long before they were invented in Europe. This fact is brought out clearly in Masudi,[2] where it is narrated that the Persian slave who assassinated Omar knew how to construct windmills. To-day in Persia these windmills are found only in the districts where this wind blows.

The Climate of Ancient Persia.—The importance of climate in its effect alike upon the configuration of a land and upon its people, its government, and its history is so great that it is of considerable interest to know whether there has been any change in historical times.

---

[1] *Journal R.G.S.* for October 1906.
[2] *Vide* Chapter XLVI.

Huntington[1] has devoted a chapter to this very question, in which in addition to noting the changes towards aridity in the basins of Lop, Turfan, and Sistan, all of which he carefully examined, he has quoted my views to the effect that Persian Baluchistan and Kerman must have been more fertile when Alexander the Great traversed them some 2200 years ago than they are to-day.[2] Take, for instance, one section of the Mighty Greek's journey, from Bampur in Baluchistan to the district of Rudbar in the Kerman province.[3] Throughout the distance of one hundred and fifty miles I did not find a single village or hamlet, and the whole country is now only fit for occupation by nomads. It is impossible to believe that the Greek army could have traversed the desert as it is to-day without great difficulty ; whereas Arrian shows that when once the Bampur Valley had been reached the army found enough supplies to feed it for two months. After this the refreshed heroes marched in comfort across Southern Persia, by the route which our party was enabled to traverse only by means of forage and all other supplies laid out in advance at every stage. Huntington also gives other examples drawn from various sources, all of which tend to show that the aridity of Persia is increasing. It is of course difficult to distinguish between deforestation caused by man and continued by his flocks and the deforestation which is due entirely to change of climate. In any case it is of interest to note that in the central portion of Khorasan, termed Kuhistan in ancient times and mentioned in the Avesta,[4] there was a great forest known as the "White Forest," of which not a vestige is left to-day. And yet, were the rainfall a few inches heavier, forests would be able to reproduce themselves. To take a second instance in the history of Mohamed Ibrahim,[5] the Chief of Jiruft stated that he was quite safe against attack from Kerman, "owing to the rugged ranges and thickly wooded spurs." This was in the eleventh century of our era : and to-day, in the whole of the splendid mountains to the south of Kerman, which are referred to in the passage quoted above, there are only a few old junipers which are not reproducing themselves.

There is of course the hypothesis that war and mis-

---

[1] *The Pulse of Asia*, chap. xvi.   [2] *Ten Thousand Miles, etc.*, chap. xiv.
[3] *Vide op. cit.* p. 144.   [4] William Jackson's *Zoroaster*, p. 215.
[5] For Mohamed Ibrahim *vide* Chapter LI.

government, the effects of which are shown in deforestation and in other ways, have caused the depopulation of Persia ; and to a certain extent this is true, as will appear in this book. Moreover, the traveller who sees the ruins of deserted towns does not always realize that in Persia the sites of towns and villages were frequently changed after an earthquake or an outbreak of plague, or for other reasons. Again, if he visits Persia in the winter he is apt to take an exaggerated view of its aridity. But no theory based on considerations such as these can weigh against the absolute proof that, in the Lop basin for instance, there was in the Middle Ages a dense population living on lands irrigated from a river which has now ceased to flow, and that in the Turfan basin the underground channels termed *Kanat* were not introduced until comparatively recently.

Again, many years ago, when travelling from Panjgur on the Perso-Baluch frontier to Quetta,[1] I traversed a country devoid of all inhabitants ; yet the hillsides for mile after mile were carefully terraced and had evidently supported a dense population whose crops were rain-fed, where to-day there are only wells of bad water at long intervals, and where rain-fed crops would be quite out of the question. Nor had this population disappeared before the dawn of history. On the contrary, the pottery which littered the sites of their towns was of about from the tenth to the thirteenth century of our era. At the time I attributed the disappearance of all population from a tract measuring two hundred miles from west to east to deforestation and war, and I did not realize that this was but one illustration of a larger question which included the whole of Central Asia. Similar deserted tracts have also been noted in Kharan, now a hopelessly arid district, and they perhaps supply the strongest of all proofs that aridity has increased on the Iranian plateau.

Population.—The present population of Iran is estimated to be about ten millions,[2] and there may be perhaps two million Persians living in the Russian, Turkish, and Indian empires. Before the era of sea transport there is no doubt

---

[1] *Ten Thousand Miles, etc.*, p. 234. I have also consulted Sven Hedin's *Overland to India*, chap. l.; Stein's *Ruins of Desert Cathay, passim*; and *Is the Earth drying up?* by Prof. Gregory (*Journal R.G.S.* for February and March 1914).

[2] Divided into nine million Shias, nine hundred thousand Sunnis, eighty thousand Christians (Armenians, Nestorians, Greek Orthodox, Roman Catholics, Protestants), thirty-six thousand Jews, and ten thousand Zoroastrians. *Vide* article on "Persia" in 11th edition of the *Encyclopædia Britannica*.

that the cities of Persia were generally larger and more prosperous than at present, as the greater caravan traffic must have provided a living for thousands of families along the main routes apart from the benefits conferred on the agricultural class. Moreover, as already explained, it is at least possible that the rainfall was heavier and the agricultural capabilities of the country were greater at earlier periods than to-day. Again, certain districts such as Astrabad are suffering from being overrun by nomads. But after making these allowances it is difficult to believe that the plateau has ever been more than sparsely peopled, and in my opinion it is an error to suppose that in respect of population it ever resembled modern Europe. It is impossible to make an accurate estimate ; but, if we consider the much larger volume of traffic which passed across " the Highway of the Nations " before the era of sea transport, and the fact that Persia was generally the seat of a great empire, even although the capital was rarely on the plateau, I am inclined to suggest that fifteen millions may have lived in the country which now supports but two-thirds of that number.

The Mountains of the Iranian Plateau.—Persia is not, as is sometimes stated, merely a vast plain surrounded by exterior mountain chains. On the contrary, practically in every part there are detached parallel ranges with valleys averaging twenty miles in width, this formation being repeated with a monotony which is exasperating to the traveller whose journey lies at right angles to their trend. Limestone is the prevailing rock material from the Elburz in the north to the Baluchistan ranges in the south ; but gypsum, saliferous beds, conglomerate sand, and alluvial shingle are frequently found. The central masses of the hills are occasionally formed of red sandstone and arenaceous shales : limestone is, however, much more frequent. As the gypsum and saliferous deposits are soluble, and are thus affected by the melting snows, these substances have been carried down into the plains and have thereby produced the dreary areas covered with salt crystals, of which there is a good example near Nishapur.

The gigantic gravel slopes are a striking feature. That which extends from the Elburz is enormous, having a width of some sixteen miles. Its depth, too, is great. When experiments were made at Teheran, which is built on the slope, with a view to obtaining water by means of artesian wells, the boring at 500 feet was still on the gravel, and so the attempt was abandoned. As Teheran is some ten miles from the range, what must be the depth of the gravel at the base?

The Northern Ranges.—Of the great frontier ranges, those to the north start from the Pamirs, the most elevated valleys in Asia, which in Persian phraseology are well termed *Bam-i-Dunia*, or "The Roof of the World." Thence, under the names Hindu Kush, Kuh-i-Baba, and other terms, they run south of west, forming a great natural rampart across the entire length of Afghanistan until, north of Herat, they subside into rolling downs. It is of interest to note that the Greeks realized the magnitude of this range; for Arrian writes: "This range of mountains stretches out so far that they say even that Mount Taurus, which forms the boundary of Cilicia and Pamphylia, springs from it, as do other great ranges."[1]

To resume, on the western side of the Tejen, the ranges recover their original height and, under various names, run in a westerly direction for some hundreds of miles. South of the Caspian Sea the chain is termed the Elburz and the stupendous volcanic peak of Demavand is thrown up. Rising to an altitude exceeding 19,000 feet, this is the loftiest mountain of the continent of Asia west of the Himalayas, the height of historical Ararat not exceeding 17,000 feet. The trend of the range in this section changes from west to north-west as it passes to the south of the Caspian Sea and, after being pierced by the Kizil Uzun, the longest river in Persia, it terminates in the superb ranges which culminate in the crown of Ararat. In the elevated basin of the Lake of Van the mountains of the Armenian plateau, with their approximate west to east trend, of which the main range of northern Iran is a continuation, meet the Persian orographic system with its parallel chains running from north-west to south-east. It is to be noted that, although this northern range is the most important from the point of view of altitude, it is narrow and does not constitute a belt of mountainous

---

[1] *Vide* Chinnock's *Arrian*, Book III. chap. xxviii. p. 197. Arrian terms the range the Caucasus, whereas the Indian Caucasus was a more usual term; but Parapamisus or Parapanisus is the more correct name for the range, and Caucasus was vaguely applied to it as being at the end of the known world. Strabo, Book XI. chap. viii., states that the "heights and northern parts" of the Parapamisus were called Emoda. This name is akin to the modern Himalaya and is derived from a Sanscrit word parallel to the Greek $\chi\epsilon\iota\mu\omega\nu$ and the Latin *hiems* (winter).

country in the same sense as the parallel ranges of the Zagros. Consequently on the southern slopes, in the eastern section at any rate, the water-supply barely suffices to support a few scattered oases, and the desert sometimes actually touches the skirt of the mountains.

The Southern Ranges.—Starting again from the Pamirs, the main southern range, under various names, runs south-west through Afghanistan and Baluchistan towards the Arabian Sea. Here it diminishes in height and runs westward, parallel to the coast, for some hundreds of miles, until, to the south-east of Kerman, the regular north-westerly trend parallel to the Persian Gulf begins. High peaks exceeding 13,000 feet, such as Kuh-i-Hezar and Kuh-i-Lalazar, are thrown up in this section where the system constitutes the central range of Persia. The western frontier of Persia also maintains a generally high altitude in its regular parallel ranges, until at the Ararat range, after having formed the segment of a circle, these great parallel ranges unite with the northern system.

Although the interior ranges cannot vie in importance with those which hold up the great plateau, yet they are often of considerable altitude. One of the most interesting is that of Kuh-i-Taftan,[1] which is a volcano in the solfatara stage and rises to a height of 13,268 feet close to the Perso-Baluch frontier. Farther west in the middle of the desert is situated Kuh-i-Bazman, an extinct volcano consisting of a singularly beautiful peak with an altitude of 11,175 feet. On the western side of Persia, Mount Alvand, the classical Orontes, which towers above Hamadan, is much better known than any of the ranges in Eastern Persia, because it is the most striking mountain on the historical route from Babylonia to Rhages. Elsewhere there are ranges which rise to considerable altitudes and provide numerous streams of water on which the crops depend. Indeed, in almost the whole of Persia there are a succession of ranges which generally decrease in height the farther they are from the outer walls : and even in the Lut the traveller crosses range after range of hills, most of which are parallel to the higher surrounding mountain chains.

One point I have not touched on. There are no glaciers in Persia, however high the mountains may be, although

[1] *Ten Thousand Miles, etc.*, pp. 132, 140.

KUH-I-TAFTAN.

(From *Frontiers of Baluchistan*, by G. P. Tate.)

traces of them have been found on the more important ranges. None of the many mountains I have climbed retains snow throughout the summer except where steep valleys with a northern aspect protect it from the powerful rays of the sun. Thus in the Kuh-i-Lalazar, which rises to nearly 14,000 feet to the south of Kerman, I have travelled on a snow bridge up the valley in July ; but higher up there were only large patches of snow and the summit was quite bare. Demavand has its crater filled with snow for the same reason. In Khorasan at an altitude of 9000 feet large patches of snow last occasionally through the summer, but no eternal snow, in the sense of a permanent snow-line, is to be found anywhere in Persia.

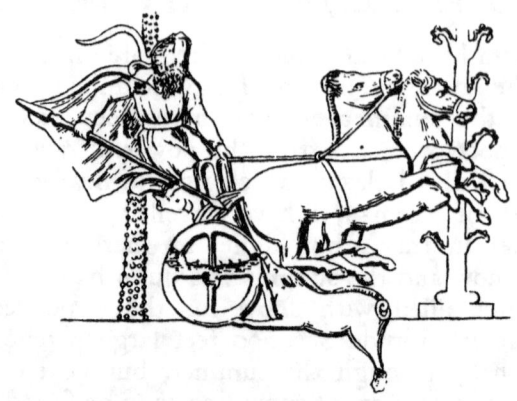

PART OF A PERSIAN HUNTING SCENE.
(From a Polychrome Terra-cotta Vase in the Hermitage Museum.)

CHAPTER II

DESERTS, RIVERS, FLORA, FAUNA, AND MINERALS

A desert of surpassing aridity . . . ; here are neither fruits nor trees to be seen, and what water there is is bitter and bad, so that you have to carry both food and water. The cattle must needs drink the bad water, will they nill they, because of their great thirst.—MARCO POLO on the Lut.

The second portion of Northern Asia begins from the Caspian Sea, which is a bay extending from the Ocean to the south.—STRABO, Bk. XI. chap. vi. § 1.

The Lut, the Desert of Persia.—A most important feature of Persia, which has impressed itself forcibly on the character, religion, and life of the people and also on its government, is the Great Desert. There has been a good deal of discussion as to whether there is a general name for this vast waste, and the facts appear to be that in the south of Persia the word Lut is used to indicate the whole desert, in which there are saline wastes termed *Kavir* ; whereas, in the north, there is much more water running into the desert, and consequently more and larger saline wastes, and there *Kavir* is the term generally used.[1] At the same time it appears that the word Lut is gradually becoming recognized as the one general name for the desert, while it is also used to express dry desert in opposition to salt desert.

The word, which is comparatively modern — the Arab

[1] This question is dealt with in my " Fifth Journey in Persia " (*Journal R.G.S.*, November and December 1906). Sven Hedin in his *Overland to India* also discusses the desert in great detail.

DESERTS, RIVERS, ETC.

geographers using the term *Mafazeh* or "wilderness"—originated from the circumstance that in more than one locality stories are told of ancient cities, or "Cities of Lot," which were destroyed by The Almighty with fire from heaven in the same manner as the cities of the plain where now roll the waters of the Dead Sea. The latter, it is to be noted, is locally termed "The Sea of Lot," Lut being the Koranic form of the name. The traveller who visits these "Cities" will see that they are merely bluffs worn by the elements until they—

> Form'd turret, dome, or battlement,
> Or seemed fantastically set
> With cupola or minaret.[1]

Taking into consideration the extent to which the Koran influences nomenclature in Persia, I have very little doubt that this is the true derivation of the term Lut.

The etymology of the word *Kavir* is uncertain, but it signifies a saline desert, whether dry or wet. During the course of my travels I have seen it under many forms. Sometimes the ground is white, level, and solid as ice. Again, it is hummocky, pock-marked, and almost impassable; to venture on it would mean to be engulfed in a bog of slime. These differences depend mainly on the quantity of water, and there is no doubt that if the water supply ceases the *Kavir* tends to become *Lut*. Almost every river or stream in Persia has on its banks a white efflorescence, which is composed of chloride of sodium with traces of alkali and is akin to *Kavir*.

The Lut is the manifestation in an extreme and concentrated form of the general aridity of Persia, itself surrounded by arid countries. It is more arid than other parts simply because of its position, which, being more central, is more unfavourable, both for rainfall and for receiving water from the high mountain ranges which encircle the comparatively low-lying plateau and keep off moisture from it. I have mentioned above how the inadequate water supply dries up and disappears, being unable to form trunk river systems powerful enough to force their way to the sea. Failing signally to do this, the scanty streams which, as a rule, are utterly undrinkable owing to their saltness, are lost in basins. Within these are immense gravel slopes, occasional salt lakes, and square miles of sandhills backed by naked,

[1] Scott, *The Lady of the Lake*.

jagged ranges or Persian Sierras, which complete a melancholy and depressing picture. Pierre Loti's description in *Le Désert* is so true and so beautifully expressed that I cannot refrain from quoting it :

C'est la désolation absolue, le grand triomphe incontesté de la mort . . . on est là comme dans les mondes finis, dépeuplés par le feu, qu'aucune rosée ne fécondera plus.

To cross the Lut means at the best bad water and the carriage of all supplies, including forage. At its worst it means being caught in a storm which is equally to be dreaded for its cold in winter or for its parching effect in summer; and the toll of the desert, levied on man and beast alike, is indeed a heavy one, whether the caravan sinks into the ochrous slime of the *Kavir* or is lost amid the terrible moving sandhills. In either case there are few survivors.

Among the agencies which produce such dire results are wind and the process of disintegration. In a humid country vegetation and moisture alike protect the surface of the soil ; but in a land where nothing more than a few stunted bushes can grow the force of moving air is powerful to a degree that is only beginning to be realized. Disintegration, too, is rapid. The extremes of temperature co-operate powerfully with wind and rain in breaking up the misnamed " eternal " hills.[1]

This huge desert has left a deep mark on its inhabitants. Separating north from south and east from west more effectively than high ranges of snow-clad mountains or a gulf of equal size, it has necessarily made government very difficult ; for a distant chief could always rebel and take refuge in the desert if defeated. Again, the dualism of Zoroastrianism was undoubtedly affected by the desert, as will be shown later on, and it has influenced the habits, the outlook, and even the physique of the Persian ; for it lies close to his cities, to Teheran and Meshed on the north, to Kum and Kashan on the west, to Yezd and Kerman on the south, and to Kain and Birjand on the east. In short, the desert is the "Dead Heart of Persia."

Rivers.—Owing to the scanty rainfall and the high ranges surrounding the plateau, there is not a single river of import-

---

[1] There are some remarkable illustrations of wind erosion in Sir A. Stein's *Ruins of Desert Cathay.*

ance in the many hundred of miles of coast which lie between the mouths of the Indus and the Shatt-al-Arab.

One of the affluents of this latter river is the Karun, which will be dealt with fully in connexion with the empire of Elam : here it is enough to say that its modern importance consists mainly in its being the only navigable river in the whole of the huge Persian Empire. The most important river in the western basin of Persia is the Zenda Rud, which, rising close to the Karun in the Bakhtiari Mountains, irrigates the Isfahan district. It discharges its surplus waters into a swamp known as the Gaokhana or "Hollow" some forty miles below Isfahan. Farther north the Aras, which for part of its course, as mentioned above, forms the Russo-Persian frontier, is an important river : it is the classical Araxes, and flows down past great Ararat. Proceeding eastward, we cross the longest river of Persia, the Kizil Uzun, the classical Amardis. Rising near Lake Urumia, it breaks through the Elburz and, under the name of Safid Rud, discharges its turbid silt-laden waters into the Caspian Sea east of Resht. It is identified by Williams Jackson as the "River of the Law."[1] Still farther east is the Tejen, which has been referred to in Chapter I. Its volume is not great, and its water is almost undrinkable, except in time of flood. Its importance, therefore, is small so far as Persia is concerned, although under the name of the Hari Rud it irrigates the fertile Herat valley and is thus of value to Afghanistan. In Eastern Persia there are no rivers until the historic Helmand is reached ; and this can scarcely be claimed as Persian, for it rises in Afghanistan and remains there as far as Sistan, where it discharges its waters into the famous lake and irrigates both Afghan and Persian lands. Except during the spring, travellers can traverse the Iranian plateau from east to west and from north to south, and nowhere meet with rivers. If they come across a brook and happen to taste it, the chances are that its waters will prove so salt as to be useless ; and nothing is more depressing than the constant presence of the white efflorescence already described, which speaks forcibly of an insufficient rainfall.

The Oxus.—The River Oxus now lies far away from the borders of shrunken Iran, but for many centuries it formed its eastern frontier, and consequently, to complete

[1] *Zoroaster*, p. 211.

this brief survey, some mention of this great river is called for. It rises in the Pamirs and, after making a bend encircling Badakshan, runs approximately north-west and now discharges into the Sea of Aral. Writing in the fifth century B.C., Herodotus referred vaguely to the Oxus and perhaps also to the Jaxartes in his description of the Araxes, mentioning that one branch discharged into the Caspian Sea. More than a century later Aristobulus is quoted by Strabo as stating that the Oxus " is navigable with ease, and that large quantities of Indian merchandise are conveyed by it into the Hyrcanian Sea, and are transferred from thence into Albania by the Cyrus, and through the adjoining countries to the Euxine."[1] When Alexander the Great conquered Western Asia the Oxus still flowed into the Caspian Sea ; but at some period at present unknown to us it adopted in the main the course it follows to-day, and discharged into the Sea of Aral. In A.D. 1220, however, the Mongols, after the capture of Urganj,[2] the capital of the state now known as Khiva, overwhelmed the city with the waters of the Oxus, and the flood thus caused found its way back in time to the ancient bed leading to the Caspian Sea. This once more became the main channel, and so remained for about three centuries, during which it was lined with villages. What caused the Oxus to alter its course yet again is unknown, as is also the exact date of the change : but Anthony Jenkinson, to whom belongs the great honour of being the first Englishman to visit Khiva and Bokhara, travelling in A.D. 1558, mentions that the Oxus had changed its course and " falleth into the lake of Kithay," under which name he obviously refers to the Sea of Aral.[3]

The nomenclature of the two rivers has changed greatly during the centuries. Oxus, the name used by the Greeks, is still preserved in Wakhsh-ab, the Wakhsh River, which is now one of the upper affluents. At this period the sister river was termed the Jaxartes. The medieval Arab conquerors called the two rivers Jayhun and Sayhun respectively, apparently adopting a corruption of the Gihon and Pison of Genesis ii. 11, 13. Here it is interesting to note that the two frontier rivers of Cilicia were given the almost identical names of Jayhan

---

[1] Strabo, xi. 7. 3. Albania is the valley of the Cyrus, the modern Kur, on which the picturesque city of Tiflis is situated.
[2] *Vide* Chapter LV.
[3] *Vide Early Voyages and Travels to Russia and Persia* (Hakluyt Society), i. 68. *Vide* also Chapter LXII.

and Sayhan. In both cases the second name was brought into a jingling rhyme with the first, just as in Yajuj and Majuj, or Gog and Magog. About the time of the Mongol irruption the Oxus received its present name, Amu Daria, and the Jaxartes became the Sir Daria.[1]

The Oxus is the historical river of Central Asia, and I recollect the thrill which I felt when I first saw its yellow waters, although where I crossed it at Charjui or Amu Daria it ran between low banks and the scenery was by no means striking. Yet I felt that to see the Oxus was a great event in my life, and I thought of Matthew Arnold's noble lines:

> But the majestic river floated on,
> Out of the mist and hum of that low land,
> Into the frosty starlight, and there moved,
> Rejoicing, through the hush'd Chorasmian waste,
> Under the solitary moon.

Lakes.—In the preceding chapter it was mentioned that an inland sea once extended over what is now the Iranian plateau. This disappeared when the plateau was upheaved; and the lake of Urumia, the salt lakes of Shiraz, the *hamun* of Sistan, the Jaz Morián and other isolated patches of water are all that is left of it. The wide-spreading sea is now *Kavir* or *Lut*, with numerous quicksands. Hence the intense salinity of the water is the most remarkable feature of these lakes, wherever they are not greatly affected by rivers.

The most important body of inland water lies near the north-western frontier, and is one of three great lakes, which lie comparatively close together, at a considerable height above sea-level. Of these, Lake Van is in Turkish territory, and Lake Gokcha in Russian Armenia. The Persian Lake Urumia or Urmi is the third and most important of all. Situated 4100 feet above sea-level and measuring some eighty miles from north to south and about twenty from east to west, this large body of water, which is studded with islands, is famous for its saline characteristics, in which it surpasses even the Dead Sea. The town of Urumia, twelve miles to the west of the lake, is the reputed birthplace of Zoroaster, the Great Prophet of ancient Iran.

Other lakes are the Daria-i-Mahalu, an important body

---

[1] *Vide Lands of the Eastern Caliphate*, by Guy le Strange, p. 434. This work is one which I shall allude to frequently, and no single book is of equal value in connection with the mediaeva geography of the Caliphate.

of water, to the south-east of Shiraz, and, farther to the north-east, the fantastically shaped Daria-i-Niriz, which is almost bisected by a projecting promontory. All these lakes, as may be supposed, are very salt, and they are also extremely shallow. We now come to the famous lake or *hamun* of Sistan. This is replenished by the snows from the sources of the Helmand and its tributaries, and consequently varies at each season of the year. For instance, during the winter months the whole area is occasionally dry and lifeless; but more usually is half covered with water, which increases steadily as the floods come down, until the whole country appears to be in imminent peril of submersion. In years of exceptional flood the surplus overflows by a wide channel termed the Shela into the Gaud-i-Zirreh or "Hollow of Zirreh," which, to judge by its size, about one hundred miles by thirty, must have taken the entire discharge of the Helmand in bygone days. In the spring of 1911 the Shela was 200 yards wide, 30 feet deep and running at about four miles an hour, a truly formidable volume of water. Another of these *hamun* is termed the Jaz Morián, and is formed by the united discharge of the Bampur and Halil rivers.

The Persian Gulf.—The south-west and south coasts of Iran are washed by the Persian Gulf. This landlocked body of water is seven hundred miles in length, with a width varying between three hundred and one hundred and fifty miles. At the Straits of Hormuz, by which it is entered from the Arabian Sea, the width is only thirty-five miles. It is a shallow depression, and, at its western end, its waters are annually receding. Even since the dawn of history the deltas of the rivers of Mesopotamia have advanced considerably.[1] The sea bottom is, for the most part, flat or gently undulating, and numerous islands dot the surface. There are many shoals and reefs, especially around the Bahrein islands. Among its earliest names were Nar-Marratum, or the "Bitter River," "The Eastern Sea" and the Erythraean or Red Sea. To-day Persians term it the Gulf of Fars.

If the traveller is fortunate, he will enter this land-locked sea by moonlight, past Musandam Cape, the black cliffs of which rise in sombre majesty and bear a decided likeness to an anvil, as the name implies. In the morning, as he steams up the Persian coast, he everywhere beholds sun-scorched,

[1] *Vide* Chapter III.

serrated ranges, running parallel to the trend of the Gulf and hindering access to the interior. The shores of Arabia, too, are sun-stricken and scorched. Whenever the steamer stops, the squalor of the roadsteads seems to intensify the ever-present heat : and the traveller's only wish is to start again and pass through the uninviting region without unnecessary delay.

Yet there is another side, and one that may well stir the blood of the most sluggish. Not only are there vague indications that this torrid Gulf was the home of a civilization earlier than anything of which we know, but there is the possibility that its waters witnessed the first attempts at navigation made by mankind. The Egyptians launched ships upon the Red Sea for the voyage to Punt (Somaliland) about 2700 B.C., and upon the Mediterranean Sea about 3100 B.C. The Babylonians probably navigated the Persian Gulf still earlier, their legends referring to voyages to the Land of Dilmun, which is either Bahrein or the opposite coast. Their chief object was stone.

Later on, in historical times, Sennacherib describes in detail an expedition by sea across the head of the Gulf, and, later, Nearchus keeps a log-book with such curiously modern accuracy and illuminating comment that most of his mooring-grounds have been identified. Farther on in the ages Sindbad the Sailor voyages from Zubair near Balsora or Basra, meeting junks from distant China ; and again a new epoch is born, and European fleets appear on its waters. Finally, after stubborn contests with Portugal and Holland, Great Britain acquires the supremacy and, by continuous effort and at a heavy cost of blood and money, pacifies this pirate-swept sea, which Persia has at no period of her history controlled. To-day the British Resident, whose post is one of great importance, is entrusted with the preservation of peace ; and few people living comfortably at home can realize how difficult the task now is. Added to the many problems of the past are new ones created by new conditions. Many of these are of extreme delicacy, and they have to be handled in a climate where for at least half the year life is a burden.

The Caspian Sea.—There are few more interesting bodies of water than the Caspian Sea, which washes the northern maritime provinces of Persia. Its length from north to south is some six hundred miles, and its width three hundred miles in the northern portion, but much less in the southern. It is divided into three distinct basins, that to the north being very shallow owing to the discharge of the Volga. The middle basin is deep, but a submarine ridge runs across it from east to west at a depth of only thirty fathoms. The southern basin is the deepest of all. The harbours as a rule are bad and very shallow.

Few bodies of water have been called by so many names, but each of them recalls some interesting historical fact. According to Williams Jackson[1] it may have been the Zrayah Vourukasha or " Sea of wide Bays " of the time of Zoroaster. The Avesta refers to it as " The gathering of waters," and again as " Beyond all waters " ; and undoubtedly it was the largest body of water within the ken of these Aryans. To quit the dim ages of the past, the name by which it is known in Europe is derived from the Caspii, a tribe that dwelt on its western shores. But among Persians it is known as the Bahr-al-Khazar, or " Sea of the Khazar," from the kingdom of the Khazars, which, in the earlier Middle Ages, existed to the north. Other names, such as the Sea of Hyrcania and the Sea of Gilan, have also been used at various periods.

In the days before Herodotus it was vaguely understood to be a bay of the great " Stream of Ocean " surrounding the then known world ; but the " Father of History " stated definitely that it was " a sea by itself."[2] Later writers, however, as the quotation from Strabo at the head of this chapter indicates, believed in an outlet stretching away to the dim north, and the fact that this belief lasted until the Christian era shows how little advance was made in the exact knowledge of the world during those four centuries.

But the most interesting problem connected with the Caspian Sea is the fluctuation of its level in historical times. At present it is 85 feet below that of the Black Sea. We cannot connect abandoned strands observed by Huntington at 600 feet above present Caspian sea-level with any historical period ; but we do know of a surprising change in the conditions prevailing at various times. Huntington produces evidence to show, what is indeed probable on other grounds, that at the time of Alexander the surface of this inland sea

---

[1] *From Constantinople to the Home of Omar Khayyam*, p. 83.
[2] Herodotus, i. 203.

was about 150 feet higher than at present. Associated with this higher level was a vastly larger area, especially on the east, where the Central Asian line now runs across what was once the sea-bed of the Caspian. The same observer saw two strands at a point one hundred miles east of Krasnovodsk, situated respectively 250 and 150 feet above the present sea-level. Indeed, it is not certain that the Caspian did not at that period include the Sea of Aral.

To continue our survey, the route up the Oxus was abandoned about the beginning of the Christian era, almost certainly because of its change of course, and the great caravan route between India and the west was diverted to Abaskun, a port at the south-east corner of the Caspian near the mouth of the Gurgan River. The site of Abaskun is in the neighbourhood of Gumesh Tappa,[1] from which runs the great wall known as the Kizil Alang or "Red Wall," or, again, as the "Barrier of Alexander," which I have examined in two sections.[2] O'Donovan, who visited Gumesh Tappa, states that the foundations of this wall can be traced running westwards until they disappear into the sea :[3] a caravanserai which lies under water is also spoken of. At Derbent, where the great ranges which run across the Caucasus terminate, there is also a celebrated wall, and this too runs down into the sea. Finally, one of the sights of Baku is a solid building, the towers of which show up above the sea, at some distance from the present shore.

To summarize, there is no doubt that the waters of the Oxus have affected the level of the Caspian ; but the evidence collected by Huntington tends to prove that this by itself would not have been sufficient to cause the great changes of which proofs have been given. The American geographer believes that this basin has "passed through a double series of great climatic changes during historical times," the climate being alternately damper and drier. At present the tendency is towards dryness, and I have read recent reports according to which the depth of water in the Gulf of Krasnovodsk was decreasing to a marked extent ; and this decrease was also noted at Chikishliar, where ships have to lie three miles farther out than they did five years ago, and in other parts.

[1] This was the port at which the ex-Shah landed in 1911 in his attempt to win back his throne.
[2] *Journal R.G.S.* for January 1911. *Vide* also Chapter XXXVIII.
[3] *The Merv Oasis*, i. p. 205.

If the process, which is attributed to a decrease in the volume of the Volga and other rivers, continues, the navigation of the Caspian Sea will become a serious problem.

Communications.—The question of communications is of such great importance that it is strange it should have been ignored by the historian until comparatively recently. The earliest great route in Persia ran from Babylonia up the defiles of the Zagros to Kermanshah and so to Hamadan, the classical Ecbatana. Under the Achaemenians this royal route indeed ran from Sardes to Ecbatana and thence to Rhages and so eastwards to distant Bactria. It was along this route that Darius retreated before Alexander, and from time immemorial it has been the chief highway in Asia between east and west; for farther south lies the great desert, and the route passing between the northern slopes of the Elburz and the Caspian was always very difficult. In mediaeval times the great trade thoroughfare from Europe passed through Tabriz, the Tauris of Marco Polo. Then, however, India as well as High Asia was the goal of the journey, and so the Venetians travelled mainly between parallel ranges past Yezd and Kerman to Ormuz, *the* emporium of the "Gorgeous East."

As already stated, Persia is exceedingly difficult to enter from the Persian Gulf on the south, the Bushire-Shiraz route being one of the very worst in the world.[1] It is also difficult of approach from the Caspian Sea on the north, from Arabistan on the west, and from Baluchistan on the east. Indeed, few countries are by nature more isolated; while, as if that were not enough, the Lut serves to disintegrate the whole country into scattered, loosely connected provinces. Perhaps the easiest access is from the north-west, where, as already stated, the great trade routes from Trebizond and Tiflis unite at Tabriz. The south-east route is also an open one, and as far as Herat there are no natural difficulties; a carriage can be easily driven the whole way across a country without a mile of made road.

Persian communications are still those of an undeveloped land, where "the mules are the only engineers," and, as

---

[1] To show how the road from Bushire to Shiraz struck Pierre Loti, I give the following extract from *Vers Ispahan*, p. 31 :

"Et il est fou pour sûr mon *tacharvadar* qui fait mine de grimper là, qui pousse son cheval dans une espece d'escalier pour chèvres, en prétendant que c'est le chemin ! . . .

" Or c'est bien le chemin en effet, cet escalier inimaginable."

Hogarth aptly points out,[1] they have relatively deteriorated owing to the immense improvements effected elsewhere. It is indeed discreditable to Persian energy that merchandise is still carried on camels, mules, and donkeys, and that the waggon, which was known more than 2000 years ago, is only just beginning to oust pack-traffic from the main routes.

Flora.—The vegetation of the Iranian plateau is everywhere meagre and scanty. In few districts do trees grow freely, and except where irrigation brings life and verdure, the prevailing feature is steppe and desert. Turf is unknown except in rare marshy patches, and nowhere do the bushes cover the ground. Indeed, here again the prevailing note is aridity. For a short period in the spring the bushes are in flower, the hills especially producing thousands of Alpine plants: but when once the heat of summer has set in, everything is parched and stunted, and yellow becomes the dominant colour. As a rule the hills are bare, except for a few stunted trees from which exude the valuable ammoniacum and tragacanth gums. There are also a few areas covered with a scanty growth of junipers or wild pistachios; but these are fast disappearing. Along the Zagros range, however, starting from near Shiraz, there is a belt of dwarf oaks some two hundred miles in length and in places a hundred miles wide. Elsewhere on the plateau the trees are either grown by irrigation or else found along river-courses. The most frequently grown tree is the poplar: then come the aspen, the oriental plane, the elm, the ash, the willow, and the walnut: the pine and cypress are rare. The poplar is in great demand for building, the oriental plane for doors, the elm for ploughs, and the other trees for fuel. The wood of the walnut and ash is too hard for the native carpenter. The cypress, the acacia, and the Turkestan elm [2] are planted mainly for ornament and, in the case of the last named, for shade. Lilac, jasmine, and red roses [3] are alone common in the gardens. Hawthorn abounds in the hill valleys, as also does the Judas tree, which is used for weaving baskets. It was much the same 400 years ago, as we learn from Josafa

---

[1] *The Nearer East*, p. 216.

[2] This tree is more correctly termed *Ulmus nitens*. It is mentioned by Baber in his description of the gardens of Samarcand.

[3] Attar of roses is manufactured from the *mahmudi*, a strongly scented rose resembling a dog-rose.

Barbaro, who visited Persia at the end of the fifteenth century. His account runs :

> In those parties arr no woodes nor yet trees, no not so much as one, except it be fruite trees, which they plante, whereas they may water them ; for otherwise they wolde not take.[1]

Persia is especially rich in fruit, which grows to considerable perfection in spite of the lack of scientific cultivation. Pears, apples, quinces, apricots, black and yellow plums, peaches, nectarines, cherries, and black and white mulberries are grown everywhere in great abundance. Figs, pomegranates, the famous almonds and pistachios grow best in the warmer districts ; and the date-palm, orange, and lime are confined to the " Hot Country." The grapes and melons of Persia are famous.

The main crops are wheat, barley (which is the staple horse food), millet, beans, cotton, opium, lucerne, and tobacco. Sesame and other oil seeds grow everywhere, as do onions, beetroot, and turnips. Rice and maize are as a rule grown extensively only in the Hot Country, or in the Caspian provinces. Potatoes, cabbages, cauliflowers, artichokes, tomatoes, cucumbers, spinach, egg-plants, lettuces, and radishes are the chief vegetables ; but many of them are not regularly grown. For instance, when I first lived in Kerman, potatoes were hard to procure, and cauliflowers and tomatoes were almost unknown : but, thanks mainly to European colonies at various centres, there has been some improvement in this respect of late years.

The products of the Persian hills are not to be despised. An edible thistle, rhubarb, and large mushrooms are all additions to the table ; manna, highly esteemed by the Persian faculty, exudes from the *Cotoneaster nummularia* ; and *turanjabin*, a similar product, from the camel-thorn. Manna is also collected from the tamarisks which grow in the watercourses. The valuable carraway seeds are found more especially in the Kerman province : " to take carraway seeds to Kerman " is a proverb. Finally, the odoriferous asafœtida is highly valued in India by the Hindus, and it is of interest to note that Arrian, on the authority of Aristobulus,[2] mentions its existence on the Hindu Kush, and the fact that sheep were very fond of it.

[1] Josafa Barbaro (Hakluyt Society), p. 71.
[2] Chinnock's *Arrian*, Bk. II. chap. xxviii. p. 198.

In the Caspian provinces the contrast in vegetation is extraordinary. There everything is luxuriant, and owing to the humidity elms, beeches, oaks, maples, ash, limes, and other trees, including the valuable box, grow to perfection. I shall never forget the wild vines festooning the trees, the ferns, and above all the carpeting of snowdrops, which I saw near Astrabad. Violets, too, and primroses flourish luxuriantly. The flora, it is to be observed, is not a tropical one ; rather it is that of Southern Europe and of the Caucasus. Its intensity is due to the protection from all cold and to the abundance of moisture. Along the shores of the Persian Gulf the climate is very hot and dry, and the date palm is a pleasing, though rare, feature of the landscape. At Minab, however, near Bandar Abbas, there are extensive date plantations, and in Persian Baluchistan these afford relief to the eyes in a country which is almost entirely desert.

To conclude this brief notice, lucerne, *Medicago sativa* or *Herba Medica*, was introduced into Europe from Persia, as we learn from Pliny.[1] Moreover, Sir G. Birdwood considers that Mazanderan was the primeval habitat of the vine, and the legend of the discovery of wine given in Chapter XII. supports this theory. The pistachio, almond, and various flowers and vegetables reached Europe and also China from Persia and, in many cases, have retained their Persian names in Europe. The apricot and the peach actually came from China, although the latter signifies the "Persian" fruit *par excellence* in European languages. Finally we know that Persians of all classes, from the monarch downwards, took great pride in laying out gardens and in the cultivation of fruit.

Fauna.—The fauna of Persia[2] include the tiger in the Caspian provinces, the "Hyrcan tiger" of Shakespeare, and the almost extinct lion of the South-West provinces, of which I saw a dead specimen floating down the Karun. In the north the bear is the *arctos* and in the south the *syriacus* ; but they are rare. Wolves, leopards, hyenas, lynxes, wild cats, foxes, and jackals exist in considerable numbers. Magnificent stags and roebuck roam the forests of the Caspian

---

[1] *Vide* Pliny, *H.N.* xviii. 144. " medica (herba) externa etiam Graeciae est, ut a Media advecta per bella Persarum quae Darius intulit."

[2] The best book dealing with this subject, and one of the most delightful books on sport ever written, is Lieut.-Colonel R. L. Kennion's *By Mountain, Lake, and Plain—Sport in Eastern Persia.*

provinces, and the fallow deer is found in the Zagros on the confines of Mesopotamia. But the usual quarry in the hills are the wild sheep and ibex, which are found throughout Persia and at every elevation. The wild boar, probably the most plentiful game, is little shot, as according to Moslem law its meat cannot be eaten. It swarms in the Caspian forests, and in every range or river-bed where there is any cover available. The plains are the haunt of gazelles, and the wild ass inhabits the vicinity of the salt marshes and is occasionally captured and ridden. Hares are generally scarce owing to lack of cover.

To turn to domestic animals, Persia, or rather Media, was the home of the Nisaean horse referred to in Chapter X. The cattle, which are very small and underfed, are the *Bos taurus*. The humped cattle, *Bos indicus*, are met with in the Caspian provinces and in Sistan. The buffalo is common in the Caspian provinces and in Arabistan, but is rarely seen on the plateau, which is not suitable for it. The fat-tailed sheep, *Ovis aries steatopyga*, is the sheep of Persia. The tail weighs up to 19 pounds in the late spring, but shrinks away during the winter. There is but one species of goat—*Capra hircus*, with its valuable *kurk* or down from which the finest fabrics are woven. The one-humped camels of Khorasan are famous for their strength, and the dromedaries of Baluchistan for their speed. The two-humped Bactrian camel is occasionally seen in caravans travelling in Northern Persia.

The game birds include bustard of three species, the rare snow-cock, which is found only on the summits of mountains above 9000 feet, and pheasants of more than one species.[1] The common birds of the plateau are partridges of two species ; the *Perdix pondiceranus*, a third species, is confined to the south. The francolin is somewhat rare in the Caspian provinces, but abounds in the Jiruft valley and elsewhere in the " Hot Country " of Southern Persia wherever there is scrub. Sand-grouse of three species are to be found ; but the " Imperial " is the most common on the plateau. In the Gurgan valley I have seen thousands of pin-tailed sand-grouse. Duck, mainly mallard, teal, and snipe appear in fair quantities in

[1] The authorities of the Natural History Museum have named the pheasants of the Gurgan Valley *persicus* as opposed to the *principalis* which is found on the Hari Rud. They also consider the Talish pheasant to be a distinct species and have named it *talischenis*. Specimens of the two former species have been presented by me to the Natural History Museum.

the winter, and quail are snared in the spring. Pigeons are plentiful everywhere in the vicinity of cultivation.

Of non-game birds, eagles, hawks, and vultures abound. The bee-eater, the hoopoe, and the blue jay make the spring and summer bright; and the crow, raven, chough, magpie, starling, sparrow, lark, and wagtail are common. Scarcely less so are the nightingale, the thrush, and warblers of various species. Nightingales are caught in large numbers and kept in cages. Finally, in the Caspian provinces almost every species of water bird is to be found. The same is true in a lesser degree of Sistan, where the noise of their wings resembles surf beating on a shore. Near Meshed pelicans are common, and I have occasionally seen swans, which, with geese, abound in Sistan.

Minerals.—Persia is not specially rich in minerals and, owing to the lack of good communications, no successful effort has been made in modern times to work the mines. In ancient days it was otherwise. De Morgan points out that in the old world there were two centres of inventions in metallurgy: the oldest was Elam, whose mountains were rich in copper, and the second was Central Asia.[1] It thus appears probable that the earliest metal age depended on these mines, which were perhaps the first ever worked by man, and which, so far as I know, have not yet been rediscovered. Later, if, as is probable, the Magan of the cuneiform inscriptions is the Sinai peninsula, copper was obtained from mines in its arid ranges both by the Babylonians and the Egyptians. In this connexion it is to be noted that the earliest metal age in Babylonia was a copper and not a bronze age, there being no tin mines to which the primitive miners had access.

To turn to the Assyrian inscriptions, the stone most frequently connected with Media was the highly-prized lapis lazuli, which is mentioned as being found in Mount Demavand; indeed, in the Assyrian inscriptions, Mount Bikni, as it was termed, is described as a mountain of *Uknu* or lapis lazuli.[2] But nothing is known as to the locality of this mine, which must have been one of the most ancient in the world.

---

[1] *Études sur la préhistoire et l'histoire*, p. 169. The view that the copper age of Sumer, Akkad, and Elam was of greater antiquity than that of Egypt is supported by Professor Gowland in "The Metals in Antiquity," *Journ. Anthrop. Instit.* vol. xlii., 1912.

[2] *Vide The Passing of the Empires*, by Sir G. Maspero, p. 453. De Morgan in his *Mémoires sur la Délégation en Perse*, vol. viii. p. 53, states that lapis lazuli was originally worked near Krahan, which is not so very far distant from Demavand. The site of the mine is unknown.

Other metals of classical times were iron, lead, gold, and silver. The topaz, emerald, sapphire, and cornelian were the precious stones. It has to be remembered in considering the working of the ancient mines that the labour was probably that of prisoners or slaves who were given the scantiest fare and whose life was of very little value. Also it is improbable that the cost of even this very cheap labour was carefully reckoned against the output of ore, which in all probability could not be procured elsewhere. Consequently deposits were then worked which to-day, from a combination of economic reasons, are quite valueless.

Shah Abbas tried to work the mines of Persia, apparently with free labour, but found that the cost was greater than the profit. Tavernier, who travelled in the middle of the seventeenth century, mentions that "the silver mines of Kerven where they spend ten to get nine" had become a proverb. This has been the invariable experience down to the English Mining Corporation, which found minerals in plenty but failed to make them pay, mainly owing to lack of good communications and of fuel.

Iron, copper, lead, mercury, coal, silver, gold, manganese, borax, asbestos, turquoises, and petroleum exist in various parts of the country. No attempt is now made, so far as I know, to work the iron; but the copper mines behind Sabzawar are worked, as also mines which I visited on the eastern edge of the Lut. At Kala Zarri, as these mines are termed, I found deep cuttings and series of galleries connected by shafts some 50 feet deep. No mention is made of these mines by Moslem writers. The fort which guards them does not appear to be of extreme antiquity, and it is interesting to speculate as to their origin.[1] Lead, mercury, silver, gold, manganese, and borax are not worked to-day so far as I am aware; but coal is extracted regularly near Teheran and Meshed. In the case of Meshed, although the mines are only a few miles from the city, the price works out at about £4 per ton. Yet the belt seems to be very extensive, and in a country where fuel can be grown only by means of irrigation an abundant supply of cheap coal would be of enormous benefit to all classes.

Finally there is the question of petroleum. In 1907, at a point thirty miles east of Shuster, successful borings

---

[1] *Ten Thousand Miles*, etc., p. 412.

were made, and the industry is now being developed. This oil-bearing zone is believed to run from the Caucasus to the Persian Gulf, where there is oil in the island of Kishm, and borings were once made, without success, at Daliki near Bushire. In the Gulf, where communications by water affect the situation favourably, red ochre is found in large quantities, and is worked in Hormuz, Bu Musa, and Halul ; salt is mined in Kishm ; and sulphur is worked intermittently to the east and west of Lingah.

To conclude, if Persia were opened up by railways, it is probable that mines which are now quite valueless would become remunerative and would contribute to the prosperity of the country.

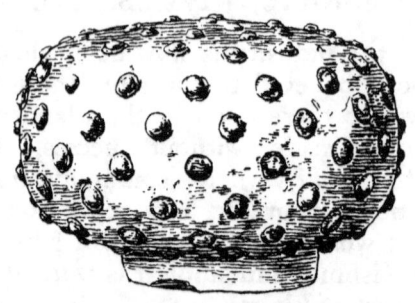

HEADPIECE OF GLAZED STONEWARE.
(From statue of Elamite period. De Morgan's *Délégation, etc.*)

CHAPTER III

THE GEOGRAPHY OF ELAM AND BABYLONIA

And it came to pass, as they journeyed from the east, that they found a plain in the land of Shinar; and they dwelt there.—Genesis xi. 2.

Early Civilization.—It is generally accepted that civilization first came into existence in the valleys of the great rivers of the world, and thence spread gradually into the mountains which bordered them. The dweller in such a valley would usually be assured of his food supply so long as he tilled the land. He would also enjoy the inestimable benefits of intercourse by river as well as by land; and intercourse is certainly an important factor in the foundation of civilization.

Moreover, the valley was, and is, the permanent centre of the life of a country; for periodical droughts, such as occur all over the world, would drive the pastoral dwellers in the mountains down to the valleys, where the perennial rivers would, at any rate, save them and their flocks from dying by thirst. Even to-day the primitive nomad of Sarhad, on the eastern borders of Persia, migrates whenever drought dries up the scanty springs in his barren hills; and I have seen families driving their flocks and herds to Sistan just as the patriarchs under similar conditions took refuge in Egypt. Indeed it is certain that from time immemorial the influence of drought has been enormous in determining migrations; and yet, until quite recently, this question has not been studied by the historian with the attention its importance merits.

CHAP. III GEOGRAPHY OF ELAM & BABYLONIA 37

In the eastern hemisphere there is a broad belt of desert, which runs from the Atlantic Ocean across the north of Africa to Asia. There it is continued in the deserts of Arabia, and farther eastwards, with a northerly trend, to the paralysing waste of the great desert of Persia. Indeed deserts extend nearly across Asia to the Yellow Sea. At the point where the low-lying Arabian desert gives place to the high-lying plateau of Iran the waters of the Euphrates, the Tigris, and the Karun, at the time when our survey commences, flowed into the Persian Gulf by separate mouths. This huge depression, with its great navigable rivers running south-south-east into the landlocked Persian Gulf, is one which is of great natural importance, and to it our attention must now be turned.

Nowhere else throughout the entire world do great rivers discharge into a landlocked sea. Nowhere else could be found in equal degree those favourable conditions which were required for the early beginnings of civilization. The great rivers of Babylonia made cultivation easy, and provided facilities of communication by river and in the Gulf.

In these valleys, then, the civilization of the world as we know it took shape. China and the Far East were remote, and made progress on their own distinctive lines at a later date. Egypt, although it developed in a similar way and is believed to have derived its ancient and marvellous civilization in part from Asiatic sources, was shut in by natural obstacles. Moreover, the Nile discharged into an open sea; and, consequently, Egyptian influence in those early days found considerable difficulty in passing beyond its sandy deserts. It is true that, at least as early as the Third Dynasty (*circa* 3100 B.C.), Egyptian ships navigated the Mediterranean coast, making voyages to fetch timber from the Lebanon, yet we cannot trace any very early Egyptian influence in ancient Palestinian and Syrian culture, whereas Mesopotamian influence is evident from the beginning. Thus we have Babylonia as the centre of West-Asiatic civilization, but affecting an area which extended to the Mediterranean on the one hand and included Persia on the other. The influence during the period of its greatness was Sumerian in character exercised by Semites, for the civilization of the Semites was acquired by the desert tribes who from time to time swarmed into the Euphrates valley and there learned the culture of the

Sumerians. The latter had no racial or linguistic connexion with the Semites, but may have been akin to the Elamites. A second and later fact of capital importance is the Aryan influence which included Central Asia and the Iranian plateau from about 1500 B.C. The effect upon the world of other countries is secondary and accessory to that of these two centres.[1]

Elam, the Home of the Earliest Civilization of Persia.— For the reasons just stated we do not seek for the earliest civilization of Persia on its plateau, where there are no important rivers. In the whole of the vast area of Iran there is, as we have seen, but one navigable river, the Karun, and it is in its valley that we find the earliest civilization in what was generally known as the kingdom of Elam. This was a state bordering on ancient Sumer and Akkad, the two Babylonian lands; like them it was situated, partly at any rate, on a rich alluvial plain, faced with somewhat similar problems, leading a similar life, and, if not related in similarity of origin or in language, yet connected from the first by raids and counter-raids, and later on by intercourse of every description. I propose, in the first place, to ascertain what has been discovered about these neighbouring lands of hoary antiquity. Next I propose, so far as is possible, to trace briefly the history of Elam, not only independently but as forming one of these very ancient states. Later, we shall come down to the period when the inhabitants of the Iranian plateau conquered these developed civilizations, which, in their turn, deeply affected their conquerors, who adopted the arts and civilization of Babylonia and of Elam, and made their chief capital at Susa, the centre of the oldest civilization in what is still the Persian Empire.

Physical Changes in Elam and Babylonia since the Dawn of History.—The formation of the great alluvial valleys of the Euphrates, Tigris, and Karun has already been referred to briefly in the first chapter. Here it is important to consider what was their physical condition in the fourth millennium B.C. when historical civilization was dawning in those regions, and again at later periods; for few countries have seen greater physical changes.

The first point to note is that the coast has advanced

---

[1] In dealing with these very early periods I am especially indebted to the works of King, Hall, and de Morgan.

enormously, and that it then lay about one hundred and twenty miles farther north than to-day. The importance of this fact cannot be over-estimated, and it must be borne in mind in considering every question in these early days; moreover, it circumscribes the area in which these epoch-making events occurred. It must also be recollected that land recently formed by deltaic action is generally of little agricultural or other value.

The Rivers of Babylonia and Elam.—At the earliest historical period in Babylonia and in Elam the rivers which were the makers of the country were those which exist to-day; but their courses were somewhat different, and they all reached the Persian Gulf independently by one or more mouths.

The Euphrates.—Starting from the west we first consider the Sumerian Zimbir or Buranum, now the Euphrates, the Babylonian Puratta, and still locally termed the Frat. Rising in the Taurus not very far from the Tigris, it followed a course in its lower reaches mainly to the east of the bed it now occupies, and thus diminished the area of Babylonia as compared with to-day; for the country to the west has always been in historical times hopelessly sterile. The Euphrates, which, unlike its sister river Tigris, receives few tributaries of any value, played a greater part in the earliest stages of civilization; its banks being lower, its stream less swift, and its waters falling more slowly during the summer. Also cities on the Euphrates would be less exposed to attack from the Elamite highlands. It is thus not surprising to find that not only Babylon but every city of Sumer and Akkad, with the sole exception of Opis, was situated on the Euphrates or on one of its offshoots. Its waters discharged by two main branches, on the southern of which " Ur of the Chaldees " was the great emporium for trade moving east and west; but it does not appear that at this very early period there was any commerce with India, though there may have been with Egypt.[1]

The Tigris.—We next come to the Tigris,[2] which, rising

---

[1] Kennedy demonstrates that the trade between Babylonia and India arose at the commencement of the seventh century B.C.; *vide* his " Early Commerce of Babylon with India," *Journal R. As. Soc.* 1898, art. xvi.

[2] The earliest name of the river was the Sumerian *Idigna*, semitized by the Babylonians as *Diglat*, which occurs under the form of Hiddekel in Gen. ii. 14. The meaning of the original name is uncertain, but it was assimilated by the Persians to the word *Tighra*, an arrow (the same word as *tigh*, the modern Persian for a razor), from which the Greek form Tigris is derived. To-day it is termed the Dijla, the Arabic form of the Babylonian Diglat.

near Diarbekr, receives constant accessions from the rivers draining the Zagros, of which the Great and the Lesser Zab are among the most important. It pursued its rapid course parallel to the Euphrates for some hundreds of miles, and discharged independently many miles east of the sister river. Owing to its high banks and rapid current, none of the earliest settlements were formed near it; moreover, dwellers on the Tigris would be more exposed to attack than dwellers on the Euphrates. It carried, and indeed still carries, a larger volume of water to the Persian Gulf than the Euphrates, which is not navigable for steamers.

The Kerkha.—We now come to the river on the left bank of which Susa, the capital of Elam, was situated. Known as the Uknu, and by the Greeks as the Choaspes, it springs from Mount Nahavand, where it flows near the rock inscriptions of Bisitun under the name of Gamasiab. Ever an impetuous river, it rushes through the defiles of Luristan and does not appear as the Kerkha, so called from a town of that name on its right bank, until the plain is reached. In early days it discharged into the Persian Gulf, but its waters are now lost in the swamps of Hawizeh.

The Ab-i-Diz.—The Ididi, known as the Koprates in classical times and as the Ab-i-Diz to-day, rises in the mountains of Luristan near Burujird. After being joined by another river called the Kazki, it flows past Dizful and joins the Karun, of which it is the main affluent, at Band-i-Kir.

The Karun.—The Ulai, termed Eulaeus by the Greeks and Pasitigris or the "Lesser Tigris" by Nearchus, was named Dujayal by the Arabs.[1] It is now the Karun, and at the fourth millennium before Christ flowed into the Persian Gulf at a point near the modern Ahwaz, where what is now a prominent rocky ridge was at a still more remote period an island in the Persian Gulf.

In the heart of the Bakhtiari country there is a culminating mass of ranges. From this, on one side, springs the Zenda Rud, which runs east to Isfahan, while on the southern slope the Karun takes its rise. From its source the Karun dashes down at an incredible speed, falling 9000 feet before it reaches Shuster. On its way it passes through some of the grandest scenery in the world. The rugged mountain gorges are

---

[1] *Lands of the Eastern Caliphate*, pp. 232 ff. Dujayal means "Lesser Dijla" and is thus the equivalent of Pasitigris.

GEOGRAPHY OF ELAM & BABYLONIA

frequently inaccessible and the river appears like a riband thousands of feet below. At one point the gorge is so narrow that it can be jumped by an ordinarily active man. The river flows in every direction by turn, and often parallel to its original course. Indeed the windings between its source and Shuster measure two hundred and fifty miles, although as the crow flies the distance is less than one-third of this total.

The Karun—or rather its artificial branch, the Ab-i-Gargar—is navigable from a few miles below Shuster, where the mountains end. At this point the banks are very high and the bed is narrow. Until the Ab-i-Diz joins it, there is no appearance of a fine river. Throughout the plain is absolutely treeless, and the inhabitants are nomads of a distinctly low type. The navigable portion of the river is bisected by the natural barrage at Ahwaz, where steamers are changed, and the lower reach is extremely uninteresting and tortuous until the date groves around its mouth are reached. At a point some two miles above Mohamera there is an old channel known as the Bahmeshir which connects with the Persian Gulf direct and has been navigated. The present channel, termed the Haffar, by which the Karun joins the Shatt-al-Arab, is generally believed to be artificial. To-day the Karun, which increases at its mouth to a width of nearly half a mile, discharges its waters into the majestic Shatt-al-Arab and adds sensibly to its volume.

At the earliest historical period we thus have the chief rivers directly connected with the Persian Gulf, each forming a separate delta and bringing down millions of tons of soil. This fact and the shorter courses of the rivers made for the quicker formation of land than the conditions of the present day. It is also probable that the rainfall in the hills was heavier, and the quantity of mud-laden water consequently greater.

The Expedition of Sennacherib.—In the seventh century B.C., or, to be more exact, in 694 B.C., there is a detailed account given by Sennacherib of a campaign which he waged against the Chaldaeans, who had taken refuge in the towns of the sea-coast of Elam. This is of the utmost value from the geographical point of view.[1] The great Assyrian describes how he sent for Syrians to Nineveh to build great

---

[1] Maspero, *The Passing of the Empires*, p. 301; also de Morgan, *Mémoires*, etc., vol. i. p. 17.

ships in the manner of their country. This flotilla was constructed partly on the Euphrates and partly on the Tigris. The ships built on the Tigris were rowed down to Opis and thence dragged on rollers to the Euphrates by their crews of Syrians and Greeks. The united fleet then moved down the Euphrates to the port of Bab-salimeti, distant a few miles from its mouth, which has a truly modern Arabic ring and means the " Gate of (divine) Mercies." There the camp was flooded by a high tide, and for five days the army was cooped up in the ships. The fleet was then got ready, and, when it was about to start, Sennacherib sacrificed victims to Ea, God of the Abyss, on the shore of the " Bitter River," into which he also threw a golden model of a ship, a fish made of solid gold, and a golden ring.

The expedition proceeded across the head of the Persian Gulf to the mouth of the Karun River, a distance of perhaps one hundred miles if there were no mud islands to be avoided. The force was landed on the first firm ground, probably close to Ahwaz. The surprise was complete, various towns were sacked, and the Chaldaean settlements were broken up, after which the Assyrians looted the country towards the delta of the Tigris, and finally returned in triumph to the presence of the Great Monarch, who had prudently remained behind at Bab-salimeti.

The Voyage of Nearchus.—Close on four centuries after this memorable expedition, namely in 325 B.C., we have a still more valuable description of the head of the Persian Gulf from Nearchus, the intrepid admiral of Alexander the Great, whose high place in the roll of fame was won not only by the then unparalleled feat of conducting a fleet of river-built ships from Karachi across the Arabian Sea and up the Persian Gulf to Susa, but also by his accurate observations, which have fortunately been preserved to us in the pages of Arrian.

The Greek admiral mentions the fact that between the mouths of the Euphrates and the Tigris there lay at the period of his famous journey a lagoon into which the Tigris then discharged. Of still greater interest with reference to Elam is his statement that one hundred and fifty stadia, or seventeen miles, from the mouth of the Karun the bridge of boats leading from Persepolis to Susa is reached.[1] He adds

---

[1] It is owing to this statement that it can be laid down that Ahwaz was at or near the mouth of the Karun at the time of the earlier expedition.

that this point was six hundred stadia, or sixty-eight miles, from Susa. As this is the exact distance from Susa to the modern Ahwaz, which not only lies on the direct Susa-Behbehan-Persepolis route, but is situated at a point where the famous natural barrage facilitates a crossing, the identification of this centre is of primary importance; for, working down from it, we can accurately fix the position of the coast. To-day, if we measure the distance of seventeen miles downstream from Ahwaz, we come to Kut Omeirah, which thus in the fourth century B.C. lay at the mouth of the River Karun. To continue our identifications, the mouth of the Tigris lay six hundred stadia, or sixty-eight miles, from that of the Karun, and the mouth of the Euphrates was situated three thousand stadia, or three hundred and forty miles, below Babylon itself, also a fixed point. This works out at some seven miles above Kurna. Here or hereabouts was the mouth of the Euphrates at that period.

Taking then these observations of Nearchus, which not only are those of an author on whom reliance can be placed, but are corroborated in other ways, we have a sufficiently accurate delineation of the coast-line at a most important period. For, if we take the earliest historical era of Babylonia to be the middle of the fourth millennium, from that period to the present day is about 5400 years. Now the voyage of Nearchus was undertaken some 2240 years ago, and thus gives us a faithful geographical description of Babylonia and Elam at a period which is almost half-way between the days when Lagash was a flourishing seaport and the twentieth century, when it is more than one hundred miles inland.

The Rivers of Babylonia and Elam at the Present Day.—To-day the relatively small stream of the Euphrates and the much larger volume of the Tigris unite at a point a short distance north of Basra in the suburb of Magil. Until a few years ago the confluence took place at Kurna, which Moslems look upon as the site of the Garden of Eden, but which is of course comparatively newly-formed land. The united waters become a broad river, termed the Shatt-al-Arab or "River[1] of the Arabs," which flows in majestic beauty past Basra to Mohamera, where the Karun swells its stream to a width of half a mile. From Mohamera it is a distance of fifty miles to the Persian Gulf. The stately river with

[1] *Shatt* really signifies "bank of a river."

its great historical associations, exceeding the Nile in volume, lined throughout on both banks with dense palm groves, and attaining the ample width of a mile opposite Fao, will ever remain in my mind as an impression of ineffaceable beauty.

The Boundaries of Elam.—I now propose to give some description of the historical province of Elam, which included the modern provinces of Arabistan, Luristan, Pusht-i-Kuh, and the Bakhtiari mountains. Dieulafoy holds that it stretched down the Persian Gulf as far south as Lingah, while to the north its approximate boundary was the trunk road running from Babylon to Ecbatana. On the east the Bakhtiari mountains and part of the modern province of Fars were included within its limits, which obviously varied as the state was strong or weak. On the west the Tigris formed the frontier when Elam was powerful ; but at other periods much of the fertile land to the east of this natural boundary, as far as the lower slopes of the mountains, was held by the Sumerians.

Its Cities, Ancient and Modern.—When Elam was at the zenith of its prosperity we read of Madaktu, situated on the middle course of the river Kerkha, rivalling Susa in strength and importance ; of Khaidalu, probably on the site of modern Khorramabad, and of other large walled cities scattered about in the fertile valleys to the north of the plain.

At Ahwaz, as already mentioned, is the natural barrage. Indeed the site has been of great importance from very ancient times. The present name is abbreviated from Suk-al-Ahwaz, signifying the " Market of the Huz or Khuz." Modern Ahwaz is little more than a village situated on the left bank above the rapids, with Nasiri, developed by English enterprise, below the rapids, opposite to Aminia, the port on the right bank. But, if the potential wealth of Arabistan be developed, Ahwaz will regain its former prosperity.

Shuster, too, with its picturesque castle, is historically of great interest, as in A.D. 260 the Emperor Valerian, who fell into the hands of Shapur I. as narrated in Chapter XXXVI., was employed, according to Persian historians, to build the great weir across the river. This weir still stands, though at the time of my visit in 1896 a great gap in the centre had destroyed its usefulness. The climate of Shuster,

GEOGRAPHY OF ELAM & BABYLONIA

as mentioned in the previous chapter, is terribly hot. Ahwaz I found comparatively cool, with a maximum temperature of 118°.[1] In mediaeval times it was otherwise, and the climate of Ahwaz, owing to the large amount of cultivated land, was damp and, according to Mukaddasi, execrable; for hot winds blew all day, and by night the noise of the rushing water, the mosquitoes, and bugs which "bite like wolves" rendered sleep impossible.

Some thirty miles north-west of Shuster, near the river Kerkha but actually on the left bank of the little river Shaur (a corruption of Shapur), lie the mounds of Sus, the site of Susa, which will be described in detail later on. Farther north, on the main route leading to the mountains, is Dizful, or the "Bridge Fort," which derives its name from a second splendid example of Sasanian work that spans the Ab-i-Diz.

Some sixty miles to the south-east of Shuster is the small mountain plain of Malamir, which contains remarkable bas-reliefs. This district was apparently that of the Hapardip, and the large mound on the eastern part of the plain was probably the capital, Tarrisha. Most of the figures in the rock sculptures have no inscriptions; but one of them forms a happy exception, and we learn that it was chiselled in honour of a certain Prince Khanni, whose effigy dominates the scene, the figures of a priest, of the attendants, and of the sacrificial rams being disproportionately small. Above these tiny figures three musicians march in procession.[2] Ruins of the Sasanian period have also been discovered; and to the north-west are the remains of the famous bridge Khurrah Zád,[3] so named after the mother of Ardeshir, the founder of the Sasanian dynasty.

Ram Hormuz on the Ahwaz-Behbehan road was also a site of antiquity, its founder under its present name being Hormuz, grandson of Ardeshir. It was also celebrated as the site of the last and decisive battle which sealed the fortunes of the house of Sasan and ended the Parthian dynasty. It is probable that all these sites, and others like Band-i-Kir, are extremely ancient, and that the Sasanian and mediaeval remains cover Elamite foundations.

The Natural Fertility of Elam.—In mediaeval times

---

[1] *Ten Thousand Miles*, etc., p. 253.
[2] *The Passing of the Empires*, p. 228; also *Etudes*, etc., p. 225, note 3.
[3] *The Lands of the Eastern Caliphate*, p. 245.

Khuzistan, as it was then termed, was perhaps the most fertile province of Persia, its sugar-cane being especially celebrated. But an influx of nomads, following on ruthless conquest, has destroyed a once teeming population, which depended for its living on the splendid irrigation works. This system of canals every government until comparatively recent times kept in order, even if it did not enlarge it; but now ancient Elam, like Babylonia, awaits the engineer who, given a free hand and a stable government, could in a few years, as in Egypt or on a still larger scale in the Panjab, settle millions of prosperous peasantry on land which now supports only a few thousand nomads and their flocks.

The Boundaries of Babylonia.—Having given some account of the province of Elam both in ancient and modern times, I now turn to Babylonia. As already explained, owing to the much greater northern extension of the Persian Gulf and the more easterly course of the Euphrates, Babylonia was formerly of smaller extent than the study of a modern map would lead the student to suppose. On the north, the natural division was one between the dead level plain and the slightly undulating country, which would be represented by a line drawn from near Samarrá on the Tigris to Hit on the Euphrates. On the east the Tigris was the boundary when Elam was strong; but when Elam was weak, Babylonia occupied fertile districts to the east of the river. On the west, the Euphrates was a natural boundary and defence; and on the south lay the Persian Gulf. Canon Rawlinson calculates the area as being rather less than that of the Netherlands.[1]

Meaning of Sumer and Akkad.—Before proceeding further it would seem desirable to explain the various terms used in connexion with this ancient country. At the very earliest period it was referred to simply as " The Land." At a later but still early period the name Sumer was applied to the district at the head of the Persian Gulf, and Akkad was the neighbouring district to the north-east. There was no marked geographical or other division between the two countries;[2] but Erech, Ur, Larsa, and Umma formed part of Sumer, which is referred to as the land of Shinar in the book of Genesis,[3] the verse running, " And the beginning

---

[1] *Ancient Monarchies,* i. 6.   [2] *Sumer and Akkad,* p. 13.
[3] Genesis x. 10. Calneh may perhaps be Nippur. See also the quotation at the head of this chapter.

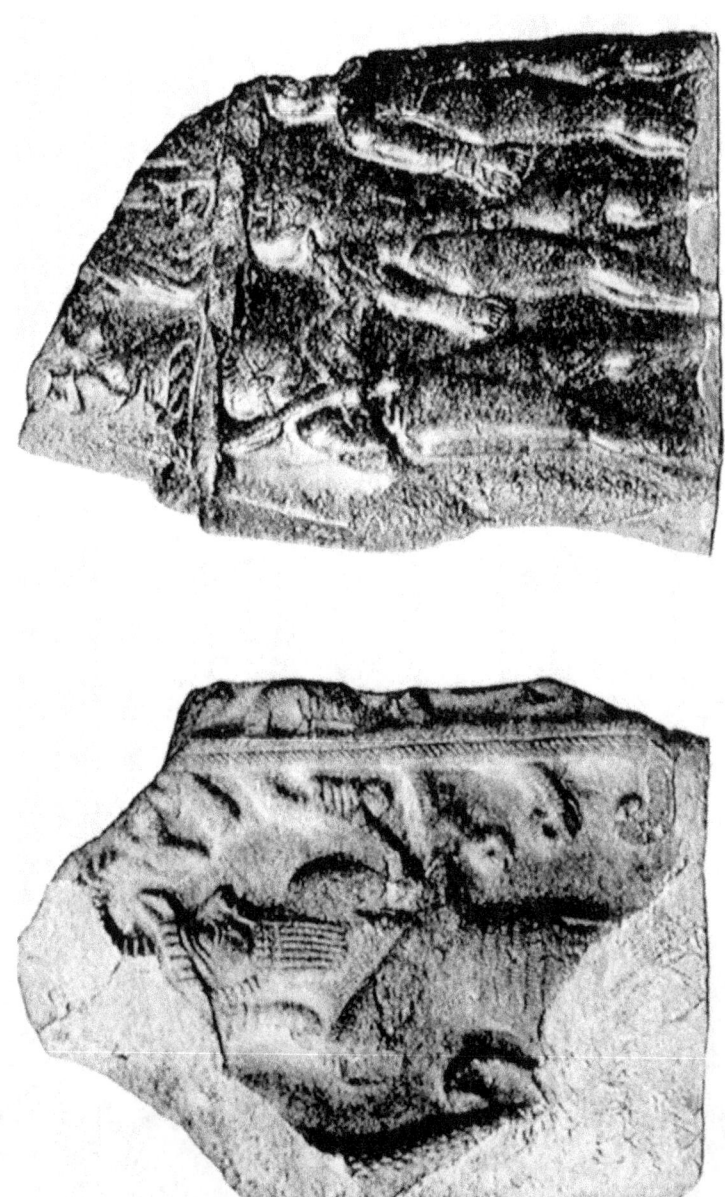

ELAMITE (?) GOD AND PRISONERS.
(From bas-reliefs found at Susa.)
(From J. M. de Morgan's *Mémoires de la Délégation en Perse*. Ernest Leroux.)

of his (*sc.* Nimrod's) kingdom was Babel, and Erech, and Accad, and Calneh, in the land of Shinar." Akkad or Agade, on the other hand, had Sippar, Kish, Babylon, and Borsippa within its boundaries. Nippur, in some respects the centre shrine of the Sumerians, stood almost on the frontier between Sumer and Akkad.

Chaldea and Babylonia.—The term Chaldea was formerly used in referring to this ancient land ; but, as Rawlinson points out, the word is not found at all before the ninth century B.C., and then in Assyrian inscriptions. Consequently, owing to the fame of Babylon and its comparative antiquity, it appears to be most convenient to employ Babylonia as the geographical term during all periods of its history.

Description of Babylonia.—And what sort of a country was it that saw the birth of a civilization which has affected mankind so intensely ? Then, as to-day, it was so absolutely featureless and flat, and on such a vast scale, that dwellers in Europe can hardly realize what the description of it means. Everywhere the land touches the sky, with only rare palm groves to break up the landscape, and no mountains are visible. As in Egypt, civilization had its birth between the sea and the dry land, on alluvial soil interspersed with vast marshes and flooded annually by its rivers. These rivers, indeed, as is shown above, formed it and, as also in the case of Egypt, kept it alive ; although the marshes, with their fevers, must have taken, then as now, a heavy toll from the wild population.

Climate, Flora, and Fauna.—The climate of this rich land is one in which snow is unknown and frost hardly ever severe, although the nights are at times bitterly cold. In the early winter there are heavy rains, which were in all probability more abundant in those early days. The winter upon the whole is bracing and healthy; but it is succeeded by six months of heat that is trying to Europeans, and affects the value of the man unit to some extent. To-day the desert winds are much dreaded ; and this was equally the case in early days. The soil was and is fertile, and it is generally believed that, while rice was first cultivated in India, this historical land can claim to have given wheat and barley as its main contributions to the sustenance of man. As residents in the East know well, the wheat-fed man is almost invariably superior in energy and vigour to the man whose chief support is rice, the Japanese perhaps supplying the one exception to this rule. The date-palm supplied many needs, including food, drink, and building materials. Next perhaps in general utility to the date-palm were the enormous reeds, from which huts, matting, and boats were alike constructed. Fish, too, formed a staple article of food, especially the barbel and carp. There is also the amphibious fish termed the goby, which is equally at home in the water or out of it.

Of big game we know that the elephant and the urus were hunted by the early monarchs; and the hippopotamus had at this period but recently disappeared. The lion, the leopard, the wild ass, the wild boar, the gazelle survive, and are still plentiful, except the first named, which is gradually becoming extinct. Jackals are common, but wolves and hyenas are rare. Of small game, the common francolin and the quail inhabit the scrub in the vicinity of the crops, and the ostrich and bustard may be found on the borders of the desert, though the ostrich is very rare to-day; but above Babylon it was abundant and hunted by the soldiers of Cyrus the Younger, as may be read in the pages of Xenophon.[1] The marshes during winter teem with geese, duck, and snipe. Cranes, herons, and other aquatic birds abound.

[1] *Anabasis* i. 5. 3.

GILGAMES AND EABANI IN CONFLICT WITH BULL AND LION.
(Cylinder Seal in British Museum.)

CHAPTER IV

ELAM AND SUSA, THE CAPITAL

The children of Shem ; Elam, and Asshur, and Arphaxad, and Lud, and Aram
—Genesis x. 22.

Recent Study of Origins.—Nothing is more striking in recent archaeological research than the scientific and successful manner in which the origins of civilization have been studied, and nowhere is this more noticeable than in the Near East. To-day the three great civilizations of Greece, Egypt, and Babylonia have been traced back, the two former to the Neolithic age and the last named to the primitive race which then occupied the lower plains of the Tigris and Euphrates. Nor is this all ; as a fourth civilization of the Hittites, differing in some aspects from the other three, is shown to have existed in Central Asia Minor at least as early as 2000 B.C. In the case of Elam, which was closely connected with Babylonia, a Neolithic period has been discovered ; and, although no purely Neolithic remains have, as yet, been found in Babylonia, this is due, in all probability, to the incessant activity of its rivers, which not only make, but destroy, and above all cover up. A Neolithic period can therefore be reasonably assumed, notwithstanding the absence of remains. It is impossible to fix even an approximate date for its commencement in this part of Asia ; but de Morgan considers that it ended towards the sixth millennium B.C., both in Babylonia and in Egypt. The succeeding stage of culture, termed " Chalcolithic " or " Aeneolithic," when stone and copper were used side by side, is well represented both in Elam and in Babylonia. In the latter country the recent excavations of Captain R. Campbell Thompson, in 1918, and of Mr. H. R. Hall, in 1919, at Abu Shahrein (the ancient Eridu), and of Hall at Tell-el-Ma'abed or Tell-el-Obeyd, near Ur, have yielded valuable examples of the Chalcolithic period, which the same explorers have also found at Ur. The pottery of this period is especially interesting, as it is of much the same type of ware and decoration as that found by de Morgan at Susa and Tappa Musyan. Specimens of this ware and also of the small flint saw-blades and scrapers that accompany it at Abu Shahrein and el-Obeyd have been met with sporadically at other Babylonian sites and in Assyria also, but, until now, have not been identified as belonging to the Chalcolithic period. The ware also connects with the early pot-fabrics of Asia Minor, but appears to be older. Its appearance in Babylonia, where it certainly antedates Sumerian pottery, is due to a westward extension of a proto-Elamite population, which, in Thompson's opinion, was afterwards driven out by the Sumerians.

The Meaning of Elam.—It is desirable at this point to refer to the various names of the country with which we are dealing, as much assistance is frequently to be obtained by such means. And first the name Elam, or Elamtu, the classical Elymais, requires explanation. Its signification is "mountains." The Assyrians came into contact with Elam in its mountain section, and as in ancient times its plains were far less extensive than to-day and the mountains predominated, this name needs no further comment.

The people of Susa termed their country Anzan-Susunka, and distinguished the various tribes given below. Strabo and the historians of Alexander similarly distinguish Susiana or Susis, the plain country, from the mountains of Cossia (or Kissia), Paraetakine, Mardia, Elymais, and Uxia. The book of Ezra, too, distinguishes between the Susanechians, or inhabitants of the plains round Susa, and the Elamites, or hill people.[1] Under the Persians the province was known as Ouvaja. Finally, in mediaeval times it was called Khuzistan or "The Country of the Huz or Khuz," and this name has recently been revived by a decree of Shah Riza.

[1] Ezra iv. 9 : "Susanchites, the Dehavites, and the Elamites."

Negrito Aborigines.—Dieulafoy[1] and de Morgan, who both headed expeditions to Elam, and who studied the question most exhaustively on the spot, concur in the opinion that there was a very ancient occupation of the Susian plain by Negritos, and that, so far as is known, these were the original inhabitants. In support of this view Herodotus writes: " The Ethiopians from the direction of the sunrising (for the Ethiopians were in two bodies) had been appointed to serve with the Indians, being in no way different in appearance from the other Ethiopians, but in their language and in the nature of their hair only ; for the Ethiopians from the East are straight-haired, but those of Libya have hair more thick and woolly than that of any other men." [2] Again, there is the fact that in the most ancient bas-reliefs, figures of Negritos appear with frequency. More especially is this the case in the famous stele of Naramsin, referred to in the next chapter, where the monarch, who is of Semitic type, is portrayed as leading Negritos to victory. Some years ago, during the course of my travels, I was puzzled by the extremely dark populations of Bashakird and Sarhad, very remote and mountainous regions bordering on Persian Baluchistan. The solution may be that the whole country was originally peopled by Negritos, the Anariakoi or Non-Aryans of the Greeks, who probably stretched along the northern shores of the Persian Gulf to India, and that their descendants have survived in those distant parts, which are scarcely known even by Persians, and where, in some districts, I was the first European traveller. Hall would derive the dark section of the inhabitants of Elam and the Sumerians from this stock, and, in my opinion, this would appear to be the soundest view to take of a very difficult problem.

The Legend of Memnon.—But Elam, in addition to the rich alluvial plain, also included the hill districts to the north and east, and here there is no question of a Negrito race. Consequently there were in effect at least two races inhabiting Elam—the Negritos of the plains, who were very dark, and the white hill-men. This would appear to have been vaguely recognized by the Greeks.[3] They describe Memnon, who came to the aid of Troy, as the offspring of a white mountain

---

[1] *L'Acropole de Suse*, by Dieulafoy, with appendix by Houssaye.
[2] Herodotus vii. 70.
[3] *Vide* Strabo xv. 3. 2 : also Herodotus v. 54, where Susa is termed " the city of Memnon." Hesiod calls him the Ethiopian king.

woman Kissia and of black Tithonos. He leads an army of Susians and Ethiopians—Tithonos is the Ethiopian god Didun—to the assistance of Priam, who is his paternal uncle, and is slain by Achilles. There are brief references to Memnon in Homer, and he is evidently regarded as an important personage ; for we read in the *Odyssey*, when Ulysses is speaking to Agamemnon of his son :

> To Troy no hero came of nobler line,
> Or if of nobler, Memnon it was thine.

In another passage he is given the epithet of swarthy.[1] It is of interest to note that there is no mention of Babylon or Nineveh in these early legends preserved by the Greek writers, which, although probably without historical foundation, are yet of some value from the ethnological point of view. When the Greeks found a black population in Elam, they would naturally compare it to the Ethiopians, of whom they knew through Egyptian sources, and this explains the transfer of Tithonos to Persia.

At a rather later period there was first a Sumerian, and then a considerable Semitic influx, which in time, as in Babylonia, dominated and absorbed the earlier inhabitants of the country. As far as Babylonia is concerned, this Semitic invasion was mainly peaceful and perhaps should be described rather as penetration : but in the case of Elam, probably owing to the mountain fastnesses, no permanent conquest was effected by the Semitic kings of Akkad, and it was not until the establishment of the second Sumerian Empire by the later kings of Ur that Elam became really subject to Babylonia, and then only for a short time.

The Various Tribes of Elam.—Apart from the general ethnological divisions given above, Elam was the home of several tribes among whom were the Hussi or Uxians, and the Hapartip ; the Umliyash, who inhabited the district between the Kerkha and the Tigris ; and the people of Yamutbal and of Yatbur, whose districts lay between the Tigris marshes and the mountains.

The Hussi or Kussi are the Uxians of the Greeks who demanded toll from Alexander the Great for his passage from Susa to Persepolis, and in return were surprised and subdued, as mentioned in Chapter XX. Their name survives in

---

[1] *Odyssey*, xi. 522 and iv. 188.

Khuzistan. The Hapartip or Hapirtip[1] appear on the rock sculptures of Mal Amir, and are perhaps the Amardians or Mardians of the Greeks, whom Herodotus mentions as nomadic Persian tribes ranged with the Dahae, Dropini, and Sagartii under the banners of Cyrus.

Anzan or Anshan —Among the most important districts was Anzan or Anshan, which probably, in course of time, included Susa and the neighbouring hills, and finally became synonymous with Elam, as shown in a cuneiform tablet.[2] The passage from Isaiah,[3] "Go up, O Elam ; besiege, O Media," distinctly bears out this view ; and the fact that the Achaemenian monarchs would only drink the water of the Kerkha, points clearly to that river as flowing through their homeland. Anshan is especially celebrated as being the principality of Cyrus the Great.

The Ancient Language.—A few words are called for concerning the ancient language of Elam. Like Babylonia, Elam furnishes us with Sumerian inscriptions containing Semitic words, and also with Semitic inscriptions containing Sumerian words. But in Elam there are found in the earliest period proper names which are neither Sumerian nor Semitic ; but which belong to a language somewhat vaguely described as Turanian, and known among scholars as Anzanite, Susian, or simply Elamite. This language, which was subordinate during many centuries of foreign rule, suddenly reappeared towards 1500 B.C. at the time when Elam became an independent nation. Consequently in Elam there were several languages, of which Anzanite was the oldest, but of this only traces were left. Thanks to the devoted labours of Father Scheil, who was attached to the de Morgan mission, we know that the Elamite monosyllabic roots were agglutinous,[4] and that the simple inflexions associated with derived words are due to the influence of a higher language.

One of the most striking proofs of the independent lines on which Elam developed is furnished by the so-called " proto-Elamite " system of writing, which was discovered during the course of the excavations at Susa. This consists, so far as

---

[1] The " p " in the name is merely the plural termination.
[2] *Vide* "Anshan" in *A Dictionary of the Bible*, edited by James Hastings.
[3] Isaiah xxi. 2.
[4] " The true test of agglutination is the power of the particles to become detached and shift their places in the combined form, as when *ly* in the English word *man-ly* makes room for *ful* in *man-ful-ly*."—Quoted from Keane's *Ethnology*, p. 209.

we know it, of either signs or ideographs for various objects impressed on rough clay tablets. These tablets have not been fully deciphered, but enough is known to prove that the system is quite independent, and evolved by the Elamites. A very few of the signs, as for example those used for " tablet " and " total," resemble the corresponding Babylonian characters ; but, beyond this, there is no connexion, and it is noteworthy that, although the signs for " total " are the same as in the Babylonian script, the Elamite figures are different, being based on a decimal system, whereas the Babylonian numeration is sexagesimal.

Basha-Shushinak, who probably reigned before the Babylonian dynasty of Ur established Sumerian rule for a while in Elam, dedicated a stone statuette seated on a throne. On each side of the figure is an inscription, that on the left being in Semitic and that on the right in proto-Elamite characters. This proves that at that period the two scripts were employed together. Finally Susa, forced to use the Semitic script during the many centuries of her existence as a vassal state, forgot her ancient script, and, when her independence was recovered, used the Semitic signs in writing her own language. According to de Morgan, Anzanite died out some three thousand years before our era.

The Religion.—Very little is known about the religion of Elam. As in the case of Sumer, there was a world full of vague forms and spirits. The chief deity, whose name was sacred and secret, and who was referred to as Shushinak or the " Susian," dwelt in a forest sanctuary which was sacred, and to which only the priests and the King were admitted. Associated with Shushinak were six other deities of the first rank, grouped in two triads. Of these, Amman Kasibar may possibly be the Memnon of the Greeks. The names of a considerable number of other deities have been recovered from inscriptions, but beyond their names little is known of most of them.[1] We have few data for determining their characters and attributes. We read that on certain solemn days or in celebration of victories, the statues were brought out to receive the devout homage of the people, and from various facts in their history we know how strongly they cherished their deities. As in Babylonia, the priesthood was both powerful and wealthy, and, although we have as yet but little informa-

[1] Gautier, *Rec. de trav.* xxxi. pp. 41 ff.

tion as to the details of Elamite cult and ritual, it is clear that in many features they bore a general resemblance to the Babylonian rites. The votive and dedicatory inscriptions that have been deciphered do not suggest a completely independent system or organization, and the readiness of the Elamite priesthood to borrow from Babylonia is well illustrated by the bronze votive plaque of Shilkhak-in-Shushinak, representing a rite of purification performed at sunrise, which, as its name implies, was directly taken over from the Semitic Babylonians. The disturbed condition of the mounds at Susa has prevented the recovery of trustworthy archaeological and architectural evidence on the religious side ; but this defect may at any moment be remedied by the finding of native Elamite religious texts. These might throw as much light on the religion and ritual of Elam as the purely votive and building inscriptions have already thrown upon the succession of her kings.

Susa, the Ancient Capital.—We owe practically all our knowledge of the ancient history of Elam to excavations conducted at Susa. It is therefore desirable to give some account of the famous capital of Elam and of the important secrets it has yielded.

The mounds of Shush or Susa are situated some thirty miles from the hills, and are, to judge from their position, of great antiquity. Indeed, Susa may claim to be the oldest known site in the world. It has already been shown that in the days of Sennacherib the coast-line was not more than sixty miles from it. Consequently, the possible sites for an ancient city were limited to a comparatively narrow fringe of plain lying at the foot of the great mountains ; for land recently formed would not have been suitable for occupation by a large population.

Excavations by Loftus.—These ruins of Susa were first visited by Loftus[1] and Churchill in 1850. The reception given to the travellers was unfriendly, and after Churchill had made the first plan of the sites, they withdrew and reported to General Williams, who was the chief British representative on the Turko-Persian Frontier Commission, at that time assembled at Mohamera. The next winter General Williams visited the ruins in person, and, as the result of excavations carried out under his instructions, a great Achaemenian palace

[1] *Travels and Researches in Chaldea and Susiana.*

was discovered. Loftus returned later, and with the wholly inadequate sum of £500, which had been placed at his disposal, continued the excavations.

The Dieulafoy and de Morgan Missions.—Englishmen were thus the pioneers in this truly magnificent task, and the name of Loftus will ever be honoured in connexion with Susa ; but it is to the talented sons of France, supported generously by their Government, that the chief credit belongs of drawing back the veil from a totally forgotten past of glorious history, and of adding yet another to the list of Great Oriental Monarchies.

The French Government despatched two expeditions, the first of which, under Dieulafoy, who was accompanied by his gifted wife, took up, in 1884, the work of Loftus, and discovered that the palace of Darius had been destroyed by fire and that, more than a century later, Artaxerxes Mnemon had raised on its ruins a still more splendid edifice. Dieulafoy merely continued the excavations of Loftus, and it was reserved for another Frenchman to complete the achievements of his fellow-countrymen by discovering Elam and its history in the lower strata of the same mound.

The Four Quarters of Susa —To the traveller crossing the level plains, the mounds of Susa appear to rise to a great height, and it is not difficult to imagine how imposing they must have been, crowned with splendid edifices, and probably set in palm-groves amid a sea of waving corn, the whole picture being backed by range after range of grim mountains rising in sombre majesty to snow-capped peaks.

To-day the city is represented by desolate mounds covering a considerable area on both banks of the Kerkha. This river flowed past the citadel, and the space now existing between the Shaur and the Kerkha was covered with buildings, which have been partly demolished by the wayward river.

De Morgan divides the ruins into four chief quarters, corresponding with the most important mounds :

(1) The Citadel, which was the fort in Achaemenian times.

(2) The Royal City with the palaces of the successors of Darius.

(3) The Commercial quarter.

(4) The quarter on the right bank of the present course of the River Kerkha. This formerly included the whole of the area now existing between the Shaur and the Kerkha.

The so-called Citadel is the smallest in area, but the most important owing to its altitude. It rises 38 metres above the plain and measures 450 metres by 250. It dominates the plain more than its mere height would suggest, owing partly to its steep sides, which are difficult to ascend. The Citadel would appear to have been inhabited without interruption from prehistoric times down to the Graeco-Persian period.

The Royal City, which stretches from south-east to northeast of the Citadel for 1500 metres, is separated from it by a large depression known locally as the Bazaar, and was never joined to it. The *Apadâna* or throne-room of the Achaemenian Palace at the north-east is a square of some 350 metres. Although extensive, the ruins of Susa are small compared with those of Babylon or Nineveh, which were the capitals of worldwide empires. Elam, although an independent and mighty kingdom, never seriously aspired to the empire of the known world, as did her rivals.

The Prehistoric Period.—We now come to the earliest periods into which de Morgan divides the history of Elam. First of all there is the prehistoric period, subdivided into two, in neither of which have metals been discovered : though, of course, this negative information is not conclusive. Pottery of a good class was dug up in the lowest stratum 20 metres below the surface, whereas the pottery found in the stratum above is of a coarse and less artistic type. Bricks were also found resembling the segment of a ring, badly baked and equally badly shaped.

De Morgan compares the pottery of the prehistoric strata with similar ware found in Egypt, which he dates back to 8000 B.C. ; and he holds that the fragments found at Susa are certainly as old. It is, however, pointed out by King that the absence in the intervening countries of any pottery similar to that of Egypt, makes this method of reckoning unsafe, and the pre-dynastic Egyptian pottery is not really at all like that of Susa, except superficially. King in an appendix to his *Sumer and Akkad* deals with the excavations made by Pumpelly, near Askabad, and holds that the pottery of the earlier periods found in the North *Kurgan* or mound at Anau " may well point to some connexion between the stone and early metal-using cultures of Transcaspia and Elam." Similar buff-coloured pottery with geometrical designs was discovered by me in the neighbouring district of Darragaz, which fact strengthens this view ; the vase, which appears as an illustration, is now in the British Museum. But there is, even stronger confirmatory evidence in the treasure discovered near Astrabad[1] in the Turang Tappa or " Pheasant Mound," situated perhaps two hundred and fifty miles to the west of Anau, in a country studded with mounds containing ruins of ancient towns and villages similar to the Anau *Kurgan* ; indeed the intervening country bears traces throughout of such ruins.

The discovery was made in 1841, but has hitherto not received the notice its importance merits. It consisted of a number of golden objects, worked stone vessels, and copper weapons. The most remarkable piece was a golden goblet, on which two unmistakably Sumerian figures are engraved, the heads and faces clean-shaven with the characteristic " puffin " look.

At Anau and Darragaz nothing better than coarse pottery has been found, but here we have a treasure which, taken in conjunction with the ware discovered at Anau and Darragaz, proves that the culture of Elam covered a much wider area than was previously supposed.

It would be idle to press the argument further until more ample materials are forthcoming, as will probably be the case before long from the ruined sites of Mesopotamia where, as mentioned on page 50, Hall and Thompson found quantities of similar pottery at Ur and Eridu. This ware is known to occur farther north, and it will eventually appear that there was a line of connexion between Elam and Transcaspia through Mesopotamia, and possibly also directly north. As to date there is no doubt that the pottery found at el-Obeyd is proto-Sumerian or earlier than 4000 B.C. But this is much later than the dates given to their finds by de Morgan and Pumpelly. Enough, however, has been said to show that the earliest period discovered by de Morgan dates back to a hoary antiquity undreamed of a generation ago.

The Archaic Period.—Just above the prehistoric zone the French Mission discovered a layer of earth some 6 feet thick, in which nothing was found ; and the theory was formed that the prehistoric city had been destroyed by a

---

[1] " The Sumerian Treasure of Astrabad," by Professor M. Rostovtzeff, in *The Journal of Egyptian Archaeology*, vol. vi. part i., January 1920.

higher race, which covered up the ruins with earth before commencing the construction of a new city. In the next, or Archaic, zone were found tablets of unbaked clay with archaic writing and also unguent vases, but very little pottery. Almost all the articles made of alabaster were pitted with holes as the result of its having been burnt. De Morgan believed that this period should be dated about 4000 B.C.

Elam in the Legend of Gilgames.—One of the greatest, and certainly one of the most interesting, epics in the history of mankind is that of Gilgames, containing a legend of the Deluge, from which that in Holy Writ was inspired, Gilgames himself being possibly the Nimrod of the book of Genesis. In it the subjection of Elam is dealt with, and although the mists of antiquity lie low over the episodes, there is no doubt that these legends possess an historical basis, and are therefore of considerable value.

The first of these old-world stories is to the effect that Khumbaba, King of Elam, had invaded Babylonia, had razed its temples, and had substituted the worship of Elamite gods for the local deities. In this crisis all hopes rested on Gilgames and his devoted monster Eabani. The heroes set out to meet the Elamite invader, and heard from a female magician that the foe was concealed in a sacred grove. Undeterred by fear they pressed on " and stopped in rapture for a moment before the cedar trees ; they contemplated the height of them, they contemplated the thickness of them, the place where Khumbaba was accustomed to walk up and down with rapid strides ; alleys were made in it, paths kept up with great care."[1] The Elamite king, surprised when about to take his outdoor exercise, was slain and the heroes returned in triumph to Erech, the well-protected. Here, apart from the extraordinarily modern habit of the Elamite monarch in taking exercise in a well-kept pleasaunce and the evident wonder and joy shown in the sacred grove, we note that Elam, as in the earliest historical times, raided the rich lowlands.

A second Elamite sovereign, Khumbastir, also appears, but merely as a name. Kudur-Kuku-Mal, yet a third Elamite monarch, whose name is also preserved to us, was more successful, as he defeated the Babylonian forces and ravaged their country. No details are forthcoming, nor

[1] Haupt, *Das babylonische Nimrodepos*, p. 24.

is it possible to fix even an approximate date for these monarchs ; but there is no doubt that, in these delightful legends, we obtain glimpses of the great struggle in which Elam was probably the aggressor for many generations, but which ended in her subjection to the higher organization of Babylonia.

HEROES TENDING CATTLE.
(Seal of Sargon's scribe, from *Menant*.)

CHAPTER V

ELAM, SUMER, AND AKKAD AT THE DAWN OF HISTORY

And they said one to another, Go to, let us make brick, and burn them throughly. And they had brick for stone, and slime had they for mortar.—Genesis xi. 3.

Sumerians and Semites.—It was pointed out in the last chapter that Elam was closely connected with neighbouring Sumer and Akkad; and in this chapter I propose to trace the growth of all three states and, by this means, to give a sketch of the development of Elam and its relations with Babylonia.

It is now known that there were two races inhabiting Sumer and Akkad which were distinct not merely in race and speech, but also in personal appearance. The Sumerians shaved both the head and face, whereas the Semites grew their hair and wore a beard. The dress also differed, that of the Sumerian consisting of a mantle worn over the left shoulder, whereas the Semite wore a long, narrow plaid wrapped round the body, with the end thrown over the left shoulder.

There has been much discussion as to whether the Sumerians or the Semites were the earlier inhabitants of Babylonia; but the question may now be regarded as definitely settled in favour of the Sumerians. They, however, were themselves perhaps preceded by a proto-Elamite race which made the pottery that so much resembles the primitive ware of Susa. And so far as the evidence goes, it would appear that, at the earliest period of which there is any record, Semites had been long settled in the north of the country, the land of Akkad, by the side of the Sumerians.

The Legend of Oannes.—Of considerable importance in connexion with this discussion is the legend of Oannes, as narrated by Berossus, a Babylonian priest, who wrote a few years after the death of Alexander the Great, and who diligently collected ancient traditions. According to his chronicle, of which unfortunately only fragments have been handed down, the ancient inhabitants of Babylonia lived like beasts without any laws. During this era a monster, half-fish, half-man, and endowed with reason, Oannes [1] by name, appeared out of the sea and taught the use of letters, laws, arts, and sciences. He also instructed mankind to plough, to sow, and to reap. At night he disappeared into the sea ; for he was amphibious. Oannes and his successors, we are told, taught the people of Babylonia during a period of 691,200 years which preceded the great flood. Now this legend has generally been held to point to the arrival of a higher race by sea, and, as the Semites ultimately predominated, it has been argued that it was they who entered Babylonia from the south. But King, to whose work I am specially indebted in this chapter, looks upon this legend as merely implying that the shores of the Persian Gulf were the earliest centre of the Sumerian civilization, and believes that, as there are but slight traces of Semitic influence in Sumer during the earlier periods, the Semites came from the north-west and not from the south ; and this view holds the field at present.

Of the Sumerians themselves, and whence they came, until quite recently the earliest traces of cultural development consisted of the remains of a bronze age culture. It was therefore held that the arrival of the Sumerians in the Euphrates valley was sudden, and that they had brought their culture with them from the country to the south-east of the Caspian, where finds of treasure with Sumerian figures and pottery had been discovered, as noted in the previous chapter. But fresh light has been thrown on this very important subject by American discoveries at Nippur, the recently published tablets giving us some ten dynastic lists which precede the earliest of the hitherto known lists. We must therefore modify our previous view, as we now hold the proof that, before the close of the third millennium, the Sumerians had strong traditions, if nothing more, which pointed to Babylonia being in their possession at the dawn

---

[1] Oannes is believed to be a corruption of Ea, the God of the Abyss.

of history. Thanks to Mr. Woolley our knowledge of this subject is steadily increasing.[1]

The Sumerian Language.—The language of the Sumerians, in which the oldest records we possess are written, is agglutinative, and is thus entirely unlike the Semitic. King states that "the two races of Elam and Sumer do not appear to be related either in language or by physical characteristics." But he adds that "until the phonetic elements of the language are finally established, all theories based upon linguistic comparisons are necessarily insecure."

Religion.—No account of a people, however brief, is complete without some reference to religion. The special characteristic of the Sumerian temples was the "ziggurat," composed of immense cubes of sun-dried brick piled up one on the other, and diminishing in size up to the small shrine set on the summit. Apart from this striking feature, which impressed itself on mankind in the legend of the tower of Babel, and is reproduced in our church steeples, their architecture was commonplace; the temples were built of sun-dried bricks, and, if speedily constructed, speedily fell into decay. They cannot be compared with the granite and limestone temples of Egypt, which took generations to complete. And what was the Sumerian idea of his gods? A striking feature is that, whereas most of the greater gods were beneficent, there was a host of spirits and demons hostile to mankind and requiring constant appeasement. In Egypt the gods were, upon the whole, beneficent; but in Babylonia, to some extent, the opposite view prevailed, and constant terror and unhappiness must have resulted from the odious and detestable ideas associated with many of the higher powers. Most cruel of all the lesser host of heaven was the demon of the south-west wind, which struck down man and beast and destroyed trees, harvests, and pasturage in his rage against life. To combat these terrors a multitude of beneficent genii, monsters of noble and benign aspect, were imagined, and it was the colossal figures of these which were set to protect the entrance to palaces and form such typical and striking examples of Babylonian art. The Cherubim described more particularly by Ezekiel[2] are the lineal descendants of these colossi.

---

[1] *Vide* the Preliminary Essay.
[2] Ezekiel i. 4 ff.

The gods of Babylonia were men, with their violence, their cruelty, and their boldness accentuated, just as the goddesses were glorified women. Each had its special city-state in which the *patesi* or priestly ruler governed by virtue of being the representative and interpreter of the god's will. Other gods, however great, were merely allies and subordinate to the particular god in his own city, just as he himself ranked below the chief god in a neighbouring state. Nevertheless, Anu, the heaven ; Ea, the Abyss ; and Bel, the earth, formed a supreme triad in later times.

The next world was painted in depressing colours ; for hunger, thirst, and misery were the lot of those who were fortunate enough not to be sentenced to eternal torments. Consequently every one prayed for health during his lifetime, for a large family, and for wealth, as a reward for devotion to the local god. The latter, if his worshippers displayed any lack of zeal in his service, would overwhelm them with crushing disease and calamities of every kind. The priest who presided at the burial of a Sumerian demanded as a fee for himself " seven urns of wine, four hundred and twenty loaves of bread, one hundred and twenty measures of corn, a garment, a kid, a bed, and a seat." In a temple there were included treasuries, store-rooms, granaries, and pens for cattle and sheep ; in fact, everything was ordered as if the god were an earthly monarch who lived surrounded by a great retinue.

It is clear that the Sumerians were, in doctrine, terribly priest-ridden ; but the extent and severity of their thraldom become still more apparent when we know that the god, through his servants, was a great land-owner and also a great merchant, facts which seem to imply a priestly trade monopoly.

The Earliest Sumerian Settlements.—The houses of the dwellers in Babylonia were probably at first constructed from reeds, which are still a prominent feature of the country, and these were gradually succeeded by hovels of clay or sun-dried bricks. The early Sumerian's greatest friend and enemy was the river on whose low banks he had pitched his settlements. While it gave him abundant water for irrigation, it was his constant terror in time of flood. An interesting light has lately been cast upon this remote period by the discovery of the oldest version of the Deluge story, which reflects the conditions of a primitive Sumerian settlement.

The text is composed in the Old Sumerian language, and although the tablet on which it is written dates only from about 2000 B.C., the legend itself goes back to the dawn of history. The hero of the tale is a certain Ziudsuddu, a priest-king or head-man of a Sumerian village, whose piety was such that his god Enki warned him of the coming flood. So he builds a boat, probably a *guffa* or circular pitched coracle, and, having loaded it with his live-stock, survives the rain-storm which rages for seven days and seven nights. The boat is carried away on the flood, but finally the storm ceases, the sun comes out, and when its light shines into the boat, the priest of Enki sacrifices an ox and a sheep. At the end of the text we find the old priest worshipping Enlil, the chief god of his country, whose anger against men has now abated. So Enlil grants the priest immortality and an eternal soul like that of a god.[1] Ziudsuddu, the priest, is the prototype of the Babylonian Ut-napishtim and of the Hebrew Noah. He is here revealed as the original Deluge-hero, an old priest-king who ruled one of the earliest Sumerian settlements in Babylonia.

Apparently from the earliest times the centre of each of these lowly hamlets was the shrine of the local god. In the course of time the hamlets developed into highly organized city-states, whose constant struggles resulted in the temporary hegemony of the victor. Nothing is more striking than the strength of the theocratic position; for the *patesi* makes war and gains the victory entirely at the bidding of his city-god, and this fiction is fully maintained in the subsequent treaty of peace. In short, the *patesis* are merely the human agents of the gods. There is reason to believe that these city-states were common to Babylonia and Elam, and that Susa and Anshan were ancient city-states coeval with Lagash, Erech, Ur, and Larsa. It is also reasonable to suppose that the mountain tribes were much less advanced than the inhabitants of the plains.

Eannatum, King of Lagash, before 3000 B.C.—The most striking figure among the earliest Sumerian Kings whose date

[1] See Arno Poebel, *The Museum Journal (University of Pennsylvania)*, vol. iv. No. 2 (June 1913), pp. 41 ff., and *Historical Texts* and *Historical and Grammatical Texts* (Univ. of Penns. Mus. Publ., Bab. Sect., vol. iv. No. 1, and vol. v.), Phila., 1914, and L. W. King, *Legends of Babylon and Egypt* (Schweich Lectures for 1916), *passim*. On another fragment of a supposed Deluge-legend, discovered by Prof. Langdon among the Nippur tablets, see King, *ibid.* p. 125, and Langdon, *Le Poème Sumérien du Paradis*, Paris, 1919. In this legend we find parallels to the Biblical story of the Fall of Man.

is known is Eannatum, *patesi* of Lagash by inheritance from a line of ancestors. He acquired fame and power through the defeat of the neighbouring city-state of Umma ; and it is deeply interesting to read the details of his campaigns and their results. These are graven on the famous " Stele of the Vultures," erected as a memorial of victories which won him the hegemony of Sumer some forty-eight centuries ago. The sculptured fragments give a picture of the Sumerians advancing to the attack in a solid phalanx of spearmen protected by shield-bearers. The Great Conqueror himself is represented driving in a chariot drawn by asses, horses being at that time unknown in Babylonia. The burial customs, too, are vividly portrayed, the dead being piled up in horizontal layers to form a mound.

Nor did Eannatum neglect the peaceful task of developing the resources of his state ; for numerous canals were dug, apparently during the latter years of his reign, when, to use his own expression, " his might had borne fruit."

Victories of Eannatum over the Elamites.—It would appear that in the reign of Eannatum the Elamites were regarded by the agriculturists of Sumer and Akkad as the natural enemy : indeed, their rulers could never be sure of immunity from the attack of the hardy mountaineers. This feeling is well expressed by Eannatum in his reference to Elam as " the mountain that strikes terror." However, the great Sumerian was able to record victories over the hereditary foe, in lines which run : " By Eannatum was Elam broken in the head, Elam was driven back to his own land," the metaphor being taken from a mace which was then a favourite weapon. Elsewhere Eannatum states that " he heaped up burial mounds," apparently referring to a severe defeat of the foe. It is to be noted, however, that these victories accomplished nothing more than the driving back of an Elamite expedition ; there was apparently no following up of the enemy into his own country. In other words, the policy of Sumer was defensive and not offensive.

The Earliest-known Letter and Elam.—The earliest example of a letter which has been found in Babylonia relates to Elam. It is written in Sumerian and probably belongs to the reign of Enannatum II., one of the later kings of Lagash. The writer, who was chief priest of the goddess Ninmar, informs his correspondent that a band of Elamites had raided Lagash

THE STELE OF NARAM-SIN.

The Conqueror is portrayed in the dramatic act of lowering his spear in token of acceptance of the surrender of his puny foemen, whose eyes are fixed on him.

territory, and that he had defeated them with heavy loss. The date of this document must be about 3000 B.C.

Elam and the Kish Dynasty, 2900–2800 B.C.—Upon the downfall of Sumerian Lagash rose the Semitic dynasty of Kish in Akkad. Manishtu, one of its warrior kings, conducted a campaign against Anshan and records its success ; not only were the people subdued and forced to pay tribute, but the captive king of Anshan graced the conqueror's triumph. Again, on a vase found at Nippur an inscription has been deciphered which states that the vase was booty from Elam, and was dedicated by another warrior king termed Urumush, " when he had conquered Elam." From this it appears that the agricultural states are at last assuming a forward policy, and that, no longer content with beating off the raids from Elam, they aim at the subjection of that country.

The Empire of Akkad, 2800 B.C.—We now turn to Akkad, or Agade, which, some two centuries after the death of Eannatum, was not only the leading state, but welded the collection of city-states into an empire ruled by a Semitic dynasty. To accomplish so much, a great man was needed ; and a great man appeared in the person of Sargon, who boasted that " he poured out his glory over the world " and that the Western Land (Syria) and the Eastern Sea (the Persian Gulf) formed the boundaries of his empire. Indeed, there is a tradition to the effect that he subdued the island of Dilmun in the Persian Gulf, and we know that he conquered not only Elam, but many districts of the Zagros to the north.

Sargon was equally distinguished for the arts of peace ; and it was under his influence that the old laws, the religious writings, and the works of magic were compiled and translated into the Semitic language. All these documents were stored in the temple of Erech, where, 1500 years later, they were copied by order of the Assyrian monarch Assurbanipal ; and it is owing to the enlightened action of this sovereign that a store of priceless knowledge has been preserved for the use and profit of mankind. Moreover, Sargon is the first monarch who is known to have organized a regular system of communication throughout the empire, an achievement which alone is sufficient to mark him out as a great man.

The Campaign of Sargon against Elam.—Sargon has recorded his campaigns against Elam. The most important was that in which the Great Warrior gained his victory partly by devastating the country and destroying the crops. There is, however, no proof that either in the time of Sargon or in that of Naram-Sin, who also waged war with Elam, that country was annexed by Akkad, although tribute was probably exacted for periods of varying length. On the other hand, from the newly-published historical inscriptions referred to above, we learn that Awan is shown as an important city of Elam during the dynasty of Akkad, and this may mean that the country passed temporarily under Elamite rule.

The Stele of Naram-Sin.—The famous stele of Naram-Sin, one of the most splendid trophies of the de Morgan mission, which has been mentioned in connexion with the Negrito question, was erected in memory of the conquest of Lulubi, a district in the Zagros between modern Baghdad and Kermanshah. It represents the king and his allies triumphing over the enemy in a hilly country. Moreover, in the same district, in the valley of the Hulvan (or Holwan), there are also important sculptures, which represent an early Semitic monarch, by name Anu-banini, and also his goddess Ninni or Ishtar.[1] The conquests of these two warrior monarchs undoubtedly tended to develop the intercourse between Elam and the Babylonian empire, of which there is some mention in the tablets. Elam, it is true, appears mainly as supplying contributions, and not as trading ; but, no doubt, commerce was developed even by this sort of intercourse. From the point of view of the history of Babylonia the dynasty of Akkad marks the supreme expression and culmination of Sumer and Akkad, both in civilization and in art, during the earlier period of their history. Out of a loose confederacy of city-states a great empire had been founded, and, although it was not destined to last long, its memory must have remained as an inspiration and a guiding star in after years, which were to see even greater power swayed by the rulers of Babylonia.

The Kingdom of Guti.—The close of the Akkad dynasty is no longer wrapped in the total darkness by which, until recently, it was surrounded. Indeed the names of its last seven kings have been recovered, although we are ignorant of their achievements or of the state of Babylonia and Elam under their sway. We now know also that the dynasty of Akkad was succeeded by another with its capital at Erech in

---

[1] *Sumer and Akkad*, p. 250 ; also de Morgan's *Mission Scientifique en Perse*, vol. iv. p. 161.

the south, which was short-lived. But the most interesting historical fact which has lately come to light is the complete domination of the country, at the close of this line of Erech Kings, by the Semitic Kingdom of Guti, which lay to the east of the Lesser Zab. The Gutian invasion led to the subjugation of both North and South Babylonia, and there can be little doubt that Elam itself acknowledged the suzerainty of these vigorous rulers, who had long been established in the mountainous regions upon their western border. The domination of these Gutian Semites was brought to an end by the valour of Utukhegal, King of Erech, who defeated and captured the Gutian King Tirikan, after having sought the assistance of the great Babylonian gods in their shrines upon his line of march. The success of this monarch marks the first wave of the Sumerian reaction, which reached its high-water mark under the Third Dynasty of Ur.

Gudea, Patesi of Lagash, 2500 B.C.—As the generations go by we see Lagash once again powerful as a city-state under the famous Gudea, whose reign became the golden age of this already ancient city. Gudea was not renowned as a conqueror, although he repulsed Anshan; but he is fully entitled to his position in the temple of Fame for his love of justice and his championship of the weak and poor at a period when such enlightened conduct was almost unknown. He will also be remembered by his buildings, for which he obtained materials from distant Syria, from Arabia and from Elam, the last-named country supplying the timber. He also states that the Elamite came from Elam and the Susian from Susa, presumably to take part in the building of the temple of Ningirsu, god of Lagash, which was his chief work.

The Rise of the Third Dynasty of Ur.—As we come down the centuries, we find the city-state of Ur, about 2450 B.C., reassuming the hegemony of Sumer and Akkad, which had largely sunk back into the position of separate city-states. This revival was Sumerian, as is shown by the fact that the Sumerian language is again employed, in contrast to the Semitic texts dating from the time of Sargon and Naram-Sin. Under Dungi, the second monarch of the dynasty, the bow, hitherto used exclusively by the Semites, was adopted,[1] and it was possibly by this means that he extended his empire over Elam, Lulubi, and other countries to the east of the Tigris.

[1] This is now known to be incorrect. *Vide* Preliminary Essay, p. xxxiii.

These and other conquests were maintained with great difficulty and at the cost of constant expeditions, Simuru and Lulubi, for instance, being invaded nine times.

The Administration of Elam by Dungi.—Elam now, for the first time, came under the permanent administration of Sumer. Tablets have been found at Tello, the site of Lagash, which contain orders for supplies, to be given to officials passing through that city on their way between Ur and their posts in Elam. The tablets give a list of supplies assigned to these representatives of Dungi for use during their stay at Lagash or for their onward journey. The functions of these officers were mainly the recruiting of labour for the king's great buildings, the transport of material, and the control of supplies. From the number of places mentioned, it is clear that Dungi's authority in Elam was not confined to a few cities, but was established practically over the whole country. Susa was in all probability the local capital, and Dungi rebuilt the temple of Shushinak, the national god. A fact of considerable interest in connexion with this conquest is that one district of Elam was ruled by a daughter of the Sumerian monarch. From the tablets just referred to we learn the names of several of the *patesis* of Elam, none of whom is a native of the country. This would account for the constant attempts at revolt, and it is quite likely that it had something to do with the progress of Elam towards nationality and the downfall of the dynasty of Ur.

The Overthrow of the Third Dynasty of Ur.—The fall of the dynasty of Ur was caused by an Elamite invasion, its last king being captured and taken as a prisoner to Anshan. Few details are known, but it is reasonable to suppose that, as the dynasty became weak, Elam recovered its liberty and finally turned on its oppressor.

The Sack of Erech by Kudur-Nankhundi, circa 2280 B.C.— Connected with the downfall of Ur is the sack of Erech by an Elamite king. The knowledge of this event reaches us in a way that is truly remarkable. When Assurbanipal captured Susa in *circa* 645 B.C. he recovered and restored to Erech the image of the goddess Nana, which Kudur-Nankhundi had carried off 1635 years before. This amazing piece of history is accepted as genuine, and it points to 2280 B.C. as the approximate date of the campaign. As King observes, the sack of Erech could not have occurred when the dynasty of Ur was in possession of Elam, and he is consequently of opinion that no more probable epoch for this event can be found than that of the Elamite invasion which brought about the destruction of Ur.

The Dynasty of Nisin, circa 2339–2115 B.C.—Little is known about the dynasty of Nisin, which reigned for a period of 225 years after the downfall of the house of Ur. It was composed of Semites who first rallied Sumer against Elam and then ruled the country. What little is known is derived from the Nippur dynastic list, which gives the names of sixteen kings. During most of this period the empire probably included Sumer and Akkad, and possibly for a time Elam also, although we read that it was Rimsin the Elamite King of Larsa who overthrew Nisin in 2115 B.C., the seventeenth year of his reign. Sumerian power and prestige, which were already shaken, never recovered from this blow.

The Influence of Sumerian Civilization.—The dynasty of Nisin fell, and with it the old order passed away. The race of the Sumerians was nearly run, and as a political factor they soon ceased to count. At this moment let us pause and take stock, before proceeding to outline even more dramatic periods in the history of the ancient races of Elam and Babylonia.

All nations that have passed away must be tested at the bar of history by their deeds ; and Sumer can face the trial without fear. The most important achievements of this great race which have come down the ages as a legacy to mankind are the invention of cuneiform writing, one of the greatest intellectual triumphs of the ancient world, and the code of laws on which the famous code of Hammurabi was based. Nor is our indebtedness confined to these two great boons. We owe the beginnings of art and science also to this hoary civilization. The more the mists that hang over the past are lifted, the more clearly shall we discern how astronomy, medicine, and art were learned by the Greeks from this ancient land. One legacy from Sumer we all carry in our pockets in the shape of a watch, whose face is a direct reproduction of the twelve double hours of the Sumerians, with its further divisions of sixty minutes and sixty seconds. Indeed, it is profoundly impressive to follow the archaeologist deeper and deeper into the past of Sumer and to find, in the fourth millennium B.C., organized communities enjoying a civilization which even then was clearly old ; and it is impossible not to express profound admiration and gratitude to those workers, through whose untiring labours and lucid exposition we of the twentieth century are receiving such gifts of fundamental knowledge.

ANZANITE TEXT OF SHILKHAK-IN-SHUSHINAK ON A HILT OF GLAZED POTTERY.
(From J. de Morgan's *Études, etc.* [Ernest Leroux.])

CHAPTER VI

ELAM AND BABYLON

I Shilkhak-in-Shushinak, son of Shutruk-Nakhunta, a valiant chief, for the blessing of my life, the blessing of the life of Nakhunta-Utu, my beloved wife, and the blessing of the life of our family.

The Rise of Babylon.—The triumph of the Semite over the Sumerian was finally sealed by the rise of Babylon. The victory of the Semite in the long racial contest was perhaps due to the fact that Arabia, the cradle-land of the Semitic race, was not only close by, but was constantly throwing out fresh waves of hardy tribesmen, who were anxious to settle in the fertile well-watered lands. Arabia was then undoubtedly less arid than to-day, when it can only support a scanty population, but the waves of racial movement may have been caused by periods of aridity, or by the weakness of the inhabitants of the settled districts, owing to war or pestilence, or perhaps, most of all, by the greater virility of the nomad. The rise of Babylon introduces one of the greatest epochs of history, and that city gradually became a centre of such imposing might that its grandeur and influence filled the old world.

A Retrospect.—Before we consider the relations of Elam with the earliest dynasties of Babylon, it will be interesting to look back and gain a general impression of its internal condition. It may be accepted that Elam was, throughout, more backward and less developed than its western neighbours. This we naturally infer from its hilly formation, which prevented easy communication, and provided few large tracts of fertile land, and the scanty information at our disposal tends to prove that the inference is correct. Raids and not conquest were the aim of its endeavours, and until a foreign yoke welded the loose congeries of tribes into a nation, it does not appear that Elam obeyed a single ruler. Nor is it at all certain that the hill tracts were subdued when the cities of the plains were brought under the rule of the Babylonian monarchs; indeed de Morgan holds that the Elamites of the hills never lost their independence. In any case, the length of time under review is so great, covering, as it does, a period equal to that separating the Norman Conquest from the twentieth century, that there was ample time for the wild tribesmen to unite with the inhabitants of the plain and develop into citizens of an empire which was a worthy antagonist, first of Babylonia, and later of Assyria.

The Difficulty of connecting Early Elamite Dynasties with those of Sumer.—One of the greatest difficulties in connecting the earlier dynasties of Elam with those of Babylonia is the want of a fixed point common to both. Some of the texts recovered by de Morgan give a succession of Elamite princes who had successively repaired or rebuilt the temples of Susa. Until the close of the First Dynasty of Babylon, however, it is impossible to fix the date of any one of these princes. Consequently, until the requisite information be forthcoming, we have to be satisfied with mere lists, arranged, it is true, in chronological order, but yet of little value until some fortunate discovery enables us to fix their place in relation to the history of Babylonia.

Of these early dynasties, that of Basha-Shushinak, who, as we have seen, employed the Semitic tongue in recording his votive offerings, is held to precede the Third Dynasty of Ur, whereas the dynasty of Khutran-tepti is supposed to be later. As the members of the latter dynasty were termed *patesi* of Susa, it is possible that they were vassals of Babylonia during the period of the empire of Ur. Later dynasties can be traced, but their place in history has not been determined.

The one certain Synchronism between Elam and Babylonia.—The only fixed point we can be sure of is the fact that a certain Kukka-Nasher governed Susa under Ammi-zaduga, the last monarch but one of the first Babylonian dynasty. But it is reasonable to suppose that those rulers, whether earlier or later, who were termed *sukkals*,[1] acknowledged the overlordship of Babylonia. Probably the control was loose and

---

[1] A *sukkal* signifies a minister or a governor, and not an independent prince.

varied by local wars and raids, such as we see to-day in more than one part of Asia. Indeed, this state of affairs is indicated by an inscription of a ruler of Dir, who claims that " he broke the heads of the men of Anshan and Elam. . . ." He probably lived during the period of the dynasty of Nisin.

The Elamite Conquest and its Results.—It is interesting to mark, under de Morgan's guidance, the results of the Elamite reaction, which was undoubtedly violent, and even savage : so much so that whole bodies of the inhabitants of Babylonia fled to save their lives. According to the views of the French writer, it was on this account that the worshippers of Assur fled up the valley of the Tigris, and founded the Assyrian nation. Again, according to him, to the south, the inhabitants of the country at the head of the Persian Gulf and of its islands, among them the Bahrein islanders, emigrated to the coast of Syria, and under the name of Phoenicians became celebrated as navigators, colonizers, and traders.[1] Yet, again, it was this same movement which caused the Hyksos invasion of Egypt ; and, finally, it was responsible for the departure from Ur of the Chaldees of Abraham's tribe, which ultimately followed in the wake of the Hyksos to Egypt, and was well received by the Shepherd Pharaoh. King, on the other hand, is cautious, and holds that there is no evidence that Elam controlled Babylonia for any long period. His view is that Elam threw off the foreign yoke as the result of the victories of her monarch, and then probably broke up into a number of independent states. But we can well believe that the Elamite outburst was fierce, and it is quite probable that its effects were felt far beyond the boundaries of Babylonia.[2]

Chedorlaomer, King of Elam.—An echo of these obscure but troublous times, which incidentally accentuates the closer relations existing at this period between Babylonia and the West, may be read in the 14th chapter of Genesis, which is believed to be one of the oldest parts of the book. An account is given of a campaign known as the battle of four kings against five, verse 9 running : " With Chedorlaomer the king of Elam, and with Tidal king of nations, and Amraphel

---

[1] This tradition is not now generally accepted as historically accurate.
[2] Winckler's view is that it is possible that the Hyksos dynasty was formed by the same wave of Arabian immigrants which founded the First Dynasty of Babylon. See his *History of Babylonia and Assyria*, p. 60. Hall regards it as caused by the Aryan invasion of Northern Mesopotamia, which drove the dispossessed Syrians into Egypt. See *Ancient History of the Near East*, p. 212.

king of Shinar, and Arioch king of Ellasar ; four kings with five." The " nations " are the Goyyim or Northern Barbarians. They are the non-Semitic peoples of Asia Minor. Thus it is probable that Tidal was king of the Khatti or Hittites ; that Amraphel was Hammurabi king of Sumer, and that Arioch of Ellasar represents the dynasty of Larsa. The four kings overthrew the kings of Sodom, Gomorrah, and other neighbouring city-states, and incidentally carried off Lot, who was rescued by Abraham. Chedorlaomer is not otherwise known to history, but his name is good Elamite, being obviously Kudur-Lagamar, and we have no reason to doubt that an Elamite king of this name was allied with Hammurabi in an attack on the West, even though our sole authority is the Hebrew tradition.

The Decay of the Elamite Empire.—The Elamite empire was short-lived, and few details can be gleaned of its history. It appears that Elam, albeit formidable in war, lacked the capacity to administer her conquests, and that each country was allowed to retain its organization and ancient rulers, subject to the payment of a heavy tribute. So far as can be gathered, first of all Syria was lost, and gradually, one by one, the neighbouring states recovered their liberty. Then the dynasty of Nisin, in its turn, conquered Elam. Such evidence as we have is based on the names of Elamite princes found by de Morgan in the building-inscriptions already mentioned. The whole period is still very obscure, in spite of the advance that has been made on our previous knowledge.

The First Dynasty of Babylon, 2225-1926 B.C.—The rise to power of the Semite kings, under whom Babylon attained the rank of a capital, was an event of immense importance, and fortunately we know more about this period than any that preceded it. King gives eleven names of monarchs who made up the first dynasty, and, thanks to the discovery by Professor Clay of a tablet containing a list of the kings of Larsa and the length of reign of each monarch, and of other tablets showing connexion between Larsa and Nisin, we have the necessary connecting links for the reconstruction of the chronology back to the middle of the third millennium.[1]

The Laws of Hammurabi.—The greatest monarch of this dynasty was the sixth, Hammurabi, the law-giver and conqueror, who reigned from 2123 to 2081 B.C. The defeat

[1] *History of Babylon,* p. 89.

of Rimsin, the Elamite king of Larsa, and the capture of his city in 2093 was the most important military event in Hammurabi's reign, and shows Babylon victorious in her struggle for mastery over rival city-states. Hammurabi was the author of the famous code of laws named after him, which is the most ancient in existence, although fragments have been discovered of the Sumerian code, on which it was undoubtedly based, and which show a standard almost equally high. When it is remembered that the laws of Hammurabi were codified centuries before those of Moses, which, in the view of some scholars, were to a considerable extent based on them,[1] we realize the magnitude of the debt we owe to de Morgan for recovering the priceless stele on which they are inscribed. The code as a whole is remarkable for its high moral tone, and also for the fact that it is a royal, or secular, and not a religious code. Among the subjects of legislation are the status of judges and other officials, farming, irrigation, and grazing, navigation, purchase of slaves, their relation to their masters, marriage laws, penalties in case of assault, the condition of women, inheritance, and brigandage. While the Empire endured, these laws continued to be the foundation on which the whole civilization of Babylonia rested.

The Second Dynasty of the Sea-Land, circa 2068–1710 B.C. —It is now known that the First Dynasty was brought to an end by an invasion of the Hittites, after having been weakened by continual conflicts with the earlier rulers of the so-called " Second Dynasty " recorded in the List of Kings. The eleven rulers of this dynasty controlled the extreme south of Babylonia, known as the " Sea-Country," Iluma-ilu, its Sumerian founder, having secured his independence in the reign of Samsu-iluna, Hammurabi's son. But the Hittites do not seem to have retained their hold on Babylon, for they were shortly succeeded as conquerors by Kassite tribes from Elam, who had already made raids into Babylonia during the period of the later Kings of the Hammurabi dynasty. Under the leadership of Gandash or Gaddash, the Kassites established themselves as the so-called Third Dynasty of the Babylonian King-lists in 1760 B.C. The earlier of these

[1] The earlier opinion that this was the case has now been given up in many quarters. The more striking points of resemblance which have been noted are, it is pointed out, such as would naturally characterize two codes in vogue among kindred peoples in a similar stage of culture whereas the specifically Babylonian features of the Hammurabi Code have left no trace on the Mosaic legislation.

Kassite Kings were contemporaneous with the later rulers of the "Second Dynasty," who continued to hold the southern part of Babylonia. Ea-gamil, the last in this line of southern monarchs, was not content with holding the district at the head of the Persian Gulf, but invaded Elam itself. He was signally defeated by Ullam-Buriash, the son of King Burna-Burariash, a relation of the Kassite chief, and henceforth these tribesmen, who had continued to maintain their connexion with Western Elam, enjoyed undisputed rule throughout the whole of Babylonia.[1]

Contemporary Elamite Dynasties.—Little can be gleaned about the internal condition of Elam during the period of the First Dynasty after Hammurabi and his son Samsu-iluna, who finally succeeded in defeating the son of the Elamite Kudur-Mabug. But there are traces of an independent kingdom with a predominant Anzanite element. Chief of these sovereigns are Khumban-numena and his son. The father evidently spent his life working for the consolidation of Elam. The son occupied himself in the reorganization of the country and the repair of its ruined sanctuaries, and it is thanks to these pious labours that numerous bricks bearing his name have been discovered.

The Kassite Dynasty of Babylon, circa 1925-1185 B.C.— We now return to the Kassite dynasty, which had its origin among the mountains of the Zagros to the north of Elam, and which ruled Babylonia for close on six centuries. The Kassites are believed to have been an Aryan tribe having as their chief god Suryash, the Sun.[2] They apparently formed the advance-guard of the invading tribes referred to in Chapter VIII. As might be supposed, the influence of the great capital asserted itself in time, and the successors of the first conquerors became Babylonian in outlook, being assimilated by the superior civilization of their subjects.

During the rule of the Kassite dynasty Assyria appeared as a rising power in the middle reaches of the Tigris, and we have the record of a treaty concluded in the fifteenth century B.C. between a Kassite monarch and the King of Assur. In 1275 B.C. the northern power temporarily

---

[1] On the interrelation of the first three Babylonian dynasties and the successive interference of the Hittites and Elamites with Babylonian affairs, *vide* King, *Studies in Eastern History*, ii. chaps. iv.-vi. pp. 76 ff.

[2] Suryash is the same word as the Indian Surya and the Greek Helios. *Vide* Hall, *op. cit.* p. 201.

conquered Babylon, and again about 1100 B.C. there was a second, but equally ephemeral, occupation ; the attempt in both cases proving in the end disastrous to the arms of Assyria.[1]

With Egypt intercourse was maintained, and letters exchanged between the two monarchs are still preserved. When the Kassite power waned Elam possessed the greatest influence, and the dynasty at its close acknowledged the overlordship of Elam. It was under the Kassite dynasty that the horse was introduced into general use in Babylonia to draw chariots, although there is now evidence that it was already known at the time of the First Dynasty, when Kassites served in the armies under the name of " the ass of the mountain."

The Position of Elam.—During this long period of time the position of Elam is but slightly known. We read of a war waged in the later period of the Kassite dynasty, by Khurbatila, King of Elam, against Kurigalzu, King of Babylon. The former, who was invading Babylonia, was defeated and made prisoner. Susa, too, was apparently captured. Some generations later Elam, under Kidin-Khutrutash, devastated and conquered Babylonia and carried away many of its inhabitants.

Shutruk-Nakhunta, King of Elam, circa 1190 B.C.—Among the famous warrior-kings of this period was Shutruk-Nakhunta, who not only conquered Babylonia, but removed to Susa the choicest works of art from the cities he laid waste. It is thanks to this action that de Morgan's labours have been so richly rewarded, the famous stele of Naram-Sin, for example, having been transported by this monarch from Babylon, to be found by the French archaeologist some 3000 years later. Marduk, the chief Babylonian deity, was also carried off in triumph to Elam and remained in captivity for 30 years. This invasion by Elam finally brought about the overthrow of the Kassite dynasty.

Shutruk-Nakhunta was succeeded by Shilkhak-in-Shushinak, a great administrator who was also a great builder. De Morgan owes much to him, for he never inscribed his name on a restored temple without also mentioning the original founder. Even better, he transcribed word for word the old commemorative inscriptions in the Semitic language

[1] *Vide* Chapter VII.

and added the Anzanite translation, with the result that we have, with an interval of 2000 years between them, two editions of the first text, and marvel at the antiquity of the people of Elam. This was their golden age in art and literature ; and stelae, columns of bronze, bricks, and inscriptions belonging to it abound.

The Pashe Dynasty of Babylon, circa 1184-1053 B.C.—A new dynasty gained a victory over the Elamites, and Marduk was brought back to Babylon. The victor, Nebuchadnezzar I., was a leading member of the Pashe dynasty, so called from one of the quarters of Babylon. He for the last time carried the arms of Babylon as far as the Mediterranean. From the close of his career to the end of the period, about 1053 B.C., very little trustworthy information can be gleaned. It is probable that during most of it Elam was the overlord.

The Sea-Land and Bazi Dynasties, circa 1052-1032 B.C.— Three kings belonging to a second dynasty of the Sea-land ruled for twenty years, to be succeeded by another, of three kings, which endured for two decades and was known as the Dynasty of Bazi. Then the Elamites again appear in Babylonia, and we find an Elamite ruler on the throne, but only for a brief period of six years (*circa* 1011-1006 B.C.).

This fact in itself is sufficient evidence of the state of impotence into which Babylonia had fallen in consequence of the invasion of the country by the nomadic Gutians in the reign of the usurper Adad-aplu-iddina, one of the successors of the powerful Nebuchadnezzar I. They devastated both Sumer and Akkad, plundered the cities and destroyed the great temples, with the result that the land lay prostrate and without stable government. Adad-aplu-iddina had attempted to secure Assyrian aid, and, probably with this object in view, had given his daughter in marriage to the reigning Assyrian monarch. It was not unnatural that Elam should endeavour to take advantage of this state of affairs, but she effected no permanent control over the country. The solitary Elamite ruler who ascended the throne (and possibly adopted the Babylonian name of Ae-aplu-utsur) failed to found a dynasty. The circumstance that Babylon, although overshadowed at this time both by Assyria and by Elam, managed to retain a semi-independence may be connected with the continual menace of invasion by fresh Semitic hordes.

The Chaldaeans, circa 970-732 B.C.—Babylonia, spoiled

ELAM AND BABYLON

by Elam and coveted by Assyria, was now overrun by a horde of Semitic immigrants, known to history as the Chaldaeans, whose appearance marks the beginning of a new epoch. Issuing from Eastern Arabia, they entered Mesopotamia from the south, and thenceforward a third power joined in the contest for Babylonia. It is impossible to enumerate the various campaigns waged during this period. Winckler describes it as being characterized by "the attempts of the Chaldaean princes, with the assistance of Elam, to obtain the throne of Babylon, and the superiority of Assyria when not engaged in other quarters."[1] In short, constant strife and anarchy followed, until, during the reign of Nabu-natsir (747–732 B.C.), who is famous as having introduced a new era, Babylonia fell under the domination of the New Assyrian Empire.

[1] *Op. cit.* p. 107.

INSCRIPTION OF ASSURBANIPAL.
(From Sir H. C. Rawlinson's *Cuneiform Inscriptions of Western Asia*, 1861, vol. v. plate 6, col. 6, lines 96-106.)

CHAPTER VII

THE ASSYRIAN EMPIRE AND THE DOWNFALL OF ELAM

The dust of the city of Shushan, of the city of Madaktu, and the rest of the cities, I have taken it all away to the country of Assur. During a month and a day I have swept the land of Elam in all its width. I deprived the country of the passage of cattle and of sheep and of the sound of joyous music. I have allowed wild beasts, serpents, the animals of the desert and gazelles to occupy it.—*Inscription of Assurbanipal.*

The Rise of Assyria.—The " land of Assur " was originally the territory belonging to the city of the same name. Like the city-states of Babylonia, it was ruled by *patesis*, who, as in the case of the older civilization, in time developed into puissant monarchs. The first mention of the city of Assur is in a letter of the time of Hammurabi, when it apparently formed part of the empire of that great monarch.[1] Between 1800 B.C. and 1500 B.C. Assyria won its independence. As it expanded it moved steadily northwards. The ancient capital, Assur (the modern Kala Shergat), was superseded, as the seat of empire, first by Kalkhi or Calah (Kalakh), on the site of the modern Nimrud, and finally by Nineveh. Situated on the only route connecting Babylonia with the west, Assyria, in the course of its development, naturally

[1] Winckler, *op. cit.* p. 180. I am specially indebted to this work in the present chapter.

conquered the neighbouring states ; and it is interesting to note how it was that Assur rose to such a splendid height as to subjugate the mother-country and to make the neighbouring states her humble tributaries.

Unlike Babylonia, which was based on a feudal, ecclesiastical system, Assyria drew her strength from a free agricultural class ; and this system led to the formation of the most formidable army known in the Near East. Indeed, Assyria rested entirely on her army ; and when the free-born cultivators of the soil were exhausted, steps were taken to employ mercenaries, who fought well for Assyria as long as pay and booty were forthcoming, but deserted her in the hour of need.

The Old Empire.—Owing to the document termed the " Synchronous History," on which important past events in Assyria and Babylonia were tabulated by the official scribes of Assurbanipal, it is possible to follow the history of Assyria from the fifteenth century without difficulty. The first event recorded is a compact between Karaindashi, a monarch of the Kassite dynasty, and Assur-rimnishishu of Assur. A generation or so later there is a letter which a King of Assyria, Assur-uballit II., sent to Amenophis IV. of Egypt. In this the Assyrian refers to letters that his grandfather, Assur-nadin-akhi, had written to Amenophis III., a fact of considerable interest. About 1300 B.C. Adad-Nirari I. overthrew the kingdom of Mitani to the north-west and obtained possession of Mesopotamia. His son Shalmaneser I., about 1270 B.C., continued his father's conquests, and during his reign the second capital, Kalkhi, was founded between the Tigris and the Upper or Greater Zab. At this period Mitani was finally subdued ; and Babylonia, the great state to the south, which at that time was harassed by Elam, was conquered by Tukulti-Ninibi in or about 1248 B.C.[1] The Babylonians, however, in the end drove out the invaders, and as the result of internal troubles Assyria lost her empire and reverted to her original position of subordination to Babylonia.

About 1100 B.C. Assyria again became a great power under Tiglath-pileser I., who carried the Assyrian arms to the source of the Tigris, where his effigy is still preserved with an inscription telling of three campaigns in the district.

[1] Hall, *op. cit.* p. 370.

He also overran the western portion of the Iranian plateau, as will be narrated in Chapter X. Among other exploits he defeated the Hittites and penetrated to the Mediterranean Sea, and it is most interesting to read of his embarking for a cruise at Arvad. During this campaign gifts were exchanged with the monarch of Egypt, who presented him with a crocodile. He finally marched his victorious army against Babylonia and obtained possession of the capital; but, as in the case of the earlier conquest, the wheel of fortune turned, and Assyria, once again, sank to her dependent position.

The Aramaean Immigration.—The great event of this period both for Assyria and for Babylonia was the immigration of the Aramaean hordes which, issuing from Arabia, had already overrun the country as early as 1300 B.C. They now swept across Mesopotamia down the Tigris, and, although in Babylonia they were opposed by the Chaldaeans who were still moving north and also by their own kinsmen, the Suti, who had already occupied much of the country, they were henceforth a factor to be reckoned with. In Assyria they apparently took possession of the entire land, and it was this human avalanche which brought the Old Assyrian Empire to an end that is enveloped in darkness. It is of considerable interest to note that about 1200 B.C. the Aramaeans absorbed Damascus, Aleppo, and other kingdoms in Syria. They became great traders, and by 1000 B.C. were using alphabetic writing adopted from the Phoenicians. Their commercial influence and their writing spread throughout the Near and Middle East, and slowly, but surely, their writing displaced cuneiform signs.

The Middle Assyrian Kingdom, circa 900–745 B.C.—When Assyria regained the upper hand she first subdued the Aramaean tribes and then broke into amazing military activity in every direction, from the source of the Tigris to the Nahr-ul-Kalb near Beirut, where Assyrian sculptures may still be seen by the traveller.

The reign of Adad-Nirari II. (911–890 B.C.) is of special importance, as from 893 B.C. a continuous record is preserved, or, as Hall puts it, " accurately dated history begins." [1] Consequently, when the monarch refers to his grandfather, Tiglath-pileser III., we know that the latter was a con-

---
[1] *Op. cit.* p. 445.

THE ASSYRIAN EMPIRE

temporary of Solomon and of Shishak. The greatest conqueror of this dynasty was Assur-natsir-pal (884–860 B.C.), who restored the kingdom to the limits ruled by Tiglath-pileser I. His fame is tarnished by the fiendish cruelty with which he treated his prisoners, all children, both boys and girls, being burned alive at the stake. His son, Shalmaneser II., failed to conquer Damascus, the ally of whose monarch was Ahab of Israel, but his success in Babylonia made him overlord of the country. To these two monarchs was due the military organization of Assyria, which soon made her the great conquering power of the Near East. At this period, Elam, inaccessible and warlike, and Egypt, weak but distant, alone were free from attack, and Assyria again reached the height of fame ; but, owing mainly to the rise of the kingdom of Urartu or Ararat, she again found herself unable to hold the conquered states, which broke away and regained their liberty, and a mutiny ended the dynasty.

The New Assyrian Kingdom, 745–606 B.C.—Under Pul or Tiglath-pileser IV., by which title the general commanding the mutineers ascended the throne, Assyria became the ruling power of Anterior Asia from the Iranian plateau to the Mediterranean Sea, a position which she maintained for more than a century. This great conqueror made his first campaign in Babylonia, where he defeated the Aramaean and Chaldaean tribes. He assumed the overlordship of Babylonia, whose monarch Nabu-natsir reigned under the protection of Assyria. In the north he waged several campaigns against Urartu, and although unable to capture Van, the capital, he annexed her southern provinces. But his campaigns to the west excite our interest still more, inasmuch as, by the ultimate conquest of Damascus in 732 B.C., Palestine was deprived of the help of the state which alone stood between it and Assyria. And finally, after a series of successful campaigns, he entered Babylon as a victor and "took the hands of Bel" as king of Sumer and Akkad.

Sargon II., 722–705 B.C.—Sargon II. came to the throne of Assyria as the founder of a new dynasty. It would appear that his immediate predecessors had opposed the privileges of the priests, who not only were exempted from taxation but owned a very large proportion of the land, with the result that the free agriculturist class had been driven away to make room for gangs of slaves or prisoners of war. The priests, however, were able to bring about a revolution, and Sargon II. ascended the throne as their nominee. The monarchy henceforth was supported by mercenaries and the army ceased to be a national force.

The First Battle between Assyria and Elam.—It was under this monarch that Assyria for the first time met Elam in a pitched battle. Tiglath-pileser had fought with the wild hill tribes in the mountains to the north of Susa, and other Assyrian monarchs had come into conflict with the semi-independent tribes which formed buffer states between the two powers; but it was not until Aramaean districts east of the Tigris had been annexed and Babylon conquered by Tiglath-pileser IV. that the two powers came into direct contact, which was bound to develop into hostilities sooner or later. On the one hand was the comparatively civilized and organized state of Assyria, which annexed other countries and administered them, and on the other was Elam, which, like most independent and secluded peoples, lacked all knowledge as to its relative strength and felt confident of victory. Moreover, Elam suffered from the fact that the Assyrian advance interfered with its immemorial custom of raiding. In these circumstances it is not surprising that an alliance was concluded between Elam and Babylonia; but the energy and genius of Sargon had not been sufficiently realized. Hearing from his spies that the army of Elam had crossed the frontier, he resolved to take the initiative and to crush the two powers separately. Consequently, while the Elamite monarch was awaiting a junction with his ally, the Assyrian army most unexpectedly appeared in sight.

The two armies, which were to meet for the first time, were unequally equipped. The Elamite infantry soldier possessed no armour, whereas mail coats were worn by the heavy Assyrian archers; he carried a light shield as against the big Assyrian shield, while his head was protected by a low helmet without a crest and a large horse-hair plume. His arms consisted of a bow smaller than that used by the Assyrians, a lance, a mace, and a dagger. His chariot was much lighter than that of Assyria and his force of cavalry very small. Finally, as the Elamite army was mainly composed of independent or semi-independent allies from the mountain ranges surrounding the plain of Susa, it is obvious that, while bravery was not lacking, there could not have been the same cohesion or organization as in the host of Assyria, which had marched to victory all over the Near East. Even so, the Elamite proved a brave, tenacious enemy to the armies of Assyria.

The first engagement was stubbornly contested and sanguinary. Both sides claimed the victory, but the Assyrians had to retire and so the battle of Durilu constituted a defeat, though not a crushing one, for the Assyrian army. There, for the time being, the contest rested, and Sargon commenced his marvellous career, in the course of which he inflicted a severe defeat on the armies of Egypt, while the land of the Hittites became an Assyrian province and the Greek " Kings " of Cyprus sent gifts to Nineveh. It was during this reign that Samaria was captured and the Ten Tribes were sent into captivity.

Sennacherib, 705–682 B.C.—We now come to the reign of Sennacherib, the son and successor of Sargon, who, as mentioned in Chapter III., raided the sea-coast of Elam. His object was to attack Chaldaean refugees who were trying to found a new state, and to some extent he succeeded ; but, while his army was plundering the sea-coast of Elam, Northern Babylonia was being laid waste as a reprisal by the active Elamites under Khalludush, who even captured the King's son.

His Campaigns against Elam.—A revolution in Elam, in which Khalludush was besieged in his palace and put to death, gave Sennacherib an opportunity of which he did not hesitate to take advantage ; and for the first time the Assyrian army was able to ravage the rich plain on which Susa stands. The Assyrian monarch recorded the result as follows : " Thirty-four strongholds and townships depending on them whose number is unequalled, I besieged and took by assault, their inhabitants I led into captivity, I demolished them and reduced them into ashes. I caused the smoke of their burning to rise into the wide heaven, like the smoke of one great sacrifice."

Kudur-Nankhundi, who had been elected to occupy the vacant throne, retreated into the mountains, where he remained a passive spectator throughout the campaign. Encouraged by this sign of weakness, Sennacherib determined to march upon Madaktu in the hill country ; but violent storms of rain and snow drove the Assyrian army back to the plains, whence it returned to Nineveh. Kudur-Nankhundi became unpopular owing to his failure to attack the Assyrians, and was murdered in 692 B.C.

His younger brother Umman-Minanu was his successor, and under his rule the army of Elam soon recovered its formidable character. Seeing this, the Babylonian monarch thought the opportunity favourable for a combination against the common oppressor. To provide money with which to pay Elam for contingents from the Iranian plateau, the treasuries of the gods of Babylon were emptied, and soon a very large force was collected and met the Assyrians on the Tigris. Again the field was stoutly contested, with heavy loss on both sides. The Elamite general was killed, and many perished " of those who wore golden daggers at their belts." Finally, both armies retreated to their respective bases, without any decisive advantage to either.

The Capture and Sack of Babylon, 689 B.C.—In 689 B.C. Sennacherib again took the field and advanced on Babylon; and on this occasion Elam failed her ally, her monarch having been struck down by paralysis. Babylon apparently did not stand a long siege, and when it was captured, instead of being dealt with leniently as on former occasions, it was handed over to the pitiless soldiery, with orders to massacre and sack. These instructions were obeyed but too well, and Babylon was levelled to the ground, a canal being turned on to the ruins as a punishment for the constant revolts of its inhabitants.

Esarhaddon, 681–669 B.C., and his Relations with Elam.— The first act of the new monarch was to commence the rebuilding of Babylon, and in the tenth year after its destruction the walls, towers, and gates were completed. In 674 B.C. Khumban-Khaldash II. of Elam suddenly raided Babylonia, pushing forward as far as Sippar, while the Assyrian monarch was engaged elsewhere. As the Assyrian garrisons were too weak to meet the Elamites in the field, the raiders returned in triumph to Susa, where their monarch died a few days later. Urtaku, his brother, who succeeded to the throne, restored the gods which had been carried off from Sippar; in return he received aid from Esarhaddon when Elam was suffering from famine.

The Conquest of Egypt, 670 B.C.—The crowning feat of Esarhaddon's reign was the conquest of Egypt, which had indeed suffered defeat before at the hands of the Assyrians, but had never seen her cities captured, her lands devastated, and her princesses carried off into slavery. The power of Assyria culminated after this campaign, which brought the whole of the civilized world, except Elam, under its stern sway; and the fall of Elam was soon to follow.

Assurbanipal, 669–626 B.C.—Upon the death of Esarhaddon, Assurbanipal succeeded to the empire; and his brother Shamash-shum-ukin to the kingdom of Babylon. The attention of the new monarch was first taken up with the suppression of the Egyptian revolt in 668 B.C. under Tirhakeh, the Ethiopian king who had retreated into Nubia. In 665 B.C., when the bulk of Assyrian forces were still in far-off Egypt, the Elamites, who evidently thought the opportunity too good to be lost, suddenly crossed the Tigris under Urtaku and devastated the land far and wide. Babylon was too strong to be captured, and so the Elamites, following their usual practice, returned to Susa, laden with booty. There, however, Urtaku died, and the coincidence of his death with that of other leaders left Elam a prey to anarchy. Urtaku was succeeded by his brother Teumman, whose attempts to murder his nephews caused sixty royal princes, with a considerable following, to flee to the court of Assurbanipal. There they were received with honour, as it was hoped, through their instrumentality, to weaken Elam by means of civil war. The policy was successful, for these family feuds were the ultimate cause of the downfall of Elam. In the meanwhile, the Nile was again ascended by Assurbanipal in person and Thebes was sacked, two of the obelisks which adorned the temple of Amen being transported to Nineveh.

The First Campaign against Elam.—Teumman, firmly seated on the throne of Elam, made an alliance with the Gambula, who occupied the Tigris fords, and thus opened the road to Babylon. Before crossing the frontier he offered Assurbanipal the choice between war and the surrender of the refugees from Elam. The Assyrian monarch could not agree to a demand which would have been looked upon as a confession of utter weakness, and so war became inevitable; though, as the inscriptions show, Assurbanipal did not enter upon it with a light heart. However, the gods, when consulted, gave reassuring replies; and the Assyrian army was sent to the frontiers of Elam.

The Battle of Tulliz, 659 B.C. ?—Teumman, disconcerted

by this unexpected rapidity of action, concentrated his forces, and slowly withdrawing to Tulliz, a town close to Susa, prepared to fight a decisive battle with his left flank resting on the Karun, and his right protected by a palm-grove. At the same time, as all his troops had not arrived, he despatched one of his generals, by name Ituni, to open up negotiations with a view to gaining time. The Assyrian commander, however, saw through the ruse, and gave orders for the envoy to be decapitated. The battle hung in the balance for a long while; but at length the Assyrians swept the Elamite left wing into the Karun, until the river was choked with the corpses of men and horses. The remainder of the beaten army tried to escape under cover of the groves to the mountains. Teumman fought like a hero, leading charge after charge until he was wounded. He then attempted to escape in a chariot, but one of its wheels broke against a palm-tree and he was thrown out. The Assyrian pursuers were close at hand, under the command of an exiled Elamite prince thirsting for revenge. Teumman was again wounded, and, feeling furious that an Elamite should lead the foe, cried out to his son to shoot him. The young warrior, having missed his mark, was himself wounded by darts and despatched by a blow from the mace of the Elamite prince, while Teumman's head was cut off and sent to Nineveh.

The scene is vividly represented in the illustrations, taken from originals which are in the British Museum. They show that the pursuit passed through a grove of date palms, and the figures are very lifelike. This decisive victory was duly celebrated, as was customary, by beating the rank and file to death, and flaying alive the generals and other superior officers, the chiefs alone being reserved to grace the triumph.

The Revolution at Susa.—The news of the disaster, which reached Susa the same day, brought about a revolution. The adherents of the exiled princes threw their opponents into chains, and met the victors in a solemn procession, in which the sacred eunuchs took the leading part. In accordance with instructions sent by Assurbanipal, Khumban-igash, the eldest son of Urtaku, was presented to the populace as their monarch, and the Assyrian army, after receiving tribute, returned to Nineveh.

The Triumph of Assyria.—The joy of Assurbanipal is some proof of the terror that Elam had inspired. The captured

THE LAST ARROW OF TEUMMAN.

(From the slab in the Nineveh Gallery in the British Museum.)

leaders were flayed alive, and their bodies were quartered and sent to various parts of the empire. The head of Teumman, after being hung on a tree at a banquet, was fixed over a gate of Nineveh. Although Elam had not beaten Assyria in any campaign, it had defied Esarhaddon, had repeatedly ravaged Babylonia, and was the only power which had hitherto remained free and a standing menace to Assyria. Consequently we can imagine the delight of Assurbanipal at having reduced the country of the hereditary foe to tribute, and we can admire his successful diplomacy, which encouraged the exiled Elamite princes from their secure retreat in Nineveh to create divisions at home. But it is difficult to understand why the Assyrian army stayed its hand when Susa was apparently within its grasp.

The Rebellion of Babylon.—After the crushing defeat inflicted on Elam and the accession of an Assyrian protégé to its throne, it seemed unlikely that there would be trouble from that quarter for many years. But Assurbanipal by his unbounded arrogance alienated his brother, whom he treated as a mere viceroy of Babylon removable at will, with the result that, in 652, the latter revolted and formed a coalition against the Assyrian monarch, which included the chief feudatory states. Khumban-igash, king of Elam, would naturally have remained loyal to Assyria; but Assurbanipal had demanded that the statue of Nâna should be restored to Erech. To comply with this demand and keep the throne was impossible, the statue being intensely venerated by the whole Elamite nation; and, as the Babylonian envoys offered the treasures of the gods, Khumban-igash threw himself into the alliance, which was undoubtedly popular.

The Second Campaign against Elam, 651 B.C.—The campaign opened, and the opposing forces watched one another throughout the year 651. Assyria again reaped the benefit of internal dissensions in the Elamite royal family. Tammaritu, brother of Khumban-igash, conspired against him, and after putting him to death seized the throne; but, to prove that there was no change of policy, he at once despatched more troops to join the army in the field. His reign was short; for one of the great feudatories of Elam, by name Indabugash,[1] was encouraged by the state of affairs to rebel, and was so successful

---

[1] This name is clearly an Aryan one, as it contains the Slav *buga* or god, the modern Russian *bog*. *Vide* Hall, *op. cit.* p. 201.

that Tammaritu was forced to flee to the marshes bordering the Persian Gulf, where a ship was seized by the refugees. But a storm drove the ship ashore, and Tammaritu was made prisoner and sent to Nineveh. There he was kindly treated by Assurbanipal, who hoped, no doubt, to make use of him in the future. Meanwhile the successful rebel withdrew the Elamite forces from the field and left his ally to his fate.

The Capture of Babylon, 648 B.C.—Assurbanipal was thus free to deal with Babylon, which, after a long siege, was captured and dealt with in exactly the same way as it had been by Sennacherib forty years before, its inhabitants being massacred by thousands in front of the great winged bulls.

The Third Campaign against Elam.—The Assyrian monarch now wisely determined to take advantage of Elamite divisions to make an end of the independence of this turbulent state, and, as may be imagined, Tammaritu was the chosen instrument. Even before the fall of Babylon a demand had been made for the surrender of the Chaldaeans who had taken part in the rebellion, but no definite answer had been given. Upon the fall of the great city, which it was to the vital interests of Elam to have prevented, Assurbanipal dismissed the Elamite ambassadors with the following message to the neighbouring monarch : " If thou dost not surrender those men, I will go and destroy thy cities and lead into captivity the inhabitants of Susa, Madaktu, and Khaidalu. I will hurl thee from thy throne, and will set up another thereon : as aforetime I destroyed Teumman, so will I destroy thee."

Meanwhile Indabugash had been murdered by his nobles, who had set up Khumban-Khaldash in his place. Thus the moment was specially favourable for Assurbanipal, who openly espoused the cause of Tammaritu, and the latter, aided by the Assyrians, re-entered Susa, and was again crowned king. No sooner was this successfully accomplished than Tammaritu with incredible folly attempted to massacre his grasping allies ; but the plot was revealed, and he was again seized and thrown into prison. The Assyrian army, however, not feeling strong enough to maintain its position unsupported, retired to Nineveh, laying the whole country waste.

The Capture and Sack of Susa, circa 645 B.C.—Assurbanipal, dissatisfied with the meagre results of the campaign, sent the treacherous Tammaritu to demand the surrender of the Chaldaeans and of the goddess Nana ; but Khumban-Khaldash knew that to accede would mean his own death, and preferred to resist to the bitter end. On this occasion, however, the Assyrian forces were too strong, and, after burning fourteen royal cities, found Susa at their mercy. An Assyrian army had twice before entered Susa in the guise of allies; but now the soldiers of Assur were able to gratify their ancient hatred and to satisfy their lust of pillage to the full. The booty was rich. Apart from treasures looted in bygone days from Sumer and Akkad, there was the gold and silver of the temples of Babylon, which had been used to secure the Elamite alliance. The gods, too, whose sanctuaries were violated and whose treasures were sacked, were sent to Nineveh, together with thirty-two statues of Elamite monarchs in gold, silver, bronze, and marble. Finally, the tombs of the ancient heroes were broken open and their bones despatched to Nineveh, where, in a supposed exquisite refinement of cruelty, libations were offered, by means of which the souls chained to the crumbling bones were kept alive to taste to the full the bitterness and humiliation of exile! In short, everything was done that malice or cruelty could suggest to fill the cup of bitterness of fallen Elam. To quote the words of Ezekiel, " There is Elam and all her multitude round about her grave, all of them slain, fallen by the sword." [1]

The Statue of Nana restored to Erech.—And at last Assurbanipal was able to carry out his purpose and send back the statue of Nana to Erech, after a captivity lasting 1635 years. Is there any parallel in history comparable to this?

The Assyrian army finally marched back in triumph, taking with it not only the wealth of Susa, but also a large proportion of its surviving population as well as that of the surrounding districts. Khumban-Khaldash escaped for a while; but he was finally driven to surrender, and the culminating triumph was reached when Assurbanipal harnessed him and Tammaritu, with two other conquered kings, to the chariot which bore the great monarch, now at the zenith of his glory, to the temples of Assur and Ishtar.

The Disappearance of Elam.—Elam as a kingdom had fallen, and, even if there still remained independent hill tribes, her memory passed away and was lost in a mist of fable and legend. It is not unprofitable, before we leave it, to look back for a moment at her history. Elam in her

[1] Ezekiel xxxii. 24.

earliest days was a predatory power, and so she remained throughout. At the same time she developed her own system of writing, her own art,[1] and to a certain extent her own civilization. But she raided rather than subdued, and made little serious attempt at empire ; and when she tried to organize her conquests she signally failed. In relation to Babylon her behaviour might perhaps be compared with that of the " thresher " to the whale : she raided the great kingdom relentlessly, and although her resources were incomparably more slender, she almost invariably succeeded in bringing booty safely back to Susa. Brought face to face with Assyria, when the intervening buffer states had been absorbed, Elam fought heroically against superior organization, forces, and equipment. Even so, thanks to her inaccessibility and valour, she might well have survived Assyria but for civil dissensions, which again and again paralysed her arms at the most critical juncture. In the end she fell, and so entirely was her greatness forgotten that in the pages of Strabo we read that Cyrus placed the capital at Susa because of its situation and the importance of the city, and also because " it had never of itself undertaken any great enterprise and had always been in subjection to other people."[2] *Sic transit gloria mundi !*

[1] In the making of jewelry and in casting metal the Elamites excelled the Babylonians.
[2] Strabo xv. 3. 2.

A MEDIAN HORSEMAN.
(From Lujard's *Culte de Mithra*.)

CHAPTER VIII

THE ARYANS OF PERSIA—THEIR ORIGIN AND TRADITIONS

The first of the good lands and countries which I created was the Aryanem-Vaejo.—*Vendidad,* i.

The Contrast between the Plains and the Uplands of Persia.—One of the most pleasant experiences of a traveller in Persia is to quit the plains, already disagreeably hot in spring, and to ascend to the uplands, where the sun has no sting and where everything is fresh and green. He reaches, indeed, a different country. Hitherto, in the course of our survey, civilization has been concerned almost entirely with the low-lying plains where primitive man developed until great cities such as Susa, Babylon, and Nineveh were built, and where, finally, the whole of the Near East and Egypt were irresistibly swept into the orbit of a great predominant Semitic state.

The Uplands dominated by the Aryans.—Leaving these plains, with their comparatively old and developed civilization, we ascend to the Iranian plateau, where, just as the physical characteristics differ, so also do the inhabitants. Upon reaching the plateau we have passed from areas dominated by Semitic influence to a country where the Aryan is the ruling race, although deeply influenced by the more civilized powers of Babylonia and Assyria. The history of the ancient world is henceforth destined to be a struggle between the Semitic races of the South and the Aryan races of the North, which finally ended in the complete victory of the northern races.[1]

[1] *Vide Ancient Times*, by J. H. Breasted, p. 172.

The Aryan Question.—The "Indo-European" question, more commonly termed the Aryan question (although the term Aryan is strictly applicable only to the Indo-Iranian group), excited controversies without number at a time when the study of these absorbing problems was in its infancy. The original idea was that from some primitive home swarms of Aryans peopled the uninhabited parts of the northern hemisphere. We have travelled far from those early conceptions and know that the world was already, at the time we speak of, inhabited by other races. Consequently, it is now generally admitted that it is more correct to speak of a "*family of Aryan languages* and perhaps of a primitive *Aryan civilization*, which had preceded the separation of the different Aryan dialects from their common stock." [1]

We may, indeed, be proud to be descended from this Aryan stock, but let us not forget the debt we owe to the Sumerians, to the Semites, and to that wonderful Mediterranean race, whose civilizations the barbarous Aryans adopted and developed. The more the origins of our civilization are examined, the more certain it becomes that we inherit from all the civilizations of all the ages.

The Cradle-land of the Aryans.—The identification of the centre from which the Aryan races issued is a point on which the greatest diversity of opinion has prevailed; yet there are some indications to guide us. The Aryans were evidently inhabitants of a land with a continental climate, as they recognized only two or three seasons. Their language shows that they were steppe-dwellers, that there was a marked absence of mountains and forests, and that only a few hardy trees such as the birch and the willow were known. Now we know that the Aryans came from the north, and, as nomads range widely, it is the view of some that their home may be sought in the vast region of the steppes to the far north of Khorasan—then, in all probability, more fertile—and in the adjacent and similar, but better-watered, plains of Southern Russia. Others regard the district to the southwest of the Caspian Sea as the original home. In any case, the question is not one for dogmatic pronouncement.

The Tradition of the Aryans of Persia.—The Aryans of the Iranian branch, with whom we are here concerned, were the first to be civilized and to acknowledge one god, and conse-

[1] *The Races of Man*, by Deniker, p. 318.

THE ARYANS OF PERSIA

quently they have special claims on our interest. They possessed a tradition that they quitted their ancient home because the Power of Evil made it ice-bound and uninhabitable. Perhaps this may mean that they were irresistibly urged forward by a change of climate, just as aridity possibly caused the hordes of Mongolia to swarm westwards, and incidentally to blast the civilization of the countries they overran.

Special legends [1] refer to a lost home termed Aryanem-Vaejo. When cold compelled them to leave this terrestrial paradise, they moved to Sughda and Muru (the classical Soghdiana and Margiana), the former being Bokhara and the latter the modern Merv. Locusts drove them from Sughda and hostile tribes forced them to Bakhdhi, "the country of lofty banners," which was later known as Balkh. From Balkh they proceeded to Nisaya, which has been identified with Nishapur, but in my opinion erroneously; for the district of Nasa or Nisa to the south of Askabad fits in much better. Haroyu (Herat) and Vaekereta (Kabul), "the land of noxious shadows," were reached in the farther stages of the migration. Later, the chroniclers divided these countries into two groups, namely, Arahvaiti (Arachosia), Haetumant (the Helmand), and Hapta-Hindu (the Panjab) to the east; and Urva (Tus), Vehr-Kana (the Gurgan), Rhaga (Rei), Varena (Gilan), and other districts to the west. This grouping may well have been devised to explain the Indian and Persian divisions of the Aryan.

The site of Aryanem-Vaejo has been placed in the northern portion of the modern province of Azerbaijan; but de Morgan [2] points out most pertinently that, if the northern or any other part of Azerbaijan had been the original Aryanem-Vaejo, the Aryans would have been brought into contact with the tribes inhabiting what is now Armenia, who knew the art of writing and were comparatively civilized. In truth we cannot fix this centre with precision, although, owing to the discovery of Tokharic,[3] the most ancient form of Indo-European in Siberia, the south-western portion of that vast land may well be held to have claims that merit deep consideration. The entire legend, as it has come down to us, is too detailed to be very ancient, and it is quite

---

[1] Cf. especially Farjand I. of the *Vendidad*. [2] *Études, etc.*, p. 415.
[3] Meyer, *Geschichte des Alterthums*, i 801.

possible that, at the time when it assumed its final form, Azerbaijan was regarded as the Aryanem-Vaejo, and the original home in the north was forgotten. Nevertheless, Avestan scholars set much store upon it ; for there can be little doubt that it is based on tradition from the remote past.

The Arrival of the Aryans in Persia.—It is believed that the Medes migrated into Persia from Southern Russia, and finding the kingdom of Urartu or Ararat too strong to be attacked, avoided it, and gradually occupied the western side of the Iranian plateau. Another Aryan branch, that of the Persians, entered Eastern Persia from the steppes to the north of Khorasan and, traversing the province of Kerman, occupied Fars, from the neighbourhood of the valley of the Zenda Rud, possibly already held by the Medes, to the Persian Gulf. Their western frontiers would touch those of the tribes under Elamite influence. A third migration took a south-easterly direction from Aria or Bactria, the invaders crossing the Hindu Kush and conquering the Panjab. Behind these three great bodies we hear of the Hyrcanians, who inhabited the modern district of Astrabad ; and behind the Persians came the Carmanians, whose name survives in Kerman ; the Gedrosians of the littoral of Baluchistan ; the Drangians and Arachosians, inhabiting the northern districts of Baluchistan and part of Southern Afghanistan respectively ; and, finally, the Margians of Merv and the Bakhtrians of Balkh.

The Dates of the Migration.—Among the cuneiform inscriptions recently discovered at Boghaz Kyoi, the ancient Pteria, and the capital of the Hittites, are some which contain treaties between the Hittites and the Mitannians, a people whose aristocracy at least was of Aryan race. On one of these, oaths taken by the Vedic deities, Indra, Varuna, and the Násátya-twins (Asvins), show most clearly not only that the Mitannians venerated these gods, but that by 1350 B.C., the date of the document, the Iranian and Hindu elements of the Aryans had not yet become differentiated. Incidentally this document disposes of any claims for extreme antiquity in the civilization of India.

De Morgan[1] holds that the Aryan invasion of Bactria took place before 2500 B.C., and that the Medes entered

[1] *Études, etc.*, p. 314.

North-western Persia about 2000 B.C. The fact that, as mentioned in Chapter VI., the Kassites were an Aryan tribe which founded a dynasty about 1900 B.C., and were heard of during the First Dynasty of Babylon, helps to date this migration more definitely than could be done until the identity of the Kassites, who were probably a Median tribe, had been established.

The Medes and the Ancient Inhabitants.—The ancient inhabitants were, in all probability, partly massacred, partly driven into the hills, and partly permitted to live side by side with the conquerors. If we consider the heavy losses which the defending tribes must have sustained, the wide area affected, and its mountainous character, this appears to be a reasonable hypothesis, and history shows it to be in accordance with the procedure of most conquering nations. It is also corroborated by Herodotus, who gives the names of the tribes that were welded into a nation as the Busae, the Paraetaceni, the Struchates, the Arizanti, the Budii, and the Magi.[1] It is possible that the first four of these were Aryans and that the Budii and Magi were Turanians. The last-named tribe was found by the invaders to be possessed of a form of worship which, fused with that of the Aryans, developed, under the influence of Zoroaster, into the religion which still bears his name.

The Aryan invaders were a primitive pastoral folk owning horses, cattle, sheep, goats, and the watch-dog. They travelled in rude waggons with axles and wheels roughly hewn from a single stem. The bride was captured, and the family was based on patriarchal authority and polygamy. They knew gold, electrum,[2] and bronze : but their art was limited to a very few simple line patterns and to ornaments. They were ignorant of writing. Gradually they settled down and, learning agriculture, founded villages and towns ; and for a long time they continued to be a number of loosely organized clans, independent of one another but usually ready to unite in case of danger.

Aryan Myths.—It has been well said that no religion is ever invented, a characteristic which it shares with language.

---

[1] Herodotus i. 101.
[2] In the *Revue d'Ethnographie et de Sociologie*, vol. ii. p. 5, de Morgan points out that electrum (a compound of gold and silver) was obtained from the nuggets and dust collected by washing, and that, as the process of separating the metals was unknown, the first Greek coins contained as much as fifty per cent of silver.

Both are the results of growth and transformation, and since religion is founded on beliefs which themselves are deeply affected by myths, if not based on them, it is of primary importance to study, if we can, these fundamental old-world ideas. Most fortunately the Aryan legends have been preserved for their descendants and appeal to us, if only for the light they throw upon modern civilization in its primitive phases.

Our earliest glimpse of the Aryans shows them to be at the stage of pure nature-worship. The bright heavens, light, fire, the winds, and the life-giving rain-storm were all worshipped as divine beings, whereas darkness [1] and drought were held to be accursed demons. To the heavens in this polytheistic system pre-eminence was granted, and the sun is termed Heaven's eye, and lightning Heaven's son. It may be urged that most religions contain these myths, which are, indeed, widespread; but with the Aryans there was not, as in the case of the Sumerians, the propitiation of the evil spirits. Rather they had to be faced and overcome by the good spirits, who, in their turn, depended largely for success on the prayers and sacrifices of man. It is thus evident that, from the beginning, the position of man was one of assured dignity, with a manly attitude towards his deities, to whom he prayed for help, to whom he sang hymns of praise, to whom he offered sacrifices and, above all, drink offerings of the sacred *haoma*.[2] By such prayers and by such sacrifices he felt that he aided the beneficent deities to fight on his behalf against the powers of drought and darkness. It is indeed of extraordinary interest to read how the Sky-god Varuna, the Ouranos of the Greeks, was worshipped as the Supreme God to whom prayers should be addressed, how moral attributes gathered round him, and how he, in particular, hated the lie, a fact which was deeply impressed on the Iranians, as can be seen from the inscriptions of Darius and also from the pages of Herodotus.

Associated with the Heaven is the luminous ether, personified under the name of Mithra. Together they watch the hearts and deeds of mankind, both being all-seeing and all-knowing. Again fire, in its original form as lightning,

---

[1] The Gathas and Later Avesta differ as to darkness. Ahura Mazda created darkness according to the Gathas, *Yasna*, xliv.

[2] The *haoma*, identical with the *soma* of India, is a mountain plant, but there is doubt as to its identity.

plays a prominent part in the eternal combat which the gods of Light are waging with the powers of Darkness; and it is in describing these sublime natural phenomena that the poetical exuberance of the Aryan was specially displayed.

PART OF A PERSIAN HUNTING SCENE.
(From a polychrome terra-cotta Vase in the Hermitage Museum.)

CHAPTER IX

THE RELIGION OF THE MEDES AND PERSIANS

They (the Persians) are in the habit of ascending the highest mountains and offering sacrifices to Zeus—they give the name Zeus to the whole celestial circle. Moreover, they sacrifice to the sun, moon, earth, fire, water, and winds. To these alone they were accustomed originally to sacrifice.—HERODOTUS i. 131.

Zoroaster *loquitur* : "This I will ask ; tell it me right, O Ahura, 'Will the good deeds of men be rewarded already before the future life for the good comes ? '"

The Common Religion of the Aryans of Persia and of India.—In the last chapter reference was made to the Aryan worship of the great forces of nature, and the present chapter [1] is mainly a development of this theme. This nature-worship, as described by Herodotus in the passage quoted above, was characteristic of all the Aryan peoples, but with the Aryans of India the Iranians shared a common religion and culture throughout a long period, which came to an end not very long before the time with which we are now dealing. The Aryans of India possessed revealed scriptures termed *Vedas* or "Knowledge," consisting of a collection of more than 1000 hymns preserved by the ancient Aryan conquerors of the Panjab. Now, especially in the early Vedic period, we find among them the same general stage of development as in Iran, and the same worship of the Nature-powers.

[1] In this chapter I have consulted Professor Williams Jackson's *Zoroaster, the Prophet of Ancient Iran.* Mr. Edwards very kindly sent me a proof of the masterly article on God (Iranian), contributed by him to Hastings' *Encyclopaedia of Religion and Ethics.* During revision I have consulted *Early Zoroastrianism*, by J. H. Moulton, which work gives a carefully reasoned and moderate opinion on the various difficult questions.

CHAP. IX RELIGION OF MEDES & PERSIANS 103

Similar terms were employed for a god, indicating, as Edwards points out, that the character of the objects of worship was similar. One name was *asura* (Sanscrit, *asura*, Avesta, *ahura*), signifying "the Lord"; another was *daiva* (Sanscrit, *deva*, Avesta, *daeva*), from the Indo-European word denoting "heavenly ones." The latter has continued to be an Aryan word for god, in such forms as *theos*, *deus*, and the latter's derivatives, *dieu*, and *deity* in Greek, Latin, French, and English respectively.

Even in early Vedic times the two classes of gods, *ahuras* and *daevas*, were looked upon as rivals in their claims on the veneration of the tribesmen. In India the *daevas* were in the ascendant, and in the later Veda the *asuras* are regarded as demons. In Iran, on the other hand, the *ahuras* were in the ascendant, and it is in relation to Ahura that the religious consciousness of the Iranians developed, the *daevas* being relegated to the position given to the *asuras* in India.

Indo-Iranian Legends, Yama or Jamshid.—There are also legends common to both countries.[1] Of these perhaps the most interesting is that of the hero Yama, originally one of the names of the setting sun. He was held to be the first "to show the way to many," and, being the first to arrive in "the vasty halls of death," as Matthew Arnold beautifully expresses it, he not unnaturally becomes transformed into the King of the Dead. He possessed two dogs, "brown, broad-snouted, four-eyed," who went forth daily to scent out the dead and to drive them into the presence of their monarch. We can trace a reminiscence of these dogs in Persia in the Zoroastrian custom known as *Sagdid*, or "The Seeing of the Dog." The Avesta prescribes that "a yellow dog with four eyes or a white dog with brown ears" shall be brought to the side of every person who dies, as its look drives away the demon which attempts to enter the corpse. To-day the Parsis, who, in Persia at any rate, are ignorant of the great antiquity of the custom, place a piece of bread on the chest of the man supposed to be dead. If the dog eats it, the man is pronounced to be dead, and is carried off to the *Dakhma*, or Tower of Exposure, by members of the community who are held to be permanently impure and are condemned to a miserable life.

Zoroaster, the Prophet of Iran.—The founder of the

[1] This subject is referred to again in Chapter XII.

ancient religion of the Persians was Zoroaster, around whose name and personality have gathered bitterly conflicting opinions. It has been denied that he was an historical personage, and, not so very long ago, it was held—among other theories—that he was a product of the ubiquitous storm-myth. Here again, as in the case of the Aryan problem, an immense advance has been made on the theories of the early pioneers, to whom, however, all honour is due. In spite of legend and fable which obscure his figure, the Great Reformer, the Prophet of Iran, now stands out, through the mists of antiquity, as an actual historical person.

The origin of the name Zarathustra—Zoroaster is merely a Latin corruption—is not known in its entirety, but it contains the word *ustra*, a camel, which still exists in modern Persian in a slightly different form. There is reason for accepting the tradition that the Prophet was a native of Azerbaijan, the classical Atropatene, in both forms of which may be discerned the ancient word *athar*, fire, in which connexion in pre-Zoroastrian days the priest was known as *atharvan* or "guardian of the fire." His birthplace is believed to have been Urumia, to the west of the lake of the same name. His youth was given up to meditation and retirement, in the course of which he saw seven visions and endured various temptations. Ultimately he proclaimed his mission, but for many long years he met with little success; indeed, in the first decade he gained only one convert.

Gushtasp, the First Royal Convert.—Zoroaster was then inspired to travel to Eastern Persia, and at Kishmar[1] in the province of Khorasan he met Vistasp, the Gushtasp of Firdausi's epic. At this ruler's Court he first converted the two sons of the Vizier and then the Queen. There was a formal disputation between the Prophet and the wise men, during the course of which they tried to overcome him by their magic; but Zoroaster triumphed and gained the King himself as a fervid convert to the new religion. To quote from the Farvardin *Yasht*:

> He it was who became the arm and the support of the Religion of Zarathushtra, of Ahura; He, who dragged from her chains the Religion that was bound in fetters and unable to stir.

---

[1] *Vide Journal R.G.S.* for January and February, 1911.

RELIGION OF MEDES & PERSIANS

The conversion of Gushtasp and his Court was followed by invasions of the Turanian tribes of Central Asia, perhaps provoked by crusades of the converts. These " Holy Wars," as they may be considered, were waged mainly in Khorasan, and, if the legend can be trusted, the deciding battle was fought to the west of the modern town of Sabzawar.[1] Zoroaster, full of years and honours, was slain at Balkh when the Turanians made their second invasion. The tradition runs that he died at the altar, surrounded by his disciples.

The Date of Zoroaster's Birth and Death.—Zoroaster was an inhabitant of Azerbaijan and perhaps a Magian, although this is doubtful. There is also much doubt as to when he lived. Some authorities consider that the Prophet was born about 1000 B.C., whereas the traditional view, that is accepted by Williams Jackson, places his birth in 660 B.C. and his death in 583 B.C. In favour of a later, rather than an earlier date, is the fact that Darius was, we believe, the first strongly Zoroastrian monarch. Owing to these striking divergencies of opinion, it seems desirable to await fresh evidence on this important, but difficult, question.

The Avesta.—In the eyes of a Moslem, the inhabitants of the world are divided into those nations which have revealed scriptures and those which have not. The Zoroastrians can certainly claim to belong to the former class, as they possess the Avesta, which, or part of which, was revealed to Zoroaster. This sacred work, written in a language which is generally termed Avestic and which differs from the language used by the Achaemenian monarchs in their inscriptions, is believed to have consisted of twenty-one books inscribed in letters of gold on 12,000 ox-hides. It is understood to have been destroyed after the downfall of the Achaemenian dynasty, and but little of it has been recovered. Volagases I., the Parthian monarch who reigned about the middle of the first century A.D., is believed to have begun a reconstruction of it, which was, however, mainly the work of Ardeshir, the founder of the Sasanian dynasty; and it is probable that it received additions for the next two or three generations.

Antiquity appeals strongly to mankind, and when we

---

[1] *Vide Journal R.G.S.* for January and February, 1911.

recollect that Zoroastrianism, which is a living religion still, was contemporary with the religions of Baal, of Assur, and of Zeus, which have all been forgotten for many centuries, we can sympathise with the eagerness and zeal of students who devote their lives to tracing it back to its remote source amid the mists of legend and myth.

The extant portions of the Avesta contain only one complete book, the *Vendidad* (more correctly *Videvat*), or "Law against the Demons." Portions of some of the other chapters enter into the composition of the *Yasna* or liturgy, and other fragments are preserved in Pahlavi books. The latter bear much the same relationship to the Avesta as patristic literature does to the New Testament. What exists of the Avesta is divided into four sections as follows :

(*a*) The *Yasna*, subdivided into seventy-two chapters, and consisting of hymns, including the *Gathas*.

(*b*) The *Vispered* or collection of doxologies, used in conjunction with the *Yasna*.

(*c*) The *Vendidad*, the ecclesiastical law-book prescribing penances, purifications, and expiations.

(*d*) The *Yashts* or hymns in honour of the angels who preside over the various days of the month.

The oldest portion is represented by the *Gathas*, which have been aptly compared with the Hebrew Psalms and are believed to represent the actual teaching and utterances of Zoroaster and his immediate followers. In these the Prophet stands out as an historical personality, teaching lessons of pure morality, which must excite profound reverence when we bear in mind how deep was the darkness around him.

Ormuzd the Supreme God.— In connexion with the subject of Aryan myths reference was made to Varuna (Uranus), the old Aryan Sky-god. Under the spiritualizing influence of Zoroaster's teaching, which may be defined as the attribution of a moral character to the powers of nature, Varuna became Ahura, "the Lord," or, more commonly, Ahura Mazda (Ormuzd), "the Lord of Great Knowledge," the Supreme God and the Creator of the World. This appears in one of those conversations with Zoroaster which embody the revelation that was made to him. Ahura Mazda says, "I maintain that sky there above, shining and seen afar, and encompassing the earth all round. It looks like a palace that stands built of a heavenly substance, firmly established with ends that lie afar, shining in its body of ruby over the three worlds; it is like a garment inlaid with stars made of a heavenly substance, that Mazda puts on." [1]

It is important, even in this brief account, to distinguish between the conception of the supreme God as taught by Zoroaster and that which prevailed at later periods. The Gathic conception is that of a beneficent Spirit, the great and sole Creator. The attributes of Ahura Mazda—"the good spirit," "righteousness," "power," "piety," "health," and "immortality"—are constantly personified and addressed as if distinct from Ahura Mazda; and yet again they are often referred to as common abstract nouns and not as separate personalities. Thus under the Gathic conception we have what is undoubtedly monotheism.

In the later Avesta Ahura Mazda is still supreme, but he is no longer the sole object of worship. By this time the six attributes had become the "Immortal Holy Ones," and were worshipped as such. More than this, practically all the Nature-gods, which the Great Reformer had abolished, were brought back and worshipped side by side with Ahura Mazda and his archangels: Mithra may be quoted as an example of this phase; and the worship of Anahita, modelled on Ishtar, the Semitic goddess of fecundity, was also introduced. Thus the reforms and the monotheism preached by Zoroaster were gradually forsaken and a return was made to the old polytheism. It remains to add that for the Achaemenian monarchs Ahura Mazda was their tribal god, represented as a warrior standing in a winged (and also bird-tailed) solar disk, as figured in the illustration of the bas-relief at Bisutun. This representation of the deity, termed the *ferwer*, was an exact copy of the Assyrian god Assur, which itself was ultimately derived from Egypt.

Ahriman, the Spirit of Evil.—Coeval with Ahura Mazda, fundamentally hostile to him and having the power to thwart his beneficent actions for a while, is Angra Mainyu or Ahriman, the Spirit of Evil, who thus limits the omnipotence of Ahura Mazda. As Edwards puts it, he is "the dark background" against which our lofty conception of Ahura Mazda must be set. Later, when the good spirits are personified, evil spirits are created to oppose them, and the

[1] *Yasht*, xiii.

fight between the powers of Good and Evil is waged grimly with alternations of victory and defeat. It must, however, be remembered that for Zoroaster *Druj* or the Lie summed up all evil as it did for Darius, and that Ahriman is a somewhat later conception.

The Three Principles of Zoroastrianism.—In the *Vendidad* there are three fundamental principles underlying an immense accumulation of priestly ritual and formality :—

(1) That agriculture and cattle-breeding are the only noble callings.

(2) That the whole creation is a combat between Good and Evil.

(3) That the elements—air, water, fire, and earth—are pure and must not be defiled.

To illustrate the first principle, I cannot do better than describe what may be termed the ideal life according to Zoroastrianism. In reply to a question put by the Prophet, we are informed that : " It is where one of the faithful erects a house with cattle, wife, and children, and where the cattle go on thriving ; the dog, the wife, the child, the fire are thriving . . . where one of the faithful cultivates most corn, grass, and fruit ; where he waters ground that is dry or dries ground that is too wet." The precepts are singularly sane and wholesome. Among other things, they forbid fasting, on the ground that " Whoso eats not, has no power either to accomplish a valiant work of religion, or to labour with valour. . . . ; it is by eating that the universe lives, and it dies by not eating." Contrast this with the curse of fasting in modern Persia which yearly adds thousands to the number of opium-smokers, the half-starved men and women being weakened to such an extent that they are unable to resist the deadly drug : moreover, the ordinance presses lightly on the rich, who sleep all the day, and heavily on the poor. The good physique of the Zoroastrians in Persia is, I am sure, due mainly to the absence of all unnatural restraints. To continue, marriage was strictly enjoined, as also polygamy. Herodotus notes that the King awarded a prize yearly to the subject with the largest family.

The second principle is a statement of the somewhat dualistic nature of Zoroastrianism. Ahura Mazda created all that is good, such as the ox, the vigilant dog, and the cock, whom it was the duty of all believers to cherish.

Ahriman, on the other hand, created all noxious creatures, such as beasts of prey, serpents, and all flies and insects, which it is the bounden duty of the faithful to destroy. In this latter category are the ant, which it is meritorious to kill as eating the farmer's grain, the lizard, and the frog. The position of cattle needs no comment; it is illustrated by the sanctity which still attaches to cattle in India. The explanation of the dog's position, as placed in the mouth of Ahura, is delightfully poetical : " I have made the dog self-clothed and self-shod, watchful, wakeful and sharp-toothed, born to take his food from man and to watch over man's goods. . . . And whosoever shall awake at his voice, neither shall the thief nor the wolf steal anything from his house without being warned ; the wolf shall be smitten and torn to pieces. . . . For no house could subsist on the earth made by Ahura, but for those two dogs of mine, the shepherd's dog and the house-dog." When living at Kerman I noticed that the Parsis shrank from dogs owing to the example of their Moslem neighbours, in whose eyes the dog is impure ; and I never failed to point out how contrary to the precepts of their religion was their action. These precepts occasionally went too far in placing the dog on an equality with man. This appears in the phrase " the murder of a dog or of a man," and in the ideal of a Zoroastrian life quoted above, wherein the dog is mentioned before the wife and children.

The position assigned to the cock, which arouses the slothful, would certainly have flattered Rostand's *Chantecler*. It runs : " The bird that lifts his voice against the mighty Dawn . . . And whosoever will kindly and piously present one of the faithful with a pair of these my birds, it is as though he had given a house with a hundred columns." It also perhaps tends to prove that domestic poultry were rare in Persia at that time. The water-dog, presumably the otter, was held to be extraordinarily sacred. The penalty for killing one was ten thousand stripes, the highest laid down for any crime. Perhaps its modern name of *Sag Mahi*, or " dog fish," is reminiscent of the period of its sanctity.

The third principle involved the sacredness of fire as a symbol, and caused the priest to cover his mouth when officiating at the altar. It also led to rules against defiling running water which are still known in Moslem Persia, although mainly honoured in the breach. Again, the dead

Zoroastrian is exposed on a tower to prevent pollution of the earth. But, further, since all sickness is looked on as possession by the powers of Evil, the dying Zoroastrian is frequently neglected by the members of his family and deprived of even the necessaries of life. The treatment of sickness, indeed, and the disgusting ablutions and purifications with the urine of cows are among the weak features of this wonderful religion.

Turanian Influences on Zoroastrianism.—Even in a brief review of Zoroastrianism it is impossible to neglect the question of Turanian influences on the Aryan religion. It is, of course, natural and, indeed, almost inevitable that an invading tribe which takes possession of a new country, without exterminating or driving out its original inhabitants, should be more or less influenced by their religious beliefs. The history of the tribes of Israel furnishes an excellent example of the rule. The most salient instance in Zoroastrianism is the profound reverence paid to fire; for this feeling was almost certainly intensified by the fact that the Aryans in the country to the west of the Caspian Sea found it springing out of the ground and revered by the surrounding populations. I shall never forget my visit to see this phenomenon near Baku. I arrived at the place at sunset to find it covered with snow, and yet flames were springing out of the ground, the whole scene being impressive and weird beyond description. Thus the nature of the country positively suggested the institution of sacred fires, and one cannot but feel that it was not unfitting to regard this pure element as a symbol of the Creator of the world. No doubt, as time went by, the reverence paid to it became excessive, so that the title " Fire-Worshippers " was applied to the Zoroastrians. The cult has survived to this day; for no Persian Parsi will either blow out a candle or extinguish a burning log. Smoking, too, is forbidden.

The use of the *barsom* or bundle of twigs is probably taken from the divining rods of the Turanians; and certainly the hosts of evil spirits continually assailing mankind, the long incantations necessary to defeat them, the superstition that the parings of nails should be buried with prayer to prevent their being " spears, knives, bows, falcon-winged arrows and slingstones in the hands of the Daevas," were pre-Zoroastrian superstitions. In modern Persia nail-parings are carefully buried underneath the threshold by Moslems, as it is believed that, if so placed, they will form a barrier and prevent the family from joining Dajjál or Anti-Christ when he appears. It seems probable that this superstition has descended from the older one.

The Magi.—It is supposed that the Magi [1] were a non-Aryan and possibly Turanian tribe which was absorbed by the Aryan conquerors. In historical times we see that they became the Levites of the Zoroastrians, and that it was they alone who slew the victim, prepared the sacred *haoma*, and held the bundle of *barsom* ; moreover, they were deeply versed in astrology, and through this science are connected in the legend of the Wise Men from the East with the birth of Christ. Their influence, as the generations passed, became supreme, and it is possibly owing to this fact that the pure beliefs taught by Zoroaster, who was, however, himself believed to be of Magian descent, were overlaid with superstition and rigid formalism. The Persians do not seem to have readily adopted the observances of the Magi, and it was apparently not until the Sasanian period that the religion was embraced in its entirety.

The Doctrine of the Resurrection.—The belief in a future life which was to constitute reward or punishment after death was an ancient fundamental Aryan belief. In the *Gathas*, this doctrine is not defined with precision, but in the *Vendidad* the somewhat vague speculation of the *Gathas* became more definite. The doctrine is given in the usual form of a revelation. In reply to the question whether the believer, and the unbeliever too, have to " leave the waters that run, the corn that grows and all the rest of their wealth," Ahura says that it is so, and that " the soul enters the way made by Time and open both to the wicked and the righteous." We next learn that for three nights after death the soul has its seat near the head of the body it has just quitted and, according to its deserts, enjoys pleasure or misery in an extreme degree. When the fourth dawn appears, a sweet-scented wind blows from the south and the soul of the faithful is met at the bridge of Chinvat, or Bridge of the Separation, which is thrown across the abyss of hell, " by a fair, white-

---

[1] Magus is believed to signify a " slave." It occurs, once only, in a compound word, in the Avesta. It may sound improbable that members of a subject tribe would be employed as priests by the conquerors, but examples of similar action are given by Moulton on the excellent authority of Sir J. G. Frazer.

armed maiden as fair as the fairest things in this world." The soul inquires who she is and receives the reply, " O thou youth of good thought, good words and good deeds, I am thy own conscience." Led by this beauteous guide, the soul of the faithful is brought to the presence of Ahura and is there welcomed as an honoured guest. The wicked soul, after meeting a hideous woman, cannot cross the bridge and falls into the Abode of Lie, there to become the slave of Ahriman.

In the pages of Herodotus [1] there is a most interesting passage which bears upon this topic. Cambyses, who has heard of the rising in favour of the supposed Bardiya, whom he had put to death, reproaches Prexaspes, who had been ordered to carry out the sentence. The latter defends himself by saying that there is no truth in the news, and then makes the following statement : " If of a truth the dead can leave their graves, expect Astyages the Mede to rise and fight against thee ; but if the course of nature be the same as formerly, then be sure no evil will ever come upon thee from this quarter." A truly remarkable passage.

The Iranian Paradise.—The Paradise of the Zoroastrians lay on the mountains of Hara-Berezaiti or " Lofty Mountain," known in the Pahlavi period as Alborj, the modern Elburz. This mysterious mountain rises from the earth above the stars into the sphere of endless Light, to the paradise of Ahura Mazda, " the Abode of Song." It is the Mother of Mountains, with its summit bathed in everlasting glory, where there is no night, no cold, and no sickness. Surely this poetical idealization of the peerless peak of Demavand may appeal to us all, and perhaps with special intensity to those who, like myself, have watched the glory of a sunset shining upon it in midwinter. When the setting sun has left the main range deadly white, the cone of Demavand is suffused with rosy-coloured light, which gradually recedes until only the summit is touched with the flame. Suddenly the sun sets and all is dead. No sight I have witnessed is more beautiful or more impressive. It is one of the recollections which I shall cherish most, now that my connexion with Iran is severed.

The Influence of Zoroastrianism on Judaism.—To go deeply into the question how far Zoroastrianism influenced

[1] iii. 62.

RELIGION OF MEDES & PERSIANS

Judaism, and thereby Christianity, is beyond the scope of this work; but it is worth pointing out that the Ahriman of Zoroastrianism is almost identical with Satan. In both religions alike they are malignant demons, whom the Supreme God cannot destroy immediately, as obviously he would if he could. Again, the purity and loftiness of conception of Ahura Mazda, as preached by Zoroaster, exceeds that of Yahveh, the tribal god of Israel, who is represented as exclaiming, " If I whet my glittering sword, and mine hand take hold on judgement, I will render vengeance to mine enemies and will reward them that hate me. I will make mine arrows drunk with blood, and my sword shall devour flesh."[1] On the other hand, the God whose sublime nature is depicted in the lofty passages of Isaiah surpasses the highest conception of Ahura Mazda.

We now come to a still more important question. It is perhaps going too far to claim that the doctrine of the immortality of the soul was first preached by Zoroaster and adopted by the Hebrews, who were placed by Sargon II. "in the cities of the Medes," as they disappeared and were lost to Israel. We do, however, know that the priestly and aristocratic families of the Jews, represented by the Sadducees, held, at the beginning of the Christian era, that there was nothing in the Scriptures to warrant the belief in angel, spirit, or resurrection. Thus we have, on the one hand, the Zoroastrians, with whom the doctrine of the immortality of the soul was a fundamental article of belief, and, on the other, the Jews divided among themselves on this vital doctrine many centuries after the death of the great Prophet of Iran. Space forbids me to enlarge further on the immense influence which Zoroastrianism must have had, both directly and indirectly, on Judaism : even if it was not the pure religion of Zoroaster, it was undoubtedly an influence which tended to the discouragement of the idea of the tribal god and to the strengthening of the grand ideal of a god of all nations. It remains to point out that the tone of the Hebrew prophets towards the Persians is remarkable, and, to give a single example out of many, we read in Isaiah, " Thus saith the Lord to his anointed, to Cyrus." Indeed, the Persians, alone of the great dominant races, are never doomed to Hell by the Prophets ; and are to some extent recognized by

---

[1] Deuteronomy xxxii. 41-42.

the Hebrews as a people whose religion was akin to their own.

Summary.—We have traced the Aryans in their migration and their occupation of the land of Iran, to which they have given their name. We have seen them first as rude nomads, worshippers of nature; and then appears the stately figure of Zoroaster, who spiritualized their myths and evolved a deity whose sublimity approaches that of the God of Isaiah. It was Zoroaster who preached the Aryan belief in the immortality of the soul, and whose message of hope has surely come from the remote past along the whispering-galleries of time, and has influenced this twentieth century in which we live, both directly and indirectly. According to his teaching, man, in the eternal combat between Good and Evil, is free to take his choice, is supported by the good spirits and assailed by the evil; but knows that in the end Good will triumph over Evil just as the rain-cloud dispels drought. In my humble opinion, it is difficult to improve on the tenets of this religion, as repeated by every lad when he is old enough to don the mystic girdle and, instructed by his elders, says, *Humata, Hukhta, Hvarshta,* " Good Thoughts, Good Words, Good Deeds."

IRANIANS FIGHTING SCYTHIANS.
(From *R.A.S. Journal*, vol. lii.)

CHAPTER X

THE RISE OF MEDIA AND THE FALL OF ASSYRIA

And it shall come to pass, that all they that look upon thee shall flee from thee, and say, Nineveh is laid waste: who will bemoan her? whence shall I seek comforters for thee?—Nahum iii. 7.

A Description of Media.—The Aryan empire of the Medes came into being earlier than that of the kindred Persians, owing to their closer proximity to the predominant Semitic power of Assyria, and the fact that the one great natural route from Mesopotamia to the Iranian plateau runs across the Zagros range, through the heart of the country occupied by this tribe. We read of Assyrian expeditions traversing Media for generation after generation, apparently with ease, and again we hear of the tribute which was paid; and nothing seemed more unlikely than that the loose congeries of tribes should, within a few years, develop into a formidable power.

The kingdom of the Medes arose in the centre of the Zagros range and the fertile plains to the east of it. It was formed, as mentioned in Chapter VIII., by the union of the six most important tribes under one rule. At first the district around Hamadan was organized; but the rising power soon extended its territories until its northern boundary was the Caspian Sea. To the north-west it included the modern province of Azerbaijan; to the east there was the Lut, with a scanty nomadic population; and on the west and south the kingdom touched the Assyrian border provinces of Ellipi and Kharkhar. Later on, Media was subdivided into three great provinces, namely, Media Magna, now Iraki-Ajami; Media Atropatene, the modern Azerbaijan; and

Media Rhagiana, the country around modern Teheran. At this period the northern boundary appears to have been the river Aras, which is also the modern boundary of Persia. Gilan and certainly part of Mazanderan were inhabited by Medes, the boundary to the east being considered to be the Caspian Gates, some miles east of Rhages or Rei, and, to the south of this pass, the great desert. Southward the modern boundaries of Fars and Pusht-i-Kuh perhaps constituted the frontier line, and to the west the Medes held the Zagros ranges, which afforded them security from attack and were well watered. Indeed, this part of the Iranian plateau is the best watered and most fertile, the country becoming arid as the Lut is approached.

The Nisaean Horses.—In dealing with Media it is not proposed to make any special reference to its products, since these have already been described for the whole of Persia; but an exception must be made in the case of its horses, which were famous throughout Asia. Their grazing grounds were chiefly in the Zagros range, and the breed, which has been made famous by Herodotus, Arrian, Ammianus Marcellinus, and other writers, was termed Nisaean. These horses were dun, grey, or white,[1] and were universally regarded as unrivalled for speed, endurance, and beauty. The leading part played by the cavalry in Median battles was due to the possession of thousands of good remounts.

The Expedition of Tiglath-pileser I., circa 1100 B.C.—Tiglath-pileser I. directed a campaign across the Zagros against the Medes and kindred tribes, but in his annals we have merely a bald list of the places he took. It was, no doubt, one of a series of campaigns which, at this period, carried the arms of Assur in every direction.

The Expeditions of Shalmaneser, 844 B.C.—Some three centuries later, Shalmaneser II. led an expedition into Namri, the modern Kurdistan, a country which, it is of considerable interest to note, had been under Babylonian influence for a long time. Its prince, who bore the Semitic name of Marduk-

---

[1] The white horses were considered sacred and were offered in sacrifice by the Achaemenian monarchs. According to Strabo the Parthian horse was the descendant of the Nisaean, and so presumably is the modern Persian horse. Curiously enough in modern Persia a white horse is generally the best. In *The Origin and Influence of the Thoroughbred Horse*, Professor Sir W. Ridgeway lays down somewhat dogmatically that the Nisaean was the ancestor of the Turkoman horse. I hardly think that he proves his case. The Turkoman horse, which is found only on the borders of north-east Persia and in Turkestan, is entirely distinct from the Persian horse.

Mudammik, escaped to the hills ; but his people and treasure were captured and carried off by the conquerors. Shalmaneser also appointed a king of Kassite origin, Ianzu by name, to rule over the district.

Seven years later he again marched into Namri, as Ianzu had revolted. On this occasion he surprised the rebels and drove them into the forests. He then bore down on Parsua,[1] the neighbouring district to the east, and plundered twenty-seven princes. Finally, he skirted Amadai and Kharkhar (the district of Kermanshah), and at length overtook and captured Ianzu, whom he brought back to Assyria in triumph. This expedition is of special interest, as the Madai or Medes are mentioned for the first time in the inscription recounting this campaign, and thus make their humble entry on to the stage of history. In this connexion, in Genesis x. 2, we read : " The sons of Japheth ; Gomer (the Cimmerians), and Magog (Armenia), and Madai (Media), and Javan (Ionia)," etc.

During the reign of Shalmaneser's successor, Shamsi-Adad IV., the Medes are again mentioned as being conquered and paying tribute, and it would appear, from the frequency with which expeditions raided the Iranian plateau and from the number of towns destroyed, that it was then a distinctly fertile and well-populated country. The inference is confirmed by the number of prisoners and the thousands of horses, cattle, and sheep that were captured.

The Invasion of Adad-nirari III., 810 B.C.—Adad-nirari III., whose wife Sammuramat, a Babylonian princess, is possibly the Semiramis of legend, led an expedition into Media in 810. It was the earliest of at least four campaigns conducted by this energetic monarch, who extended the Assyrian Empire until it included the greater part of the western side of the Iranian plateau.

The Campaigns of Tiglath-pileser IV., 744 B.C.—Pul or Tiglath-pileser IV., who ranks high among the many warrior-kings of Assur, invaded Media in 744 B.C. Like his predecessors, he found the various tribes disunited and was therefore able to attack them one by one. The nearest districts he converted into an Assyrian province, and the success of the campaign may be estimated from the fact that 60,500 prisoners and enormous herds of oxen, sheep, mules, and dromedaries were led back in triumph to Calah. One of his

---

[1] It is not known whether the inhabitants of Parsua were the ancestors of the Persians.

generals had pressed on as far as the slopes of Bikni, or "the lapis mountain," the modern Demavand, considered by the Assyrians to be the extreme boundary of the world. This exploit, curious as it may seem, decided the success of the campaign, and the victor was met by every chief in the country, all equally anxious to pay homage to the man who had achieved such an exploit. Later in his reign, in 737 B.C., the districts of Media were again ruthlessly swept bare of every living thing ; not even the most remote valley or the most rugged mountain range saved the chiefs and their subjects from capture by the ubiquitous enemy, whose most valuable booty was, in all probability, the multitude of captives, destined to be employed in building the Assyrian works of peace.

Israel carried Captive into Media by Sargon II., 722 B.C.—A generation passed and Sargon II. captured Samaria, which, relying on help from Egypt, had withheld the onerous tribute. This event is narrated in the book of Kings as follows : " In the ninth year of Hoshea the King of Assyria took Samaria, and carried Israel away into Assyria, and placed them in Halah and in Habor by the river of Gozan, and in the cities of the Medes." [1] Halah is Calah, at that period the capital ; Habor is the Khabur, a main tributary of the Euphrates ; Gozan lay to the east of the Khabur, and " the cities of the Medes " were the districts which had been formed into an Assyrian province by Tiglath-pileser IV.

The same sovereign, a few years later, during the course of a campaign with the Mannai, who inhabited Azerbaijan to the south of Lake Urumia, and were akin to the Medes, captured one of their chiefs, Dayaukku, whose name is apparently identical with that of the classical Deïokes, the founder of the Median Empire. Contrary to the Assyrian custom, the prisoner's life was spared and he was sent with his family into exile at Hamath. As the result of this campaign the Medes once more acknowledged the suzerainty of Assyria, and twenty-two of their chiefs swore the oath of allegiance at the feet of the monarch.

Esarhaddon's Expeditions, circa 674 B.C.—Under Esarhaddon, the Assyrian expeditions penetrated as far as Mount Demavand and the "Salt Deserts," a country rich in lapis lazuli, which no Assyrian army had hitherto reached. It is related that the monarch captured two petty kings and

---

[1] 2 Kings xvii. 6.

deported them to Assyria, with their subjects, their two-humped camels, and their thoroughbred horses. Owing to the successful results of this expedition, other Median kings followed Esarhaddon back to Nineveh with gifts of lapis lazuli and horses, and begged for his protection. This was graciously accorded, and thus the empire of Assyria expanded its borders towards, and even beyond, Media. The exact date of this campaign cannot be fixed, but it is known to have been before 673 B.C.

The brief summary I have given of the various campaigns and expeditions made during a period of some five hundred years in the western half of the Iranian plateau is, I would urge, of considerable value, as it proves clearly that, on every occasion, the Assyrians were able to attack the inhabitants of each district separately, and that between Armenia, then the kingdom of Urartu, on the north, and the hill districts of Elam to the south, there was no organized power to be reckoned with. Moreover, it shows that the western half of the Iranian plateau had been, to some extent at any rate, under Babylonian influence, and that the whole district was tributary to Assyria when that power was strong. It is, however, reasonable to suppose that the more remote and inaccessible districts were always ready to rebel when the opportunity arose; for the Assyrian tribute was no light impost. Throughout this long period the whole country must have been more or less permeated with Assyrian influence; and it was thanks to the severe education it was forced to undergo that Media became a powerful empire.

The Tradition of the Medes.—The meteoric empire of the Medes was, so they themselves believed, the work of one man of no high lineage. At the time when the reign of Sennacherib was drawing to a peaceful close, this race of mountaineers, who had hitherto been but one of many barbarous hill tribes leading mainly a nomadic existence, or at best dwelling in scattered villages, had begun to establish an organization which was destined to culminate in a glorious, though short-lived, empire.

Deïokes, the Founder of the Royal Dynasty.—We read in the pages of Herodotus that the founder of Media as a separate kingdom was Deïokes, son of Phraortes, whose justice became so famous that, first, his fellow-villagers, and then all his fellow-tribesmen, flocked to hear his decisions. Seeing his power, Deïokes gave out that he could not continue to spend all his time judging his countrymen to the obvious detriment of his private affairs, and thereupon he ceased to administer justice. As he had probably anticipated, robberies and disorders of every kind again broke out, which the Medes contrasted with the order previously maintained. To quote Herodotus : " We cannot possibly, they said, go on living in this country if things continue as they now are ; let us set a king over us, so that the land may be well governed, and we ourselves may be able to attend to our own affairs, and not be forced to quit our own country on account of anarchy." [1]

Ecbatana, the Capital.—An election was held and, as had in all likelihood been carefully prearranged, Deïokes was chosen king. His first act was to surround himself with a powerful bodyguard. He then proceeded to build a capital, selecting for the purpose the town of Hamadan. This historical city is first mentioned, under the name of Amadana, in the inscription of Tiglath-pileser I., and in ancient Persian inscriptions it appears as Hagmatana or " The meeting place of many roads " ; the Greeks termed it Ecbatana. Hamadan is situated at the foot of Mount Alvand,[2] the classical Orontes, a mighty granite range rising more than twelve thousand feet above sea level, or just six thousand feet above Hamadan, the climate of which, though severe in winter, is delightful in summer. Its situation marked it out for a capital. It is protected by Alvand to the south and south-west, and commands the route to Babylonia and Assyria and also the plains of upland Persia. Placed at a point where many roads meet, and surrounded by a fertile, well-watered plain, it is not surprising that through all its vicissitudes Hamadan has invariably been an important centre. The modern city, with its thirty thousand inhabitants, among whom are a number of Jews, is exceptionally squalid.

The Musallah hill, on which once stood the famous capital of Media, lies to the east of the modern city. The walls, seven in number, were concentric and so arranged that they rose one above the other by the height of their battlements. The royal palace and treasuries were situated within the seventh wall, which had its battlements gilded,

---

[1] i. 97.
[2] Alvand is the Aurant of the Avesta. The classical Orontes is nearer the old Median name than the modern Alvand.

the other walls being decorated in various colours. The whole design was derived from Babylonia, where, in the Birs Nimrud of Borsippa, each stage was coloured differently, to symbolize the sun, the moon, and the planets. Deïokes also instituted a ceremonial, probably modelled on that of Assyria, by which it was forbidden to see the king face to face, all petitions being conveyed by messengers. This and other rules were established to inspire awe by the feeling of remoteness, as otherwise the new monarch feared that his peers would rebel against him.

This account is drawn from Herodotus and is believed to be true. Moreover, as already mentioned, a certain Dayaukku, a chief of the Mannai, was deported to Hamath in 715 B.C. ; and two years later what corresponds to the province of Hamadan is termed Bit-Dayaukku. Inasmuch as the epoch assigned by tradition coincides closely with the date of Dayaukku, it is probable that Deïokes was the actual founder of the royal family of the Medes.

The Language of the Medes.—According to Strabo, the language of the Medes closely resembled that of the Persians, the Arians, the Bactrians, and the Soghdians.[1] Unfortunately we have no inscriptions in this language, in spite of the excavations that have been made. At Hamadan, where the soil has been searched most thoroughly by the treasure-seeker, no remains of a Medic language have been discovered.[2] In these circumstances, is it not reasonable to believe that the Median was only a spoken language and was not used for writing ? Examples of this distinction are common, as, for instance, in Afghanistan, where Pashtu is the national and Persian the written language. It seems possible that the written tongue of the Medes was the Assyrian language. Oppert's view is that it is the language which occupies the second place in the trilingual inscriptions, generally believed to be Susian, whereas Darmsteter holds that it is identical with the language of the Avesta. To go into these questions is beyond the scope both of this work and of my powers ; and I chiefly refer to them to show what very divergent views have been propounded. The *spoken* language was, of course, Aryan and closely akin to Persian.

[1] xv. 2. 8.
[2] In 1913 a French Mission excavated the Musallah, but failed to discover anything of value.

Sennacherib and the Medes.—The welding of the Medes into a nation began, as we have seen, during the reign of Sennacherib ; and only one expedition to the Iranian plateau —against Ellipi, the district of Kermanshah—is recorded. Thus the Medes, guided by the astute Deïokes, had leisure to develop along the path of progress, while Sennacherib was far too busy with Babylon and Elam to give much thought to the obscure and distant mountaineers of the Zagros. The proud monarch could never have dreamed that these mountain shepherds would, at no very distant date, sack great Nineveh and cause the name of Assyria to disappear from among the nations.

The Expansion of Media.—Dayaukku or Deïokes reigned for fifty-three years, and his son, Fravartish, the Phraortes of the Greeks, succeeded him about 655 B.C.[1] At this period we may believe that Media was not yet strong enough to think of refusing to pay the Assyrian tribute, more especially as Assurbanipal was at the height of his power. It appears that Phraortes continued his father's policy of annexing the few remaining petty states which had not been absorbed by Deïokes ; and he then set to work to conquer the kindred tribes of the Persians, whose territory was the modern province of Fars.

The Conquest of the Persians by the Medes.—The Persians had probably, like the Medes, partly absorbed and partly driven out the older occupants of the soil. At this period, being divided up into independent tribes, they were apparently unable to offer a successful resistance to the relatively well-organized Medes, and were absorbed, so far as is known, without any desperate contests. But it is necessary to bear in mind that the Medes have left no authentic documents of any kind, and in piecing together their history we have to rely mainly on the work of Herodotus.

The Later Years of Assurbanipal.—During the reign of Phraortes, in 645 B.C., Assurbanipal had dealt Elam its death-blow ; and he was now devoting himself to peaceful development and, if tradition may be trusted, to inglorious ease. As already mentioned, it is to this monarch that we owe the priceless library collected by his orders, which included, not only the classics of the period, but also copies of

---

[1] In *The Passing of the Empires*, p. 447, reference is made to an untrustworthy tradition embodied in the work of Ctesias of Cnidus, which doubles the number of kings.

the tablets that filled the libraries of Babylonia. It is perhaps the greatest archaeological treasure of the British Museum. Temples, too, were rebuilt, and the splendid palace of Sennacherib, which had become unsafe owing to the unsatisfactory nature of its foundations upon an artificial mound, was remodelled on still more grandiose lines.

The First Attack by the Medes.—However, by warlike mountaineers, this discontinuance of constant campaigning would inevitably be regarded with contempt. The Medes, moreover, had received no severe lesson from Assyria for a considerable period, and were probably full of self-confidence on account of their success in attacking and conquering the Persians. These facts, coupled with much ignorance as to their real military strength, were probably responsible for the invasion of Assyria, which failed utterly before the valour and discipline of the Assyrian veterans. The result was the death of Phraortes and the destruction of the greater part of his army.

The Accession of Cyaxares.—Huvakshatara, whose name is known to us in the classical form Cyaxares, succeeded to the throne at this critical juncture. He was one of those rare leaders in war and administrators in peace who, from time to time, have appeared on the stage of the world. Convinced by bitter experience that he could not hope for success until his army was modelled on Assyrian lines, he broke up the feudal levies which had hitherto fought independently, and in their place organized regular bodies of troops. The infantry was armed with bow, sword, and one or two javelins. But the bow was more deadly in the hands of the cavalry, which was of greater importance in the Median than in the Assyrian army. Accustomed from childhood to ride and to shoot from horseback, these hardy horsemen, like the Parthians of a later date, kept just out of reach of their enemy and poured in a ceaseless stream of arrows which was demoralizing even to the best-trained veterans. Cyaxares, while organizing his army, trained it to war by stubbornly resisting the Assyrians; and at length a victory was won over the generals of Assurbanipal and Assyria was invaded for the second time.

The First Siege of Nineveh.—Nineveh, it might be thought, was too strongly fortified for the Medes to attempt to capture it. Nevertheless Cyaxares laid siege to it while his troops devastated the fertile plain, and the feelings inspired by his attempt to overthrow Assyria may be read in the book of Nahum. "The burden of Nineveh," begins this splendidly realistic book, and who does not feel the spell of its burning lines? "The noise of a whip, and the noise of the rattling of the wheels, and of the pransing horses, and of the jumping chariots. The horseman lifteth up both the bright sword and the glittering spear: and there is a multitude of slain, and a great number of carcases; and there is none end of their corpses; they stumble upon their corpses." [1]

The Scythian Invasion.—Just when it seemed probable that the great robber nation would at last be dealt with as it deserved, a horde of Scythians, possibly as allies of Assyria, flung themselves on Media and compelled Cyaxares to raise the siege of Nineveh and to return to defend his own country. There he was defeated, to the north of Lake Urumia, and forced to accept the victors' terms. The Scythians, intoxicated by success and aware of the weakness of Assyria, which had succumbed to the power they had themselves vanquished, overran the whole country. The fortresses alone resisted the tempestuous charge of these wild horsemen, who destroyed everything they could capture. Meeting with little resistance and finding insufficient booty in Assyria, they swept through it like a cyclone and then overran province after province, as far as the Mediterranean Sea. It is to this invasion that the prophet Jeremiah referred when he wrote: "They shall lay hold on bow and spear; they are cruel, and have no mercy; their voice roareth like the sea; and they ride upon horses, set in array as men for war against thee, O daughter of Zion." [2]

Cyaxares finally overthrew the invaders by inviting Madyes, their monarch, and his principal officers to a banquet where they were first made drunk and then slain. The Scythians, weakened by the death of their leaders, were attacked and finally driven out, after desperate fighting. In the meanwhile Assurbanipal, the last great monarch of Assyria, had died in 626 B.C., and his successors were not men of a stamp that could restore the fame and power of the war-worn and exhausted country.

The Second Siege of Nineveh.—A proof of the disintegration of the empire may be found in the fact that Nabopolassar, who had apparently been appointed Governor of Babylon by Assurbanipal, assumed the title of king under his successor.

---

[1] Nahum iii. 2 and 3.　　　[2] Jeremiah vi. 23.

A host of invaders marched up from the mouths of the Tigris and Euphrates and, instead of being attacked, were joined by Nabopolassar. To ensure success Cyaxares was asked to lead the united forces of Media against the common foe. The ambitious Mede readily complied, and the last Assyrian sovereign, deserted by his tributaries, was unable to face his enemy in the field. He shut himself up in Nineveh, where he was besieged.

The Fall of Nineveh, circa 606 B.C.—The fall of Nineveh was dramatic. Its monarch defended it till further resistance was impossible, and then, seeing that there was no hope, caused a great pyre to be erected and perished with his family amid the flames rather than fall into the hands of his foes. Ctesias, whose account is not deemed generally trustworthy, relates that the waters of the Tigris swept away part of the city wall, and Rawlinson quotes from the prophet Nahum, " The gates of the rivers shall be opened, and the palace shall be dissolved." Thus in or about 606 B.C. fell Nineveh, and so utter was its ruin that the Assyrian name was forgotten and the history of the empire soon melted into fable, in which the names of mythical Sardanapalus and mythical Semiramis vaguely attracted to themselves something of the splendour, might, and prestige of Assyria. How swiftly the waves of oblivion swept over Assur may be judged by the fact that, two centuries later, Xenophon's army passed by the vast deserted cities of Calah and Nineveh, misnamed Larissa and Mespila by their guides ; and, although they marvelled at them, they never suspected that these were the great cities of Assyria.[1]

The Verdict of History on Assyria.—And what is the verdict of history on Assyria ? It is this : that, although Babylonia and Egypt were merciless in the hour of triumph, yet Babylonia bequeathed to mankind law, astronomy, science, and Egypt erected buildings which still challenge the admiration of the world ; whereas Assyria, merely borrowing such arts of peace as she adopted, shone only as the great predatory power, and when she fell, she passed away into utter and well-merited oblivion.

[1] Xenophon's *Anabasis*, iii. 4. 7.—The passage begins, " There was a deserted city of large extent, the name of which was Larissa ; but Medians of old inhabited it." *Vide* also Chapter XIX. of this work. For new light on the downfall of Assyria *vide* Preliminary Essay, pp. xxxvi, xxxvii.

EARLY LYDIAN COIN.

CHAPTER XI

MEDIA, BABYLONIA, AND LYDIA

> There Babylon, the wonder of all tongues,
> As ancient, but rebuilt by him who twice
> Judah and all thy father David's house
> Led Captive, and Jerusalem laid waste,
> Till Cyrus set them free.
> — MILTON, *Paradise Regained.*

The State of the Ancient World after the Fall of Nineveh.—Whenever a great empire falls, a readjustment takes place in the relations of the neighbouring states both to one another and also to the possessions of the fallen power. Consequently, the fall of Nineveh affords a suitable occasion for surveying the state of the ancient world.

The Position of Media.—The most virile and formidable power was undoubtedly Media, the conqueror of the Scythians and the leading confederate in the attack on Assyria. The alliance between Media and Babylonia was cemented by the marriage of the daughter of Cyaxares with Nebuchadnezzar, son of Nabopolassar and heir to the throne of Babylon. The terms of this alliance were adhered to throughout the life of Cyaxares and his successor, although at times the wealth of Babylon must have sorely tempted the Medes.

The New Kingdom of Babylonia.—If the downfall of Assyria was an immense benefit to Media, the gain to Babylon was still greater. Indeed, it was owing to the annihilation of Assyria that the new kingdom of Babylon was formed and speedily showed an amazing vitality sufficient in itself to claim our notice. But its interest for us is intensified by the knowledge that it is the traditions of this kingdom which have come down to us from the classical and other writers.

The Campaign of Necho II.—Nabopolassar had resigned

CHAP. XI   MEDIA, BABYLONIA, AND LYDIA   127

the active direction of affairs to Nebuchadnezzar during the campaign against Assyria, and after its fall he apparently arranged with Cyaxares that the western provinces should be joined to Babylon. Their inhabitants were unable, of themselves, to offer any resistance ; but Necho II. of Egypt had first to be reckoned with. While Nineveh was being attacked, this energetic monarch had, in 608, marched north and had taken possession of Palestine and Syria, being opposed only by Josiah, king of Judah, who, in spite of friendly warnings, threw himself across the formidable Egyptian army at Megiddo near Mount Carmel and there met his fate.[1] Necho continued his march as far as the Euphrates, where he halted at Carchemish. This was his farthest point. Hearing, probably, of the fall of Nineveh and not wishing to try conclusions with the victors, he marched leisurely back, receiving tribute and posting garrisons at important centres. Upon his return to Egypt he received the acclamations of his people, who were delighted at the revival of the military glory of Egypt. This triumph was hardly justifiable as Necho had not met the forces of Babylon. Three years later Nebuchadnezzar, who had been engaged in securing his position nearer home, marched towards Carchemish, and thereupon Necho again set out, this time really to try the fortunes of war.

The Victory of Nebuchadnezzar over Necho II., 604 B.C.—The two armies met at Carchemish and, in spite of the bravery of the Greek contingent, the Egyptians were defeated. Their disaster formed the theme of a mordant passage in Jeremiah, who, describing the campaign, wrote : " Come up, ye horses ; and rage, ye chariots ; and let the mighty men come forth ; the Ethiopians and the Libyans, that handle the shield ; and the Lydians that handle and bend the bow. . . . For the Lord God of hosts hath a sacrifice in the north country by the river Euphrates." [2] Nebuchadnezzar was following up the beaten Egyptians and was close to Egypt when he received news of his father's death ; whereupon, fearing hostile intrigues at the capital, he made peace with Necho, who ceded Syria and Palestine.

The " Hanging Gardens " of Babylon.—The victor marched across the desert to Babylon and ascended the throne. Thence-

[1] *Vide* 2 Chronicles xxxv. 20-24 ; also 2 Kings xxiii. 29. Josiah was acting in the interests of Assyria.
[2] Jeremiah xlvi. 9, 10.

forward the reign of Nebuchadnezzar was prosperous and comparatively peaceful. During the ensuing years Babylon, as the Greeks knew it, was built with the wondrous terrace gardens, which became famous as "the hanging gardens of Semiramis," the splendid Ishtar-Gate, and the great processional way which ran from the citadel to the temple of Ishtar. Nebuchadnezzar also constructed the great fortified dam, known as the "Median Wall," stretching from the Tigris to the Euphrates, which allowed him to flood the whole country north of Babylon, and a similar dam which protected the city to the south. He was, indeed, a great monarch, and it is only due to his memory to say that nothing is to be found in history to justify the grotesque description of his alleged madness given in the book of Daniel, which was merely one of those wonder-tales that are told of every famous ruler in the East.

The Campaigns of Cyaxares.—It is unfortunate that so little is known of the splendid career of Cyaxares after the downfall of Assyria. Apparently he ceded to Babylon the richest and most easily subdued provinces of Anterior Asia. He reserved as his own share the uplands of Persia which already formed part of the Median Empire, Armenia, recently conquered by another Aryan people, and, in the west, hilly Cappadocia and other regions which had never been included within the Empire of Assyria even at her zenith. His reason for abandoning the richest provinces is hard to guess; but perhaps the Medes as a mountain people feared the enervating heat of the plains and preferred to possess regions which closely resembled their own rugged highlands.

The countries which Cyaxares now slowly but surely conquered were in a state of anarchy and exhaustion owing to the devastation wrought by the Cimmerians and Scythians, who had been ravaging and massacring incessantly for more than a century without evolving any tolerable form of government. Indeed, it is certain that all these lands had lost much of the civilization which they had with difficulty acquired. Cyaxares subdued race after race in his westward career until, upon reaching the right bank of the Halys, he found himself confronted by the powerful and warlike state of Lydia.

The Empire of Lydia.—The origin of the Lydians is one of the questions on which recent research has thrown considerable light, and still more may be expected from the excavations

MEDIA, BABYLONIA, AND LYDIA

of the American Mission at Sardes. Originally the belief set forth in the book of Genesis [1] that they were of Semitic origin was accepted, but it is now held that this interesting people belonged to the indigenous population of Asia Minor, which was neither Semitic nor Aryan.[2] It must be remembered that the Biblical allocation of various peoples to the different sons of Noah is political rather than racial. The sons of Shem represent the political family, of which Assyria was the centre and, as we know, Lydia was a vassal of Assurbanipal.

Anatolia was overrun from Thrace by the Aryan tribes of the Bryges or Phrygians, who were akin to the Hellenic Greeks and were gradually absorbed by the subject population. These invasions took place in the tenth and ninth centuries, and in the eighth century the monarch of this kingdom was Midas, the historical " Mita of Mushki." About 720 B.C. Mita, in alliance with Rusas, King of Urartu, came into conflict with Sargon II. of Assyria, and this campaign, being historical, supplies us with a fixed point of considerable value. The establishment of the Phrygian kingdom was followed by the consolidation of the Lydian tribes into a powerful state under the Heraclid dynasty, which absorbed Phrygia. It was this state which was destined to meet Media on equal terms, and finally to succumb to the rising power of Iran.

The Mermnad Dynasty.—It is beyond the scope of this work to detail the curious legends connected with the earlier monarchs of Lydia, which may be read in the pages of Herodotus; and we come to Gyges, who founded a new dynasty by the assassination of Sadyattes of the Heraclid dynasty, with whose bride he had fallen in love. The well-known story of Herodotus deals with this same event, but in a somewhat legendary fashion. Gyges was a great ruler and developed the strength of Lydia, and more especially its cavalry, which became famous throughout the East. Conscious of his strength, he subdued some of the Greek cities on the coast and made treaties with others. His constant preoccupation, however, was the invasion of the Cimmerians, which was threatening Phrygia and finally swept over it like

---

[1] x. 22 : "The children of Shem; Elam, and Asshur, and Arphaxad, and Lud, and Aram."
[2] It is particularly interesting to compare Hall's views in *The Oldest Civilisation of Greece*, published in 1901, with his later views in *The Ancient History of the Near East*, 1913. In the former he doubts the identity of Midas with Mita; in the latter he accepts it without question, and thus shows the steady increase in our knowledge of these subjects. *A Commentary on Herodotus*, by How and Wells, has been consulted in this and following chapters.

a devastating tornado. In 667 B.C., with the object of appealing for aid, he despatched an embassy to Assurbanipal, who was much flattered and stated that the name of Lydia had never been heard of before in Assyria. The Assyrians were most anxious to avoid complications ; and so, though polite messages were sent, no help reached Gyges, who was left to his own resources and was overthrown and killed by the terrible Cimmerians. His son Ardys rallied the refugees and, in alliance with the Greek contingents of the sea-coast, who possessed war-dogs trained to attack horses, drove off the Cimmerians, who turned eastwards and were defeated with crushing losses by the Assyrian troops in the Cilician gorges. Lydia, freed from this incubus, speedily recovered until, under Alyattes, the dynasty of the Mermnadae reached its zenith, having conquered all the districts up to the Halys, which thereby became its eastern boundary.

The Invention of Coinage.—The civilization of the Lydians is not without importance. They occupied a rich country abounding in minerals, and it is generally believed that to Ionian Greeks employed by them the world is indebted for the invention of coinage, developed from a system of Babylonian weights. This invention undoubtedly ranks, after writing, as the greatest achievement of civilization in those early days. The Lydians were also famous traders, if not the first retail dealers, as Herodotus states ; and they invented many games. They were capable, cultivated people, to whom the epithet of " luxurious "[1] was invariably applied by the Greeks. At the same time they were splendid fighters, and as at that period, when the Medians appeared on the Halys, their power was at its zenith, it was only a question of time when these two expanding empires would try conclusions with one another.

The War between Media and Lydia.—The cause assigned by tradition for the actual outbreak of hostilities is curious. Cyaxares, it is said, maintained a band of Scythians as huntsmen and entrusted some of the young nobles to their charge. One day, upon their returning empty-handed, the king so insulted them that, in revenge, they cut up one of the young nobles and served him as a dish at a banquet, and then fled to Alyattes, who refused to give them up. Whether there is

---

[1] 'Αβροί or ἁβροδίαιτοι. The usual translation of this word is " delicate," which would imply effeminacy.

any truth in this or not, a trial of strength between two such aggressive powers brought face to face was inevitable. The Medians were certainly more numerous than their opponents; but they were a long way from their base, and they possessed no troops comparable with the Greek hoplites or the famous Lydian cavalry.

The Battle of the Eclipse, 585 B.C.—For six years the war was waged without decisive advantage to either side. A total eclipse of the sun, foretold, it is said, by Thales of Miletus, interrupted a seventh contest and made the rank and file of both armies unwilling to meet again. In the peace negotiations that followed, wherein Babylon played the part of arbitrator, the Halys was fixed on as the boundary between the two empires. Again a marriage sealed the contract, the Median monarch bestowing his daughter on the heir-apparent of Lydia. One result of this treaty was the absorption by Media of the kingdom of Urartu.

The Death of Cyaxares, 584 B.C.—The year after the eclipse, Cyaxares, whose genius had raised Media into a powerful empire, died. When we recall that he inherited the throne at a time when aggressive Media had been beaten down by Assyria, that he organized an army only to be defeated by the Scythians, and yet not only overcame these wild horsemen but within a few years played the leading part in the overthrow of Assyria and afterwards built up a great empire, it is impossible not to feel that he was one of the great figures on the stage of the world. At the beginning of his reign the paramount power of the East was Semitic, but when he died, it was Iranian. Cyaxares is thus the leader in one of the great movements in history.

Astyages, the Last King of Media.—Ishtuvegu, generally known to us by the Greek form of his name, Astyages, succeeded to a splendid inheritance at a time when its prospects seemed altogether bright. But, so far as can be gleaned from the scanty available information, he was a degenerate and unworthy son of a noble sire, and spent his time in voluptuous idleness, immersed in semi-barbarous luxury and indulging in excesses of every kind.

The Luxury of the Median Court.—The account of the Median Court, with its elaborate ceremonies and myriads of officials, the red and purple robes of the courtiers, their chains and collars of gold and all their luxury, shows that it was modelled on the Court of Assyria. At both alike the chief pastime was sport. Sometimes great drives of game were organized in the open country, but, more frequently, the quarry was hunted in a " paradise " or park near the capital.

The Defeat of Astyages by Cyrus the Great.—The long reign of Astyages was peaceful until just before its close. This fact probably caused rapid deterioration in his soldiers, who shared in, and suffered from, the general surfeit of prosperity. The king had no son, and this must have weakened his position. So unpopular did his rule become that when he was attacked by an army of Persians under Cyrus, his own subjects, instead of rallying round him, surrendered him to the foe. Thus in 550 B.C. the empire of Media passed into the hands of the kindred Aryan people of Persia. The Greeks did not regard Media as having fallen, and, indeed, it is more correct to look upon it as having undergone internal transformation. A century later, the wars against Persia were referred to by the writers of Hellas as " The Median Events," although it is true that Aeschylus named his great tragedy *The Persians*.

The Later Kings of the New Babylonian Kingdom.—Before concluding this chapter we must glance for a moment at the affairs of Babylon. Nebuchadnezzar, full of years and honour, died in 561 B.C. During the next six years three monarchs ruled Babylon in succession, and after them came Nabonidus, the last of all. The son of a rich merchant, and called to the throne in 555 B.C. as a docile tool of the priesthood, this sovereign was an antiquarian born entirely before his time and was utterly unsuited to occupy the throne at a critical period such as this. But his excavations in the ruined temples, which have fortunately been rescued from oblivion, are of priceless value, and, since Babylon was destined to fall before the new power of Persia, it was perhaps a piece of good fortune that it should be ruled by a monarch who, at any rate, would not arouse resentment in a conqueror. The fall of Babylon belongs to the history of the Persians, headed by Cyrus the Great. Here it need only be recorded that everything was ripe for the new order which was about to come.

ACHAEMENIAN KING BETWEEN TWO SPHINXES, WITH THE SYMBOL OF AHURA MAZDA.
(From a Seal in the Louvre.)

CHAPTER XII

THE HEROIC AGE OF PERSIA

*Deem every day in thy life as a leaf in thy history;
Be careful, therefore, that nothing be written in it unworthy of posterity.*
          A Maxim of Feridun.

The Legendary Nature of Early Persian History.—The rise of the Persians, who have given their name to the great empire which, albeit with vicissitudes, has existed for more than 2400 years and has been a leading power for more than half its existence, was an event of the greatest importance to mankind. As previous chapters have shown, the country can claim through Media, inhabited by a kindred Aryan people, and through Elam, the home of the founder of the empire and still a province of Persia, an existence of close on 6000 years.

In this chapter we are dealing with the heroic age of Persia, which, as given by Firdausi in his great epic the *Shahnama* or "History of the Kings," is practically the only early history ever read or believed by Persians. And yet what Firdausi wrote is a mixture of legend and fable even after the historical period is reached. Not that the poet did not use the best information at his disposal;[1] but, viewed in the light we possess to-day, his sources were limited and, in many cases, entirely untrustworthy.

The Pishdadian Dynasty.—The history of Persia, so far as its inhabitants know it, begins with a legendary dynasty, termed Pishdadian or "Early Law Givers." The founder of this was Keiomarz, the Zoroastrian Adam, who, with his

---

[1] This question is also dealt with in Chapters XLI. and LIV.

two successors Hushang and Tahmurz, is supposed to have laid the foundation of civilization in Iran.

Jamshid and Zohak.—But the most famous of these legendary monarchs was Jamshid.[1] To his credit is placed the building of Persepolis—termed to this day *Takht-i-Jamshid* or "The Throne of Jamshid"—the introduction of the solar year, and the invention of most of the arts and sciences on which civilization is based.[2] His invention of wine is stated to have been due to an accident. He had preserved some grapes which fermented and were believed to be dangerous to life. One of the wives of Jamshid was suffering from a painful malady and drank of the fermented beverage in the belief that she would die; but, on the contrary, she fell into a delightful sleep and was cured. Persians from this date have termed wine "sweet poison," and in spite of the prohibitions of the Koran many of the upper classes are addicted to drinking it.

Jamshid, after reigning for many years, was uplifted with pride. He became a tyrant and declared himself a god. For his impiety the mystical Glory or Royal Splendour was lost by the great monarch, as we read in the XIXth Yasht:

> Ere he first to lies and untruth
> Bent his thought and tongue . . .
> Then before all eyes the Glory
> Bird-like fled away from Yima.

Zohak, a Syrian prince, was incited by the Heavenly Powers to attack him, and although he fled to Sistan, to India, and even to distant China, he was in the end made captive by his relentless foe. He was put to a barbarous death, being fastened between two boards and sawn in two with the backbone of a fish. Zohak, at whose hands he perished so miserably, and who conquered Persia, is legendary, the name being a corruption of the primeval serpent, Aji-Dahak. In Persian legend he is represented as an Arab prince invading Persia from Syria, and as a monster from whose shoulders hissing snakes grew. The daily rations of these snakes consisted of the brains of two human beings; and the levying of this blood-tax led to the overthrow of the invader.

---

[1] The first portion of the name is identical with that of Yama or Yima, who is mentioned in Chapter IX. *Shid* signifies brilliant.

[2] The Persian argument runs that whoever erected the buildings at Persepolis and Pasargadae must have been aided by the Divs. As only Jamshid and Solomon had power over them, they alone could have built these gigantic works.

Feridun and Kawa.—Kawa, a blacksmith, whose sons had been doomed to feed the snakes, excited a popular rising, and seeking out Feridun, a scion of the royal race, set him at the head of it. After many campaigns, during which the blacksmith's apron [1] was used as the royal standard, Zohak was captured and chained up inside the crater of Mount Demavand, there to undergo a lingering death, just as Prometheus was bound on Caucasus ; indeed, this legend of Zohak closely resembles that of Prometheus. Feridun is the ancient Thraetona, and appears as Traitana in the Veda, where he earns renown by cutting off the head of a mighty giant.

The Three Sons of Feridun.—According to the legendary history, Feridun had three sons. To Selm he gave the West, to Tur the East (henceforward termed Turan) ; while to his youngest son, Erij, he promised the throne of Persia after his own death. This arrangement, not unnaturally, was displeasing to the elder brothers, who threatened to invade Persia to make good their demands. Erij visited his brothers and offered to resign his rights to the throne, hoping by this means to avoid civil war during the last days of his father's reign. Selm and Tur, however, resolved to put Erij to death, and refused to listen to his pathetic pleading for life, which, as given by Firdausi, runs :

> Will ye ever let it be recorded
> That ye, possessing life, deprive others of that blessing ?
>
> Pain not the ant that drags the grain along the ground ;
> It has life, and life is sweet and pleasant to all who possess it.

Erij was murdered, and, to complete the horror of the fratricide, his head was embalmed and sent to the aged Feridun, who was impotent to avenge the crime. Some years passed and Manuchehr, son of Erij, grew up and, "attended by armies and clad in steel," killed both his uncles in single combat.

Sam, Zal, and Rudabah.—Manuchehr succeeded his grandfather, and his chief adviser was Sam, Prince of Sistan, who, with his son Zal and his still more famous grandson Rustam, the Hercules of Persia, fills the stage of Persian legend, even the kings playing but secondary parts. None of these figures appear in the Indo-Iranian legends ; but it

---

[1] The apron, richly adorned with jewels, became the royal standard of Persia, and was known as the *Durufsh-i-Kawani*.

is quite likely that they embody a nucleus of truth, which succeeding generations overlaid with much fiction ; and the genius of Firdausi welded the whole into a grand epic. It is related that Zal was born with white hair, which convinced Sam that the infant was not his own, but the offspring of a Div. Consequently, he gave orders to expose it on Mount Elburz ; but it was nourished by the *Simurgh*, a fabulous eagle, and after a while Sam, hearing a divine voice, repented of his conduct and recovered his son. Zal grew up to be a mighty warrior, and, when hunting in the wilds of what is now Afghanistan, came to a castle where he saw the beauteous Rudabah, daughter of Mehrab, King of Kabul. It was a case of love at first sight on both sides, and the ardent lover scaled his mistress's tower by using her long tresses as a rope.

Rustam the Champion.—The offspring of the marriage was Rustam, the great champion of Iran, whose fabulous exploits as a warrior, as a hunter, and as a trencherman still loom immense in the minds of Persians. Closely connected with the hero was his charger Raksh, whose size and courage are legendary ; in Sistan, ruins situated a mile apart are pointed out as having been the " manger " and " heel-ropes " of Raksh ! Rustam's prowess was mainly displayed in the wars waged between Turan and Iran, which began after the death of Manuchehr and the accession of his unworthy son Nozar, and lasted for more than a generation. The Turanian leader was Afrasiab, who slew Nozar and ruled Persia for twelve years, and this period of gloom saw the end of the Pishdadian dynasty.

The Keianian Dynasty.—We now come to what is the first historical, or perhaps semi-historical dynasty, known as the Keianian. To-day there is a family of chiefs in Sistan who claim descent from this illustrious stock, although, as in the case of the probably allied tribe in Baluchistan, it seems more likely that they are descended from the Saffar dynasty.[1] In India some of the Parsi families make the same claim, which is generally conceded.

The first monarch of this dynasty was Kei Kobad, a lineal descendant of Manuchehr, whose retreat was the Elburz range, and who was brought from his place of retirement by Rustam. The great champion now took the field against the hereditary foe for the first time and covered himself

---

[1] *Vide* Chapter LI. ; also *Ten Thousand Miles*, etc., p. 229.

with glory by defeating Afrasiab in single combat, from which, however, the Turanian monarch escaped alive because the girdle by which he was held gave way. Thereafter peace was concluded on equal terms, and it was agreed that the Oxus should remain the boundary of Iran, as before.

Kei Kaus to some extent identified with Cyaxares.—Kei Kaus, who succeeded his father, invaded Mazanderan against the advice of his councillors, and was there defeated in a great battle by the Div-i-Sufid or "White Div," a legendary name that evidently refers to some specially white nation. During the battle the army was struck with blindness, and it is reasonable to see in this legend a reference to the eclipse which occurred during the battle between Cyaxares and the Lydians, described in the preceding chapter. This being so, we may, to some extent, identify Kei Kobad with Deïokes and Kei Kaus with Cyaxares. But it would be a mistake to press the matter too far, and there is no resemblance in the name.

Sohrab and Rustam.—Afrasiab again invaded Persia, and again Rustam was the protagonist. To this period is assigned the famous and tragic combat between Rustam and his unknown son, which is familiar to English readers through Matthew Arnold's stirring poem. As Firdausi declares, the episode is "full of the waters of the eye."

Siawush and Kei Khusru.—The next incident in the drama is that of Siawush, heir of Kei Kaus, who deserted his father's court after trials similar to those which befell Joseph at the hand of Potiphar's wife. He took refuge with Afrasiab, who at first received him as an honoured guest. A few years later, however, false charges were brought against the young prince, and he was executed; but his infant son Kei Khusru was hidden and ultimately restored to Persia, where he succeeded to the throne.

Kei Khusru not Cyrus the Great.—Many European writers on Persia, and almost all Persians who have heard of Cyrus the Great, identify him with Kei Khusru; but the theory, pleasing as it is, cannot stand, for the simple reason that this Kei Khusru is the Kava Husrava of Indo-Iranian legend, and belongs to a period before the dawn of history. After several dramatic vicissitudes of fortune, Kei Khusru, thanks mainly to Rustam, conquered Afrasiab, who was finally taken captive and put to death in revenge for the death of Siawush. Kei Khusru lived to a great age, and died full of years and honours.

Lohrasp and Gushtasp.—Lohrasp, who succeeded Kei Khusru, after ruling for some years, resigned the throne to Gushtasp, who, as has already been narrated, was Zoroaster's royal convert and patron. Again wars with Turan followed, and again the Persian forces suffered great reverses, in the course of which Lohrasp, the old king, and Zoroaster were killed at Balkh.

Isfandiar.—On this occasion Isfandiar, whom his father Gushtasp had imprisoned, came to the rescue and recovered not only the lost provinces of Persia but also the famous national standard. Isfandiar had been promised the throne by Gushtasp, who falsely proclaimed his intention of following the example of Lohrasp. When he claimed it, he was persuaded by his crafty sire to accept the mission of bringing Rustam, who was alleged to have thrown off his allegiance, to the foot of the throne in bonds. Again heroic combats ensued, and again the Champion of Persia slew his adversary, winning thereby his last great fight. A few years later he fell into a pit prepared by his treacherous brother and there ended his heroic life.

Bahman or Ardeshir Dirazdast.—Gushtasp was succeeded by his grandson Bahman, who is known to history as Artaxerxes Longimanus, the Latin equivalent of Ardeshir Dirazdast. According to Firdausi, this monarch made a speciality of keeping himself informed about the affairs of his empire through secret agents. He was also, according to the same authority, a great conqueror. The historical Artaxerxes Longimanus is dealt with in Chapter XVIII.

The End of the Heroic Period.—Here this description of early Persian history as known to and fully believed in by Persians of every class, who in no wise despise their pre-Moslem heroes, may be concluded. Indeed, but for this intense belief in legends, which contain, at most, but a modicum of history, and omit all mention of Cyrus the Great and Darius, the period would have been treated still more succinctly. As it is, they are so interwoven with the national history and the national mind that I shall have occasion to refer to them again and again.

PERSIAN KING FIGHTING BARBARIANS.
(Cylinder of Chalcedony, British Museum.)

CHAPTER XIII

THE RISE OF PERSIA

By divine decree destiny was potent of old, and enjoined on Persians to engage in wars, and cavalry routs, and the overthrow of cities.—AESCHYLUS, *The Persae.*

The Early Organization of the Persians. — The heroic period of the history of Iran described in the previous chapter is mainly legendary, although towards its close we are dealing with historical personages obscured by the mists of fantastic myth. In the present chapter we have to do with historical figures only.

We have seen, in connexion with the empire of the Medes, that the ancient inhabitants of the country were to a considerable extent absorbed, and the same thing probably occurred in the case of the Persians. This view receives support from Herodotus, who, referring to the tribes into which the Persians were divided, writes as follows : " The principal tribes, on which the others depend, are the Pasargadae, the Maraphians and the Maspians, of whom the Pasargadae are the noblest. The Achaemenidae, from which spring all the Persian kings, is one of their clans. The rest of the Persian tribes are the following : the Panthialaeans, the Derusiaeans, the Germanians, who are engaged in husbandry ; the Daans, the Mardians, the Dropicans, and the Sagartians, who are nomads." [1] It is generally supposed that the first three tribes were the Aryan conquerors, and that the Achaemenidae were the royal family belonging to the

---

[1] Herodotus i. 125 ; also *The Passing of the Empires*, p. 458.

Pasargadae, and did not form a separate tribe. Of the others, the nomads are believed to have been non-Aryan and in some cases their territory is known ; but very little has been gleaned about the agricultural tribes except that the Germanians are the Carmanians.

The Persians were governed by the members of seven noble families, among whom the Achaemenians were originally first among equals ; but, in course of time, they became the royal family. The other chiefs became subjects, but preserved, among other privileges, the right of access to the monarch and formed his council.

Owing to the voyage of Nearchus we hear the names of some ports on the Persian Gulf, among them being Harmuza, the mediaeval Hormuz, and in the interior were Pasargadae, Istakhr (Persepolis), Gabae, and Carmana. Gabae may possibly be identified with Achaemenian ruins I visited to the east of Shiraz, where are also Sasanian bas-reliefs ; and Carmana I have identified with ruins situated to the north of the Jiruft valley. Generally speaking there were few cities at this period in Persia.

The Rise of Cyrus the Great according to Herodotus.—The account given by Herodotus of the coming of Cyrus is well known.[1] Astyages, we are told, dreamed that from his daughter Mandane " such a stream of water flowed forth as not only to fill his capital, but to flood the whole of Asia." The Median monarch thereupon feared to marry her to a nobleman of her own country, lest the dream should be accomplished. Instead, he gave her to a Persian " of good family, indeed, but of a quiet temper, whom he looked on as much inferior to a Mede of even middle condition." Cambyses, the Persian, took away Mandane to his home. Shortly afterwards Astyages dreamed another dream, in which he saw a vine growing from Mandane which overshadowed the whole of Asia. Terrified at this second warning, he summoned his daughter to the capital and, when her son was born, entrusted him to Harpagus, " a man of his own house and the most faithful of the Medes," with instructions to slay and bury the infant Cyrus. Harpagus, not caring for many reasons to sully his own hands with such an infamous deed,

---

[1] I have not referred to the account given by Ctesias, whose authority is much discredited. It is given in *The Passing of the Empires*, p. 596 ; and, according to it, Cyrus started life as a *farrash* or sweeper of the palace.

made the child over to one of the royal herdsmen, with orders to expose him " in the wildest part of the hills where he would be sure to die speedily." The herdsman's wife, who had just given birth to a still-born infant, persuaded her husband to make an exchange, and her child was shown to Harpagus as the corpse of the dead prince. Cyrus was brought up by this woman, whose name was Spako—signifying a bitch—and he was ultimately identified by his grandfather, who, recognizing the family likeness, made inquiries and was glad to learn that his grandson was alive.

The Tragedy of Harpagus.—Harpagus, however, was cruelly punished. At a royal banquet he was served with the flesh of his own son, whom Astyages had sent for and killed, and the child's head, hands, and feet were presented to him in a basket. Harpagus showed himself submissive at the time ; but a few years later he opened up correspondence with Cyrus, who had been sent home to his parents, and in the end he became the chief instrument in the overthrow of Astyages, by persuading Cyrus to revolt and by gaining him adherents among the Median nobles. Astyages, when he sent an army to crush the Persian rebellion, fatuously confided it to Harpagus, who prevented it from opposing Cyrus and so finally satisfied his vengeance and hatred.

It is surmised that the settlement of the family of Harpagus in Karia, a province in South-West Asia Minor, gave rise to this story, in which he plays such a leading part. The legend is open to criticism on several points. For one thing, Herodotus was not aware that Cyrus was (as will be shown later) King of Anshan. The story, too, of the woman Spako obviously contains the Iranian legend that their great king was suckled by a bitch, just as Romulus and Remus were nursed by a she-wolf or *lupa*. Herodotus would not be likely to know that dogs were held in special honour by the tenets of Zoroastrianism. The sacred bitch of the real legend is transformed through the ignorance of the Greek historian into a woman named Spako, as was Lupa in the parallel instance. But this very mistake is a striking testimony to his honesty and shows how truthful and accurate he strove to be. Indeed, but for the " Father of History," there would be many lacunae in our knowledge of this obscure period.

Fresh Light on Persian History.—Until comparatively recently the account just given was generally accepted :

but the discovery of the famous cylinders of Nabonidus and of Cyrus has changed the whole situation ; and I now propose to deal with the question in the light of these important documents. It appears that, just as in the case of Media, a strong man arose and welded the loose congeries of tribes into a nation, although, in the case of the Persians, their remoteness from the civilized powers of the Tigris and Euphrates hindered the process of organization and development.

Achaemenes, the Founder of the Royal Family.—The founder of the Persian monarchy was Hakhámánish or Achaemenes, Prince of the tribe of Pasargadae ; his capital was the city bearing the same name, ruins of which, dating from the era of Cyrus the Great, still exist. No definite acts can be traced to Achaemenes, after whom the dynasty was named ; but the fact that his memory was highly revered tends to prove that he did in truth mould the tribes of rude Persians into a nation before they stepped on to the stage of history.[1] His son Chishpish or Teispes took advantage of the defenceless condition of Elam, after its overthrow by Assurbanipal, to occupy the district of Anshan, referred to in Chapter IV., and assumed the title of " Great King, King of Anshan." Upon his death one of his sons succeeded to Anshan and another to Fars.

The Double Line of Achaemenian Monarchs.—This division started the double line, a reference to which by Darius in the Behistun inscription greatly puzzled its decipherers. This double line continued, and examination justifies the statement of Darius : " There are eight of my race who have been kings before me ; I am the ninth. In a double line we have been kings."

To make this matter clear I append the following genealogy :[2]

[TABLE

---

[1] Achaemenes is held by some to be a semi-legendary figure fed, like Zal, by an eagle during infancy ; but I cannot help feeling that we are dealing with an historical personage, as Achaemenes headed no long line, but, on the contrary, was only four generations removed from Cyrus.

[2] Lehmann-Haupt, *Klio*, viii. 495.

THE RISE OF PERSIA

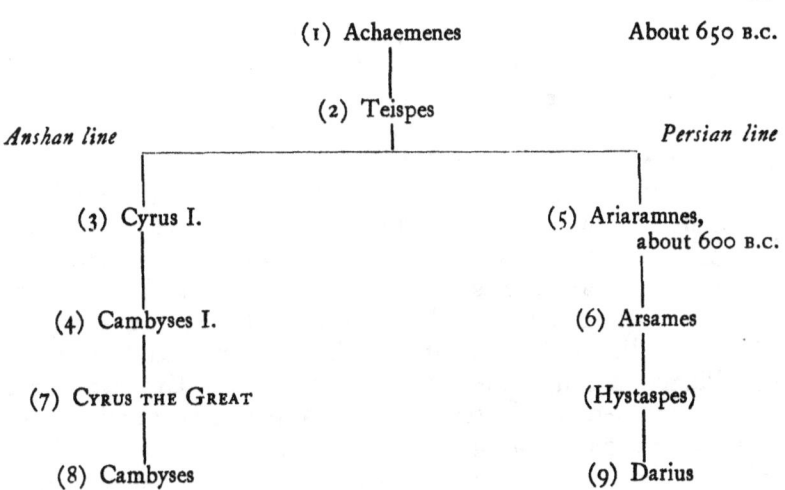

The Defeat of Astyages by Cyrus.—We now come to the historical account, so far as it is known, of the campaign against Astyages. The famous tablet of the Annals of Nabonidus runs : " [His troops] he collected, and against Cyrus, king of Anshan, . . . he marched. As for Astyages, his troops revolted against him and he was seized (and) delivered up to Cyrus. Cyrus (marched) to Ecbatana, the royal city. The silver, gold, goods, and substance of Ecbatana he spoiled, and to the land of Anshan he took the goods and substance that were gotten."[1] No details are given ; but we learn from the Median traditions, as preserved by the classical writers, that there were three battles before the final victory of Cyrus. The date of the capture of Ecbatana is 550 B.C.[2]

Cyrus, King of Anshan, becomes King of Persia.—One important question on which no light has hitherto been shed is at what period, and by what means, Cyrus became King of Persia. If we turn to the tablets we see that he appears in 549 B.C. as " King of Anshan," and in 546 B.C. he is referred to as " King of Persia." The inference is that he succeeded to the throne of Persia without serious fighting, of which there is no mention ; though the absence of mention does not amount to proof. Possibly upon his capture of Ecbatana he was asked to accept the throne, which was after all in his family. In any case, we know that Hystaspes, father of Darius, never reigned, though he was the son of Arsames. He may have

---

[1] *Light from the East*, p. 219.   [2] Hall, *op. cit.* p. 552.

been a minor and passed over ; but, failing fresh evidence, the situation must remain obscure. It may, however, be accepted that Cyrus occupied the throne of Persia before he started his career of conquest in the West, and that the evidence of the tablets is perfectly trustworthy.

Croesus of Lydia.—The position of Cyrus after taking possession of the throne of Media was by no means assured. Fortunately for him, peace-loving Nabonidus reigned at Babylon, so that he was reasonably safe from active hostility in that quarter ; but with respect to Lydia the situation was very different. Alyattes, who had ratified the treaty of alliance, strengthened by marriage with Cyaxares, had been succeeded by Croesus, whose name is proverbial among Western nations for a man of fabulous wealth, just as Moslems talk of Karun or Korah. This monarch, whose accession to the throne was contested, carried on the work of Alyattes and brought Miletus and afterwards the other Greek colonies of the littoral under his sway. Eastwards, too, he fought successfully, and in less than ten years he had made good the position of Lydia up to the left bank of the Halys, these conquests being completed just at the time when Astyages was being attacked by Cyrus.

The overthrow of Media must have deeply affected Croesus, who, instead of having an ally as his neighbour, had now to face an entirely altered state of affairs. In these circumstances, inasmuch as he possessed a fine war-hardened army with superb cavalry, which he could strengthen with large numbers of Greek mercenaries, and might reasonably rely on the support of Babylonia and of Egypt, it was probably a sound decision to invade Cappadocia and fight the Persians before they had consolidated their power. The alternative would have been to allow them to develop their strength and attack at their own convenience.

We learn from Herodotus that Croesus, whose failing was overweening confidence, felt certain of success ; but, to fortify his opinion, he sent ambassadors to the famous oracle of Delphi to inquire what would be the result if he crossed the Halys and attacked the Persians. The reply was that " if Croesus attacked the Persians, he would destroy a mighty empire." He was moreover recommended to " see who were the most powerful of the Greeks and to make alliance with them," Delighted with what he regarded as the favourable reply, he sent again to inquire whether his kingdom would endure. The oracle gave the following answer:

> Wait till the time shall come when a mule is monarch of Media;
> Then, thou delicate Lydian, away to the pebbles of Hermus;
> Haste, oh! haste thee away, nor blush to behave like a coward.

The injunctions of the first oracle were carefully followed. Croesus sent an embassy with rich gifts to the Spartans, who readily agreed to his proposals and prepared to despatch an expedition to join his forces. In addition, alliances were made with Amasis of Egypt and Nabonidus of Babylonia, both of whom were unfavourably affected by the overthrow of Media, which had ceased to be a predatory power and was allied to Babylonia as well as to Lydia. Indeed, everything appeared to be working for the realization of the astute policy of the Lydian monarch, when an agent to whom he had entrusted large sums of money for engaging Greek mercenaries fled to Persia and revealed the secret of this formidable coalition.[1]

The Perso-Lydian Campaign.—Cyrus determined to forestall Croesus and to attack Lydia before the arrival of his allies. The daring decision to quit Media and Persia for a long period, to march one thousand miles mainly across lands which were either outlying provinces of Babylonia or independent, and then to surprise a powerful military state, proves him to have been a great general.

The result justified his calculations. Upon entering Cappadocia he found Croesus unsupported by his allies, and negotiations were opened, Cyrus offering the Lydian monarch his life and kingdom on condition that he swore to become his loyal vassal. These terms were naturally refused, and the first battle proved to be a victory for the Lydians.[2] A truce of three months was negotiated, and then, upon the resumption of hostilities, the Lydians were apparently overpowered at Pteria by the superior numbers of Cyrus. Croesus retired under cover of night towards Sardes, laying waste the country to impede the march of the Persians, and hoping that Cyrus would not dare to lengthen still further his line of communications, with hostile Babylon in his rear and the winter coming on. But Nabonidus deserted his ally and accepted terms of

---

[1] Diodorus Siculus ix. 32. It is, however, improbable that Cyrus was altogether ignorant of the formation of the coalition.

[2] *Vide* Maspero's *The Passing of the Empires*, p. 616, note 3, where good reasons are brought forward for not following the account of the campaign as given by Herodotus.

peace as soon as they were offered, without perhaps realizing that his own independence was just as much at stake as that of Lydia. Cyrus, freed from anxiety as to his rear, again showed his genius by making a rapid march on Sardes. This unexpected advance utterly surprised Croesus, who, feeling sure that the winter would completely stop all operations, had, with supreme folly, disbanded part of his own forces and arranged for his allies to defer their arrival until the spring. However, nothing daunted, he prepared to face the invader with his cavalry on the open plain of the Hermus. But Cyrus employed the now world-renowned ruse of covering the front of his army with camels, the smell of which terrified the horses [1] of the enemy and made them unmanageable. The gallant Lydians dismounted and fought to the death on foot; but the Persians outnumbered them, and their shattered remnant was forced to retreat to Sardes.

The Capture of Sardes, 546 B.C.—In his impregnable capital Croesus, aided by the winter, might have defied the Persians until his allies assembled ; but again fortune declared against him. The story in Herodotus is well known. When the city had been blockaded for fourteen days Cyrus offered a rich reward to the first man who should enter it. A Mardian soldier saw a member of the garrison descend what looked from a distance like an inaccessible cliff, pick up his lost helmet, and return. He noted the track, and, with a few comrades, surprised the careless garrison, which trusted to the strength of their position, and opened the gates to the Persian army. Thus fell Sardes in 546 B.C.,[2] and the campaign may fairly claim to be of signal importance ; for, had Croesus won, as he should have done but for his own folly, the course of the world's history would have been profoundly modified. His defeat removed the only strong organized state which could fight on equal terms for the mastery of Anterior Asia ; and it gave to Cyrus the Great an empire far exceeding in extent any of its predecessors.

The Fate of Croesus.—Like his fellow-monarch at Nineveh half a century before, Croesus, it would seem, disdaining to fall into the hands of his enemy, erected a funeral pyre in his palace and mounted it with his family and choicest possessions.

---

[1] I recollect most vividly that some thirty years ago a young Australian horse I was riding literally roared with fright and nearly collapsed under me upon seeing, or more probably smelling, a camel for the first time.

[2] For this date *vide Études, etc.,* p. 412.

Greek legend, as preserved by Herodotus, represents that the pyre was indeed built and set alight, but by the orders of Cyrus. The Lydian monarch, we are told, sighed and repeated the name of Solon thrice, in recollection of the warning he had received from the sage that no man should be called happy until his death. Cyrus, moved to pity, ordered the pyre to be extinguished, but in vain, until Apollo came to the rescue of his worshipper and saved him by a heavy fall of rain. Perhaps what actually occurred was that Croesus mounted the pyre of his own free will and was taken from it by the Persians in time to save his life. The belief of the Greeks that he ended his days as a great noble at the Court of Persia strengthens this view.[1]

The Geographical Position of Hellas.—The geographical position of Hellas, turning towards the East, was singularly favourable for development and progress, in view of the fact that none of the early great states of Asia had approached the sea, or developed sea-power. The Greek city-states bordered the Aegean Sea, which was studded with islands so close to one another that the navigator was seldom out of sight of land. The great powers were too far off to be feared, but one of them, Egypt, was accessible. Consequently the Greeks were bound to be navigators and pirate traders, and as such they could benefit by the older civilization of Egypt and, in a lesser degree and mainly indirectly, by that of Babylon, without fear of being conquered. On the other hand, the physical characteristics of Greece, and perhaps this very security, gave rise to a multiplication of small states and a spirit of mutual rivalry and jealousy. Thus impeded, its inhabitants never developed into a great nation, and it is left to us to admire the splendid conceptions and great deeds of tiny isolated states, whose energies, for the most part, were wasted in fighting petty rivals. As de Morgan puts it, " their destiny would have been sublime if, by their divisions, they had not paralysed the soaring of their genius." [2]

Recent Progress in Knowledge of Greek History.—A generation ago our knowledge of Greek history did not extend farther

---

[1] This question is dealt with by E. Edwards under " Human Sacrifice " (Iranian), *Encyclopedia of Religion and Ethics*. In this article reference is made to a recently discovered poem of Bacchylides (born 507 B.C.) and to a vase of the sixth or fifth century preserved in the Louvre, both of which tend to show that Croesus elected death rather than submit to capture. *Vide* also *Adonis, Attis, Osiris*, by Sir J. G. Frazer, p. 89.
[2] *Études etc.*, p. 380.

back than the beginning of the seventh century B.C., Thucydides and Herodotus being the limits beyond which the student could not pass ; and Homer, even to the select few who were not content to rest satisfied, was separated by a fathomless gulf from the era of Herodotus. The historical outlook was, in fact, so narrow that the epoch-making discoveries in Egypt and the Near East were not supposed to bear upon Greece, and were treated with a conspicuous lack of interest. Now, however, all this is changed, and we are able to connect the classical age with the period of Homer, and even to survey Greek civilization before the Homeric era ; indeed, almost as far back as its inception. In other words, Greece is now treated as part of a vast field of study in which the parts are not isolated but to a great extent influence one another.

The Aryan Invasion of Greece.—Although there are still many points on which the authorities on Hellenic history are not agreed, it is generally accepted that the earliest known inhabitants of Greece, and indeed of the countries bordering the northern coast of the Mediterranean Sea, were a dark-haired group of tribes which were neither Semitic nor Aryan, and were sometimes known as " Pelasgi." These were the people who created the wonderful civilization that was discovered by Schliemann at Mycenae and by Evans at Knossos. At dates which cannot be fixed with certainty they were conquered by Aryans from the north, and it is believed that in Greece the invaders mixed with the older inhabitants and imposed the Aryan tongue upon them ; but there is little doubt that the latter continued to exist and to form, at any rate, a very important section of the population. The Aryan Greeks adopted from them a great number of non-Aryan words, and it is evident that the artistic capacity of the Greeks was mainly derived from the Mediterranean race.[1]

The Greek Colonies in Asia Minor.—The Greek colonies in Asia Minor were believed by the Hellenes themselves to have been founded as a consequence of the Dorian invasion, which was an event of first-rate importance. The Dorians, who came from the north, conquered a large part of the Peloponnesus and other parts of Hellas. This great movement, which reacted on the whole of Greece, is believed to have occurred about 1000 B.C. Its result was to set in motion

---
[1] Hall, *op. cit.* p. 537.

a wave of emigration, which broke not only on the islands, but also on the Asiatic coast of the Aegean Sea. The process of colonization was spread, no doubt, over a long period; but it is not unreasonable to suppose that the Dorian invasion was the chief cause of a departure which had far-reaching effects. These colonies throve marvellously in Asia Minor, their development surpassing that of the home country, with its narrower scope and sterile soil. On the other hand, their position was precarious, and their independence was likely to be threatened as soon as a power appeared in the hinterland of Asia Minor. Thus the rise of Lydia resulted in constant attempts on Greek independence; but, fortunately for the colonies, the Lydians, who worshipped the same gods and who differed but little from the Greeks, were bent only on securing influence and control over the colonies and not on ruining them. Indeed, when Croesus was on the throne, the Greeks liked him well, and they bitterly regretted his fall.

Their Conquest by the Persians.—After the overthrow of Croesus, the Phrygians, Mysians, and other Asiatic tribes submitted to Cyrus, who wished to complete his task by securing the submission of the Greek colonies that lined the coast of Asia Minor, some of which had attained considerable strength. Their conduct had been entirely lacking in foresight. They had refused to ally themselves with Cyrus; but they had not lifted a finger to aid Croesus, and now they had to reckon with his conqueror. In their hour of need they appealed to Sparta; but the Spartans contented themselves with sending an ambassador, who arrogantly demanded of Cyrus that he should respect the Hellenic cities, under pain of incurring the hostility of Sparta. The Great King, whose sense of humour was higher than that of the Spartans, conveyed his thanks for the good advice; but added, "Take care that I do not soon cause you to babble, not about the misfortunes of the Ionians, but of your own calamities." The Greek cities were subdued piecemeal, thanks to skill in the art of conducting sieges inherited by the Persians from the Assyrians,[1] and in spite of a revolt during which Sardes was besieged. So intense in certain cases was the feeling for liberty that the inhabitants of Phocaea and Teos quitted their cities in a body and sailed off westwards to found Marseilles

---

[1] Hall, *op. cit.* p. 558.

and Abdera respectively, a circumstance that bears striking testimony to the range and excellent organization of their fleets.

The Eastern Campaigns of Cyrus.—Shortly after the capture of Sardes, and before securing the submission of the Greek cities of Asia Minor, Cyrus hastened due east ; and for a period of five or six years, from 545 B.C. to 539 B.C., he is almost lost to sight, waging distant wars against almost unknown tribes.[1] Perhaps his campaigns were mainly necessitated by rebellions in the provinces in favour of the Median dynasty, as movements of this nature would have been encouraged by his long absence in the West. Such information as we possess concerning this period of his career is of slight historical value ; but the legend according to which Bactria was first attacked and peace was made when it was known that Cyrus had wedded the daughter of Astyages may contain some nucleus of fact. The Sakae, too, were subdued, and the greater part of what is now Afghanistan. The tradition that the Great King lost an army in the wastes of Makran is of little weight ; but this barren country was added to the Persian Empire, possibly after one or more successful expeditions.

The Surrender of Babylon, 538 B.C.—It is clear that a conqueror like Cyrus would not tolerate the existence of Babylonia as an independent state for very long, and, as a proof of his intentions, we have the fact that, in 546, an attack on Southern Babylonia had been launched from Elam and that, as a result, a Persian bore rule at Erech, though possibly only temporarily. We have seen that the last king of Babylon was a tool of the priesthood. His ruling passion was the discovery of the foundation-cylinders of the ancient sanctuaries and their restoration at the cost of much levying of taxes. Such a man would tend to become a mere cypher, and it appears that the real power lay in the hands of his son, Belshazzar. The Babylonians seem to have been weary of the prevailing discord. We know that the Jews were excited by their prophets to expect the downfall of Babylon, the oppressor, and we can imagine that this feeling was shared by thousands of exiles from other lands. Moreover, Nabonidus alienated a large section of the priests and people

---

[1] How and Wells, in *op. cit.* i. p. 135, are of opinion that this expedition took place after the capture of Babylon.

by bringing into Babylon the gods of Ur, Uruk, and Eridu, which lay outside the defended area of Nebuchadnezzar, as is clearly shown in the so-called " cylinder of Cyrus." In this, his proclamation to the people of Babylon, he represents himself as the servant of Merodach, chosen to repair the evil deeds wrought by Nabonidus.

To quote a few lines : " In wrath because he brought them (*i.e.* the gods of Ur, etc.) to SHU-ANNA (Babylon), Merodach . . . showed compassion upon all the lands together. . . . Yea he sought out an upright Prince, after his own heart, whom he took by the hand, Cyrus, king of the city of ANSHAN ; He named his name ; to the kingdom of the whole world He called him by name." [1] Had Cyrus been opposed by a united people ready to rally to the support of their monarch, it seems improbable that the Persians could have taken Babylon, with its triple lines of fortification and its immense resources, without a long siege ; but, as it happened, everything played into the hands of the invaders.

Cyrus began operations by draining off the waters of the Tigris and of the Diyala at a time when these rivers were at their lowest levels, and in this manner forced his way into the protected area. He himself then moved north to attack the Babylonian army, which, through supreme incompetency or treachery, had remained at Opis and was thus cut off from Babylon. This force he defeated with ease. Meanwhile his general Gaubaruva (Gobryas) marched south and, driving Nabonidus from Sippar, entered Babylon, " without skirmish or battle." The king, as might have been expected, tamely surrendered. In pursuance of the strict orders of Cyrus, the temples were protected and no pillaging was allowed ; and when the Great Conqueror finally arrived in person, he was welcomed as a deliverer. As the cylinder runs, " when I had entered TINTIR (Babylon) peacefully, with rejoicings and festal shouts in the King's palace, I occupied the Seat of Sovereignty." Belshazzar, who had not surrendered, was surprised and slain by Gobryas, who was made Viceroy of Babylon ; and this final success decided all those who were hesitating whether they should proffer allegiance to the Conqueror. Seldom has a great prize been more easily won than when

---

[1] Ball's *Light from the East*, p. 224. The almost identical language used in Isaiah, chapter xlv., is of considerable interest for its parallelism to this quotation. It runs : " Thus saith the Lord to his anointed, to Cyrus, whose right hand I have holden . . . I have even called thee by thy name."

Babylon, the holy city, whose gods and whose laws were the oldest and most highly respected throughout the known world, surrendered without a fight to the power of the conquering Persians. With great diplomacy Cyrus [1] "took the hands of Bel," which gratified his new subjects immensely. Furthermore, he restored to the cities the gods which Nabonidus had collected at Babylon.

The Traditional Account.—There is no part of Persian history which has suffered such remarkable vicissitudes as the fall of Babylon. Until the discovery of the tablets, the dramatic account given by Herodotus and supplemented by the book of Daniel, how Cyrus diverted the waters of the Euphrates and marched along the dry bed, in which the gates had been left open upon the occasion of a feast, was fully accepted.[2] A massacre ensued, the drunken Babylonian monarch, paralysed by the writing on the wall, was slain, and the city was given over to fire and the sword. The prophecies, moreover, were fulfilled, the finest of them being that given in the book of Isaiah : "Hell from beneath is moved for thee to meet thee at thy coming : it stirreth up the dead for thee, even all the chief ones of the earth ; it hath raised up from their thrones all the kings of the nations. All they shall speak and say unto thee, Art thou also become weak as we ? art thou become like unto us ? "[3] Actually, although there was no siege of Babylon, the citadel apparently held out for some months, and was stormed in the presence of Cyrus. It is possible that the above legends may have sprung from some such attack.

The Latter Years of Cyrus.—Lydia had fallen, Babylon had fallen, and Egypt alone, among the powers of the old world, remained unsubdued. We may feel sure that Cyrus, while organizing his newly-conquered dominions, which included the cities of Phoenicia with their valuable fleets, often gave this matter his most earnest consideration. Indeed, it is probable that during this period of perhaps eight years he was steadily preparing the necessary resources.

The Repatriation of the Jews.—It has been suggested that the remarkable generosity displayed by Cyrus towards the Jews, which may have been due to a desire to requite services

---

[1] This action has been used to show that Cyrus was not a follower of Zoroaster, and perhaps he may be best described as a worshipper of Ahura Mazda, his national god.
[2] *Five Monarchies*, iii. 513 ff.   [3] Isaiah xiv. 9, 10.

rendered during the course of the campaign against Babylon, or, again, from a recognition of the striking similarity of Judaism with Persian beliefs, was also partly due to his desire to have a body of loyal adherents close to the confines of Egypt. Indeed, when it is remembered that not only was permission given to rebuild both Jerusalem and the temple, but the gold and silver vessels of the sanctuary were restored and help of all kinds was enjoined in the solemn edict recorded in the book of Ezra, it seems certain that some special motive actuated the Great Conqueror. He was justified in his calculations; for the few Jews who were sufficiently fervid in their yearning for Jerusalem to leave their properties and business in Babylonia formed but a small colony among hostile tribes, and, without the support of the Persian governor, they could not have maintained their position. Thus, apart from any sentiments of gratitude, they were necessarily loyal from motives of self-interest.

The Death of Cyrus, 529 B.C.—The last campaigns of Cyrus and his death are wrapped in mystery. It appears probable that he was called upon to beat back one of those invasions from the East which have constituted the chief factor in the history of Central Asia. In this campaign he was killed, in 529 B.C. Tradition, of course, has woven many legends. The best-known is that of Herodotus, who narrates that he demanded the hand of Tomyris, Queen of the Massagetae, in marriage, but was refused with disdain. Thereupon he invaded her country, defeated her advance-guard and captured her eldest son and heir, who immediately killed himself. In the great battle which ensued and was fiercely contested, Cyrus was defeated and slain. The Queen, to avenge the death of her son, dipped the hero's head in gore, exclaiming, "I give thee thy fill of blood." This legend is to some extent discounted by the fact that the Great King's body was brought back to Pasargadae, where it was interred in the tomb described in Chapter XV. According to Berossus, Cyrus was waging war against the Dahae of Parthia.

His Character.—Cyrus, who from being king of a petty state rose to be the Lord of the mightiest empire the world had up to that time seen, is one of the most attractive figures in history. As a general he excites our wonder by his victories, Lydia and Babylon each falling within a few months after the campaign had opened. His conquest of Lydia was perhaps his most magnificent achievement; and he owed it to the lightning initiative by which, in the first stage, he surprised Croesus with half his troops absent, and, in the second, again surprised his adversary and captured Sardes. His manly beauty, his soldierlike qualities of bravery and activity, were apparently conspicuous throughout his life, and he never lost his virility through luxury and self-indulgence, as so many great men have done. His ideals were high, as he laid down that no man was fit to rule unless, by his own qualities, he was more capable than all his subjects. As an administrator Cyrus was not conspicuous, but his sagacity was great, and he showed himself both intelligent and reasonable, and thereby made his yoke incomparably lighter than that of previous conquerors. As a man he was admirable. He married Cassandane, daughter of Pharnaspes, an Achaemenian, and when she died he lamented her deeply. His humanity was equalled by his freedom from pride, which induced him to meet people on a level, instead of affecting the remoteness and aloofness which characterized the great monarchs who preceded and followed him. His sense of humour was shown in his reply to the Ionian Greeks, who, after refusing his overtures to join him in his attack on Croesus, came, after the fall of Sardes, to proffer their submission. To them Cyrus replied, "A fisherman wished the fish to dance, so he played on his flute; but the fish kept still. Then he took his net and drew them to the shore, whereupon they all began to leap and dance. But the fisherman said, 'A truce to your dancing now, since you would not dance when I wished it.'"

I would now give the considered opinion of Xenophon in the *Cyropaedia* : " He was able to extend the fear of himself over so great a part of the world that he astonished all, and no one attempted anything against him. He was able to inspire all with so great a desire of pleasing him, that they ever wished to be governed by his opinion." With this view I am in entire sympathy, but I cannot endorse Gobineau's fantastic summing up : " Il n'eut jamais son égal ici-bas. . . . C'est un Christ en effet, un homme prédestiné par-dessus tous les autres."

In conclusion, the evidence of Holy Writ, of the classical writers, and of the Persians themselves, all tends to show

THE TOMB OF CYRUS THE GREAT.
(From Dieulafoy's *L'Art antique de la Perse*.)
(Published by Ch. Eggimann, Paris.)

that Cyrus was indeed worthy of the title "Great." His countrymen loved him and termed him "father"; and we, too, may feel proud that the first great Aryan whose character is known in history should have displayed such splendid qualities.

PERSIAN CUNEIFORM INSCRIPTION.

CHAPTER XIV

THE PERSIAN EMPIRE AT ITS ZENITH

I am Darius, the Great King, the King of Kings, King of lands peopled by all races, for long King of this great earth, the son of Vishtasp (Hystaspes), the Achaemenian, a Persian, son of a Persian, an Aryan of Aryan descent.

The Accession of Cambyses, 529 B.C.—Cambyses was the eldest son of Cyrus and Cassandane his queen. Being, moreover, born in the purple, he was the undoubted heir to the vast empire created by his illustrious sire. Indeed, during his father's lifetime he had been associated with him as King of Babylon.[1] But Cyrus had expressly laid down that his second son Bardiya, termed Smerdis by the Greeks, should retain the rule of Khorasmia (Khiva), Bactria, Parthia, and Carmania (Kerman), the eastern provinces of the empire, which, cut off by the barren Lut, were even more remote from the centre of power than would appear from the many intervening degrees of longitude. This, in an Oriental monarchy, was an almost impossible arrangement in any case ; but the violent and jealous nature of Cambyses made it certain that, unless Bardiya rebelled, his life would, sooner or later, be sacrificed to his brother's fears and mistrust. These feelings were accentuated by the knowledge that Bardiya was popular and beloved, whereas Cambyses himself

---

[1] Several of the tablets of the Egibi family, the great Babylonian financiers, have been found showing Cambyses as " King of Babel." It may be added that the expression " son of Egibi " may denote merely an inhabitant of Bît-Egibi, and not a lineal descendant of the founder of a family of that name.

was known by the harsh name of the "Master." Of his severity the classical instance is the story given by Herodotus, that, having proved corruption in Brexaspes, one of the seven supreme judges, he sentenced him to be flayed; and, not content with this, had his judicial seat covered with his skin, and ordered the son of the unjust judge, who succeeded him, to sit in that seat when trying cases.[1]

The Death of Bardiya, 526 B.C.—In the last chapter we saw reason to believe that Cyrus had for years been working to organize the campaign against Egypt. Risings are known to have taken place which occupied the attention and energies of his successor, and it was not until the fourth year of his reign that everything was ready. But to leave his huge empire with his popular brother Bardiya ruling the eastern provinces seemed unwise, and we can imagine how his courtiers kept working upon his fears until the jealous monarch gave the order for his supposed rival to be secretly assassinated. Great as the crime seems to us, it was not so regarded at the time; and the annals of Persia and other Oriental states furnish frequent examples of the wholesale extirpation of all relatives upon the accession of a new monarch.

The Egyptian Campaign.—Amasis of Egypt, like his fellow-monarchs, had watched the rise of Persia with anxiety, which had deepened when he saw first Lydia and then Babylon succumb to the irresistible might of the new power after short campaigns. Throughout the period of grace he steadily organized his forces, and he strengthened his position by making an alliance with the Greek islanders who had maintained their independence, whose fleet would, he hoped, form a valuable counterpoise to the navies of the Phoenicians and subject Greeks. Owing, however, to internal troubles, this aid was not only withdrawn but given to the enemy, and Amasis, when war broke out, faced it without allies.

Cambyses, with a splendid army trained by Cyrus, marched to Gaza, the last city of any importance before the desert was entered. Fortune favoured him throughout the campaign; for, while he was considering how to cross the waterless belt, he was joined by the mercenary leader, Phanes of Halicarnassus, who had deserted Amasis and induced the desert chiefs to collect thousands of camels laden with skins of water, and thus create depots at the various stages. Finally,

---

[1] Herodotus v. 25.

to crown his good fortune, Amasis himself, the great soldier and administrator, who would have proved a formidable adversary, died, and was succeeded at this critical moment by his untried son Psammetichus III.

The Battle of Pelusium, 525 B.C.—In these circumstances, it is small wonder that the Egyptians and their Greek mercenaries were depressed. They fought desperately, but the Persian forces were superior in numbers and overwhelmed them. The panic-stricken Psammetichus, instead of defending the passages of the canals and thus gaining time to collect a second army, fled with no thought of anything but his own safety. Cambyses, after capturing Pelusium, from which the battle has taken its name, marched on Memphis, which held out for some time, but finally surrendered. Its fall completed the conquest of Egypt.

This campaign, which was fought in 525 B.C.,[1] brought about the overthrow of the third great power of the old world, which had, indeed, been weaker from the military point of view than the great powers of the Tigris and Euphrates valleys, but had generally played a leading rôle, thanks in part to its remoteness and inaccessibility. With Egypt added to his dominions, Cambyses became the ruler of an empire more colossal than any known before. It stretched from the Nile to the Jaxartes, from the Black Sea to the Persian Gulf, and included countries like Lydia on the one hand, and Bactria on the other, which had never been approached by an Assyrian army.

The Suicide of Cambyses, 521 B.C.—Cambyses had suffered as a child from epileptic fits, and four years after the conquest of Egypt the failure of expeditions to Nubia and to the Ammon oasis unhinged his mind. He quitted Egypt in 521 B.C., and was marching through Syria when he heard that a revolution had broken out, headed by a Magian. This man closely resembled the murdered Bardiya, whose assassination was not known to his mother and sisters, much less to the common people. Cambyses was on his way to meet the rebels when, hearing probably of some important defection, he killed himself in despair. With him perished the last male scion of the family of Cyrus. A legend exists to the effect that he wounded himself in the thigh when mounting his horse, but the manner of his death is clearly stated by

---

[1] Regarding this date, *vide The Passing of the Empires*, p. 661, note 4.

Darius in the Behistun inscription, and may be accepted with confidence.

Gaumata, the Pseudo-Smerdis of the Greeks.—The recognition of Gaumata the Magian as Bardiya appears to have been almost universal. Nor is this surprising, since, after the death of Cambyses, all claims would unite in Bardiya, whose murder was a state secret known to very few. As may be supposed, a diligent search was made by the emissaries of the impostor for every one who either knew Bardiya or had been connected with his murder ; and those who possessed such dangerous knowledge were secretly put to death. Moreover, in order to win popularity, the usurper proclaimed freedom from war-service and remission of taxes ;[1] and, to further the imposture, he withdrew as far as possible from public life and ordered the members of his harem to break off all relations not only with the outside world, but also with one another. It was not possible to execute these orders, as any one with a knowledge of the East will realize ; and their only result was to increase the suspicion, already entertained by the nobles, that this new monarch was no descendant of Cyrus, but a usurper.

As we have already seen, there was a second royal line of Achaemenian princes whose leading member was Darius, son of Hystaspes. With him were associated the heads of the other six great Persian tribes, whose right it was to have access to the king at all times, and who resolved to attempt the overthrow of the Magian by the exercise of this privilege.

The Slaying of Gaumata, 521 B.C.—In pursuance of their design, they presented themselves without their retinues at the castle gate of Sikayauvatish in Media, where the Magian then was, were admitted, and immediately slew Gaumata and his attendants. The conspirators, after striking this blow, rode post haste to Ecbatana, exhibited the head of the impostor, and organized a massacre of the Magi who had aided and abetted the late usurpation, which was perhaps an attempt by the priestly caste to regain ascendancy. But Darius was not vindictive, and the massacre ceased at nightfall.

There is a well-known story connected with the usurpation of the Magian. Gaumata had suffered the loss of his ears, and one of his wives was instructed by her father, a leading

---

[1] As to his action in extinguishing the pyres of the great families, *vide The Passing of the Empires,* p. 671.

nobleman of Persia, to test the imposture by ascertaining whether her husband's ears had been cut off. This, at infinite risk, she did, and so convinced the conspirators that they had in truth been deceived by a clever impersonation. Another equally famous story is that the seven conspirators agreed to choose as king him whose horse neighed first after sunrise. Darius, it is said, had an ingenious groom, who contrived that his master's horse should neigh, and thus won for him the lordship of Asia. It is more probable that Darius ascended the throne upon the death of the usurper as the heir of Cambyses, his father Hystaspes being probably passed over on account of age.

The Accession of Darius, 521 B.C.—The claims of Darius did not meet with unquestioned recognition. The usurper, by his remission of taxes and of war-service, had won the populace to his side. Again, the Governors of the distant provinces, thinking possibly that the empire of Persia would share the fate of Media, desired to carve out kingdoms for themselves. Darius, therefore, had to conquer, and in some cases to reconquer, the many kingdoms of which the Empire consisted; and there were times when only his army and a few of the provinces remained true to him.

The Eight Rebellions.—The provinces of Elam and Babylonia were the first to break into open revolt, almost as soon as the death of the usurper was known. In Elam, Atrina, the rebel leader, was descended from an old royal family; but he was not supported and, being taken prisoner, was sent to Darius, who slew him with his own hand. In Babylon, Nidintu-Bel claimed to be the son of Nabonidus, and assumed the illustrious name of Nebuchadnezzar. Darius took the field in person, but was at first unable to cross the Tigris in the face of a strong fleet supported by a powerful army. But after mounting his troops, and deceiving the enemy by numerous feints as to his intentions, he succeeded in throwing his army across the Tigris into the defended area. There he twice defeated the Babylonians; but Nidintu-Bel escaped into the city of Babylon, and a regular siege became necessary. Meanwhile Media, taking advantage of the embarrassments of the new monarch, tried to recover her old position under the leadership of a certain Phraortes, who claimed to be a descendant of Cyaxares; and a second pretender, Martiya, arose in Elam.

Darius, without raising the siege of Babylon, despatched columns both to Media and to Armenia. In the latter country a great victory was ultimately gained; but this was more than counterbalanced by rebellions in Sagartia, in Hyrcania, the province governed by his father, Hystaspes, and in Margiana. As if this were not enough, even Persia revolted and followed a second impostor, Vahyazdáta by name, claiming to be Bardiya. But the genius and courage of Darius were proof against all reverses and by sheer force of personality he triumphed. He had recognized that Babylon was the most important centre, and when at last, through the devotion of Zopyrus[1] and after a siege of nearly two years, the great city fell in 519 B.C., Darius was free to attack his opponents in detail. Leading the splendid regiments of war-hardened veterans in person, he speedily crushed the Medians, Phraortes being captured at Rei. As a grim warning to rebels, his nose, ears, and tongue were cut off, his eyes were gouged out, and in this horrible condition he was chained at the royal gate for a time and then impaled. Victories in Armenia and over the Persian pretender followed. The appearance of a second Babylonian pretender threatened to nullify the capture of the city, but the garrison was strong enough to quell this revolt. With the capture of the second Pseudo-Smerdis, in 518 B.C., these rebellions, which had served to exhibit Darius as a master of men, came to an end, and peace at length reigned over the vast empire.

Darius the Administrator.—The victor proceeded to punish those governors whose behaviour had displeased him and to reward those who had helped him. During the crisis, Oroites, Satrap of Lydia, who was suspected of aiming at an independent monarchy, had been put to death by his Persian guard, acting on secret orders from Darius; and this step had probably prevented a rebellion in that province. The Great King visited Egypt in person, and, having executed its Governor summarily, set to work to win over the priests to his side by benefactions of every description.

Having thus pacified the outlying provinces, he began to organize his immense empire under a uniform system of administration. The old method, which the Assyrian monarch Tiglath-pileser III. had introduced, and which had ever since remained in operation, rested partly on the transportation

---

[1] *Vide* Herodotus iii. 151 for this story.

of thousands of families to districts far from their homes, and the bringing in of others to take their place. The newcomers were looked on as alien intruders and naturally supported the Assyrian Governor. Each country, when conquered, was either added to a neighbouring province or made into a separate province and assessed in a primitive fashion for tribute. Babylon, however, was never absorbed. The system, indeed, was very imperfect, owing to the almost complete independence of the Governors, and was possible only so long as the empire was of moderate dimensions. Constant rebellions and revolts proved that the control of Assyria was extremely difficult to enforce.

The Satrapies.—Under Darius, the principle *divide et impera* was adopted and strictly applied ; any tendency towards unification was avoided. To prevent the concentration of power in one man's hands, a Satrap,[1] a General, and a Secretary of State were appointed in each province, these officials being independent of each other and reporting to headquarters direct. Under this system of divided powers, the three great officials would be hostile to one another and consequently most unlikely to organize a rebellion. As a further precaution, inspectors of the highest rank were sent out at irregular intervals, supported by strong bodies of troops and armed with full powers to investigate and punish any abuses and to report on the Satrap and other officials. It may be objected that the weakening of the hands of the Governor might paralyse him in case of a sudden emergency when rapid action was vital ; but in practice the system worked well so long as the officials were virile, and Darius was justified in the belief that the greatest danger was that of a rebellion organized by the ruler in a distant province.

The satrapies varied from twenty to twenty-eight at different periods of the reign. Persia, the cradle of the race, was not generally regarded as a satrapy, and its inhabitants paid no taxes, but were bound to make a gift to the sovereign when he passed through the country. The provinces may thus be divided into the eastern, on the Iranian plateau, and those to the west of Persia.

Of the Persian satrapies, the chief was Media, and then followed Hyrcania, Parthia, Zaranka or Zarangia, Aria, Khorasmia, Bactria, Soghdiana, Gandara, the land of the

---

[1] Satrap is the contracted form of a Persian word signifying " Lord of the Country."

From a photograph by King and Thompson.

DARIUS AND THE REBEL LEADERS IN THE BAS-RELIEF AT BISUTUN.

The King supported by a Persian grandee, who is possibly Gobryas, triumphs over his enemies. Above hovers the representation of Ahura Mazda, to whom Darius raises his right hand in adoration.

Sakae, Sattagydia, Arachosia, and the land of Maka (whence probably came the modern word Makran). To the west lay Uvaja or Elam (Susiana) ; then Babylonia and Chaldaea ; Athura (ancient Assyria) ; Arabia (including most of Syria and Palestine) ; Egypt (including the Phoenicians, Cypriots, and the Greek islanders) ; Yauna or Ionia (including Lycia, Caria, and the Greek colonies of the coast) ; Sparda (Lydia and the lands west of the Halys) ; Armenia, and Cappadocia.[1]

These satrapies were assessed partly in money and partly in kind, and it is interesting to note that this system still obtains in Persia. The lowest revenue was that paid by the land known in modern times as Baluchistan, then, as now, poor and sterile, which was assessed at 170 talents of silver. Babylon, on the other hand, was assessed at 1000 talents, and Egypt at 700 talents of gold, and the total revenue in money was £3,708,280.

Darius was the first Persian monarch to coin money, and the " daric," a gold coin weighing 130 grains, was famous for its purity and soon became the only gold currency of the ancient world. Silver coins were also stamped. It is of interest to note that the English pound and shilling are almost the exact equivalents of the daric and siglos [2] respectively. The taxes in kind were also heavy, Babylon feeding one-third of the army and of the court, and Egypt providing corn for the army of 120,000 men. The Medes furnished horses, mules, and sheep ; the Armenians foals ; the Babylonians eunuchs, and so forth. In addition, the provinces were called upon, after defraying these royal taxes, to support the Satrap, his court, and army ; and as there was no fixed salary for the officials, who, moreover, probably bought their posts, the burden laid on the provinces was great, if not intolerable. On the other hand, there were the checks already mentioned,

[1] For further details of these satrapies *vide* How and Wells, *op. cit.* i. p. 405.
[2] *Vide* " Notes on the Imperial Persian Coinage," by G. F. Hill (*Journal of Hellenic Studies*, vol. xxxix., 1919). " Daric," the term by which the Greeks knew the coins, is derived from Δαρεικοὶ στατῆρες. There is a word *dariku* used in contracts of the reign of Nabonidus, but its meaning is obscure. *Siglos* is the same word as the Hebrew *shekel*. The royal *weight* system of the Babylonians and Persians was 1 talent = 60 minae = 3600 shekels. But for weighing precious metals they used a mina of only 50 instead of 60 shekels ; thus the system for gold and silver was 1 talent = 60 minae = 3000 shekels. The daric was a gold shekel ; a talent of gold weighed 390,000 grains, and, being about 960/1000 fine, must have been equivalent to about 3313 British sovereigns of 22 carat gold. The silver coin (siglos) weighed about 86½ grains, *i.e.* *half* a shekel of the special Babylonian silver system (which was not the same as that used for gold), and was worth $\frac{1}{20}$ of the daric ; a Persic talent of silver (6000 siglos) was worth 300 darics or about 331 British sovereigns. It should be remembered that estimate of this kind, however correct mathematically, are economically misleading, because of the different values of commodities in relation to money at different periods.

which, so long as a capable monarch reigned, made the Satrap careful not to exceed the customary limits, and forced him to be zealous in maintaining order and improving communications. It must also be remembered that the lower classes in every country were accustomed to be taxed to their utmost capacity by their native rulers. Moreover, the arrangement gave the monarch a regular budget, and thus lessened excessive demands on any one province ; and, finally, the new system was much better than that which it superseded. As Maspero points out, it was mainly defective from the point of view of military organization. Darius maintained a bodyguard consisting of 2000 cavalry and 2000 infantry, whose lances bore gold or silver apples ; and under them ranked the ten thousand " Immortals," divided into ten battalions, the first of which had its lances decorated with golden pomegranates. This guard was the nucleus of an imperial army, supported by Persian and Median levies and by garrisons placed at various important centres, constituting imperial, as distinct from local, troops. When a great war broke out, untrained levies, differing from one another in language, in manner of fighting, and in equipment, poured in by thousands ; and it was this undisciplined force which was ultimately a main cause of the overthrow of the Persian Empire.

The Royal Road.—Darius, like most great rulers, realized the importance of good communications, and we read of the Royal Road constructed between Sardes and Susa, by means of which officials were kept in touch with the Court. The distance was about 1500 miles, which constituted a three months' journey for a man on foot, but, in view of the rapid movement of mounted couriers in the East and the extraordinary swiftness of the service, despatches were probably carried in fifteen days. The route, for it was not a made road, except perhaps in marshy or mountain sections, ran through the heart of Phrygia, making a detour across the Halys to Pteria, the ancient Hittite capital, and thence southwards across the Taurus, reaching the Euphrates at Samosata. The Tigris was struck at Nineveh, and the road, after following the course of the river for some distance, crossed the country of the Kissians to Susa.

The influence of the Royal Road in widening the horizon of the provinces through which it ran must have been considerable, and its importance in the eyes of the Greeks is shown by the prominence given to it in the earliest maps of the Ionian geographers.

The Expansion of the Empire.—Darius, even had he been content with his immense possessions, would have known that his name would not be famous unless it could be recorded of him that he had extended the Persian Empire ; he was also obliged to keep his forces employed, as was ever the case in the ancient monarchies. To the north its limits were fixed by definite geographical boundaries difficult to overstep, such as the magnificent Caucasus range, which still defies the Russian railway engineer, the Caspian Sea, and the steppes of Central Asia. To the south lay the deserts of Africa and Arabia and the Indian Ocean. Consequently the directions in which expansion was practicable were limited.

The Object of the Scythian Campaign.—The object of Darius in undertaking the campaign against the Scythians has been interpreted in various ways by different writers. Grote,[1] for example, terms it " that insane expedition," whereas Rawlinson held that it was a well-thought-out scheme to protect the line of communications in the advance on Greece —the great object which, in his opinion, Darius kept before his mind throughout. Maspero entertains somewhat similar views, but thinks that Darius was ill-informed as to the distance of the country of the Scythians from his intended line of march. Holm refers very briefly to the campaign and considers that it strengthened the supremacy of Persia in Western Asia.[2] Finally, Nöldeke sees in it merely the desire to conquer an unknown country.

Grote's view may, I think, be dismissed as entirely out of keeping both with the character of Darius and with the manner in which the campaign was conducted. Let us turn next to the views of Rawlinson. The terrible raids of the Scythians in Media and in Asia Minor a century before must have given them a prestige far above their actual military strength at this period. But for Darius to have " embarked on a campaign against these elusive-nomads simply from fear that they would cut his communications when he was marching on Hellas," would show that he was very badly informed, both as to their effective power and as to their distance from

---

[1] *History of Greece*, vol. iii. p. 188. [2] *Ibid.* vol. i. p. 417.

his line of march. Moreover, we learn that, although Darius traversed Southern Russia for two months, it was not until he heard that the Greek cities of Thrace had revolted that he detached against them a force of 80,000 men, which incidentally conquered Thrace and received the submission of Macedonia. Finally, after the Scythian campaign, Darius returned to Sardes, remained there about a year, and then left Asia Minor for his capital.

With these facts before us, it is difficult to believe that the Scythian campaign was intended to be a preliminary to the conquest of Hellas. Had it been so, what was there to prevent the Great King from either marching on Greece in person or doubling his army in Thrace for an invasion of Greece? In any case, why did he remain a year at Sardes inactive, although his troops had paved the way most successfully for an advance on Hellas by annexing Thrace and Macedonia? It is difficult to avoid the impression, in studying the views set forth above, that, just as there has been a lack of proportion in dealing with the history of the children of Israel, so, in dealing with the history of Greece, the rôle of Hellas has, through intense and repeated study, been exaggerated.

Looking at the question from the point of view of Darius, who would hardly have organized a campaign on such a big scale in order to meet a very problematical danger to a line of communications, I am inclined to think that the Great King did not make Greece his objective, but rather wished to annex Thrace up to the Danube and to raid the Scythians, who had devastated the Near East about a century previously, and loomed large in the Persian Empire ; a further incentive was that gold was reported to be plentiful in the country. He may also have had reasons, of which we are ignorant, to fear a fresh irruption into his provinces, and may have hoped that his action would remove all danger of any serious movement. Finally, we know that " the Scythians beyond the Sea " are enumerated in the Nakhsh-i-Rustam inscription, and we can understand that to attack such distant foemen in their own home would add lustre to the name of the Great King.

The Course of the Campaign, circa 512 B.C.—Darius throughout this campaign showed his usual military capacity. Before setting his great army in motion, he ordered the Satrap of

Cappadocia to make a raid on the northern coast of the Black Sea, mainly with a view to capturing some prisoners. This preliminary operation was carried out with complete success, and among the captives was the brother of a local chief, whose information must have been of considerable value.

The great expedition started about 512 B.C., crossing the Bosphorus, in the neighbourhood of modern Constantinople, on a bridge of boats built by the Greek cities of Asia Minor and guarded by the Greek cities of the neighbourhood. Thence, keeping near the coast of the Black Sea and receiving the submission of the Thracians, of whom only one tribe attempted resistance, the huge force, accompanied by the fleet, marched to the delta of the Danube. At the head of the delta, a second bridge of boats was constructed by the tyrants of the Ionian cities, to whose care it was entrusted; and Darius, after crossing it, launched into the unknown steppe. Had the campaign been made in connexion with a future expedition to be undertaken against Greece, it would seem extraordinary that the distance already traversed and the magnitude of the Danube should not have proved to the Great King that the Scythians were extremely unlikely to raid down to the Hellespont in force. In the march beyond the Danube there was apparently no adequate objective, although many flocks and herds must have been captured. The Scythians, whose mobility, like that of all nomads, was great, kept away from his line of march as far as possible. Had serious operations eastward been intended, the fleet would obviously not have been left in the Danube.

Herodotus,[1] whose delightful pages deal somewhat fully with this campaign, states that Darius sent an emissary to the Scythian king with the following message: " Thou strange man, why dost thou keep on flying before me, when there are two things thou mightest do so easily? If thou deemest thyself able to resist my arms, cease thy wanderings and come, let us engage in a battle. Or if thou art conscious that my strength is greater than thine, even so shouldest thou cease to run away: thou hast but to bring thy lord earth and water, and to come at once to a conference." To this message the Scythian king replied: " This is my way, Persian, I never fear men or flee from them. . . . Earth and water I do not send; but thou shalt soon receive more suitable

[1] iv. 126.

gifts." These were sent by a herald, and proved to be a bird, a mouse, a frog, and five arrows. The herald, questioned as to their signification, replied that the Persians, if wise, would find out themselves. At a council, Darius expressed the opinion that the Scythians intended to surrender, and that the mouse and frog symbolized earth and water respectively. His father-in-law, Gobryas, however, explained that the real meaning was as follows : " Unless, Persians, ye can turn into birds and fly into the sky, or become mice and burrow underground, or make yourselves frogs and take refuge in the fens, ye will never make your escape from this land, but die pierced by our arrows." The fact appears to be that the expedition became a military promenade,[1] as the Persians were unable to secure a decisive engagement. After a march of some two months, during the course of which its losses might have been considerable from desultory attacks, lack of supplies, and sickness, the army returned to the Danube, where the Scythians had tried to induce the Greeks to destroy the bridge. The "tyrants" debated on this question, but came to the sapient conclusion that their own position depended on the support of the Great King, and they consequently remained loyal to their trust.

The Annexation of Thrace and the Submission of Macedonia.—Darius recrossed the Danube in safety, albeit with somewhat diminished prestige. On the way back to Sardes he detached a force of 80,000 men for service in Europe. These troops not only reduced the Greek cities of Thrace which had revolted, but also received the submission of Macedonia, and thereby with little effort brought the boundaries of the Persian Empire into contact with northern Greece. The conquest of Thrace was the main result of the campaign.

The Indian Campaign, 512 B.C.—In 512 B.C. the conquering Persians, like their predecessors the Aryans of India, looked down from the eastern edge of the Iranian plateau on to the vast plain of the Panjab and annexed large districts of it and of Sind. Scylax, the Greek admiral, descended the Indus and, undismayed by the tides, launched out on the Indian Ocean and explored the coasts of Arabia

---

[1] Since this account was written I have consulted *Scythians and Greeks* by E. H. Minns. The author writes (p. 116) : " Darius can hardly have done more than make a demonstration against the northern barbarians, with a view to securing his frontier on the Danube." Minns also gives instances of messages exchanged between Scythians which closely resemble that quoted above from Herodotus.

and Makran. A satrapy was carved out of these conquests, and immense quantities of gold poured into Persia. So important was this invasion to India that it has been stated that the chronology of that country commences with the preaching of Buddha and this event. It must be confessed that little is known about this campaign, and at one time the authenticity of the great voyage of Scylax was doubted.[1] To-day we realize how well organized were these grand old monarchies, and can thus believe that the main facts of the narrative were correct, even if to some extent the glory of the expedition of Alexander be diminished by the fact that Scylax had navigated the Indus and the Indian Ocean some two centuries before his illustrious fellow-countryman.

Summary.—We have now followed the fortunes of the Persian Empire from the annexation of Egypt, the last great power to be conquered, and through the period of desperate revolt brought about by the madness of Cambyses and the remarkably successful imposture of the Magian Gaumata. Next we have seen Darius refounding the Persian Empire on more solid foundations than it had ever before possessed, by welding the loose collection of provinces into a system which, if not in all respects a good one, was yet a great improvement on the organization it superseded; and we realize that, but for this monarch, who undoubtedly merits the title " Great," the huge empire would, like that of Media, have swiftly dissolved. Finally, the Panjab with Sind, to the east, and Thrace with Macedonia, to the west, were annexed apparently without any special difficulty. We thus see an empire which included the whole of the known world and a good deal of territory till then unknown, which stretched from the burning sands of Africa to the ice-bound borders of China, vast but obedient; and we may well say that here we reach the zenith of Persia, and indeed of all the great empires that the world had as yet seen. Nevertheless, in Hellas were to be found a few thousand warriors, who, preposterous as it might appear, were destined to repel the collective might of this immense power, and in time to requite tenfold the invasion of their territories.

---

[1] Herodotus iv. 44. Scylax published an account of the expedition, which was still extant in the lifetime of Alexander.

ACHAEMENIAN KING IN CONFLICT WITH TWO LIONS.
(Cylinder seal in British Museum.)

CHAPTER XV

THE ANCIENT PERSIANS—THEIR CUSTOMS, LANGUAGE, AND ARCHITECTURE

The barbarians many times seized hold of the Greek spears and brake them ; for in boldness and warlike spirit the Persians were not a whit inferior to the Greeks.—HERODOTUS ix. 62.

> Those black granite pillars, once high-reared
> By Jamshid in Persepolis to bear
> His house, now, 'mid their broken flights of steps,
> Lie prone, enormous, down the mountain-side.
> MATTHEW ARNOLD.

The Virility of the Persians.—During the course of my journeys in Persia I have frequently observed encampments of a dozen or more black tents woven from goats' hair and set down in a wide valley. Their occupants, whose livelihood depends on their flocks, are forced, and have been forced for untold generations, to move from district to district in search of pasturage, which is ever meagre in these lands of scanty rainfall. In the winter the flocks sometimes suffer terribly even when the camp is pitched in a well-protected spot ; but when spring has come, the *Iliat* or Tribesmen, as they are generally termed to-day—albeit the word is a Turkish one—make for the mountains. There they graze the higher parts in the summer, descending again as the autumn sets in to their winter grounds, where they probably sow their crops. These nomads are extremely ignorant. To go upstairs in a house would frighten them ; but on their own mountain-side they are a fine virile race, ready as occasion may serve to raid, to fight, or to shoot the ibex or wild sheep, and rendered by their environment and circumstances absolutely hardy and tireless.

It is reasonable to suppose that the Medes and Persians to a great extent led a similar life ; and, inasmuch as the climatic and social conditions have not materially changed, we cannot go far wrong if we assume that they were just such a free, warlike, manly race as are the nomads to-day, some of whom at any rate are their descendants. This view of their character was held by the Greeks themselves ; and, if the Greeks won deathless fame in their defence of Hellas, surely some share of it was earned by the gallant Persians, who, in spite of inferior weapons and armour, attempted at Plataea to break the spear-shafts of the Greeks and so force a way in, regardless of their lives.

Customs.—Virility, expressed in valour and energy, is the best stock on which to graft other virtues, and the ancient Persians were taught more especially " to ride, to draw the bow, and to speak the truth." They were also careful to avoid incurring debt and were hospitable and generous. To give an example of the latter virtue, Herodotus tells us of a Greek who had fought until covered with wounds to prevent the capture of his ship. The Persians, admiring his valour and seeing that his wounds were not mortal, dressed them and treated him as a hero. To continue, they regarded buying and selling in the market-place as ignoble ; and even to-day no Persian of position will condescend to enter a shop.

Against these good qualities must be set off a lack of self-control, whether in prosperity or adversity, intense vanity, and a love of luxury, which, however, is common to all prosperous nations alike. As a race they were, and are, remarkable for keenness of perception, for smart repartee and for humour, sometimes of a very subtle kind. Persians have apparently ever been lavish in their expenditure, particularly upon their food ; and we read in Herodotus that they ate " few solid dishes, but many served up after as dessert, and these not in a single course." The magnificence of their banquets will be referred to in connexion with the life of their monarchs.

Like the Greeks and the Scythians, Persians were devoted to the wine-cup, and Herodotus states that they deliberated on an important question when intoxicated in the evening, and then in the morning, if they saw no reason to change their views, they decided the matter. To be the father of many sons was, and still is, deemed a proof of good fortune, and in this their attitude is surely more sane than that of the modern European who shirks the duties of a family. A well-known example of philoprogenitiveness was Fath Ali Shah, who had three thousand descendants when he died, a fact which gave him extraordinary prestige among his subjects.

Laws.—" The law of the Medes and Persians which altereth not " was, as may be supposed, extremely severe ; but certainly not more so than that of the earlier empires. The King could do as he willed, except that he could not change an order once given, and the life and property of his subjects were at his mercy ; at the same time, abuse of rights was tempered by fear of assassination. The criminal code, which, rightly enough, made death the penalty for murder, rape, treason, and such serious crimes, seems to have visited minor offences with equal severity. But in a wild country, with a wild people to deal with and no organized prisons, it is impossible to condemn death sentences or mutilation in the case of brigands, thieves, and other bad characters. To do so would be to ignore the severity of our own code, by which sheep-stealing was a capital offence even after the accession of Queen Victoria. Punishments such as throwing into the ashes,[1] burying alive, flaying, and crucifying are horrible enough to modern ideas, but equally horrible were punishments in mediaeval Europe.

The Position of Women.—As to the position of women, polygamy was encouraged, and then as now the upper classes kept their wives secluded, litters with closely-drawn curtains being always employed on journeys. Neither in the inscriptions nor in the sculptures does a woman appear. On the other hand, it is unlikely that the nomad women were ever veiled, and their position was probably much better than that of their jealously-guarded sisters, who were not even allowed to receive their fathers or brothers.[2] As this has apparently been the general rule in the East, the Persians were no worse off than their neighbours ; but their decay as a great empire can be traced in no small degree to the intrigues of eunuchs and women in the *anderun*, as the harem

---

[1] This punishment consisted in throwing the criminal into a pit filled with ashes, in which he was slowly suffocated.

[2] As a result the nomad women are incomparably more capable and thus bear more capable and efficient children.

is termed in Persia, where to do any work was looked upon as degrading. Their ideals in this respect were noticeably lower than those of Greece, where the women, albeit secluded, spent their days in spinning and other domestic tasks; and until Eastern women come out into the world and learn to distinguish between good and evil, it is hopeless to expect their children to compete on equal terms with the offspring of a father and a mother who are both well-educated. This question is fundamental.

The King and his Court.—In no country has the national life centred more intensely round the King than in Persia; and consequently a description of the position and life of the monarch will show better than anything else the conditions prevailing in Iran after the empire had been established. There is no doubt that, just as the Medes copied their ceremonies and their etiquette from Assyria, which had itself copied from the older empires, so we may rightly regard Persia as the inheritor of all the previous ages. Even to-day the Shah follows the etiquette and bears the high-sounding titles which have descended from the remote past; they are given as a heading to Chapter LXXXI.

The sovereign was the absolute master, the sole fountain of law and honour, blessed himself with infallibility, the one man on whose character and capacity the weal or woe of the entire country depended. At the same time there were some limitations to his power. He was expected to observe the customs of the country and was bound to consult his great nobles. He was equally bound by his own decisions.

The royal robe of purple worn by the Great King was the dignified flowing garment of the Medes, and on his head was set the high kydaris or tiara of bright colour, which the monarch alone might wear and which is figured in the sculptures of Persepolis. He wore ear-rings, bracelets, chains, and a girdle all of gold, and appears in the sculptures seated on an elaborately-wrought throne, wearing a long beard and curled hair. In his hand he holds a pointed sceptre having a golden apple at the butt. Behind stands an attendant with the necessary fly-flapper. At the head of the court stood the commander of the bodyguard, whose position was naturally one of the greatest importance. The great officers included the chief steward, the master of the house, and the chief eunuch. The King's " eyes " and " ears," or secret police, chamberlains, cup-bearers, huntsmen, messengers, musicians, and cooks completed the list of the more important members of the Court. Ctesias mentions that fifteen thousand people were fed daily by the king, and that sheep, goats, camels, oxen, horses,[1] and asses were all used as food. Ostriches and geese were also eaten, and small game of every kind. The monarch was generally served alone, but occasionally the Queen and his favourite children were admitted to the meal; and this custom still prevails in Persia. Reclining on a golden couch, the King drank deeply; in the case of great banquets he presided at the table. Gold and silver plate abounded and was displayed with ostentation, as in modern England, where, however, there is little of pure gold.

War and the chase were the pursuits of the monarchs, and so long as these were strenuously followed manhood was fully maintained. In battle the King occupied the centre of the line and was expected to display courage; in hunting, even with the aid of dogs, to face a lion or a boar with bow and arrow must have required twice the nerve demanded from the big-game shot of to-day. Moreover, in adoption of the Assyrian custom, game was preserved in " paradises " or huge walled parks;[2] and naturally sport of this kind was tame compared with the tracking of a lion to its lair. Wild asses, ever a favourite quarry, were apparently pursued by relays of horsemen and gradually run down.[3]

Within the palace, the monarch amused himself with dice; but, as may be supposed, the kings who left everything to their ministers suffered from boredom, just as much as the modern pleasure-seeker; and we read of cases in which carving or even planing wood was a royal distraction. Except for the listening to " the Book of the Chronicles of the Kings of Persia and Media " recorded in the book of Esther, no literature is mentioned, and, unlike the Assyrian kings and their subjects who could read and write, the Persian monarchs were generally illiterate. Since, however, we know that even Alfred the Great " could not write and perhaps could not read,"[4] this ignorance is not extraordinary. Even to-day in Persia I have known men holding high positions who could

---

[1] Horses are not eaten to-day in Persia, but camels occasionally are. I have eaten an excellent camel steak.
[2] The word in Old Persian is *Pairi-daexha*, from the Arabicized form of which the title of Firdausi, the Poet, was derived.
[3] Xenophon, *Anabasis*, i. 5. 2.
[4] *The British Empire*, by Professor A. F. Pollard, p. 23.

neither read nor write, and, as their letters were not signed but sealed, their ignorance was by no means easily discovered.

Below the King were the heads of the great families, known as the "Seven Princes," whose right it was to demand admission to the monarch's presence at any time, unless he were in the women's apartments. They generally filled the great offices and formed a permanent council. Below them, again, were the younger scions and adherents of the great families. The trading community was held in great contempt; and consequently there was no intermediate class between the nobility and the commonalty. A subject admitted to an audience prostrated himself on entering the presence and his hands remained hidden throughout. This custom still survives.[1]

The equipment of the Persians, which may be studied on the bas-reliefs, is given by Herodotus: "About their heads they had soft felt caps called *tiaras*, and about their body tunics of various colours with sleeves, presenting the appearance of iron scales like those of a fish, and about the legs trousers; and instead of the ordinary shields they had shields of wicker-work, under which hung quivers; and they had short spears and large bows and arrows of reed, and, moreover, daggers hanging by the right thigh from the girdle."

The Queen was supreme in the women's quarter She had the right to wear the royal tiara and lorded it over the other wives. She possessed large revenues of her own and a personal staff of officials and servants. When a woman of character filled the position her influence was necessarily great, and to this history bears full evidence. The inferior wives, it would seem, had relatively little influence, and the hundreds of concubines, unless they attracted the monarch's special notice, shared the royal couch for only one night. The position of the Queen herself was liable to be overshadowed by that of the Queen-Mother, who took precedence; and the acts of Amestris show how great was her power. Eunuchs swarmed in these huge establishments, and when the dynasty became luxurious and effete, their pernicious influence, which still persists, corrupted the young princes who were in their charge. The cost of a court such as I have described

---

[1] When I first came to Persia I was surprised to see servants all standing with their arms crossed, until I learned that they were hiding their hands out of respect.

must have been a serious drain on the empire, as it has been ever since. Even the late Nasir-u-Din, who ranks among the most enlightened monarchs of Persia, married some fifty wives, all of whom had to be provided for on a more or less costly scale.

Such were the chief customs of the Persians. The good in them far outweighed the bad, and when their religion with its lofty and sane ideals is taken into consideration, it is little wonder that these enlightened Aryans founded an empire and held in subjection the lower Semitic and Turanian races whose civilization they had absorbed.

The Language of the Ancient Persians.—We have travelled far from the days of Hyde, whose work, published in 1700, summed up the entire knowledge of the subject at that period. In his *History of the Religion of the Ancient Persians, Parthians, and Medes,* he declared the Old Persian inscriptions to be hardly worthy of attention, and laid down with equal emphasis that they were not written in the language of ancient Iran. Thanks to the labours of Grotefend, of Lassen, and above all of Sir Henry Rawlinson, the language of Cyrus has been deciphered, and it is of special interest to learn that many of the words, such as those for horse, camel, etc., used by these old-time heroes still survive in modern Persian ; in fact, the language was Old Persian. The theory of Oppert, that the writing was derived from the Assyrian ideograms, which is given in his *Le Peuple et la langue des Mèdes,* seems quite in keeping with the immense influence of Assyria on Media and Persia already referred to in Chapter X. This can be traced also in their social organization, their laws, and their architecture.

The Trilingual Inscriptions at Behistun.—By way of illustrating the language of the Achaemenians I propose to describe briefly the great rock inscriptions of Behistun or Bisitun. The former name occurs in the pages of Yakut, and was adopted by Rawlinson ; the latter name is that used by the Persians of to-day.[1]

Upon leaving Kermanshah the traveller bound for Hamadan sees a range broken up into a series of isolated peaks, as is so common in Persia, and at the foot of the last

---

[1] I am indebted to *The Inscription of Darius the Great at Behistun,* by L. W. King and R. C. Thompson, who sat in rough cradles and swayed against the face of the rock while copying the inscriptions.

peak, which rises precipitously to a height of some 4000 feet, are a number of springs which have made this a favourite camping-ground for caravans, probably from times before the dawn of history. This was the site chosen by Darius for the commemoration of his great exploits, and indeed he chose well.

The earliest mention of the famous records is by Diodorus Siculus, who, writing in the first century of our era, states that the sculptures were the work of Semiramis, and identifies the bearded figure of Darius as that of the great mythical queen. Even European travellers of the early nineteenth century have not been more illuminating, and the figures have been described by Gardanne [1] as those of the twelve apostles, and by Sir Robert Ker Porter [2] as celebrating the conquest of Israel. The credit both of copying these inscriptions and of translating them correctly is due to Rawlinson, and it was not until he had copied the long trilingual record that any progress was made in deciphering the cuneiform script, although Lassen and others had succeeded in identifying correctly the values of many of the Persian characters.

The difficulties surmounted by Rawlinson in copying the inscriptions on the almost perpendicular rock make thrilling reading, and it is satisfactory to know from King and Thompson, whose work on the subject is the most recent and fullest, that his translation holds good to-day. The sculptures, which owe their present good condition mainly to their inaccessibility, represent Darius, attended by two of his great officers, one of whom is believed to be his father-in-law, Gobryas, triumphing over his enemies. The Great King stands with his left foot firmly planted on Gaumata the Magian, represented as lying on his back with his arms raised in an attitude of entreaty. In front stand nine rebel leaders, roped together with their hands bound, all of whom are named by epigraphs.[3] Above hovers the god

[1] *Journal d'un voyage*, Paris, 1809, p. 83.
[2] *Personal Narrative of a Journey from India to England*, 2nd edition, vol. ii. pp. 80 ff., London, 1827.
[3] Taken from left to right, as shown in the illustration, are:—
    I. Atrina, the first Susian pretender.
    II. Nidintu-Bel, the first Babylonian pretender.
    III. Phraortes, the Median pretender.
    IV. Martiya, the second Susian pretender.
    V. Citrantakhma, the Sagartian pretender.
    VI. Vahyazdata, the second Pseudo-Smerdis.
    VII. Arakha, the second Babylonian pretender.
    VIII. Frada, the Margian pretender.
    and IX. Skunka, the Scythian leader, whose figure was added at a later period.

Ahura Mazda, and to him the right hand of Darius is raised in adoration. The famous trilingual inscriptions, in Persian, Susian or New Elamite, and Babylonian, give the titles of Darius and the extent of his empire. They next refer to the murder of Bardiya or Smerdis by Cambyses and the revolt of the Pseudo-Smerdis, Gaumata the Magian, during the absence of Cambyses in Egypt. The death of the pretender at the hands of Darius is described in some detail. Then the revolts against Darius are enumerated at length, and the inscriptions end with an adjuration to future rulers to beware of liars and to the reader to preserve the sculptures. The curse on whoever destroys the memorial of the Great King runs : " Saith Darius the king : If thou shalt behold this tablet or these sculptures, and shalt destroy them and shalt not preserve them so long as thy line endureth, then may Ahura Mazda slay thee, and may thy race come to nought, and whatsoever thou doest may Ahura Mazda destroy ! " It is impossible to over-estimate these trilingual inscriptions, not only for their extraordinary historical value, but perhaps even more for the light they shed on the Babylonian and Assyrian cuneiform inscriptions, the decipherment of which became possible through the elucidation of these Persian records.

The Ruins of Pasargadae. — I now turn to the architectural glories of the Achaemenians.[1] Pasargadae was admittedly the ancient capital of Parsa, better known under the Greek form of Persis, when it was a small state, and can thus claim precedence in the brief account I propose to give of the ruins of old-world Persia. In dealing with them I shall imagine that, as happened in my own case upon the occasion of my first visit, the traveller is coming from the north. The site of Pasargadae differs from that of the later and more splendid capital. For the original city a site secluded in a small valley[2] was chosen, whereas splendid Persepolis looks across a wide plain. In other words, Pasargadae was the chief city of a small, weak state, and Persepolis the capital of a mighty empire.

---

[1] I have especially consulted Lord Curzon's great work for this section. I have also referred to Perrot and Chipiez, *Histoire de l'Art*, vol. v., and O. M. Dalton's *Treasure of the Oxus*. Mr. Dalton has kindly helped me to select illustrations from his work.

[2] In 1917, when opening up a route for wheeled traffic to the east of the Polvar valley, the ruins of a large dam, locally termed Kala Jask, were discovered near the Tang-i-Kamin. The stored-up water was led to the old Achaemenian capital by a canal some thirty feet wide, termed *Jub-i-Dukhtar*, this work explaining how the lands around Pasargadae were able to support a relatively large population.

The first ruin to be visited consists of a platform built out from the summit of a low, rounded hill, and is known locally as Takht-i-Sulayman, or "the Throne of Solomon," that potentate occupying quite as high a position in the minds of Persians as in those of his own countrymen. The terrace is a parallelogram about 300 feet in total length. It is built of huge blocks of white stone, originally fastened together by metal clamps, all of which apparently have been scooped out; and, from the absence of any staircase and of any ruins of buildings, it appears not to have been finished. Passing on, we come to a limestone monolith, on which, sculptured in low relief, is the famous winged figure of Cyrus the Great, or of his *fravashi* or genius. The inscription, "I (am) Cyrus, the King, the Achaemenian," was copied by earlier travellers, but has been broken off, and indeed the whole figure is now becoming very indistinct. The bas-relief of the hero, which is rather more than life-size, is in profile, and the treatment is Assyrian in conception so far as the wings and the fringed robe are concerned; but the triple crown is Egyptian. The face, however, is distinctly Aryan in type, and we may therefore believe it to have been a portrait of the first great Aryan whose features have been preserved to us down the ages.

We come finally to the most famous monument of all, the sepulchre of Cyrus the Great, which I have elsewhere described as follows: "The tomb, which has been the cause of so much discussion, and was certainly designed by a Greek architect, was originally surrounded by a colonnade, of which Dieulafoy gives a restored plan; indeed the bases of many of the columns are still visible. Known for centuries as Mashhad-i-Madar-i-Sulayman, or 'The Tomb of the Mother of Solomon,' the mausoleum stands on seven courses of white limestone, composed of enormous blocks, the lower steps being hard to climb, but the upper ones being shallower. The walls and roof are built of great blocks, beautifully fitted together, and still standing, in spite of the fact that the metal clamps have been scooped out by the nomads. To effect an entrance, we had to crawl through a very narrow doorway, which has been graphically described by Arrian. The interior, which is blackened with smoke, was found to be ten feet five inches long by seven feet six inches wide and six feet ten inches high. This chamber was quite empty but for

---
[1] *Vide* illustration facing p. 154.

a string of votive offerings, and an Arabic inscription adorned the wall. Arrian says that the following inscription was on the tomb, ' O Man, I am Cyrus, the son of Cambyses, who founded the Empire of Persia, and was King of Asia. Grudge me not therefore this monument.' " [1] Thrice have I visited this tomb, which I have also been privileged to repair,[2] and on each occasion I have felt how great was my good fortune in seeing the actual tomb of " Cyrus, the King of the World, the Great King." Indeed, I doubt whether there is any single monument which for historical interest to us Aryans can surpass the tomb of the founder of the Persian Empire, who was buried some 2440 years ago.

The Palaces of Persepolis.—Pasargadae is situated in the upper valley of the Polvar, and separating it from the later capital is a lofty range which is traversed by a most romantic gorge down which speeds the same river ; this opens out and again closes in, and throughout the whole forty miles separating the two capitals there is a belt of mountainous country. The plain of Mervdasht, in which Persepolis is situated, has always been fertile, and, as it was visited by the Great King more especially in the spring, it was well chosen. There is more than one set of ruins to be described, including the grandiose rock-sculptures of the Sasanian dynasty which will be dealt with later in this work. But none of the relics of a mighty past compare with the great platform termed Takht-i-Jamshid, or " The Throne of Jamshid," alluded to in the well-known lines in FitzGerald's *Omar Khayyám* :

> They say the Lion and the Lizard keep
> The Courts where Jamshyd gloried and drank deep.

I have already referred to the platform at Pasargadae, which is on a much smaller scale, but appears to greater advantage inasmuch as it is not, like the platform of Persepolis when seen from a distance, dwarfed by its surroundings ; for, whereas Pasargadae is built amid low, rounded hills, Persepolis is set against a mountain range. The mighty platform, which rises 40 feet above the plain, forms three sides of a parallelogram. Its main length is 1500 feet, against the

---

[1] *Ten Thousand Miles*, etc., p. 328.
[2] On the roof a chance-sown seed had grown into a small tree, whose roots were forcing the great slabs apart and letting in the damp. The roots were cut out and the opening filled with cement.

BAS-RELIEF AND INSCRIPTION IN THE PALACE OF XERXES.

From a photograph by Sir P. Z. Cox.

300 feet of Pasargadae; its breadth is 900 feet. The workmanship resembles that of its forerunner at Pasargadae, the immense limestone blocks, quarried close by, exciting wonder. At the same time, had it not been directly inspired by the stupendous artificial platforms of Assyria, it seems improbable that this enormous platform would ever have been made, although in the preparation and utilization of the hill-side an advance on the Assyrian prototype is effected. The labour was, of course, considerably less than in the great earthworks of Assyria; for in the case of Koyunjik, to give a single example, it is estimated that the platform alone must have employed 20,000 men for six years.[1]

The steps of the main double staircase, although cut out of blocks large enough to form step after step, are so shallow that I rode my sixteen-hand horse up them with ease. Gaining the platform opposite the head of the staircase, I saw the wonderful porch of Xerxes, with its massive portal flanked by winged bulls which are Assyrian in character and most impressive. Above them are trilingual inscriptions, which state, among other things: " I am Xerxes, the Great King, the King of Kings, the King of many-tongued countries, the King of this Great Universe, the son of Darius, the King, the Achaemenian. Xerxes, the Great King saith: 'By the grace of Ormuzd I have made this portal, whereon are depicted all the countries.' "

Passing the first pair of colossi we find two columns out of the four which originally supported the central hall still standing, and at the entrance facing the mountain is another pair of colossi, keeping ceaseless watch and ward. Here, in spite of the destroyer, it is evident that these colossi were human-faced, their great beards being still clearly visible.

This splendid porch evidently constituted the entry to the great palace which was the chief glory of Persepolis, and which was also built by Xerxes. Leading up to it is a second staircase, most richly sculptured. The main wall of the terrace, some 12 feet in height, is occupied by three rows of bas-reliefs. Those upon the left, with chariots and horses, represent armed men, the guard of the Great King, advancing in triumph to the sound of music. Those upon the right, divided into groups by sculptured cypresses, represent the many-tongued peoples of the empire bearing gifts

[1] Rawlinson's *Five Monarchies*, i. p. 317.

and tribute from every quarter.[1] Ascending this splendid staircase, we enter the Hall of Xerxes. To-day but a dozen of the seventy-two columns, which terminated in two demi-bulls supporting the architrave, are standing; but it is easy to reconstruct the great hall, which had a roof of cedar and lofty porticoes, the whole superb building being approximately a square of 150 feet. Whether it had walls is doubtful, and it seems more likely that, as in the case of the palace at Susa, described in the book of Esther,[2] there were curtains in front, with walls perhaps at the sides and rear. This was the style adopted in Persia down the ages, as witness the halls of audience described in this work; and to-day the huge *talar* or archway, open to the front but closed behind and at the sides, is the most noticeable feature of Persian architecture.

The palace of Darius, although smaller, is still of importance, and probably included only the living-rooms of the monarch. But at the back of the platform is the magnificent Hall of a Hundred Columns, the largest of all the structures, whose roof was sustained, as the name implies, by one hundred columns, with a great portico on the northern side. This portico was guarded by colossi, and two great doorways led to the interior of the hall. The bas-reliefs are the finest on the platform, and represent the Great King seated on his throne supported by rows of his subjects, while above hovers the god. Perhaps what makes this, the magnificent audience-chamber of Darius, of greater interest than all the other buildings, is that it was in all probability in this very hall that Alexander feasted. We read how, in order to avenge the wrongs of Hellas, he burnt it to the ground;[3] and some confirmation of the story may be found in the discovery of a thick layer of cedar ash when excavations were made.

The Rock-Tombs.—The palaces of Persepolis proclaimed the grandeur and power of the Great King; but the rock-tombs, situated farther west, which drew their inspiration from Egypt, strike a more solemn note. From a distance four cruciform cuttings are sighted high up in the face of the perpendicular mountain, with a black gaping aperture in each, where the entrance stone has been destroyed. Externally the tombs are identical and represent the façade

---

[1] In 1916, I found that some of these bas-reliefs had fallen on to their faces.
[2] Esther i. 6, "Where were white, green, and blue hangings, fastened with cords of fine linen and purple to silver rings and pillars of marble."
[3] *Vide* Chapter XXII.

of a palace with four semi-detached columns, between which is the entrance. Above is an entablature which sustains a throne consisting of two stages, each supported by figures in the style of the Hall of a Hundred Columns. The King stands holding a bow in his left hand, while his right is raised in adoration to the god Ahura Mazda, who hovers above. One of them, which I examined with deep reverence, is proved by inscriptions to have been the tomb of Darius. With interior dimensions of 60 by 20 feet it was arranged to hold nine corpses, and a few of the stone lids which covered the deep cavities cut in the rock for the reception of the remains of Darius and his family were still in position, albeit in a broken condition.

Below the tombs are carved the Sasanian rock-sculptures, which will be referred to in their proper place, and opposite is a building which is obviously a copy of a Lycian tomb. The list of ruins is completed by several fire-altars, hewn out of the living rock. These speaking relics of a hoary religion are perhaps the oldest of all.

At my first visit I found these ruins bewildering, although I had carefully studied the detailed description given in Lord Curzon's monumental work. It was not until, some years later, I was able to spend two or three days on the spot that I grasped the greatness of the privilege I was enjoying.

Enamelled Brick-work, etc.—We now come to the splendid brick-work excavated by Dieulafoy in the palace of Artaxerxes Mnemon at Susa. Dieulafoy's most interesting discovery consisted of two superb friezes. The Frieze of the Archers, which constitutes by far the finest-known specimen of enamelling in polychrome on brick, is some 5 feet in height, and represents a procession of warriors in relief and almost of life-size. The men are of different complexions, varying from white to black; and their gold-knobbed spears identify them as The Immortals, who, in the eyes of the then civilized world, represented the glory, the magnificence, and the might of the Great King. The Frieze of the Lions, also in many colours, represents these beasts as advancing with open jaw to the attack. I have seen both these friezes in Paris; but, much as I admired them, I felt that they must have appeared to still greater advantage when they decorated the façade of an Achaemenian palace under a cloudless sky. It is doubtful whether these enamelled bricks can be considered to belong to Persian art, or whether they should be attributed to Babylon. But in the glyptic art it is remarkable to note to what height artistic execution was carried in seals, specimens of which are reproduced as head-pieces to some of the chapters. This art is Persian and is still flourishing to-day, thanks in part to a continued use of seals in Iran.

The Achaemenian Goldsmiths' Work.—Two generations ago, by a fortunate chance, a small section of the river bank of the Oxus fell in and revealed the now famous treasure,[1] most of which was taken to India and finally reached the British Museum. To illustrate this portion of my subject, I have given four examples. The gold model of an ancient Persian chariot is of striking interest, not only as a specimen of the goldsmith's work of the period, but as showing the ancient Persian chariot in the round, as no other representations do. To continue, the gold armilla is equally interesting, and proves to what a high pitch the art of the Achaemenian goldsmith had reached. The cloisonné work was executed, not with enamel, but with blue stone, apparently of the variety known as lazulite. The third example consists of a small silver disc, probably the umbo of a shield. It is embossed with thin plates of gold lapped over the embossed figures. In the centre is a boss pierced by five holes. Round the edge is a guilloche border. The three riders are represented as hunting stags, ibex, and a hare. The diameter is 3.8 inches. Finally, facing page 228, is the beautiful gold jug with its elegant shape enhanced by the lion-head on the handle, which is so characteristic of the Achaemenian goldsmith.

The Bronze Implements of Khinaman. — Several years ago, when I was stationed at Kerman, one of my Persian friends informed me that while trenching land he had discovered a number of bronze weapons and implements, and invited me to visit him.[2] The discovery was made in a district termed Khinaman, to the west of Kerman, which was totally unexplored, and included two bronze axe-heads, vessels, pins, javelins, and spear-heads, and two implements the use of which remains a mystery. Great jars containing yellow dust were also found, and had been thrown away before my arrival: two small jars were secured. The most striking

---

[1] *Treasure of the Oxus*, by O. M. Dalton, for whose kind assistance I am much obliged.
[2] *Ten Thousand Miles*, etc., p. 441. The second axe-head was secured two years later, and so does not appear in the first notice of the find.

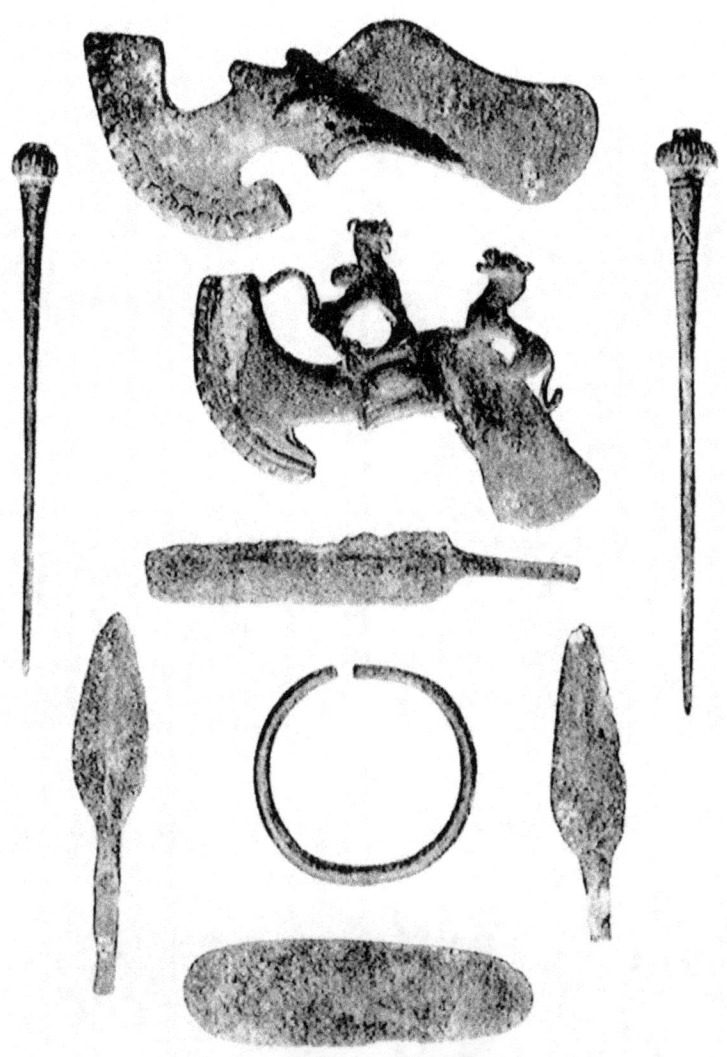

BRONZE AXE-HEADS, ETC., FROM KHINAMAN.

objects are the two axe-heads, which were undoubtedly ceremonial, their shape proving that they were not designed for warfare. The vessels included a lamp and a little vessel, which resembled that which the Persian still carries for drinking purposes. Canon Greenwell wrote a paper [1] on this interesting find, which I read before the British Association in 1906. The collection, which I have presented to the British Museum, was also examined by Sir Hercules Read and other leading archaeologists, none of whom was able to assign a definite date to the various objects, partly owing to the fact that, inasmuch as they were the first to be discovered on the Iranian plateau, it was impossible to make any comparisons. Since that date, however, a Bactrian bronze ceremonial axe of singular design has been obtained for the British Museum. This axe is entirely composed of the figures of a bear, a tiger, and an ibex, and Sir Hercules Read thinks it highly probable that it is a specimen of the art of Bactria of about the time of Alexander the Great.[2] Consequently, although I do not presume to date my collection, it seemed desirable to refer to it in this chapter.

Summary.—In concluding this brief survey, in which I have for the most part limited myself to describing the principal Achaemenian ruins, which I have visited more than once, I would sum up my impressions still more briefly. Persia borrowed, and borrowed freely, from the great nations with which she was brought into contact, from Babylon, from Assyria, from Egypt, and from Hellas, but she did not copy slavishly. Even the Assyrian colossi take a secondary place in the superb palaces built by the architects of the Achaemenian monarchs, in which, although the theme is limited to the glorification of the Great King, the general effect when thronged with the court and army must have been imposing to the most critical and artistic citizen of Athens. Even in its ruin the Throne of Jamshid challenges our wonder and admiration.

[1] *Notes on a Collection, etc.*, published by Royal Anthrop. Instit. *Vide* also *Archaeologia*, vol. 58, p. 1, for paper by Sir Hercules Read.
[2] *Man*, vol. xiv., No. 2, February 1914.

A DARIC.

CHAPTER XVI

PERSIA AND HELLAS DURING THE REIGN OF DARIUS

> They were the first of the Greeks who dared to look upon the Median garb, and to face men clad in that fashion. Until this time the very name of the Medes had been a terror to the Greeks to hear.—HERODOTUS vi. 112.

The Issues at Stake. — The invasion of Hellas by the myriads of the Persian Empire and their ultimate repulse constitute an event in the history of the world which is unsurpassed alike in importance and in dramatic grandeur. It was, indeed, the first attempt of the organized East to conquer the less organized West, and in its later phase not only did the Persian Empire invade Hellas, but through Persian influence Carthage made an equally deadly assault on the Greek colonies of Sicily. Fortunately for the cause of mankind, both invasions failed signally.[1]

The Greek Subjects of Persia.—By the conquest of the Greek cities and islands of Asia Minor, and the later annexation of Thrace and Macedonia, the Persians had acquired control over at least one-third of the entire race of the Greeks. These, from their training and equipment, were a formidable military force, and they possessed a navy equal to that of the Phoenicians, whose commercial monopoly they had broken. At the same time, the intense love of liberty and other qualities which gave the Greeks their strength also made them extremely difficult to control; and it is certain that none of the early Persian monarchs understood their value or the best methods of dealing with a race which differed so profoundly from any other

---

[1] It must never be forgotten that our knowledge of the Persian campaigns against Hellas is drawn entirely from Greek sources. Herodotus, indeed, used Persian sources to a limited extent; but the point of view is invariably that of the Greek. The authorities consulted in this and the following chapter are Macan's *Herodotus*, How and Wells's *Commentary on Herodotus*, Grundy's *Great Persian War*, and Bury's *History of Greece*. These works constitute a notable advance in our knowledge of the subject.

which had been subdued by the might of Iran. Moreover, as the Greeks lived on the extreme confines of the Persian Empire, it is not probable that they attracted much attention.

The Intercourse between Hellas and Asia Minor.—Intercourse of every kind with Hellas, especially in such matters as commerce, travel, and marriage, had not been affected by the substitution of a lenient Persian Satrap for a Lydian monarch at Sardes. Refugees from Asia Minor still found support in Hellas, just as they had done in the reign of Croesus, and deposed Greek rulers appealed to their brethren in Asia Minor or to the Persian Satrap. This state of affairs, foreshadowed in the message of Sparta to Cyrus, grew more and more intolerable to a world empire like Persia, till it culminated in the Ionic Revolt. At the same time, the constant appeals from Hellas would naturally tempt an ambitious Satrap to earn distinction by augmenting not only the prestige, but the territories, of the Great King. It seems probable that the Satraps of Sardes, if not Darius himself, had contemplated such an expansion of the empire for some years.

The Position in Greece.—Before we approach the events which actually caused the invasion of Greece, the position of affairs in Hellas itself demands our attention. Athens, which was the objective of the campaign and the key of Hellas, had been in a state of disunion for many years. Hippias, the tyrant of the family of Pisistratus, who had been expelled in 510 B.C. by the Spartans, had taken refuge at Sigeum in the Troad. There he sought the aid of the Persian Satrap at Sardes and intrigued against Athens in every possible manner.

After the downfall of the tyranny, Cleisthenes, a member of the noble Alcmaeonid family, reformed the constitution of Athens on democratic lines. This aroused the resentment and antagonism of the aristocratic party, which appealed to Sparta as the leading state of Hellas. Sparta responded by an invasion, and Cleisthenes had to yield to force. The Athenians, enraged, rose against the Spartans garrisoning Athens, who surrendered their Athenian allies and quitted Attica. But they soon returned with a still greater force of Peloponnesian allies, and Athens in despair despatched ambassadors to the Satrap of Sardes, who demanded earth and water in recognition of Persian suzerainty. These terms the ambassadors accepted, but, on their return in 508 B.C., the Athenians repudiated their action. Meanwhile Attica was ravaged by the Peloponnesians until the coalition dissolved upon the withdrawal of Corinth. In 506 B.C. the Athenians again sent ambassadors to Sardes, begging that Artaphernes, the Satrap, would cease from supporting Hippias. In reply they were sternly summoned to recall Hippias, and their refusal to do this made an ultimate invasion almost certain ; for the permanent temptation towards expansion was strengthened by the fact that the Persians could now reasonably count on active assistance from the adherents of the Pisistratidae. Spies apparently were despatched at this period to report on the fortifications, harbours, and armaments of Hellas. The attempt on Naxos, which will be referred to presently, formed part of a scheme for seizing various islands in the Aegean to serve as naval stations in connexion with the projected invasion.

The Ionic Revolt, 499-494 B.C.—There is no doubt that the Ionic Revolt was the direct cause which set the Persian forces in motion against Hellas. It was started by the personal ambitions of two Greek tyrants. The more important figure was Histiaeus of Miletus, who had been in charge of the Danube bridge, and had been rewarded by Darius with the gift of a city in Thrace. Having aroused the suspicions of the Persian representative by fortifying this town, he was summoned to Susa by Darius, and there interned, although treated with honour. Miletus was ruled by his son-in-law, Aristagoras. To him Histiaeus despatched a slave, who stated that his head was to be shaved in secret, and when this was done a message instigating a revolt against the Persians was found tattooed on his scalp. The communication thus ingeniously conveyed arrived at an opportune moment. An attack which Aristagoras had induced the Persian Satrap to make on Naxos had just failed through treachery, and the Greek was daily expecting to be dismissed from his post, if not put to death. In every city there must have been a party, small or large, in favour of throwing off the Persian yoke; and, when Aristagoras resigned the tyranny, Miletus was speedily won over to the popular cause. Other tyrants, who were on board the fleet which had returned from Naxos, were seized by the rebels. Aristagoras visited Sparta and applied for assistance in the revolt, but in vain. The Athenians, however, supplied a squadron of twenty ships and the

Eretrians five ships; and, encouraged by this somewhat meagre support, the rebels in 498 B.C. made a sudden attack on Sardes and captured the town. But they made no impression on the famous fort, and, unable to hold the town, had to retreat. They were overtaken near Ephesus by Persian troops and were apparently defeated. In consequence of this failure Ionia was deserted by Athens. The action of the Athenians in espousing the cause of liberty, in despatching twenty ships, and in then withdrawing, was not only ignoble but impolitic.

The capture of Sardes resounded throughout Asia Minor and encouraged the Greek cities to rebel. On the other hand, it aroused the wrath of Darius to such a pitch that at every meal a slave was ordered to call out, " Sire, remember the Athenians." Such, at least, is the legend. The revolt was quite unjustifiable from the military point of view, as the Persians operated throughout on interior lines, and could attack separately any city or group of cities they wished, leaving the others to await their punishment in turn. At the same time the rebels gained some successes, notably in Caria, where a Persian army was annihilated.

The Battle of Lade and the Fall of Miletus, 494 B.C.— The decisive engagement took place at sea. A Greek fleet of three hundred and fifty-three vessels was collected, but, upon its being attacked by six hundred Phoenician and Cypriote ships acting under Persian orders, the Samian squadron, followed by the Lesbian, deserted the common cause, and the Persians won the battle of Lade.[1] Miletus, the leader of the revolt and the foremost city in the Hellenic world, was taken by the Persians, its males were almost all killed, and its women and children were transported to Ampe at the mouth of the Tigris. Thus the revolt was broken. Its immediate result was to rivet the Persian yoke still more firmly on the Ionian Greeks of Asia Minor, who had given a display of disunion, of incapacity, and of treachery which would justify Darius and his advisers in the belief that the conquest of Hellas would not present any extraordinary difficulty. On the other hand, the revolt allowed Athens time to construct a fleet which was destined to be the decisive factor in the great war and thus to save Hellas. Moreover, Thrace and Macedonia had benefited by the withdrawal of the Persians, and had regained their liberty.

[1] It was named from an island opposite Miletus.

The Campaign of Mardonius in Thrace, 493 B.C.—After the successful issue of the operations against the Ionian Greeks, Darius decided to reconquer Thrace and Macedonia and apparently to punish Athens and Eretria. Two routes lay open to the Persian forces. The most direct lay across the Aegean Sea, which was studded with islands all the way to Athens, distant some two hundred miles from the ports of Asia Minor. It was undoubtedly the most convenient route ; but, with the fleets of Hellas undefeated, the risk of transporting a huge force of men, horses, equipment, and stores by sea was considerable. The land route, on the other hand, was already known. Persians, then as now, had no aptitude for the sea ; and they were justified in considering the forces of the Great King invincible on land. For these reasons the land route was selected. The first stage in the proceedings was the despatch to Thrace of Mardonius, the nephew of Darius, who reasserted Persian authority and forced Alexander of Macedon to renew the pledges made by his father Amyntas. Mardonius had intended to march into Hellas, but a great storm caused the loss of half of the fleet which supplied his army, and no further advance was possible. In pursuance of the invariable policy of Darius, who allowed no general to remain in permanent command, Mardonius was recalled in 492 B.C., and the further operations were entrusted to Datis and Artaphernes, the latter being a son of the Satrap of Lydia.

The Punitive Expedition against Athens and Eretria, 490 B.C.—The expedition of Mardonius having failed to include the chastisement of Athens and Eretria, it was decided, in 490 B.C., to despatch a second expedition. Its objects were to place Athens once again under the despot Hippias, who was no doubt ready to execute the leaders of the anti-Persian party, and to bring the vengeance of the Great King to bear upon Eretria. The destruction of the Persian fleet off the promontory of Mount Athos made that route one to be avoided ; this, and the fact that Aegina and other islands had submitted, led to the choice of the direct sea route for the armada. The Aleian plain in Cilicia was selected for the assembling of the force, which, after being embarked in transports, made for Ionia, with Samos as the actual rallying-place. The fleet of six hundred ships first crossed the Icarian Sea to Naxos, whose inhabitants were reduced to slavery. After this initial success the expedition headed for Delos, which was spared on account of its shrine, and then for the coast of Euboea, instead of making direct for Attica, as sound strategy would have dictated.

The Destruction of Eretria.—The fleet, on reaching the mainland, moved up the channel separating Euboea from Attica. A force was landed and besieged Eretria, which was captured by treachery and burned in punishment for the part its citizens had played in the raid on Sardes. Many of its inhabitants escaped to the hills; those who were captured were deported to distant Elam. Apparently no attempt was made by Athens to give effectual aid to the unfortunate city, which drained to the dregs the cup of Persian vengeance.

The Battle of Marathon, 490 B.C.—The leaders of the expedition, instead of making Athens their first objective, had wasted priceless days in devoting their entire strength to a minor operation which tended to exasperate and to unite their chief enemy. Hippias, who had meanwhile joined the Persian armada, advised the invaders to sail round to the bay of Marathon, which is situated in Attica about twenty-four miles to the north-east of Athens. The suggestion was sound; for it was a good station for the fleet and was also within reach of the Acropolis, where Hippias hoped that his adherents would gain the upper hand. It possessed the further advantage that the ground was not unsuitable for cavalry. But at this moment of supreme crisis no rising in favour of Hippias occurred; and the Athenian force of nine to ten thousand men, reinforced before the battle by a contingent of Plataeans, was able to mobilize without distraction.

The Athenian army marched to meet the invader, and an excellent position was taken up on broken ground across the tracks leading into the interior, pending expected help from Sparta. This, however, was delayed on the contemptible excuse that the Spartan army must await the full moon before taking the field. Never was a situation met with greater folly than this crisis by the Spartans, whose one-sided system of training apparently deprived them of all sense of proportion.

For several days the two armies faced one another, and we learn from the pages of Herodotus how, in view of the numerical superiority of the invaders, whose force was perhaps between forty and fifty thousand strong, a council of war was held by the Greeks to decide whether an attack should be made. The ten generals were evenly divided on the subject. But Miltiades, who knew the Persians well, persuaded the Polemarch, or War Lord, and his colleagues that the offensive was all-important, and he was apparently given the command in order to execute his scheme. His tactical disposition included two strong wings, and to prevent outflanking by the superior numbers of the Persians his centre was extended.

The attack was made at the double,[1] down the valley of the Vrana, and as the distance separating the two hosts was just a mile, the interval must have been covered in about eight or nine minutes. Before the Persian host had recovered from its surprise, not unmixed with contempt, that a Greek force unsupported by cavalry should attack a Persian army drawn up in battle array, the Athenians were among them. The fight was not long drawn. The Persians and Sakae in the centre at first more than held their own ; but the Athenians were victorious on both wings and wheeled inwards on the centre. They inflicted heavy losses, estimated at six thousand, on the army of the Great King, whereas on their side but two hundred fell. When the Persians fled, the Greeks pursued them to their ships. As Byron writes :

> The flying Mede, his shaftless broken bow ;
> The fiery Greek, his red pursuing spear ;
> Mountains above, Earth's, Ocean's plain below,
> Death in the front, Destruction in the rear !
> Such was the scene. . . .

The Persian cavalry and part of the other troops appear to have been already on board, if not on their way to Phaleron, and the fleet made off with a loss of but seven galleys. Datis, who was possibly caught when preparing to transfer his base to Phaleron, anchored that night off the coast, and the watchful Athenians sighted a shield being used on Mount Pentelicus for signalling to the enemy. In the morning the Persian armada sailed south and, doubling Cape Sunion, made for Phaleron ; but to their chagrin, upon their arrival, they found the victorious army drawn up in grim array—and they feared to face it. After all, the losses of the Persians had barely exceeded ten per cent, and, if they had been caught at a

---

[1] Grundy translates the word δρόμῳ as " quick-step."

disadvantage at Marathon, as at least seems possible, their *moral* should not have been greatly affected; but, to the eternal discredit of Persia, her general was cowed and set sail for Asia Minor.

Perhaps no battle in the world has had a moral importance so great as that of Marathon, even if there has been exaggeration in the versions handed down to us. Until then the might of Persia had been irresistible, and Greek troops had invariably in the last resort suffered defeat. Let us then pay due homage to the heroism which animated the Athenians, who, left to bear the brunt by Sparta, might well have abandoned their homes and retreated into the interior before a force estimated at four or five times their number. Even now, after a lapse of more than two thousand years, it is impossible not to be deeply moved when reading in the pages of Herodotus how the heroes charged down on the hitherto invincible foe. The intensity of their exultation can scarcely have been matched in the annals of warfare as desperation gave way to triumph, and they realized that, alone and unsupported except by Plataea, they had battled down the Great King's warriors in fair fight, and made them afraid, although still vastly superior in numbers, to face again the Athenian hoplites. Such was the superb achievement of Marathon, as we clearly see, looking back across the centuries. But to Darius it would seem nothing more than a regrettable check which need have no serious effect upon his policy.

The Rebellion in Egypt, 486 B.C.—Possibly one of the first fruits of the defeat at Marathon was a rebellion in Egypt. Under Darius this ancient kingdom had flourished, and its trade had increased enormously since the whole Persian Empire was open to it. Moreover, he completed or reopened the canal connecting the Nile with the Gulf of Suez, and he also encouraged trade with the interior of Africa. But heavy war-taxes were now imposed, at a moment when Persian prestige had suffered severely; and in 486 B.C. a serious rebellion broke out under a certain Khabbisha, who claimed to belong to the family of Psammetichus, and was proclaimed king.

The Death of Darius, 485 B.C.—Darius, who was great to the end, prepared to deliver a still more serious attack on Hellas, and at the same time to quell the rebellion in Egypt. Had he lived five years longer, it would have gone hard with Greece; but in 485 B.C., in the thirty-sixth year of his reign, the Great King died.

His Character.—Happy indeed was Persia to have been blessed with two great kings in successive generations. Cyrus the Great was the conqueror and founder of the Persian Empire. Darius, equally deserving the title "Great," won constantly against desperate odds, but, more than this, he had the genius for organization. His personal character stood very high. He was remarkably intelligent and reasonable; and even his bitter enemies, the Greeks, wrote of him with the utmost respect. The Persian grandees, whose extortions he limited and checked, sneeringly termed him the "huckster"; but this epithet was in reality high praise. Indeed, but for his organizing genius, superadded to signal capacity for war, the empire would not have lasted, as it did, through generation after generation, until Alexander the Great defeated the craven Darius who then occupied the throne of his mighty forbears. The number of great kings who have ruled over Persia is not small; but, due weight being given to the conditions of the time, Darius is among the greatest of them all; indeed, he ranks very high among the greatest Aryans of history.

COMBAT OF GREEKS WITH PERSIANS.
(Frieze from the Temple of Athena-Nike at Athens.)

CHAPTER XVII

THE REPULSE OF PERSIA BY HELLAS

> A King sate on the rocky brow
> Which looks o'er sea-born Salamis;
> And ships, by thousands, lay below,
> And men in nations—all were his!
> He counted them at break of day—
> And, when the sun set, where were they?
> BYRON.

The Accession of Xerxes, 485 B.C.—According to Persian custom, Darius had many wives. Among them was the daughter of Gaubaruva or Gobryas, one of his fellow-conspirators in the attack on the false Gaumata. By her he had three children, the eldest of whom, Artabazanes, had long been regarded as heir to the throne. But Atossa, daughter of Cyrus, ranked supreme, and her influence on the old king was so strong that just before his death he nominated as his successor her son Khshayarsha, better known by his Greek name Xerxes, and he ascended the throne without opposition. The new monarch, the Ahasuerus of the book of Esther, was famous for his radiant beauty and superb physique, but he was indolent, weak, and easily swayed by his advisers. Voluptuous and fond of luxury, he had no desire for glory, and to these defects in his character Greece, in all probability, owed her salvation. From the first he was inclined to treat the failure in Hellas as of no importance; but Mardonius insisted that the prestige of Persia would suffer, and remonstrated with such effect that in the end he gained his point, and the great invasion was undertaken.

The Rebellion in Egypt crushed, 484 B.C.—But first Xerxes

marched on Egypt to put down the rebellion, and although Khabbisha had been busily preparing to face the coming storm for two years, the Egyptians were crushed. The pretender disappeared, but his supporters were severely punished and the delta was ravaged. Achaemenes, the king's brother, was appointed Satrap, and Egypt settled down as before, the hereditary princes and the priests being left in full possession of their powers and properties.

The Revolt of Babylon, 483 B.C.—Egypt was not the only cause of anxiety to Xerxes. There was a short-lived rebellion in Babylon, where a pretender of unknown origin, Shamasherib by name, was crowned king. A siege of a few months, however, sufficed for the capture of the great city, and on this occasion not only was Babylon sacked, but the temples were plundered and the people carried into captivity. Xerxes showed no fear of Bel-Marduk, whose treasury he looted and whose golden statue he carried off. Babylon never recovered. From the time of this siege her commerce, her religion, her influence and her glory gradually passed away. But the work of the great city was accomplished ; and when we reckon up what our modern civilization owes to Babylon, we cannot fail to be astonished at the greatness of our debt.

The Composition and Numbers of the Great Expedition.—In 481 B.C. the preparations for the greatest of recorded expeditions in ancient times were completed, and in the autumn of that year the various contingents assembled in the province of Cappadocia and marched to Lydia, where Xerxes spent the winter. The force under his orders, drawn from every quarter of the enormous Persian empire, was so impressive that, vast as the numbers undoubtedly were, they have become legendary and exaggerated. The best account of the various elements that made up the army is supplied by Herodotus. It is not only delightfully graphic, but of great value to the ethnologist as well as the historian. The Persians and Medes head the list, armed with lance, bow, and sword ; the Kissians and the Hyrcanians are mentioned next, as being armed like the Persians ; the Assyrians with bronze helmets follow ; the Bactrians, Arians, Parthians, and neighbouring tribes with javelins and spears ; the Sakae, noted warriors with curious pointed caps and battle-axes ; the Indians with their cotton coats ; the Ethiopians of Africa with painted bodies, and armed with long bows and stone-tipped arrows; the Ethiopians of Asia—probably the aborigines of Southern Persia and Makran—with extraordinary helmets made of horses' heads; and others, down to the remote islanders of the Persian Gulf. Over each levy was set a Persian, and the army was divided roughly into divisions, regiments, companies, and sections. The supreme command of the infantry was vested in Marduniya or Mardonius, but the " Immortals " had a separate commander.

The mounted troops, including in this category the tribes which fought from chariots, consisted mainly of Persians and Medes, and included some 8000 Sagartians from Northern Persia, armed with lassos. There were also Kissians and Indians, the latter with chariots drawn by wild asses, which could hardly have been of much military value; Bactrians, Caspians, and Libyans who fought from chariots; and there was besides a force of Arabs mounted on dromedaries.

The twelve hundred and seven warships, with crews averaging 200 men, were supplied by the Phoenicians, Egyptians, and subject Greeks, and each vessel carried a few Persians or Sakae, who acted as marines and supported the Persian commanders. There were 3000 transports.

Herodotus gives the composition of the grand army as follows :

(*a*) Infantry 1,700,000
(*b*) Mounted troops 100,000
(*c*) Sailors and marines. 510,000
                                    ─────────
                                    2,310,000

Reinforcements in Europe and servants bring up the figures to over five millions, a total which it is impossible to accept. In view of the reliance the Persians placed on numbers and the size of the empire, we are perhaps justified in assuming that the land and sea forces combined, inclusive of followers, aggregated about one million. After deducting the crews, this total would give at the most 200,000 fighting men, so numerous are camp followers in an Eastern army, and, allowing for strong detachments posted on the lines of communication, for sickness, and other causes, the actual numbers that met the Greeks at sea, and finally on land, were not overwhelming. But it is clear that no invasion on such a scale had ever before been attempted, and its immensity constituted the highest compliment to the valour of Hellas. Yet in its very numbers lay its weakness; for such an army could not be used for any lengthy turning movement, owing to the ever-present difficulty of supplies, nor could it be separated from the fleet for more than a few days at a time.

The Military Position in Greece.—As in the case of the former invasion, Athens was the main objective, and upon Athens the brunt of the attack was intended to fall. On the other hand, the Persians, unless opposed at sea, could with the utmost ease turn the flank of the defence of the Corinthian Isthmus or any other line; consequently, in the last resort, Sparta's fate was wrapped up in that of Athens, although this was not generally grasped by the obtuse Spartans and their confederates, who were committed to the defence of the Isthmus. Through the exertions of Themistocles, the Athenians during the last decade had developed their sea-power to a remarkable degree, not only by building triremes, but also by the creation of the fortified base of the Piraeus. They were thus able, when the invaders came, to remove the population to the neighbouring islands, and in the last resort they could have sailed away to found a new Attica in Italy, as indeed Themistocles at one time threatened to do.

An attempt had been made to heal all internal feuds and to form a grand league of the entire Hellenic world against the invader. In the first place, Argos was approached, but the negotiations failed owing to the claim of the Argives that their state should be placed on an equal footing with Sparta so far as the command was concerned. Argos, however, did not declare openly in favour of Persia, although her attitude caused grave anxiety. Gelon, tyrant of Syracuse, was also approached, and, according to Herodotus, insisted on commanding either the land or sea forces of Hellas in return for his co-operation. But, in spite of the large number of troops and warships he controlled, the envoys refused even to consider the proposal. It is, however, possible that Gelon proposed terms unlikely to be accepted, as he realized the probability of an invasion of Sicily by the Carthaginians. Finally, neither Crete nor Corcyra (Corfu) rendered any assistance to the common cause.

The March of the Great Army.—The departure from Sardes of the great army, as described by Herodotus, must have been a wonderful sight. Intervals were maintained only by the picked troops; the rest were armed mobs and marched in no set order. But the mere fact that such a force could be successfully moved and fed proves that the Persian Empire was highly organized. Its power, too, in other directions was great; for not only were two solid bridges of vessels constructed across the Hellespont, but the Strymon was bridged and a canal was cut through the promontory of Athos—no slight engineering task at such a distance from the heart of the empire. In addition, vast supply depots were formed at the various stages, and the only vital point on which there was occasional failure was the supply of water for such a host.

The crossing of the Hellespont was a great feat. The two bridges of boats, across which a solid causeway was made, were constructed with cables of exceptional strength, and the passage was made under the eye of the Great King, who sat in state upon a marble throne erected on a hill near Abydos. At sunrise, Xerxes poured a libation into the sea from a golden cup and prayed that he might conquer Europe. The golden cup, a golden bowl, and a Persian sword were thrown into the sea, and the "Immortals," wearing garlands on their heads, led the way across the bridge, which was strewn with myrtle branches. The enormous host crossed into Europe, contingent by contingent, under the ever-present lash, and in the plain of Doriscus the army was numbered. From Doriscus it marched to Acanthus, where it broke up temporarily into three divisions, to unite again at Therma.

In reply to an appeal from Thessaly for help to defend the passage of Mount Olympus, the Greeks had in the first place despatched a force of ten thousand men to Tempe; but according to Herodotus they found that the position could be outflanked, and they consequently retreated, leaving the Thessalians to make their own terms with Xerxes, which they promptly did. The Persian army thus advanced unopposed through Macedonia and Thessaly, and before the first action was fought most of the Greek states of Northern and Central Hellas had submitted, with the honourable exceptions of Thespiae and Plataea.

The Defence of Thermopylae, 480 B.C.—The Spartans, as we have seen, were committed to the defence of the Isthmus of Corinth, and wished the Athenians to leave Attica to the enemy and retire to the south. This proposal of a passive defence was rightly rejected, and finally, after the retreat from Tempe, a foolish compromise resulted in the despatch of a force aggregating seven thousand men, under Leonidas, to hold the narrow pass of Thermopylae, with some idea of strengthening it after the inevitable festival. This was *the* strong position of Hellas, situated between cliffs and the sea, and it was guarded on the right flank by the Greek fleet of some three hundred ships, posted off the promontory of Artemisium in Euboea. Had the Greeks held the position with the full strength of Hellas, it is probable that the might of Xerxes would have been broken by force of arms, as happened to Brennus and his Gauls in 279 B.C. On this occasion, the fatal policy of the *petit paquet* was attempted, and failed, and an important division was annihilated without materially delaying the advance of the enemy. On the other hand, the moral effect on the Persian army of the valour that was displayed must have been enormous ; and the faulty strategy does not detract a whit from, but rather heightens, the immortal fame of Leonidas and his band of heroes.

Xerxes with his huge host marched forward from Therma, but halted and sent out a reconnoitring party upon receiving information that the pass was held. To-day the coast-line has advanced considerably, but in 480 B.C. there was only a strip of ground 100 feet wide at the base of the cliffs, and between the two narrowest points was encamped the Greek force. The reconnoitring party reported that the enemy were calmly engaged in athletic exercises and in combing their long hair as if for a festival. Xerxes, who waited for four days, apparently in the expectation that his fleet would force the passage of the Euripus, finally ordered the Medes and Kissians, and then the "Immortals," to attack. Their short spears and indifferent armour, in spite of their courage, made no impression on the heavily armoured Greeks, who slaughtered them by hundreds. The following day the combat was resumed, with the same result, and Xerxes was in despair. The situation was saved for the Persians by a track across the mountains, which was revealed by a traitor to Hellas. The "Immortals" were sent along it, and the Phocian contingent which had been stationed to guard it betrayed their trust, offering no resistance and retreating off the track. Warning was given of this treachery, and all the contingents retired [1] except the Spartans, three hundred strong, the Thespians, and the Thebans, the last named being detained by force. Then the band of heroes, not waiting to be surrounded, advanced on the Persians and fought, against hopeless odds, that fight to the death which has earned them deathless fame.

The Naval Engagements off Artemisium.—Meanwhile at sea much had been happening. The Persian fleet waited at Therma for twelve days after the departure of the army, as there was no harbour between this port and the Pagasaian Gulf. It then advanced, preceded by ten fast-sailing vessels which came upon three Greek ships engaged in reconnoitring duties off the mouth of the River Peneius. Two of these were destroyed. The squadrons of the invaders arrived on the Magnesian coast in safety, but owing to its numbers the armada had to lie in eight lines parallel to the coast, and while it was at anchor in this dangerous position a sudden storm arose and wrecked four hundred ships. After the storm had subsided, the battered Persian fleet moved across to Aphetae, situated on the mainland opposite Artemisium.

The Persians, who were by no means lacking in initiative, and who never dreamed of defeat, detached two hundred ships to sail round Euboea with a view to sealing up the straits that separated that island from the mainland, hoping thereby to capture the whole of the Greek fleet. This move having been reported, the Greeks, under the command of the Spartan Admiral Eurybiades, attacked the main fleet and captured thirty vessels; the battle was, however, indecisive. On the following night, the elements again warred in their favour and annihilated the Persian squadron which had been sent round Euboea. This welcome intelligence was brought by a strong reinforcement of fifty-three Athenian ships, which had probably been guarding the strait at Chalcis. In the final encounter the Persians, who were presumably receiving repeated orders from Xerxes to break through the

---

[1] Grundy suggests that Leonidas detached a strong force to deal with the "Immortals" and faced the main Persian army with the reduced force. This theory has something to recommend it, and would explain the presence of the Thespians and Boeotians. As, however, Leonidas abandoned the defensive for the offensive, which he would surely not have done had his plans been those suggested by Grundy, I prefer to keep to the old story and think that the personality of Leonidas fired the Thespians to share his fate.

Greek fleet and regain touch with the army, engaged the enemy all along the line, and a desperate struggle ensued. The battle was going against the Greeks, many of whose ships were damaged, when news came of the forcing of Thermopylae. This disaster changed the situation and at night an order to retire was given. Had the Persian fleet pursued in force, many of the damaged Greek ships would have been captured; but the Persians were ignorant of the retirement, although they should surely have anticipated it, and the Greeks sailed leisurely along the coast of Euboea, the Athenians acting as rearguard.

The Advance of the Persian Army and the Capture of Athens. —So far the campaign had gone well for the Persians. The most formidable pass had been forced, the Greek fleet, after two engagements, had retreated, and Central Hellas lay open and unprotected before the invaders. Xerxes marched into Phocis, which was devastated, and then the great host turned towards Attica. The Athenians, who had hoped for success at Thermopylae, had not vacated Athens; but this operation was now hurriedly effected, the women and children being sent to Troizen, Aegina, and Salamis. A few misguided individuals, relying on an ambiguous Delphic oracle that Athens should trust to its wooden walls, held the Acropolis; but after a desperate defence they were overcome and massacred. Athens was at last in the hands of the invaders, and in revenge for the destruction of Sardes its shrines were burnt. The Great King, having carried through with success the devastation of Attica and the capture of Athens, no doubt felt that the whole campaign would soon be crowned with victory; but he reckoned from false premises.

The Battle of Salamis, 480 B.C.—The Greek fleet, upon the urgent representations of Themistocles, whose ability to persuade the Spartans by arguments that would appeal to them was remarkable, after leaving Artemisium made for Salamis, on the plea of allowing the Athenians to save their families. At this island it received its last reinforcements, which brought the numerical strength of the fleet, on which depended the salvation of Hellas, up to about four hundred vessels; the number of the enemy's ships was considerably greater.

The capture of Athens and the advance of the Persian fleet to Phaleron caused such a panic that the Peloponnesian contingents urgently insisted on a retreat of the fleet to the Isthmus of Corinth, regardless of the fate of the Athenians, whose families would have been thereby exposed to capture. The argument was that, if defeated at Salamis, they could not hope to escape the Persians, whereas at the Isthmus they would be protected by the united forces of Hellas. So general was this feeling that Themistocles was in despair: but at the council of war, held under the presidency of Eurybiades, his personality again triumphed, and he secured an unwilling adhesion to his views by pointing out that the only hope for Hellas was to fight in narrow waters, and that off Corinth the numerical superiority of the Persian fleet would unquestionably tell. The Corinthian admiral tried to force a quarrel on Themistocles by declaring that, since the Athenians had lost their country, they were no longer in the position to give an opinion. This attack was skilfully parried by a telling threat that, if the Athenians sailed off to found a new Attica in Italy, they would be missed at this juncture.

Matters were in this state, and the defection of one or more contingents seemed probable, when Themistocles made his winning stroke and saved Hellas by an act of disloyalty to his colleagues. He sent a messenger to Xerxes with the intelligence that the Greeks were contemplating retreat, and that his opportunity to destroy them had at last come. Accustomed to Greek treachery, Xerxes decided to trust this information, and despatched his Egyptian squadron of two hundred ships to close the western passage between Salamis and Megara. His main fleet then advanced from Phaleron, and took up station for the great battle in three lines on each side of the island of Psyttaleia, which was occupied by a Persian force. Xerxes thought success assured, and the main object of his dispositions was to prevent the escape of the Greeks.

Information of the movements of the Persian fleet, which made it clear that victory alone could save Hellas, was brought to the Council by Aristides, who had recently returned from exile. The Greeks fully realized that their own lives and the lives of their families were at stake. They had the advantage of homogeneity, and the fact that the battle was to take place in narrow waters was an additional point in their favour. The Persian fleet, on the other hand, was composed of various contingents, and, although there was at first ample sea-room, it came into contact with the enemy in an area which was too small for its numbers, and where an advance had to be made in column, in face of an enemy drawn up in line. But no lack of courage was shown by the subjects of the Great King, who realized that they were fighting under the eye of their merciless master.

The famous sea-fight opened favourably for the Persians. When morning dawned the Greeks, appalled by the odds, backed their ships almost to the shore ; but suddenly the courage of despair nerved them to heroism of the highest order, and they advanced on the enemy. The Phoenician column, which moved between Psyttaleia and the mainland, was faced by the Athenians and Aeginetans ; and the Ionian Greeks, who advanced between Psyttaleia and Salamis, were opposed by the Peloponnesian squadrons. The battle was desperately contested. The Persian numbers were a hindrance rather than a help in the narrow fairways, and, although they gained ground on their left wing, their right wing was finally defeated by the valour and skill of the Athenians and Aeginetans, to whom, by common consent, the honours of the day belonged. At last the Persians gave way all along the line and retreated to Phaleron with a loss of two hundred ships, not counting those which were captured with their crews; the Greeks lost forty ships. There was no pursuit by the victors.

Thus ended the great naval battle, which is one of the decisive battles of the world ; for I hold, with Grundy, that its claims to be so classed exceed those of Marathon, admitted by the historian Creasy.

The account of the battle given by Aeschylus, who fought in one of the ships, deserves to be quoted :

> At first the Persian navy's torrent-flood
> Withstood them ; but when our vast fleet was cramped
> In strait space—friend could lend no aid to friend,—
> Then ours by fangs of allies' beaks of bronze
> Were struck, and shattered all their oar-array ;
> While with shrewd strategy the Hellene ships
> Swept round, and rammed us, and upturned were hulls
> Of ships ;—no more could one discern the sea,
> Clogged all with wrecks and limbs of slaughtered men :
> The shores, the rock-reefs, were with corpses strewn,
> Then rowed each bark in fleeing disarray,
> Yea, every keel of our barbarian host.
> They with oar-fragments and with shards of wrecks

Smote, hacked, as men smite tunnies, or a draught
Of fishes ; and a moaning, all confused
With shrieking, hovered wide o'er that sea-brine
Till night's dark presence blotted out the horror.[1]

The Greeks, who under-estimated their victory, had spent the night on the beach of Salamis, prepared to renew the struggle in the morning ; but when day dawned the Persian fleet was nowhere in sight, and Hellas was saved.

The Retreat of Xerxes.—Towards the end of the battle Xerxes had hastily summoned a council of war and, heedless of Persian honour and prestige, had readily allowed himself to be persuaded by Mardonius to return to Sardes and to leave him with 300,000 troops to complete the subjugation of Greece. The unworthy monarch withdrew unmolested from Attica, as the Spartans took advantage of an eclipse of the sun, which occurred on 2nd October 480 B.C., as an excuse for not quitting their position at the Isthmus.

After halting in Thessaly, Xerxes continued the retreat, losing thousands of men on the road from hunger and disease. Finding the bridge at the Hellespont destroyed by a storm, he was glad to escape in a ship to the safety of Asia, where it is stated that thousands more of his famished soldiers died from surfeit. The Greeks pursued the Persian fleet, but in vain. Upon reaching Andros they held a council of war, at which Themistocles urged that they should sail north and destroy the Hellespont bridge. Eurybiades, however, as might have been expected, strongly objected, and on the defeat of his proposal the crafty Athenian made capital out of it and sent his servant to Xerxes with the information. It was actions like these which tarnished the lustre of the great Athenian's glory.

The Carthaginian Invasion of Sicily, 480 B.C.—Another act in the great drama was played in Sicily. The Carthaginians, probably instigated by Persian diplomacy, organized a powerful force to attack Hellas in Sicily, and after losing its cavalry and chariots in a storm the expedition reached Panormus. From this port Hamilcar the leader marched along the sea-coast to his objective, Himera, which he besieged. Gelon, tyrant of Syracuse, promptly came to the rescue of Theron of Himera with a force of 50,000 infantry and 5000 cavalry. The decisive battle was prefaced

---

[1] *The Persae*, translated by A. S. Way. A Persian is represented as speaking.

by the destruction of the Carthaginian sea-camp and the death of Hamilcar. This operation was carried out by Syracusan cavalry, who were admitted under the mistaken belief that they were allies. Gelon then attacked the panic-stricken Carthaginians, who offered little resistance and were cut down or captured almost to a man. The battle of Himera thus resulted in another decisive victory for Hellas.

The Campaign of Mardonius.—The curtain was now raised on the third and final act of the long, heroic struggle between the numbers of Asia and the highly disciplined and patriotic valour of the Greeks. While halting in Thessaly, Xerxes had entrusted to Mardonius the picked troops through whose instrumentality the gallant Persian general hoped to add Hellas to the long list of the provinces of the Great King. He was at last freed from the encumbrance of the undisciplined contingents, and, more important still, from the presence of the monarch and his courtiers, whose large retinues, while not adding materially to the fighting line, had to be fed before the warriors received their rations. Moreover, nothing is more true in war than that disaster almost certainly attends military operations when their conduct is interfered with by a court.

Before making any movement, Mardonius, whose experience of the Greeks was now considerable, not only consulted various oracles, but opened negotiations with the Athenians through King Alexander of Macedon, offering them the honoured position of allies of the Great King. The Spartans, hearing of this, despatched a special embassy to Athens, and although in the past the leading land power had played but a sorry rôle, the solemn oaths of the ambassadors were accepted by the sorely tried Athenians, who nobly refused the tempting offer, in the following terms : " So long as the sun runs his course in the heavens, we will never make terms with Xerxes." Mardonius, upon realizing that he could not detach the Athenians, marched south from Thessaly and reoccupied Athens ten months after its first capture ; and once again the Athenians, unsupported by their allies, transported their families to Salamis, where, this time, they were absolutely safe. At this point Mardonius again opened negotiations both with the Argives and with the Athenians, but without result. The Spartans, in face of these facts, continued to fortify the Isthmus before the necessity for offensive action dawned on their dull minds. They had, indeed, strained the loyalty of the Athenians very nearly to breaking point. At last, possibly owing to the death of Cleombrotus and the accession of Pausanias to the command, an active policy was adopted, and the army of the Peloponnesus, when once the order was given, marched swiftly north to meet the foe.

Mardonius, who had destroyed what was left of Athens, retired to Boeotia, where he was supported by allies and could use his cavalry to greater effect than in hilly Attica. The Greek army, which included no mounted troops, followed, and at first took up its position on the lower slopes of Mount Kithaeron, where it was less exposed than in the open plain to the attacks of the Persian cavalry. Mardonius sent all his cavalry, under Masistius, to harass the Greeks, and by charging in the Persian manner division after division, it inflicted considerable loss. Finally, however, the horse of Masistius was wounded and threw him. The Greeks then rushed forward and killed the prostrate leader. The Persian cavalry charged with the utmost fury to recover his body, but in vain ; and after incurring serious losses returned to camp much dejected.

The Battle of Plataea, 479 B.C.—Elated by this success, and influenced no doubt by the important matter of the water supply, the army of Hellas quitted the protection of the hills and took up an advanced position, with its left resting on a tributary of the Asopus River, and its right near the spring of Gargaphia. The main stream of the Asopus lay between the Greeks and the Persians. The Persian cavalry could now be employed more effectively. The new Greek position had ceased to protect the two passes across which their lines of communication ran, and as a result a convoy of five hundred pack animals, with its drivers, and presumably its escort, was cut to pieces by the Persians.

Mardonius, possibly owing to shortness of supplies, was anxious to fight a decisive battle. His plan was to weaken the Greek *moral* by a free use of his mounted troops, and in this he partially succeeded. His active horsemen "harassed the whole Greek army by hurling javelins and shooting arrows, being mounted archers who could not be brought to close combat. The spring of Gargaphia, too, from which the entire Greek army obtained water, they spoiled and filled up ! " This quotation from Herodotus indicates that the position of affairs was most favourable to the Persians. The Greek leaders, abandoning the offensive, decided to effect a night retreat to a better position near Plataea. This, the most difficult of all the operations of war, nearly proved disastrous; for one of the Spartan generals refused to retire for several hours, and the centre, composed of small contingents, lost touch with the wings. Consequently, daybreak found the main bodies of Spartan and Athenian troops out of effectual supporting distance of one another, the former being much nearer the foe; while the other allies were nowhere to be seen.

Mardonius must have believed the battle as good as won; for he had about 200,000 Persians and some 50,000 Greeks, to attack at most 100,000 Greeks,[1] who were split up into at least three divisions, none of which was able to support the other. Eager to close, he launched the cavalry, and followed with the "Immortals" to attack the Spartans, who, finding the omens unfavourable, at first supported passively the showers of arrows. At last the omens changed, and they fiercely charged their lightly armed enemy, with whom they came to close quarters. The Persians exhibited splendid courage, but their lack of armour made all their efforts fruitless. The battle was finally decided by the death of the gallant Mardonius, killed at the head of the "Immortals," who fell in thousands around his corpse. The loss of the commander, as so often happens with Asiatic armies, produced a panic; and the Persians fled in confusion back to their entrenched camp. Meanwhile the Athenians, who were marching to the help of the Spartans, were attacked by the formidable Hellenic contingent of Mardonius, which, however, with the exception of the Boeotians, displayed little zeal in their assault. Upon its retreat, the Athenians led the way in the successful assault on the stockade, for they were regarded as the engineers of Hellas, and the Spartans were awaiting their arrival.

In the Persian camp the slaughter was prodigious. The unnerved Asiatics offered little resistance, and Herodotus relates that only 3000 Persians escaped. He states, however, that an entire corps of 40,000 men under Artabazus, who had opposed the views of Mardonius and had advised a waiting game, retreated in perfect order from the battle-

---

[1] The numbers on both sides are probably exaggerated.

field, without even engaging the Greeks. Moreover, it is not to be believed that the large force of cavalry was overtaken by the Greek infantry.

Thanks mainly to Spartan valour, the victory of the Greeks was of the most decisive kind. Their army had been caught in the open and at great disadvantage, with only two divisions out of three on the battlefield, and these unable to support one another; and yet, in spite of these serious drawbacks and in the face of great odds, Greek training and armament had triumphed completely.

The Battle of Mycale, 479 B.C.—Just about the date of this epoch-making battle, if not on the same day as the Greeks would have it, the Persian fleet stationed off Samos was destroyed by the Greeks. Unwilling to face the victors of Salamis, the Persians drew their ships up on the mainland at Cape Mycale, where they were protected by a force of 60,000 men and an entrenched position. But the heroes of Hellas were not to be baulked of their prey, and following up the enemy on shore they won yet another glorious victory and burned the whole of the ships. This final blow shattered the power of Persia over the Greek islanders. Rebellion broke out in a blaze and spread like wildfire. The Athenians, who now assumed their rightful position as leaders at sea, aided this revolt, until the Hellenes in Europe and those of the islands were alike free and able to assist their brethren on the Asiatic mainland to regain their liberty.

The Capture of Sestos, 478 B.C.—The concluding feat of arms in this wonderful campaign was the capture of Sestos, which, from its situation on the European side of the Hellespont, served as an admirable *tête-de-pont* for the Great King. The Spartan squadron, whose leader was unable to realize the strategical necessity for the enterprise, sailed home, and to the perseverance of the Athenians was due the final capture of this important fortress. The Persian garrison escaped, but was pursued and overtaken. The capture of Sestos ended the Great Persian War, and is thus the final act of the stupendous drama.

The Final Results.—These titanic campaigns, in which the leading Aryan nation in Asia attacked its distant kinsmen in Europe, merit some retrospect, and the first question to be asked is why the Greeks won. Apart from their wonderful *moral*, they had the advantage of fighting on rugged ground with which they were familiar, and which suited their training and constitution, whereas the Persians were accustomed to the vast open plains of Asia, where infantry unsupported by cavalry is hopelessly inferior to a mobile mounted force. In addition to this, there was the difference in armament. The Greeks were trained to carry heavy armour with relative ease, and also to wield heavier weapons than their adversaries, who trusted to quantity rather than quality. Finally, although the organization of the Persian army was in itself remarkably efficient, the remoteness of Hellas from the Persian base stood her in good stead. It is possible to exaggerate the importance of the military results of these campaigns, inasmuch as, even if Xerxes had conquered Hellas, such a distant province could not have been held effectively for very long. As Grundy well puts it, " It was the war itself rather than its issue which proved the salvation of Greece." In other words, the bitter hostility aroused by the invasion saved the civilization of Hellas from being orientalized.

Many writers have assumed that the Persian Empire was doomed because of its repulse by the Greeks ; and there is no doubt that the miserable survivors of the Great Army carried the tale of defeat to every corner of the empire. Yet we see Persia play the leading rôle on the world's stage for another century and a half, and this proves that her race was by no means run. Indeed Greece, split up into small and generally rival states, was not, even after Marathon, Salamis, and Plataea, an equal opponent of the Lord of Asia ; and it was not until the rise of Macedonia and its paramountcy that Hellas, represented by a great genius for war, perhaps the greatest of all time, was strong enough to throw down the gauntlet of the challenger with success. Until then it was only the fringe of Asia Minor that was operated against by the Greeks, and the populations of the interior continued to obey the Satrap of Sardes.

But if writers on Greek history have exaggerated the force and weight of the blows inflicted on Persia in the repulse of the Great King, it is almost impossible to exaggerate the importance of the victories to Hellas and to modern civilization. Cyrus, after the defeat of Croesus, had annexed with conspicuous ease the Greek colonies on the coast of Asia Minor and the adjacent islands, and Darius after the Scythian War had detached a force which had extended Persian suzerainty to the borders of Northern Greece. Then, when the great expedition was launched, most of Northern and Central Hellas submitted, and practically only heroic Attica and the Peloponnesus (where, however, Argos was in favour of the Persians) were left ; and the enemy ravaged even Attica at will, and twice destroyed Athens. The victories of the Greeks at once freed the whole of Hellas and almost all her colonies in Europe and Asia Minor ; the islands simultaneously regained their liberty, and many of the cities on the mainland also. Indeed, thanks to the feebleness of character displayed by Xerxes, who, during the remainder of his inglorious reign, refused to face the Greek problem, Hellas ceased to act on the defensive and was able to assume the offensive. This rôle she maintained until Alexander burned the capital of Iran and became Lord of Asia. But there is the wider aspect of the case, the world aspect ; and, from this point of view, Marathon, Salamis, and Plataea were victories not only for Greece but for mankind. It was the triumph of the higher ideal, and even to-day we cannot estimate fully what we owe to those intrepid heroes, who wrought and fought as few have done before or since.

ACHAEMENIAN EAGLE.
(From a Gold Medallion, British Museum.)

CHAPTER XVIII

THE PERSIAN EMPIRE AFTER THE REPULSE FROM HELLAS

> This is Ahasuerus which reigned, from India even unto Ethiopia, over an hundred and seven and twenty provinces.—Esther i. 1.

Xerxes after the Retreat from Hellas.—Herodotus is our sole trustworthy authority for this period, and after the conclusion of his great work with the capture of Sestos the history of Persia becomes for a time somewhat obscure; for, although in the pages of Thucydides important events connected with Persia are referred to, no details are given. Xerxes spent more than a year at Sardes after his ignoble retreat, and apparently there were plans, which came to nothing, of leading a new expedition to overcome the Greeks. Meanwhile the licentious monarch became passionately enamoured of the wife of his brother Masistes; but, meeting with a rebuff, he transferred his affections to her daughter, and endeavoured to compass his evil ends by marrying the latter to his son Darius. Amestris, his royal consort, mad with jealousy, succeeded in getting her rival's mother into her power, and inflicted upon her horrible mutilations. Her fiendish action led Masistes to attempt to excite a revolt in Bactria; but he was overtaken on his way there and slain. Xerxes proceeded from Sardes to Susa and was lost to view for some years.

The Greek Raids on Asia Minor and the Battle of the Eurymedon, 466 B.C.—The expeditions of the Greeks, when once the King had retired to the centre of the empire, must have lost much of their importance from the Persian point of view; while for the Greeks it was impossible to strike a blow at the heart, the distance from their base being too great. At the same time, to Athens the continuance of hostilities was of vital importance. Through the instrumentality of the League of Delos, by the terms of which she organized and commanded the forces of her allies, a really formidable sea power was created. In 466 B.C., after twelve years of constant fighting, the efforts of the Greeks, under the inspiring leadership of Kimon, son of Miltiades, culminated in a splendid victory on the Eurymedon in the Gulf of Pamphylia, where, as at Mycale, they landed a force and defeated an entrenched Persian army, besides destroying the enemies' fleet. This victory was completed by the capture of a reinforcement of eighty Phoenician ships; and we may well believe that the Asiatic seamen, after these crushing losses, never willingly faced a Greek naval force, unless the odds were heavily in their favour.

The Assassination of Xerxes, 466 B.C.—The incapacity and viciousness of Xerxes apparently brought their own punishment; for, after a disastrous reign of twenty years, he was murdered by Artabanus, the captain of his guard.

His Character.—Of Xerxes, who, as already mentioned, is generally identified with the Ahasuerus of Holy Writ, little good can be said. He succeeded to the mightiest empire that the world had until then seen, together with a magnificent army and immense resources. In spite of this splendid inheritance, he allowed the Hellenes to frighten him away after a naval repulse; and, instead of continuing the war in order to wipe off the stain of defeat, he fled from rugged Hellas back to Asia, where, for the remainder of his reign, he abandoned himself to debauchery, and allowed eunuchs to direct the affairs of state.

The Accession of Artaxerxes I., 465 B.C.—Artabanus, according to one probable account, had as an accomplice the chief eunuch, who, after the murder of his master, roused the young prince Artakhohayarsha (Artaxerxes), then a mere boy, accused his elder brother Darius of the crime, and extracted an order for the execution of the latter, which was instantly carried out. Under such sinister conditions did

Artaxerxes I., known to history by the epithet of "Long hand,"[1] ascend the throne. For seven months Artabanus was the real king, and his name even appears in some chronologies; but his triumph was short-lived. Not content with the murder of his master and of his master's son, he aimed at the assassination of the young King also. On this occasion, however, he overreached himself and paid the penalty with his own life, the avenger being Bágathukhsha (Megabyzus), who was destined to play a leading part during the long reign of Artaxerxes.

The Rebellion of Hystaspes, 462 B.C.—Persia was by no means breaking up, in spite of these domestic convulsions, and when Vishtáspa (Hystaspes), an elder brother of the young King, rose in distant Bactria, he was attacked by the royal forces, with whom was Artaxerxes himself, and defeated in two battles about 462 B.C. These defeats evidently ruined his cause, for nothing more is heard of him.

The Revolt of Egypt, 460-454 B.C.—We have seen that, after the last revolt in Egypt, the hereditary princes were not deprived of their power; and in consequence, when the province of Libya rose under Inaros, son of Psammetichus, he was able to collect a considerable force. The Delta declared for him, but the Nile valley, in which the Persian garrison held all the important positions, did not rise. So far as can be judged, the revolt would have been crushed by the regent Achaemenes, but for the fact that the Athenians came to the assistance of the Egyptians. At this period Athens was at the zenith of her greatness, and a remarkable record still exists in the shape of a monument erected to the citizens of one tribe of the city, which bears 168 names of Athenian heroes, all of whom fell in battle in 459 B.C. (the year that the fleet went to Egypt), in Cyprus, Egypt, Phoenicia, Halieis (in the Argive Peninsula) and Aegina and Megara. Yet another naval battle, that of Kekryphalea, was fought in the same year. Surely such a record has seldom been equalled in the annals of any nation.

The fleet of 200 triremes now despatched to Egypt

---

[1] Nöldeke contends that the epithet expressed his great power; but it seems reasonable to connect it with a physical peculiarity. As an example, Yasht XVII. may be cited as follows:

> Beauteous art thou, Zarathustra,
> Shapely art thou, O Spitama;
> Fair of limb and long i' th'arm thou,
> Glory to thy body is given.

constituted a formidable force, capable of fighting by land as well as by sea ; and the allies met the Persian army at Papremis in the Delta, with the result that Achaemenes was slain and his army exterminated. At this juncture a second division of the Athenians fell in by chance with the Phoenician fleet, and the latter lost fifty ships sunk and captured. The Athenians, who were naturally elated by these victories, attacked Memphis, which they speedily took ; but the Persians held its fortress, known as the White Wall, and defied the assailants, who were forced to undertake a regular siege.

In the following year, 456 B.C., a Persian army numbering 300,000 men, supported by a fleet of 300 Phoenician ships, appeared on the scene under the capable leadership of Megabyzus. The allies raised the siege of the White Wall and met the enemy ; but, as almost invariably happened when they fought in the open, the Egyptian army suffered defeat, the pretender Inaros being wounded and captured. The Greek contingent retreated to the neighbouring island of Prosopis and withstood all assaults for a year and a half after the beginning of 455 B.C.

The Persian army, meanwhile, had laboured to divert a branch of the Nile, and one day the fleet was left high and dry and was burned by the desperate Greeks, most of whom perished in the subsequent Persian assault. The survivors, some six thousand strong, capitulated on honourable terms and were taken to Susa pending ratification of the agreement by the Great King. The Phoenicians now had their revenge for former defeats by sinking half of a tardy and quite inadequate reinforcement of fifty Greek triremes, which had entered one of the mouths of the Nile.

The defeat of the Greeks brought the rebellion to an end ; but a guerilla warfare was successfully maintained by a band of patriots who took refuge in the marshes and there proclaimed a reputed scion of the house of Amasis, by name Amonrut (Graecized as Amyrtaeus), as their king. Looked at from the military point of view, this campaign shows that even large bodies of Greek troops were not necessarily able to defeat the armies of Persia, and makes it probable that, had Artaxerxes been a man of character, the Greek colonies in Asia Minor would again have become subject to Persia, and the independence of Hellas would have been seriously menaced.

The Peace of Callias, circa 449 B.C.—The heavy blow dealt to the power of Athens in Egypt was, indeed, followed up to a certain extent by the attempt of the Persians to recapture Cyprus. The Athenians rose to the occasion, and in 449 B.C., after concluding a five years' peace with Sparta, despatched Kimon, Commander-in-Chief of the League, with a fleet of 200 triremes; but this able leader died before any decisive success could be claimed. The fleet was apparently forced by scarcity of supplies to raise the blockade of Kition in Cyprus, but when passing Salamis, in the same island, it fell in with a Phoenician fleet, three hundred strong, which had been disembarking troops. As on two previous occasions, the Greeks not only defeated the fleet, capturing 100 triremes and sinking others, but completed their success by a victory gained against the forces on land.

The Athenians promptly took advantage of this brilliant achievement to come to terms with the Great King. Callias, a leading statesman, proceeded to Susa and an agreement was effected, by the terms of which Artaxerxes recognized the independence of all the Greeks who were members of the League of Delos, and at the same time agreed that no warships but only merchantmen should enter Hellenic waters. The Greeks, on their part, renounced all ideas of freeing the remaining Greeks from the Persian yoke, and, hardest of all, they gave up their claims to Cyprus.[1] But they showed extreme prudence in ratifying the treaty; for they ran the greatest risk of exhausting Attica's scanty population, on which heavy calls were constantly being made to maintain the power of Athens at home. Moreover, Cyprus was too far from Attica and too near Phoenicia for a continuance of the struggle to be profitable. Thanks to this peace, Athens suffered no apprehension of attack from Persia until the fear of that empire as an aggressive power had entirely passed away.

Spain and England compared with Persia and Athens.—If we look down the ages and substitute Spain for Persia, which in some respects it closely resembles from the physical point of view, and England for Athens, we see a powerful empire, which included many rich countries of Europe and

---

[1] Holm (ii. p. 176) denies that there was such a treaty and advances various reasons. It would appear possible that there was no formal treaty, but that the Great King sealed an order embodying these terms and thereby saved his face.

drained the wealth of the New World, assailing a country which was relatively as poor as Athens, though numerically stronger. As in the earlier case, the overwhelming might of the great empire was repulsed at sea by the dauntless valour and seamanship of our ancestors, and although, as in the war with Persia, after the defeat of the Great Armada other battles were fought with varying success, the defensive was then exchanged for the offensive. Like the Athenians after Salamis, the English sailors after 1588 were always ready to attack their foemen even in the face of apparently hopeless odds.

The Rebellion of Megabyzus.—The career of Megabyzus throws considerable light on the state of Persia under one of its most incompetent monarchs. He had granted honourable terms of capitulation to the remnant of the Greek forces in Egypt and had promised to spare the life of Inaros. Amestris, however, had to be reckoned with, and after five years' incessant importunity on her part, Inaros was impaled to avenge Achaemenes, and some fifty Greeks were at the same time beheaded to satisfy this fiendish woman. This was a deadly offence in the eyes of Megabyzus, who revolted and defeated successively two armies that were sent against him. He was thereupon pardoned and reappeared at Court. Having, however, been invited to take part in a lion hunt, he came between the monarch and his quarry, and for this high offence was sentenced to death: but the doom was commuted into banishment to the shores of the Persian Gulf. After spending five years in this desolate part of the empire, he gave out that he was suffering from leprosy and returned to Persia, no one taking the risk of stopping him. Finally he was again pardoned by the Great King, and lived to a green old age as his trusted adviser.

A Period of Anarchy, 425 B.C.—Artaxerxes, in spite of his incompetency and the evil influence of the Queen Mother, reigned for many years without any serious breach of the peace. Indeed, during this period the Athenians were fighting against Sparta for their very existence as a state, and this effectually prevented them from attempting any distant adventure. When he died in 425 B.C. he was succeeded by his son, Xerxes II., who was quickly murdered when drunk by his brother Soghdianos. This prince in turn was attacked by Ochus, another son of Artaxerxes, the husband of Parysatis, daughter of Artaxerxes. The Persian nobles flocked to his standard, and Soghdianos, to whom a proposal was made to rule in common, was treacherously seized, and suffered capital punishment in the Persian mode by being thrown into the ashes.

The Reign of Darius Nothus, 424-404 B.C.—After the overthrow of his brother, Ochus ascended the throne under the title of Darius II.[1] As Parysatis and three eunuchs were his chief advisers, it is not surprising that his reign was a constant series of insurrections. The first of these was raised by his brother Arsites, who was joined by Artyphius, a son of Megabyzus; and with the co-operation of Greek mercenaries he won two victories. The Greeks were then corrupted by the gold of the Great King, which was destined thenceforward to be Persia's most powerful weapon. The rebels foolishly surrendered on promise of good treatment, but oaths were no longer binding in Persia, and they too like Soghdianos were thrown into the ashes. Yet another rebel, Pissuthnes, the Satrap of Lydia, was deserted by his Athenian mercenaries, who could not resist the gold of Darius. Forced to surrender, he met the same terrible fate. Tissaphernes, thanks to whose devices he was successfully captured, was appointed Satrap of Lydia in his place, and for many years employed his remarkable talent for intrigue with such success that he acquired a very powerful influence in the politics of Greece. Pharnabazus, Satrap of Daskyleion, was also a very important Persian Governor at this period.

Tissaphernes and the Alliance with Sparta, 412 B.C.—It was at this period that the Athenian expedition to Sicily ended as disastrously as that of the Carthaginians at the time of Salamis and Plataea. The wily Tissaphernes quickly appreciated the new conditions, and made an agreement with Sparta, by the terms of which the two powers undertook to levy war on Athens. Thus the old order, according to which the two chief states of Hellas set aside their local divisions and united to oppose Persia, gave place to the new, and we see Sparta, followed by Athens, and later by Thebes, making agreements with Persia, each in turn, for an attack on home rivals. Tissaphernes played his part with consummate skill, and by not carrying assistance so far as to enable any one of the combatants

---

[1] The epithet "Nothus," signifying a bastard, was bestowed in reference to the fact that his mother was a concubine.

to defeat another decisively and so upset the balance of power, he maintained Persian influence and interests, and even extended them in Asia Minor, without great military effort or heavy expenditure. From this period dates the weakening of Persian military spirit. Sapped by their monarch's example and by too much prosperity, the army had to be stiffened by Greek mercenaries, who were introduced in large numbers, and whose leaders were allowed to fill the highest commands both by land and by sea. This new departure was to have sinister consequences.

The Story of Terituchmes.—The complete degeneration of the Persian Court from the high ideals of Cyrus and Darius I. is illustrated in the reign of the unworthy Darius II. by the story of Terituchmes. This infamous creature was the son-in-law of the Great King; but, having fallen in love with his half-sister, Roxana, entered into a plot against his father-in-law in order that he might be freed from his wife, Amestris. The leading conspirators all swore to plunge their swords into a sack in which the hapless Amestris was to be fastened, in order that they might realize that there was no possibility of going back. But the plot failed and Terituchmes was killed. This revolt gave Parysatis full scope for her cruelty. First of all Roxana was cut in pieces, and then all the relations of the rebel, including his mother and sister, were buried alive. Such was the Persian Court under this degraded monarch.

DOUBLE SILVER SHEKEL OF SIDON.
(Obverse—war galley. Reverse—the Great King in chariot followed by an attendant. Coin attributed to Abdastart (Strato II.).)

CHAPTER XIX

THE DECLINE OF THE PERSIAN EMPIRE

A man, of all the Persians who existed after the ancient Cyrus, the most kingly and worthy to command, as is acknowledged by all those who seem ever to have had an opportunity of judging.—XENOPHON on Cyrus the Younger.

Cyrus the Younger.—There is no single campaign in Asia which has excited greater interest than that of Cyrus the Younger, mainly owing to the famous exploits of the Greek force which served under him and the genius of Xenophon; but there is also the sympathy excited by the refreshingly virile and energetic nature of the Great Adventurer, which contrasts so favourably with that of the effete Persian monarchs and strikes the reader as gratefully as a cool breeze does the dweller in the tropics.

Cyrus the Younger was the second son of Darius II., his elder brother being Arsaces, who afterwards reigned as Artaxerxes II.; but whereas Arsaces had been born while his father was holding the post of Satrap of Hyrcania, Cyrus was born in the purple. He was also the favourite of his terrible mother, by whose influence he was appointed Viceroy of Asia Minor with practically independent powers, and assured that during his absence from Court she was working in his interests.

His Relations with Sparta.—The youthful ruler was resolved from the first to strengthen his position, and as he realized the immense superiority of Greek troops, he determined to make full use of his official position to collect and organize a formidable army. After studying the situation

DECLINE OF THE PERSIAN EMPIRE

with care, he came to the conclusion that the Spartan confederacy was more likely to serve his ends than a sea power like Athens; and he accordingly favoured the Spartans. The financial support which he gave to their extremely clever leader Lysander helped the latter to win the decisive battle of Aegospotami in 405 B.C.

Tissaphernes, whose position was weakened, and who realized that Cyrus was preparing to rebel, conveyed a timely warning to the Great King. The ambitious prince was summoned to Susa to justify his conduct; but he arrived just in time to be present at the death of his father, in 404 B.C.

The Accession of Artaxerxes Mnemon, 404 B.C.—Arsaces, in spite of the influence of Parysatis, was acknowledged heir, and ascended the throne as Artaxerxes II., with the sobriquet of Mnemon or "The Thoughtful." He was crowned at Pasargadae,[1] and Cyrus, it is stated, determined to murder his brother at the altar during the ceremony; but Tissaphernes was warned and the would-be assassin was seized. The King, enraged, ordered his instant execution; but the Queen-Mother shielded him with her arms and finally obtained his pardon. The foolish Artaxerxes, with true Persian magnanimity, allowed his madly ambitious brother to return to Asia Minor, where, as was to be expected, he immediately prepared to fight for the throne.

His Greek general was Clearchus, a Spartiate of character and experience, and he speedily enrolled a formidable force of Greek mercenaries. Cyrus also applied to Sparta and, although open support was not granted, a body of 700 hoplites was despatched to serve under him. His army ultimately attained the considerable total of 13,000 Greeks and 100,000 Asiatics; and in 401 B.C. the Great Adventurer started from his headquarters to fight for the lordship of Asia.

The March of Cyrus on Babylon.—Upon quitting Sardes, Cyrus, careful to conceal his objective from all but his chief advisers, gave out that the expedition was intended to subdue the Pisidians. He marched through Phrygia and Mysia, meeting on his way Epyaxa, wife of Syennesis, King of Cilicia, who gave him large sums of money. He then made a wide semicircle and bore down on the famous Cilician Gates, which according to Xenophon " were exceedingly precipitous and impracticable for an army to enter, if any one should oppose

---

[1] *Vide* Plutarch's *Life of Artaxerxes*, where an interesting account is given of the occurrence.

their passage."[1] Upon his arrival he found the heights occupied ; but Syennesis made the fact that the troops of Menon, Cyrus's Thessalian general, had already landed in Cilicia an excuse for withdrawing his force during the night ; and the army reached Tarsus without striking a blow.

Cyrus now experienced considerable difficulty with his Greek troops. Xenophon, who was destined to play so important a part in this famous expedition, describes how, at first, they refused to proceed, and indeed stoned Clearchus ; but they were finally persuaded by an increase of pay to march forward, although their consent was reluctantly given. Cyrus now gave out that his objective was the army of Abrocomas, Satrap of Syria, who, it was believed, would dispute the passage of the Euphrates ; and he marched swiftly through the Gates of Syria, the Thermopylae of Asia, keeping touch with his fleet and prepared to land troops in the rear of any defending force. But Abrocomas had no intention of opposing the Great King's brother, who, traversing fertile Syria, reached Thapsacus on the Euphrates. There he learned that Abrocomas had retreated, after burning all the boats he could find.

At Thapsacus the Greeks found themselves finally committed without hope of retreat to a campaign against the Great King ; and again there were serious divisions, the soldiers being enraged with their generals for deceiving them. But an appeal to their love of money once more won the day. For an increase of pay they decided to run all risks ; and this was readily granted by Cyrus, who was a gambler, staking everything on success.

The unusually low state of the Euphrates favoured the invaders, who forded it and pressed on rapidly, marching at the rate of nearly twenty miles a day and neither seeing nor hearing anything of the enemy. As Xenophon points out, the object was to prevent the Great King from mustering his full strength.

The Battle of Cunaxa, 401 B.C.—Upon entering the rich province of Babylon they met some light cavalry ; but found no signs of the Persian army as they continued their march steadily southwards. After advancing in battle array for three days Cyrus, who does not seem to have been well served by his spies, came to the somewhat natural conclusion that

[1] *Anabasis*, translation by Wheeler, i. 2. 21. The "Gates" are graphically described in David Fraser's *The Short Cut to India*, p. 71.

DECLINE OF THE PERSIAN EMPIRE

Artaxerxes had abandoned Babylon and retreated to the uplands of Persia. But he was mistaken, and on the fourth day, when his troops were marching in somewhat careless order, there suddenly appeared a horseman with the warning that the huge army of the Great King would be upon them in a few hours. Thanks to this timely notice, Cyrus was able to form line of battle. The Greek contingent under Clearchus he posted on the right, resting on the Euphrates. Cyrus, following the invariable Persian custom, took post himself in the centre, surrounded by a mounted guard of six hundred heavily armed men. Ariaeus commanded the left, where the greater part of the cavalry was massed.

The immense army of Artaxerxes, numbering, it is stated, half a million, overlapped that of Cyrus; but he, realizing that everything depended on defeating the centre, where the Great King was posted, ordered Clearchus to lead the Greeks at the heart of the enemy. Clearchus did not rise to the occasion, but, fearing to leave both his flanks unprotected, replied evasively that "it would be his care that all should be well," and kept close to the Euphrates.

The battle opened by an advance of the Greeks at the double against the scythed chariots that faced them, and of which great things were expected. The result was most extraordinary, for the drivers of the famous chariots and the whole of the line turned and fled, pursued by the Greek hoplites for two or three miles.

Cyrus saw the rout of the Persian left wing; but realized that until the centre was broken the action could not be decisive. Great general that he was, he curbed his natural impetuosity until he saw the Persian centre bear down on the rear of the Greeks, and then made his grand charge, leading his gallant six hundred against the six thousand Cadusians of the Great King. With his own hand he slew the leader of the opposing force, and the drama heightened in intensity as they wavered and the way lay open to where Artaxerxes was stationed. Mad with hatred and the lust of battle, Cyrus shouted out, "I see the man," and, hurling a javelin, struck his brother full on the breast, pierced his cuirass, and unhorsed him. The lordship of Asia must have seemed to him already gained, when he was suddenly wounded by a javelin near the eye, and in the mêlée which ensued he was slain. Artaxerxes, who was but slightly wounded, hearing of the death of his brother, advanced against the Asiatic troops. They, learning that Cyrus was dead, retreated northwards.

Tissaphernes, on the extreme left of the Persian line, had charged through the light-armed contingent of the Greeks without inflicting loss, and had attacked their camp, from which he was repulsed. Clearchus returned from the pursuit on hearing that his camp was in danger, and in anticipation of an enveloping attack the Greeks formed up with their back to the river and charged a second time. Again the craven Persian host, unlike their brave forefathers, refused to face the terrible hoplites. Consequently the Greeks, after pursuing their cowardly opponents, returned to camp victorious so far as they knew; though actually the day was lost, owing mainly to the bad generalship of Clearchus.

The result of Cunaxa, by which name the battle was known, was stupendous, as the Greeks now learned that they could drive a Persian host before them like a flock of sheep, and although advantage was not taken of their immeasurable superiority for many years, it is certain that Alexander based his calculations on the experience of Cunaxa. For Persia the death of Cyrus the Younger was a great misfortune, as, with his great capacity, his energy, and his varied experience, he would have been an ideal Great King, and might even have restored the empire to the position it held under Cyrus the Great and Darius. In any case, he would have revitalized Persia and, with his knowledge of the Greeks and skill to play off one state against another, might have destroyed the independence of Hellas. *Dis aliter visum.*

The Retreat of the Ten Thousand.—Few of the exploits of mankind challenge our admiration more than the retreat of the immortal Ten Thousand. The morning after the battle the Greeks were on the point of advancing to effect a junction with Cyrus, when they were informed of his death and of the flight of his Persian adherents. Nothing daunted, Clearchus sent to offer the throne to Ariaeus : but he prudently declined it on the ground that the Persian nobility would not accept him. Later in the day heralds arrived from Tissaphernes summoning the Greeks " to deliver up their arms and to proceed to the King's porte,[1] to obtain any favourable terms they could." This summons provoked

---

[1] It is extraordinary how widespread is this idea of the Sublime Porte. The terms Pharaoh and Mikado both convey a similar meaning.

DECLINE OF THE PERSIAN EMPIRE

intense indignation, but after discussing the situation and receiving the refusal of Ariaeus, the Greeks decided that to advance farther would be unwise. Their celebrated retreat began by a night march which brought them back to the spot they had left the day before the battle, and here they rejoined the troops of Ariaeus. A council was held, at which the Persian general pertinently pointed out that the question of supplies made a retreat along the route which they had come impossible, and he recommended a longer route to the north. He added that two or three forced marches would make them safe from the Great King, whose vast army moved slowly, while he would not dare to attack with a small force.

In the morning, accordingly, the united forces marched north, but to their surprise fell in with the Great King's army. The Persians were more alarmed than the Greeks, who, however, were in a state of panic all night. The next day negotiations for a truce were opened by Tissaphernes, and after much discussion it was agreed that the Greeks should be allowed to return home unmolested. Finally they marched off, the forces of Tissaphernes and Ariaeus—the latter had meanwhile made his peace with the Great King—accompanying them, and reached the Tigris, which they crossed by a bridge of thirty-seven boats.

Four more stages brought them to Opis, the site of which is now known, and passing it they reached the Lesser Zab. Here Tissaphernes enticed Clearchus and the other generals to a meeting at which they were treacherously seized. This trial, perhaps the severest that a body of men in their situation could undergo, did not cause the heroic Greeks to surrender, as most troops would have done. They chose the leader of the Spartan contingent as their commander, with Xenophon as his Chief of Staff, and the march was resumed, with the Persian host now openly hostile. The little army, passing, and marvelling at, the ancient cities of Assyria, was, in spite of the agreement, intermittently harassed by Tissaphernes, whose attacks, however, were feeble and half-hearted, and whose force invariably retired early, in order to camp at a distance from the dreaded Hellenes.

The Persians were finally shaken off; but the difficulties experienced in the mountains of the Carduchi or Kurds and in the highlands of Armenia were greater than those from which they were relieved. The attacks of the wild tribesmen were invariably defeated by a display of fine hill tactics, in which the Greek highlanders were past masters, and supplies were generally obtainable, but they had to face great physical difficulties, such as heavy snowfalls and intense cold, and it speaks highly both for the *moral* of the troops and for the influence of Xenophon that their losses were so small. Onward they marched, passing to the west of Lake Van and across the backbone of Asia Minor, until at last, on a happy day, they climbed a pass from which the sea was visible and arrived at Trapezus, the modern Trebizond, after accomplishing a feat which has never been surpassed.

It is now more than twenty years since I first visited Trebizond, but never shall I forget the thrill I experienced when there was pointed out to me the distant pass from which resounded the joyous shouts of θάλασσα ! θάλασσα ! " The Sea ! the Sea ! " or when I visited Campos, the alleged site of the historical camp in which those heroes of all time rested, after their unparalleled hardships and magnificent feats of valour.

Persia and Hellas after Cunaxa.—It was a natural result of the defeat of Cyrus that the alliance of Persia with the leading power of Hellas was broken off, on account of the assistance given to the Pretender. Far from craving pardon, Sparta, after the experience gained at Cunaxa, ultimately engaged the Ten Thousand to protect the Hellenes of Asia against the Satraps Tissaphernes and Pharnabazus, who were so jealous of one another that each was ready to pay heavily for the assistance of Greek arms against his rival. Again, however, Persian gold was the supreme factor. At one time it seemed possible that not only the Greek colonies, but the whole of Asia Minor, would shake off the Persian yoke ; but Persian gold prevailed. Agesilaus, who was conducting the operations with great skill, and who gained a decisive victory on the Pactolus which led to the execution of Tissaphernes, was summoned home to meet a league which had been formed by Thebes, Argos, Corinth, and Athens, against Sparta, as a result of Persian intrigue supported by Persian money.[1]

Athens in her turn became the ally of Persia, and Conon,

---

[1] Agesilaus made the witty remark that a thousand Persian archers had driven him out of Asia, referring to the daric, which was stamped with the figure of an archer, as figured in the headpiece to Chapter XVI.

who after the disaster at Aegospotami had fled to Cyprus and had entered the Persian service under Pharnabazus, defeated the Spartan fleet at Cnidus in 394 B.C., and thereby indirectly restored to Athens the command of the sea. As a sequel to this victory a Persian fleet under Pharnabazus and his Athenian admiral ravaged the coast of the Peloponnesus, and the long walls of Athens were rebuilt under its protection and by means of the all-pervading gold of Persia. How completely the situation had altered is shown by the fact that Thebes, the erstwhile deadly foe of Athens, in common with other states, helped on the work.

The Peace of Antalcidas, 387 B.C.—In this manner the Persian Viceroy, by skilful diplomacy which consisted mainly in playing off the weak states of Hellas against Sparta, re-established the balance of power in Greece. The prestige of Persia was restored most of all by the manifestation of the Great King's sea power in Peloponnesian waters, to which it had never previously penetrated, and in the end Sparta appealed for peace. For some years negotiations dragged on, partly at any rate, in order to enhance the dignity of the Persian monarch, and finally, after the Spartan ambassador Antalcidas had spent some time at Susa, peace was made, not by a treaty but by an edict of the Great King, who proclaimed that all the continent of Asia Minor, together with Cyprus and Clazomene, formed part of the Persian Empire, but that every state of Hellas not under Persian domination should be autonomous, with the exception of Lemnos, Imbros, and Skyros retained by Athens. This peace, to which the leading states subscribed, was very favourable to Persia, inasmuch as it restored her lost possessions, and prevented future interference by Hellas in Asia Minor. In short, the peace of Callias was annulled. The prestige of the Great King must have been immensely augmented, and the constant drain of defending Asia Minor ceased.

To Hellas this edict was humiliating, but to Sparta individually it was favourable, for she retained all her territory and was thus enabled to play the leading rôle in Hellas until, the cup of her tyranny being full, her arrogance received a humbling lesson at the battle of Leuctra in 371 B.C., through the instrumentality of Epaminondas of Thebes.

The Egyptian Campaigns.—The weakening of the central

government naturally reacted on the position in Egypt, where the descendants of the ruling families had retained their powers, and when about 405 B.C. a second Amonrut, or Amyrtaeus, grandson of the first, headed a revolt in the Delta, his cause was strongly supported. As Egyptians figure prominently on the roll of troops that fought at Cunaxa, it would appear that Amyrtaeus ruled only a portion of Egypt ; but his short reign of six years was so much of a reality that his name was inscribed by the chronologists of the sacred colleges in the list of the Pharaohs. Upon his death a Mendesian dynasty, founded by Naifaaurut (called by the Greeks Nepherites), completed his work and succeeded in regaining liberty for Egypt. Directing their policy with great capacity, they encouraged with money and troops every conspiracy and every rebellion that might occupy Persia ; and alliances were formed with Cyprus, Caria, and even with distant Hellas. Nor were preparations for war omitted. Large numbers of Greek mercenaries were engaged, and the most experienced generals of the age, the Egyptians realizing as fully as the Persians their marked inferiority to the warlike and well-disciplined Hellenes.

Fortunately for Egypt, the after-effects of Cunaxa included rebellions among most of the warlike tribes of Asia Minor. Cyprus, too, under Evagoras, with the support of both Greece and Egypt, became a centre of hostility to Persia, and in a sense an outwork of the kingdom of the Nile. Hakor, or Achoris, the successor of Nephorites, had between 390 and 386 B.C. repulsed a Persian attack, of which the details are not known. Instead of resting on his laurels, he strengthened the King of Cyprus with consignments of corn and money, while Athens sent a strong force under Chabrias, one of her leading generals. So strong did Evagoras consider his position that he raided the mainland and actually captured Tyre.

The position of affairs appeared to be growing steadily brighter for Egypt when the peace of Antalcidas changed the entire situation. Cyprus was the first to suffer, Artaxerxes collecting a huge force for its recapture as a preliminary to the attack on Egypt ; and Evagoras, after occupying the armies of the Great King for some ten years and thereby rendering great service to Egypt, obtained most favourable terms and was permitted to retain Salamis and the title of King.

ACHAEMENIAN GOLD JUG IN THE BRITISH MUSEUM.
(From *Treasure of the Oxus*.)
(For description *vide* Chapter XV.)

DECLINE OF THE PERSIAN EMPIRE

Artaxerxes was at last free to deal with Egypt, and for three years preparations on an immense scale were made at Acre, which was selected as the base. King Nekhthorheb, who now ruled Egypt, did all he could to meet the coming storm by hiring Greek troops and by building fortifications with the skill Egyptians have always shown. The Athenian general Chabrias was engaged as his Commander-in-Chief and the Delta was transformed into an entrenched camp. In the spring of 374 B.C. the expedition was ready. It consisted of 200,000 Asiatic troops and 20,000 Greeks, supported by 300 triremes, under the supreme command of Pharnabazus. The influence of the Great King was strong enough to secure the recall of Chabrias and to obtain for Persia the services of Iphicrates, the most famous general of Athens.

The fortifications of Pelusium, strengthened by inundations, were found too formidable to attack, and consequently, on the advice of Iphicrates, a force was secretly landed at the mouth of the Mendesian branch of the Nile. The enemy made a sortie from their fort, and upon their retreat the Persian troops gained an entrance with them. By this initial success, the line of defences was pierced, and if the advice of Iphicrates had been followed to press on to Memphis, which had been denuded of its garrison, Egypt would in all probability have been conquered. Pharnabazus, however, was too old to take great risks, and in consequence of his procrastination the Egyptians resumed the offensive. Iphicrates, indignant, returned to Greece, and when the Nile began to rise, the Persian army retreated and Egypt was saved.

The Expedition against the Cadusians.—During this period the Cadusians were in revolt, and Artaxerxes in person took command against them with the usual unwieldy army. This tribe inhabited the modern province of Gilan, which is almost impassable from its dense forests, its rugged ranges, and its many rivers. The Cadusians, who confined themselves to a guerilla warfare, cut off the supplies of the Persians and reduced them to serious straits. But the two leading chiefs were played off against one another and terms were arranged. The Persian army returned to the Iranian plateau safe but unsuccessful.

The Latter Days of Artaxerxes Mnemon.—In spite of the entire failure of the expedition against Egypt, the Greeks, blinded by mutual jealousies, sent Antalcidas again to Susa in 372 B.C. to obtain a fresh edict for putting an end to the existing hostilities in Hellas. In 367 B.C. envoys from Thebes approached the Great King, and in the following year others from Athens, for in spite of his real weakness he was universally accepted as arbiter in the quarrels of the Greeks—so low had Hellas fallen.

In remarkable contrast with the estimation in which he was held by the Greek states was the position of Artaxerxes at home during the closing years of his reign. First one and then another Satrap revolted, through fear of royal disfavour or from personal ambition. Tjeho or Tachós, the new Pharaoh, took advantage of the general disquiet to invade Syria; but during his absence a revolution, aided by the aged Agesilaus, who appears at his worst in Egypt, forced Tachós to flee to Susa, and local disturbances paralysed Egypt for some years. At one time it seemed as though the break-up of the Persian empire were imminent; but bribery, treachery, and the good fortune which caused the enemies of Artaxerxes to fight among themselves saved the situation.

Artaxerxes died at a great age, in 358 B.C., after a reign of forty-six years. He appears to have been a mild monarch, very generous and always ready to pardon; but he was entirely dominated by the terrible Parysatis, who maintained her hold upon him even after poisoning his wife, Statira, to whom he was fondly attached. It was on her evil advice that her weak son married his own daughter Atossa, an act which led to future calamities. It remains to add that Artaxerxes set up images to Anahita, goddess of fecundity, and thereby marked a development in the national religion, into which the Semitic-Babylonian idea of a nature-goddess had now penetrated. Of still greater importance was the revival by this monarch of the worship of Mithra. After a long eclipse during the period of the Gathas and Achaemenian inscriptions, we find the god of compact developing into the great warrior god. As Moulton writes, " Whatever the origin of the duality, he was also on the way to the *sol invictus* of Mithraism." [1]

The Accession of Artaxerxes III., 358 B.C.—The old King is believed to have had more than one hundred sons by the

---

[1] *Early Zoroastrianism*, p. 138. An inscription found in the palace of Artaxerxes Mnemon at Susa runs, " By the grace of Ahura Mazda, Anahita and Mithra, I built this palace."

hundreds of concubines in his harem; but most of them died before their father, and only the three sons of the Greek lady Statira, Darius, Ariaspes, and Ochus, were regarded as legitimate and eligible for the succession. Darius had been nominated heir-apparent some years before, but Ochus, an arch-intriguer and a worthy descendant of Parysatis, induced him to attempt the murder of the old King, who, Ochus alleged, intended to pass him over in the succession. Darius fell into the trap, failed, and was executed. Ochus also terrified Ariaspes by declaring that he was to be executed for complicity in the plot, and the unhappy prince committed suicide to avoid this disgrace. By these acts of treachery Ochus, assisted by Atossa, to whom he had promised marriage, became the heir-apparent, and upon the death of the King, whose end was hastened by these domestic tragedies, he ascended the throne with the title of Artaxerxes III. He inaugurated his reign by massacring all the princes of the blood; and even, it is said, the princesses were not spared.

The Capture of Sidon and the Reconquest of Egypt, 342 B.C. —The throne of the new monarch was by no means secure. The failure of his father to reconquer Egypt had turned that country into an anti-Persian centre, from which aid of every kind poured out to rebellious Satraps or to states attempting to shake off their allegiance. It was clear to Ochus that he could not hope to deal successfully with other rebellions until Egypt was once more conquered. The first attempt was a complete failure. The army of the Egyptian king Nekhtnebf (Nectanebo) under Greek commanders inflicted a crushing defeat on the Persian forces, and drove them to a precipitate retreat. At no period had Egypt been so strongly fortified, and the *moral* of even her native troops must have been excellent. In consequence of this disaster not only Syria, Asia Minor, and Cyprus, but even the Phoenicians rebelled, and under Tennes, King of Sidon, burned the royal palace on the Lebanon and the depots of supplies collected for the Egyptian campaign. The Athenian general of Ochus was successful in Cyprus; but in Asia Minor the rebellious Satrap of Phrygia, supported by both Athens and Thebes, held his own; and Tennes gained a victory in Syria which secured the support of Nectanebo, who placed four thousand Greek mercenaries at his disposal.

Ochus was not a weakling like his father. Raising

another huge force, he advanced in person on Sidon, which was defended by high walls and a triple trench. Tennes, hoping to save himself thereby, basely betrayed the leading citizens into his hand, and the Greek mercenaries sent from Egypt were corrupted by the all-powerful daric. The Sidonians thereupon gave up all thought of defence. Their representatives to the number of five hundred were slain by the bloodthirsty monarch, and the rest of the townsmen resolved to make one holocaust of themselves, their families, and their homes. They carried out their dreadful purpose, and when Ochus entered the city he found only a heap of ruins. These he sold for a large sum to treasure-hunters. The infamous Tennes was executed as soon as Sidon had been captured, and the other Phoenician cities submitted.

The Persian army, having suffered little delay at Sidon, resumed its southward march along the ancient route to Egypt. Pelusium was reached, and the invaders drew off the water in the protecting canal and erected battering-rams; but the Egyptians saved the situation by constructing a second wall behind that which was threatened. As before, the invasion made no headway, and it seemed probable that the floods would again baffle the Persian army. But a Greek general in the Persian service with much daring made his way up a canal to the rear of the Egyptian army, where he was attacked but repulsed his assailants. Nectanebo, realizing that his communications were threatened, retreated upon Memphis, and the garrisons of Pelusium and other important centres, believing that they were deserted, capitulated. In consequence of these disasters, Egypt fell again into the hands of Persia in 342 B.C. Ochus treated the country with pitiless and wanton cruelty. Following the impolitic example of Cambyses, he not only slew the bull Apis, but had it served up at a banquet which he gave to celebrate the capture of the White Walls of Memphis. He spoiled temples, destroyed cities, and killed thousands of Egyptians. Having thus inspired terror of the Persian name, he returned to Babylon.

The Murder of Artaxerxes III., 338 B.C.—The triumphant success of the campaign in Egypt had a pacifying effect upon the western portion of the Empire. Artabazus, who had been in rebellion for several years, fled to Macedonia; and other kings and princes hastened to make submission. The rival states of Hellas fawned upon the Great King, hastened to carry out his orders, and thirsted for his darics. Yet the state of the satrapies had much changed since the time of Darius. The Caspian provinces, which were almost inaccessible, retained their independence, and the Panjab had entirely thrown off Persian suzerainty. Elsewhere there was a slackening of the strict control which was necessary for maintaining the integrity of an empire so huge. Ochus was, however, strong and capable, and, under the able administration of the eunuch Bagoas, not only did the machinery of government improve, but the rising power of Macedonia was jealously watched and thwarted. The policy of this statesmanlike eunuch was frustrated by intrigues, which became so serious that in the end he found himself compelled, in 338 B.C., to assassinate his master as the only alternative to being himself put to death. Most of the King's sons he murdered with him, but Arses, the youngest, he placed on the throne. Even this youth upon showing dangerous signs of independence was also murdered by the merciless eunuch.

The Accession of Darius Codomannus, 336 B.C.—He now selected a certain Codomannus, whose birth was obscure, but who was probably a scion of the Achaemenian race, and he ascended the vacant throne under the title of Darius III. The last member of an illustrious line, he excites a certain amount of sympathy. He had gained a reputation for bravery in the Cadusian campaign by slaying a gigantic tribesman in single combat, and had been appointed Satrap of Armenia as a reward. He appears to have been in character more generous and less vicious than any of his immediate predecessors, and had the circumstances of his reign been normal, he might have ruled with credit. Unfortunately for him, a new power, led by the greatest soldier of all time, had arisen in the West, and Darius, although backed by all the resources of the Persian Empire, quailed and fell before the fiery onset of Alexander the Great.

COIN OF PHILIP OF MACEDON.

CHAPTER XX

THE RISE OF MACEDONIA UNDER PHILIP AND ALEXANDER

What a man had we to fight! For the sake of power and dominion he had an eye thrust out, a shoulder broken, an arm and a leg mortified. Whichever member fortune demanded, that he cast away, so that the rest might be in glory and honour.
—DEMOSTHENES on Philip of Macedon (*De Corona*, 67).

The Geography of Macedonia.—To those who, like myself, believe that the influence of geography on history is profound, it is of interest to observe that Nature, by breaking up the Peloponnesus and Central Greece into small isolated tracts of country with very indifferent land communications, prevented Greece from being the home of a united people, but fashioned it into a congeries of petty states, looking mainly to the sea for a living. A reference to the map, however, shows that the position is different in the case of Macedonia with its great valley of the Vardar, which is rich, is easily traversed, and ends in a very fertile delta, formed by its own and other waters. That these advantages are realized to-day is shown by the situation of Salonica,[1] the chief port of this part of Europe, which lies at a point where communications with the interior up the Vardar are best, and where it can tap the agricultural wealth of the region. In short, Macedonia possessed what the other states of Greece lacked—the physical configuration and the wide area of fertile land required for the support of a large population; and it succeeded to the Greek inheritance for somewhat the same reason that Portugal, in the sphere of maritime exploration and colonization, succeeded to Venice, Genoa, and other small republics.

[1] Salonica was founded in 315 B.C. on the site of the ancient Therma and was named after Thessalonica, half-sister of Alexander the Great and wife of Cassander.

The People.—It is probable that there were two strains among the Macedonians. The first and dominating element was Hellenic, and consisted, according to Greek belief,[1] mainly of a band of immigrants from Argos. The older population was Aryan, but to the Greeks "barbarian," and was driven away from the fertile lands to the rugged hills. In course of time there was fusion, but this was not complete.

Valour and virility were the leading characteristics of the people as a whole. A man who had not proved his manhood by slaying an enemy was forced by custom to wear a cord round his waist, and he could not even sit at table with men until he had killed a boar with his own hands. Alexander, the typical Macedonian, held that the chase was the finest possible preparation for war and much to be preferred to training for athletic contests; and there is no doubt that he was right. As a set-off to these splendid virtues was a great love of drinking, which led to deplorable tragedies, as will be seen in Alexander's career. Polygamy, too, prevailed, with its attendant family hatreds and murders.

The Macedonians, in their isolation and rustic surroundings, were far removed from the highly polished and travelled Athenians. But they were not classed as barbarous; and both Philip and Alexander were so devoted to art and literature that Macedonia became the torch-bearer of Greek culture in Asia. Again, just as the geographical formation of Greece, reacting on the people, made for separate states with the highly developed individualism of its citizens, who were, moreover, sea rovers perforce, so the larger area of Macedonia, its distance from the sea, its relatively good communications, and its greater resources, made for the formation of a united nation of farmers and shepherds ruled by a king. It has been well said that the Macedonians, when they began to play their great rôle, were politically in the Homeric stage.

The Early History.—The early history of Macedonia is the attempt of the comparatively civilized and probably Hellenic rulers of the plains to conquer and organize the wild tribesmen of the mountains. Indeed, little is known of the country until the Persians after the Scythian campaign

---

[1] I would acknowledge my indebtedness to Professor D. G. Hogarth's *Philip and Alexander of Macedon*, a most suggestive work.

received the submission of Amyntas, who was, as mentioned in Chapter XIV., at that time the king. In the pages of Herodotus we read of the fate of the first Persian ambassadors, who at a banquet given in their honour insisted that Amyntas should send for the ladies of his household. His son Alexander was furious at the insult, and when the Persians were drunk substituted for the women youths armed with daggers, who despatched the insolent Asiatics. Their attendants shared the same fate, and it required a great deal of diplomacy to hush up the massacre. This was, however, successfully accomplished by the heir of Amyntas, who gave his sister in marriage to the leader of the mission which was sent to investigate the matter ; and when the great invasion took place Alexander, who had succeeded his father, joined the Persians, though as far as possible he befriended the Hellenes.

Perdiccas, who reigned from 455 to 413 B.C., appears in the accounts of the Peloponnesian War as a capable, crafty ruler, and his successor, Archelaus, was a great organizer and created a fine army. He also welcomed Greek poets and artists to his Court, including Euripides, Agathon, and Zeuxis. A long obscure period of anarchy, with numerous assassinations, followed until, his brother having been slain by an invading horde of Illyrians, Philip became King of Macedonia in 359 B.C.

Philip the Organizer, 359-336 B.C.—The exceptional capacity of Philip is proved by the manner in which, in the course of a few years, he raised Macedonia from the position of a weak state constantly threatened by her neighbours to that of the dominant power of Hellas. He had spent three years of his youth as a hostage at Thebes, then the leading military power of Hellas, and the lessons he there learned, in close intercourse with Epaminondas, were never forgotten. His genius was shown not only in his statesmanship, but in the creation of the famous phalanx,[1] which, although requiring protection on the flanks, could pierce through every other formation of the period. Moreover, he improved his cavalry until it became irresistible, and created an efficient siege train and also a fleet. Nor did this extraordinary man

---

[1] The phalanx was composed of a column sixteen deep. Its weapon was the *sarissa*, a pike about sixteen feet in length ; this, when levelled by the first five ranks, projected and protected the front of the formation.

neglect the important question of the "sinews of war," and it was only through his exploitation of the gold and silver mines of Macedonia that the vast wealth necessary to carry out his ambitious plans was provided. His rise to power was opposed by various states of Greece, especially Thebes and Athens, the latter being swayed by the eloquence of Demosthenes. Who in his school days has not read the famous Philippics and formed the opinion that the patriotic orator, though supremely eloquent, was lacking in a sense of proportion, and failed to realize that polished, ease-loving Athens, even when allied to military Thebes, was a most unequal match for Philip, the soldier and man of action?

The wars of this great captain were extraordinarily successful. Campaign after campaign was waged against Illyrian tribesmen whom he massacred, against Amphipolis which he captured, against Thessaly which he absorbed, and against the Phocians whom he defeated. He then conquered Thrace up to the Propontis; though he failed signally to capture Perinthus, a strongly situated city to the west of Byzantium. Not only did all Greece seem to be arming against him, but the Great King had to be reckoned with, and Philip, seeing that his dream of controlling the Dardanelles could not be realized, withdrew to conquer Hellas.

The Battle of Chaeronea, 338 B.C.—Thebes and Athens, in alliance, faced him at Chaeronea, and found their day of reckoning. But it was more than this; for it was the first occasion on which a veteran national army met the old system of civic militia and hired mercenaries. After a stubborn contest Philip gained a complete victory, the battle being finally decided by the youthful Alexander, who led a charge of the heavy cavalry and broke the right wing of the enemy, where the stubborn Thebans fought. The losses of the allies were crushing. The Athenians alone had three thousand killed or captured and the Thebans at least as many. The victor treated Thebes with severity. Not only was she deprived of the leadership of the Boeotian towns, but her own autonomy was destroyed, and a body of exiles, supported by a Macedonian garrison, was put into office. On the other hand, with Athens at his mercy, Philip not only released her citizens, but concluded an alliance with the "Theatre of Glory," as he termed her. He then marched into the

Peloponnesus where Sparta alone resisted, and as a consequence had her territory reduced to the original Laconia.

The Election of Philip as Captain-General of Hellas, 337 B.C.
—A year after the battle of Chaeronea, a meeting of all the states except Sparta was convened at the Isthmus of Corinth. Philip explained to the assembled delegates that he wished to form a new Hellenic League on the terms that all the states should retain their autonomy and join in a war on Persia under his leadership, to avenge the impious wrongs inflicted on them by the barbarous invader. The Greek states felt no special bitterness against the Great King, who was now little feared. But they were obliged to elect Philip Captain-General, and perhaps they preferred to have his energies diverted to Asia rather than concentrated on Hellas. Their hostility to him was necessarily masked, but Philip was probably aware of it. What he wanted was to be chosen the official Captain-General of Hellas, and, this done, he returned in triumph to Macedonia to prepare for the invasion of the Persian Empire.

Olympias.—The first wife of Philip was Olympias, the daughter of an Epirote prince, a woman of striking beauty and of primitive passions which occasionally drove her to deeds of abhorrent cruelty ; yet a great woman, and famous in history as the mother of Alexander. He was her only son, and to his interests she devoted herself with fervour. As time passed Philip came to detest his wife, and upon his return from Greece married a fellow-countrywoman. At the wedding banquet Attalus, the bride's uncle, insulted Alexander by casting doubts on his legitimacy. The young Prince threw his cup in the face of Attalus, and Philip, under the influence of wine, drew his sword on his son, who sneered at his father and then left the court with his mother. This quarrel was made up, but a second began when Alexander wished to marry the daughter of the Satrap of Caria. Philip was very angry, and not only broke off the match but exiled four friends of Alexander's, who, he believed, were working against him. Two of these were Harpalus and Ptolemy, the latter destined to play a large part on the stage of history and to die a king.

The Assassination of Philip, 336 B.C.—The political situation was at its brightest and Philip was making his final preparations for the great campaign when, in 336 B.C., he was assassinated by a certain Pausanias, who had also been insulted by Attalus, and to whom Philip had refused redress. Assassination was common in Macedonia and, although Alexander was charged with parricide, it is improbable that he instigated the crime. Olympias, on the other hand, may well have wished for vengeance on her faithless husband, and may have felt that the succession of her son would be hopelessly imperilled unless she cut the knot by a bold stroke.

Thus in the prime of life died Philip, who not only originated the grand scheme of conquering Asia, but forged the weapon with which the battles were won. Had he lived longer he might have been known to history as the Conqueror of Asia; but, even though fate was unkind to him and contemporary evidence is lacking, the fact that " he evolved the first European power in the modern sense of the word, an armed nation with a common national ideal,"[1] constitutes a claim to greatness which cannot be disregarded. His epitaph may well be, " Europe had borne no such man, take him for all in all, as the son of Amyntas,"[2] until, as Hogarth adds, " She bore Amyntas' grandson."

The Extraordinary Fame of Alexander the Great.—There is little exaggeration in the statement that Alexander the Great was the most famous man ever born; and even to-day throughout Asia as far as the confines of China his name is one by which to conjure. Striking examples of this meet the traveller in the East almost everywhere, and by way of illustration I give two instances from countries many hundreds of miles apart. I would, in the first place, invite the reader to accompany me to Kashmir, to cross the stupendous ranges of the Himalayas to Gilgit, and then to proceed to Hunza, certainly among the most remote states in the world, which was never visited by any European traveller until a few years ago. In this isolated valley rules a petty Raja who claims descent from Alexander. Nor can we dismiss his claim with ridicule. Marco Polo tells us that a similar claim was made by the King of Badakshan, and it is reasonable to believe that in both cases the claims are based on a tradition of the Graeco-Bactrian kingdom which still lingers in these upland countries.[3]

---

[1] *Philip and Alexander of Macedon*, p. 3.
[2] Theopomp. 27, quoted from *op. cit.* p. 145.
[3] *Vide* Yule's *Marco Polo*, vol. i. p. 157.

From Hunza it is a far cry to the coast of Makran, where, in 1897, a Telegraph official, while inspecting the line which runs along its barren coast, was murdered by the wild tribesmen of Karwan,[1] who had hitherto regarded an Englishman's life as sacred. They murdered this man mainly because they had heard that their co-religionists, the Turks, had defeated the Greeks, the nation of Iskandar Zulkarnain or Alexander, the Lord of the Two Horns,[2] and they considered this defeat to be a blow to the power and prestige of all European nations alike. It is thus with no ordinary interest that the career of Europe's mightiest son is to be regarded. In my own case this interest is heightened by the fact that for many years I have been engaged in tracing out the routes followed by the illustrious Greek in Persia, and in one section, at any rate, I have been the first European to follow in his footsteps.

The Alexander Romances.—It is necessary here to point out that the Great Macedonian's career was in time overlaid with myths. So far has this process gone that the Alexander known to the East is, for the most part, an almost legendary being. The earliest form of the many romances is in Greek, and can be traced to the second century A.D. According to this, Alexander was the son of a King of Egypt. But for us the most important work dealing with Alexander from the Persian point of view is the famous epic of Firdausi. In it the poet describes Iskandar as a scion of the Persian royal family, and he describes how Dara or Darius married the daughter of Filigus of Rum,[3] or Philip of Greece. He divorced his wife, who became the mother of Alexander, and Darius Codomannus was his son by a second wife. Thus the Macedonian was half-brother to the Great King, and his campaigns in Asia were undertaken to wrest the throne from his kinsman. I would add that this version of history is devoutly believed by most Persians, who delight above all things in the improbable. These fascinating romances must have been the joy of European and Asiatic alike, and they were incorporated into literature both sacred and profane, including the Koran.

---

[1] *Vide Ten Thousand Miles, etc.*, chap. xxiv.
[2] "Lord of the Two Horns" is an epithet referring to his supposed descent from Ammon, in virtue of which he is represented in art as having a ram's horn on each temple.
[3] Rum is Rome, and to the Asiatic, Constantinople, a Greek city, was the capital of the empire of Rome; actually it was named "New Rome" by Constantine.

His Youth and Accession.—It is universally agreed that Alexander showed brilliant natural gifts even as a boy. Plutarch tells the story how he entertained ambassadors from Persia in his father's absence and how deeply he impressed them, with the result that they "looked upon the ability so much famed of Philip to be nothing in comparison with the forwardness and high purpose that appeared thus early in his son." Another celebrated story is that, when Bucephalus was brought for sale, Philip refused to buy it, on the ground that it was vicious and unmanageable. His son, however, who had noted that the horse was really only afraid of its own shadow, turned its head towards the sun and, leaping lightly on its back, completely mastered it, to the joy of Philip, who exclaimed, "O my son, look thee out a kingdom equal to and worthy of thyself, for Macedonia is too small for thee."

So much for stories of the famous youth. To come to firmer ground, we know that Alexander had the extraordinary good fortune to be taught by Aristotle, and it was he who implanted the passion for knowledge which never weakened throughout his strenuous life. Moreover, he was for the most part kept away from the undesirable atmosphere of the Court and was encouraged and enabled to devote his energies to study and to sport.

The young Prince obtained his first experience of war at Perinthus. At the age of sixteen he was appointed Regent during the absence of Philip and led a successful expedition against the rebellious Maedi. When eighteen years old, as already mentioned, he commanded a wing at Chaeronea, and is said to have been the first man to charge the famous Sacred Band. Thus when he succeeded his father not only had he considerable experience in war and administration, but owing to the fact that Olympias was out of favour he had known for some years that he might have to fight for the throne. Consequently, although but twenty, he bore an old head on his young shoulders.

His Recognition by Hellas.—Naturally enough, his capacity was not fully realized by the hostile factions in his own country or by the enemies of Macedonia abroad, but it did not take long to teach them the necessary lesson. After the usual murders of relatives, probably due to the influence of Olympias, Alexander marched to Thermopylae, where his succession to the chief command against Persia was acknowledged by all the important states of Hellas with the exception of Sparta, which, as before, remained aloof but unimportant. This matter having been satisfactorily settled, the young monarch turned his attention to his hostile neighbours in the north; and in the year following his succession he led his army into the Balkans. It is related that during this campaign he averted a disaster in a narrow gorge by a display of extraordinary resourcefulness. The tribesmen started their heavy waggons down the pass with a view to crushing the invaders, but with lightning-like decision Alexander ordered his men to lie down in their ranks covered by their shields, and over this improvised roadway the waggons passed without doing any harm. His objective the Danube was crossed without loss in the face of the enemy, and having by the exploit impressed the neighbouring tribes with a sense of his power, he marched through Illyria and finally returned to Macedonia, followed by numerous ambassadors who sued for peace.

The Destruction of Thebes, 335 B.C.—The next campaign was of value not only in exercising Alexander's capacity and valour but also as showing how little he could rely on the support of Hellas. A rumour of his death had reached Greece, and without waiting for its confirmation the Thebans, who in common with the Athenians and other Greeks had received subsidies from Sardes, revolted and blockaded the Macedonian garrison. The other Greeks sent messages of sympathy and Demosthenes went as far as to supply arms; but before any alliance was organized, Alexander had reached Boeotia with a victorious army. Lenient terms were offered, but foolishly refused; and the Macedonian army, supported by the garrison in the Cadmea (the citadel of Thebes), attacked the Thebans, killing 6000 and taking 30,000 prisoners, or practically the whole male population. The fate of Thebes was similar to that meted out by her in the days of her power to other cities of Boeotia. The city was destroyed with the exception of the temples and Pindar's house, the population was enslaved, and Thebes ceased to exist. Throughout Alexander showed statesmanlike moderation and self-control. He gave a severe lesson which resounded in Hellas like a thunder-clap and thereby strengthened his position; at the same time he avoided all cruelty or outrage such as would have shocked the sentiment of Hellas. These campaigns, which were necessary for a young monarch who had recently ascended the throne and who wished to quit his dominions, had the intended effect ; for during the long absence of Alexander from Europe the Regent was able to cope with all local risings and never required help from the army in Asia.

PART OF A PERSIAN HUNTING SCENE.
(From a Polychrome Terra-cotta Vase in the Hermitage Museum.)

CHAPTER XXI

THE BATTLES OF THE GRANICUS AND OF ISSUS

> Lordynges, Alisaunder the kyng,
> No hath in eorthe non evenyng :
> Hardy is his flesch and blod,
> His ost is muche, wyght, and god.
> Bothe in palys, and in bataile,
> He doth by Aristotles counsaile :
> By him, he is so ful of gynne,
> That alle men he may wynne.
> From the *Romaunce of Alisaunder*
> (Weber, i. p. 126).

The Situation before the Great Expedition.—Before we enter upon what are among the greatest campaigns in the world's history, let us consider for a moment the principal factors in the situation. In the preceding chapters we have followed continuously the relations between Persia and Hellas, and it is clear from these that whereas the Persian Empire was old and tending to decrepitude, Alexander represented a young and vigorous power. Furthermore, he stood for a higher civilization than that of Persia, where blind obedience to the Great King stifled progress and contrasted unfavourably with the remarkably free individuality of the Greeks.

With regard to the military situation, it is unlikely that Alexander, who was like all great generals a student, underrated the difficulties that lay before him, although in face of the enemy his youth and the lust of battle tempted him to run the greatest risks. It is, I think, a mistake to look upon the Persian Empire as utterly rotten and an easy prey to the first bold adventurer. Darius Codomannus, whose rule was unchallenged inside the empire, was a man of experience and had gained a reputation for bravery. He was certainly more capable than many of his predecessors. It must also be remembered that the resources at the disposal of the Satraps of Asia Minor were quite as great as those of Alexander, and included large numbers of Greek mercenaries, who fought with the utmost bravery against the Macedonians. Indeed, from the military point of view, not the mercenaries alone but the entire Greek population of Asia Minor constituted the backbone of resistance, and, as will be seen later on, the death of Memnon, who commanded for the Great King, was a stroke of extraordinary good fortune for the invaders. The Persian fleet was supreme at sea, as was very clearly shown at the siege of Miletus, and thus even the crossing of the Hellespont must have been an operation involving immense risk. Again, it was the Macedonian King's good fortune that the straits were not guarded by a Phoenician squadron. Alexander, moreover, until after the conquest of Phoenicia, must always have borne in mind the possibility that a strong Persian expedition might be despatched to Hellas, where hatred of Macedonia and greed for Persian gold would at any time have created a serious situation. No ordinary leader would have risked taking almost his entire army to Asia, with a hostile Greece in his rear and a Persian fleet commanding the sea. The Persians might reasonably suppose that the expedition of Alexander, who was unknown and very young, would not be more serious than that of the veteran Agesilaus. They would recall the fact that Philip's generals Parmenio and Attalus, who had invaded Asia Minor with 10,000 men in 336 B.C., had at first met with success; but that when Memnon took the field against them, they had not been able to make good their position, and had finally retreated to Europe upon hearing of the assassination of their master. In short, if we eliminate the genius of Alexander, the chance of the Macedonian army doing more than conquering and holding some of the coast provinces of Asia Minor would appear to have been remote; it would have been worn away by the distances and by attrition. It was Alexander's genius alone, using the splendid weapon forged by Philip, that won the lordship of Asia.

The Start of the Expedition, 334 B.C.—It was springtime in 334 B.C. when the great expedition started from Macedonia. Perhaps the most striking fact about it was the paucity of its numbers for the magnitude of the enterprise. The total force consisted of but 30,000 infantry and 5000 cavalry, and of these only about one half were Macedonians. Thessaly and the surrounding tribes provided large contingents, but few Greeks served in the ranks, although mention is made of a contingent of Peloponnesians and other Greek allies. On the other hand, it was an army trained by warfare both against regular troops and against hill tribes, its *moral* was high owing to its almost uninterrupted record of victories, and its confidence in its leaders was strong and well founded. Finally, its training and equipment were in advance of anything that the world had hitherto seen. As to its small numbers, Alexander counted on success to bring him recruits whose enrolment would more than compensate for losses in action and by sickness. He was, moreover, unable to provide the pay of a larger force until he had conquered some wealthy provinces. We know that his war chest was very light, as he stated himself that he started on the expedition heavily in debt.

The road as far as the Hellespont was well known and had been recently trodden by Macedonian troops. The march was made rapidly, probably to prevent the news from reaching the Persians; and much anxiety must have been felt for the safety of the fleet of 160 triremes and attendant transports on which the force depended for crossing to Asia. On the twentieth day Sestos was reached, and, as Abydos on the opposite shore had been retained by the Macedonians after their last campaign, the army was speedily transported to Asia, where it landed unopposed. It may be imagined with what fervour the Macedonian monarch sacrificed to Zeus, to Athene, and to his supposed ancestor Heracles.

The Battle of the Granicus, 334 B.C.—After performing a pilgrimage to the tomb of Achilles at Ilium, Alexander, who had undoubtedly heard that a large force had been assembled to oppose him, marched northwards along the coast from Abydos and fought his first great battle at the Granicus, a river flowing into the Sea of Marmora near the then important city of Cyzicus. It is stated by Arrian that Memnon, who commanded the large force of Greek mercenaries, proposed to the Persian generals a policy of devastation and retreat; but this was overruled by the proud Iranians, who never showed a finer spirit than in this battle. Had their dispositions been as good, it might have gone hardly with Alexander. The Persians were posted on the right bank of the river, which was difficult to cross, and although fordable had deep holes and high banks. They placed the whole of their cavalry, to the number of 20,000, in the fighting line, and kept the formidable body of 20,000 Greek mercenaries entirely in reserve. In fact, they were determined to win the fight themselves, and were too proud to employ their infantry, which possibly in their hearts they despised.

On the Macedonian side full use was made of all arms. The heavy infantry, divided into two phalanxes and carefully flanked by Thessalian cavalry, formed the left wing under Parmenio. Alexander massed the heavy cavalry on the right wing, and by threatening to outflank the Persian line induced the enemy to prolong it at the expense of the left centre. He led the main attack to this point, taking care not to lose touch with the phalanx. At first the advantage was with the Persians, who hurled javelins at the light cavalry, struggling below them through the river in face of superior numbers; but the heavy cavalry was brought up in support, and a fierce struggle ensued between the Persians with their javelins and the Macedonians with their long spears. In the mêlée Alexander's spear was broken, but being supplied with a fresh weapon, he charged Mithradates, the son-in-law of Darius, and aiming at his face bore him to the ground. In turn he received a blow on his helmet, but quickly struck his assailant dead. He was again attacked, and this time was saved by Clitus. Meanwhile his troops were gaining the bank and pressing back the Persians, whose weapons were no match at close quarters for the Macedonian spears, until their centre was finally pierced. This decided the battle. The Persian cavalry broke and fled, leaving the mercenary Greek troops to face the attack unsupported. Alexander allowed no pursuit of the Persians, but bringing up the terrible phalanx, attacked the mercenaries from every side with foot and horse. These fought bravely, but nevertheless the entire body was speedily cut to pieces, only 2000 prisoners being made.

The Surrender of Sardes, 334 B.C.—After this battle no

organized Persian army was left in Asia Minor, and Sardes was surrendered by its cowardly Persian Governor. This was another piece of good fortune; for its inaccessible site, strengthened by a triple wall, should have enabled the garrison to sustain a protracted siege. Its possession enhanced still further the great prestige of the Macedonians, and gave them a strategical position and material resources of the utmost value. Having conquered Lydia, Alexander showed that he intended the conquest to be permanent by the careful and thorough manner in which he reorganized its administration. Owing to the weakness of the Court, the Satrap had managed to unite the three originally separate posts of Civil Governor, Commander of the Troops, and Secretary-General into his own hands. Alexander separated the military and the financial control, entrusting them to different officials, who were independent of one another; and this arrangement he adopted throughout the empire as its provinces were won.

The Campaign in Caria, Lycia, Pamphylia, Pisidia, and Phrygia.—After the capture of Sardes, Alexander determined to reduce the Greek colonies on the coast of Asia Minor, that he might make his position secure before moving eastwards. Ephesus surrendered and a democracy was established in place of an oligarchy; but Miletus resisted, its garrison being encouraged by the proximity of the Persian fleet. This powerful squadron, however, was badly handled, its commander allowing the Macedonian ships to forestall it and shut it out from the port. Every effort was made to induce the Macedonian fleet to give battle, and Parmenio advised the acceptance of the challenge. But Alexander prudently declined to run the risk, and in the end he disbanded his navy owing to its heavy cost and its inferiority to the squadrons in the Persian service.

Miletus was captured by assault after a short siege. The inhabitants and mercenaries who escaped were well treated, and the latter enlisted in the Macedonian army. Halicarnassus was the next objective. The headquarters of Memnon, it was strongly fortified and well garrisoned; its capture was therefore of the utmost importance and likely to call for great efforts. The ditch was filled in and a powerful siege train was brought up. Sallies made by the garrison resulted in heavy losses, and Memnon finally set fire to the city and evacuated it, retreating with the garrison to two strongholds.

Alexander, whose losses had also been considerable, did not attempt to capture these fortresses, which were reduced in the following year by Antipater. From Halicarnassus Alexander sent back those of his men who were newly married with orders to rejoin in the spring, bringing as many recruits as possible ; he also despatched a recruiting party to the Peloponnesus. He then continued his march along the coast, subduing the various cities of Lycia and Pamphylia, in order to deprive the Persian fleet of possible bases. Indeed, it was this problem which must have called for the most serious consideration.

The army next marched northward across Pisidia, where it encountered the fierce mountaineers and repulsed their attack with heavy loss. Thence it entered Phrygia, which was occupied and administered, and at Gordium, the capital of the ancient Phrygian kings, the newly married men and recruits rejoined the main army, to the number of 4000 men, not enough one would think to make good the losses caused by casualties, sickness, and the garrisons that had to be provided.

Alexander's principal motive in leaving the coast with the Persian fleet supreme and advancing into the heart of Asia Minor appears to have been to follow the great route to Persia which ran through it ; but he was no doubt attracted also by the prophecy that the lordship of Asia would fall to him who untied the knot of the waggon of Gordius, the first ruler of the land. There was something fantastic in his character, and this drew him to Gordium, where, as every schoolboy knows, he cut the knot, while heaven signified its assent by thunder and lightning.

The Death of Memnon, 333 B.C.—Meanwhile Memnon, in pursuance of his plan of carrying the war into Macedonia and Greece, had obtained possession of Chios. He had then turned his attention to Mytilene, but during the operations fell ill and died. This was a great blow to the cause of the Great King. After his death a Persian squadron which was sent to the Cyclades suffered defeat ; and it was mainly from lack of Persian support that a Spartan revolt, which broke out in 332 B.C., never assumed serious proportions but was crushed at Megalopolis in 330 B.C. by Antipater, the Regent.

The Battle of Issus, November 333 B.C.—The second stage in the campaign began with Alexander's departure from

Gordium to encounter the Great King. Hitherto he had crossed swords only with distant Satraps ; but his advance would now, he well knew, be opposed by the united forces of the Persian Empire. The passage through Cappadocia was uneventful ; but upon reaching the famous Cilician Gates after a forced march he, like Cyrus the Younger, found them strongly held. He prepared to attack the almost impregnable position by night, hoping thereby to effect a surprise. In this hope he was disappointed, but the movement more than achieved its purpose ; for the guard, upon hearing the advance, withdrew rapidly, and Alexander, marvelling at his good fortune when he saw how easily the pass could have been blocked,[1] descended into Cilicia and occupied Tarsus by yet another forced march. Here he was delayed by a dangerous illness caused by bathing in the cold waters of the Cydnus ; but, soon recovering, he despatched Parmenio to seize the Syrian Gates, already mentioned in connexion with Cyrus the Younger, while he himself marched slowly after him, consolidating his position as he advanced. Hearing on his way that Darius was awaiting him two days' march to the east of the Gates, he prepared for battle and marched confidently forward.

Meanwhile the Great King, concluding from the delays of the Macedonian army that Alexander would decline a battle, had broken up camp and crossed the same range by a pass farther north known as the Amanic Gate. He suddenly appeared in the rear of the Macedonians and, advancing on Issus, captured and cruelly tortured to death the sick who had been left there. Alexander, who had passed the Syrian Gates, at first refused to believe the report of this movement. When it was confirmed he assembled his officers and explained to them that the deity was evidently fighting on their side by persuading Darius to draw up his vast host in a narrow plain between mountains and the sea, where there was enough room for the Macedonian army to manœuvre, but where the Persian advantage in numbers would be wholly thrown away. He also recalled the glorious exploits of the Ten Thousand which were well known to all.

The battle of Issus, one of the decisive battles of the world, was fought near the city of that name, on a plain less than

---

[1] Until the rocks were blasted in the middle of the nineteenth century, camels had to be unloaded and their loads carried by hand owing to the narrowness of the famous defile.

ALEXANDER CHARGING DARIUS CODOMANNUS AT THE BATTLE OF ISSUS.

(From the mosaic at Pompeii now in the Museo Nazionale, Naples. Photo. Brogi.)

two miles broad [1] lying between the hills on the north-east and the Gulf of Iskanderun to the south-west. A little river ran down to the sea, and, protected by it, the Persians had drawn up their vast, heterogeneous host, estimated at 600,000 men, which included 30,000 Greek mercenaries, a force by itself nearly equal to that of Alexander. Sixty thousand Cardaces, a people who have not been identified, formed the left wing and the Greek mercenaries the right wing, where the cavalry also was massed. The lower hills were strongly held by a body of 20,000 men, and had any initiative been shown by the leader of this force, the Macedonian rear would have been seriously embarrassed. The remainder of the Persian force was ranged in support and took no part in the battle. Darius, according to invariable custom, took post in the centre.

Alexander, upon marching back through the Syrian Gates, formed up his force as soon as the ground permitted, with the heavy cavalry headed by himself on the right wing and Parmenio with the phalanx and the rest of the infantry on the left. Seeing the Persian cavalry massed on the right of its line, Alexander modified his dispositions to the extent of detaching the Thessalian cavalry to protect the flanks of the phalanx. His anxiety as to his rear was soon set at rest by the supineness of the Persian outflanking force, and we read in the pages of Arrian that he first rested his men and then led them forward very slowly to the river-bank where the Persian host passively awaited the attack. As at Cunaxa, the Persian troops would not stand the Greek charge and fled like sheep; but the Greek mercenaries stood firm, and as the ranks of the phalanx were thrown into disorder by crossing the river the contest was desperate. The deciding factor was the cowardice of Darius, who when the tide of battle surged towards him was seized with panic and fled, throwing away his shield to lighten his chariot. In the mosaic battle-scene Alexander, the bare-headed figure on the left, is shown as charging Darius, and his lance has transfixed a Persian. The face of the Achaemenian monarch expresses horror and fear, and his charioteer is lashing the horses. In the centre of the picture a Persian has dismounted and offers his horse to

---

[1] Holm, iii. 239, states that the plain was about three miles broad; but Callisthenes, who accompanied Alexander, makes it fourteen stadia, or say rather more than a mile and a half, and, although the distance varied, it was probably at that period less than two miles.

Darius. It is stated that the craven Shah had caused mares whose foals were left behind to be posted along the route, and that finally quitting his chariot he rode for his life. Meanwhile the victorious Macedonian right came to the help of Parmenio, on the left, where as at the Granicus the steady Greek mercenaries, deserted by their Persian comrades, fought magnificently, but in vain, unless indeed they helped to save the worthless Great King, whom Alexander did not pursue until he saw that the battle was won. The slaughter of the Persian troops, fleeing in panic along the hill tracts, was enormous, and is said to have exceeded 100,000. The camp of Darius, with his mother, wife, and two daughters, became the spoil of the victor, who showed his magnanimity by treating his prisoners with respect and courtesy. Less than the equivalent of a million sterling was captured, but the main treasury was subsequently seized at Damascus by Parmenio.

The results of the battle of Issus were stupendous. Not only had the Macedonians defeated an army more than ten times their own number, but they realized that no Persian force, however great, would face them resolutely in battle. The tide of Asiatic conquest had indeed been turned when the Great King fled panic-stricken before Alexander, leaving the western provinces of his huge empire either to resist entirely unsupported or to submit to the invader. Issus ranks as one of the decisive battles of the world.

The Siege of Tyre and its Capture, 332 B.C.—From Issus Alexander advanced towards Phoenicia, which was his next objective, receiving as he proceeded the submission of Aradus, the Arvad of Ezekiel, of Sidon, which had to some extent recovered from its sack by Ochus, and of other cities. The conquest of Phoenicia meant for him the destruction of Persian sea power, and the consequent removal of danger to his rear. It also meant the formation of a new base from which he could operate. It would result in the submission of Cyprus, which was also an important naval centre, and finally it was a necessary preliminary to the annexation of Egypt.

Tyre was now the chief city of Phoenicia, the destruction of Sidon having considerably increased its power and wealth. The "crowning city" of Isaiah stood on an island distant half a mile from the shore, and was defended by very high walls. Relying on their strength, as they had successfully done in the case of Persia, its rulers, after first agreeing to submit, declined to allow Alexander to enter the city with his army in order to sacrifice to Melkarth, the Tyrian Heracles, who was recognized as a separate hero from the Heracles worshipped in Hellas. This refusal was not to be borne, and Alexander resolved to deprive the city of its inaccessibility by constructing a mole from the mainland, no easy task in the face of a desperate enemy. At first the work progressed rapidly, unlimited labour being available ; but as soon as it reached water deep enough for the Tyrian triremes, the workers were constantly harassed. To protect them, two towers mounting engines were erected on the mole, but these were destroyed by a fireship supported by triremes. The mole was then constructed wider than before, and more towers were erected. Meanwhile the Sidonians and other Phoenicians, deserting from the Persian fleet with 80 ships, made terms with Alexander. They were joined before long by the Kings of Cyprus with 120 ships, the Tyrian fleet was overmatched, and the siege entered on its final phase.

The engines mounted on the completed mole did little harm, owing to the strength of this section of the wall, so that the construction of the mole did not justify itself ; but other engines were mounted in ships and attacked weaker parts of the wall. Finally, a general assault was ordered. Alexander entered Tyre through a breach made by a shipborne engine, and, after seizing some of the towers on the wall, he descended into the city. A massacre ensued, the Macedonians being exasperated by the stubborn resistance and by the killing of some of their comrades on the city walls. The women and children were safe in Carthage, but 8000 Tyrians were killed, 30,000 were sold as slaves, and thus Tyre " whose merchants are princes "[1] was laid desolate.

The Annexation of Egypt, 332–331 B.C.—The fall of Tyre was the first step towards the invasion of Egypt. Gaza came next, and resisted, in spite of the terrible warning so recently given. Owing to its situation on rising ground, an embankment 250 feet in height and 1200 feet broad had to be constructed all round the city, truly a colossal earthwork. The wall was then undermined and, after three unsuccessful assaults, Alexander triumphed, the garrison fighting to the death. Egypt was annexed without a struggle, the Persian Viceroy realizing that resistance was useless. Like Cyrus the

[1] Isaiah xxiii. 8.

Great, Alexander paid extraordinary respect to the Egyptian deities and treated the natives with the utmost consideration. Alexandria, the most successful of the many cities planned by him, was founded. Finally, impelled by the fantastic strain in his blood, he visited the mysterious oasis of Ammon, where, according to the official account, he was recognized as the son of Ammon. After appointing Egyptian rulers to govern in his name, Alexander retraced his steps to Tyre, where he met his fleet and immediately began preparations for the advance into the heart of the Persian Empire.

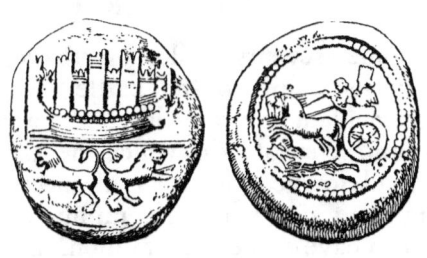

SILVER COIN OF SIDON ABOUT 400-384 B.C.

CHAPTER XXII

THE CAREER OF ALEXANDER THE GREAT TO THE DEATH OF DARIUS CODOMANNUS

> His city there thou seest, and Bactra there ;
> Ecbatana her structure vast there shows,
> And Hecatompylos her hundred gates ;
> There Susa by Choaspes, amber stream
> The drink of none but kings.
> MILTON, *Paradise Regained.*

The Battle of Arbela, 331 B.C.—Upon quitting Tyre Alexander marched eastwards to Thapsacus on the Euphrates, just as Cyrus the Younger had done. There he found two bridges of boats which had been constructed by his orders. A small Persian force of 3000 cavalry which had been posted without support to defend the passage had withdrawn. Indeed it is an extraordinary feature of this campaign that Darius, who had large bodies of light horse at his disposal, made no attempt whatever to harass the Greek troops, who were heavily armed and possessed only a small force of light cavalry. In these vast open plains the Macedonian host should have been constantly assailed, as was done with complete success a few centuries later by the Parthians, who in this way laid low the pride of Rome.

After crossing the Euphrates, Alexander marched through the fertile district of Mesopotamia past Carrhae, to the Tigris, which Darius with fatuous negligence made no attempt to defend, although owing to its swiftness it was not crossed without great difficulty. He then proceeded down the left bank, traversing ancient Assyria, which at that period was termed Athuria. At Gaugamela, close to the ruins of

Nineveh and some seventy miles north-west of Arbela, which has given its name to the battle, he found Darius awaiting him on a plain specially levelled for the evolutions of the cavalry and chariots on which he placed his chief reliance. He had learned the folly of meeting the Macedonians in a cramped area where his numbers could not tell. His army is said to have exceeded a million, drawn from every corner of his empire. There was a body of Greek mercenaries, but not as numerous as at Issus. Fifteen elephants were marshalled in the fighting line, their first appearance in an historical battle.

The Macedonians, whose only formidable opponents at Issus had been Greek mercenaries, must have felt serene confidence in their own valour, their long training, and the superb leading of their general. This confidence is exemplified by the leisurely though careful movements of Alexander, who, after receiving information as to the exact position of the Great King, rested his men for four days and fortified his camp, in which he left his heavy baggage, the sick, and a small garrison. He thus prepared a position to fall back on if necessary, and ensured the absolute freedom of his fighting force.

The two armies were encamped some seven miles apart, separated by a low range of hills; and when these had been crossed by Alexander and the huge Persian host lay before him, a council of war was held to decide whether battle should be joined immediately. Parmenio, whose opinion had most weight, advised a careful reconnaissance of the battlefield in case of pitfalls or ambushes, and a study of the dispositions of the enemy. Consequently camp was pitched and Alexander made a detailed examination of the whole ground, apparently without interference from the enemy. Parmenio furthermore suggested that, in view of the overwhelming numbers of the Persian host, a night attack should be made. Alexander replied with the famous remark, "I do not steal a victory."

The Persian army, which had been kept under arms all night, was drawn up with Darius in the centre, supported by a *corps d'élite* known as the "King's kinsmen" and the "Immortals." The two divisions of Greek mercenaries were distributed one on each side of the Great King. To the front were stationed the royal horse guards, with the elephants and fifty chariots. The right and left wings, composed of various detachments, horse and foot, must have extended a considerable distance on either side. The Macedonian army, consisting of 40,000 infantry and 7000 cavalry, was drawn up in its usual formation, with Parmenio in command of the phalanx on the left wing, supported by a powerful force of Thessalian cavalry. Alexander commanded the right wing, composed mainly of the superb Macedonian cavalry.

In view of the overwhelming numerical superiority of the Persians, a strong reserve was formed to protect the rear. So well trained was his force, and apparently so contemptuous was he of the enemy, that Alexander boldly exposed his left flank and marched towards the Persian left, almost parallel to the huge army, thereby forcing Darius, who should have taken advantage of the movement to order a general attack, to conform, much to the disorganization of his unwieldy array. At last, when the carefully prepared battlefield was being quitted and rough ground entered, Darius, seeing that his chariots would soon be useless, ordered the mounted troops on his left wing to attack. The movement was at first successful, and the cavalry combat which ensued was fierce, until discipline prevailed and the organized Greek squadrons broke the ranks of the enemy. Meanwhile the scythe-bearing chariots, of which great things were again expected (although their uselessness against trained troops had been clearly demonstrated at Cunaxa), were launched against the foe. Their charge, which was apparently not effectively supported by cavalry or light-armed troops, was a complete failure, as the Greek light infantry hurled javelins at them, cut the reins, and pulled off the drivers. The phalanx opened out when necessary, and any chariots which passed through were dealt with by the guards and grooms in rear. The charge of the Persian left wing and the reinforcements sent to it had caused a gap in the line near Darius, and towards this Alexander charged at the head of the Companion Cavalry, supported by part of the phalanx. A short hand-to-hand fight ensued, which was ended by the flight of the dastardly Darius, who, craven as he was, turned to flee while the issue still hung in the balance.

The field of battle was so enormous that the news did not spread at once. Parmenio was enveloped by masses of the enemy, and being hard pressed sent a message to

Alexander,[1] who returned to his aid, meeting on the way bodies of Parthian, Indian, and Persian cavalry now in full flight. Their desperate efforts to break through caused the heaviest losses of the day to the Macedonians. Upon reaching the phalanx, Alexander found that Parmenio, with the assistance of the Thessalian cavalry, had defeated the Persian right wing, which was in full flight. He therefore started again in pursuit of Darius, and reached the Great Zab that night, where he bivouacked for a few hours to rest his men and horses. The next day he continued the pursuit as far as Arbela, the modern Erbil, seventy miles from the field of battle ; but he failed to capture Darius, and men and horses being worn out, he allowed the defeated monarch to retreat towards Ecbatana without further molestation.

The issue of the battle of Arbela, though on a field chosen by the Great King, who was supported by the entire force of his empire, was, from a military point of view, almost a foregone conclusion, but for the chance that Alexander might be struck down in the mêlée. Thereafter the armed resistance of Darius was a thing of the past, and the capitals of the empire, particularly Susa and great Babylon, with all their hoarded wealth and material resources, lay at the victor's mercy. Darius became a fugitive, and could not hope to do more than maintain a guerilla warfare on the outskirts of the empire. Even this was denied to the last of the Achaemenian line, owing to treachery of the basest kind. Creasy, in his account of this battle, quotes the following remark made by Napoleon : " Alexander deserves the glory which he has enjoyed for so many centuries and among all nations ; but what if he had been beaten at Arbela, having the Euphrates, the Tigris, and the deserts in his rear, without any strong places of refuge, nine hundred leagues from Macedonia ? " Surely the reply is that Alexander could have done what Xenophon had already shown to be possible.

The Capture of Babylon and Susa.—From Arbela the victor marched on Babylon, where he was welcomed by its governor, priests and people, who knew the respect he had shown to the gods of Egypt. Like Cyrus the Great, Alexander apparently " took the hands of Bel," and gave orders that the temples which Xerxes had destroyed should be rebuilt.

---

[1] Perhaps Parmenio sent these messages to prevent pursuit until the victory was won. Forgetfulness of this precaution lost the Greeks Cunaxa.

The Babylonians were pleased and thenceforth served him loyally.

From Babylon Alexander marched in twenty days to Susa. The Greeks looked upon Susa as the capital of the Great King; and there Aeschylus laid the scene of the *Persae*. In the city 50,000 talents, or £16,550,000,[1] were found, with other treasure of inestimable value. It included the brazen statues of Harmodius and Aristogeiton, and these Alexander restored to Athens, where, many centuries later, they were seen by Arrian.

The Occupation of Persepolis and Pasargadae.—Alexander celebrated his triumph at Susa with great splendour, by offering sacrifices, by a torch race, and by a gymnastic contest. Having been joined by a welcome reinforcement of fifteen thousand men, which must have been sorely needed to make good his losses by death and sickness, and the necessity of leaving garrisons at important strategical centres, he again set forth. He decided to ascend the Iranian plateau, to the sacred home of the Persians, the occupation of which would prove to all the world that their empire had indeed fallen.

Crossing the Karun at the site of modern Ahwaz, he followed the route connecting the two capitals *via* Behbehan, which was then well known, but has seldom been traversed by modern travellers, owing probably to the destruction of both the great cities. The Uxians, who inhabited the rugged hills and were accustomed to receive toll from the unwarlike Great Kings whenever they passed that way, demanded the same from Alexander, who bade them in reply come to their defiles to receive it. He then followed an unfrequented route with the swiftness which will ever be associated with his operations, and falling suddenly on their villages surprised the tribesmen, who fled in all directions. Meanwhile Craterus by a forced march had occupied the heights commanding the pass. Alexander's own column made a second great effort and occupied the pass before the Uxians, who found themselves obliged to yield without attempt at resistance.

Parmenio with the main body and baggage was sent by the so-called carriage road lying farther south, which is still as unmade, except in so far as it is worn by traffic, as it was more than two thousand years ago. Alexander himself

---

[1] In the case of silver talents the sum is as given above, but if golden talents are meant, the sum works out at £132,400,000.

marched with his wonted celerity through the mountains to the "Persian Gates," where the Viceroy of Persis had built a wall to block the pass, and was defending it with a force of forty thousand men. The tactics of Thermopylae were now repeated, this time by the Macedonians, who were led by a hill track to the rear of the pass and fell on the Persians before dawn. Their trumpets gave the signal to Craterus, who had been left in command at the mouth of the defile, and thus the Persians were surrounded, and a terrible massacre ensued. This was the only organized resistance encountered in Persia.

Alexander then marched to the Kur, the Band-i-Amir, where he had ordered a bridge to be built. Crossing this, he reached Persepolis, the Persian capital of the Great King, where he seized 120,000 talents, equivalent to £28,290,000, and other booty in vast quantities. We learn from Plutarch that ten thousand mule carts and five thousand camels were needed for its transport. There is nothing incredible in these immense figures when we remember that, generation after generation, from every quarter of Asia, huge sums were received by the Great Kings, whose tradition it was to amass treasure against a day of need. We also know that the effect on commerce throughout the civilized world was extraordinary when this treasure was dispersed. Pasargadae was subsequently occupied.

The splendid palaces of Persepolis were burned and a general massacre of its inhabitants was ordered. Arrian represents this as a reprisal for the wrongs inflicted by Persia on Hellas, and especially on Athens ; and it is not unlikely, for we know that a large band of mutilated Greek prisoners met the conqueror at Persepolis, and their clamour for vengeance would naturally be taken up by the army. Plutarch's account is reproduced in Dryden's well-known lines :

> Revenge, revenge, Timotheus cries,
> See the Furies arise ;
> See the snakes that they rear,
> How they hiss in their hair,
> And the sparkles that flash from their eyes !
> Those are Grecian ghosts, that in battle were slain,
> And unburied remain
> Inglorious on the plain :
> Give the vengeance due
> To the valiant crew.

> Behold how they toss their torches on high,
>   How they point to the Persian abodes,
>   And glittering temples of their hostile gods.
>   The princes applaud with a furious joy;
>   And the king seized a flambeau with zeal to destroy;
>   Thais led the way,
>   To light him to his prey,
>   And, like another Helen, fired another Troy.

The Capture of Ecbatana, 330 B.C.—Alexander was now in possession of Babylon, of Susa, of Persepolis, and of Pasargadae; and only Ecbatana, the summer capital, was left. Following his invariable custom, he marched with extreme rapidity towards Media, having heard on the way that Darius intended to fight a third battle. But upon approaching Ecbatana he learned that the Persian king had fled to the Caspian Gates, whither he had previously despatched his women and heavy baggage. So a halt was made and the army was reorganized, the Thessalian cavalry and other Grecian allies being sent home loaded with gifts. Arrian states that not a few of their number elected to follow the fortunes of Alexander, whose forces were now entirely professional, looking to their leader and to no one else. The enormous treasure, estimated by Diodorus at 180,000 talents, or some forty millions sterling, was left at Ecbatana, which was garrisoned by a force of six thousand Macedonians. It thus became the most important military centre in the newly conquered empire, and was particularly well chosen owing to its central position and its approximately equal distance from Babylon, Susa, and Persepolis. It also served as a new base for the main army. Parmenio was detached northward to march through the difficult country of the Cadusians with orders to rejoin in Hyrcania, and this operation, the need for which is not apparent, he duly carried out.

The Pursuit and Death of Darius Codomannus, 330 B.C.— When arrangements had been completed, Alexander with a strong force of picked men started in pursuit of the hapless Darius, whom he hoped to overtake at Rhagae, the Rhages of the book of Tobit, the ruins of which lie a few miles to the south of Teheran.[1] Alexander rested his men for five days at Rhagae, and then marched east along what is to-day the post road between Teheran and Meshed, which throughout

---

[1] From Ecbatana, the modern Hamadan, to Rhagae, the modern Rei, is just under two hundred miles.

skirts the southern slopes of the range then known as the Taurus. It is seldom out of sight of the great desert of Persia, which almost throughout comes up close to the foot of the mountain range, and has thus through all the ages fixed the course of the great route connecting Ecbatana with Bactria. The first march brought him to the famous Caspian Gates,[1] and the second led him beyond them. He then heard that Bessus, Satrap of Bactria, Barsaentes, Satrap of Arachosia, and Nabarzanes, commander of the mounted troops, had made a prisoner of the fugitive king, and the information spurred him to redouble his efforts. Two more extremely long marches brought his weary troops to a stage where information reached him that all the Persians had approved of the infamous act of Bessus, but that the faithful Greek mercenaries, unable to prevent the treachery, had quitted the Persian army and made for the mountains. The fifth forced march brought Alexander to a village where the Persians had encamped the night before. Discovering that there was a shorter route to the next stage, he mounted some officers and picked infantry on five hundred of his cavalry horses and, starting off again in the afternoon, overtook the Persians just before daybreak after a march of nearly fifty miles. No resistance was attempted. Bessus, finding Alexander in close pursuit, gave orders for the hapless Darius to be put to death, and then took to flight. Alexander found the waggon with the body of Darius, covered with wounds and just dead, drawn up at a spring and deserted by its driver. Thus miserably ended the last of an illustrious dynasty, the lords of Asia for more than two centuries.

The exact spot where Alexander overtook Darius is not known; but Persian legend places it in the neighbourhood of Damghan, a position which fits in very well with the facts. The town is some two hundred miles east of Rhages, or six very long marches, such as those recorded by Arrian, averaging thirty miles for five marches and fifty for the final effort. In the heat of the Persian summer even Alexander could not have accomplished more. The site, moreover, is indicated approximately by the fact mentioned by Arrian, that when the waggons and heavy baggage were sent into Hyrcania they crossed the

---

[1] In Curzon's *Persia*, i. 293, the question of the exact site is gone into at length. Williams Jackson, who has made a special study of the question, agrees with Curzon's conclusion that the Sardarra Pass is the defile referred to by Arrian.

Elburz range by the main route, which was longer. Now the only main route across this section of the range runs from Shahrud to Astrabad,[1] and had Alexander overtaken Darius at Shahrud the remark would not have held good. Moreover, Shahrud is some fifty miles east of Damghan, or two hundred and fifty miles east of Rhages. The evidence at our disposal, therefore, all points to the neighbourhood of Damghan. The murder of Darius by treacherous subjects was yet another stroke of good fortune for Alexander. Not only did it discourage guerilla operations, which might easily have become formidable, but the odium of the deed fell upon Bessus and not upon Alexander. True to his chivalrous instincts, the victor had the body buried with all pomp at Persepolis.

[1] "A Sixth Journey in Persia," *Journal R.G.S.*, Feb. 1911.

SPHINX.
(Gold Medallion from British Museum.)

CHAPTER XXIII

THE LIMIT OF CONQUEST

> Comparisoun myght never yit be maked
> Betwixe him and another conquerour;
> For al this world for drede of him hath quaked,
> He was of knyghthode and of fredom flour.
>   CHAUCER, *The Monkes Tale.*

The Conquest of Hyrcania, Parthia, and Areia.—The heritage of the empire of Persia was now Alexander's, and he might well have deputed others to subdue the outlying eastern provinces. But lust of conquest and ambition were his ruling passions, and the death of Darius produced no abatement of his thirst for universal dominion, which his wonderful successes had merely whetted. From the neighbourhood of Damghan the Macedonian army turned north into the main range to attack the Tapuri, whose name is perhaps preserved in Tabaristan, the mediaeval nomenclature of the province of Mazanderan. Alexander's objective being Hyrcania, he divided his army into three divisions in order to subdue as wide an area as possible, and also to prevent the hill-men from uniting to attack any one column. He himself took the shortest and most difficult route, and, crossing to the Caspian watershed, was met by the most distinguished of the Persian nobles who had been in attendance on Darius, including the Viceroy of Hyrcania and Parthia. The three columns united again at Zadracarta, the capital of Hyrcania, which probably occupied a site at or near Astrabad. Hereabouts he received the submission of other Persian nobles, including the Satrap of the Tapuri, and of the fifteen hundred Greek mercenaries.

During the halt of the main body in Hyrcania a raid was made on the Mardi, who lived farther west than the Tapuri under Demavand; they were easily subdued and placed under the Viceroy of the Tapuri, who was reappointed to his post.

At Zadracarta, upon his return from the Mardian expedition, Alexander offered sacrifice and held a gymnastic contest. We then read in the pages of Arrian that "after these celebrations he began his march towards Parthia; thence to the confines of Areia and to Susia, a city in that province." The general opinion has been that Alexander recrossed to the south side of the Elburz and rejoined the main Teheran-Meshed road at Shahrud; but, as often happens, this view, formed originally, perhaps, with inadequate knowledge of the country, has been adopted by writer after writer without sufficiently careful and thorough examination. It is much more reasonable, in the absence of precise information, to suppose that the Great Conqueror marched up the fertile valley of the Gurgan in which Astrabad is situated. From this valley there are two exits: one by the No Deh valley, which leads through the heart of the range to Pursian and Nardin, and the other up the Gurgan defile. Both these routes pass the famous meadow of Kalposh, where an existing legend represents that Alexander camped and rested his army. The route by which the valley of the Kashaf Rud was entered, containing Susia or Tus and modern Meshed, is fixed by the fact that there is only one break in the wall of mountains which could be used for the passage of an army with wheeled transport. This I traversed in 1908, and there is little doubt in my mind that it was the very route that Alexander trod.[1] Satibarzanes, the Satrap of the Areians, offered his submission at Susia. Here Alexander learned that Bessus had assumed the title of the Great King, under the name of Artaxerxes, and he decided to pursue him. Traversing Areia, now Northwest Afghanistan, which he had restored to its Viceroy, he was already well on his way towards Balkh when he heard that Satibarzanes, acting in collusion with Bessus, had rebelled, had killed the Macedonian representative and his escort, and

---

[1] To deal fully with this question would take an undue amount of space and would be out of place in this work, although I have made two journeys mainly to study it.

had collected the people to the capital, named Artacoana. As usual a forced march was made, some seventy miles being covered in two days, and the rebellion collapsed. The site of Artacoana is unknown, but it was probably on the Hari Rud. This view is strengthened by the fact that Alexander founded an Alexandria in the neighbourhood, which is generally believed to be close to modern Herat. Not that Herat was a new site. On the contrary there is the quatrain which runs :

> Lohrasp had laid the foundations of Herat :
> Gushtasp on them raised a superstructure :
> After him Bahman constructed the buildings,
> And Alexander of Rum completed the task.

The Annexation of Sistan and the March up the Helmand.—This rebellion changed Alexander's plan of campaign, and instead of marching eastwards to Balkh, he decided to go south and attack Barsaentes, Satrap of Drangiana or Zarangiana,[1] who was one of the accomplices in the murder of Darius. Alexander feared that Barsaentes might cut his line of communications, which was kept open with marvellous success, notwithstanding the enormous distances and the fact that the downfall of its old-established dynasty must have thrown the country into a state of anarchy.

The capital of the province was then Farrah, on a river of the same name, still a place of some importance. But the centre of population must always have been the delta of the Helmand. This river has changed its course so frequently that until archaeological proof is forthcoming, it is impossible to identify with certainty the delta that was inhabited at this period. Sir Henry McMahon,[2] whose authority is most weighty, concludes probably by a process of elimination that it was the delta of Tarakan, and selects the ruins of Ramrud as being the site of the capital of the Ariaspae, whose country was visited by the Macedonians after Drangiana. It is mentioned that Cyrus had given this tribe the honourable name of Euergetae, or " The Benefactors," in return for aid rendered to him ; and Alexander also treated them with honour and increased the extent of their territories.

---

[1] These names are the classical form of Zaranj (now known as Nad-i-Ali), which name is still preserved in Zirrah, one of the great depressions.
[2] *Vide* " Recent Survey and Exploration in Sistan," in *Journal Royal Geographical Society* for September 1906. Tate, in his *Memoir on Sistan*, Part I. p. 8, would identify the Reis tribe with the Euergetae. This work contains valuable information collected at first hand.

This was the most southerly point reached in Eastern Iran. A great section of the Lut separates Sistan from the province of Carmania or Kerman, which was traversed on the return from India. Alexander now swung eastwards and marched across Arachosia, a district situated on the middle Helmand. He probably crossed the river at the modern Girishk, following what has been the main route from time immemorial, and then marched up the Argandab and founded yet another Alexandria, the Kandahar of to-day. Thence he turned nearly north, by what must have always been a main route, to Kabul. The same road was trodden in the opposite direction more than two thousand years later by another European force, an English army under Lord Roberts.

The Crossing of the Hindu Kush and the Annexation of Bactria, 328 B.C.—North of Kabul, close to the main range of Asia, which had been already crossed to reach Hyrcania, yet another city was founded, near the village of Charikar, a site of great importance at the junction of three routes across the various passes from Bactria. This was termed Alexandria *ad Caucasum*,[1] and was garrisoned with Macedonian colonists, for whom one cannot but feel deep sympathy; for their chances of seeing their homes again were slight. Indeed, when 20,000 infantry and 3000 cavalry who had been settled in Central Asia attempted to return home after the death of Alexander, they were ruthlessly massacred by the orders of Perdiccas, the Regent, being apparently regarded as deserters.

Alexander probably crossed the Hindu Kush by the Panjshir pass, which is longer but easier than the others and only 11,600 feet high, whereas the Kaoshan pass rises to 14,300 feet. The army suffered both from cold and from scarcity, and mention is made of the fact that nothing grew on the mountains except the terebinth or wild pistachio tree and the silphium or malodorous asafœtida. The Macedonians descended unopposed into what is now Afghan Turkestan, and great Balkh, venerated by Persians on account of its antiquity and its close connexion with Zoroaster, offered no resistance, but together with Aornos, an unidentified city, fell into the hands of the conqueror. The capture of Balkh is specially noteworthy, for apart from its fame which gave it the title of "Mother of Cities" in later days, it was the last

---

[1] This range, now known as the Hindu Kush or "Hindu Killer," was then termed the Indian Caucasus or, more usually, the Paropanisus.

remaining great city of the Persian Empire, which was now entirely annexed.

The Capture of Bessus.—When Balkh fell, Bessus was deserted by his Bactrian cavalry and fled across the Oxus. Alexander, though the country had been laid waste, pressed after him to the river and crossed it, probably at Kilif, on rafts made of skins stuffed with straw, the passage taking five days. All doubt as to the possibility of Alexander extending the Macedonian operations to the right bank of the Oxus being now dispelled, Bessus was betrayed by Spitamenes, who was the commander of the Soghdian cavalry, and was punished by being crucified at Ecbatana.

The Advance to the Jaxartes or Sir Daria.—Alexander then marched north to Maracanda, now Samarcand, the future capital of Tamerlane. After resting his army there he beat the eastern boundaries of the Persian Empire by advancing to the Jaxartes, the Sir Daria of to-day, on which he founded Alexandria Eschate or "the Extreme," the modern Khojand. To give some idea of the size of the Persian Empire and the distance travelled by the Macedonians, it is only necessary to state that Khojand is fifty degrees of longitude, or about 3500 miles, east of Hellas. What that meant before the era of modern communications can hardly be grasped by the European of the twentieth century, unless, indeed, he has travelled in Persia, where fifteen miles a day is the average stage for a caravan, or from ninety to one hundred miles a week, including halts.

The First Macedonian Disaster.—While Alexander was thus engaged he learned that Spitamenes, who had submitted to him, had rebelled. Acting with his usual energy, he crossed the Jaxartes, and defeated the Scythians, who had collected on its right bank to help the insurgents. Meanwhile a division he had sent to raise the siege of Samarcand had been cut to pieces in the valley of the Polytimetus (now the Zerafshan) by Spitamenes, supported by a large body of Scythians from the steppes. Alexander started off immediately, but arrived only in time to bury the fallen, and to avenge the disaster he ravaged and massacred throughout the fertile valley. Thence he returned to Zariaspa,[1] where, during

---

[1] Identified by Sir T. Holdich (*vide Gates of India*, p. 90) with Anderab; but as this district is in the hills it could hardly have served as the winter quarters of Alexander. Moreover, we know that Spitamenes raided Zariaspa with some Scythian horsemen, and, if modern analogy serves, they would not have entangled themselves in the hills. Zariaspa was more probably in

midwinter 329-28 B.C., he rested his army and received large reinforcements from Greece, which must have been extremely valuable at this juncture.

The Capture of the Sogdian Rock.—After its rest, the Macedonian army again crossed the Oxus. Alexander himself marched to Maracanda; four other columns were formed to subdue the country thoroughly, and this they did without much difficulty. While these operations were in progress Spitamenes, the most energetic of Alexander's opponents, made a raid, in which he penetrated as far as Zariaspa; but he was pursued and driven away by Craterus. In attempting another raid he was defeated, and the Scythians ultimately sent his head to Alexander as a peace-offering. Bactria and Sogdiana were then organized in peace.

This campaign was marked by a striking feat in the capture of the Sogdian rock. Its garrison, believing it to be inaccessible, taunted the Macedonians and boasted that only winged men could take the fort. Alexander offered immense rewards for the first men who scaled the cliffs, and a band of heroes achieved the seemingly impossible by climbing up iron pegs driven into the rocks. When they appeared on the cliff overlooking the fort, the garrison forthwith surrendered. Among the prisoners was Roxana, the beautiful daughter of Oxyartes, the Bactrian chief, whom Alexander afterwards married. The late winter of 328-327 B.C.[1] was spent at Nautaka, a fertile oasis between Samarcand and the Oxus, evidently the modern Karshi, there being no other oasis in the mountains south of Samarcand; and, in the following spring, Alexander completed his conquests in those parts by conquering the Paraitakai or mountain tribes of Badakshan.

The Invasion of India, 327 B.C.—Nearly two years had been spent in subduing and organizing the warlike eastern provinces of Persia. Consequently it was not until the summer of 327 B.C. that everything was ready for the invasion of India, a country which had attracted Alexander with irresistible force, just as it attracted the Portuguese, the

---

the open plain not very far from the Oxus, and may possibly be identified with Balkh itself. *Vide Bactria*, by H. G. Rawlinson, pp. 10-12.

[1] Hogarth, in his Appendix to *Philip and Alexander of Macedon*, demonstrates most clearly that Alexander took some fourteen months in the section of the expedition which commences from the death of Darius and closes with the arrival at the Hindu Kush; and I have no hesitation in accepting the dates he gives.

Dutch, the English, and the French some nineteen centuries later. Recrossing the Hindu Kush to the Alexandria of the Indian Caucasus, the Macedonian army, now 120,000 strong, marched thence to Nicaia, identified by Sir Thomas Holdich [1] with Kabul, where King Taxiles made his submission. The main body was then despatched under Hephaestion north of the Khyber [2] pass
identified with the lower Swat valley, to the north of Peshawar. Alexander, with a picked force, attacked the tribes living on the southern slopes of the main range, in accordance with his usual custom of protecting his lines of communication by attacking and overpowering the local tribesmen. The capture of a second Aornos in this campaign has given birth to an immense controversial literature concerning its site; and Holdich considers that the question of its identity is by no means finally settled. The Macedonian army besieged several towns, and although their losses were not heavy, the effort would appear to have been somewhat out of proportion to the results, especially as Alexander himself was wounded in the shoulder by a dart and in the ankle by an arrow. Probably the report that Hercules had not been able to capture Aornos was the main cause of the whole campaign. The moral effect of these successes must, however, have been considerable.

Nysa, a Colony founded by Dionysus.—One extraordinary incident of the campaign was the arrival at a city termed Nysa, whose inhabitants claimed to be descendants of the army of Dionysus, pointing in proof of their statement to the fact that ivy grew in their neighbourhood and nowhere else. Alexander, delighted to hear this legend, which would act as an incentive to the Macedonians to rival the exploits of the god, treated the Nysaeans with marked kindness, and in honour of Dionysus the army wove ivy chaplets and sang hymns, invoking him by his various names.

The Passage of the Indus.—Meanwhile Hephaestion had reached the Indus at Attock, where its width narrows to about one hundred yards, and constructed a bridge of boats some time before Alexander rejoined the main body. Taxiles, too, had sent a gift of money, elephants, oxen, and sheep, together with a force of seven hundred mounted men; at the same time he formally surrendered his capital of Taxila,

---

[1] *Vide The Gates of India*, chaps. iv. and v., which deal with the routes of Alexander. McCrindle's *Ancient India* also commences at this point. Both works are valuable.

[2] *Vide* Preliminary Essay, pp. xxxvii, xxxviii.

the largest city in the Panjab, whose ruins lie half-way between Attock and Rawal Pindi. Alexander recognized the importance of the occasion by offering sacrifices and celebrating contests; and he waited to cross the Indus until the omens proved favourable. He then advanced on Taxila, where he was received with demonstrations of friendship, and in return he added to the territory of the state.

The Battle with Porus, 326 B.C.—A Macedonian garrison was left at Taxila and the ever-victorious army marched towards the Hydaspes, now the Jhelum, where it was known that Porus, a mighty monarch, had collected a large force strengthened by many elephants to withstand the invaders. Upon reaching the river they saw his camp on the opposite bank. The situation was difficult, as the Jhelum was in flood and unfordable, and Alexander's horses could not be trusted to face the elephants. But his genius shone most brightly when dealing with difficulties, and after lulling the suspicions of Porus by constant marches and counter-marches, he crossed from a point seventeen miles above his main camp where a wooded island screened his movements. During the operation there was a violent storm of rain and wind, which, however, ceased before daybreak. The troops were embarked in boats, and after passing the island steered for the opposite bank, where they were detected by the scouts of Porus who rode off to give the alarm.

Upon landing, the Macedonians found that they were not on the mainland after all, but on another island, and they had to ford a swift stream reaching higher than the chest before they formed up on the left bank of the river. There Alexander encountered the son of Porus with a force of 2000 men and a detachment of chariots; but after a sharp skirmish the Indians were driven back with the loss of their commander. Porus, meanwhile leaving a few elephants and a small force to contain the Macedonian troops who had been left in camp, formed a line of battle with his main body in the immediate neighbourhood of Chillianwala, where in 1849 British troops met valiant Sikhs, many of whom were probably the descendants of the soldiers of Porus. Trusting to the terror inspired by his elephants, he distributed them to the number of two hundred in front of the line, a hundred paces apart. Behind these was a force of 30,000 infantry. His cavalry and chariots were posted on the flanks.

Alexander, whose troops must have been weary after their long march in heavy rain and the passage of the Jhelum, ordered rest to be taken while he studied the dispositions of the enemy. Seeing the elephants covering the whole line, he decided not to make a frontal attack, but, taking advantage of his superiority in cavalry, to make his main attack against the left flank of Porus. He detached Koinos with a brigade to work round by the Greek right [1] to the rear of the enemy, with orders to harass them when they moved to meet the main attack. The commanders of the phalanx were instructed not to advance until the cavalry charge had produced its effect. The Indian cavalry, upon seeing their rear threatened, were preparing to wheel part of their force to meet the unexpected danger when Alexander charged home, and they broke and fled for shelter behind the elephants. The phalanx now advanced, and as the elephants crashed through it the situation was for a while serious. The Indian cavalry attempted a second charge ; but the better disciplined Macedonians drove them back upon the elephants, and following them up hemmed them in. The elephants, as the battle progressed, became unmanageable from their wounds and attacked friend and foe indiscriminately ; but, whereas the Macedonians could retreat and open out when charged, the Indians were so closely wedged in together that their losses were very heavy. At last, when the elephants refused to charge any longer, the Macedonians, advancing in close order, cut the Indians to pieces. At this juncture Craterus, who had crossed the Jhelum, appeared on the battlefield, and as his troops were fresh they engaged in a vigorous pursuit which turned the defeat into a rout.

Porus, conspicuous on a huge elephant, had fought throughout with the utmost bravery, and not until his troops were defeated did he seek refuge in flight. Being captured he was brought before Alexander, who asked him how he wished to be treated. " Like a King " was the proud reply. Asked if he had any further request to make, he rejoined, " Everything is comprised in the words ' Like a King.' "

Alexander was at his greatest in this battle. Throughout the operations he made no mistake ; his army faced elephants in large numbers for the first time, after a long night march

---

[1] Plutarch, who was not very accurate in military questions, makes Koinos attack the right wing of the Indians.

in a storm and the trying passage of the Jhelum; the victory was absolutely decisive, and, to crown all, he displayed great generosity to the vanquished monarch. The words attributed to him by Quintus Curtius run : " I see at last a danger that matches my courage. It is at once with wild beasts and men of uncommon mettle that the contest now lies." These words furnish an accurate epitome of this famous battle.

The Limit of Conquest.—The Macedonians, in spite of their splendid victory, felt depressed at the stubborn valour displayed by the Indians and also on account of their losses, which were comparatively heavy.[1] Alexander, however, after founding Nicaia on the battlefield in celebration of the victory, and Bucephalia at the point where he crossed the river, in memory of his famous charger which died shortly after the battle, led on his army, without heeding the heavy monsoon rains. The Acesines (the Chenab) and the Hydraotes (the Ravi) were crossed in succession, and everywhere the fertile country was subdued until the army camped on the right bank of the Hyphasis (the Beas).

The Macedonians, hearing that the country farther east was governed by powerful monarchs whose war elephants and armies were stronger and more numerous than those of Porus, began to hold meetings at which the speakers all declared that they had gone far enough, that they were tired of endless marches and battles, and wished to return home to enjoy what they had so hardly earned. A fine speech by Alexander, who declared his ideal to be " no other aim and end of labours except the labours themselves, provided they be such as lead to the performance of glorious deeds," fell flat on men in this mood. Koinos, a general of the second rank, in a very sensible reply pointed out that there must be some limit set to human achievement; that but few of the soldiers who had started from Greece were left; and that, if Alexander wished to conquer the whole world, he should first return home to celebrate his triumphs and then recruit a fresh army with which to undertake fresh conquests.

Alexander, who listened with not unnatural resentment to these unpalatable truths, broke up the assembly, and for three days secluded himself entirely, in the hope that the soldiers' mood would change. Finally, as they showed no

[1] Arrian makes the casualties about three hundred, but Diodorus estimates them at a thousand.

sign, he sacrificed and, the omens being unfavourable to an advance, the greatest soldier of all time permitted himself, as the Macedonians put it, to be vanquished by his own men. The order to march back was given [1] and received with demonstrations of heartfelt joy. Twelve enormous altars were erected to serve as thank-offerings to the gods and as memorials of the toil endured, and after celebrating a festival in the usual manner, the army marched back to the Ravi, which was probably crossed near Lahore, and to Wazirabad on the Chenab, which is now a prosaic railway junction. Alexander then proceeded to the Hydaspes, where he halted to construct sufficient ships to carry 8000 men, and when these were ready, the armada started off to conclude the most important of all early voyages. It is safe to state that until the present generation no other European had trodden many of the routes which are mentioned by the Greek writers, but which can now be identified from the accurate descriptions that have come down to us, more especially in the pages of Arrian.

[1] In *Ten Thousand Miles, etc.*, chap. xiv. is devoted to the march of Alexander from India to Susa.

MEDALLION OF ALEXANDER THE GREAT.
(From the Tarsus Treasure in the Cabinet de France.)

CHAPTER XXIV

THE DEATH OF ALEXANDER THE GREAT—HIS
ACHIEVEMENTS AND CHARACTER

He taught the Hyrcanians the institution of marriage, the Arachosians agriculture; he caused the Sogdians to support, not to kill, their parents; the Persians to respect, not to wed, their mothers. Wondrous philosopher, who made the Scythians bury their dead instead of eating them.—PLUTARCH on Alexander the Great.

The Voyage to the Indian Ocean.—To term the expedition of Alexander to the Indian Ocean a retreat is surely incorrect. Just as of his own will he made the Jaxartes his limit of conquest in the north, so in India his army made the Panjab his limit to the south. But he descended the Jhelum and the Indus as a conqueror, and as a conqueror he traversed the deserts of Gedrosia, subduing and organizing his conquests, until he reached the South-eastern provinces of Persia. Thus he completed an expedition during the course of which, as an examination of the map will prove, few if any centres of importance between Egypt and the Panjab had failed to hear the footsteps of his warriors and feel their might.

The great armada started down the Jhelum in the autumn of 326 B.C., on a journey which to the sea alone was about nine hundred miles in length, and took nearly a year to accomplish. Nearchus, destined to earn immortal fame as the first of all scientific naval explorers, was in charge of the fleet, which kept carefully defined stations, while divisions of the army marched along both banks. The Chenab was entered, not without danger from the eddies, and Alexander, ever thirsting for fresh laurels, left the river to attack the

Malloi, whom he severely harassed. In storming their chief city, generally identified with Multan, he leaped down alone into the stronghold with only three devoted followers, and when the Macedonians came to his assistance he appeared to be mortally wounded. The dismay of the army, to whom it was reported that Alexander was dead, may be imagined, and so may the transport of joy with which he was greeted when sufficiently recovered to endure the fatigue of returning to his camp, where he mounted a horse to prove his convalescence to his soldiers.

From Patala, at the apex of the Indus delta, Craterus was dismissed in charge of three brigades, the invalids, and the elephants, with instructions to travel to Persia " by the route through the Arachosians and the Zarangians." Alexander sailed down to the Indian Ocean and, in spite of a storm and the still more alarming phenomenon of the tide, which ebbed and left the fleet stranded, he advanced into the open sea, where he sacrificed to Poseidon, and after offering libations threw the goblet into the water as a thank-offering, praying the god to grant Nearchus a successful voyage.

The March from the Indus to Susa, 325 B.C.—The direction of Alexander's march through almost the entire length of what is now termed Makran was undoubtedly determined by the knowledge that his fleet, on which he relied to complete this epoch-making expedition, would require assistance ; throughout it is clear that his movements were subordinated to this consideration. Knight-errant as he was, his conviction that Semiramis and Cyrus had barely escaped from the deserts of Gedrosia with the loss of almost all their men would naturally furnish him with an additional incentive to win fresh laurels. Crossing the Arabius, now the Purali, he turned towards the sea to dig wells for the use of the fleet, and then swept the country of the Oreitai to the west, where he followed the same course. He next entered Gedrosia, and for some marches maintained touch with the coast ; but even thus early the pinch of hunger was felt, and his soldiers took for their own use the corn which he had collected for the revictualling of the fleet. It was during this stage of the journey that the abundant myrrh and nard, so valued in that age, was collected by the Phoenician sutlers.

About one hundred miles from the Arabius the Ras Malan forced the army to turn inland up the Hingol River.

This range entirely prevents all access to the sea, and here it was that the sufferings of the troops really began. As Arrian puts it, "the blazing heat and want of water destroyed a great part of the army. . . . For they met with lofty ridges of sand not hard and compact, but so loose that those who stepped on it sank down as into mud . . . tortured alike by raging heat and thirst unquenchable." In October 1893 I travelled from Chahbar, on the coast of Makran, to Geh and Pahra, in the interior ; nowhere have I made so trying a journey, and I appreciated the truthfulness of Arrian's description. So difficult, indeed, are the conditions in Makran that, but for the dates and palm cabbages which, on the authority of Strabo, saved the army, it is unlikely that a single survivor would have been left to tell the tale.

Alexander regained the coast near Pasni, where he obtained fresh water by digging wells on the sea-shore, which he followed as far as Gwadur. From this port a natural route leads up a river to the interior, and, realizing that to continue along the coast would involve the total destruction of his force, Alexander led the way to the fertile valley in which Pura was situated. Here his worn-out men were able to rest.

Pura,[1] now termed Pahra by the Baluchis and Fahraj by the Persians, lies in the only really fertile valley of Persian Baluchistan. In the neighbourhood are ruins of two older forts, and the site is generally believed to be ancient. Arrian states that Pura was reached in sixty days from Ora, and, as the map makes the distance perhaps six hundred miles, this would, in all the circumstances, be a reasonable distance to be covered in the time. Moreover, the army would naturally recruit at the first fertile district it reached, and would certainly not pass by the valley of the Bampur River. Therefore we may confidently assume that the mid-winter was spent in this valley of Baluchistan, and here Alexander regained touch with his Persian Satraps. From Pura the river was followed down to where its waters commingle with those of the Halil Rud in a *hamun* or lake known as the Jaz Morian, which I discovered in 1894 when I followed the footsteps of Alexander in this section of his great journey. A standing camp was formed in the valley of the Halil Rud, probably in the modern district of Rudbar. Higher up this valley, in 1900, a Greek alabaster unguent vase, dating from the fourth century B.C.,

---

[1] For the identification of Pura *vide Ten Thousand Miles*, etc., p. 172.

was found by me. It is now one of my greatest treasures, as it may well have belonged to Alexander.

It was at this standing camp, where an Alexandria was founded which has been identified with modern Gulashkird, that the weather-beaten and ragged Nearchus appeared. Alexander, seeing him in a miserable plight, feared that his fleet was lost, and we can imagine the joy of all when its safety was announced, and with what fervour sacrifices were offered and honours bestowed.

In the valley of the Halil Rud the army was joined by Craterus, with the baggage and elephants, after a march down the Helmand and across the Lut; and the journey was resumed under the most agreeable conditions, with abundant supplies, and no hostile force to be expected. Nearchus returned to the fleet, which he safely conducted to Ahwaz, and Hephaestion marched along the coast, keeping in touch with it. Alexander, with a picked force of light troops, traversed the districts of Sirjan and Baonat to Pasargadae, where we read of his distress upon finding that the tomb of Cyrus had been desecrated. The great army was reunited at Ahwaz, and crossed the Karun by a bridge. Thence it marched to Susa; and here the greatest expedition recorded in history terminated in triumphal rejoicings and in weddings between the noblest Macedonians and Persians.

The Voyage to Babylon.—After a while Alexander, ever chafing at inaction, sailed down the Karun to the Persian Gulf, and, skirting the low-lying coast to the mouth of the Tigris, travelled up this great river to Opis situated above modern Baghdad. The voyage took many months to accomplish and was completed in the summer of 324 B.C.

At Opis he announced that he intended to dismiss many of his veterans with rich rewards to their homes. This brought to a head the feelings of discontent and jealousy which had been constantly inflamed by the knowledge that thousands of Orientals were being trained to take their places in the ranks, and by the supposed change in Alexander from the mighty War Lord of a free people to an Oriental Despot surrounded by thousands of attendants. The war-worn veterans, deeming themselves slighted, collected in a vast throng and cried out to the King to dismiss them all, and then jeeringly advised him to continue the war in company with his father, the god Ammon. This mutinous behaviour enraged Alexander, who ordered the ringleaders to instant execution. He then harangued the army in a stirring speech, demonstrating with much force how he had raised his kingdom from penury to opulence ; and then, retiring to his palace, he began to organize Persian footguards, to choose Persian companions, and to give high posts to Persians. This was too much for his men, who implored with tears to be forgiven, and a great banquet marked the reconciliation with their commander.

Alexander then marched to the uplands of Media, where he found that the famous breed of Nisaean horses had been seriously diminished through neglect. The death of his friend Hephaestion at Ecbatana was a grievous blow to him ; and, finding in strenuous action the best alleviation of his grief, he made a winter expedition against the Cossaeans, who occupied the rugged ranges of Luristan. In spite of the cold and the elusiveness of the enemy, this, his last campaign, was as successful as every other war that he waged. In savage mood he offered up the Cossaeans as a sacrifice to the ghost of Hephaestion.

The Great Conqueror now marched towards Babylon, arranging on the way for ships to be constructed in Hyrcania for the exploration of the Caspian Sea. There was at that time no certainty that it was an inland sea, and the Volga was quite unknown. Embassies from many lands, including Carthage, Libya, Ethiopia, Italy, and Gaul, came to offer their congratulations, and such widespread homage must have tended to flatter the pride of the Great Soldier. When he approached Babylon, the priests of Bel begged him not to enter the city ; but he rejected their advice, as interested, and marched in triumph into the ancient capital of Asia.

The Death of Alexander the Great, 323 B.C.—Not content with the vast empire he already possessed, Alexander began almost immediately to prepare for an expedition to Arabia by means of reconnaissances and the construction of a powerful fleet to be manned by Phoenicians. He also made a voyage down the Euphrates and began the construction of a dockyard at Babylon. Suddenly, in the midst of his preparations, he was stricken with fever, probably contracted in the marshes of the Euphrates. He continued to give orders and to offer sacrifices as usual ; but at last he became speechless, and after greeting his grief-stricken soldiers as they filed past him, Alexander the Great passed away at the early age of thirty-two, in the height of his fame and the splendid plenitude of his power.

An Analysis of Hellenism.—It is important to grasp the effect produced on the Persian Empire by the Greek Conquest ; and in order to do so it is necessary to consider for a moment the nature of Hellenism, which was imposed on the East. Bevan, who devotes a brilliant and most suggestive chapter to this subject,[1] lays down that the epoch-making achievement of the Greeks was to bring freedom and civilization into unity ; and this is profoundly true. As has been pointed out in dealing with Sumer and Akkad, the dwellers in Babylonia, in consequence mainly of the physical conditions, were certainly not free in the Greek sense of the word ; indeed each of the old powers not only rested on slavery but held that even its free subjects were bound to obey any and every order without demur. In Hellas, on the other hand, the physical conditions always made for freedom ; but the intense love of freedom prevented Hellas from developing into a great power, and to the end of the history of Greece there was no continuous unity of effort.

Macedonia was not strictly a Greek state, being composed of a number of mountain tribes who served an absolute monarch ; but that monarch was strongly imbued with all that Hellas could teach, and thus Alexander the Great was the torch-bearer of Hellenism, and the *Diadochi* or " Successors " founded dynasties which were Greek in mind and speech. But, as absolute monarchs, both he and they conflicted with the spirit of Hellenism, which implied a certain type of character and a certain cast of ideas entirely opposed to absolutism. The life of the Greek citizen was dominated by his sense of duty to the state, of which he was himself a part, and it was this which gave him his love of freedom, his individuality, and his spirit of enterprise, priceless qualities that raised him above the Asiatic. But the lack of other qualities hindered the Greeks from the steady co-operation necessary to make a united Hellenic people. The Macedonian kings were absolute rulers, and consequently would be regarded as tyrants by the Greeks ; yet they were Hellenes, who looked to Athens for fame, and who treated

---

[1] *The House of Seleucus,* chap. i.

A Comparison between the Hellenized and the British Empire.—It is interesting to compare the Greeks with ourselves, and their empire with that of Great Britain. It can certainly be maintained that the class from which the administrators of Great Britain have been mostly drawn is trained at the Public Schools both mentally and physically to produce an average type which in many respects must resemble the best Greek ideals more closely than any other since the downfall of Hellas. Indeed in some ways it even surpasses the highest Greek ideals. This training, in a society which is from many points of view a model republic, produces a certain type of character and a certain cast of ideas which no other European race can rival; and this explains the fact that the Englishman is so often an able administrator who, thanks to his love of sport and of physical exercise, can live all over the globe and maintain his health and with it his sane outlook, his initiative, and his energy. Just as Alexander the Great built cantonments at strategical points, where he posted garrisons who led their own lives, so the British of to-day hold India by a mere handful of administrators and soldiers also living their own lives in cantonments distributed at strategical centres, albeit with their task facilitated of late years by railways and the telegraph.

To conclude this comparison, would it be far-fetched to compare the Macedonians with the Scotch, who, descended from wild clansmen, have yet played almost as leading a part in empire-building as was played by the tribesmen of Macedonia under their ever-famous King?

The Fruits of Hellenism.—Given then the Greek character, it is reasonable to suppose that in ordinary conditions the position of the subject races would be better than under the rule of Persia, just as the Englishman shows incomparably greater consideration to the Indian than the Indians do to their fellow-countrymen. The Greek generals, we know, followed the example of their king in subduing robber tribes and in introducing law and order. But when once the master mind had been removed by death, furious rivalries and wild ambitions were let loose and the Macedonians spoiled their splendid heritage by incessant campaigns. And yet the spirit remained, and, if the era of strife never entirely passed away, it is to be remembered that the armies engaged were small and the area enormous ; and thus we can well believe that, as in India during the Mutiny, quiet progress was constantly made in districts which were not affected by the fighting.

A matter of no little importance was the dispersal of the hoards of the Achaemenians. Although in the first place the money was given to Macedonian officers and men and was mainly spent on building temples and on public works in Greece, this unlocking of the treasure-house of Asia increased the trade of the known world enormously. As the roads to the East were open for intercourse of every kind, it is reasonable to suppose that the beneficent power of commerce was stimulated and increased to an extent we cannot easily appreciate.

One further point remains for notice. Alexander the Great is made to figure in Persian legend as the destroyer of the Zoroastrian religion. This is in fact a complete misrepresentation. Strabo [1] mentions that he prohibited the barbarous custom of exposing persons at the point of death to the sacred dog, and perhaps it was this and similar actions which make the policy of Alexander appear to be the very reverse of what it actually was. It must also be remembered that it was through priestly and consequently hostile sources that legends concerning his actions were handed down.

The Achievements and Character of Alexander the Great.—It has been well said that Alexander the Great represents the culminating point of Greek civilization both in his achievements and in his character. His achievements were to lead the forces of the poor but virile kingdom of Macedonia, threatened as it constantly was by the states of Hellas and the surrounding tribes, over the known world, conquering, organizing, and civilizing wherever he went. He held together his conquests by justice, by founding cities at strategical points which were occupied by Greeks, and above all by his genius, which was not merely dazzling but attractive. And this gigantic work, which was accomplished in eleven years, held good in many cases for centuries ; so that after his death, Arrian tells us, from Hellas to India, Semitic, Aryan, and Turanian states were alike ruled by Greek dynasties permeated with the Hellenic spirit. Again, this extraordinary

[1] Strabo xi. 517.

personality worked to break down the barriers between East and West, and had he succeeded in yoking all Hellas to the noble task the results would have been incomparably greater and more lasting than they were ; but even Athens could not rise above local jealousies, and Sparta was ever hostile. This temper in Greece only heightens the achievements of Alexander, which, when the age, the short time, and the circumstances are all considered, stand unrivalled among the deeds of men.

In studying his character no one who reads with care the pages of Arrian and of Plutarch can fail to notice the judicial frame of mind in which they are written. The errors and defects of Alexander are neither concealed nor extenuated but set forth plainly, and we are impressed with the fact that we have a truthful, detailed, and impartial account of his life. This being so, does the character of any great conqueror appear finer than that of this fearless knight, who in Makran poured away a precious draught of water in the sight of his army ? He was courteous to women, ever athirst for knowledge, and surely worthy of the chief seat at any court of chivalry ; true to all, generous, humane, and greedy only of renown. Were he impeached before any conceivable tribunal, could we not fancy him exclaiming, like the great Englishman, Clive, " By God, Mr. Chairman, at this moment I stand astonished at my own moderation " ? Moderation, self-control, and the cult of the " proper mean " of Aristotle were among his marked characteristics in all his dealings with his fellows.

Alexander was not only the greatest of all soldiers, he was a statesman whose plans were constantly successful, and his love of exploration and of knowledge of all kinds was a ruling passion throughout his life. In parting with perhaps the most famous man who ever trod this earth, I quote the words of his great historian, Arrian : " For my own part, I think there was at that time no race of men, no city, nor even a single individual to whom Alexander's name and fame had not penetrated. For this reason it seems to me that a hero totally unlike any other human being could not have been born without the agency of the deity."

SELEUCUS NICATOR.
(From a Coin of Philetaerus of Pergamum, 281–263 B.C., in the British Museum.)

CHAPTER XXV

THE WARS OF THE "SUCCESSORS"

Of all those who succeeded to the sovereignty after Alexander, Seleucus became the greatest king, was the most kingly in mind, and ruled over the greatest extent of land after Alexander himself.—ARRIAN.

The Problem of the Succession.—The sudden and unexpected death of Alexander the Great before he possessed an adult son unchained a conflict of interests which convulsed the known world for two generations. Roxana was expecting an heir, Alexander had only recently married Statira, a daughter of Darius, and there was Heracles, falsely alleged to be his son by Barsine, widow of Memnon. Another claimant to power was his illegitimate half-witted brother, Philip Arrhidaeus. Olympias, beloved as being the mother of the hero, had to be reckoned with, and also his sister Cleopatra, the widow-queen of Epirus. Cynane, a daughter of Philip, and her daughter Eurydice, who subsequently married Philip Arrhidaeus, were also prominent figures on the stage.

The first fight for power took place almost before the King's body was cold. Perdiccas, the senior officer of the Court, who had served with much distinction and in high posts under Philip as well as under his great son, but was selfish, cruel, and narrow-minded, took the lead at a meeting of generals, at which it was decided to govern the empire by means of a council pending the birth of an heir. The infantry, on the other hand, representing a lower class without personal ambitions and more loyal to the throne, proclaimed Philip Arrhidaeus king.

CHAP. XXV   WARS OF THE "SUCCESSORS"   285

The moment was critical, but a compromise was made, and, in accordance with ancient custom, the whole army was purified by marching between the divided halves of a dog which had been sacrificed [1] and then engaged in a sham fight, the infantry opposing the cavalry and the elephant division. The infantry was overpowered, and, as the contest threatened to become grimly earnest, surrendered the leaders of the party favouring Philip Arrhidaeus, who were thereupon trampled to death by the elephants. In the end it was settled that Philip Arrhidaeus should be king until the expected heir was old enough to succeed, and that Perdiccas should be regent of the whole empire. The generals were appointed to various countries, to which they proceeded, meaning undoubtedly in most cases to carve out kingdoms for themselves, a fact history has recognized by bestowing upon them the title of *Diadochi* or " Successors."

Meanwhile Roxana had enticed Statira, the daughter of Darius, to Babylon, where she murdered her, and her own position was shortly afterwards strengthened by the birth of a son, known as King Alexander.

The Death of Perdiccas, 321 B.C.—The clash of conflicting interests ended speedily in war. Perdiccas, after many intrigues, strengthened his position by betrothal to Cleopatra, which gained him the support of the masterful Olympias. This fresh development so alarmed Antigonus of Phrygia that he fled to Antipater, who, in the previous year, had succeeded in crushing a Greek rising in what is known as the Lamian war. Perdiccas now attempted to remove Ptolemy from his path, and summoned him from Egypt, hoping that his order would be disobeyed. But the astute Ptolemy promptly appeared before the army, the sovereign tribunal, which duly acquitted him, and he returned in safety to his province. Angered by this want of success, Perdiccas invaded Egypt, where he failed signally in three attempts to force the passage of the Nile. The Macedonians turned on him and he was murdered by his own officers. Peace was then made with Ptolemy, and the army marched away to join the forces of Antipater.

The Rise of Seleucus.—Among the leaders in this mutiny was Seleucus, who was destined shortly to play a leading part. A favourite of Alexander, who had noted his splendid

[1] *Folklore in the Old Testament,* by Sir J. G. Frazer, i. 408.

physique and great courage, Seleucus, although comparatively young, had served with distinction throughout the long series of campaigns, and in India had been appointed Commander of the Royal Hypaspistai or Medium Infantry.[1] At the triumphal celebration at Susa he had been awarded the hand of Apama, the daughter of Spitamenes, who with Oxyartes had been so doughty an opponent of Alexander in Bactria, and thus the famous Seleucid dynasty, of which he was the founder, sprang from both Macedonian and Iranian stock.

After the death of Alexander and the assumption of the regency by Perdiccas, Seleucus was appointed to the command of the Companion Cavalry, and in Egypt he led the cavalry officers who forced their way into the Regent's tent.

The Macedonian infantry, which had been ignored in the mutiny, rose against Antipater when the two armies met. He attempted to reason with the men but was greeted with stones, and had not Antigonus and Seleucus intervened it would have gone hard with him. When a redistribution of posts was made, Seleucus, possibly in reward for his services on this occasion, was appointed to Babylon, where he immediately began to assert his authority and to extend his power.

The Fight for Power.—During the twenty years of constant warfare following the second distribution of posts, which was in reality a partition of the empire, events were complicated, and I propose to deal with them very briefly. Pithon, Satrap of Media, and Peukestas, Satrap of Persis, were both among Alexander's greatest and most trusted officers ; but the former was too ambitious and impatient, and no sooner had he returned to his province after reappointment to it than he seized Parthia, making away with its Satrap. This false step gave Peukestas an opportunity of heading a force supplied by himself and other neighbouring Satraps, which drove Pithon out of Media and forced him to flee to Babylon for help.

Antigonus and Eumenes.—Meanwhile Antigonus had been fighting against Eumenes, the late King's secretary, who alone at this period represented the family of Alexander in Asia, and had forced him in 320 B.C. to shut himself up in a fort in Cappadocia. The following year the loyal Antipater

---

[1] These troops were used when the phalanx could not be employed, and were less heavily armed.

died, and as he had bequeathed his office of regent not to his son Cassander but to Polyperchon, a brother-in-arms, the latter, in order to secure support against Cassander, espoused the cause of Olympias with great zeal, and Eumenes was thereby enabled for a short time to play a leading part in the ceaseless struggle for power. The command of the famous "Silver Shields" and also the disposal of the royal treasure were entrusted to him. Indeed, the prospects of the royal family seemed to be distinctly brighter; but in 318 B.C. its fleet was defeated off Byzantium by that of Antigonus and Cassander—a very serious blow. Eumenes, a man of strong character, thereupon marched inland and called upon the Satraps who had attacked Pithon to recognize his authority and to join him. He spent the winter of 318–317 B.C. in Mesopotamia, and in the spring encamped only thirty miles from Babylon, on his way to Susa. Seleucus tried to corrupt the "Silver Shields," but in vain, and Eumenes joined the Satraps at Susa.

Meanwhile Antigonus had effected a junction with the forces of Seleucus, and in pursuance of their concerted scheme he marched on Susa, which was ultimately surrendered. Eumenes opposed him as he was attempting to cross the Karun, and inflicted a serious defeat on him, filling the river with the dead and capturing four thousand men. In a second engagement the "Silver Shields," who were now men of over sixty, carried all before them, but lost their baggage. They thereupon disgraced themselves by an act of treachery seldom paralleled in military history. They handed over their undefeated general Eumenes to Antigonus; and, in spite of the remonstrances of Nearchus, one of the very few generals who kept his high reputation in prosperity, he was put to death. The date of this crime was 316 B.C.

The Supremacy of Antigonus on the Death of Eumenes, 316 B.C.—Antigonus next judicially murdered Pithon, whom he lured to a friendly conference, and Peukestas was also mysteriously removed. Laden with the treasures of Ecbatana and Susa to the value of some millions sterling, Antigonus returned in triumph to Babylon, where he intended to complete his successes by making away with his host, Seleucus. He, however, fled to Egypt, where Ptolemy received him and granted him protection. Antigonus now overshadowed all his rivals, and, as his fleets were supreme and he occupied a central position which made concerted action on the part of his enemies extremely difficult, it seemed probable that he would overcome them one by one.

The Destruction of the Family of Alexander the Great.—The savage hatred and jealousy of Olympias and Eurydice, prototypes of the equally barbarous and cruel Fredegonde and Brunhild, were the main cause of the final destruction of the royal family. At the same time, the character of the " Successors " appears in a very evil light ; for, with the exception of Antipater, who was loyal to his trust, none of the generals who owed everything to Alexander rallied round the throne to protect his helpless heir. Cassander, who had been passed over by his father, had joined forces with Antigonus, and as a result of the naval battle in the Bosphorus he had been able to conquer Hellas from Polyperchon, the Regent. Then followed the first of the royal tragedies. Olympias returned suddenly to Macedonia from Epirus and contrived to seize Philip Arrhidaeus and his intriguing wife Eurydice. With savage cruelty she put them to torture and finally to death, Philip being shot with arrows and Eurydice being graciously permitted to hang herself. The old Queen then arrested hundreds of the adherents of the family of Antipater, and they too were mercilessly dealt with. Upon the return of Cassander the tide turned, and Olympias, besieged and captured in Pydna, was stoned to death in revenge for her many crimes.

The youthful Alexander and Roxana now fell into the hands of Cassander, who, having himself married a daughter of Philip, aspired to the throne. He kept the young King and his mother close prisoners for a few years ; but in 311 B.C., hearing that the people were murmuring, he basely murdered the deserted son of Alexander the Great, whose fate is surely one of the most pathetic in history. Cleopatra, the widow-queen of Epirus, and Heracles, the illegitimate son, were also murdered, and the extirpation of the royal family was continued until the usurpers had no fear of a hostile claimant to the throne who could boast that he was of royal descent.

The Battle of Gaza, 312 B.C.—To return to the chief actors, there were in 315 B.C., or only eight years after the death of Alexander the Great, but four Macedonians who had maintained their power, the others, namely, Perdiccas, Eumenes, Peukestas, and Craterus, having disappeared from the stage, while Seleucus was a fugitive. Antigonus ruled from the Mediterranean Sea to Bactria ; Ptolemy held Egypt firmly ; Cassander ruled in Hellas and Macedonia, and Lysimachus was carving out a kingdom for himself in Thrace and in Asia Minor.

The balance of power having been upset by the preponderance of Antigonus, the three weaker rulers made common cause, and down to the decisive battle of Ipsus, in 301 B.C., they constantly endeavoured to undermine and weaken his position. The first great blow was struck by Ptolemy, who, accompanied by Seleucus, marched into Syria and inflicted a heavy defeat on Demetrius, the brilliant son of Antigonus. This entirely upset a plan for invading Europe which Antigonus had been maturing.

The Reoccupation of Babylon by Seleucus, 312 B.C.—The effects of this defeat were made much greater by the daring venture of Seleucus, who set out with a body of only one thousand men to recover his lost province. There was a strain of knight-errantry in Seleucus that recalls his great master. When his little force quailed and faltered, he sustained it by an oracle which hailed him king and by speeches touched with a fire like Alexander's. Following the route through Carrhae, where he was joined by some Macedonian soldiers, he boldly traversed Mesopotamia and marched on Babylon, hoping that his adherents would come to his side. Nor was he disappointed, as everywhere he was warmly welcomed, even by the Macedonian officials. Carrying all before him, he re-entered Babylon in triumph on October 1, 312 B.C., from which date the Seleucid era is, according to the most generally received opinion, held to begin.

He set to work at once to organize an army, knowing that the supporters of Antigonus would challenge his position. He had not long to wait before Nicanor, Satrap of Media, advanced to attack him at the head of 17,000 men. Though his own force numbered one-fifth of this, he made a series of forced marches and surprised Nicanor, whose army came over to him. The defeated Satrap himself barely escaped with his personal following, but was pursued into Media and killed.

The Raid of Demetrius on Babylon, 311 B.C.—Antigonus, after the battle of Gaza, rightly considered that Ptolemy was his chief enemy, and prepared to invade Egypt ; but in order to effect a diversion in favour of Nicanor, he despatched a flying column of 19,000 men under Demetrius, with orders to recover Babylon and to return as quickly as possible to join the great expedition. This raid was not opposed. Patrocles, who commanded in the absence of Seleucus, sent his small force far away to prevent the soldiers from being tampered with, while he himself merely observed Demetrius. The latter entered Babylon but had to return without producing any permanent impression ; indeed the pillaging committed by his army only damaged his father's cause.

The Making of the Empire of Seleucus, 311–302 B.C.—Seleucus, after the withdrawal of Demetrius, returned from Media in triumph, and, realizing that Antigonus was too much occupied to attempt a serious invasion of Babylonia, employed his great abilities in annexing the eastern provinces of the Persian empire. By 302 B.C., after nine years of successful warfare, his empire extended to the Jaxartes in one direction and to the confines of the Panjab in the other. In India he came into contact with the famous conqueror Chandragupta, better known to us by his classical name of Sandrocottus, grandfather of the still more famous Asoka. At first he prepared to attack this monarch ; but realizing that the advantages to be gained were far outweighed by the risks, he came to terms with him, ceding the Greek possessions in India up to the Hindu Kush, in exchange for 500 trained war elephants and large sums of money. Seleucus sealed the treaty by giving his daughter to the Indian monarch, and it was faithfully observed on both sides.

During this period Seleucus organized his vast empire into seventy-two satrapies, an arrangement which lessened the chances of revolt by preventing any single subject from becoming too powerful. Furthermore, he had moved the capital to Seleucia, a city which he founded on the Tigris some forty miles north of Babylon. His object in building it was probably to strengthen the influences of Hellenism, which must have been weak in face of the great traditions and associations of Babylon.

Antigonus and Ptolemy.—In the west, meanwhile, the struggle had continued with varying success. Demetrius was subduing Cyprus when a fleet commanded by Ptolemy in person came in sight. In the battle which ensued the Egyptians suffered complete defeat, forty ships of war, 8000 soldiers, and immense booty being captured ; and many ships besides being sunk. Following up this success, Antigonus invaded Egypt; but the expedition failed, Antigonus, like Perdiccas, being baffled by Ptolemy. He was baffled also at Rhodes, which Demetrius was unable to take. Here, too, the assistance in men and money afforded by Ptolemy contributed not a little to the successful defence.

The Battle of Ipsus, 301 B.C.—During these last years Antigonus had been barely holding his own, and when in 302 B.C. the forces of Lysimachus and Cassander carried the war into Asia Minor, Demetrius was recalled from Greece, where he had been conducting a brilliant campaign. It was Seleucus who now decided the issue. At the end of 302 B.C. he marched into Cappadocia with a veteran army of 20,000 infantry, 12,000 mounted troops, 480 elephants, and 100 scythed chariots. In the spring of 301 B.C. he united his forces with those of Lysimachus and a decisive battle was fought at Ipsus, in the province of Phrygia, on the great route running from Sardes to Susa. In the first phase Demetrius routed the opposing cavalry commanded by Antiochus, son of Seleucus; but he, like Prince Rupert in later times, carried the pursuit too far, and Seleucus, whose elephants were used to great effect, won the battle. The success was rendered all the more complete by the death of the veteran Antigonus, who to the end was expecting the return of his impetuous son. This victory was a most important one; for, although Demetrius still maintained his hold on parts of Hellas and on Cilicia, Cyprus, Tyre, and Sidon, and possessed an unbeaten fleet, Syria was annexed by Seleucus and Asia Minor by Lysimachus.

Seleucus became thenceforward the paramount king, as Antigonus had been before him, and consequently, to preserve the balance of power, Ptolemy and Lysimachus united against him. Probably it was on this account that the Seleucid capital was again transferred, this time from the centre of the empire to the Orontes, where Antioch arose in great splendour foreshadowing its future importance.

The Career of Demetrius Poliorcetes after Ipsus.—Reference has already been made to some of the brilliant exploits of Demetrius, best known by his title Poliorcetes or "Taker of Cities." Plutarch compares him aptly with Antony, and their lives were indeed, as he says, "each a series of great successes and great disasters, mighty acquisitions and tremendous losses of power, sudden overthrows followed by unexpected recoveries." No one was more conspicuous than he for some years after the battle of Ipsus, and a brief account of his later career is necessary, as he was connected with almost every important event.

When Seleucus practically succeeded to the paramount position of Antigonus, Lysimachus and Ptolemy, as we have seen, were forced into opposition. Seleucus consequently made overtures to Demetrius, and asked for his daughter Stratonice, the grand-daughter of Antipater, in marriage. This pleased Demetrius, who came to Syria with his daughter, and the two monarchs remained on excellent terms until Seleucus tried to purchase Cilicia, and demanded Tyre and Sidon, the possession of which had become a matter of great importance to him since his establishment at Antioch. Demetrius replied by augmenting their garrisons, and shortly afterwards returned to the West.

His Accession to the Throne of Macedonia.—In 297 B.C. Cassander died, and in the following year his son Philip also; the kingdom of Macedonia was then held by his two remaining sons, who reigned conjointly. But again the barbarous Macedonian spirit showed itself in Antipater, who murdered his mother; and Demetrius, taking advantage of his opportunity, seized the throne of Macedonia in 293 B.C. Soon afterwards, his vast preparations for a campaign in Asia aroused Lysimachus and Ptolemy, who incited Pyrrhus of Epirus to join the former in a concerted invasion of Macedonia, while Seleucus turned the situation to advantage by annexing Cilicia. The Macedonians had come to despise the luxuriousness of Demetrius, and, regarding Pyrrhus as the bravest soldier of the day and the most like Alexander,[1] desired him for their king. They consequently deserted Demetrius, to whom Plutarch applies the words put by Sophocles into the mouth of Menelaus :

> For me, my destiny, alas, is found
> Whirling upon the gods' swift wheel around.

After a period of eclipse this truly great adventurer collected a force, and, landing in Asia Minor, captured Sardes.

[1] Plutarch writes: "They thought his countenance, his swiftness and his motions expressed those of the Great Alexander, and that they beheld here an image and resemblance of his rapidity and strength in fight." What a splendid memory Alexander bequeathed to the Macedonians !

WARS OF THE "SUCCESSORS"

Agathocles, son of Lysimachus, now appeared on the scene, and although he gained no success, the army of Demetrius suffered from lack of supplies and forage and lost a number of men in the passage of the Lycus. So, after following the route of Alexander as far as Tarsus, he opened up negotiations with his son-in-law. Seleucus was at first inclined to meet him generously; but, convinced by the arguments of Patrocles that it would be dangerous to allow such an ambitious and restless personage to reside within his borders, he changed his mind and marched to Cilicia at the head of a large force. Demetrius, at bay, fought splendidly, and had more than once defeated the troops of Seleucus when he was prostrated by sudden illness and deserted by many of his soldiers. Rapidly recovering, however, he made a daring raid into Syria at the head of the band which had remained faithful. Seleucus followed, and with great courage rode up alone to the diminished army of Demetrius, which recognized him and at once came over to him.

His Captivity and Death.—Demetrius then attempted to reach the sea-coast but failed and surrendered to Seleucus. At first he was treated royally; but afterwards was sent into dignified confinement at Apamea on the Orontes. There he died two years later, a worn-out drunkard.

The Defeat and Death of Lysimachus, 281 B.C.—The power and prestige of Seleucus were greatly enhanced by his capture of Demetrius, and other events which occurred at this period enabled him to overshadow his two rivals still more effectually. Ptolemy, now very old, abdicated, not in favour of his eldest son, Ptolemy Keraunus, but of his son by Berenice, known to history by the title Philadelphus [1] because of his marriage with his full sister. Keraunus fled to the court of Lysimachus,

---

[1] To show the various complicated relationships I append the following table from Professor J. P. Mahaffy's *Empire of Alexander* :—

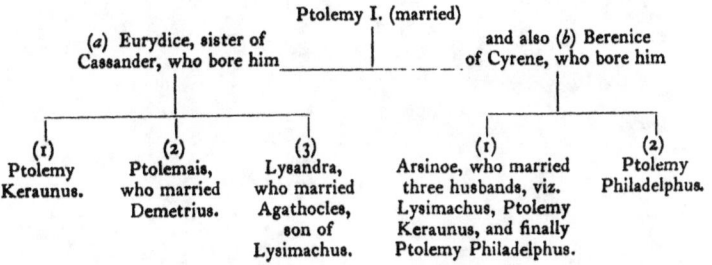

where he was received most kindly. But he intrigued against his brother-in-law Agathocles, who, on a false accusation, was put to death by his father, and Keraunus then left his court for that of Seleucus. The murder of Agathocles, whose innocence was subsequently proved, raised a storm of indignation against Lysimachus, and Seleucus took advantage of it to attack him. The issue of the campaign, whose theatre was in Asia Minor, was hardly doubtful, as the subjects of Lysimachus were completely alienated. In a battle on the plain of Koros, the site of which has not been identified, Lysimachus was killed. Thus at last Seleucus won where both Perdiccas and Antigonus had failed ; but, in view of his extreme age, he decided to surrender his vast empire to his son and to spend his few remaining years as King of Macedonia, his dearly loved home.

The Assassination of Seleucus Nicator, 281 B.C.—But the fates were against the realization of his desire. As he was proceeding towards Macedonia, after crossing the Hellespont, he was assassinated by Keraunus while listening to the legends connected with an ancient altar. Thus fell Seleucus Nicator, or " the Conqueror," who was perhaps the greatest and most attractive of the " Successors." His death may be said to close a chapter of history.

SILVER COIN OF SELEUCUS III. SOTOR (KERAUNUS)

CHAPTER XXVI

THE SELEUCID EMPIRE TO THE RISE OF PARTHIA

And the soldiers made ready for battle and sounded the trumpets. And they distributed the elephants among the phalanxes and for every elephant they appointed a thousand men, wearing coats of mail, and on their heads helmets of brass. . . . And the rest of the horsemen they set on the two wings of the army to strike terror into the enemy and to serve as protection for the phalanxes. And when the sun shone upon the shields of gold and brass, the mountains glistened therewith and blazed like torches of fire.—The Seleucid Army, from 1 Maccabees vi.

The Accession of Antiochus Soter, 281 B.C.—The house of Seleucus was shaken to its foundations by the foul deed of Keraunus : and the defection of the army and of the fleet to the assassin seemed to presage its overthrow. Probably the great distances and the lack of good communications gave a respite and thereby proved the salvation of Antiochus, who moreover, it must be remembered, was no raw youth but a man with considerable experience both in war and in administration. For a considerable period the energies of the new monarch were entirely devoted to securing his position in Syria. Meanwhile his brother-in-law Antigonus Gonatas, son of Demetrius, promptly espoused his cause, and attacked Keraunus, partly, it may be imagined, in order to defend Macedonia, but he was defeated and retired to Central Greece.

The Invasion of the Gauls and the Death of Ptolemy Keraunus, 280 B.C.—Keraunus was not destined to enjoy his ill-gotten power very long but to perish and that speedily. A terrible inroad of Gauls, or as the Greeks termed them Galatians, spread desolation far and wide, and on Keraunus fell the brunt of the invasion, which resulted in his defeat and death in the spring of 280 B.C. That year Macedonia was overrun by the terrible invaders, who, not content with murdering, ravishing, and burning, apparently even ate the Greek children. The following spring they turned the pass of Thermopylae and ravaged Hellas; but they were at length defeated at Delphi, whereupon they retreated and Greece was saved.

Asia Minor so far had remained inviolate: but the Northern League, consisting of Bithynia and the powerful city-state of Heraclea, made a sinister alliance with the Gauls and ferried across a large body of these savages, who spread far and wide ravaging and massacring, and finally occupied districts in the province of Phrygia.

The Defeat of the Gauls by Antiochus I.—Antiochus I. gained his title of Soter or the " Saviour " by a great victory gained over these invaders. Lucian tells us that the Gauls, who possessed forty thousand cavalry and many war chariots, were preparing to charge when the elephants of Antiochus moved to the front and by their mere appearance terrified the horses and caused a mad stampede. The Macedonian victory was complete, and Antiochus celebrated it suitably by a trophy bearing the figure of an elephant. As time passed we hear of the Galatians enlisted as mercenaries and fighting as such on opposite sides, until gradually they settled down and became partially civilized, although gangs of them levied blackmail for many years to come.

The Divisions of the Empire of Alexander after the Invasion of the Gauls.—The " Celtic Fury " ended the epoch of the contemporaries of Alexander the Great, and when its force was spent there were only three empires or kingdoms left, with a fringe of independent states. The most important in area, population, and resources was ruled by the house of Seleucus, which was united to that of Macedonia by ties of special strength. Seleucus Nicator had, as we have seen, married Stratonice, sister of Antigonus Gonatas, and then, to gratify his love-sick heir, the son of another wife, had committed the horrible deed of handing her over in marriage to him. Again, a daughter of Seleucus by the first marriage was subsequently married to her Macedonian uncle in order to strengthen still further the bonds uniting the two families. The kingdom of Macedonia, by far the smallest and poorest in resources, possessed the prestige and warlike population of the mother-country, but remained weaker than the other two. The empire of Egypt was very strong, from its fertility, its compactness, its inaccessibility, its sea-power, and its trade. It included Cyprus and a protectorate over the confederation of the Cyclades; and when hostilities broke out with the Seleucids, its latent powers developed and enabled it to control most of the Greek ports on the coast of Asia Minor. At the same time it resembled Athens, to whose hegemony it had succeeded, in not usually attempting to hold anything but islands and some of the ports on the mainland. The houses of Ptolemy and Seleucus were united by the marriage of Apama, a daughter of Seleucus, to Magas, the half-brother of Ptolemy II. These three empires alike depended mainly on Greek mercenaries to supply their armies, and it was consequently of great importance to them to bear a good reputation in Hellas. This reliance on foreign troops rather than on a national army naturally encouraged intrigues which threatened the stability of the throne in all three empires.

The secondary powers were established for the most part in hilly and comparatively inaccessible regions. To the east was Atropatene, now the province of Azerbaijan. Adjoining it to the west was Armenia, generally independent; then came Cappadocia in the heart of Asia Minor, ruled by a great Persian family, as also was Pontus farther north, which was to achieve great renown in later years. Finally there was Bithynia, supported by Galatian brigands, and Pergamus, a new state, founded by Philetaerus, a general who had served Lysimachus. In Europe there was a Celtic state in Thrace, and also the confederacy of the Aetolians and the other states of Hellas, which, although now relatively poor and weak, were yet independent and useful as allies. In Europe, too, during the reign of Pyrrhus, Epirus had to be reckoned with. In short, there was an unbroken chain of lesser states in touch with one another from Atropatene to Hellas, and forming an important factor in the political situation.

The Death of Antiochus Soter, 262 B.C.—The later years of Antiochus are wrapped in some obscurity, the chief event to record being an indecisive campaign waged with Egypt, which began in 274 B.C. Ptolemy apparently used the cry of Hellenic autonomy with much effect, and for the most part was successful during the first two years; but when

Antigonus intervened the Egyptians were defeated off Cos. The life of Antiochus until its close was one of constant struggle to keep his vast possessions together. The task was enormous; for Asia Minor, his real home, was far from the centre of the empire, and between Syria and Persia lay great separating wastes. After nineteen years of constant effort with varying success he died, full of honours and years, a not unworthy prince of the house of Seleucus. His reign and that of his contemporary Ptolemy in Egypt constitute the golden Hellenistic age, and it is thanks to his enlightened patronage that Berossus published the history of Babylonia, based on the cuneiform records, of which, alas! only fragments have come down to us. Dr. Mahaffy was of opinion that the early Greek version of the Pentateuch was also made at this period, for the benefit of the Jews settled in Egypt.

Antiochus Theos, 262-246 B.C.—The reign of Antiochus II., whose title of the "Deity" was bestowed by the city of Miletus, was marked for some years by a continuance of the dreary war with Egypt; but at last this terminated not only in a peace, but in a close alliance. By its terms Berenice, the daughter of Ptolemy, was married to Antiochus, who undertook to divorce Laodice, to whom he had been married for many years and by whom he had a family. Laodice's influence, however, brought Antiochus back to her, and in 246 B.C. she poisoned him. It is recorded of him, probably with truth, that he was hopelessly sensual and depraved.

The Revolt of Bactria, 256 B.C., *and of Parthia*, 250 B.C.— It was during this reign that Bactria, in conjunction with Sogdiana and Margiana, broke away from the empire under its governor Diodotus, who was allowed to organize his kingdom undisturbed for many years before a Seleucid monarch attempted to reassert his claims. A few years later Parthia also revolted and established its independence. Little did the Seleucids realize that the small cloud on the northern confines of the empire was destined before long to overcast the whole horizon of Anterior Asia. Atropatene also, under its Persian ruler, increased in strength, and we see the chain of secondary powers now stretching uninterruptedly from distant Bactria to Hellas.

The Third Syrian War and the Invasion of Syria and Persia, 245 B.C.—The death of Antiochus II. was the signal for a bitter civil war, in which during the first phase the protagonists were Laodice and Berenice. The influence of the former, whose eldest son Seleucus had almost reached manhood, was naturally great ; but, if her rival could gain time, the armed support of Egypt was assured. Laodice struck the first blow by arranging to kidnap Berenice's infant son. The mother showed great spirit, and succeeded in establishing herself in a fortified part of the palace ; but she lost this advantage by her folly in trusting herself to the oath of her adversary, and she was murdered.

Ptolemy Philadelphus had in the meanwhile been succeeded by his son Ptolemy III., known as Euergetes or the "Benefactor." A brilliant soldier, he speedily collected a powerful army, with which he appeared on the scene, and the operations that followed are known as the Third Syrian War. Our chief authority for this campaign is an inscribed stone seen near modern Suakin by the Egyptian monk Cosmas Indicopleustes and copied by him. This most important inscription runs : " He marched into Asia with foot-soldiers and horse and with a fleet and with Troglodytic [1] and Ethiopian elephants, which he and his father had first captured in those parts and equipped for war. After having made himself master of all the countries on this side of the Euphrates . . . he crossed the Euphrates, and after the subjugation of Mesopotamia, Susiana, Persia, Media, and all the remaining districts as far as Bactriana . . ., he sent troops through the canals." [2] Here the inscription breaks off, and we learn from other sources that events in Egypt compelled Ptolemy to return. Although he left an army behind, the campaign was rather a brilliant raid than a serious attempt at permanent conquest. The naval operations were more successful, and many ports and coast provinces were occupied, but, as in the case of the former war, there was no finality.

The second phase of the civil war was entered upon when Seleucus II., as to whose operations during the raid of Ptolemy we know very little, was defeated decisively in Palestine after having lost his fleet in a storm.

The Battle of Ancyra, circa 235 B.C.—At this crisis Seleucus appealed to his brother Antiochus Hierax, now fourteen years of age and his mother's favourite. Hearing of this and ascertaining that the army of the north had started, Ptolemy

---

[1] The word " Troglodytic " refers in this passage to the coast of the Red Sea.
[2] *Vide* Holm, vol. iv. p. 211.

concluded a ten years' peace with Seleucus. Antiochus, however, or perhaps rather the Queen-Mother, had no intention of supporting Seleucus ; on the contrary, claim was laid to the whole empire and a desperate civil war began. At first Seleucus carried all before him ; but when Mithridates of Pontus declared in favour of Antiochus and joined his army with a large force of Galatians, the odds against Seleucus were too heavy. At Ancyra in Phrygia, about 235 B.C.,[1] these grim mercenaries swept away the army of Seleucus, whose losses are said to have aggregated twenty thousand. He was himself reported as slain ; but the news was false, and he escaped to Cilicia, where he rallied the fragments of his broken forces.

The provinces north of the Taurus were definitely lost to Seleucus II., but Antiochus Hierax was not on that account secure in the possession of his kingdom ; for the Galatians, who realized their power, turned on him, and made his position precarious. A peace was therefore concluded between the two brothers, and Seleucus was able to turn his attention to Parthia and Bactria.

The Campaign of Seleucus II. against Parthia. — The campaigns of Seleucus II. in the north of his straggling empire belong to the history of Parthia, and will be dealt with in the following chapter. Here it is enough to state that Seleucus, whose title of Callinicus or " Splendid Victor " does not appear to have been particularly well earned, defeated Arsaces of Parthia, who fled northward to the steppes. Thence he speedily reappeared and Seleucus retired to Syria, constrained, perhaps, as much by troubles in the western provinces as by fear of the Parthians. Little more is recorded of him, and a few years later, in 227–226 B.C., he was killed by a fall from his horse, after a reign crowded with failures and disappointments.

Attalus of Pergamus and Antiochus Hierax.—The fortunes of the house of Seleucus were considerably influenced by the rise of Attalus of Pergamus, who succeeded to the throne in 241–240 B.C. Early in his reign he rendered an immense service to Hellenism by his crushing and repeated victories over the Galatians, whom he drove from the coast into the hills. As a result he extended his power over Asia Minor

---

[1] *Vide* Holm, vol. iv. p. 242, note 2 ; for this date Bevan, vol. i. p. 285, writes "soon after 240."

at the expense of Antiochus Hierax, who maintained his position at Sardes with difficulty.

The events of this period are extremely difficult to follow: but it appears that Antiochus Hierax, finding himself unable to cope with Attalus, attempted to conquer Syria by an invasion of Mesopotamia. There, however, he was defeated by the forces of Seleucus, and he escaped into Cappadocia. In 229–228 B.C. he again fought Attalus, and being defeated in a series of four battles fled to Thrace, where in 228–227 B.C. he was killed by a raiding band of Gauls, a year before the death of his brother. The result was to leave Asia Minor entirely at the mercy of Attalus; for the death of Seleucus Callinicus prevented any attempt to reunite the vast but unwieldy possessions of the house of Seleucus. As Holm well puts it, the state of affairs in Anterior Asia during this troublous period must have closely resembled that in Germany during the Thirty Years' War.

Seleucus III., 226–223 B.C.—The burden which fell upon the heir to the throne of Seleucus, who is also known as Seleucus Soter, was crushing; but he appears to have faced it with energy and courage. Indeed the whole of his short reign was spent fighting for his inheritance against Attalus of Pergamus, with what results we do not know. His career was cut short by murder, in 223 B.C.

The Close of a Great Period.—The historian Polybius chose 221 B.C. as the opening year of his great work, on the grounds that it marked a distinct turning-point in the history of the world. Ptolemy Euergetes of Egypt, Cleomenes of Sparta, and Antigonus Doson of Macedonia, men of great personality, had all recently died, and the vacant thrones were filled by youths without experience, none of whom, except Antiochus the Seleucid, showed any capacity, and he too fell ingloriously after achieving a splendid reputation. We shall have occasion to touch upon his career in connexion with Parthia. For in the history of Persia, too, this was a time of change, the rising state of Parthia having already embarked on a career of conquest which was soon to embrace the whole of Iran. In the west also a new period was opening, when Rome, after absorbing the Greek cities of Italy, and the greater part of Sicily, appeared in Hellas at Corcyra, in connexion with attacks made on her merchantmen by Illyrian pirates. Had Antigonus Doson lived, after defeating Cleomenes, to consolidate what he had won, united Hellas might have formed a bulwark strong enough to beat back the rising might of Rome : but it was not so ordained.

Iran under Macedonian Rule.—Before we quit this period it will be well to give some idea of the state of Persia under the dominion of Alexander and the " Successors." If we compare the character of the Persians as described by Herodotus and that of the Macedonians, we find considerable similarity both in their mode of life and in their pleasures. Both nations were equally fond of sport, which included a love of horse and hound. Both, too, were equally addicted to drinking-bouts. Above all, love of war and booty was a ruling passion in Macedonian and Persian noble alike. The high ideals of the Persian religion as regards speaking the truth, and other matters also, was recognized by the Greeks, and Alexander regarded them as a race worthy of all respect, and even of inter-marriage. In this he set the example by marrying Roxana, who became the mother of his heir. He also married Statira, daughter of Darius ; and these two Oriental women were his only legal wives. Seleucus, too, whose family afterwards ruled Persia, married Apama, daughter of Spitamenes, and her descendants occupied the throne. This fusion of race necessarily reacted powerfully on the general attitude of the house of Seleucus, which must have been rather Graeco-Iranian than purely Greek in its ideals. Consequently, it is by no means surprising that many satraps were Persians or Medes, and that Persian troops were employed and fully trusted. We have few details to go upon, but there is little doubt that the policy of Alexander the Great was, to some extent, maintained, that the Persians of the upper classes were, on the whole, content with their position, and that intermarriage and the fusion of races continued. Had it been otherwise, we should surely have heard of many revolts, whereas in fact there were but few.

The position of the lower classes was little affected by the Greek conquest except near the great centres and the Greek cities. There was probably considerable freedom for those whose life was nomadic, and oppression of those who dwelt in villages. It has been my invariable experience that under an Oriental Government nomads are bound to be free owing to the difficulty of effective control. On the other hand, villagers being tied to one place and unable to move off at an hour's notice, have always been more easily oppressed ; and oppression has ever marked the rule of the strong in Asia, and indeed in Europe too until quite recently.

To what degree Iran was hellenized, we are unaware. We know, however, from various Greek writers that many Greek cities were founded in the west of Persia, among them being Europus and Heraclea, both at strategical points in the neighbourhood of Rhages. Polybius says : " Media was covered with Greek cities after the plan prescribed by Alexander to form a defence against the neighbouring barbarians."[1] It is probable that there was a chain of Greek cities or posts between Media and Bactria, and we know what a large number of colonists were settled by Alexander in those utterly remote regions, and with what pitiless severity they were treated when attempting to return home. In Persis, which remained somewhat apart, we hear of Antioch-in-Persis. In Carmania, the modern province of Kerman, an Alexandria was founded, which, as already mentioned, has been identified with modern Gulashkird, a small village which I have visited to the north-east of Bandar Abbas. In Sistan the capital had been made a Greek colony by Alexander under the name of Prophthasia, and farther north he founded an Alexandria on the Hari Rud ; two other Greek cities were built in this comparatively fertile district under Seleucid auspices. Finally Hecatompylus, the capital of Parthia, and Eumenea in Hyrcania must be mentioned.

The Greek Cities in the Persian Empire.—Let us, in conclusion, consider for a moment the position of the Greek cities. If we bear in mind the numerical paucity of the Macedonians and Greeks, together with the sanguinary wars in which they were constantly engaged, it is clear that, unless they maintained their ideals with the utmost constancy and remained like flints in chalk, they must within a few generations have merged into the surrounding populations. To a certain extent this actually was their ultimate fate. The consciousness of a similar danger prevails very strongly in India to-day among the English community, where experience proves that children educated in India are almost invariably inferior in type to those brought up in England. As the Greeks in Asia could not send their children back to Hellas for education, it was of the utmost importance that they should be brought

[1] Polybius x. 27. 3.

up in cities which were typically Hellenic, even if situated on the banks of the Tigris or on the Iranian plateau. Even so there was undoubtedly rapid degeneration, partly owing to the fact that the Greeks were settled among peoples whom they used as servants, and who probably did all the work. As a consequence, the Greeks of Hellas despised the Greeks of Syria, just as, in India, a so-called "country-bred" is sometimes looked down upon by Englishmen bred in Great Britain.

Posidonius of Apamea (*circa* 135–51 B.C.) depicts the life led by the Greek colonists, and shows clearly how luxury had ruined their manhood. "The people of these cities," he says, "are relieved by the fertility of their soil from a laborious struggle for existence. Life is a continual series of social festivities. . . . In the public eating-halls they practically live, filling themselves there for the better part of the day with rich foods and wine. The cities are filled from end to end with harp-playing."[1]

If this was the case in Syria, which maintained constant intercourse with Hellas, the degeneracy must have been still greater in cities where there was no chance of regular intercourse; and it is a remarkable tribute to the vitality of Hellenism that, even when Bactria was cut off by Parthia from the empire, it survived for several generations as a centre of Greek culture.

[1] Posidonius ap. Athen. v. 210 f and xii. 527 e.

EARLY PARTHIAN SILVER COIN, WITH PORTRAIT OF ARSACES I. OR TIRIDATES I.

CHAPTER XXVII

THE RISE OF PARTHIA AND THE APPEARANCE OF ROME IN ASIA

> Parthia is not an extensive tract of country ; for this reason it was united with Hyrcania for the purpose of paying tribute under the Persian dominion and afterwards. . . . Besides its small extent, it is thickly wooded, mountainous, and produces nothing.—STRABO xi. 9. 1.

Parthia Proper.—Parthia, the home of the warrior race which for so many centuries divided with Rome the empire of the world, is familiar to me, as lying mainly within the modern provinces of Khorasan and Astrabad, in which I have travelled extensively. Its original boundaries cannot be ascertained with exactitude ; but it is known that Parthia marched with Hyrcania on the west, and that the latter state occupied part of modern Mazanderan and part of the Astrabad province. It seems certain that the lower reaches of the Gurgan and Atrek valleys were included in Hyrcania, and that their upper valleys belonged to Parthia. Along the southern slopes of the Taurus, Parthia, even in ancient times, appears to have stretched considerably farther to the west than on the northern side. There can be little doubt that its capital lay in the neighbourhood of Damghan, which was the chief city of Kumis in mediaeval times ; and Kumis is the classical Comisene mentioned by Ptolemy[1] as being that part of Parthia which adjoins Hyrcania. On the east it was bounded by the Tejen River, which in part of its course marks the frontier of Iran to-day. The northern boundary was the desert, then termed Chorasmian, and to-day the Kara Kum. To the south there were the settled districts of Zarangiana and Arachosia, but the Lut was the principal boundary. Conse-

[1] Ptolemy vi. 5. 1. *Vide* also Strabo xi 9.

quently we have a country which, from the Tejen on the east to its western extremity, measured in length some five hundred miles, but was nowhere proportionately broad. Within the limits above described, the upper valleys of the Atrek and Gurgan are extremely fertile. The Kashaf Rud, too, on which Meshed is situated, waters a rich valley; and both Nishapur and Turshiz, if we may count the latter as having been in Parthia, are distinctly productive districts. To-day the wooded area starts from the Gurgan Defile and runs in a continuous belt right across the Caspian provinces, but is confined to the northern slopes of the Elburz range. Elsewhere there is no timber to-day, and although there may probably have been a growth of junipers on the southern slopes in ancient times, I am confident that these have never within the historical period been thickly wooded. There is no tradition to suggest it, and the writings of the classical authors all tend to show that there was a marked difference between the exuberant fertility of Hyrcania and the comparatively arid provinces of the Iranian plateau.

The Authorities for Parthian History.—Gardner[1] begins his sketch of Parthia by laying down that "there is scarcely any branch of history to which more aptly than to the Parthian can be applied the old saying that history consists of recognized fictions." This statement is certainly true. Where there is contact with Syria or Rome, contact represented chiefly by war, a stream of light is poured on Parthia, but at other periods there is only a chance reference or the evidence of coins to depend upon. The only history of the earlier Arsacid kings is that of Justin, which is both scanty and contradictory; for the later Arsacid kings we have no consecutive history, but only a few scattered references. Nor can any information of historical value be gleaned from the Persian or Arabian historians. The coins, unfortunately, bear no dates until the close of the first century of the Christian era, when the race of Parthia was more than half run. But as there are almost invariably portraits on the coins, and as there are dates on the later tetradrachms, the value of their evidence is considerable, more especially since there are practically no rock sculptures

---

[1] The chief authorities for this somewhat difficult period, in which many of the dates are only approximate, are Rawlinson's *Sixth Oriental Monarchy*, 1873; P. Gardner's *Parthian Coinage*, 1877; Wroth's *Catalogue of the British Museum Collection*, 1903; *Geschichte Irans und seine Nachbarländer*, by A. von Gutschmid; and the article on "Parthia" in the *Encyclopædia Britannica* (eleventh edition).

or inscriptions to furnish materials for the use of the historian. In the earlier reigns the question of dates presents considerable difficulties.

The Arsacid Dynasty.—The origin of the Parthian dynasty cannot be ascertained with certainty, and divergent statements are given by the classical writers. But some facts are known. The Arsacids were not a native dynasty which rose in revolt, but came from outside. The native Parthians are mentioned by Darius with the Varkana or Hyrcanians in the Behistun inscriptions, and were apparently as much Aryans as their neighbours. The invaders were a Turanian tribe from the north, termed Parni, a division of the nomadic people known as the Daae or Dahae, whose habitat was that of the modern Yamut Turkoman to the east of the Caspian Sea, and who fought in the left wing of the Persian army at Arbela.[1] In the Akhal oasis to the north of the River Atrek there is a district which in the tenth century A.D., and probably in much earlier times, was termed Dihistan. It included a town of the same name, which according to the Persians was founded by Kei Kobad of the heroic age. To-day the name is still known. Moreover, during the course of my inquiries I was informed that the Daz tribe of the Yamut cherish a legend, according to which they are descended from kings, and among the Yamut Turkoman they are regarded as the noblest section. They connect the ruined Kala Maran, to which subsequent reference will be made, with the period of their greatness. It is at least possible that these names are derived from the Dahae, but it would be a mistake to press the point too far.

The Chief Arsaces, who is the somewhat shadowy founder of the dynasty, appears to have settled in Asaak [2] in the district of Astabene, which seems to be identical with the Akhal oasis, although Gutschmid identifies it with Kuchan; Asaak is possibly connected with the term Ashkani, which is invariably applied to the dynasty by the Persians, and which survives in place-names noted by me in this district and also as far south as Tabas.[3] On the other hand, Ashkani may be identical with the name of the dynasty. The name Arsaces, by which the dynasty is known to the west, is believed not to have

---

[1] *Anabasis*, iii. 11. The Dahae are mentioned as being one of the chief tribes of Persia in chap. xiii.
[2] *The House of Seleucus*, l. 285.
[3] "A Fifth Journey in Persia," *Journal R.G.S.* for Nov. and Dec. 1906. According to Persian historians, the founder of the Parthian dynasty was Ashk, who was descended from the ancient kings of Iran.

been a personal one, but to have been adopted deliberately in order to connect the Turanian dynasty with the royal Achaemenian line. It will also be remembered that Artaxerxes II. (Mnemon) was named Arsaces, and we are expressly told that the Arsacid dynasty was descended from Artaxerxes.[1] It is worth noting that the Achaemenian Arsaces was born when his father was Satrap of Hyrcania and probably also of Parthia, and this fact strengthens the theory just mentioned.

The Birth-Year of the Arsacid Dynasty, 249–248 B.C.—The Parthians themselves gave for the birth-year of their dynasty a date corresponding to 249–248 B.C. This we may believe was in memory of some victory won by Arsaces, but it is by no means certain, and the question is certainly not one for dogmatic pronouncement.

The Career of Arsaces I., 249–247 B.C.—The Chief Arsaces, with whom was associated his brother Tiridates, attacked a Seleucid representative, probably the sub-governor of the district of Asaak, in revenge for an insult offered to the younger brother. The official, who is variously termed Pherecles or Agathocles, was killed, and as, just before this period, the provinces of Bactria, Margiana, and Sogdiana had broken away from the empire, the opportunity was favourable for a bold nomad chief or the leader of a body of bandits [2] to occupy an outlying district and then make a bid for a province. Here again the situation is not clear in its details; but apparently the leading figures on the stage of this part of Asia were Diodotus, the rebel Satrap of Bactria, Andragoras, Satrap of Parthia, and the nomad chieftain already newly established in Astabene and apparently attacking Parthia. Arsaces I. disappears from the scene, probably being killed in battle in 247 B.C. Though a shadowy figure, he was nevertheless the founder of a mighty dynasty.

Hecatompylus, the Capital.—The site of the capital of Parthia presents considerable difficulties. Rawlinson, who was well acquainted with the classical writers, located it somewhere in the neighbourhood of the city of Jajarm.[3] On the other hand, Apollodorus of Artemita places it one thousand two hundred and sixty stades, or one hundred and

---

[1] Syncell. p. 539, quoted by Bevan in *op. cit.* i. p. 286.

[2] Justin xli. 5, writes : " One Arsaces, a man of uncertain origin but undoubted courage, arose at this period. He was accustomed to make his livelihood as a bandit. . . ." Perhaps Justin was unable to appreciate the somewhat narrow line separating a nomad chief from a robber.

[3] *Vide* map to *The Sixth Oriental Monarchy.*

forty-four miles, east of the Caspian Gates. Polybius, too, in narrating the campaign of Antiochus the Great against Arsaces III., states that he took Hecatompylus and then marched to Tagi in the mountains and descended into Hyrcania. Now Tagi, or Tak, was a well-known fortress in the Elburz range, the last refuge of the *Sipahbud* of Tabaristan, and considered at that period to be ancient. Much other evidence has been marshalled by Schindler [1] and Williams Jackson, and the site of Hecatompylus may now be identified with that of the ancient city of Kumis. This lies some eight miles to the south of the modern city of Damghan, and about sixteen miles from Tak. But it is curious that the Parthians should have had their capital at the western extremity of their country, and this fact misled me at one time ; perhaps the site was selected because their most formidable enemy was the Seleucid monarch, or possibly they occupied a Greek city cuckoo-fashion.

The Conquest of Hyrcania under Arsaces II., 247–214 B.C.— Tiridates, who is conjectured to be Arsaces II., succeeded his brother. He is probably the first Parthian monarch of whom we possess coins.

Tiridates was perhaps the real founder of the Parthian Empire ; certainly his claim to the honour has a substantial basis. Fortune favoured him shortly after his accession, Seleucus Callinicus remaining a helpless spectator while his eastern empire was being overrun by Ptolemy Euergetes, who claimed to have subjugated the countries as far as Bactria, but actually penetrated in person no farther than Babylon. Although the occupation of that city was temporary, the blow was heavy to the house of Seleucus, which instead of uniting in face of danger wasted its strength in civil war, and the defeat at Ancyra must have been disastrous for Callinicus. These favourable conditions were turned to good account by Tiridates, who attacked and annexed Hyrcania.

Arsaces II. and Seleucus II.—But Seleuces II., whose courage in adversity was admirable, finally made peace with his brother and marched a large army across Media with the intention of regaining the eastern provinces of his empire. There are conflicting accounts of the course of the campaign ; but it is clear that Tiridates, in the first instance, fled to the region between the Oxus and the Jaxartes, where he was well

---

[1] *Journal Royal Asiatic Society*, 1876, p. 427.

received by the nomadic Aspasiacae. He then returned, but whether he fought a decisive battle with Seleucus is unknown. The fact remains, however, that that unfortunate monarch retired to the western portion of his empire with his object unachieved, and the Parthians considered the issue to have sealed afresh their independence. The memory of the victory they claimed was kept green by a solemn festival for many generations. It is reasonable to believe that Tiridates did defeat the troops of Callinicus, but that it was not a serious disaster and the main body was probably not involved.[1]

Dara, the New Capital of Parthia. — Tiridates, upon the retirement of Callinicus, devoted the remaining years of his life to organizing his conquests. He fortified the Parthian cities, and selected a site for a new capital. This was found in the district of Apavortene or Apavarta.[2] It was surrounded by precipitous rocks, which enclosed a very fertile plain ; in the neighbourhood were thick woods and many running streams ; and, finally, the soil was very rich, and there was an abundant supply of game. This city, named Dara by Tiridates, was subsequently known as Dareium. Its site has not hitherto been identified. It seems probable that it lay in the Gurgan Valley, for nowhere else, I think, can the necessary conditions as to woods and running streams be found. In the course of a journey in 1912 I visited a high mountain, resembling Gibraltar in shape, and termed Kala Maran. Situated some fifty miles east of Astrabad in the Gurgan Valley, it contains important ruins, and it may have been the site in question. In any case, Dara was found to be unsuitable, perhaps because the springs dried up, as had happened at the time of my journey, and Hecatompylus after all remained the capital down to the first century B.C.

The Early Career of Antiochus the Great, 223–213 B.C. — Antiochus III. was a youth of eighteen when he unexpectedly succeeded to the throne of the Seleucids. Achaeus, his able cousin, remained loyal at this critical juncture, and the young monarch was received with acclamation by the

---

[1] Justin quotes Trogus, who flourished in the Augustan era, as saying, "Quem diem Parthi exinde solennem, velut initium libertatis, observant."

[2] According to Brunnhofer, Apavarta is preserved in Bavard. If so, Kalat-i-Nadiri may be referred to, as it is close to Abivard, the modern Doshakh ; but I hardly imagine that Parthia stretched so far east at this period as to have its capital in this district. Nor was this district well wooded.

THE RISE OF PARTHIA

Macedonians in Syria upon his arrival from Babylon. He rewarded Achaeus by appointing him Viceroy with full powers in Asia Minor. Molon, the Satrap of Media, and his brother Alexander, Satrap of Persis, were also given full powers east of the Tigris. Unhappily the young monarch was at this period under the influence of Hermias, a corrupt and jealous minister of the familiar type, and fearing for their own safety the Satraps of Media and Persis in 221 B.C. rebelled, partly in self-defence, but influenced, no doubt, by the success of Diodotus and Arsaces. Epigenes, the capable general of Antiochus, pressed his master to attack the rebels in person; but Hermias persuaded him that kings should war only against kings, and a force was despatched under an incompetent leader, who was defeated with heavy loss. This disaster roused Antiochus, who had already started upon a campaign against Egypt, but had been quite unable to force the pass between the Lebanon and the Anti-Lebanon. Consequently he was ready to deal with the situation. Epigenes was put to death as the result of a plot, but even so the mere presence of the head of the house of Seleucus was sufficient to induce the troops to return to their allegiance. Molon and some of his adherents committed suicide.

Antiochus proceeded to Seleucia on the Tigris, where Hermias desired to gratify his cruelty and avarice to the full; but the king determined to be clement and mitigated the severities he proposed. From Seleucia he marched across the Zagros range into the province of Azerbaijan, where the Persian dynasty bowed to the inevitable and accepted his terms.

Meanwhile Hermias, who was plotting to murder his master, was himself assassinated by some of the King's companions. Antiochus, released from his baneful influence, returned to the west to meet Achaeus, who had resolved to make a bid for the empire. But the troops remained loyal, and Achaeus was forced to abandon his treasonable design, though not before he had betrayed its existence.

Antiochus was now free to carry out an invasion of Coele-Syria, which was initiated by the capture of Seleucia, a city only twelve miles from Antioch, and commanding its communications with the sea. The "golden key" opened the gates of this indispensable harbour, and Theodotus the Aetolian, who had foiled Antiochus in 221 B.C., handed over Ptolemais (the modern Acre) and also Tyre. Antiochus now hoped that the much-coveted province of Coele-Syria would soon be in his possession. For two years the campaign on the whole went in his favour; but in 217 B.C. the Egyptian preparations, which included the engagement of large numbers of Greek mercenaries, were completed, and Ptolemy marched northwards across the desert. He met Antiochus at Raphia, on the northern edge of the waste. The fighting was severe. The Indian elephants of Antiochus drove back the African elephants on to the Egyptians, and thereupon Antiochus broke the Egyptian left by a charge and pursued it for miles. On the other flank the situation was reversed. There the two phalanxes met, and at the first charge the Seleucid army fled in disorder. Ptolemy was satisfied with this success and readily made peace, leaving the discredited Antiochus to face the unscrupulous Achaeus.

In 216 B.C. Antiochus marched across the Taurus, and although no details have reached us he was evidently successful; for two years later we read of his besieging Achaeus in Sardes. In the end, through an act of treachery, the details of which are more thrilling to read than many a romance, Achaeus was thrown bound into the royal tent at night and put to a cruel death. This campaign re-established the supremacy of the house of Seleucus in Central Asia Minor, and led to an agreement with Attalus which left Antiochus free to turn his arms eastwards.

Arsaces III. and Antiochus the Great, 209 B.C.—We now return to Parthia. Arsaces III., like his father, took advantage of the difficulties of the house of Seleucus, at this period engaged in fighting Achaeus, to extend the sway of Parthia. The Mardian territory was first overrun, and the Parthians then passed the famous Caspian Gates, on the west side of which lay Media Rhagiana, with Rhages and other important cities. Media Magna, with its capital, Ecbatana, was next occupied; and it seemed probable that Arsaces would descend the gorges of the Zagros, when his advance was effectually checked. After the death of Achaeus, Antiochus first invaded Armenia, and in 209 B.C. he marched into Media and occupied Ecbatana, which was not defended by the Parthians. The capital of Astyages still boasted of the immense old palace with its colonnades of wood, which had escaped fire, by a miracle it would seem, although the gold and silver plates had been stripped off after Alexander's death. The temple of the goddess Anaitis had also been spared, and furnished rich treasure to the hard-pressed Antiochus, who realized the immense sum of four thousand talents by his act of sacrilege.

Arsaces III., meanwhile, had disappeared from Media, hoping that he would not be followed, and by way of precaution he attempted to fill up the *Kanats* or underground water-channels. But Antiochus was too quick for him, and marching with a force of cavalry spread out far ahead to prevent the water supply from being tampered with, passed through the Caspian Gates and seized Hecatompylus, which the Parthians, aware of their weakness, made no attempt to hold. After resting his men, Antiochus probably followed Alexander's footsteps into the Taurus, where, although the Parthians had every advantage of position, his light troops forced the passage, and from the summit of the range the army marched down into Hyrcania. Arsaces there engaged in a determined guerilla warfare, for which the country was favourable. Finally he induced his powerful antagonist to make terms and accept him as an ally.

The March of Antiochus through Bactria, the Panjab, and Kerman, 208-204 B.C.—Upon the conclusion of the Parthian campaign Antiochus marched on Bactria, which was ruled by a Magnesian named Euthydemus, who had overthrown the house of Diodotus. A cavalry engagement was fought on the right bank of the River Tejen, in which Antiochus displayed great bravery, and the defeated Bactrian army was shut up in the capital. After a long blockade which had no definite result, a treaty was concluded and sealed by a marriage; and Antiochus, following still in Alexander's footsteps, crossed the Hindu Kush and, moving down the Kabul valley past Alexandria *apud Caucasum*, marched through the Khyber Pass into the Panjab. The successor of Asoka wisely bought off the invader with rich gifts of elephants and money ; and the Seleucid monarch continued to beat the boundaries of his empire, following down the River Helmand to Sistan, and thence crossing the Lut to Narmashir by the same route that Craterus had taken rather more than a century before. Wintering in the Kerman province, probably where Alexander had halted, Antiochus ended this great expedition, which included Gerrha in the Persian Gulf, at Seleucia on the Tigris.

By it he increased the prestige of his dynasty and regulated its interests in more ways than one.

Early Relations between Hellas and Rome.—It may seem to be going far afield in a History of Persia to give any account, however brief, of the early relations between Hellas and Rome ; but the latter was destined to exercise such an important influence on the history of the Persian Empire that if all mention of the subject were omitted, it would be impossible to bring certain aspects of the question into proper focus.

It is certain that envoys from various Italian states, if not from Rome, travelled to the court of Alexander the Great as far as Babylon, and possibly dreams of adding Italy and Carthage to his Empire were indulged in by the Great Conqueror. The fight for power among the " Successors " interested Rome but little, and the first relations established with a Greek state consisted of a commercial treaty concluded in 306 B.C. with Rhodes, then at the zenith of her prosperity, a year before the famous siege by Demetrius Poliorcetes.

It was Pyrrhus, the leading soldier of his age, who first led a phalanx against Roman cohorts and thus began those direct relations on which, as Mommsen well says, " the whole subsequent development of ancient, and an essential part of modern civilization are based." Pyrrhus invaded Italy in 280 B.C. Thanks mainly to the fear inspired by his elephants alike in their soldiers and their horses, he won two great though costly victories over the Romans. In 275 B.C., after an unsuccessful campaign in Sicily, he returned to Italy and was defeated by the splendid valour of the legions which drove " the Eagle " back to its eyrie.

The First Macedonian War, 215–205 B.C.—After the campaigns of Pyrrhus had ended, Rome was too much occupied with affairs in Italy and the First Punic War to concern herself with Hellas. However, upon the close of the first phase of that gigantic contest, in the course of which the Greeks both of Italy and of Sicily had felt the might of Rome and had come under her sway, the Senate desired to have its new position recognized in Hellas. The first step actually taken was to follow up and punish some Illyrian pirates, and as a consequence of these operations Corcyra, Apollonia, and Dyrrachium were received as subject allies. This was in 229 B.C., and further interference had taken place in 219, just before the life-and-death struggle with Carthage recommenced, and for twenty years Rome was fighting for her existence.

The chances of another invasion from Hellas were serious. On hearing of the crushing defeat of the Romans at Trasymene (217 B.C.), Philip V.[1] of Macedon determined to aid Hannibal, and it seemed possible for a while that he would lead a united Hellas. But the monarch whose maxim was " Whoever kills the father must also slay the sons " had not the necessary qualities to play so big a part. He was dilatory, and at first very little was effected beyond the conclusion of a treaty with Hannibal. The truth is that the sea power of Rome made him shrink from crossing the Adriatic ; instead, he employed himself in attacking the Roman possessions in Epirus, and that in a half-hearted and ineffectual fashion.

Rome was not content to remain a passive spectator of these operations, but landed a force in Epirus, which attacked the Macedonians. Moreover, Roman diplomacy succeeded in combining the Aetolians and minor Greek states against Macedonia, and the coalition was joined by the Thracians and Illyrians and by the astute Attalus of Pergamus. Philip in the end emerged victorious, but weary of the war, and made peace with Rome on the basis of the *status quo*. This was a turning-point of history ; for had Philip promptly thrown his veteran army into the scale by landing in Italy, it might have gone hard with exhausted Rome, even after the defeat of Hasdrubal at the Metaurus in 207 B.C. Instead of this, he had shown hostility but stayed his hand, and thereby sealed not only his own doom but that of the Hellenic world.

The Spoliation of Egypt by Philip V. and Antiochus the Great.—Philip V., shortly after making this impolitic peace with Rome, agreed with Antiochus in 202 B.C. to divide the outlying possessions of Egypt, and in pursuance of this design attacked the Thracian possessions and islands belonging to the House of Ptolemy. Pergamus and Rhodes united to repel him, and in the first naval battle they were victorious, although the losses on both sides were heavy. A second engagement was won by Philip. On the whole, he had added to his possessions and power when he returned to Macedonia in the late autumn of 201 B.C. ; and in the

---

[1] He was son of Demetrius the Fair, and father of Perseus.

following year he completed his conquests on the coast of Thrace.

Antiochus, on his side, was equally active. He naturally burned to avenge his defeat at Raphia and to add Coele-Syria to his possessions. This apparently he accomplished by 199 B.C. ; but no details of the operations have been preserved. He then invaded the territory of Pergamus, which was undefended by Attalus, who was absent co-operating with Rome against Philip. The Romans protested against this attack on their ally, and Antiochus promptly withdrew. Meanwhile an Egyptian army invaded Coele-Syria and drove out the Seleucid garrisons. But Antiochus marched to the rescue, and near the sources of the Jordan gained a decisive victory, which finally substituted his rule for that of Egypt in Palestine. The defeated army was besieged in Sidon, which surrendered ; and the campaign ended with the siege of Gaza, where the Philistines maintained to the full the glory of their Minoan descent,[1] and made a defence that is memorable in military history. Nevertheless it was at last stormed by Antiochus.

The Second Macedonian War, 200–197 B.C.—The position of Rome in the year 200 B.C. was very different from that of five years before. The Second Punic War had been carried to a successful conclusion by the crushing defeat of Hannibal at Zama in 202 B.C., and the Republic was free once again to develop its policy eastwards, or in other words to win a wider empire at the expense of Macedonia.

The Senate, which had made a treaty of friendship with Ptolemy Philadelphus the year after Pyrrhus had quitted Italy, had maintained these relations ever since ; and they culminated at this period in the acceptance of the protection of Rome by the boy Ptolemy Epiphanes. The agreement with Philip had probably been concluded in 205 B.C. only as a temporary political expedient, until the Punic peril had been overcome ; and although the new campaign against Macedonia was unpopular in Rome, where the Second Punic War had naturally made the whole nation long for peace, two legions were embarked at Brindisi and hostilities were begun. For some time Philip held his own, as the Romans suffered from lack of supplies and from other difficulties ; but the campaign culminated in the decisive battle of Cyno-

[1] *The Ancient History of the Near East*, p. 72.

scephalae, fought in the hills near Tempe in 197 B.C. Here the phalanxes were at a disadvantage and 13,000 Macedonians were killed. Peace was then made on terms that were by no means harsh, not only because Philip could have continued a guerilla warfare, but because Antiochus the Great, who had stood aloof, was now preparing to take the field.

Antiochus the Great and Rome, 200–191 B.C.—The first authenticated communication between Antiochus the Great and Rome took place in 200 B.C. In this year the embassy which was charged to carry the ultimatum to Philip V. of Macedon was instructed to visit the courts of Antiochus and of Ptolemy. Nothing definite was arranged with the former, but, as already mentioned, the boy-king of Egypt was placed under the protection of Rome. Had Antiochus been a really great man, he would certainly have aided Philip to repel the Roman legions. Instead, he sent a complimentary embassy to Rome ; and in 197 B.C., the year of Philip's final overthrow, he marched into Asia Minor to secure his own position while his rival was fighting for his throne.

The result of the battle of Cynoscephalae was apparently not unwelcome to Antiochus, who foolishly fancied that now he could not only regain Asia Minor, but even mount the throne of Macedonia. Pending the realization of these fantastic dreams, he continued to restore his power over the coast cities of the Hellespont and Northern Ionia. One of these, Lampsacus, situated on the Asiatic side near Abydos, appealed to Rome, claiming kinship with Massilia.[1] As that city also sent an embassy to support the representations, the appeal was successful in enlisting the sympathy of the Senate. Moreover, the Massilians, who were in close relation with the Gauls of the Rhone Valley, wrote to their kinsmen of Asia Minor, the Galatians, begging them to befriend Lampsacus.

In the spring of 196 B.C. Antiochus crossed into Europe and began to rebuild Lysimachia, which Philip had abandoned to the Thracians, and appointed his son to rule there as his Viceroy. The Roman general Flamininus and the Ten Commissioners who had pronounced the liberty of Hellas had also declared the freedom of the Greeks of Asia, and had summoned Antiochus to surrender all the cities he had taken from Philip and Ptolemy. Consequently the advance of Antiochus into Europe was viewed with strong resentment.

---

[1] Both colonies were descended from Phocaea. *Vide* Chapter XIII.

Philip, who was affected more closely still by this act of his quondam ally, naturally ranged himself on the side of his late enemies when hostilities finally broke out. A Roman embassy was sent to protest; but Antiochus merely expressed astonishment at their pretensions, and, a rumour having reached Lysimachia that the young Pharaoh was dead, both parties hurried off to Egypt. On the way Antiochus learned that the rumour was false, and, his fleet having been shattered by a storm, he retired to Antioch. About this time he was joined by Hannibal, who unreservedly placed his services at his disposal, and had he been guided by the genius and experience of the great Carthaginian, the issue might well have been different.

In 194 B.C. the conquest of Thrace by Antiochus was completed, and in the same year the Romans, who for once in their splendid career gave way to sentimentality, withdrew all their garrisons from Hellas, failing to realize that the numerous petty states would speedily call in another power. At this juncture Hannibal framed a plan, according to which he would once again invade Italy at the head of an army, while Carthage would rebel and Antiochus would invade Hellas. But Antiochus could not grasp the necessity of meeting the danger by careful forethought and large preparations, and he drifted somewhat aimlessly, sacrificing policy to side-issues. Nor does it appear that he made any adequate military preparations for the trial of strength that was imminent. However, upon hearing that the Aetolians had captured Demetrias, the important city of Magnesia, Antiochus, in spite of the lateness of the season, decided suddenly to cross into Hellas with the troops at his immediate disposal, about 11,000 strong. This was in truth a puny army for the Master of Asia, and it could not be reinforced until the spring.

It is unnecessary to describe in detail the intrigues of the various Greek states, which had very little influence on the issue of the campaign. In the spring of 191 B.C. the Roman army took the offensive, and in conjunction with Philip marched into Thessaly. Antiochus, who received few or no reinforcements, retreated to Chalcis in Euboea and finally took up his position at world-renowned Thermopylae. As in the days of Leonidas, the main position was too strong to be forced; but a Roman detachment was able to utilize the hill tracks, which were inadequately guarded, and when the rear of Antiochus was threatened, his force became demoralized. The defeat was decisive, and Antiochus with a body of fugitives hastened back to Ephesus, leaving his adherents in Hellas to their fate. Thus ingloriously ended the first phase of his contest with Rome.

The Battle of Magnesia, 190 B.C.—Antiochus, it would seem, after his safe return to Asia, was disposed to believe that, while he had indeed failed to defend Hellas, it was open to him to make a second and more fortunate attempt when circumstances were propitious. But Hannibal, whose opinion was now as eagerly listened to as it had previously been lightly disregarded, pointed out that the tenacious Romans would not rest until they had attacked their foe in his own country, and that he must be prepared to fight for his throne. The Romans, on their part, viewed the campaign with apprehension, owing to the distance from their base and the difficulty of marching by land through Thrace with the forts of Antiochus barring the route. Furthermore, not to speak of raids by the Thracian highlanders, there was the fact that Sestos and Abydos, the strongly guarded portals of the Hellespont, were garrisoned by Seleucid troops. Above all, so difficult was the question of supplies that the command of the sea would clearly play a decisive part in the approaching contest.

The Romans did not waste time, and before Antiochus could develop his resources, it was known that their fleet had reached Delos. The island states of the Aegean, although not conquered by Antiochus, felt their liberty threatened and consequently joined the invaders. Of still more importance were the adhesion of Rhodes and the steady alliance of Pergamus. So strong, indeed, was the position of Rome from the first that Chios, though close to Ephesus, was selected as the base of supplies. By these alliances Antiochus was entirely cut off from his Thracian possessions by land. His communications by sea depended on his sea power, which was vital to the maintenance of his empire. His admiral, Polyxenidas, determined to attack the Roman fleet before it was joined by the allied squadrons; but he failed to carry out his purpose, and the Roman commander, after the junction with the Pergamene squadron, was as anxious to meet his antagonist as he had previously been to avoid him. As in Greece, Antiochus again failed to place a superior force in the field, and the Roman fleet of 105 vessels easily defeated the 70 smaller ships which were all that Antiochus had contrived to collect. For the time, at any rate, the command of the sea passed to the victors.

During the winter Antiochus, at last fully alive to the peril, strained every nerve to collect an army at Magnesia, situated in the valley of the Hermus about half-way between the sea and Sardes. At the same time his fleet, although defeated, was not destroyed, and he hoped by building fresh ships in the dockyards of Ephesus to be ready to fight again in the spring. Hannibal was sent to Tyre and the other Phoenician cities to organize a formidable naval force—a step that should have been taken in the first instance.

When the spring came the Roman commander sailed north, and received the capitulation of Sestos. Abydos was besieged, and was being hard pressed when the siege was raised by news that the Rhodian squadron had been annihilated by a clever ruse on the part of Polyxenidas. After this the Roman fleet confined its activity to watching that of the enemy, while Antiochus ravaged the territory of Pergamus. All the while a Roman army of 13,000 infantry and 500 cavalry was approaching through Macedonia. On the other side the Phoenician squadron, under Hannibal, was due to appear.

A fresh Rhodian squadron was detached to seek out the Phoenicians, and off the mouth of the Eurymedon, at Side, close to where the Athenians had won their glorious victory over a Phoenician fleet and an entrenched Persian army, a Greek fleet again signally defeated a superior Phoenician force. In spite of receiving no reinforcements, Polyxenidas made a final bid for victory, but, although he was still slightly superior in numbers, his Syrian crews would not face the Romans. Thus the command of the sea, which was vital to the legions, who could not hope to cross into Asia without it, was finally won by the Republic.

Antiochus drew in all outlying garrisons in such haste that the stores of Lysimachia were left to the enemy. Moreover, he attempted to make peace, on the basis of the evacuation of Europe and an indemnity for half the cost of the war. But the Romans proved their intention to fight by demanding the whole cost of the campaign and the evacuation of Asia Minor north of the Taurus. Such terms it was impossible for Antiochus to accept while still undefeated, and the two forces met at Magnesia. Antiochus commanded on the right, and driving before him the weak Roman force of cavalry, pursued it regardless of the fate of the main body, just as he had done at Raphia. His left wing was broken by the retreat of his own force of scythed chariots upon the cavalry, which in its turn threw the infantry into confusion and masked the phalanx. In short, the defeat was as complete as if Darius Codomannus had been commanding against Alexander. Antiochus, like his predecessor on the throne of Iran after Arbela, fled without further hope of resistance.

The Peace of Apamea, 188 B.C.—The terms finally agreed to were similar to those demanded before the battle. Antiochus gave up his possessions in Europe and evacuated Asia Minor north of the Taurus and west of the Halys. The indemnity was fixed at 15,000 Euboic talents or £3,600,000. Twenty hostages, selected by Rome, were handed over, and Hannibal, Thoas, Chief of the Aetolian League, and others were required to be surrendered. Hannibal, however, had already escaped to Crete, but eventually was forced to end a glorious though unsuccessful career by taking poison.

The peace of Apamea had far-reaching results ; for it showed beyond doubt that there was no power able to withstand Rome. The Seleucid dominions shrank into a comparatively weak but compact kingdom, and Pergamus, their rival, to which most of the ceded provinces were handed over, rose to great power. Antiochus, having no more hope in the West, turned his thoughts to a further campaign in the East and left Syria never to return. He was killed in 187 B.C., in an expedition organized for the purpose of robbing a shrine of Bel in the Elymean hills. The sentence in the book of Daniel referring to his death runs : " Then he shall turn his face toward the fort of his own land ; but he shall stumble and fall, and not be found."[1]

Parthia until the Reign of Mithradates I., 209–170 B.C.— To return to Parthia, after the departure of Antiochus, Arsaces devoted his energies to developing his war-worn country, as also did his son and successor Phriapatius. In 181 B.C. Phraates I. succeeded to a kingdom which had fully

---

[1] Daniel xi. 19.

recovered. He extended his sway over the Mardi who lived under Demavand, and built Charax on the western side of the Caspian Gates in the territory of Media Rhagiana. But it was reserved for his brother and successor Mithradates to enlarge the state of Parthia into an empire.

Bactria, 205–170 B.C.—To complete the narrative of events connected with Persia, a few lines must be devoted to the Hellenic kingdom of Bactria. This state was bounded to the south by the Hindu Kush and to the north by the Oxus Valley. Under Euthydemus and his able successor Demetrius the Hindu Kush was crossed, and in a series of campaigns the Greek state annexed not only Eastern Afghanistan but part of the Panjab. Commercial relations, too, were extended in every direction. But the prosperity of Bactria did not last long ; for Demetrius was overthrown by a pretender, and the little state, already strained by distant campaigns, was further weakened by internal convulsions.

From the point of view of Parthia it was of the utmost importance that the aggressive energy of Bactria should be diverted towards India instead of to the West, and at the close of the period under review the Hellenic state was not in a condition to do more than defend part of its original possessions, while holding on for a time to some of its recent conquests.

Summary.—The foregoing chapter deals with countries lying far apart, Parthia in the East being separated from Rome in the West by many degrees of longitude. But between these two rising states lay Hellas, incapable at any time in her history of uniting in the face of a common danger : a defect which led to her destruction. Asia Minor, too, at this period was broken up into a number of secondary states. Chief among them was Pergamus, but the confederacy of Rhodes, which headed the league of free cities along the coast, had also to be reckoned with on account of its sea power. True to the Greek character, however, these two states were usually on bad terms with one another, and both appealed to Rome again and again. There were also the kingdoms of Bithynia, of Pontus and Cappadocia, and the provinces which were held by the Galatians and other barbarous tribes. In Syria there was, indeed, loyalty to the Seleucid dynasty ; but the Greeks and Macedonians of Syria were alike degenerate and incapable of facing the

Roman legions. Finally, Egypt was already a protected state, unable to do more than play a secondary part, and not even that without Roman aid. Consequently the real result of the battle of Magnesia was to make Rome the dominant power of the West, with a circle of secondary states, incapable of opposing a solid front to her and inviting absorption whenever it might suit the policy of the Republic.

In the East, on the other hand, the rising dynasty of Arsaces, with its curious veneer of Hellenic civilization, had firmly established itself in Parthia and Hyrcania, and was about to expand until its frontiers touched those of Rome. It will thus be seen that the two military systems meet in a country which is favourable to the light horseman, with the result that upon the whole the Asiatic power holds its own. But both powers benefited by intercourse, which widened the outlook of East and West alike and prepared the way for progress.

SILVER COIN OF THE PERIOD OF MITHRADATES I.

CHAPTER XXVIII

THE EXPANSION OF PARTHIA AND THE DOWNFALL OF THE HOUSE OF SELEUCUS

> Antiochus who was called *Epiphanes* came upon the Jews with a great army, and took their city by force, and slew a great multitude of those that favoured Ptolemy, and sent out his soldiers to plunder them without mercy. He also spoiled the temple. . . . And being overcome with his violent passions, he compelled the Jews to dissolve the laws of their country and to keep their infants uncircumcised, and to sacrifice swine's flesh upon the altar.—JOSEPHUS, *The Jewish War*.

The House of Seleucus, 188–175 B.C.—The death of Antiochus III. closed a period of continuous warfare ending in crushing defeat; and probably it was well for the dynasty that the defeated and discredited monarch disappeared so quickly from the scene. Peace was urgently required, but this was out of the question except under a new ruler, who could realize the imperative necessity for recuperation. The result of the battle of Magnesia, apart from the loss of Asia Minor, reacted on Armenia, which shook off the supremacy of the house of Seleucus; and the provinces which make up modern Iran probably did the same, so far as they were not already independent. On the other hand, the acquisition of the valuable provinces of Coele-Syria and Cilicia helped to round off the reduced empire, now more correctly termed the kingdom of Syria.

Seleucus IV. Philopator, who succeeded to the throne, was obliged to wring the Roman war indemnity out of his subjects at a time when the prestige of the dynasty was at its lowest. For fourteen years he ruled in a peace which circumstances imposed on him, but which was regarded as inglorious, and he was then murdered by his chief minister, in 176–175 B.C.

The Succession of Antiochus Epiphanes, 175 B.C.—He was

succeeded by his brother Antiochus IV., who had lived as a hostage in Rome for many years and whose character was full of extravagances and contradictions, so that some historians have regarded him as a genius and others as a madman. He prudently paid Rome the instalments of the war indemnity and refrained from joining the enemies of the Great Republic. He repelled an attempt on the part of Egypt to regain Coele-Syria and acquired rich spoil from the campaign, in the course of which Alexandria was besieged. Later, he undertook a fresh campaign, and this time it seemed probable that he would secure possession of the whole of Egypt.

The Battle of Pydna, 168 B.C.—Rome during this period had been engaged in what is generally known as the Third Macedonian War. Philip V. had bequeathed extensive military preparations and undying hatred of the Western Power to his son Perseus, who attempted to unite Hellas against the " barbarian " state, but as might be expected he failed. In 171 B.C. the Roman legions again landed in Greece to fight the King of Macedonia, who was unsupported by a coalition. For two years the advantage lay with Perseus, and had he been willing to spend his treasure freely Rome might have suffered a heavy defeat. But he was neither a statesman nor an able soldier. At the battle of Pydna his phalanx carried all before it, and a charge of the Macedonian cavalry might have decided the day. But the Roman legionaries were allowed time to recover and to annihilate the phalanx, which was left unsupported by Perseus, who paid the penalty of his cowardice and ineptitude by being led in triumph through the streets of Rome. Polybius dates the establishment of the Roman Empire, as we know it, from this battle ; as, with the sole exception of the desperate effort made by Mithridates of Pontus, this was the last attempt on the part of any state to challenge the might of the Republic.

The Evacuation of Egypt by Antiochus, 168 B.C.—Rome was now free to take a strong line in Egypt, and immediately despatched an embassy to Antiochus. Polybius tells us that the Roman envoy handed the king a tablet containing the formal resolution of the Senate that he should evacuate Egypt, and then, drawing a circle round him on the sand, demanded a reply before he stepped outside it. Antiochus dared not refuse. He evacuated Egypt and returned home to celebrate a triumph on a scale surpassing all records, presumably hoping thereby to "save face" and to soothe his lacerated feelings.

The Eastern Campaigns of Antiochus and his Death, 165–164 B.C.—Antiochus, realizing that he could not pursue an aggressive policy in the west, determined to reconquer the eastern provinces of his empire, one great incentive being that his extravagance had brought him to the end of his resources. Following in the footsteps of his father, he first invaded Armenia, where his suzerainty was quickly acknowledged and no doubt tribute was paid. He then marched into Media, where we know little of his doings. Apparently he met with no opposition, and Ecbatana was renamed Epiphanea in his honour. In Luristan, undeterred by the fate of Antiochus the Great, he attempted to rob the temples of their treasures; but the wild mountaineers drove him and his army out of the country. Shortly after this "shameful retreat," as it is termed in the book of Maccabees, he apparently went mad, and he died at Tabae in Persis in the winter of 165–164 B.C. His reign, in spite of some successful campaigns, must have further weakened and exhausted his empire.

Antiochus Epiphanes and the Jews.—The dealings of Antiochus Epiphanes with the Jews are an episode which would not have been regarded as important at the time; yet it is owing to his persecutions that his name is best known, and consequently the subject cannot be passed over in silence.[1] The little Jewish colony planted by Nehemiah had tenaciously maintained its position in Palestine, and more than two centuries later was still holding its own under the rule of a High Priest. It had been involved in the contest for Coele-Syria, and had become part of the possessions of the house of Seleucus.

Since the conquests of Alexander the Great, who had transported some Jewish prisoners to Hyrcania, the cities of Syria, whether Canaanite, Philistine, or Phoenician, had become hellenized, either by an influx of Greek colonists, as in the case of Samaria, or through the all-pervading influence of the dominant race. There is proof from Josephus and

---

[1] It is dealt with by Bevan in chap. xxv. *Vide* also the work of Josephus and the book of Maccabees.

from both books of the Maccabees that Jerusalem also was hellenized, a fact which was marked by the erection of a gymnasium in Jerusalem at the request of a Jewish deputation. The city was divided between those who saw with approval their youth practising Greek athletics in a state of nudity and those who rigidly maintained the old traditions. Antiochus, who was mainly concerned with the question of tribute, would in all probability have allowed the Jews to manage or mismanage their petty local affairs ; but he was forced to take action because during his absence in Egypt they rose on behalf of the house of Ptolemy. Consequently, upon his return he entered Jerusalem and not only spoiled the Temple as recorded in the quotation from Josephus at the head of this chapter, but even entered the Holy of holies. Nor was this all, for he determined to hellenize Jerusalem, and in pursuance of this policy forbade the rite of circumcision, and erected a Greek altar on the old Jewish altar in the court of the Temple, and caused swine to be sacrificed upon it. These outrages goaded the Jews to resist. They won brilliant victories under Judas Maccabaeus, and upon the death of Antiochus they were granted full liberty to worship according to the Jewish rites, together with an amnesty.

Demetrius the Saviour, 162-150 B.C.—After the death of Antiochus Epiphanes, his son, a boy of nine, succeeded to the throne under the guardianship of a certain Lysias, whose incapacity and corruption produced a hopeless state of anarchy, culminating in the murder of a Roman envoy in 163-162 B.C. Demetrius, son of Seleucus IV., who had been living in Rome as a hostage, seizing the opportunity, landed at Tripolis in Phoenicia, was welcomed by the army and the people, and occupied the throne in 162 B.C.

Timarchus the Milesian, who was then Satrap of Media, immediately proceeded to Rome, where he was well known, and petitioned the Senate that he should be recognized as king of the Medes. As a result of his efforts, which no doubt included bribery on a large scale, he received a document to the effect that " as far as Rome was concerned Timarchus was King."[1] Encouraged by this title, he apparently invaded Syria ; but, as in the case of Molon, the prestige of the royal house caused his troops to desert, and he suffered the same fate as his predecessor in 160 B.C.

[1] Diod. xxxi. 27 a.

Demetrius was hailed in Babylonia as Soter or "the Saviour," by which title he is known in history. The recognition of Rome was gained in the same year, and his future looked bright. But Alexander, a pretended son of Antiochus Epiphanes, with the support of Egypt and the patronage of Rome, marched against this soldier-like scion of the house of Seleucus, whose good qualities were quite sufficient to make him disliked by the degenerate and fickle Syrians. The first battle Demetrius won, but in the second he was defeated and killed, fighting to the last. He was almost the last creditable member of this famous dynasty, which was now nearing its end.

The Conquests of Mithradates I. of Parthia, 170–138 B.C.

We now turn again to Parthia. Mithradates I. succeeded to the throne by the desire of his brother, who during his life had assumed the title of "Philadelphus." As the headpiece to this chapter proves, the features of the new sovereign were strong and dignified, and his career was in keeping with his appearance. The Bactrian monarchs, as we have seen, had weakened their grasp on their native state in favour of conquests beyond the Hindu Kush. Of this Mithradates took advantage to annex two border districts. Eucratidas of Bactria seems to have made no effort to recover his lost possessions, being probably too much involved elsewhere.

During the lifetime of Antiochus Epiphanes, Mithradates was too prudent to provoke hostilities, but some time after the death of Timarchus he suddenly invaded Media, which he subdued in a campaign involving much hard fighting. He returned to the north to crush a rising in Hyrcania, and then from his new base overran Elymais, which was successfully reduced. Persia, cut off from any help from the West, submitted, as also did Babylonia. Thus in a short period Parthia had created an empire reaching from Bactria to the Euphrates and from the Caspian Sea to the Persian Gulf. For some years after these successes Mithradates, who was the Darius of the Arsacid dynasty, organized his conquests before attempting to carry them further.

Meanwhile Eucratidas had been murdered by his son, who drove his chariot over his father's corpse and forbade its burial. But the new monarch was assailed by Scythians and also by the Zarangians and Indians, and when, about

150 B.C., Mithradates also invaded Bactria, he was unable to offer any effective resistance.

Demetrius, whose expedition will be mentioned later, was joined by a Bactrian contingent; but his defeat and capture took away the last hope of aid from Syria. Exhausted Bactria, overrun by Sakae from the north-east, while its western provinces were annexed by Parthia, was driven from its ancient habitat. An Indo-Bactrian kingdom is, however, known to have existed on the southern slopes of the Hindu Kush for more than half a century, before it was swept away by an irruption of tribes.

The House of Seleucus, 150–140 B.C.—To revert to the house of Seleucus, Alexander the Pretender ruled for four or five years as Alexander *Balas*, under the political suzerainty of Ptolemy Philometor, whose daughter Cleopatra he married; but again the scene changed, and Demetrius II. Nicator, son of Soter, a boy of fourteen, was brought back and won a battle. Alexander fled and, after a further defeat by Philometor, was assassinated; Cleopatra was handed over to the new monarch. The ascendancy of Egypt, however, was lost owing to the death of Philometor in the battle. Yet again a claimant for the throne appeared in the person of Antiochus VI., called Diompus, the son of Alexander by Cleopatra, whose cause was espoused by a certain Diodotus, a man of low extraction. Antioch was ready to welcome the son of Alexander *Balas*, and for some time there were two monarchs in Syria, Antiochus holding Antioch and the North, and Demetrius the South. Diodotus, who assumed the name of Tryphon, murdered the young Antiochus in 143–142 B.C. and usurped the throne. The Jews now took advantage of this divided authority to strengthen their position until the erstwhile city-state developed into a kingdom, as may be read in the pages of Josephus.

In or about 140 B.C. Demetrius, who had reached the age of twenty, determined to make a bid for the eastern provinces, although Tryphon was unsubdued, hoping perhaps to return with a full treasury and an increased force of veteran soldiers.

Mithradates I. and Demetrius II.—When this surprising campaign was undertaken Mesopotamia was still a possession of his house, and Babylonia had been his in 144 B.C.; but since that date it had been added to the Parthian empire, although loosely held. The Greeks, as always, greeted the Seleucid monarch with enthusiasm, and, since the Parthian rule was both new and unpopular, adherents flocked so rapidly to his standard that Demetrius was victorious in more than one battle : the Bactrians also helped him by a diversion. Mithradates resorted to stratagem, and made proposals for peace which were being accepted when the unsuspecting Demetrius was suddenly attacked, his army dispersed, and he himself taken prisoner. He was in the first place carried round the empire in triumph, but was afterwards well treated and granted a residence in Hyrcania. An attempt to escape was unsuccessful, and he was recaptured by Phraates II., the successor of Mithradates, who, affecting to treat the matter as a youthful escapade, sent him a gift of dice. Curiously enough, the incident is described by Chaucer in *The Pardoneres Tale* :

> Looke eek that, to the kyng Demetrius
> The kyng of Parthes, as the book seith us,
> Sente him a paire of dees of gold, in scorn,
> For he hadde used hasard ther-biforn ;
> For which he heeld his glorie or his renoun
> At no value or reputacioun.

The Death of Mithradates I., 138 B.C.—The reconquest of Elymais was the last exploit of Mithradates I. The great Parthian monarch died, full of years and honour, in 138 B.C.

Antiochus VII. Sidetes, 138–129 B.C.—When the news reached Syria of the disaster that had overtaken Demetrius the cause of Tryphon benefited, but only for a short time. Antiochus, known as Sidetes from the Pamphylian port of Side where he had lived, at once claimed his brother's throne, and in the end gained it, together with the hand of the often-married Cleopatra. Again the prestige of the house of Seleucus won the day, and Tryphon was deserted by his adherents, who went over to his rival at Seleucia, distant only twelve miles from Antioch. Tryphon was captured and allowed to commit suicide—an advance on the horrible mutilations and tortures he would have suffered a few generations earlier.

Antiochus Sidetes and Phraates II., 130–129 B.C.—The new monarch, in the first place, occupied himself in putting down the old abuses and in reasserting his authority over the Jews and other subjects.

In 130 B.C., considering that his rule was consolidated, he prepared to try conclusions with Phraates II., the son and successor of Mithradates. He collected a large army, in which was included a Jewish contingent under John Hyrcanus, grandson of the first Maccabee leader. But the number of camp followers appears to have been enormous, and probably led to the final disaster. Like his brother, he was greeted with warm affection in Mesopotamia, and adherents came in by thousands. Three battles were fought and won, which gave him possession not only of Babylonia, but also of Media, and the Parthians had to retreat to their native fastnesses. Indeed, it seemed as if Antiochus were destined to repeat the exploits of his great ancestor.

During the winter, however, his army was broken up and quartered in various cities, and great discontent arose, probably on account of the host of camp followers. One of the generals, too, made an evil name by his exactions. Phraates during this period tried to negotiate, but the victor's terms were too hard, as only Parthia was to be retained by him, and that in return for tribute; and Demetrius was to be handed over to his brother.

Phraates played one trump card by releasing Demetrius, with an escort to take him to Syria; but the mistakes of his adversary made this stroke of policy unnecessary, for, at a given signal, the cities of Media attacked their garrisons and Phraates was able to march with his army to Ecbatana in support of them. Near Ecbatana he found Antiochus, whom he attacked at a considerable disadvantage in numbers, and the last warrior Seleucid, defeated and wounded, threw himself from a cliff to avoid capture and thus ended a strenuous life. The Parthian monarch enslaved the remnants of the great army and then turned with fury on Seleucia, which was punished with merciless severity.

The Downfall of the House of Seleucus.—But this was merely a detail. The dominant fact was that the death of Antiochus Sidetes was the end of the dynasty of Seleucus as a great power. Thenceforward it was destined to expend its waning energies in domestic broils. Some years later, when Rome appeared on the scene as a conqueror, it was with the Kings of Pontus and Armenia that battles were fought, and not with the degenerate and disinherited descendants of the great Seleucus.

Its Place in History.—Before we quit this dynasty, which loomed so large in the history of Persia, and even on a wider stage, we may well pause to consider the part it played. Bevan [1] points out that in the kingdom of the " Successors " there were three distinct traditions : the Oriental inherited from the previous empires, the Macedonian, and the Hellenic. Even during the lifetime of Alexander the Oriental conception of the monarch's infallibility and absolutism began to prevail, and it necessarily clashed with the Macedonian and Hellenic traditions.

On the other hand, the Seleucids claimed to be different from these Oriental monarchs, and to a limited extent their claim was justified. Perhaps it would be more correct to say that in their conduct towards their subjects they distinguished between the Asiatic, accustomed to obey passively, and the Macedonian or Greek, whose character was strongly opposed to passive obedience. In Macedonia the king was supreme, but his supremacy was in practice tempered, and in some cases controlled, by the great nobles and the army. In the East the nobles tended to give place to courtiers depending on the favour of the monarch ; but examples occur of the army's taking action. For instance, it was the army which called Antiochus the Great to the throne. In fact, the rule of the Seleucids was two-faced, inasmuch as it was absolute towards its Oriental subjects, but was tempered by the army, which was mainly a home-born and therefore a national force. Moreover, the character, and consequently the acts and policy, of the Seleucids were influenced deeply by Greek opinion, by the use of the Greek tongue, and by Greek training. Of the achievements of the house of Seleucus, the most important was that it kept alight the torch of Greek civilization and Greek ideals, so that it affected even the rude Parthians. Further, by holding the Nearer East for Hellenism, that great and important part of Asia was preserved from being overrun by barbarism, and although towards the last the dynasty became effete and helpless, it had done its work. Rome was ready to take its place and to keep back the hordes of Central Asia and the Arabian desert-dwellers, until Byzantine Rome, too, in the course of the centuries, waned and fell before the onslaught of a new power.

[1] *House of Seleucus*, chap. xxxii.

SILVER COIN OF MITHRADATES II.

CHAPTER XXIX

PARTHIA, ROME, AND PONTUS

J'ai vengé l'univers autant que je l'ai pu :
La mort dans ce projet m'a seule interrompu.
Ennemi des Romains et de la tyrannie,
Je n'ai point de leur joug subi l'ignominie ;
Et j'ose me flatter qu'entre les noms fameux
Qu'une pareille haine a signalés contre eux,
Nul ne leur a plus fait acheter la victoire,
Ni de jours malheureux plus rempli leur histoire.

RACINE, *Mithridate.*

The Nomadic Peril.—Until the present generation, there was no means of connecting the history of Iran with that of China ; but thanks to the devoted labours of a handful of scholars, to whom all honour is due, it is now possible to trace to their origin some, at any rate, of the great nomadic migrations which have so profoundly affected the history of the world.

The date 250 B.C., so close to the birth-year of the Arsacid dynasty, was most important in China, marking as it did the downfall of the Chow dynasty which had ruled for close on a millennium.[1] China was for some time after this event broken up into a number of feudal states, but a famous warrior arose in the person of Tsin, who restored the authority of the central power. This extraordinary man is generally believed to have built the great wall of China, which

---

[1] In this section my chief authorities are *A Thousand Years of the Tartars*, by E. H. Parker ; *The Heart of Asia*, by F. H. Skrine and Sir E. Denison Ross, and Kalman Nemati's "The Historic-Geographical Proofs of the Hiung-Nu-Hun Identity," *Asiatic Quarterly*, April 1910. For the Sakae, *vide* "Sakastana," by Dr. F. W. Thomas, *Journal R.A.S.* for January 1906.

was an effectual bar to raiding nomads and thereby undoubtedly influenced the course of their migration.

In 200 B.C. China first became a World Power, and at this very period the tribes termed in Chinese history the Hiung-Nu or Huns fought with the neighbouring nomadic nation of the Yue-Chi, which was defeated and fled west to the Ili river. Finding the local tribes too strong to be attacked in this district, the horde swung south on to the Sakae, who in 163 B.C. were displaced from their habitat in the Tarim basin. They in their turn advanced to the Sir Daria and Bactria, where they broke up the Graeco-Bactrian kingdom.

This movement of the Yue-Chi set in motion waves of hardy nomads, who were forced by the driving power behind to win fresh territories from the comparatively civilized kingdoms to the south, or to suffer annihilation. It is not suggested that all these movements were simultaneous. Fortunately for civilization they were not; but they had this in common, that they gave rise to an overwhelming danger, for in place of the absorption of one civilized state or some of its provinces by a neighbouring state which was also more or less civilized, the whole civilized world was threatened by hordes of Scythians or nomads who devoured their aged relations, held their women in common, and were from every point of view coarse savages whose success would have been a calamity for mankind. Even to-day a Yellow Peril is feared by some; but Japan, the leading Turanian state, has already entered the comity of nations, and China is also struggling, painfully it may be, towards the same goal. Consequently we realize with difficulty that defeat in those days meant death, probably after torture, to man, woman, and child, or a life to which death was infinitely preferable.

The Victories of the Nomads over the Parthians.—It was with this threatening state of affairs that Phraates II. was confronted after his victory over the Seleucid forces, and it was on this account that he made no attempt to conquer Syria. Far from this, he at once marched to defend Parthia, and increased his army by embodying in it the survivors of the force of Antiochus. No details of the campaign have been recorded, but apparently it lasted for some years and ended in the total defeat of the Parthians, owing to the defection of their Greek contingent, and in the death of the monarch. His successor continued his policy, but he too was defeated and died fighting against the formidable nomads.

Mithradates II. of Parthia, 124–88 B.C.—It might be thought that Parthia was doomed to succumb after this second defeat; but Mithradates II., who now ascended the throne, was a more fortunate or a better general, and his operations changed the whole aspect of affairs, the nomads receiving such severe lessons that they turned their arms to a quarter where the resistance was weaker, and poured into the state now termed Afghanistan. Indeed, so successful was Mithradates that he annexed various provinces to the eastward, and coins prove that princes with Parthian names bore rule near the Himalayas during this period. After his new provinces had been duly organized, Mithradates was free to devote attention to the west of his empire, where Himerus, the Viceroy of Babylon, was preparing to revolt. But the Parthian monarch with his seasoned army was too powerful, and Himerus was easily crushed.

Parthia and Armenia.—The state of Armenia with its capital Van has already been referred to in connexion with the campaigns of the Assyrian conquerors, when it was inhabited by the Nairi, the Urartu, and the Mannai. But about the seventh century B.C. the Armenians, who are an Aryan race, apparently entered the country from the West. Herodotus speaks of them as colonists of the Phrygians, when he mentions their contingent in connexion with the great army of Xerxes.[1] Armenia (Armina) also appears among the provinces of the Persian Empire in the Behistun inscriptions, and we hear of it from time to time in subsequent history, but generally as having no particular importance. It is to be noted that the Armenians term themselves Haykh, the plural form of Hay, their eponymous hero. When Mithradates I. extended the Parthian empire, Armenia, which had been compelled to submit to Antiochus Epiphanes, again threw off the Seleucid yoke. Apparently this was accomplished through Parthian assistance, as its new monarch, who reigned from 150 to 128 B.C., was an Arsacid prince, named Val-Arsaces. His son, who waged war with Pontus, ruled until 113 B.C., and was succeeded by Artaxias, the Artavasdes of Justin. It was about 100 B.C. when Mithradates invaded

---

[1] Herodotus vii. 73.

Armenia, and although no account of the campaign has been preserved, we learn from a remark by Strabo that Tigranes, the eldest son of the Armenian king, was for some years a hostage in Parthia. This clearly points to Parthian success; but Artavasdes kept his throne, and during the course of the two following decades Armenia under Tigranes reached the zenith of her power and ruled from the Gulf of Issus to the shores of the Caspian Sea. In the history of Parthia, the Armenian question constantly recurs as a matter of the first importance.

The Expansion of Rome, 190–129 B.C.—When the legions crushed Antiochus the Great at the battle of Magnesia in 190 B.C., it seemed inevitable that the era of independent kingdoms in Asia Minor and Syria must speedily come to a close. But Rome, perhaps inspired with statesmanlike prudence, withdrew, and for a generation pursued a policy of abstention, the different states being allowed to act much as they pleased without any armed intervention from the West. In 168 B.C. the battle of Pydna and the subsequent annexation of Macedonia changed the situation, as the curt order to Antiochus Epiphanes to evacuate Egypt clearly showed. A few years later (151–145 B.C.) a pretender appeared in Macedonia, and the Achaeans also rose; but the result was the sack of Corinth and the final reduction of Hellas to subordination under the Roman Governor of Macedonia, although at first there was no direct administration by Rome. Carthage, too, had been destroyed, its site being levelled to the ground after its capture by Scipio in 146 B.C. Yet another event, perhaps in its direct effect the most important of all, brought Rome permanently to the East. The rulers of Pergamus had always been staunch allies of the Republic, and although the services of Eumenes had not been rewarded after Pydna, his successor in 133 B.C., being without an heir, bequeathed his state to the Roman people. The legacy was accepted, and after the final defeat of a natural son of Eumenes, the kingdom of Attalus was annexed. Its Thracian possessions were united to Macedonia, which was now a Roman province, and the eastern districts were ceded to Mithridates[1] of Pontus, the ally of Rome; but the most valuable portion became a Roman province under the name

---

[1] I am using the classical spelling for Mithridates of Pontus to distinguish him from the Parthian monarchs of the same name.

of Asia.[1] This was effected in 129 B.C. Rome now occupied a position very different from that at the end of the second century, and she henceforth pursued a career which, like that of the British Empire, was not the result of carefully-thought-out schemes of aggression, but was due to the irresistible force of circumstances.

The Making of the Empire of Mithridates VI. of Pontus, 120–90 B.C.—There are few more dramatic figures on the stage of history than Mithridates VI. of Pontus, who claimed descent from the Achaemenidae on his father's side and from the Seleucidae through his mother. Left an orphan by the assassination of his father, he grew up surrounded by treason even in his own household, and the knowledge of this fact warped, while it strengthened and hardened, his character. Accustomed to a wandering life, he acquired a remarkable physique, and his mental equipment was sufficient to enable him to appreciate Greek literature and art. For falseness and cruelty few monarchs have surpassed Mithridates, but his energy, initiative, and capacity compelled the admiration of all. Starting with the remote and insignificant kingdom of Pontus, which included the country along the southern shores of the Black Sea from Sinope and Trebizond to the neighbourhood of the modern Batum, he soon built up a formidable empire, including Mingrelia and Imeritia to the east of the Black Sea and so round to its northern coasts. Circumstances favoured the young conqueror, who found the Hellenic cities too weak to withstand the exactions of the hordes roving in the interior.[2] As a result, Mithridates was welcomed as a deliverer, and created the kingdom of the Bosporus, which not only furnished him with large supplies of corn and money, but provided the finest recruiting ground imaginable. Nor did his conquests end with these successes. He annexed Lesser Armenia and made a treaty with Tigranes, who had meanwhile succeeded his father, and who sealed it by bestowing his daughter Cleopatra on Mithridates. The details of this important agreement are not known, but it evidently included a promise of mutual support and probably mapped out the respective zones of conquest. We thus have Mithridates of Pontus, an ally of Rome, united by a treaty to Armenia,

---

[1] It is used in this sense in the New Testament. *Vide* Acts xvi. 6.
[2] Mommsen (Bk. IV. chap. viii.) refers to an inscription at Olbia, situated near the mouth of the Dnieper, which gives a contemporary account of the incessant exactions and depredations of the Scythians.

which was regarded by the Parthians as at any rate lying within what nowadays we should call their "sphere of influence."

Hitherto the interests of Rome had not been directly affected, although the wiser and better-informed must have realized that this new empire boded ill for the peace of the East; but when Paphlagonia and Cappadocia were also absorbed it was inevitable that the Senate should take action. In 102 B.C. the Romans had established themselves in Cilicia, being forced to take this step by the piratical tendencies of its population, and Lucius Sulla, its Governor, was instructed to intervene in Cappadocia. On this occasion Mithridates dared not oppose the representative of Rome, and Sulla swept through the country. Thus for the first time a Roman army reached the Euphrates, a river destined to play so large a part in the future as the eastern boundary of the Roman Empire. But the expedition of Sulla had no permanent results; for upon his departure the Roman nominee was driven out by Tigranes, and Paphlagonia, which had been evacuated, was again occupied. The Senate despatched a second Roman officer, as an ambassador, and again, in 90 B.C., Mithridates yielded.

The First Intercourse between Parthia and Rome, 92 B.C.—Mithradates II. of Parthia had undoubtedly watched the growth of Armenia with deep concern, as Tigranes, who owed his throne to Parthian support and who had ceded some territory in payment for it, had not only taken back his gift, but had even annexed provinces across the Parthian border. Consequently, when Sulla reached the Euphrates, a Parthian ambassador was sent to him to propose an offensive and defensive alliance with Rome. It was a meeting full of portent, and Sulla gained unbounded prestige by assuming the place of honour between the King of Cappadocia and Orobazus the Parthian ambassador. The latter afterwards paid with his life for not maintaining Parthian honour as its monarch considered that it should have been maintained. Sulla was unable to conclude a treaty and perhaps was reluctant to do so; at all events the matter dropped. It is, however, of interest to note that the two states which were destined to champion for so long the rival interests of East and West met at first in friendly intercourse and with proposals for an alliance.

The Earliest Intercourse of China with Parthia, 120–88 B.C.
—It is at least of equal interest to know that Mithradates II. was not only the first Parthian monarch to open relations with the Great Republic of the West, but that he also received the first Chinese embassy which visited Iran.[1]

It is generally agreed by Chinese scholars that until 140 B.C. China had no knowledge of the West. But under the Han dynasty missions were despatched in every direction, and more than one of these penetrated as far as Parthia, which is termed An-Sih—the Chinese form of Arsaces, as Kingsmill first pointed out. The Chinese description of Parthia is to the effect that rice, wheat, and the vine were cultivated, that the cities were walled, and that it was a very great country. Reference, moreover, is made to the use of silver coins bearing the effigy of the reigning monarch. It was also reported that " they make signs on leather from side to side [2] by way of literary record." This evidently refers to parchment, which, as its name shows, reached Europe from the Near East, the word having been traced through the late Latin *pergamena*, or product of Pergamus. No mention whatever is made of the Roman Empire, which lay beyond the ken of China at this period. The account then refers to the " Weak Water," which, as Kingsmill points out, was originally the tradition of an inland sea in the basin of the Tarim, of which the Lop Lake is a dwindling representative. The envoys probably heard of the Sistan *Hamun* and transferred the legend to the new and more distant site, as was the invariable custom among early travellers of the East and West alike.

Return embassies bringing gifts of " great birds' eggs and clever Li-Kien conjurers to offer to Han " are mentioned. The eggs referred to must be those of the ostrich, probably obtained from the Arabian Desert, although Kingsmill suggests that the ostrich may have ranged the Lut in those days ; and Li-Kien is to be identified with Hyrcania. Parker dates these embassies, which throw the first gleam of light on the intercourse between Iran and China, between 120 B.C. and 88 B.C.

---

[1] *Vide* " Chinese Knowledge of Early Persia," by E. H. Parker (*Asiatic Quarterly*, January 1903) ; *The Intercourse of China with Central and Western Asia in the Second Century B.C.* (Shanghai, 1880), by T. W. Kingsmill, and *China and the Roman Orient*, by Dr. F. Hirth.

[2] Chinese writing runs from top to bottom, and consequently a horizontal script would strike the observant traveller.

An Obscure Period of Parthian History, 88–66 B.C.—The circumstance that Parthia applied to Rome for an alliance is in itself evidence of the conviction that the forces of Armenia, supported by Pontus, were too strong to be met. And although we now enter a period of history which is obscure, we learn that Tigranes was strong enough to defeat Parthia and to expand at the expense of the Arsacid monarch, who died about 88 B.C., and of his successors. We read that, taking advantage of the Pontic War, he annexed Upper Mesopotamia and Media Atropatene from Parthia, and westwards absorbed what was left of the kingdom of the Seleucids. These campaigns took place between 85 B.C. and 74 B.C.; and, as already mentioned, Armenia from being a small state grew into a wide-spreading empire. Tigranes only recorded an accomplished fact when he stamped in Greek upon his coins the ancient title of the monarchs of Asia, "King of Kings."

For about twenty years, from 88 B.C. to 69 B.C., Parthia played a secondary rôle under Sinatruces and other rulers, and observed with difficulty a strict neutrality, while Rome fought for empire against Pontus and Armenia; but in 66 B.C. Pompey succeeded Lucullus, and the situation once more entirely changed.

Mithridates VI. and Rome, 89–66 B.C.—The monarch of Pontus, who had yielded to Rome on more than one occasion, at length felt himself strong enough to cross swords with the Western Power. As there was no adequate force at the disposal of the Roman representatives, Mithridates overran Pergamus, and, posing as a deliverer, remitted all taxes for five years. On the other hand, he suddenly massacred all the Italians who resided in the province of Asia, to the number of eighty thousand.[1] His fleet seized Delos and the Piraeus, Athens having declared for him; and a majority of Greek cities followed her example.

Sulla landed in Epirus with 30,000 men, marched on Athens, and attempted to escalade the Piraeus, but failed signally; nor was he more successful when he resorted to regular siege operations. Athens was taken in 86 B.C.; but the Piraeus was not captured till after the departure of the fleet of Mithridates, which proceeded to Thermopylae

---

[1] This large number proves the accuracy of Seneca's observation that "wherever the Roman conquers, he inhabits."

to join the Pontic army. Sulla, who now had but 15,000 men at his disposal, met the army of Mithridates, numbering 100,000 men, at Chaeronea, where Philip of Macedon had conquered the allied Athenian and Boeotian forces. The battle was desperately contested, but the discipline of the West once again prevailed over the numbers of the East, and ended in a disastrous defeat for the army of Mithridates. Negotiations were then opened, and Sulla accepted 2000 talents by way of an indemnity and the surrender of 70 ships of war. Thus closed what is generally known as the First Mithridatic War.

The Second Mithridatic War was of little importance; but the Third was a long struggle. Mithridates, who was well informed of the state of affairs in Rome, heard of the death of Sulla and of the victories in Spain of Sertorius, with whom he opened up negotiations and made a treaty in 75 B.C. He was also aware of the exhausting war against the gladiators under Spartacus. Consequently, in 74 B.C., he marched into Bithynia, whose monarch, following the example of the last Attalid, had bequeathed his kingdom to the Roman people. Again he carried all before him at the outset, but when Lucullus appeared on the scene and blockaded the Pontic army, which was besieging Cyzicus, it was severely handled, and only a shattered remnant escaped to Lampsacus. The fleet of Mithridates, too, was lost in a storm. During 73 B.C. and the following year Lucullus operated in Pontus, until Mithridates, hard pressed, took refuge in Armenia.

Tigranes, whose pride was of the order which precedes a fall, declined to surrender his father-in-law, and when the Roman legions advanced into Armenia in 69 B.C. he contemptuously remarked, "Those Romans for ambassadors are too many, for an army too few." But his army was scattered like chaff before the Roman onset and fled eastwards. In the following year he was again defeated, and Lucullus would have completed the subjugation of Armenia, had not his soldiers refused to advance amid the high mountains of the Ararat district. He retired southwards to less elevated country, where he captured Nisibis. In the spring of 67 B.C. Lucullus returned to Pontus, where Mithridates had reappeared, and again wished to march into Armenia, but again his army mutinied. Thus Lucullus failed to complete the task he had begun, which was one of extraordinary difficulty, partly on account of the enormous distances and the mountainous nature of the field of operations.

The Career of Pompey in the East, 67–63 B.C.—Pompey was one of the greatest men produced by Rome, and his career in the East showed his extraordinary capacity to full advantage. He had already brilliantly distinguished himself in Africa and in Spain, and had arrived back in Italy in time to take a leading part in the annihilation of the gladiators of Spartacus, a difficult feat, the credit for which he shared with Crassus. He therefore stood high in the esteem of his fellow-countrymen before he even visited the East.

His eastern campaigns began with his appointment, invested with extraordinary powers, to crush the Cilician pirates, whose depredations were as fearless and as dangerous to life and liberty, not only at sea, but even on land, as those of the mediaeval Corsairs. He appears to have displayed an unusually comprehensive grasp of naval strategy, by organizing a sweeping movement which drove these formidable pirates from Italian waters. He followed them up and defeated their combined fleets in their own waters—a notable achievement.

While absent on this campaign, Pompey was appointed to conduct the Mithridatic War to the end. He started promptly. When he landed to undertake this important task, Pontus was again in the possession of Mithridates. Lucullus was still in the highlands of the Upper Halys, his successor, Glabrio, having not yet taken over the command. Operations were at a standstill in the theatre of war; and in Cilicia there were three legions equally inactive. In fact, it was clearly a case in which new blood was required.

The great Roman displayed immense energy and infused a new spirit into the war, and the renown of his name led many discharged veterans to volunteer for service. In the spring of 66 B.C. he proceeded to take up command of the troops with Lucullus, and began active operations, although the Cilician legions had not joined the main body. Mithridates was unwilling to face the famous Pompey, and retreated, until the Romans ceased to follow his very mobile army, and began to annex and subdue the country. Mithridates seized his opportunity to cut Pompey's line of communications, and the latter remained on the defensive until the Cilician legions arrived. He then invested the Pontic camp by a chain of posts, and Mithridates, after suffering from scarcity for over a month, broke away to the east, but was surprised by a night attack and utterly defeated. With the remnant of his forces he hastened up the Euphrates, intending to take refuge in Armenia; but Tigranes on this occasion not only refused to receive him, but even set a price on his head. Mithridates then made for the eastern corner of the Black Sea, pursued by Pompey up to the River Phasis, and ultimately appeared in the Cimmerian Bosphorus, where his son, who had rebelled against him, being unable to maintain his position, committed suicide.

Pompey gave up the pursuit, but not content with having driven Mithridates from his state, marched on the Armenian capital, Artaxata, close to modern Erivan. There he received Tigranes and his son of the same name, and dictated to them his terms. A payment of 6000 talents, or £1,400,000, was demanded, and also a present for the soldiers. Tigranes had to yield up all his conquests, including Cilicia, Phoenicia, and above all Syria. His territories were in fact reduced to the original kingdom, and he became a Vassal-King. The young Tigranes, having foolishly refused to accept the governorship of a province, was made a prisoner, and, with his wife, the daughter of Phraates, graced the Victor's triumph.

Few generals have had the good fortune of Pompey in this campaign. In the case of Mithridates mutiny alone had prevented Lucullus from crowning with final success the crushing blows he had inflicted on the king, whereas Pompey by a single engagement was able to drive him, almost a fugitive, out of Asia. In Armenia, without even an engagement, and partly at any rate in consequence of the awe inspired by Lucullus, he had dictated terms to Tigranes by which he not only annexed some of the richest, and strategically the most important, provinces of the Near East, but also received a huge sum of money, which enabled him to reward his soldiers and keep them contented. Not that Pompey did not merit good fortune. He was no carpet knight, and success did not weaken his energy and manhood.

After the submission of Tigranes, he marched into the valley of the Kur, and, fighting the Albanians, crossed by the picturesque pass across which now runs the railway connecting Batum with Baku into the valley of the Phasis; this he descended to the Black Sea, where he met his fleet. This march was undertaken in the hope of re-establishing contact with Mithridates; but, realizing that the old king was out of his reach, and not likely to trouble Pontus, he returned into the valley of the Kur and subdued it. Plutarch states that he wished to advance to the shores of the Caspian Sea, but that, when only three marches' distant, he was forced to retreat by the number of venomous snakes. At all events he had penetrated to districts where even Alexander the Great had not been, and he concluded these operations by returning to Lesser Armenia, where he received letters from the kings of the Elymaeans and of the Medes.

Pompey and Phraates III. of Parthia.—Upon his arrival in Asia, Pompey, who was an able diplomatist, had opened negotiations with Phraates III., son of Sinatruces, and had proposed that in return for assistance against Armenia, Corduene and Adiabene, which Tigranes had annexed, should be restored to Parthia. These terms were accepted, and as it happened that the eldest son of Tigranes with many adherents was then at the Arsacid court, Phraates III. had no difficulty in carrying out what he had promised. He invaded Armenia with a powerful army, accompanied by the refugee prince, and drove Tigranes from Artaxata to the mountains. Thinking that the campaign was ended, Phraates left the Armenian prince to besiege Artaxata; but after the departure of the Parthian monarch Tigranes swooped down on the investing army and drove it headlong from the country. As already related, Pompey afterwards appeared on the scene and dictated terms. Phraates, who had already recovered Adiabene, proceeded to repossess himself of Corduene; but Afranius, Pompey's legate, expelled the Parthians and handed over the disputed province to Armenia. This cynical breach of faith and Pompey's contemptuous refusal to address Phraates by his accepted title of " King of Kings " raised a feeling of hatred against Rome, which soon bore bitter fruit. It is probable that Pompey was contemplating an invasion of Parthia with his victorious legions; but he ultimately decided that the risk was too great, and, modifying his policy, he appointed arbitrato s who settled the outstanding questions between Armenia and Parthia.

The Suicide of Mithridates VI., 63 B.C.—Mithridates, in

whom there must have been a strain of madness such as showed itself in his kinsman Antiochus Epiphanes, at this time reached the end of his long career. He was preparing a fresh army with which to invade Italy, when his son Pharnaces headed a rising against him, which was joined by all classes who had united in opposition to this wild scheme. The old wolf, finding no hope left, first poisoned his wives, his daughters, and his concubines, and then himself drained the deadly cup. Thus dramatically died Mithridates VI. of Pontus, in 63 B.C., and with him passed away the greatest enemy that had ever withstood the might of Rome in the East. As Plutarch puts it, "The whole army (of Pompey) upon hearing the news fell to feasting, as if in the person of Mithridates alone there had died many thousands of their enemies."[1]

The Results of Pompey's Campaigns.—The campaigns of Pompey and their results can be concisely summarized. He had thoroughly subdued and partially annexed Pontus, which with neighbouring Bithynia became united to Rome; he had made Armenia a vassal state, as also the Cimmerian Bosphorus; and the Albanians and Iberians of the valley of the Kur had been conquered. Parthia had been humiliated but not subdued, and here, in his dealings with this Eastern Power, he had shown a lack of wisdom and foresight. In Syria he refused to acknowledge the puppet-princelings of the house of Seleucus, and subdued the various disturbing elements, the last resistance being offered by the Jews. Rome now marched with Parthia, but the demand of Phraates that the Euphrates should be the recognized boundary had neither been definitely acknowledged nor observed. Pompey, moreover, had received communications from states such as Elymais (Susiana), which, like Persis, was independent, and from Media, which certainly formed part of the Parthian Empire. In short, the arrangement come to was intended to be an advance and not a final settlement, and the course of events in the next generation proved that this, indeed, was its character.

[1] Plutarch's *Lives*—Pompey.

SILVER TETRADRACHM OF ORODES I.

CHAPTER XXX

PARTHIA AND ROME—THE FIRST TRIAL OF STRENGTH

Parthi, penes quos, velut divisione orbis cum Romanis facta, nunc Orientis imperium est. . . . A Romanis quoque, trinis bellis, per maximos duces, florentissimis temporibus lacessiti, soli ex omnibus gentibus non pares solum, verum etiam victores fuere.—JUSTIN xli. 1.

The Internal Affairs of Parthia, 57–55 B.C.—Phraates was assassinated by his two sons less than two years after the departure of Pompey. Mithradates, the elder, ascended the throne, but was deposed on account of his injustice and cruelty, and Orodes, the younger son, became the " King of Kings." The deposed monarch was assigned the province of Media Magna ; but he rebelled, and being defeated fled to Gabinius, the Roman Governor of Syria. This official was delighted at the chance of playing an important rôle in the East ; but just as he was about to organize an expedition he was diverted by the dazzling offer of money to the value of £2,500,000 if he intervened in Egypt. Consequently Mithradates was left to his own resources, and, as Seleucia and Babylon had declared for him, he threw himself into the latter city, where he was captured by Orodes and executed.

The Appointment of Crassus to Syria, 55 B.C.—Marcus Licinius Crassus was one of the foremost Romans at this period. He was of a very different type from Pompey or Caesar, having obtained his position mainly through the power of his purse, which was filled by nefarious means. Plutarch says that even those who esteemed him most thought of him as " a brave man anywhere but in the field." In 55 B.C. Crassus was given the proconsulate of Syria, and, jealous of the fame of his rivals, he boasted that he would lead an army to Bactria, to India, and to the Eastern Ocean. Starting at the beginning of winter from Brindisi, he lost several ships in a storm. He then marched through Macedonia and Thrace to Asia Minor. On his way to Antioch he saw Deiotarus, the aged king of the Galatians, laying out a new city. "You begin to build rather late in the day," was his remark. The caustic retort was, "And you, too, are not beginning very early in the morning to attack the Parthians."

Crassus marched across the Euphrates and gained a success, defeating the Parthian Satrap. But, instead of following it up, and taking advantage of Babylon being held by Mithradates, he returned to Syria, where he spent the autumn and winter of 54 B.C. in adding to his already colossal fortune by plundering temples and levying special imposts.

The Projected Invasion of Parthia, 53 B.C.—In the spring of 53 B.C. the Proconsul determined to undertake the much-talked-of expedition. He had been visited by Artavasdes, King of Armenia, who promised the co-operation of a force of 16,000 cavalry and 30,000 infantry. The promise was accompanied by the advice that the line of march should be through friendly Armenia, where the hills were favourable to the manœuvres of the Roman infantry and unsuitable for the Parthian cavalry. Crassus, however, decided to use the route across the plains of Mesopotamia which was in part already familiar to him, and where he had left garrisons; these to some extent committed him to this line of advance.

Orodes realized that Parthia would without doubt be invaded, and, knowing the character of Crassus, was not afraid. Indeed, in the spring, he sent an embassy to the Roman general with a provocative message, to the effect that "if the war was waged by the people of Rome, he (the king) proclaimed war to the bitter end; but if, as he understood was the case, Crassus for his own private profit had invaded his territory, he would be merciful, and taking pity upon Crassus's dotage, would send those soldiers back who had been left there as his prisoners." Crassus replied that his answer would be given at Seleucia, whereupon the leader of the embassy laughed and said, "Hair will grow on the palm of my hand before you will see Seleucia."

Crassus at last started on his great undertaking, and crossed the Euphrates without incident at Zeugma at the head of seven legions, supported by 4000 cavalry and a similar force of slingers and archers, making up a total of 42,000 men. It appears that his original plan was to follow down the left bank of the Euphrates until he reached a point opposite Seleucia where the two rivers of Mesopotamia are close together; but the influence of the Shaykh of Osrhoene, whose district he was traversing, caused him to alter his plan of campaign. This wily Arab, who was secretly allied to Orodes, explained that the main Parthian army had fled towards the East, and that the only chance of overtaking it was to march after it by the shortest route. In spite of counsels of prudence, Crassus could not resist the prospect of securing rich booty from the supposed flying enemy, and the army turned its back on the Euphrates and marched east across the open steppe of Mesopotamia.

The Plan of Campaign of Orodes.—The plan followed by Orodes was to advance in person into Armenia with all the Parthian infantry and thereby prevent Artavasdes from reinforcing Crassus with cavalry, an arm in which the Romans were very weak. He not only succeeded in this object, but made a treaty of peace with Artavasdes, which was sealed by a marriage. The main operation of attacking Crassus he left to his Surena, or Commander-in-Chief, to whom he gave the whole of the mounted troops, which were of little value in a mountainous country, but were in their element on the open plains.

This Surena, who greatly impressed the Romans, and who probably organized both campaigns, was a combination of fine qualities and extremely luxurious habits. His private baggage was loaded on one thousand camels, and two hundred waggons were required for the use of his concubines! Yet his activity, energy, and capacity were indubitable, and after the great victory was won, Orodes paid him the high but painful compliment of so fearing his personality that he had him put to death.

Parthian and Roman Troops compared.—The Parthian mounted troops consisted of light and heavy cavalry. The first was the more famous, and is referred to in the well-known lines of Horace:

> Miles sagittas et celerem fugam
> Parthi (timet).

It consisted of swarms of light horsemen armed with bow

and arrow, and trained from boyhood to shoot at full gallop while advancing or retiring.[1] Spare arrows in thousands were carried on camels, and as the field of operations was particularly suited to this mode of warfare and the Roman army consisted almost entirely of infantry, this force, both brave and devoted, was as formidable from its elusiveness as from its offensive power. The heavy cavalry, organized on entirely different lines, was armed much in the same manner as the mediaeval knights of Europe. The horses were protected by armour equally with their panoplied riders, and the chief weapon was a heavy lance. In battle they charged in line, and, unless opposed by similarly protected troops, constituted a most redoubtable force.

The famous infantry, of which the Roman army was chiefly composed, was trained for close combat, and their procedure was to hurl a javelin and then charge sword in hand in serried ranks. But against a mounted foe their charges were of little avail; nor did their javelins carry as far as the Parthian arrow, which indeed completely outranged the arrows of the Roman archers. The Roman cavalry too, although well mounted and equipped, was, in this campaign at any rate, unable to face the Parthians with success. It must, however, be remembered that its numbers were comparatively small, and that it was not well handled.

The Battle of Carrhae, 53 B.C.—Crassus had advanced some three or four stages from the Euphrates, and had approached the River Belik at a point thirty miles south of Carrhae, the Haran of Holy Writ, when the Parthian army suddenly appeared. The subtle Shaykh of Osrhoene, who, we learn from Plutarch, had kept the Surena informed of the movements of the Romans and had amused himself at their expense, now left Crassus on a specious pretext and joined the Parthians. The Proconsul, confident and ill-informed, instead of resting his weary and thirsty soldiers, led them on against the enemy, over whom he expected to gain an easy victory.

The Surena had concealed the number of his troops and the magnificence of their arms—an important matter in those days from the point of view of moral effect—by

---

[1] Persians shoot guns or rifles off horseback at full gallop with remarkable precision, their shot to the rear being one that would baffle any European cavalryman. Indeed it is impossible when using a European saddle.

coverings of skins. But as the Roman army approached the kettle-drums made an unearthly and unnerving din, and the Parthians stripping off the coverings of their armour, appeared in all their numbers and splendid appointments. According to Plutarch, their first intention had been to attack the Romans at close quarters with their heavy cavalry ; but they wisely decided to employ their special tactics in the first place. Feigning to retreat, they moved in every direction and began to surround the Roman column, which was drawn up in a square. They then gave a display of those " Parthian tactics " which thenceforward were famous, by shooting showers of deadly arrows into the solid Roman mass. Charges by the Roman legionaries were attempted, but were of no avail, as their elusive enemy retired, shooting just as rapidly and unerringly as before.

Crassus ordered his son Publius, who had joined him from Gaul, where he had served with much distinction under Caesar, to make a counter-attack before the entire force was surrounded. The gallant youth charged out at the head of 1300 cavalry, supported by some archers and cohorts[1] of infantry. The Parthian light cavalry gave way, probably to lure him on, and Publius thinking that he was victorious pursued, followed by the infantry. The enemy, however, finally turned, and raising a great dust rained arrows upon them. The heavy cavalry next came up, and in spite of the great bravery shown by the Gaulish horsemen, who crept under the Parthians and stabbed their horses, or even pulled the lances from their hands, the combat was too unequal ; the Roman detachment was annihilated, and Publius, being wounded by a dart, ordered his armour-bearer to despatch him.

Crassus had decided on a general advance, when to his dismay he learned of the disaster by seeing the head of Publius on a spear. The Parthians, encouraged by their success, redoubled their efforts, bringing the heavy cavalry into action. They continued the uneven contest until sunset, when according to custom they rode off to a distant camp, calling out that they would allow Crassus to mourn his son during the night, before completing their task by the capture of the Proconsul, which was their special object.

Crassus was, as Plutarch puts it, " altogether past helping,"

[1] A cohort consisted of 500 men.

and consequently Octavius and Cassius,[1] who were his staff officers, gave orders for a night retreat, by which they hoped to escape from the enemy. The Parthians were aware of this movement, but negligently allowed it to be executed without making any immediate attempt to harass the demoralized Romans. In the morning they began by massacring the wounded left in camp, and by the time they followed up the retreating army it was safe in Carrhae.

So utterly demoralized were the Romans that, instead of halting in this stronghold to recover their shaken *moral*, they made another night retreat, in the course of which they broke up into detachments of armed rabble. Crassus, misled by his guide, had only reached some low hills when the Parthians overtook him. Octavius came to his rescue and a small force stood at bay on an eminence, from which they drove the Parthians.

The Surena now resorted to treachery to complete his success. He proposed a truce to arrange for the withdrawal of the Roman forces unmolested. Crassus was unwilling to trust to his good faith; but the mutinous soldiers insisted, and so, with something of the true Roman spirit, he yielded with dignity and met the Surena. The latter was most friendly and said that there was now a treaty in force between the two countries, but that Crassus must accompany him to the river to sign it, adding, with pointed allusion to the bad faith of Pompey, "for you Romans have not good memories for conditions." Crassus agreed, and ordered one of his own horses to be sent for; but the Parthian told him that a horse with a golden bit was at his disposal, and he was forcibly placed upon it and carried off. His staff, suspecting treachery, attempted to come to the rescue, and in the mêlée that ensued Crassus was killed.

The Roman troops after the death of their leader broke up in panic and were hunted down by the Arabs, but few escaping. It is computed that fully one-half of the army of 40,000 men perished in the campaign. Ten thousand escaped across the Euphrates, and as many more were made prisoners and settled at Margiana, the modern Merv, where they intermarried with the women of the country. It would, indeed, be interesting if traces of this large body of Romans were some day found in this historical oasis.

---

[1] Gaius Cassius Longinus was afterwards the leader in the assassination of Caesar.

Plutarch ends his account of the life of the unfortunate Roman with a description of the scene at the Parthian Court when his head was received. The wedding between Pacorus, son of Orodes, and the sister of Artavasdes was being celebrated, and the assembled guests were enjoying the *Bacchae* of Euripides, when the head was thrown down among them. To quote from Plutarch : " The Parthians receiving it with joy. . . . Jason, a Greek actor, taking up the head of Crassus, and acting the part of a bacchante in her frenzy, in a rapturous impassioned manner, sang the lyric passage :

> We've hunted down a mighty chase to-day,
> And from the mountains bring the noble prey."

The Parthian Invasion of Syria, 51–50 B.C.—The battle of Carrhae was undoubtedly of great importance in the conflict which has been waged between East and West for so many centuries ; for it restored to the East its lowered prestige and weakened that of the great representative European power. But in many ways its results were hardly as serious as might have been anticipated, partly because the Parthian army was not formidable except in the level open steppe, and partly owing to the execution of its capable Commander-in-Chief. Cassius commanded but the remnants of the army of Crassus, and Syria was ripe for revolt, but Parthia gave the Roman authorities two years in which to recover, merely sending out a few bands of marauders to raid. On the other hand, as the civil war was imminent in Rome, no reinforcements were sent to the Roman Governor, whose defence deserves the highest credit.

In 51 B.C. the dreaded invasion occurred, and under the leadership of Pacorus swarms of light horsemen overran Syria ; but they were unable either to gain over or to capture the stronger cities. Cassius, though compelled to throw himself into Antioch, did not wholly abandon the offensive, but played " Parthian tactics " on his enemy by feigning a retreat and luring them into an ambush, where the Roman legionaries had their revenge. In spite of this reverse, Pacorus did not recross the Euphrates, but prepared to renew the campaign in the following spring. He changed his plans, however, and instead of again overrunning Syria was induced to plot against his father. But before the conspiracy had ripened Orodes heard of it and summoned his treacherous son to Court.

The Parthian army recrossed the Euphrates in the summer of 50 B.C. Thus concluded the first trial of strength with the great Western State, which had been deeply humiliated and had been unable to take any steps to restore her damaged prestige. Parthia, on the other hand, had reaped immense advantages, both moral and material, and, had her monarch been a man of first-rate capacity, Rome's eastern empire would have been in jeopardy.

SILVER DRACHM OF PACORUS I.

CHAPTER XXXI

ROME AND PARTHIA—THE SECOND TRIAL OF STRENGTH

> Now, darting Parthia, art thou struck ; and now
> Pleased fortune does of Marcus Crassus' death
> Make me revenger. Bear the King's son's body
> Before our army. Thy Pacorus, Orodes,
> Pays this for Marcus Crassus.
> SHAKESPEARE, *Antony and Cleopatra.*

The Civil War between Caesar and Pompey, 49–48 B.C. —Shortly after the termination of the first struggle between Parthia and Rome, the great civil war between Caesar and Pompey broke out, the effects of which, needless to say, reacted on distant Parthia. Pompey, whose power was based chiefly on the East, opened negotiations with Orodes in 49 B.C. or the following year, and, curious as it may appear, they were not discouraged by the Parthian monarch, who must, it would be thought, have hated Pompey from the bottom of his heart. The Roman envoy inquired on what terms Orodes would send an army to aid Pompey in the impending civil war. The answer was that Syria was the price that must be paid, but Pompey to his credit rejected the terms, whereupon Orodes threw his envoy, Hirrus, into prison.

The campaign fought between the two great Roman generals culminated in the utter defeat of Pompey at the battle of Pharsalia, in 48 B.C. He contemplated taking refuge at the Parthian Court, and according to one account was deterred from so doing only by hearing that Antioch had declared for Caesar. Plutarch, however, states that his friends thought the risk too grave, more especially for his wife Cornelia, and that it was on this account that the illustrious fugitive sought the protection of the boy-king of Egypt, by whose ministers he was treacherously assassinated.

Caesar and the Near East, 47 B.C.—In the year following his great victory Caesar visited Syria and Asia Minor, partly in connexion with the attempt of Pharnaces, son of Mithridates, ruler of the Bosphorus, to regain the entire kingdom of Pontus. This attempt had at first been successful, the local forces of Rome having been defeated. Caesar took but one legion to reinforce the beaten troops and was boldly attacked by Pharnaces, on the 2nd August 47 B.C., at Zela, where, after recovering from the surprise, the Roman troops won the day. Pharnaces fled, pursued by his illegitimate brother, who, thanks to the support of Rome, succeeded to the kingdom of the Bosphorus. Perhaps the victory of Zela is best known as being that announced by Caesar to the Senate in the three words *Veni, Vidi, Vici*. It is improbable that Caesar, whose presence was urgently needed in the West, thought at this period of attempting to avenge Crassus. But, three years later, after the successful conquest of the whole Roman Empire, he determined to seek fresh laurels by a campaign against the Eastern foe, in which connexion his supporters gave out that it was written in the Sibyl's books that the Romans would not conquer Parthia until ruled by a king. The necessary decree was passed by the obedient Senate, the legions had been collected and had even started for the East, when on 15th March 44 B.C. the daggers of the "Liberators" saved Parthia from a peril which was perhaps the greatest in all her history; for Caesar, with his splendid genius for war and diplomacy, and with the experience of previous Roman expeditions to guide him, would have conquered Orodes as surely and as completely as Alexander the Great overthrew Darius Codomannus.

The Early Career of Mark Antony.—Of the great Romans of this period none played a more important part in the Near East than Mark Antony, of whose early career a brief account is called for. In the last chapter reference was made to Gabinius, Governor of Syria, who had been bribed by an enormous sum of money to invade Egypt. The Commander of the cavalry in this expedition was Marcus Antonius, grandson of the famous pleader and son of Julia, a member of the family of the Caesars. He had already distinguished himself by the capture of Aristobulus, the leader of the rebel Jews, and his son, in which feat he displayed considerable military skill and valour.

In the campaign against Egypt he marched ahead with the cavalry division and was instrumental in ensuring the success of the Roman arms by the capture of Pelusium, the key of the whole country, which was surrendered by its garrison of Jews. In the final battle he also distinguished himself conspicuously, and when Egypt was handed back to Ptolemy he opposed the massacres by which the enraged monarch wished to signalize his recovery of the throne. Upon quitting the country he left a great name behind him and a reputation for brilliant military capacity.

Before the Civil War he aided the party of Caesar, as Tribune of the People; and when hostilities broke out he rendered Caesar signal service, being in command of the left wing at Pharsalia. After the assassination of his patron, Antony obtained possession of his papers and money and represented the family until Octavian appeared on the scene as Caesar's heir. When the two quarrelled, Octavian drove Antony across the Alps; but he speedily returned with seventeen legions which he had won over to his cause, and forced Octavian to make terms. The united forces then marched into Macedonia to meet Brutus and Cassius, and in 42 B.C. the battle of Philippi was won chiefly by Antony, Octavian being so ill that he was obliged to be carried in a litter. After this victory Antony proceeded to the East, and levied such heavy taxes that he was boldly told that "Asia has raised two hundred thousand talents for his service: 'If this has not been paid to you, ask your collectors for it; if it has, and is all gone, we are ruined men.'" Nor was his prodigality and ostentatious recklessness limited to grinding down the East. Cleopatra appeared on the scene, sailing up the Cydnus:

> The barge she sat in, like a burnish'd throne,
> Burn'd on the water: the poop was beaten gold;
> Purple the sails.[1]

And from this time forward the wishes of this most beautiful and gifted woman were the ruling influence of Antony's chequered career.

The Parthian Invasion under Pacorus and Labienus, 40–39 B.C.—It is a curious fact that a Parthian force fought at Philippi. Orodes, who believed in fishing in troubled

---
[1] Shakespeare, *Antony and Cleopatra*.

waters, had originally sent a small contingent to aid Caecilius Bassus, formerly an adherent of Pompey, who aimed at carving out an independent kingdom. In 43 B.C. Bassus joined Cassius, bringing the Parthian contingent with him, and that capable official, who was well known to the Parthian Court, took advantage of this fact to open negotiations with Orodes, sending back the Parthian soldiers with gifts. As a result a body of cavalry was sent to join him, and took part in the battle of Philippi, this being the only appearance of a Parthian force in Europe.

The defeat of Brutus and Cassius—the latter was killed by his Parthian slave at his own request—might well have produced complications between the victors and the Parthian monarch ; but Orodes, it would seem, considered his position much stronger than that of the Roman Empire, convulsed as it was by constant civil wars, and resolved to take advantage of the situation. At this period Parthia had at her disposal the services of a Roman general, Quintus Labienus, who happened to be on an embassy to the Court of Orodes on behalf of Brutus and Cassius, and who feared to return home. He was not a soldier of any special repute ; but his services were obviously of great value to the Parthians.

Orodes, who had forgiven Pacorus, entrusted him and Labienus with a large force, which crossed the Euphrates in the spring of 40 B.C., or just a decade after the close of the previous campaign. Antony would naturally have led the Roman army ; but he was summoned West to protect his interests against Octavian, and Syria was left to his incompetent subordinate, Decidius Saxa. At first the Parthians carried all before them, compelling the surrender of both Apamea and Antioch, after defeating Decidius Saxa in a pitched battle. The two generals then separated, Pacorus going south and Labienus crossing the Taurus. Pacorus subdued Syria, with the solitary exception of Tyre, and then advanced into Palestine, where two rivals, Hyrcanus and Antigonus, uncle and nephew, were fighting for power. Antigonus offered Pacorus a thousand talents, equivalent to £240,000, and five hundred Jewish women as a bribe, and was at once placed on the throne, where he reigned for three years. Labienus was equally successful, defeating and killing Decidius Saxa in a second battle. He afterwards overran the southern provinces of Asia Minor, and his success emboldened him to adopt the title of " Imperator " and to strike coins bearing his effigy and name.

The Peace of Brundisium, 40 B.C.—Meanwhile Antony had been successful in Italy, and by the peace of Brundisium a third division of the provinces had been made. Lepidus was left in possession of Africa, and Antony was given the East, the boundary of which was fixed at Scodra, the modern Scutari. Antony and Octavian entered Rome and received a joint ovation in celebration of the peace, which was further solidified by the marriage of the former with Octavia, the highly gifted sister of his rival.

The Victories of Ventidius, 39 B.C.—In the autumn of 39 B.C. Antony reached Athens on his way to resume his command. He despatched his lieutenant Publius Ventidius to act against Labienus, who was surprised without having an adequate force at his disposal. He consequently retreated on Cilicia and appealed to Pacorus, who sent him a large reinforcement of cavalry. This force, however, acted independently, and in attempting to surprise Ventidius was defeated. Labienus was consequently left to his fate and was captured and put to death. Pacorus, alarmed at the untoward trend of events, retreated to Northern Syria, but left a strong force to guard the well-known " Syrian Gates." This division was attacked by a Roman column which was reinforced during the battle by the whole army, and Ventidius gained yet another victory. Pacorus therefore withdrew across the Euphrates, and Ventidius, content with having recovered Syria, wisely made no attempt to follow up the Parthians.

The Defeat and Death of Pacorus, 38 B.C.—The Parthian prince, however, was not disposed to surrender his conquests tamely, and in the following spring he once more crossed the Euphrates. Ventidius at first adopted defensive tactics and occupied an entrenched camp on an eminence. The Parthians were enticed into an attack on it and charged up the hill with magnificent audacity, but suddenly the gates were flung open and they were driven headlong downhill by the legionaries, who pursued them. The heavy cavalry of Parthia acted as a centre round which they re-formed, and the battle was stubbornly contested. But Pacorus was killed, and this decided the day. The Parthian host broke and fled towards the bridge of boats on the Euphrates, but was intercepted, and only the division which made northwards to Commagene escaped.

The results of this apparently nameless battle were of the first importance. Until then the Parthians were prepared to fight Rome for her Asiatic provinces, which they overran more than once, and even to a certain extent administered. After this battle, however, they abandoned the offensive to Rome, and were thenceforth content to keep within their borders, the only exception being that Armenia was, to some extent, regarded as lying within the Parthian sphere of influence.

The Death of Orodes, circa 37 B.C.—The death of Pacorus was a crushing blow to Orodes. The aged monarch resigned his throne to his eldest son, Phraates IV., whose tetradrachms are the first to bear a date. He at once proceeded to assassinate his numerous brothers, and his father on remonstrating was also murdered. Thus fell Orodes after a long and glorious reign, during which the fame of Parthia had struck terror into the citizens of Rome. He was not, perhaps, a great man, and the supreme victory over Crassus was won by his Commander-in-Chief ; but he deserves much credit as the monarch who raised the status of Parthia to that of a power able to treat with Rome on equal terms. It remains to add that, under Orodes, Ctesiphon became the capital of Parthia.

The Expedition of Antony against Parthia, 36 B.C.— Phraates IV., after assassinating his brothers and his father, instituted a reign of terror which drove away from his court many of his leading nobles. Among them was a certain Monaeses, a well-known general under Pacorus, who fled to Antony and suggested to him that the conditions were favourable for an invasion of Parthia. Phraates, alarmed at this prospect, pardoned Monaeses, who was permitted by Antony to return, with instructions to state that he only desired the restoration of the Roman standards and of any prisoners who were still alive. This, however, was merely a pretence intended to blind the Parthian Court ; for Antony, jealous of the triumph decreed to Ventidius, thought the time ripe for a campaign which would place him on the pinnacle of fame. Consequently he made secret, but strenuous, preparations and soon had sixteen or eighteen legions mobilized (about 60,000 men). Ten thousand Gallic and Iberian horse and 30,000 auxiliary horse and foot made up a formidable army. Artavasdes of Armenia also entered into a secret treaty, by the terms of which he was bound to furnish 6000 cavalry and 7000 infantry.

In spite of the importance of attacking Parthia before her preparations were completed, precious time was wasted by Antony's inability to part from Cleopatra, and in consequence it was midsummer of 36 B.C. when the army, which exceeded 100,000 men, finally started. The Euphrates was found to be strongly held, and Antony thereupon moved northwards into Armenia, where he was welcomed by his ally. His plan of campaign was now changed by the advice of Artavasdes, who pointed out that the entire Parthian army was collected on the Euphrates, and that an invasion of Media Atropatene, whose king was with Phraates, and the capture of Praaspa,[1] its capital, would be a magnificent achievement. Antony agreed to make the attempt, but apparently did not fully realize the mobility of a Parthian army. He divided his command, leaving the siege-train and baggage to follow, while he pressed forward by forced marches, hoping perhaps to surprise Praaspa; but this was found to be impossible and he was forced to await the arrival of his siege-train.

Meanwhile, the Parthians, as might be expected, followed swiftly in the tracks of Antony and attacked Statianus, who was in charge of the second column. Their victory was complete, Statianus and 10,000 Romans being slain, and the important siege-train captured. The result was a terrible blow to Antony, whom the subsequent defection of Artavasdes placed in a still worse position. All his efforts to capture the naturally strong fortress failed, supplies began to run short, and, as the Parthians pursued their national tactics of envelopment and retreat, in spite of all his efforts to engage them, the situation as the autumn drew near became increasingly serious. An attempt to " save face " by agreeing to abandon the siege if the standards and Roman prisoners were restored was treated with derision and contempt, and at last Antony decided that retreat was imperative.

His choice of routes lay between one striking the eastern

---

[1] Praaspa is identical with ruins now termed *Takht-i-Sulayman*, or "The Throne of Solomon," situated about one hundred miles south-south-east of Lake Urumia. Rawlinson erroneously considered that ancient Ecbatana was to be found at this site (*vide* Chapter X. of this work). *Vide* also Williams Jackson's *Persia Past and Present*, chap. xi.; and Strabo xi. 13, where Vera, a corruption of *bir*, signifying a castle, is to be identified with Praaspa.

shores of Lake Urumia, the water of which is undrinkable, but which is surrounded by a fertile belt of open country, or a route lying more to the east through a hilly tract. Hearing that the Parthians were occupying the route across the open plain, Antony wisely took to the hills and made for the neighbourhood of modern Tabriz. This decision gave him two days' immunity from attack; but on the third day the Parthians appeared and surrounded the retreating column. The Romans had learned since the defeat of Crassus to oppose these tactics by developing a corps of slingers who used leaden bullets with considerable effect; and this device, together with an opportune charge of the Gallic cavalry, drove off the enemy. But in the morning they reappeared, and for nineteen days in succession they harassed the Roman army incessantly, causing serious losses. In addition, Antony's men suffered from the cold and from lack of food and water.

From the neighbourhood of Tabriz, where in one combat 8000 men were killed and wounded, the worn-out Romans at last reached the Araxes. After crossing this river they were safe from the Parthian terror; for Phraates was content with having driven Antony out of his territories. But the misfortunes of the Romans were not at an end, as before winter quarters were reached another 8000 of the legionaries succumbed.

Antony showed to great advantage during this retreat, and always retained the devotion of his men. Plutarch tells us that "O, the Ten Thousand!" was his constant exclamation of admiration for the manner in which the Greek heroes had surmounted even greater difficulties and dangers with trifling losses in this part of Asia.

His Campaigns in Armenia, 34–33 B.C.—It is possible that Antony had determined to continue the campaign, but in the meanwhile he returned to Cleopatra. During the winter, the king of Media, who had apparently been wronged in the division of the spoils, ventured on a remonstrance, and, well aware of the ferocious temperament of Phraates, finally decided on rebellion. He began by opening negotiations with Antony, to whom he sent an envoy at Alexandria. The Roman General, who was especially anxious to wreak vengeance on Artavasdes, accepted his proposals with immense satisfaction, and in 34 B.C. he suddenly reappeared in Armenia, where he seized Artavasdes by a stratagem. He then overran the entire country, and leaving garrisons to hold it again returned to Egypt. Once more he appeared on the scene, in 33 B.C., when he marched to the Araxes and made a treaty with the Median king, by the terms of which the dominions of the latter were enlarged at the expense of Armenia and a body of Roman infantry was placed at his disposal. Antony then turned his back on Parthia and the Parthian problem, and devoted his energies to securing his position against Octavian.

As might be supposed, Phraates, left free to deal with Media, defeated his rebellious vassal and in the end took him prisoner. He then invaded Armenia in alliance with Artaxias, the eldest son of Artavasdes. The Roman garrisons, unsupported and left to their fate, were captured one after another, and in a very short time Armenia won back her independence. As a result of these campaigns, the position and prestige of Parthia stood higher than before. The column of Statianus had been annihilated, Mark Antony had been driven out of the country with heavy losses, and did not dare to venture again across the Parthian frontier; and finally Armenia had been brought back into the sphere of Parthian influence.

Phraates IV. and Tiridates, 33-30 B.C.—The ferocious temperament of Phraates showed itself so fiercely after his successes that in 33 B.C. a revolt was headed by a certain Parthian nobleman named Tiridates. Phraates fled to the nomads of Central Asia, and Tiridates was declared king. He had ruled for about three years when Phraates returned at the head of a nomad force. Tiridates thereupon fled, taking with him the youngest son of Phraates, and appeared at the court of Octavian, who was at the time in Syria. The son of Phraates was accepted as a hostage, and Tiridates was afforded protection; but the cautious Roman was not to be drawn into a policy of adventure beyond the Euphrates.

The Restoration of the Roman Standards, 20 B.C.—Seven years later, in 23 B.C., Phraates opened negotiations for the surrender of the Pretender and the restoration of his son. Octavian, now the Emperor Augustus, declined to consider the former proposal, but agreed to surrender his son without a ransom. In return he demanded the Roman standards. Phraates received his son with much joy; but showed no inclination to give up the standards until the Emperor again visited the East three years later. Then, fearing the consequences of refusal, he duly restored them. The joy felt in Rome and the prestige which accrued to Augustus can be discerned in most writers of the time. Indeed a wave of exultation appears to have swept through the Empire, which finds expression in the well-known lines of Horace:[1]

> Tua, Caesar, aetas
> fruges et agris rettulit uberes,
> et signa nostro restituit Iovi
> derepta Parthorum superbis
> postibus, et vacuum duellis
> Ianum Quirini clausit et ordinem
> rectum evaganti frena licentiae
> iniecit emovitque culpas
> et veteres revocavit artes.

The End of the Second Trial of Strength.—The campaigns of Mark Antony constituted the second phase in the struggle between Parthia and Rome, the protagonists of the East and West. When Phraates restored the Roman standards, one of the main incentives for Rome to attack her powerful neighbour was removed, and, as Augustus was wisely averse from foreign expeditions and left it as one of the main principles of policy that the Roman Empire should not be extended, there was for the time being no fear of wanton aggression from the West, after the fashion of the invasion of Crassus. Phraates, on his side, realized that it was as well to cultivate good relations with Rome, and when his sons grew up he sent them to the Court of Augustus, mainly perhaps in order to get possible rivals out of the way, but also to pay a compliment to the mighty Emperor, who apparently allowed them to be considered as hostages. In short, a spirit similar to that which animated the British Empire before the Great War governed the relations between the two states, and there was no invasion of the territory of one by the other for almost a century, a long period in the history of two neighbouring empires.

[1] *Odes*, iv. 15.

PARTHIAN SCULPTURE FROM THE SOUTH LIWAN OF THE MAIN PALACE AT HATRA, SHOWING HELLENIC INSPIRATION.

CHAPTER XXXII

THE ORGANIZATION, RELIGION, AND ARCHITECTURE OF THE PARTHIANS

For five centuries a people, or rather a camp, without past or future, without a religion, an art, or a policy of its own, assumed the protectorate of the East, and saved Asia from the arms of Rome.—GARDNER, on the Parthians.

The Organization of the Parthians.—From the larger point of view the history of Parthia is that of Persia and Central Asia under the paramountcy of the Arsacidae, and no attempt was made by this nomadic tribe to colonize or to weld conquered peoples into a nation. The empire was divided by the Caspian Gates into the upper kingdom with eleven and the lower kingdom with seven provinces, but the Parthians were, generally speaking, content to possess the open country and their capitals, and so long as their orders were obeyed and the tribute paid, they allowed the subject populations to develop on their own lines. After the conquest of a kingdom, it was either replaced under its monarch, who ruled as a Vassal-king, or else a Satrap termed a *Vitaxa* was appointed. In the former category, generally, were the kings of Media Atropatene, of Elymais, Persis, and Adiabene, whereas Babylon was governed by a Satrap. As Gibbon[1] has pointed

[1] *Decline and Fall*, vol. i. p. 339 (Smith's edition).

out, the whole Parthian government resembled closely the feudal system of mediaeval Europe. But the Greek cities, which, as we have seen, were scattered widely throughout the empire, and were usually flourishing, were treated in an exceptional manner. These city-states, as they might be termed, enjoyed their own municipal government, and resting on old-time privileges, were practically independent. For example, the city of Seleucia, which supported the house of Seleucus so faithfully, had a population of over half a million and ruled over a considerable tract of fertile land. It paid a fixed tribute to the Parthians, but was regarded as a "free city." The Jewish communities also, though in a lesser degree, had been granted municipal independence, and some of them were "free cities" like those of the Greeks. When invasion threatened from the West these semi-independent Greek city-states were a source of weakness and even of actual danger to Parthia, as has been pointed out ; but on the other hand it was probably Hellenic influence which, permeating the Parthians, kept their empire in existence. Perhaps the value of the connexion is recognized in the title "Philhellen," which appears on the coins of many Parthian monarchs.

The Position of the Monarch.—The royal house was placed on such an exalted pedestal that, as Ammianus Marcellinus tells us, "every one avoids as sacrilege wounding any descendant of Arsaces." Owing to this veneration for the Arsacidae, no pretender without royal blood in his veins stood any chance of the throne. At the same time two hereditary councils constituted a check on the Great King. The first of these was the assembly of the adult members of the royal family ; the second was the Senate, composed of spiritual and temporal lords, very much on the same lines as our own House of Lords. There were seven great families, including that of the monarch, on the Achaemenian model. The monarch could be chosen only from the Arsacid dynasty, but his election had to be ratified by both assemblies, which constituted the *megistanes* or nobles. After he had been duly elected, the right of crowning him belonged to the Surena or hereditary Commander-in-Chief, a custom which strongly emphasized the military constitution of the empire. The lords spiritual were known as the "Magi" or "Sophi." They were specially powerful as representing religion, and also as being the most highly educated body in the empire. As in mediaeval Europe, and in Persia at the present day, the spiritual lords owned much of the best land, were granted special privileges, and constituted a powerful hierarchy. It remains to add that the king was unapproachable, and strangers were obliged to adore his golden effigy set up in the chief cities. For him too were reserved the upright tiara, inherited from the Achaemenians, and the golden couch.

The Army.—There was apparently no standing army in Parthia apart from the royal guard. Just as under the Achaemenians, when war was declared the monarch issued orders to his Vassal-kings and Satraps, who brought their levies to an appointed centre on a fixed day, each contingent being entirely self-supporting. The infantry was of small value and of less account, as is still the case in Persia. The fighting force of the nation consisted of its light and heavy cavalry, which has been described in connexion with the campaign of Crassus. We there saw the tactics of the Parthian army at their best, and also its weakness in the failure to pursue the Romans by night.

In the campaign against Antony, it appears that Phraates was most anxious for the invader not to winter in Media, as he could not have kept his army together for so long a period ; and this indicates another serious weakness. The art of waging war scientifically, as understood by the Greeks long before Alexander the Great, was never learned by the Parthians. They possessed no siege-train, though they could easily have organized and manned one with the aid of their numerous Greek subjects. Even when they captured a splendidly equipped siege-train from Antony, they destroyed it.

Everything connected with navigation was a sealed book to this typically nomadic, horse-loving race, although the Caspian Sea washed Hyrcania. We have had occasion to make the same remark about the Persians throughout their long history.

The Court.—Like the Achaemenian monarchs who moved from Susa to Persepolis and again to Ecbatana, the Parthian Court spent the winter in Mesopotamia and the summer in Media and Parthia. Its winter capital was Ctesiphon, built on the left bank of the Tigris opposite Seleucia and a few miles below Baghdad. Ecbatana was the Median capital; and Hecatompylus, the ancient capital of Parthia which borders on Hyrcania and is perhaps confused with it by Strabo,[1] was the third capital. Rhages, too, was certainly visited, and lying as it does on the direct route between Media Magna and Parthia or Hyrcania, was probably the site of a royal palace. Finally, there was a royal palace at Babylon, and of this alone a description has come down to us, from the writings of Philostratus, who says: "The palace is roofed with brass and a bright light flashes from it. It has chambers for the women, and chambers for the men, and porticoes, partly glittering with silver, partly with cloth-of-gold embroideries, partly with solid slabs of gold, let into the walls, like pictures. The subjects of the embroideries are taken from the Greek mythology, and include representations of Andromeda and of Orpheus, who is frequently depicted. . . . You behold the occupation of Athens and the battle of Thermopylae and a canal cut through Athos. . . . One chamber for the men has a roof fashioned into a vault like the heaven, composed entirely of sapphires, which are the bluest of stones, and resemble the sky in colour."

It is tantalizing to know so little about the daily life of the sovereign. We have seen from Plutarch's account the luxury of the Surena who defeated Crassus. His dress was of the Median fashion, he wore his hair parted in the middle, and his face was painted with cosmetics. He rode to battle with a guard of ten thousand horse composed exclusively of his own adherents, and his transport train was prodigious. It is safe to infer from this and from other notices that the King of Kings passed his life in similar but even greater splendour.

The Position of Women.—The position of women, as usual in the polygamous East, was subordinate. The monarch, like the Achaemenian Great Kings, had a chief wife, who was recognized as the Queen, and a multitude of concubines, many of whom were Greeks. The customs of separation and veiling generally known as the Harem system prevailed, but eunuchs never obtained the great influence that they won under the Achaemenians; nor, with the solitary exception of Musa, the Italian slave-girl, does any Queen play a part comparable with that of several of the Achaemenian royal ladies. Indeed the Parthians maintained their virility to a

[1] xvi. 1. 16.

remarkable degree, probably because they never entirely abandoned their nomadic habits.

The Life of the Parthians.—We know comparatively little as to the actual life of the Parthians, but it is not very difficult to picture it. War was of course considered the first and noblest employment, and after it came the chase. The varieties of game which then abounded have been already described, and we may feel sure that, although shooting preserves are alone mentioned, the Parthians as a nation, like the Persians and Macedonians, were devoted to sport. This is indeed borne out in a remark by Justin, who states that game formed the main article of diet. The Parthians were addicted to a wine made from dates, and at revels there was obviously much intemperance, as indeed was the case all over the world. Their music included the flute, the pipe, and the drum, and their feasts frequently closed with dancing. Like all nomadic races they originally lived sparely, but their habits changed with prosperity. They ate meat of all kinds, including pork, and various vegetables. Their bread was leavened, light, and porous, and was known and esteemed in Rome.

Their Dress.—The Parthians, like the Persians, adopted the flowing Median robe, with baggy trousers similar to those worn by Pathans to-day. For head-dress they used a ribbon terminating in two long ends or else a rounded tiara. The beard, when worn, and the hair generally were curled, but fashions changed at various periods. In war they wore armour, with helmets of polished steel. The trappings of their horses were very rich, golden bits and bosses being usual. The national weapon was a powerful bow. Swords, too, were carried, and a dagger was invariably worn by all classes. The chief weapon of the heavy cavalry was a lance. The costume of the first Arsaces as he appears on coins is described by Gardner as follows : " He wears a conical helmet not unlike that of the Assyrians, with flaps to protect ears and neck, and bound with the regal diadem of the Greeks ; his ears are adorned with earrings, and his neck with a torques of the simplest form. He is clad in a coat of mail, apparently consisting of scale or chain armour, which covers his arms to the wrist, and his legs to the ankle ; over this is thrown a short military cloak or sagum. His shoes are fastened by straps or thongs round the ankles." Later monarchs dis-

RELIGION AND ARCHITECTURE

carded the armour for "a soft under-garment and an over-garment shaped like a cloak."

Laws and Customs.—Very little is known about the laws of the Parthians. Severity was the keynote, and there was little sense of proportion in meting out punishments. But in this they are by no means singular. Their customs were originally those of the nomad, but to some extent they inherited the traditions of the Persians, and they were certainly affected by Greek civilization to no small extent. The Greek diadem, the Greek wreath, and the Greek titles of the monarch all point to Hellenic influence ; and, though an Arsacid era was introduced for time-reckoning, the Seleucid era continued in use.[1] The personal character of the Parthians was high. They treated prisoners kindly, generally observed their pledged word, and kept treaties when concluded. The *Parthis mendacior* of Horace is a misrepresentation of fact, and had probably about as much foundation as the *Albion perfide* legend.

Religion.—The religion of the Parthians, like their customs, was derived from three distinct sources. Apparently they were almost without a creed when they first rose to power and began to worship the first Arsaces, the founder of the empire. But this ancestor-worship was not the only source of their religion. Another, derived from the Zoroastrianism of the Achaemenians, recognized the eternal conflict existing between Ormuzd, the Principle of Good, and *Drug*, the Lie. The Sun was saluted at its rising, was worshipped under the old name of Mithra, and associated with the Moon. Other deities were probably the ministers of Ormuzd, who watched over the monarchs and their families just as the genii of the Achaemenians did. The common people generally worshipped little else besides the ancestral images, which were the most precious possession of every family, high or low. There was also a profound belief in magic and invocations which recalls the ancient faith of Babylon.

The Magi were held originally in great reverence, and taught the sanctity of fire and exposure of the dead. They were members of the Parthian House of Lords. As time went by, however, their power waned, until at last their

---

[1] There is a Babylonian tablet in the British Museum (No. 33009, Bab. Room, Case G, No. 343) recording the receipt of various amounts of silver. It is dated in the 154th year of the Arsacid era and in the 218th of the Seleucid era (equivalent to 94 B.C.).

influence became slight. This is partly to be attributed to the fact that the Parthians tolerated the Greek and Jewish religions, and later Christianity,[1] which made some way in the empire. It is believed that the kings of Osrhoene were Christians from quite an early date ; and it is a well-authenticated fact that a Council was held at their capital, Edessa, the headquarters of " The Church of the Easterns," in A.D. 198, to determine the date on which Easter should be observed. As a set-off to this weakening of the national religion we learn that it was a Parthian monarch, Volagases I., who collected all that was left of the Avesta, and his successors were apparently filled with the Zoroastrian spirit.

In the works of Philostratus, who flourished from A.D. 172 to about 244, we read in the description of the palace of Babylon, part of which has been quoted, that " golden images of the gods whom they worship are set up about the vault, and show like stars in the firmament. This is the chamber in which the King delivers his judgments. Four golden magic wheels hang from its roof, and threaten the monarch with the Divine Nemesis if he exalts himself above the condition of man. These wheels are called ' the tongues of the gods,' and are set in their places by the Magi who frequent the palace." [2]

Finally, from the fact that Pallas, Artemis, Zeus, and perhaps Apollo appear on the later coins, there are good reasons for supposing that some Greek deities were at one period officially recognized by the Parthians.

Literature.—The Parthians possessed no native literature, which proves how backward they were in the arts of peace. It is probable that they adopted that of Hellas when they first seized hellenized provinces, and it must have profoundly affected their outlook, just as it has affected that of millions in modern Europe. The fact mentioned by Plutarch that Greek plays were enjoyed is most significant, and there is no doubt that Greek was widely taught, and was the written means of communication throughout the empire.[3]

Architecture and Art.—Fergusson, in his well-known *History of Architecture*, lays down that Oriental architecture

---

[1] This question is dealt with in *The Assyrian Church*, by Doctor W. A. Wigram.
[2] Philostratus, *Vit. Apoll. Tyan.* i. 25 (quoted from *The Sixth Oriental Monarchy*, p. 417).
[3] The recent discovery of two ancient Greek documents in Western Media, dated *anno Seleuci* 225 (88 B.C.) and 295 (22-21 B.C.) respectively, and dealing with the conveyance of a vineyard, is of special interest in connexion with this question. *Vide* paper by Ellis H. Minns in the *Journal of Hellenic Studies*, vol. xxxiv. p. xlix, 1914, Part II.

is practically a blank from the conquests of Alexander the Great to the rise of the Sasanian dynasty, and this is generally true. But at Hatra, situated between the Tigris and Euphrates, and not many miles west of the old cities of Assyria, ruins are still extant which are held to be purely Parthian, as the city did not rise into importance till early in the second century after Christ, and is described by Ammianus Marcellinus, in A.D. 363, as long ago deserted. Hatra was surrounded by a massive circular wall, strengthened at intervals with towers, and protected by a wide and deep ditch. Its circumference exceeded three miles. In its centre are the remains of a palace. Its principal building consisted of seven halls, parallel to one another, of various sizes, ranging from 90 feet by 40 to 30 feet by 20. These halls were all vaulted. They were of various heights, and were entirely lighted from the eastern end, which was open. As Miss Gertrude Bell writes : " The great hall, in which, no matter what its size, the interior space was unbroken by pier or column, was a setting for princely state which could not be enhanced by any architectural device." This great arch "dominated the fancy of the Sasanian and of the early Mohamedan architects " ;[1] indeed, it is still their dominant feature. The eastern façade was ornamented with a series of pilasters, and some sculptures, chiselled on the arches over the entrances to the halls, represented either human heads or a female form. The entire length of the façade was 300 feet.

Behind these halls was a square building entered from one of the great halls, and surrounded by a vaulted passage. It is believed to have been the temple, and above the doorway leading into it was a splendid frieze. Internally the temple was without ornamentation, and it was lighted only by the single doorway.

These are not the only remains ; foundations of Parthian palaces and houses have been uncovered at more than one site in Mesopotamia, such as Niffer and Sherkat ; and a Parthian rock sculpture exists on the famous rock at Behistun. This was set up by Gotarzes, whose name may still be made out in the Greek inscription above the panels. It consists of two divisions or panels. That on the left, the greater part of

---

[1] *Palace and Mosque at Ukhaidir*, p. 66. For the best and latest publication dealing with Hatra, vide Andrae, " Hatra," *Wissenschaftliche Veroffentlichung der Deutschen Orient- Gesellschaft*, No. 9 (1908).

which is now destroyed, contained standing figures, three of which are still visible. The right-hand division is better preserved and contains three mounted figures on a smaller scale. That in the centre is Gotarzes, who has charged and overthrown his rival Meherdates, and is being crowned by a winged Victory. The falling figure of Meherdates and his horse is balanced on the left by the third horseman, a supporter of Gotarzes who gallops, lance in rest, to his master's support.[1] This relief, which evidently inspired the Sasanian rock-sculptures, is of little merit, but of some interest in the historical development of Eastern art.

Coinage.—A few remarks on the coinage[2] may fitly conclude this meagre list of Parthian artistic achievement. There were no gold coins, and all the drachms bear on the reverse the effigy of Arsaces seated to the right and holding a strung bow. In the earlier coins the founder of the empire is seated on the omphalos of Apollo; in the later, on a throne with a back. The use of the conical stone of Delphi is clearly taken from the coins of the Seleucid monarchs, in which Apollo himself holds the bow, and is seated on the "centre of the world." The legend was always in Greek except on the coins of Volagases V., Artabanus V., and Artavasdes (208–228 A.D.), which are bilingual, Greek and Pahlavi. In the earliest coins of Arsaces, "King Arsaces" alone appears, but Phraates I. adopts the title of "Great King." Mithradates I. becomes "King of Kings," and other monarchs adopt still higher titles. On the obverse the effigy of the reigning monarch is graven. Gardner points out that Parthian coins may be divided into two classes. The first consisted of the silver tetradrachms and a certain number of copper coins; the second includes the silver drachms, and obols and the copper coinage. It is believed that the coins of the first class were minted at some of the great Greek cities, whereas those of the second were struck at many centres held by Parthian garrisons.

---

[1] See King and Thompson, *The Sculptures and Inscription of Behistun*, Pl. IX., a photograph taken at a time when the figures in relief stand out from the field in shadow. I have specially to thank Mr. King for the above explanation.

[2] *Vide* W. Wroth's *Catalogue of the British Museum Collection* (1903).

SILVER TETRADRACHM OF PHRAATACES AND MUSA.

CHAPTER XXXIII

THE STRUGGLE FOR ARMENIA

Quin et Artabani Parthorum regis laceratus est litteris, parricidia et caedes et ignaviam et luxuriam obicientis, monentisque ut voluntaria morte maximo iustissimoque civium odio quam primum satis faceret.—SUETONIUS, *Tiberius*, 8. 66.

The Armenian Question.—The relations between Rome and Parthia would probably have continued to be friendly but for the constantly recurring Armenian question. Augustus accepted the *status quo* as arranged by the Parthians after the departure of Antony, and Artaxias was left in undisturbed possession of the throne of Armenia. On his death, in 20 B.C., the Emperor sent Tiberius to nominate his brother Tigranes as his successor. Tigranes reigned until his death in 6 B.C., when the Armenians placed his son and daughter upon the throne. This independence displeased Augustus, who despatched an army to establish a Roman nominee in place of the three natural heirs. Shortly afterwards a rebellion broke out, and Phraates, who must have watched the situation with the greatest interest, came forward as the protector of another Tigranes, who was unanimously chosen King. Augustus was now an old man, but he was determined to assert the suzerainty of Rome, and, after hesitating whom to entrust with the difficult task, despatched his grandson and adopted son Caius with full authority to the East.

The Murder of Phraates IV., 2 B.C., *and the Treaty with Rome*, A.D. 1.—Everything seemed to point to a new trial of strength between the two great powers, when the situation was entirely changed owing to the murder of Phraates by his son Phraataces—the word is a diminutive of Phraates—the child of his old age, whose mother was an Italian slave called

Musa. The parricide seized the throne, and although Augustus at one time refused to recognize him, it was ultimately arranged that he should meet Caius on an island in the Euphrates. This historical interview took place in A.D. 1, and Phraataces, whose position must have been particularly insecure, agreed to withdraw entirely from the affairs of Armenia. On these terms, which were loyally observed, a treaty was made, and celebrated by a series of magnificent festivities.

Phraataces, Vonones, and Artabanus III.—Phraataces was hated by his subjects, partly at any rate owing to the official honours paid to his mother, whose effigy was placed on the coinage. Before long he was put to death, as was also his successor Orodes, who was an Arsacid elected to succeed to the throne. The *Megistanes* then applied to Rome for Vonones, the eldest son of Phraates, who was sent back to Parthia. At first he was warmly welcomed, but his foreign habits and his foreign favourites, whom he promoted to most of the high posts, brought him unpopularity, which was increased by his dislike of hunting and drinking bouts. A revolt soon broke out, on this occasion in favour of an Arsacid, named Artabanus, who was King of Media Atropatene. His first effort failed,[1] but at a second attempt he drove Vonones out of the country. The refugee monarch fled to Armenia, where the throne was vacant, and he was elected King in A.D. 16 ; but Artabanus threatened war, and Vonones then quitted Armenia and fled to Syria, where he was accorded Roman protection.

Rome, Parthia, and Armenia, A.D. 18–35.—Rome now stepped in again to assert her suzerainty over Armenia, and Germanicus, the nephew of Tiberius, was sent on an extraordinary mission to the East, where he arrived in A.D. 18. He at once marched with a large force to Artaxata and there selected a foreign prince acceptable to the Armenians, and proclaimed him King under the name of Artaxias. Germanicus then returned to Syria, where he was visited by Parthian ambassadors, who proposed a meeting on the Euphrates similar to that between Phraataces and Caius ; but the proposal was not accepted.

[1] It is worth noting that Vonones struck coins in which he broke the usual rule of not mentioning the reigning monarch's personal name. The coins are inscribed "King Onones who has conquered Artabanus" and afford a good example of the use of coins for political manifestoes.

Artabanus during the ensuing years was so successful in his various enterprises that in A.D. 34, upon the death of Artaxias, he entered Armenia and appointed his eldest son, known only as Arsaces, to the throne. At the same time he despatched a provocative embassy to Rome. To this Tiberius replied by sending back one of the surviving sons of Phraates IV. to Syria, as he was assured that there was a strong party in Parthia ready to rise in his favour. But this scheme was foiled by the death of the prince, and perhaps it was in exultation over this that Artabanus wrote the famous letter to Tiberius, given in the heading to this chapter, in which he strongly advised the gloomy recluse of Capri to gratify his subjects by committing suicide! Incensed by this epistle, Tiberius not only despatched a second pretender to the throne of Parthia in the person of Tiridates, nephew of the prince who had died, but also stirred up the Iberians and other neighbouring tribes against his enemy. Strengthened by this support, in A.D. 35, Pharasmanes, King of Iberia, contrived the assassination of Arsaces and then marched into Armenia, where he took the capital. Artabanus sent another son, Orodes, to fight the pretender, but after a hard-fought battle the Parthian army was routed.

The Vicissitudes of Artabanus III., A.D. 36–37.—Artabanus in the following year (A.D. 36) took the field in person, whereupon the Roman Governor of Syria, by name Vitellius, marched towards the Euphrates. This caused Artabanus to retreat from Armenia with such loss of prestige that his nobles, with Roman support, conspired against him and forced him to flee to the wilds of Hyrcania. There he spent his time hunting and waiting, as he himself put it, "until the Parthians, who could judge an absent king fairly, although they could not continue for long faithful to a present one, should repent of their treatment of him." [1]

His action was shortly justified. Tiridates, unopposed and welcomed by the leading noblemen, entered Ctesiphon, where he was duly crowned by the Surena, and in the belief that his task was accomplished paid little or no attention to his rival. But before long Artabanus was, as he had anticipated, approached by a strong party of those who were discontented with the new order, and, as Tiridates did not await his attack, he regained the throne of Parthia without opposition.

[1] Tacitus, *Annales*, vi. 36.

The Peace with Rome, A.D. 37.—Tiberius was now anxious to make peace. Following the already established precedent, Vitellius, the Governor of Syria, met Artabanus on the Euphrates in A.D. 37. The treaty resembled in its terms that made between Phraataces and Cassius, it being agreed once more that Armenia lay outside the sphere of influence of Parthia. Artabanus, moreover, sent one of his sons to Rome, where he was regarded as a hostage by the Romans, if not by his father or himself. After this treaty Artabanus was again expelled by his nobles, but again returned, and shortly afterwards died. During his reign there were terrible massacres of the Jews, somewhat similar to the recent massacres of the Armenians in the Turkish Empire, and in A.D. 50, Seleucia began a revolt which lasted for seven years. Artabanus apparently died about A.D. 40 after a long and chequered reign of nearly thirty years.

Vardanes and Gotarzes, A.D. 40-51.—The history of Parthia after the death of Artabanus III. is one of internal feuds. His two sons fought for power with varying success, and in the end Vardanes, who is praised by Tacitus, was assassinated and Gotarzes ruled alone, in A.D. 46. Three years later the *Megistanes* grew weary of him, and despatched an embassy to the Emperor Claudius asking for Meherdates, son of Vonones. The request was granted, and once again a pretender from Rome crossed the Euphrates and was joined by the leading feudatories. Gotarzes, however, finally triumphed, and it was to celebrate his victory that the bas-relief at Behistun, described in Chapter XXXII., was cut.

The Struggle for Armenia.—The struggle with Rome for Armenia again became acute after the death of Gotarzes. His successor, Vonones II., reigned but a few months, and Volagases I., his eldest son by a Greek concubine, determined from the commencement of his reign to conquer Armenia, which he wished to bestow on his brother Tiridates. That unfortunate country was still ruled by Mithradates, brother of Pharasmanes of Iberia ; but the latter had an ambitious son named Rhadamistus, and, to occupy his energies, Pharasmanes suggested to him that it would be easy to murder his uncle and usurp the throne. This nefarious scheme was successfully carried out. Volagases, finding Armenia in this disturbed condition, immediately after his succession in A.D. 51 invaded it and carried all before him.

But an outbreak of sickness caused by a famine forced him to evacuate the country, whereupon Rhadamistus returned, and for three years was left in peace.

The Parthian monarch was for some time occupied with Adiabene, with whose vassal-king he had quarrelled, and was about to invade it, when an inroad of Dahae and other nomads called him away to defend Parthia. When he returned after successfully beating off the invaders, Izates of Adiabene had died, and with his brother Monobazus, who succeeded him, Volagases had no quarrel. He was consequently free to devote all his energies to the permanent annexation of Armenia. Rhadamistus was again attacked and again fled, leaving Armenia to Tiridates.

Volagases and Nero, A.D. 55–63.—These campaigns had caused considerable uneasiness in Rome, where Nero had recently ascended the throne of the Caesars, and it was decided to make strenuous efforts to restore Roman suzerainty over Armenia. Indeed, had Rome acquiesced in the proceedings of Volagases, her prestige would have suffered a heavy blow.

In A.D. 55 the Roman legions under Corbulo, esteemed the best general of the day, were ready to take the field, but Volagases, whose position was temporarily weakened by a rebellion headed by his son Vardanes, yielded for the time being and gave hostages to Rome. Three years later he had crushed his son, and was able to meet Corbulo with his hands free. He immediately insisted that Armenia must be recognized as a feudatory state of Parthia. This was tantamount to a declaration of war, and Corbulo promptly marched into the country, which had the misfortune to be the "cockpit of the Near East" for so many centuries. Volagases was again hampered by a revolt in Hyrcania, and although Tiridates opposed the legions to the best of his ability, in A.D. 58 he lost Artaxata and two years later Tigranocerta, and was forced to retire from the field. Rome bestowed Armenia on Tigranes, a prince of Cappadocia, but reduced its extent in order to reward the neighbouring monarchs who had aided her arms.

Up to this point there had been no real trial of strength, because Volagases had had his hands tied; but he now proclaimed that he was ready to give effect to the claims of Parthia, and took the field in Mesopotamia. Again, however, he consented to negotiate, and it was agreed that the troops of both countries should evacuate Armenia pending negotiations in Rome. But his ambassadors returned without having effected a settlement. In the meanwhile Corbulo had received a colleague in the person of Lucius Paetus, a favourite of Nero, who was anxious to carry on the war with vigour and to reduce Armenia to a Roman province.

In the autumn, the truce having expired, Corbulo crossed the Euphrates in the face of a large Parthian army and formed an intrenched camp near the left bank of the river. Paetus entered Armenia from Cappadocia and ravaged it without encountering any opposition. He consequently thought that the campaign was at an end, and in the autumn withdrew into winter quarters, stationing two legions between the Taurus and the Euphrates and a third in Pontus. He also granted leave to a number of the officers and men. Volagases now seized his opportunity and surprised the Roman camp. Fortunately for him Paetus was not only incapable but a coward, and instead of awaiting relief from Corbulo, who was marching to his assistance, tamely capitulated on the terms of the surrender of all the fortresses held by the Romans and the evacuation of Armenia, pending fresh negotiations with Rome. The disgraced legions retired to the Euphrates, where they met Corbulo and the relieving army.

Once more the old Roman spirit reasserted itself, the ambassadors from Parthia were dismissed, and Corbulo was given full powers to conduct the war. He marched into Armenia, where negotiations were again opened, and peace was made on the terms that Tiridates should proceed to Rome and receive his crown from the hands of the Emperor. This treaty was made in A.D. 63 and was duly observed, although Tiridates did not reach Rome until A.D. 66.

The Investiture of Tiridates by Nero, A.D. 66.—Tiridates travelled to Rome by land in great state, with an escort of three thousand Parthian cavalry, his journey costing the Roman treasury some six thousand pounds daily for a period of nine months. The actual ceremony of investiture was of extreme magnificence, and Tiridates, duly crowned, returned to Armenia in triumph and reorganized his kingdom on the Parthian model. As Rawlinson points out, the acceptance by Rome of an Arsacid ruler in Armenia far outweighed the nominal bestowal of the crown by Nero.

In any case, the peace between the two great empires was not again broken for over half a century, and, as the course of events showed, Rome was most ready to come to terms with her formidable opponent, who on her side was unwilling to incur the hostility of the Western Empire.

An Obscure Period of Parthian History, A.D. 66–108.—After the treaty with Nero, the history of Parthia, owing mainly to the peace between the two great empires, is so obscure that even the names of the Kings become uncertain. A few facts, however, illuminate this dark period. In A.D. 69 Vespasian, who was governor of Judaea, decided to bid for the empire, and Volagases offered to place forty thousand Parthian cavalry at his disposal; but his generals had already won the day in Italy, and he courteously refused the offer. Again, in A.D. 71, Volagases sent Titus a crown of gold to commemorate his conquest of the Jews.

In A.D. 75 the Parthian Empire was overrun by the Alani, a nomadic people, who, in alliance with the Hyrcanians, poured through Media and Armenia. Volagases appealed to Rome for help, but Vespasian refused it, and the Alani, after devastating far and wide, returned to their own country with immense booty. In A.D. 77 Volagases ended his eventful reign, which upon the whole had been successful, although the inroad of the Alani and the breaking away of Hyrcania brought failure at the close.

His successor, Pacorus, had a most disturbed reign, and it appears that the Parthian Empire was divided between three or four monarchs, all of whom claimed to be the " King of Kings." Pacorus, who is believed to have died about A.D. 105, was succeeded by Osroes, during whose troubled rule the long peace with Rome came to a close.

SILVER DRACHM OF ARTABANUS V.

CHAPTER XXXIV

THE DECLINE AND FALL OF PARTHIA

Trajan was ambitious of fame ; and as long as mankind shall continue to bestow more liberal applause on their destroyers than on their benefactors, the thirst of military glory will ever be the vice of the most exalted characters.—GIBBON, *Decline and Fall.*

The Roman Empire at its Zenith.—At the beginning of his great work, Gibbon lays down that Rome enjoyed " a happy period of more than fourscore years " during the reigns of Nerva, Trajan, Hadrian, and the two Antonines, and that from the death of Marcus Antoninus the decline set in. Consequently in dealing with this period we have to remember that the Parthian Empire was facing Rome at the zenith of her power and efficiency, whereas in her own case decay had already begun.

Trajan and Armenia, A.D. 114–115.—It is remarkable with what monotonous frequency Armenia constituted the *casus belli* between Rome and Parthia. Upon the death of Tiridates, about A.D. 100, the Arsacid monarch Pacorus had placed one of his sons, Exedares, on the throne without applying to Rome for recognition, and this constituted a grave infringement of the rights of the Western Power. Unfortunately for Parthia, Rome was at this period ruled by the great soldier Trajan, who from A.D. 101 to 107 was engaged in conquering Dacia, the district to the north of the Danube, which roughly corresponds to modern Roumania. In A.D. 114 the Roman Emperor had consolidated his military power, which had been increased by the training his legions had received in war, and he was ready to undertake an expedition to the East which is among the most famous in history.

Osroes, who reigned from 106 to 129, despatched an embassy with rich gifts, which met Trajan in Athens. The Parthian envoys stated that, to meet the wishes of the Roman Emperor, Exedares had been deposed, and that their master was ready to appoint Parthamasiris to the vacant throne of Armenia, with the Emperor's approval, and on the condition that the diadem should be bestowed by him. Had Trajan been desirous merely to restore the former position of affairs, these proposals would have been acceptable ; but, as he was burning to imitate the career of Alexander the Great, he declined the gifts and replied that on reaching Syria he would do what was right. This portended war.

Trajan proceeded to Antioch, where military preparations were pushed on with the utmost vigour, and where the tributary kings or their envoys were received. Parthamasiris wrote a letter, in which he assumed the title of King ; but, receiving no reply, he again addressed the Roman Emperor, on this occasion without arrogating any title. To this second communication a reply was vouchsafed, and Parthamasiris was given to understand that, if he presented himself before Trajan, he would, like his father, receive the diadem at the hands of the Roman Emperor. In the spring of A.D. 115 Trajan marched to the Euphrates, followed it up into Armenia, and there awaited Parthamasiris. The young prince appeared with a small retinue, and in accordance with the agreement took his diadem from his brow and laid it at Trajan's feet, expecting it to be returned to him immediately. But the Emperor not only deprived the Parthian prince of his throne, but after his departure even stooped so low as to have him pursued and murdered. It is satisfactory to know that public opinion in Rome condemned this gross act of treachery.

The Conquest of Mesopotamia and of Babylon, A.D. 115–116. —Trajan, having got rid of the Armenian king, decided to settle matters, permanently as he hoped, by converting Greater and Lesser Armenia into a Roman province. He also received envoys from the surrounding tribes, on whom he impressed the might and majesty of Rome. From Armenia he marched to Nisibis, where he received the submission of Abgarus, and, meeting with success wherever he turned his arms, he organized Mesopotamia into yet another Roman province. The winter was spent at Antioch, which during the period of his residence was destroyed by an appalling earthquake, accompanied by terrible loss of life. In the spring of A.D. 116 he returned to Mesopotamia, where ships had been constructed in sections, and were afterwards put together on the Tigris. Adiabene was next invaded. As Osroes did not come to the rescue no defence was attempted, and it was occupied and made into a Roman province. Instead of marching down the Tigris, Trajan recrossed it, and, after capturing Hatra, made for the Euphrates, which he followed down to Babylon. Here again no resistance was offered, and in a short time Seleucia and Ctesiphon were successively captured. As a result, the whole region watered by the two historical rivers submitted, and so secure did Trajan feel that he travelled down the Tigris to the Persian Gulf, on whose waters the Roman standards had never yet been reflected.

The Retreat of Trajan, A.D. 116.—As might have been expected, Osroes did not intend to submit tamely, although he was too prudent to face the Roman legions. He made successful efforts to raise the country, and suddenly Trajan received reports that rebellions had broken out at every centre in his rear and that his lines of communication were threatened. Realizing that he could not hold his conquests, he attempted to retain Roman suzerainty, with which purpose he installed an Arsacid prince as King of Parthia, and then began his retreat. His first objective was Hatra, which had revolted, but he was repulsed and, to his deep chagrin, was forced to retire.

In the following year Osroes reappeared at Ctesiphon and drove out the Roman nominee; but Adiabene, Mesopotamia, and Armenia remained Roman provinces which the King of Kings dared not invade, and consequently Trajan's campaign resulted in substantial additions to the Roman Empire.

The Evacuation of Armenia and Mesopotamia by Hadrian, A.D. 117.—Fortunately for Parthia, Trajan died in A.D. 117, and Hadrian, his successor, decided that the boundaries laid down by Augustus were the best. In pursuance of this policy, he gave orders for the evacuation of the three new provinces and withdrew the Roman legions across the Euphrates. In A.D. 122 the Emperor met the King of Kings at a point on the frontier, and, as the policy of Hadrian was entirely favourable to Parthia, the most cordial relations were maintained between the two monarchs.

The Inroad of Alani, A.D. 133.—The internal history of Parthia was one of unusual tranquillity for some years after these events. The most important event was the inroad of the Alani, whom Pharasmanes, King of the Iberians, encouraged to pour through the Caucasus, of which he held the passes. One section of the horde swarmed into Cappadocia, whence they were driven out by Arrian, the great historian, who was its governor. The reigning Parthian monarch, on the other hand, resorted to the fatal policy of buying off the invaders, and thereby exposed his weakness.

The Invasion of Syria by Volagases III., A.D. 161.—In A.D. 161, when Marcus Aurelius became Emperor, Parthia was ruled by Volagases III., who had ascended the throne some fourteen years before, and who was determined once again to challenge the Roman Empire as soon as he saw a fitting opportunity. As had happened so often in the past, the first blow was struck by the invasion of Armenia ; the king, who ruled under the aegis of Rome, was expelled, and a certain Tigranes of the old royal family was set on the throne.

Aelius Severianus, legate of Cappadocia and a Gaul by birth, immediately took the field at the head of one legion ; but he was overwhelmed by numbers, and his command was annihilated by the deadly Parthian arrow. The Parthians then swarmed across the Euphrates and overran Syria once more.

The Campaigns of Avidius Cassius, A.D. 163–165.—It was not until the autumn of A.D. 162 that the armies of Rome were ready to take the field. Avidius Cassius, who commanded in Syria, first stood on the defensive, but before long he was able to assume the offensive, and in A.D. 163 he defeated the Parthians in a great battle near Europus and drove them in headlong flight across the Euphrates. In Armenia, where the country favoured the Romans, Statius Priscus met with no opposition and captured Artaxata, which he apparently destroyed. Sohaemus, the fugitive king, was recalled from Rome to occupy the throne once more, and the former position of affairs was restored. Not content with this, Cassius, who was ambitious to rival Trajan, invaded the Parthian Empire and marched to Babylon, gaining another victory on the way.

He captured and plundered Seleucia, the stronghold of Eastern Hellenism, and Ctesiphon. He even ascended the historical route into Media, and thereby surpassed the achievements of Trajan. A terrible pestilence was brought back by the victorious army and swept across the entire empire; but Western Mesopotamia, with Nisibis as its capital, was regained, and the campaign had proved conclusively to the world that Parthia was now no match for Imperial Rome.

The Eastern Campaigns of Severus, A.D. 194–197.—
The unsuccessful Volagases III. died in A.D. 191 and was succeeded by a prince known as Volagases IV. In the civil war which rent the Roman Empire after the death of Pertinax, Pescinnius Niger was saluted as *Imperator* by the legions in Syria. Volagases in the first instance appears to have offered his congratulations and a force of Parthian troops to Niger, and his Vassal-kings followed his example. But when news came that Severus had been acknowledged as Emperor in Rome, Volagases prudently played a waiting game. At the same time, with typical Oriental inconsistency, he apparently permitted the Vassal-king of Hatra to despatch a body of his famous archers to the help of the Syrian claimant. In A.D. 194 the province of Western Mesopotamia, taking advantage of the civil war, revolted, and the outlying Roman detachments were massacred. Nisibis, however, was too strong to be captured.

Severus, the most capable claimant for supreme power, defeated Niger and promptly crossed the Euphrates and relieved Nisibis. He then proceeded to re-establish Roman supremacy, and even despatched troops across the Tigris and subjugated Adiabene. Volagases made no attempt to aid his Vassal-king; but after the departure of Severus in A.D. 196 he appeared on the scene and drove the Roman garrisons out of Adiabene. In Mesopotamia, Nisibis alone held out.

Severus had meanwhile defeated Albinus, another rival for the imperial dignity, in a great battle fought near modern Lyons, and in A.D. 197 he was back in Syria ready to try conclusions with the Parthians. Armenia submitted and was granted terms, and Abgarus, King of Edessa in Osrhoene, not only joined the Roman camp but gave hostages for his fidelity.

Severus, like Trajan before him, constructed a fleet to carry his supplies, and, marching down the Euphrates, crossed to the Tigris, by dredging out an old canal, and, surprising the Parthians, captured Seleucia. Volagases fought an action in defence of Ctesiphon but was defeated, and for the second time within a few years a Roman army sacked the Parthian capital. Once more, also, the difficulty as to supplies induced the conqueror to retreat. Like Trajan, too, he failed before the strong walls and heroic garrison of Hatra, although it appears that, had he assaulted when the first breach was made, the city would have been captured. From the point of view of the Emperor an assault would have meant the loss of the riches of the Temple of the Sun, which by custom would have been the soldiers' booty, and consequently Severus stayed his hand, hoping that the city would surrender. Instead, the breach was repaired, and Hatra gained the unique distinction of foiling two Roman emperors. The later course of this campaign gave another indication of the decline of Parthia, no attempt being made to harass the Roman army during its retreat, or even during the siege of Hatra. Its material results were important; for Rome annexed Adiabene, and from this period onward it was permanently incorporated in the Roman Empire. Parthia made no subsequent attempt to wrest back her lost vassal-states, and was evidently nearing her end.

Artabanus and Volagases, the last Kings of Parthia, A.D. 209-226.—Upon the death of Volagases IV. in A.D. 208-9, two of his sons, Artabanus and·Volagases, fought for the inheritance, and so evenly matched were their forces that after the initial success of Volagases they practically divided the empire, Artabanus ruling in the West and his brother in Babylonia. Of the course of this civil war we know very little, but it is on record that Caracalla, who succeeded his father Severus in A.D. 211, was able to congratulate the Senate in the following year on the fact that hostile Parthia was still rent by internal troubles.

The Treachery of Caracalla, A.D. 216.—In A.D. 215 Caracalla, who had at first acknowledged Volagases, opened up negotiations with Artabanus. He sent ambassadors provided with gifts of great value and demanded the hand of a Parthian princess in marriage, pointing out that by this alliance Rome and Parthia, the two empires which governed the known world, would be irresistibly strong, to the benefit of both powers.

Artabanus was aware that Caracalla had entrapped the King of Edessa by treachery and had acted in a similar manner towards the King of Armenia. Consequently he was afraid that treachery was intended and gave a politely vague and evasive reply, of the kind in which Orientals have ever been adepts. A second embassy, however, persuaded him of the sincerity of the Emperor; and he wrote to invite Caracalla to fetch his bride. With detestable treachery the Roman Emperor attacked his hosts, who were taken at a disadvantage; Artabanus barely escaped; his army was massacred, and his territories were plundered. But Caracalla did not enjoy his success for long, as in A.D. 217 he was murdered near Carrhae.

The last Battle between Rome and Parthia, A.D. 217.—Artabanus after his escape had collected an army to avenge the treachery of which he had been the victim. Upon reaching the frontier he heard of the death of Caracalla and was met by the envoys of his successor, Macrinus. Artabanus insisted on the restoration of Mesopotamia and an indemnity, and these terms being out of the question the two armies met near Nisibis. The battle was fought on the old lines; the Romans suffered from the deadly arrow and also from the charges of the mail-clad lancers, who were in this case mounted on camels. They retreated, but saved themselves by strewing the ground with caltrops. On the second day, too, there was no decisive advantage on either side; but on the third day the Romans were defeated and fled back into their camp. Both sides were now weary of the contest and the heavy losses, and peace was concluded by the payment of about £1,750,000 to the victors. Thus, although this sum of money was ostensibly a gift, and although some of the outlying Parthian provinces were not given up, the long roll of campaigns between the two powers closed with a signal victory for Parthia.

The Downfall of Parthia, A.D. 226.—Artabanus was now at the zenith of his power, and there was little to indicate that the downfall of his dynasty was at hand. But about A.D. 220 Artaxerxes, known to his countrymen as Ardeshir, the Vassal-king of Persia, rebelled; and after a series of campaigns, in which three great battles were fought, Artabanus, or Ardawan as he is termed by the Persian historians, was utterly defeated and slain on the plain of Hormuz, a few miles east of Ahwaz. Although he was succeeded by an Artavasdes, whose coins are extant and who was perhaps his son, the fate of the Parthian dynasty was sealed on the historical battlefield of Hormuz.

The Intercourse of China with Persia, A.D. 25–220.—In Chapter XXIX. reference was made to the earliest intercourse between China and Persia. It is of interest to know that, after an interval of about a century, Chinese embassies were once again despatched to the West ; and from the reports given in the later Han history we learn that Rome, or, more correctly, the eastern part of the Roman Empire, now came within the ken of China. In 97 A.D. the celebrated Chinese general, Pan Chao,[1] despatched his lieutenant, Kan Ying, to Parthia and Rome. This worthy travelled to Babylonia by way of Hecatompylus and Hamadan. Moreover, he contemplated a voyage down the Persian Gulf into the Indian Ocean, and apparently up the Red Sea to Aelana at the head of the Gulf of Akaba, to Petra and Syria. But as he was assured that the ocean might take two years to cross, he prudently decided not to undertake the enterprise. It is clear that the captains to whom Kan Ying applied were unwilling that a Chinaman should learn the secrets of the profitable trade which was being carried on.

The information brought back by a later embassy was that " they (of Ta-tsin or Rome) trade with An-Sih (Parthia) and Tien-Chu (India) in the middle of the Sea, making tenfold profits. . . . The (Ta-tsin) King always wanted to open up missions with Han, but An-Sih wished to do trade with them in Han silk goods, so that he was obstructed and could not get at us until the ninth year of the Emperor Hwan's period (A.D. 166), when An-tun (Antoninus),[2] King of Ta-tsin, sent an envoy *via* the parts beyond Jihnan (*i.e.* via Indo-China) with offerings of ivory, rhinoceros-horn, and tortoise-shell." This so-called embassy, bearing products of the " Straits," was, as Parker points out, obviously but the arrival of some adventurous Roman

---

[1] When at Kashgar in 1915, I found that Pan Chao's memory was kept green. It was stated that on one occasion the city was besieged and the garrison cut off from the river. Imitating the action of Moses, Pan Chao struck the ground, and springs, still known as " the fountains of Pan Chao," gushed forth.

[2] Marcus Aurelius Antoninus was Emperor at this period, and An-tun is, as Parker states invitingly similar in sound.

merchants with gifts, and no mission from Imperial Rome. Even so, however, these few details are of extreme interest, if only as showing how the central position of the Parthian Empire caused it to be affected not only by the West, of which so much mention is made in history, but also, albeit to a lesser degree, by the Extreme East. It is to be noted that this official intercourse was invariably peaceful, and was, in every case, initiated by China.

The Cult of Mithras in Europe.—The influence of Iran on the West appears most strongly in the cult of Mithras, or Mithra, which consequently calls for special notice. Mithras [1] was one of the most ancient of the Aryan deities, and in the Vedic hymns was invoked with Ahura Mazda. In the Avesta he occupied an intermediate position between Ahura Mazda and Ahriman as the greatest of the Yazatas, beings created by the Supreme God to aid in the destruction of evil and the government of the world. He was the god of Light, and, as light is heat, he was also the god of increase, of fertility, and of prosperity. By a further development, more especially in the reign of Artaxerxes Mnemon, he became the protector of monarchs, the Lord of Hosts, and the god of Victory. The seventh month and the sixteenth day of every month were sacred to Mithras, whose name appears in Mithradates and other royal names.

As the Persian Empire spread, centres of the cult were established in Babylon and elsewhere. In Babylon the god was identified with Shamash, the god of the Sun, and the cult of Mithras was affected in other ways. After the break-up of the empire of Alexander the Great, the dynasties established in Pontus, Cappadocia, Armenia, and Commagene claimed descent from the Achaemenian Kings, and, in pursuance of these claims, worshipped the gods of Iran.

For a long while the cult was unknown outside Asia. It was never attractive to the Hellenic mind, and this was the cause of its slow progress; yet it was Greek sculptors who executed the famous bas-reliefs of Mithras, whom they identified with Helios (the Sun).

It appears that Mithraism was introduced into Rome by the Cilician pirates captured by Pompey,[2] and, like Chris-

---

[1] I have consulted Cumont's great work, *Les Mystères de Mithra*, and also the article on Mithras in the *Ency. Brit.* Mithras is also referred to in Chapters VIII., IX., and XXXII.
[2] *Vide* Chapter XXIX.

tianity, it was at first confined to the lower classes. Towards the end of the first century of the Christian era it had made considerable way in Rome and began to spread rapidly, more especially among soldiers, merchants, and slaves. From the end of the second century the emperors encouraged the cult, because it supported the theory of the divine right of monarchs; Diocletian, Galerius, and Licinius proclaimed the god the patron of the Roman Empire. At this period it made such progress that *Mithraea*, or "temples of Mithraism," have been found all over Germany, and as far away as York and Chester. But the rise of Christianity was destined to crush the Iranian religion. Constantine dealt it a staggering blow, and, although it revived under Julian, the victory of Theodosius the Great in 394 brought it virtually to an end in Europe.

And what were the legends relating to this powerful god? Mithras was miraculously born out of a rock and immediately undertook to subdue all created beings. His most famous exploit was an encounter with the sacred bull of Ormuzd, which he finally overcame and sacrificed; from the dying animal sprang the life of the earth. In the sculptures Mithras is represented as slaying the bull; a dog is leaping to drag it down, and a serpent, a symbol of the earth, is being made fertile by drinking the blood of the victim.

To turn to the mysteries of the religion, there were seven degrees corresponding to the seven planets, the probation being not merely long but terrifying; an oath or *sacramentum* was administered to all initiates, and women were excluded absolutely. Special ceremonies included a sacred communion of bread, water, and possibly wine.

The religion of Mithras appealed to mankind through its mystic ceremonies, but still more through the expectation of a better life beyond the grave. As in the parent doctrine of Zoroaster, truth, courage, and purity were needed for the everlasting struggle against the powers of evil. Mithras was the champion of Good and the faithful were assured of final victory. Towards the close of the third century of our era, Mithraism, a purely Iranian religion, and Christianity, a religion of Jewish origin, but not without Iranian elements derived probably through Judaism, stood face to face. But, owing largely to its exclusion of women, its toleration of polytheism in a monotheistic system, and a certain barbarous note, Mithraism rapidly fell before the attacks of Christianity, after a struggle which was the more desperate because of the many doctrines which the two religions possessed in common. One memorial of Mithraism still remains with us in Christmas Day, which was originally the birthday of Mithras.

Summary.—The Parthian dynasty cannot claim to be great in the sense that it bestowed on the world any of the priceless boons that we now enjoy. On the contrary, no dynasty in historical times has bequeathed less to posterity. But it was remarkable for its virility. For close on five centuries it was ruled by a race of monarchs, few of whom were effeminate or under the influence of eunuchs, "that pernicious vermin of the East," as Gibbon has it. This fact makes the Parthian "King of Kings" compare favourably with the later Achaemenian "Great Kings" and with many of the Roman Emperors. The lack of organization and of education, which was so striking a defect of the Parthians, prevented stability, and it has been pointed out that they resembled closely the Ottoman Turks, whose valour is unquestioned, but who are deficient in the arts of peace.

Ardeshir I.
(Artaxerxes.)

CHAPTER XXXV

THE RISE OF THE SASANIAN DYNASTY

> Then quoth king Ardawan to his adviser,
> " What was this mountain-sheep which ran behind them ? "
> Answered the other, " That Royal Splendour,
> Which, by his lucky star, leads him to lordship."
> <p style="text-align:right">Firdausi's <i>Shahnama</i> (ed. Macan).</p>

The Origin of the Sasanian Dynasty.—The Sasanian dynasty, under which the inherited glories of the Achaemenians were revived, marked a new and splendid epoch in Persian history. It is held illustrious by all Persians, not only because of its intrinsic greatness, but owing to the fact that under it Iran recovered its independence, instead of constituting one of many provinces ruled by a Parthian King of Kings. From the point of view of the European historian it is important, as for the first time Persian chronicles become historical in place of legendary, although, as may be supposed, the origin of the dynasty is wreathed in the mists of the past.

The death of Rustam mentioned in Chapter XII. brought us practically to the end of the heroic age of Persia, Isfandiar, whom he slew in his last great fight, having left a son Bahman, identified with the Artaxerxes Longimanus of history. This late Achaemenian monarch is thus the first historical Great King in history so far as Persian historians record it, and the Sasanian dynasty claimed descent from this illustrious stock. Following the legend as embodied in Firdausi's famous epic, we learn that Bahman married his sister Humai, who bore him Dara, a posthumous son. His brother Sasan, disappointed of the succession by the birth of an heir, retired to the mountains of Kurdistan and became a shepherd. It is from him that the Sasanian dynasty sprang.

As mentioned in Chapter XXVII., the Parthians, known as the Ashkanian dynasty and generally referred to by Persians as the *Muluk-u-Tawaif*, or " Kings of the Tribes," are almost ignored in the National Epic, which devotes but a few stanzas to the many centuries of their overlordship. On the other hand, the Alexander romance referred to in Chapter XX. made so great an impression on the East that it is not surprising to find it woven into Persia's epic, Dara being represented as marrying the daughter of Philip of Macedon, and Alexander himself as being the offspring of the marriage.

These legends embody a vague recollection of a late Achaemenian king, from whose brother the Sasanian dynasty claimed descent. It is to be recollected that the Parthians equally claimed an Achaemenian descent, although Persian writers would never acknowledge the claim in the case of hated *Muluk-u-Tawaif*. The romance of Alexander is brought in from an entirely foreign source, and by an " ecclesiastical and political secret," as Masudi terms it, the period of five hundred and forty-nine years which elapsed between the death of Alexander in 323 B.C. and the rise of the Sasanian dynasty is reduced to two hundred and sixty-six years by the Persian historian. From these facts we can understand without much difficulty how very inaccurate is the knowledge of history among Persians, and also how much that is unsurpassed in historical splendour has thereby been lost to the inheritors of the glories of Cyrus and Darius.[1]

The Coming of Ardeshir. — The birth of all ancient dynasties, more especially in the East, has ever been attended by wonder-tales, and the coming of Ardeshir or Artaxerxes is no exception. It is surrounded by charming legends. So

---

[1] Two Arab historians, Tabari and Masudi, treat of the Sasanian period. Abu Jafar Mohamed Tabari, who flourished from the middle of the ninth to early in the tenth century of our era, in his great work, generally known as *The Annals* but more correctly termed *The History of the Prophets and Kings*, dealt with the history of mankind from the creation down to A.D. 915. It has been translated from the Persian edition and published in French by Professor Zotenberg. Abul Hasan Ali Masudi, who lived somewhat later, completed his famous history, *The Meadows of Gold and Mines of Precious Stones*, in A.D. 947. This has been translated into French by Barbier de Meynard. Both works possess considerable value. The great poem of Firdausi also begins to be historical in the Sasanian period. The chief European works are *The Seventh Great Oriental Monarchy*, by G. Rawlinson ; *Geschichte der Perser und Araber zur Zeit der Sasaniden*, by Professor Th. Nöldeke ; and the translation of Ammianus Marcellinus, by Yonge. In the last-named work the first thirteen chapters are unfortunately missing. Much information has been obtained from coins, especially from Dorn's *Collection des monnaies sassanides*.

far as can be ascertained, Ardeshir, son of Papak, like his mighty predecessor Cyrus, was a Vassal-king who, finding or making the opportunity, killed his brothers and overthrew the Parthian King of Kings. But the Pahlavi writers were not content with so simple a story. According to the *Karnamak*, referred to in Chapter XLI., and Firdausi, Iran was divided up into two hundred and forty states under kings, of whom Ardawan (the classical Artabanus) was the chief. A certain Papak, who was King of Fars and dwelt at Istakhr, had no son. One night he dreamed concerning Sasan, who was his shepherd, that the sun from his head illuminated the entire world. On the following night he dreamed that he saw Sasan riding on a white elephant and receiving homage and blessings ; and on the third night he saw how the Sacred Fire waxed great in the house of Sasan and illuminated the world. Amazed at these dreams, Papak summoned the wise men, who unanimously declared that the kingship would be attained by Sasan or his son. Papak, upon hearing this interpretation, sent for Sasan, who told him of his illustrious descent. He was thereupon clothed with a royal robe and was married to Papak's daughter, who bore him Ardeshir. Another delightful legend is that when Ardeshir reached man's estate he fled from Ardawan's capital at Rei to Pars or Fars, taking with him a wise and beautiful damsel who had hitherto been Ardawan's adviser, but who deserted him from love of Ardeshir. The enraged monarch pursued the fugitives, and upon inquiring at a certain village whether they had passed through, he was informed that they were riding like the wind and that a large ram was running behind them. On the second day Ardawan was informed by the members of a caravan which he met that the ram had been seen seated beside one of the horsemen, and realizing that it was the Royal Splendour he gave up all pursuit :

> And with cheeks sallow like the scorched reed-bed,
> Did he to Rei return in the dark twilight.

Though all this is legend, it is of value as showing how the Divine Right was claimed by the Sasanians. Indeed so fully was it acknowledged by their obedient subjects, that no usurper in whose veins the sacred blood did not flow could ever be successful.

Ardeshir and Ardawan.—There is no full account of the

struggle of the Vassal-king against his suzerain. But it would be reasonable to accept the Persian story, that Ardeshir was allowed to annex the conterminous province of Kerman before Ardawan took the field. It may be noted, in passing, that the chief fort of Kerman is termed "The Fort of Ardeshir," and the famous legend of the worm is connected with the same province. Ardawan, being at length roused, invaded Fars and attacked his rebel vassal, who defeated him in a hotly contested battle, the losses being heavy on both sides. In a second battle Ardeshir gained the day with greater ease, while the losses suffered by the Parthians were most severe.

The Battle of Hormuz, A.D. 226.—The final battle was fought on the plain of Hormuz to the east of Ahwaz. In this desperate encounter the Parthian army was completely defeated and Ardawan was slain. According to one account, the Persian hero engaged the Parthian monarch in single combat, pretended to flee, and then turning in the saddle shot him through the heart. This decisive battle, the date of which is generally fixed as A.D. 226 or 227, laid the foundation of an illustrious dynasty, which ruled over a proud and contented people for four centuries, until the star of Mohamed arose in the desert of Arabia and overthrew the world.

The Eastern Campaigns of Ardeshir.—We learn from Tabari that, after conquering the countries bordering on Khorasan, Merv, Balkh and Khiva, Ardeshir received messengers from the kings of Kushan, Turan, and Makran. It was not generally realized that the Sasanian monarch had embarked on an invasion of India, but Vincent Smith [1] shows that this was actually the case. Ferishta definitely states that Ardeshir marched against India and reached the neighbourhood of Sirhind, but that Junah, the reigning monarch, gave pearls, gold, jewels, and elephants as tribute and so induced Ardeshir to return to Persia. In confirmation of this statement, a brass coin has recently been found, on which the obverse is of the later Kushan type, while the reverse exhibits a fire-altar similar to that on the coins of Ardeshir. It is thus evident that the founder of the Sasanian dynasty did more than merely occupy the various provinces of Persia, for, following in the footsteps of his mighty Achaemenian predecessors, he levied tribute on the Panjab.

[1] "Invasion of the Punjab by Ardeshir Papakan," *J.R.A.S.* for April 1920.

RISE OF THE SASANIAN DYNASTY

Ardeshir and Severus Alexander, A.D. 229–232.—Ardeshir was soon firmly established, and believing himself to be in a position to throw down the gauntlet to the Roman Empire, he decided, about A.D. 228, to cross the Euphrates. From his point of view he was the victor over Ardawan, who had forced a great Roman army to purchase an ignominious peace. He might therefore reasonably hope for success against the recently defeated legions. Moreover, ir all probability he was not only urged by his natural ambition and love of glory, but forced by circumstances also, to declare himself the inheritor of the kingdom of the Achaemenians.

Severus Alexander, who sat in the seat of the Caesars at this juncture, was a singularly well-intentioned and well-meaning youth. Hearing of the Persian invasion, and perhaps realizing that it was important to gain time pending the organization of a Roman expedition, he despatched a letter to Ardeshir exhorting him to keep to his own territories and " not to attempt to revolutionize Asia." The letter added that it was unsafe, merely on the strength of vague hopes, to begin a great war ; that Ardeshir would find a contest with Rome very different from conflicts with barbarous tribes like his own, and that he should remember the victories of Augustus, of Trajan, and of Septimius Severus.

To this monition Ardeshir replied by despatching a mission consisting of 400 Persians specially selected for their fine physique, and magnificently equipped with golden trappings and weapons. They delivered an arrogant and provocative message summoning the Romans to evacuate Syria and the rest of Asia, to permit the Persians to regain their ancient inheritance, and to content themselves with the undisturbed possession of Europe. So insolent did this demand appear that the ambassadors, in spite of their privileged and indeed almost sacred position, were seized and treated as prisoners of war. Meanwhile preparations for the coming campaign were pushed on without delay, and in the autumn of A.D. 231 a formidable force had assembled at Antioch.

The Roman plan was to divide their forces into three armies. The northern army was sent to invade Media Atropatene in alliance with Chosroes of Armenia ; the southern army was ordered to threaten Persia Proper or more probably Susiana ; and the third, commanded by the Emperor in person, was destined to operate against the heart of the country. The bad strategy of employing three detached forces which could not possibly support one another effectively met with the failure it invited. The northern army was successful in its raid into Media Atropatene, where it was probably unopposed owing to the absence of the Median troops. But on the return march its losses were severe, and nothing of importance was accomplished. Ardeshir, wisely concentrating his troops, attacked and annihilated the isolated southern force. Severus, alarmed by this disaster, ordered a general retreat.[1] It might have been thought that after this victory Ardeshir would have invaded Syria. But as in reality the campaign had been undertaken by the Persians for the possession of Armenia, destined under the Sasanian as under the Parthian dynasty to be *the* bone of contention between the two empires, Ardeshir prudently contented himself with his victory, and apparently peace was concluded in A.D. 232.

The Conquest of Armenia by Ardeshir.—By the withdrawal of Rome Armenia was left to its own resources to meet the Persian army. The mountain state rose to the occasion, and, aided by the fact that the Persian army was almost entirely composed of cavalry, Chosroes defended himself so well that Ardeshir, despairing of success in the field, offered the second place in the kingdom to whoever should make away with his enemy. A Persian noble in whose veins ran the Arsacid blood agreed to assassinate Chosroes, and gained his confidence by representing himself as a refugee fleeing from the vengeance of Ardeshir, who, to support the fiction, sent a force to pursue him. The murder was accomplished, and, as the assassin was drowned in the Araxes while fleeing from Artaxata, Ardeshir achieved his object without paying the price for it. He speedily overran and annexed Armenia, but failed to seize the infant son of Chosroes, who was safely conveyed out of the country. This successful campaign ended the military career of the founder of the Sasanian dynasty.

Ardeshir, the Reviver of the Good Religion.—It has been shown in Chapter XXXII. that the Parthians who adopted the tenets of Zoroastrianism had partially forsaken it and had gradually ceased to carry out its precepts ; indeed, their religion had rather become a worship of the Sun, of the Moon, and of ancestral images, in combination with many old Semitic

[1] Nöldeke, who declines to rely on Herodian, states that when Severus marched against Ardeshir the latter gave way.

incantations and invocations. In consequence, the fire-altars had fallen into ruins, and in many cases the sacred flame had been extinguished; nor were the Magi any longer a power in the land.

Ardeshir began by restoring to the Magi their privileges, and it was laid down that the monarch was closely connected with the teachers of the Good Religion, who formed the council of the nation. He also not only gave them broad lands but instituted tithes for their benefit. As a result images were destroyed, the worship of the Sun and Moon was swept away, and the whole nation rallied to the ancient faith of Zoroaster.

To ensure a united people, an Assembly of the Magi was convoked and seven of the holiest priests were selected, who in turn chose Arda-Viraf, a young *Mobed* of noted sanctity, as their representative. According to the Persian narrative, the chosen priest, after undergoing elaborate ablutions, was given an opiate, under the influence of which he slept for seven days, watched by the King and seven great nobles. Upon awaking he dictated the entire faith of Ormuzd to a scribe, and this was accepted as wholly authoritative by the priests and people.

As may be supposed, the zeal of Ardeshir and of the *Mobeds* would not tolerate other forms of religion, and this led to religious persecutions, directed especially against the Christian Church which the dynasty found in existence, and which, after the Eastern Empire had become Christian, was regarded with marked disfavour in Persia.

His Achievements and Character.—Of the administration of Ardeshir few details have reached us, but it appears that he used every effort to abolish the Vassal-kings whose semi-independence was so dangerous to the power of the Great King. He aimed at creating a nation supported by the priesthood and strongly centralized. His system was that of Darius rather than that of the Parthians, inasmuch as he maintained a standing army and kept it under the command of officers who were independent of the Satraps. One of his sayings ran : " There can be no power without an army, no army without money, no money without agriculture, and no agriculture without justice." Would that his successors on the throne had always observed this maxim ! As a monarch Ardeshir stands out as a sane, wide-minded ruler, who was ever anxious that his subjects should be happy, who realized that the basis of good administration was justice, and who worked incessantly to carry out his principles.

Firdausi gives what may be described as the political testament of the dying monarch, addressed to his son Shapur. In it Ardeshir says, " Consider the altar and the throne as inseparable ; they must always sustain one another. A sovereign without religion is a tyrant." Again, " May your administration be such as to bring the blessings of those whom God has confided to our parental care upon both your memory and mine ! "

Such was the splendid impression and tradition left by Ardeshir, the founder of the Sasanian dynasty, and, even if the mists have to some extent gathered round his heroic figure, it is yet permissible to believe with confidence that Ardeshir, son of Papak, was worthy of a high position in the Temple of Fame.

PAHLAVI INSCRIPTION AT NAKSH-I-RAJAB.

CHAPTER XXXVI

SHAPUR I., THE CAPTOR OF VALERIAN

This is the image of the Ormuzd-worshipper, the God, Shapur, King of Kings Aryan and non-Aryan, of the race of the Gods, son of the Ormuzd-worshipper, the God Ardeshir, King of Kings Aryan, of the race of the Gods, the offspring of the God Papak, the King.

The Succession of Shapur I., A.D. 240.—Shapur[1] or Sapor I., as the western writers term him, succeeded to his great father in A.D. 240 or 241. According to Persian belief his mother was the daughter of Ardawan, who after her marriage to Ardeshir attempted to poison her husband in revenge for her father's death. The plot, however, failed and the guilty woman was ordered away to execution. As she was pregnant, her life was spared by the Vizier, who kept her and the son that was born hidden away. One day Ardeshir complained of being without an heir, and was overjoyed to hear of the existence of a son. To test his breeding, the lad was summoned with a number of his companions to play polo in the presence of the monarch, whose prowess at this ancient game was famous. A ball was intentionally thrown near the Great King, which Shapur alone dared to follow up, and he was promptly recognized by his delighted father. Seeing that Ardeshir reigned only for about fourteen years after the death of Ardawan, this account can hardly be accepted, as it makes Shapur only thirteen at the time of his succession. On the other hand, it would be a mistake to ignore a legend which shows how spirited and manly were the ideals of the founder of the great dynasty.

The Revolt of Armenia and of Hatra, A.D. 240.—Upon hearing of the death of Ardeshir, both Armenia and Hatra revolted. The rebellion in Armenia was easily crushed. In

---

[1] The name means "Son of a Shah."

the case of Hatra, Shapur, aware that its wall had successfully defied both Trajan and Severus, did not attempt a regular siege but resorted to intrigue. It happened that the rebel King had a daughter who was ready to betray the fortress in return for a promise of marriage made by the Great King. Hatra was duly captured by this act of treachery, but Shapur broke his pledge and handed over the traitress to the executioner.

The First Campaign against Rome, A.D. 241–244.—After asserting his position within the boundaries of his empire with success, Shapur determined to take advantage of the internal troubles of Rome, whose decline, it is to be remembered, had fully set in. Severus Alexander, the adversary of Ardeshir, had been assassinated, and the gigantic Thracian Maximin had for three years ruled as Emperor from his camp with such ferocity that the whole empire loathed him. He in his turn had been assassinated, and an orgy of anarchy had prevailed. When Shapur undertook his expedition, the Roman Emperor was the youth known as the third Gordian.

The first objective of the Persians was the strong fortress of Nisibis, which they captured. According to the Persian account, its walls fell down, like those of Jericho as described in the book of Joshua. This legend may perhaps relate to the calamity of an earthquake. After this striking success, Shapur carried all before him to the Mediterranean Sea, even Antioch falling into his hands. But, as with Parthian invasions, there was no permanent occupation or administration; it was a raid on a large scale.

After a while, a Roman army appeared on the scene, under the nominal command of the young Emperor, and Shapur's forces were defeated and recrossed the Euphrates. The Roman legions followed them up and retook Nisibis, after inflicting another severe defeat on the Persian army at Resaina,[1] between that stronghold and Carrhae. The pursuing army even crossed the Tigris and threatened Ctesiphon, but failed to follow up these successes. The murder of the young Emperor caused the withdrawal of the Roman legions, and Philip the usurper, speedily making peace with Shapur on favourable terms, quitted the East in A.D. 244.

The Second Campaign: the First Phase, A.D. 258–260.—

---

[1] *Vide* Ammianus Marcellinus, xxiii. 5. § 17, where Julian refers to this campaign in his speech to the army.

SHAPUR THE FIRST AND VALERIAN.
(Bas-relief at Nakhsh-i-Rustam.)
(From Sarre and Herzfeld's *Iranische Felsreliefs*)

SHAPUR I., CAPTOR OF VALERIAN

During the fourteen years which elapsed before Shapur again invaded the Roman Empire, the history of Persia is obscure. It appears that the distant province of Balkh, where a campaign was carried on, successfully maintained its independence, as later on its rulers opened up negotiations with Rome.

Shapur, as in his first campaign against the western Power, carried all before him at the outset, Antioch on this occasion being surprised while its citizens, totally unaware of any peril, were enjoying a play.

The Capture of Valerian, A.D. 260.—As before, a Roman army came at length to the rescue, this time under the aged Emperor Valerian, who retook Antioch and drove Shapur out of Syria. But treachery was at work; for the Praetorian prefect, Macrianus, who was the actual Commander-in-Chief, aspired to the throne, and, in pursuance of a scheme of personal ambition, he arranged for the Roman army to be involved near Edessa in such a manner that Shapur cut off all hope of escape. One desperate attempt at breaking through was repulsed with heavy loss, famine ensued, and Valerian, after trying in vain to purchase safety, was apparently seized at a conference exactly as Crassus had been, although, less fortunate than his predecessor, he survived his disgrace for some years.

Few if any events in history have produced a greater moral effect than the capture of a Roman Emperor by the monarch of a young dynasty. The impression at the time must have been overwhelming, and the news must have resounded like a thunder-clap throughout Europe [1] and Asia. It was commemorated in stone by the victor both at Persepolis and at Shapur, and as long as the Sasanian dynasty lasted it was never forgotten.

Moreover, legend has magnified the Emperor's downfall. The chroniclers who wrote nearest to the period state merely that he grew old in captivity and was treated as a slave; it may be noted that the fetters on his arms are clearly visible in the famous bas-relief. Later writers inform us that he was shown to gazing multitudes, clad in the imperial purple and in chains, and this is not improbable. More doubtful, though still possibly true, is the statement of Lactantius (writing about A.D. 312) that the hapless old man served as a mounting block to his ungenerous conqueror, and that his

---

[1] Even in Trebellius Pollio, *Gallieni Duo*, § 1, we read, " Erat ingens omnibus moeror, quod imperator Romanus in Perside serviliter teneretur."

body was flayed after his death and the skin kept as a trophy.

The Second Phase of the Campaign, A.D. 260.—The traitor Macrianus after carrying out his dastardly scheme assumed the purple, and marched off to fight for the Empire with Gallienus, Valerian's son. Shapur, who must have possessed considerable originality, still further complicated matters, and heightened the impression of his power, by investing a certain Cyriadis, a citizen of Antioch, who was a refugee in his camp, with the royal purple and the title of Caesar; his is the third figure in the bas-relief already mentioned.

After this investiture, Shapur once more crossed the Euphrates and seized Antioch. On this occasion he traversed the passes of the Taurus, and the whole of Asia Minor lay at his mercy. He captured Caesarea Mazaca, the greatest city in Cappadocia; but, probably from lack of a standing army, again made no attempt to organize and administer, or even to retain, his conquests. He merely killed and ravaged with barbarous severity. Indeed it appears that, having satisfied his lust of destruction, Shapur of his own free will turned his back on Cappadocia, which, with Syria, he might have added to his empire, and made for the Euphrates, leaving behind him valleys covered with dead bodies and driving off thousands of men, women, and children.

Shapur and Odenathus of Palmyra, A.D. 260-263.— Who has not heard of Palmyra, situated in the desert almost exactly half-way between the Euphrates and Damascus at a distance of about one hundred and thirty miles from both? Founded by Hadrian as a Roman frontier stronghold and with a view to opening up a southern route between Syria and Mesopotamia, Palmyra at this period had become a flourishing trade emporium under a semi-independent chief, Odenathus by name. Upon the invasion of Shapur, Odenathus had sent a letter, together with a caravan of camels bearing gifts to the Sasanian monarch, who, in displeasure at the independent tone of the letter, ordered the offering to be thrown into the Euphrates, and exclaimed, " Who is this Odenathus and of what country that he ventures thus to address his Lord ? Let him now, if he would lighten his punishment, come here and fall prostrate before me with his hands tied behind his back."

Shapur had bitter cause to regret his arrogance; for

Odenathus, who had watched events in safety, protected by the almost waterless desert, saw his opportunity when Shapur returned eastwards laden with spoil. Collecting a large force of wild horsemen, he cut off isolated parties of stragglers and harassed the Persian army with such success that he captured not only much of the loot taken in the campaign, but even some of the wives of the Great King. So demoralized did the Persian forces become under his attacks that, even when they had crossed the Euphrates and were out of reach of the Arab horsemen, they were glad to purchase a safe-conduct from the people of Edessa by the surrender of all the coined money they had carried off.

Odenathus was evidently a great man, and no mere glorified raider. Not content with driving the Persian army across the Euphrates, in A.D. 263 he invaded Mesopotamia, defeated Shapur in a battle, and even besieged Ctesiphon. His short career was extraordinarily brilliant. He seized Syria and other provinces which Shapur had overrun and forsaken, and he retained Mesopotamia. Moreover, he won the confidence of Gallienus, to whom he showed the utmost respect, with the result that the Senate conferred on him the title of Augustus and thereby legalized his position. Consequently, before assassination cut short his career, Palmyra had become, through his exertions, a powerful buffer state, hostile to Persia and allied to Rome.

Zenobia.—Zenobia, his beauteous widow, in whose veins coursed the blood of the Ptolemies and who ranks among the great women of all time, maintained her power over the conquered provinces and even added Egypt to the kingdom of Palmyra. For a few short years her career was dazzling, and, had she appreciated the genius of Aurelian, she might have kept her state; but she refused to bend, her power was broken, and, chained in fetters of gold, the proud Zenobia graced a Roman triumph. The semi-independent kingdom of Palmyra was swept away, and the frontiers of the Persian Empire once again marched with those of Rome.

The Public Works of Shapur.—The later years of Shapur were devoted mainly to the arts of peace. Fortunately his greatest achievement, the dam at Shuster, which I visited many years ago,[1] still defies the floods of the Karun, although

---

[1] *Ten Thousand Miles*, p. 252. Shushter was used as a second residence by the Sasanian monarchs.

it sadly needs repair. In connexion with the construction of this work the entire river was diverted to an artificial channel, which still exists under the name of Ab-i-Gargar, and the river-bed was solidly paved. The dam is composed of blocks of granite cramped together, and is fitted with sluice-gates to regulate the water-supply. The total length of the bridge resting on the dam is 570 yards. It appears that Shapur employed his Roman prisoners on these works, and it is of singular interest to note that the name *Band-i-Kaisar*, or " The Emperor's Dam," recalls the captivity of Valerian.

Near Kazerun, half-way between Bushire and Shiraz, are situated the important ruins of Shapur, which was originally termed Bishapur, or " The good (deed) of Shapur." Situated on both banks of one of the rare rivers of Persia, at the mouth of a gorge, its ruined fort (known as Dunbula) was extremely strong. No buildings in the ruins can be identified with any certainty, but for the magnificent series of bas-reliefs and the unique statue of Shapur I. to which reference will be made later it is well worth visiting.[1]

Nishapur, once the chief city of Khorasan, was also founded by Shapur I., although it was refounded by Shapur II. In 1909 I discovered two ancient and now almost obliterated sites which were locally believed to be the first and second Sasanian foundations. If correct, this identification is of considerable interest. At any rate, the site is one that deserves the attention of some archaeologist of the future.[2]

The Manichaeans.—Among the religions of the East which have profoundly influenced mankind must be reckoned that which Manes or Mani founded.[3] Some account of this remarkable man and of the tenets he taught is called for, as his religion, which to a certain extent succeeded Mithraism, was not only a power in the East for many centuries, but also spread westward into Europe.

Manes was born, Al-biruni tells us, in A.D. 215 or 216, and was lame in one leg. He proclaimed his mission at the coronation of Shapur, and for some years his influence was great at Court. Later on he fell from favour, was banished, and entered upon a series of wanderings, during the course of

---

[1] *Vide Ten Thousand Miles*, p. 317 ; also the *Lands of the Eastern Caliphate*, p. 262.

[2] *Vide Journal Royal Geographical Society* for February 1911. Nishapur also signifies " The good (deed) of Shapur."

[3] The best brief accounts of the Manichaeans are given in the *Literary History of Persia*, p. 154, and in the *Encycl. Brit.* ; Al-biruni's *Chronology of Ancient Nations* should also be consulted.

which he is believed to have visited India, Tibet, and distant China.

He returned to Persia in A.D. 272 upon the death of Shapur I., and was received by his successor, Hormisdas, with much favour and veneration. Permitted to preach his doctrines freely he taught especially the Christians of Mesopotamia, and in a very short time founded the Manichaean sect, which spread with such rapidity that it is evident that Mithraism had prepared men's minds for its reception. Unfortunately for the prophet, his patron reigned for only one year, and his successor, Bahram I., reversed his policy and ordered Manes to be seized, saying, " This man has come forward calling people to destroy the world. It will be necessary to begin by destroying him, before anything of his plans should be realized." Al-biruni then adds : " It is well known that he [*i.e.* Bahram] killed Mani, stripped off his skin, filled it with grass, and hung it up at the gate of Gundisapur, which is still known as the Mani Gate." [1]

What were the doctrines of this reformer ? Browne puts the matter in an epigram by stating that he preached Christianized Zoroastrianism. His religion might almost be described, if it were not a contradiction in terms, as asceticism grafted upon Zoroastrianism. As shown in Chapter IX. Zoroastrianism was essentially sane and materialistic ; it forbade fasting, and inculcated on its followers to "be fruitful and multiply." Manes, on the other hand, held that everything should be done to escape from the evil world, and consequently marriage and the propagation of the human race were in his opinion evil ; it was this doctrine to which Bahram evidently referred in the passage quoted above. Both creeds were dualistic ; but, to quote from Browne : " In Zoroastrianism the Good and Evil Creation, the realm of Ahura Mazda and that of Ahriman, each comprised a spiritual and material part. . . . According to the Manichaean view, on the other hand, the admixture of the light and the darkness which gave rise to the material universe was essentially evil, and a result of the activity of the powers of evil. . . . The whole universe would collapse and the final conflagration

---

[1] *Op. cit.* p. 191. Gundisapur is the city of Shapur near Kazerun. The fact that Manes was thus treated after death makes it more probable that Valerian's skin was also preserved in a similar manner.

would mark the Redemption of the Light and its final dissociation from the irredeemable and indestructible Darkness."

Zoroaster, Buddha, and Christ were recognized as divine messengers. In the case of Christ, a distinction is made between the True Christ, who according to Manichaean belief had no material body, and his antagonist, "the Son of the Widow," who was crucified. It is of peculiar interest to note that Mohamed adopted this view, as is shown in the Koran.[1]

The sect did not die with its Prophet. Far from it. With a Pope of its own, seated for many centuries at Babylon and later at Samarcand, this pessimistic creed flourished, developing a wonderful art and literature of its own. Even after the advent of Islam it maintained its position and extended over Central Asia to Tibet. In Europe, too, it spread as far as Southern France, where, in 1209, a crusade was led by Simon de Montfort against the Albigenses, who were accused of Manichaeism. St. Augustine belonged to the sect for many years before he embraced Christianity.

The Death of Shapur I., A.D. 271.—The Sasanian dynasty was fortunate, indeed, in having two great monarchs in succession to lay the foundations, and to erect the structure of the new empire. Ardeshir and Shapur compare with Cyrus and Darius, although they were hardly such splendid characters as the two founders of the Achaemenian dynasty. Shapur, like Darius, although a great and successful soldier, shone chiefly as an administrator. His great works at Shuster, his sculptures and other buildings at the city which he founded and elsewhere, prove his devotion to, and successful pursuit of, the arts of peace. According to Persian belief he was of striking beauty, as indeed the bas-reliefs suggest, of a noble character, and renowned for his generosity; and when he died in A.D. 271 he must have been lamented throughout his wide empire.

Hormisdas and Bahram I., A.D. 271–275.—In all dynasties the founder is necessarily an exceptionally able man, and the second and third generations usually remain virile. But the Sasanian dynasty, after its two brilliant founders, produced a series of relatively feeble monarchs. Shapur I. was succeeded

---

[1] Sura IV. v. 156. The passage runs: "And for their saying, 'Verily we slew the Messiah, Jesus the son of Mary, the Apostle of God'; but they did not slay Him or crucify Him, but a similitude was made for them."

by Hormisdas, who had served as Governor of Khorasan. He was followed after one year by his brother Varahran, or Bahram I., whose reign lasted from A.D. 272 to A.D. 275. Bahram was apparently a man of small capacity ; for, when Aurelian attacked Zenobia, instead of leading all the forces of the empire to her assistance, as the situation clearly demanded, he adopted a fatal policy of half measures, sending only an insignificant force, and allowing the invaluable buffer state of Palmyra to be destroyed. Realizing that he had incurred the just resentment of Rome, Bahram for the time being averted hostilities by the despatch of an embassy laden with valuable gifts ; among them figured purple cloth, so rich in texture that the Imperial purple of Rome looked common when compared with it.

In A.D. 275, the year after his triumph, Aurelian decided that the time was ripe for a Persian expedition. The forces of the Empire were set in motion, the Alani were subsidized to make an inroad into Persia from the north, and Aurelian himself reached the neighbourhood of Byzantium. There he was assassinated in consequence of the intrigues of a secretary who had forged an order dooming to death many of the leading officials. They in imaginary self-defence killed Aurelian. Persia, under the Sasanian dynasty, was fortunate in this ; for Aurelian would probably have annexed what he conquered. Bahram died the same year as Aurelian.

The Early Campaigns of Bahram II., A.D. 275-282.—Of Bahram II., who succeeded his father, we know a good deal, both from the Persian historians and from the bas-reliefs. He is stated to have ruled so tyrannically at first that a conspiracy was formed to put him to death. The chief *Mobed*, however, intervened ; the monarch confessed his faults, and, taking the lesson to heart, ruled justly during the remainder of his reign. He fought the Sakae of Sistan and secured their submission. He then penetrated farther east and was engaged in these distant campaigns, when a serious danger suddenly threatened the western provinces of the Empire.

The Campaign of Carus, A.D. 283.—The military prowess of Rome, which had been so splendidly revived by Aurelian, had not materially suffered when, eight years later, Carus decided to undertake the expedition planned by that great soldier. His army, which had been trained in war against the formidable Sarmatians, was led to the Persian frontier, where Carus, encamped on a hill, pointed out the fertility of the plains stretching away to the south-east which were to constitute the rich prize of success. The Persian monarch, whose main force was many hundreds of miles distant, attempted to negotiate. His envoys, instead of being conducted to an Emperor enthroned in state and surrounded by his great officers, were brought into the presence of an old man seated on the ground, enjoying a piece of mouldy bacon and a few hard peas. This was Carus, who could be recognized as the Emperor only by his purple robe. No time was wasted in compliments. Carus came to the point at once, and, taking off the cap which he wore to conceal his baldness, swore that, unless the Great King submitted, he would speedily make Persia as naked of trees as his own head was of hair. And he was as good as his word; for, sweeping away all opposition, he conquered Mesopotamia, and captured Ctesiphon. But his career was cut short. A violent thunderstorm broke over the camp, and the Emperor was found dead. Whether he died as the result of the act of God, of illness, or of foul play is not known. Public opinion, however, inclined to the view that he was struck by lightning, and that he was thereby proved to be the object of the wrath of Heaven. Alarmed by this baleful portent, the legionaries clamoured to retreat, and once again Persia was saved by extraordinary good fortune.

The Seizure of Armenia by Tiridates, A.D. 286.—In the long duel between the Roman and Persian empires Armenia was again and again destined to furnish a cause for war. For more than a generation it had remained a Persian possession, but during that period the Sasanian dynasty had not been in any way accepted by the proud mountaineers, owing partly, at any rate, to the intolerance shown towards the national religion. A striking instance of this spirit was exhibited in the destruction of the sacred images of the Sun and Moon which had been erected by Val-Arsaces, more than four centuries previously.[1] In A.D. 286, Diocletian, who had been elected Emperor in the previous year, decided to continue the campaign of Carus. In the first place he produced a candidate for the throne of Armenia in the person of Tiridates, son of the Chosroes who had been assassinated by

---
[1] *Vide* Chapter XXIX.

the orders of Ardeshir. This claimant for the throne of his Arsacid ancestors was a man of superb physique and undaunted bravery, which had repeatedly been displayed in the service of Rome ; and when he appeared on the frontier with a Roman army at his back the entire nation rose in his favour. The Persian garrisons were expelled, and Tiridates not only gained the Armenian throne, but was even able to raid with impunity across the Persian frontier.

The Campaigns of Narses against Rome, A.D. 296–297.—Bahram II. died in A.D. 282, and his successor, Bahram III., reigned for only four months. Then ensued a struggle between two brothers, who were apparently younger sons of Shapur I. Narses finally worsted Hormisdas, who disappears from the scene. In A.D. 296, some three years after his accession, Narses invaded Armenia and drove out Tiridates, who fled and sought the protection of Rome. Diocletian, who was at the zenith of his power and fame, took up the challenge and ordered Galerius [1] from the Danube to take over the command of the Syrian army. Narses had invaded the Roman province of Mesopotamia, and Galerius met him in the open steppe country, which favoured the light horseman. Two battles were fought with no decisive result, but in a third, near historical Carrhae, the Roman army was utterly defeated, and merely a handful of fugitives, among whom were, however, Tiridates and Galerius, swam across the Euphrates to safety.

The Defeat of Narses and the Cession of Five Provinces to Rome, A.D. 297.—In the following winter Diocletian sent Galerius to win back his reputation at the head of the Illyrian legions. Warned by his previous defeat he avoided the open plains and, marching through hilly Armenia, succeeded in surprising the Persian camp by night. Narses escaped with a wound, but, as his army was almost annihilated in a panic-stricken stampede, and his family and many leading noblemen were captured, he was compelled to sue for terms.

His ambassador, attempting to make out a good case for his master, compared Rome and Persia to the two eyes of a body " which ought mutually to adorn and illustrate each other." But Galerius lost his temper and, referring to the treatment of Valerian, dismissed the envoy with an answer to

---

[1] At this period the Roman Empire was governed by two emperors, having subordinate to them two Caesars, of whom Galerius was one.

the effect that in due course of time his master would be informed of the terms which would be fixed. Ultimately a Roman ambassador demanded (*a*) the cession of five provinces beyond the Tigris ; (*b*) that the Tigris should constitute the boundary instead of the Euphrates ; (*c*) the addition to Armenia of territory up to the fort of Zentha in Media ; (*d*) that Iberia should become a Roman protectorate ; and (*e*) that Nisibis should be the only emporium at which commercial transactions between the two peoples could take place. This last clause was waived at the request of Narses, and we are therefore concerned only with the other articles.

There is some doubt as to what districts were ceded to Rome, but the Tigris became the boundary below the section where Rome held both banks, and this of itself shows the importance of the acquisitions made by the Western Power. The cession to Armenia of territory up to the fortress of Zentha is obscure, as this site has not been identified. The fourth article meant that Iberia, whose king held the passes across the great Caucasus range, passed under Roman influence.

The contest with Rome which Narses himself had provoked had ended in disaster ; for Rome now came into permanent occupation of districts valuable in themselves and of still greater importance because their possession by a hostile power threatened alike Ctesiphon to the South and Media to the East. Armenia, too, passed entirely outside the orbit of Persia. The unsuccessful monarch abdicated in A.D. 301, after witnessing a greater advance of the Roman Empire than any of his predecessors, either of the Parthian or the Sasanian dynasty.

SHAPUR THE GREAT.

CHAPTER XXXVII

SHAPUR THE GREAT

At daybreak everything, as far as we could see, glittered with shining arms ; and cavalry in armour filled the plains and the hills. And Shapur himself, mounted on his charger, and being taller than the rest, led his whole army wearing, instead of a crown, a golden figure of a ram's head inlaid with jewels ; being also splendid from the retinue of men of high rank and of different nations which followed him.—
AMMIANUS MARCELLINUS xix. 1.

The Birth of Shapur II., A.D. 309.—The father of Shapur the Great was Hormisdas II., who reigned from A.D. 301 to 309, and was noted for his activity in building and also for setting up a court of justice at which the poor were encouraged to make complaint if oppressed by the rich. Upon his death, Hormisdas, his natural heir, was set aside by the nobles, who disliked his inclination towards Hellenic culture, and a posthumous son, the famous Shapur II., was elected to occupy the throne even before he was born, the coronation ceremony being performed immediately after the *Mobed's* declaration that the embryo was of the male sex ! This monarch reigned for the extraordinarily long period of seventy years and was consequently a contemporary of ten Roman Emperors, beginning with Galerius and ending with Valentinian II.

His Minority and Early Campaigns, A.D. 309–337.— This long reign may conveniently be divided into periods, the first of which covers the twenty-eight years preceding the wars with Rome. During the long minority, which continued until the young monarch had attained his sixteenth year, the Persian Empire stood upon the defensive, with the result that it was raided by its neighbours, more especially by the Arabs inhabiting Bahrein, which, at that period, included El-Hasa, El-Katif, and adjacent districts. From

Mesopotamia, too, a sudden raid was made and Ctesiphon was captured. However, when the young monarch grasped the reins of state, an active policy was adopted, and almost for the first time since the expedition of Sennacherib we read of a naval expedition in the Persian Gulf, commanded on this occasion by the King himself. His arms were completely successful, and in revenge for the frequent raids he ordered that his Arab captives should have their shoulders pierced and then be tied together with ropes. This brutal treatment earned him the title of *Zulaktaf*, or " Lord of the Shoulders," by which he is known in oriental history.

The First War with Rome, A.D. 337-350.—The relations between Persia and the Roman Empire had not been altogether satisfactory for several years. In 323 A.D. Hormisdas had escaped from prison, and had taken refuge with Constantine, who had received him with every honour. Moreover, since under this Emperor Christianity had become the official religion of the Roman Empire, and he had assumed the rôle of protector of Christians in Persia,[1] Shapur may have felt that unless he went to war soon he might be faced with internal troubles. His successes in war and his youth inclined him to an adventurous policy ; on the other hand, to throw down the gauntlet to the founder of Constantinople, who was the leading soldier of the age, was no light thing. Shapur apparently hesitated before taking definite action, and, most fortunately for him, the Great Emperor died in A.D. 337, while bound for the eastern frontier of the Roman Empire.

Constantine divided up the Roman world among his three sons, and consequently, apart from the probability of civil dissensions, Shapur was now opposed to a monarch whose resources were far less than his own, instead of facing the master of the whole Roman Empire. Other conditions, too, were favourable ; for Tiridates of Armenia, who had at one time persecuted Christians, had become a fervid convert, and by forcing the new religion on his subjects had provoked intense discontent. He had died in A.D. 314, and his successors were weak rulers, from whose nerveless hands the territory surrendered by Narses had been recovered. More-

---

[1] A letter written by Constantine to Shapur contains the following passage: " You can imagine then how delighted I am to hear that Persia too, in some of its best regions, is adorned and illustrated by this class of men, on whose behalf I write to you—I mean the Christians—a thing most agreeable to my wishes."—Eusebius, *Vita Constantini Magni*, iv. 9.

over, the legionaries displayed a mutinous spirit after the death of Constantine.

Consequently Shapur was justified in deeming the opportunity favourable, and in A.D. 337 his bands of light horsemen crossed the frontier. At the same time he incited the pagan party in Armenia to rise, and the Arabs to raid across the Roman border. Constantius, who was but twenty years old at his succession, hastened to the eastern frontier, where he found his army weak in numbers and mutinous. Shapur, however, at first contented himself with raiding, and so gave his adversary time to enrol recruits and restore discipline, while in Armenia the Roman party regained the upper hand. The year thus closed more favourably than might have been expected for Constantius.

In A.D. 338 Shapur invested Nisibis, the chief centre of the Roman power in Mesopotamia. The siege lasted for two months, and Shapur was compelled to withdraw, baffled (if we may believe Theodoret [1]) by the prayers of St. James, its bishop, in answer to which miraculous swarms of flies appeared to harass the besiegers. The war then continued, in guerilla fashion, little progress being made. Shapur raided the country and defeated the Romans in the field, but was unable to capture the numerous Roman strongholds. In A.D. 341 he made a treaty with Armenia, by the terms of which Arsaces, son of Tiranus, whom he had captured and blinded, was placed on the throne. This made the position more favourable, and in A.D. 346 a second attempt was made on Nisibis, but again without success.

Two years later Shapur invaded Mesopotamia with an immense force and found the army of Constantius in the neighbourhood of the modern town of Sinjar, the ancient Singara. The Roman Emperor at first stood on the defensive, clinging to the hills, whereupon Shapur prepared a fortified camp, from which he sallied forth to attack him. The challenge was accepted, and the legionaries carried all before them, even storming the Persian camp, which was scarcely defended. Careless after their success, the Romans were surprised by the light troops of Shapur, who finally gained a signal victory which ended in a massacre. The Roman soldiers, before they died, tortured to death one of the Great King's sons who had fallen into their hands. The result of

[1] Theodoret ii. 30.

the battle of Singara was not decisive, as Constantius was not captured, and the war continued until A.D. 350, when Shapur made his third and last attempt to take Nisibis. Constantius had departed for Europe, probably taking some troops with him, and Shapur, who was supported by a body of Indian allies, with war elephants, again invested the great fortress. He dammed the plain and created round the city an artificial lake, on which ships were placed. The defenders resisted stoutly until a breach was made by the pressure of the water. Shapur ordered an immediate attack, which was headed by heavy cavalry, supported by elephants with armour-plated howdahs. Evidently no reconnaissance had been made, and, as might have been expected, both the horses and elephants sank into the mud. The defenders showed the greatest heroism, and built a new wall behind the breach. Shapur, after losing twenty thousand men, abandoned the siege. A Turanian invasion drew him to the north-east confines of his empire, and, as Constantius was also engaged in civil war, hostilities between the two empires ceased for a period of eight years.

The Great Persecution of the Christians.—The fact that Christianity became the official religion of the Roman Empire under Constantine was undoubtedly the main cause of the hostility shown to the members of the Eastern Church by Shapur, a hostility which was increased by Constantine's somewhat tactless assumption of a protecting interest. This must have been keenly resented by the Great King and his councillors, and suspected of covering political designs, very much as European interest in the Christian inhabitants of Turkey was resented by the Turks before the Great War. Nor was Shapur without justification, for he knew that the Christians looked to the Roman Empire, gloried in its successes, and were in consequence disloyal to his rule. In short, religion, then as now in the East, proved a deep gulf separating men of the same stock.

The Persian point of view is fairly expressed in the following words : " The Christians destroy our holy teaching, and teach men to serve one God, and not to honour the sun or fire. They teach them, too, to defile water by their ablutions ; to refrain from marriage and the procreation of children ; and to refuse to go out to war with the King of Kings. They have no scruple about the slaughter and eating of animals ; they bury the corpses of men in the earth ; and attribute the origin of snakes and creeping things to a good God. They despise many servants of the king, and teach witchcraft." [1]

The first order issued against the Christians was that they should pay double taxes as their contribution to the cost of the war in place of personal service. Mar [2] Shimun, the Catholicus, who was required to collect the money, foolishly refused, on the twofold ground that the people were too poor and that a bishop was not a tax-collector. He was arrested with many of his colleagues ; and on Good Friday A.D. 339 Mar Shimun, five bishops, and one hundred priests were executed at Susa, the ancient capital of forgotten Elam. The persecution thus initiated was continued by massacres and the destruction of churches for fully forty years, monks and nuns especially being subject to pitiless persecution, because they conspicuously violated the sane tenets of Zoroastrianism. The persecution flamed up again after the invasion of Julian and the restoration by Jovian of Nisibis and the five provinces, and until Shapur concluded his long reign there was no peace for the unhappy Christians.

The Eastern Campaigns of Shâpur, A.D. 350–357.—Few details are available concerning Shapur's eastern campaigns, which lasted from A.D. 350 to A.D. 357. We know that among the invaders were the Chionites, better known as the Huns, and apparently the Euseni or U-siun. The Gelani are also mentioned, and were probably the tribe from which Gilan received its name. It appears that the Great King was generally successful, and strengthened his prestige and power by these campaigns ; for, when hostilities with Rome again broke out, the Persian army was supported by a force of Huns, a tribe which was to inflict later on such untold misery upon the peoples of the West.

The Treaty between Armenia and Rome, circa A.D. 352.— Shapur must have believed that Armenia was safely under Persian influence when, after his success against Rome, he marched away to meet the invaders of his North-eastern provinces. But Arsaces saw in his departure an opportunity

---

[1] Acts of Akib—Shima, Bedj, ii. 351, quoted from *The Assyrian Church*, by Doctor W. A. Wigram, whose authoritative work I have consulted more than once. I have also consulted *The Cradle of Mankind*, an excellent work by the above author and Mr. E. T. A. Wigram. The latter has generously placed his sketches at my disposal.
[2] Mar signifies Lord.

for escaping from a galling yoke, and sent a request to Constantinople that a bride from the Imperial house might be bestowed upon him. Constantius selected a daughter of a Praetorian prefect named Olympias, who was received with great honour and made the chief wife of Arsaces. A treaty was then concluded,[1] and Armenia once again returned into the Roman sphere of influence.

The Second War with Rome to the Death of Constantius, A.D. 359–361.—While Shapur was engaged in fighting the Huns he received news from the West that the Roman Emperor was anxious to convert the truce between the two powers into a permanent treaty of peace. The fact was that overtures in this sense had been made by the Roman frontier officials, whereas Shapur was apparently led to believe that Constantius himself was suing for terms. In support of this view may be cited the letter of the Great King, which has been preserved, and which ran as follows :—" Shapur, King of Kings, brother of the Sun and Moon, sends salutation to his brother Constantius Caesar. . . . Your own authors are witness that the entire tract within the river Strymon and the borders of Macedon was once held by my ancestors ; if I required you to restore all this, it would not ill become me . . . but as moderation delights me I will be content to receive Mesopotamia and Armenia which was fraudulently extorted from my grandfather. . . . I warn you that if my ambassador returns in vain, I will take the field against you, as soon as the winter is past, with all my forces." War was certainly intended by Shapur, as this epistle clearly demonstrates, and the return embassy sent by Constantius was unable to avert it.

The Great King was guided in principle by the advice of a Roman refugee of position, whose plan of campaign was not to waste time and strength on the reduction of the fortresses of Mesopotamia, but to invade defenceless and opulent Syria. The historian Ammianus Marcellinus graphically describes how, being despatched on a reconnoitring expedition, he saw from the summit of a high peak which overlooked the great plain, " all the circuit of the earth which we call the horizon filled with countless hosts of men." He recognized Shapur and also Grumbates, the famous

---

[1] The date of this marriage and treaty could not have been earlier than A.D. 351, as Olympias had been betrothed to Constans, brother of the Emperor, who died in A.D. 350. As this was the year Shapur left for the East, I have tentatively fixed the date as A.D. 352.

King of the Chionitae or Huns, and, after watching the army begin the passage of the Tigris, hastened back to warn his general.

Shapur marched steadily westwards towards the Euphrates without attempting to besiege Nisibis, and would certainly have invaded Syria but for the fact that floods had made that river impassable and thus upset his plans. He consequently turned north-east across Mons Masius, and having gained a victory near Amida, the modern Diarbekr, he apparently gave up his main objective and decided to besiege this important fortress. Amida occupied a site of great natural strength, situated on the right bank of the Tigris, and was defended by a force of eight thousand men. Shapur hoped to terrify it into submission, but in vain, and an attempt to carry it by assault resulted in the death of the son of the Hunnish King. Regular siege operations were perforce undertaken, and after a heroic defence, in which the Roman historian took his part, the efforts of the garrison were frustrated by the giving way of an inner mound which filled up the ditch. Shapur forced his way in, and exasperated by his heavy losses, gave orders for a massacre. The Roman leaders who were captured were either crucified or sold for slaves. After the taking of Amida, Shapur retired for the winter.

In the following spring he captured Singara with ease, and, still avoiding Nisibis, marched north and besieged and took Bezabde. As in the case of Amida, a stout defence was requited by a vindictive massacre. Continuing his career, Shapur laid siege to Virta, the site of which is not known but is described as being " on the most distant border of Mesopotamia." Ultimately, however, he retired unsuccessful from before its walls.

During this period Constantius was unable to devote himself entirely to the Persian war owing to fear of his cousin Julian, whose army had insisted upon promoting him to the rank of " Augustus," and he therefore moved very slowly. After a leisurely progress through Asia Minor he summoned Arsaces of Armenia to his presence and endeavoured to keep him true to the Roman party by means of gifts. He then decided to recapture Bezabde, but after desperate assaults failed signally. This was the last military operation of Constantius ; for at the end of the following year, A.D. 361, during which Shapur did not cross the Tigris, he died after a reign of forty years.

The Expedition of Julian, A.D. 363.—Julian succeeded his cousin, and one of the most dramatic campaigns waged between Rome and Persia followed. The new Emperor had already displayed military talent of a high order while commanding in Gaul, and only the death of Constantius had saved the empire from a civil war.

No sooner was the soldier-like and philosophical Emperor seated on the throne than he determined to follow the example of Trajan and invade the Eastern Empire. He moved his headquarters to Antioch and pressed on his preparations with strenuous activity. An embassy from Shapur appeared at his Court, but was speedily dismissed, according to some accounts, with grave discourtesy. Shapur learned from his envoys how determined the Emperor was to engage in the campaign, and how formidable an enemy he was likely to prove.

Julian was of too imperious a nature to be popular or tactful in dealing with his allies. The Saracen chiefs obeyed his orders and joined him with contingents, but as he expressly forbade the bestowal of the pay and presents to which they were accustomed, on the lofty ground that "a warlike and vigilant emperor had iron, not gold," it is not surprising that they changed sides during the campaign, and not only deprived the Romans of an arm in which they were always weak, but inflicted upon them heavy losses. Arsaces of Armenia was also treated with a haughtiness that was peculiarly impolitic ; for he and his people, being Christians, were naturally disinclined to assist the apostate Julian, apart from the fact that it was the obvious policy for the ruler of Armenia to remain neutral and congratulate the winner. In the event, an Armenian contingent did join the Roman force under Procopius and Sebastian, and served in an attack on an outlying district of Media ; but without any warning it suddenly quitted the camp and made for home, much to the embarrassment of the Roman generals.

The great expedition, which numbered about one hundred thousand combatants, started from Antioch early in March A.D. 363 and made with all speed for the Euphrates. The river was crossed, and the march continued to Carrhae, where a short halt was made. Julian, who had kept his final dispositions a secret, although the construction of a fleet on the

Euphrates must have indicated that river as his main line of advance, detached a force with instructions to co-operate with Arsaces of Armenia in ravaging the frontier provinces of Persia, and then to rejoin the main body of the army before Ctesiphon.

He himself decided to march down the Euphrates, although steps were taken to deceive the enemy by the collection of supplies along the Tigris route. The narrative of Ammianus Marcellinus is thrilling as we accompany the Roman army southwards to the Euphrates, where the Emperor was joined by his fleet of 1100 ships, and received the homage of the Saracens, a race which, according to the Roman historian, "it is never desirable to have either for friends or enemies." From Callinicus, near the junction of the Belik with the Euphrates, to its junction with the Khabur, the Roman army marched down the great river to the boundary of the Empire at Circesium, which had been strongly fortified by Diocletian.

After crossing the Khabur by a bridge of boats, strict military precautions were taken, the whole force keeping together. The cavalry, which was commanded conjointly by a certain Arinthaeus and by the Sasanian pretender Hormisdas, patrolled to the east, a picked force maintained touch with the fleet, and the main body marched between, in extended order, with a view to impressing the enemy with its numbers. Unlike Trajan, Julian was unable to capture or secure the surrender of the majority of the cities which he passed, and he was obliged to leave them unsubdued in his rear. It was much to his disadvantage that the art of fortification, neglected by the Parthians, had been studied to advantage by the Sasanian dynasty. As in the case of Cyrus the Younger, in whose steps he was treading, no attempt at resistance was made by a field army until the steppes of Mesopotemia had been left behind and the rich irrigated lands of Babylonia were entered. Even then no battle was fought by the Persian Commander-in-Chief, but outlying detachments and foraging parties were cut off.

Continuing steadily down the Euphrates, Julian reached Perisabor, or more correctly Firuz-Shapur, an important and strongly defended city, situated on an artificially-constructed island, which he determined to capture. The city wall was soon breached and the town occupied; but the citadel, of considerable natural strength, defied all attempts at storming, although the Emperor in person led an attack on one of its gates. Julian, like most great generals, was a student, and he recollected the design of the " helepolis," or high movable tower invented by Demetrius Poliorcetes. He immediately gave orders to construct one, and the garrison was so terrified on seeing it rising stage by stage that it surrendered on terms.

After this success the army proceeded down the river till it came to the " Royal Canal," which connected the Euphrates with the Tigris. Artificial inundations and the ever-present enemy delayed progress along this canal, and a second fortress, Mahoz Malka, barred the way, but was captured by mining. The Roman army then marched forward until it reached the Tigris near Coche, opposite Ctesiphon, a separate town from adjacent Seleucia, which was apparently in ruins.

Julian, to his dismay, found that the " Royal Canal " entered the Tigris below Coche, and, as he was extremely anxious to unite with the force which he believed to be marching down the Tigris, and realized that he could not work his fleet upstream between Coche and Ctesiphon, the situation was difficult. Again his studies bore fruit, as he had read of a canal which came out above Coche, and after inquiries this disused branch was discovered and reopened, and the fleet proceeded along it to the great river.

It was evident that the Persian army was prepared to dispute the passage of the Tigris, for serried ranks of panoplied warriors, supported by elephants, of which the Romans never lost their dread, were seen drawn up along its bank. Instead of imitating the tactics employed by Alexander against Porus, Julian decided on a direct attack by night. His first detachment suffered from burning darts which set fire to the ships, but finally the army made good its position on the left bank. At dawn the Romans attacked, and the Persians, after standing their ground for twelve hours, fled to Ctesiphon, the Romans pursuing as far as the gates. The spoil was rich, large quantities of gold and silver, together with other property, falling to the victors.

His Retreat and Death, A.D. 363.—It would have been supposed that after defeating the Persian garrison of Ctesiphon with but one-third of his army, and after transporting the remainder across the Tigris, Julian would immediately besiege Ctesiphon, which possessed no natural advantages of situation.

SHAPUR THE GREAT

The fact that he, the bravest of the brave, never thought of taking this step seems difficult to understand. It is true that he was disappointed of the reinforcements he expected down the Tigris ; but even so, a veteran Roman army, sixty thousand strong, encouraged by success, and possessing a powerful siege train carried on board ship, appears strong enough to have undertaken the operation, and thereby to have compelled Shapur to fight a decisive battle. The explanation may be that, just as Julian found the fortresses on the Euphrates more strongly fortified than he expected, so now he realized that Ctesiphon was too formidable to be attempted. In other words, the Sasanian dynasty, which was served far better than the Arsacid, had studied the art of fortification, and had made Ctesiphon almost impregnable. This view is supported by Ammianus.

But even though the siege of Ctesiphon may have been impracticable, it seems extraordinary that Julian did not seek out the army of Shapur, as Alexander with his lesser resources would have done. Had it been found and defeated, Ctesiphon would in all probability have surrendered. The more the facts are studied the clearer it seems that Julian had no strategical plan to meet what was, after all, the most probable and natural position of affairs ; for, in view of his speed and the comparatively short distance to be traversed, he could hardly anticipate that he would meet the army of the Great King before reaching Ctesiphon ; and he should surely have realized that in order to succeed he would have to defeat that army.

But his proceedings were wholly inconsistent with such reasonable calculations. For, after deciding to leave Ctesiphon alone, instead of seeking out Shapur he hurriedly burned his ships—an act calculated in itself to encourage the enemy—and then retreated on Kurdistan. How differently would Alexander have acted ! Gibbon accepts the view suggested by some authorities, that before the retreat was begun Shapur sued for peace, and was haughtily refused. Rawlinson points out that Ammianus makes no mention of any embassy for this purpose, but it is possible that informal proposals were made with a view to sounding the enemy and gaining valuable information as to the strength and *moral* of the Roman troops ; and it is at least equally possible that, if made, Julian refused to entertain them, just as Charles XII. did in equally difficult circumstances. Both generals had a strong fantastic strain in their characters, like that which has been noticed in their far greater predecessor, Alexander.

The fatal retreat began on June 16 in the hottest season of the year, and scarcely had the army moved off when a dense cloud of dust appeared on the southern horizon. Saracen allies, or a herd of wild asses, were supposed by some to be the cause, but it was obvious to Julian that the Great King was in pursuit. Not merely was the retreat harassed, but before long a battle was fought, and although Roman valour gained the day, the question of supplies became urgent. Julian must have bitterly rued his impolitic treatment of the Saracens, who would have kept the Persian light horse at a distance and secured provisions for the army. As it was, the slow-moving legions were unable to prevent the supplies from being burned in front of them as they advanced, and famine stared them in the face within a few days after quitting Ctesiphon.

On the 26th of June they were slowly moving north in the neighbourhood of Samarra, with apparently few or no scouts thrown out, when Julian was hastily summoned from the front to the rear by news of an attack. No sooner had he reached the rear than he was again summoned to the front, where the main attack was suddenly delivered on the right. The Emperor, who in his haste had not put on his breastplate, was heroically fighting to rally the shaken legionaries, and appeared to be gaining the day, when he was struck by a javelin in his right side and was carried back to camp mortally wounded. His soldiers, thirsting to avenge him, charged the Persians again and again, and drove them off with heavy losses. Julian, meanwhile, had attempted to mount a horse, but finding it impossible had yielded to the inevitable. When he died thus valiantly on the field of battle he was in the thirty-first year of his age, and truly, as Ammianus wrote, Julian was " a man to be classed with heroic characters." The impression that he made upon his gallant enemies is shown with sufficient clearness by the fact that in Persian paintings Julian was represented as a furious lion emitting fire from his jaws. The lion was, and is, the Persian symbol of valour.

The Restoration of the Five Provinces and of Nisibis to Shapur, A.D. 363.—Jovian, a popular official, was chosen Emperor in Julian's place, and on the day of his election fought another battle with the Persians, who throughout showed splendid spirit ; and he then marched on to Samarra. Four more marches covered only eighteen miles in all, so fierce were the onslaughts of the enemy, and the Roman troops became discouraged and clamoured to be permitted to swim the Tigris, in the belief that they would thereby evade the Persians and reach the Roman frontier by a few forced marches. Yielding to necessity, Jovian ordered a band of five hundred Gauls and Sarmartians to make the attempt, which was successful, and thereupon the army halted and hastily prepared rafts and bladders for the crossing.

Shapur, whose troops had suffered severely in their attacks on the Roman veterans, had counted on famine to give him the victory, and was not in a position to drive home a fresh attack. He therefore opened up negotiations, which were welcomed by the harassed Romans. The terms were hard, and swept away all that Diocletian had gained. First, the five provinces beyond the Tigris which had been surrendered by Narses were restored. Secondly, Nisibis, Singara, and a third fortress in Eastern Mesopotamia were ceded to Persia, and thirdly Armenia was declared to lie outside the Roman sphere of influence.

Thus gloriously for Iran closed the long series of campaigns waged by Shapur, who was deservedly termed " Great," and who raised Persia to a position higher than any it had occupied since the conquests of Alexander the Great. For Rome, the surrender of the five provinces was a heavy blow, but nothing in comparison with the evacuation and handing over of Nisibis, which had been the centre of Roman power for nearly two centuries and possessed a large European population, which had to be uprooted and removed.

The Policy of Persia and Rome in Armenia and Iberia.—
It might have been thought that after his splendid success and the treaty signed by Jovian, Shapur would have had a free hand in Armenia ; but this was not the case. Jovian's reign had lasted only a few months in all, and his successor Valentinian divided the Roman Empire into eastern and western divisions, bestowing the former on his brother Valens. The situation had therefore changed. There was no open repudiation of the treaty, but the Emperor who had negotiated it was dead and a new family wore the purple. Shapur, who

was anxious to bring Armenia under his influence without delay, lured the hapless Arsaces to his Court, where he was immediately blinded ; but as a mark of respect his fetters were made of silver. After this successful piece of treachery, Shapur overran Armenia, where the fortress of Artogerassa, in which the Roman wife of Arsaces had taken refuge with the treasure, alone held out. In the course of the same campaign he also invaded neighbouring Iberia, drove out Sauromaces, who had received his investiture from Rome, and placed a cousin of the deposed ruler, a certain Aspacures, on the throne of the valley of the Kur. Shapur then returned to Persia, leaving a force behind to complete the conquest.

Had Rome loyally observed Jovian's treaty, there would probably have been no further change in the situation ; but Para, son of Arsaces, who had fled across the frontier, returned to lead the national party and received Roman support. This brought Shapur into the field again. Artogerassa, together with the treasure of Arsaces, was captured, and Para was forced to make terms, acknowledging Shapur as his suzerain.

In A.D. 370 Rome openly interfered in Iberia, whither Duke[1] Terentius was sent at the head of twelve legions to reinstate Sauromaces. After carrying all before him, he was met on the banks of the Kur by Aspacures, and an agreement was made, according to which the kingdom was divided between the two cousins. As this arrangement was concluded without reference to the Court of Persia, Shapur was incensed. His ambassadors failed to obtain satisfaction in Rome, and consequently war again became inevitable.

In the spring of A.D. 371 the Persian monarch crossed the frontier and attacked the Romans at a place termed Vagabanta. To avoid breaking the letter of the treaty, the Romans at first acted on the defensive, but they afterwards repulsed the Persian force, and hostilities continued for some years with no decisive results.

The tragic career of Para is given in detail by Ammianus. It appears that on the representations of the Duke Terentius he was summoned to the presence of the Emperor under pretence of negotiating a new treaty. Ascertaining that it was intended to depose him, he fled, and, although pursued, reached the Euphrates in safety. He crossed on improvised

---

[1] The titles of Duke and Count are frequently used at this period. Duke was the lower title of the two.

rafts, but found both roads leading to Armenia blocked by Roman troops, and escaped by a track through the forest shown him by a chance traveller. The Roman officials who had failed to seize him solemnly reported that he had rendered himself invisible by magic, and the fatuous Valens, implicitly believing this, decided to make away with Para, although he had never broken off relations with Rome. A Roman official was employed to murder the unfortunate Prince at a banquet.

The Conclusion of Peace between Rome and Persia, A.D. 376.—A truce, followed by negotiations which were broken off and succeeded by fresh hostilities, finally led to a treaty of peace, the terms of which are obscure, but which may have bound the two contracting powers to leave Armenia and Iberia free to govern themselves. Both these countries were now divided from Persia by difference of religion, and consequently the peace would leave them attached to the West and hostile to Persia.

The Death of Shapur, A.D. 379.—The last campaign against Rome had now been fought by Shapur the Great, who passed away, after an exceptionally long and successful reign, full of years and honours. We know little of his personal character, but he was essentially a puissant monarch of superb physique and remarkable valour, and was well served by a devoted people. The manner in which he conducted the long fight with Rome to regain the five provinces lost by his grandfather Narses and to secure possession of Nisibis—a struggle which he kept free from disaster—proves that he possessed not only military talents of a high order, but also a tenacity of purpose that was lacking in many members of the dynasty. His campaigns against the Huns, so far as these are known, afford further evidence of military and diplomatic achievement. He appears to have left no sculptures or inscriptions, but he founded many cities; and the second foundation of Nishapur is believed to have been undertaken by his orders.

To judge by results, Shapur left Persia at the zenith of her power and glory, in possession of a favourable treaty with the great Western Power, at whose prestige he had dealt a deadly blow, and with no powerful enemy threatening the eastern boundaries. A quotation from Ammianus Marcellinus, which embodies contemporary foreign opinion, may fitly end this chapter. Writing of Shapur's campaigns against Constantius, he says : "The fortune of the East sounded the terrible trumpet of danger. For the King of Persia, being strengthened by the aid of the fierce nations whom he had lately subdued, and being above all men ambitious of extending his territories, began to prepare men and arms and supplies, mingling hellish wisdom with his human counsels, and consulting all kinds of soothsayers about futurity." [1]

[1] xviii. 4.

"Varahran, King of Kerman, the son of Ormuzd worshipper, divine Shapur, King of Kings of Irán and Aniran, of celestial origin from God."

AMETHYST SEAL OF VARAHRAN OR BAHRAM IV.
(From *R.A.S. Journal*, vol. iii., New Series, 1868.)

CHAPTER XXXVIII

THE STRUGGLE WITH THE WHITE HUNS

Thou shalt ascend and come like a storm, thou shalt be like a cloud to cover the land, thou, and all thy bands, and many people with thee. . . . And thou shalt come from thy place out of the north parts, thou, and many people with thee, all of them riding upon horses, a great company, and a mighty army.—Ezekiel xxxviii. 9, 15.

Ardeshir II., A.D. 379–383, *and Shapur III.*, A.D. 383–388.—As often happened after a long and glorious reign, the immediate successors of Shapur the Great were weak and unenterprising. Of Ardeshir II. little is known except that he remitted all taxation and thereby earned the title of "the Beneficent." He reigned for only four years, from A.D. 379 to A.D. 383, in which latter year he was deposed. His nephew Shapur III. concluded a treaty with Rome the year after his succession, and led an expedition against the tribe of Yad Arabs.[1] He commemorated his reign by a rock sculpture representing the great Shapur and himself, which is still to be seen at Tak-i-Bustan near Kermanshah; he died in A.D. 388.

The Partition of Armenia, A.D. 384.—After the detestable murder of Para, the Romans had nominated an Arsacid prince

[1] Masudi, *Prairies d'or*, vol. ii. p. 189.

named Varaztad to the throne of Armenia, but had entrusted the real power to a nobleman termed Moushegh, whom Varaztad, following a sinister precedent, assassinated at a banquet. This provoked a rising headed by Manuel, brother of the murdered noble, who seized the reins of power in the name of the widow and two sons of Para. Knowing that he would have to reckon ultimately with Rome, he despatched an embassy to Ardeshir, offering to pay tribute and to acknowledge Persian paramountcy. Terms were speedily arranged, and a Satrap, supported by a force of ten thousand men, was sent to rule Armenia conjointly with Manuel. This impossible dual control was brought to a sudden end by Manuel, who, being informed of an intention to capture him, attacked and annihilated the entire Persian garrison. As long as he lived he held his own, but upon his death, in A.D. 383, both Rome and Persia were called in by the contending factions, and war between the two great powers again appeared imminent. But Rome was still weak from the effects of the staggering blow dealt by the Goths at the battle of Adrianople in A.D. 378, and Persia was ruled by unwarlike monarchs. Consequently, in A.D. 384, a treaty was made, by the terms of which Armenia was partitioned, the larger or eastern part becoming a Persian province and the western districts passing into the Roman sphere of influence. Both provinces were ruled by scions of the old Arsacid dynasty ; but the independent nationality of Armenia passed away, in much the same manner, and for the same reason, as that of Poland in later times. In both cases the turbulent nobles sacrificed the interests of their country to gratify not so much their personal aggrandizement as their personal hatreds, and the result was, in the case of the older state, that the kingdom of Armenia ceased to exist, and the Armenian question began.

Bahram IV., A.D. 388-399.—Shapur III. was succeeded by Bahram, whose seal, proving that before his accession he was King of Kerman, has been preserved and forms the headpiece to this chapter. During his reign Chosroes, the Satrap of Persian Armenia, elated by his appointment to govern the Roman provinces, attempted to revolt from Persia, trusting to the support of Theodosius. That sagacious emperor, however, was not inclined to provoke war lightly, and Chosroes, left to his fate, was seized and confined in the ill-omened Castle of Oblivion—the state prison of Persia—and his brother Bahram-Shapur succeeded him. Little else is recorded of the reign of Bahram IV., who was killed by his own soldiers in a mutiny.

Yezdigird the Wicked, A.D. 399–420.—Yezdigird I. succeeded to the throne and proved to be of a peaceful disposition. Had he inherited his ancestors' love of war, he would have found a great opportunity. The Roman Empire was in a welter of barbarian invasions, revolt, and intrigue, the sack of Rome by Alaric, in A.D. 410, falling within this period. Indeed, Syria and Asia Minor would have been an easy conquest, and Yezdigird could probably have won back all the provinces which had formerly belonged to the Achaemenian dynasty. As it was, the relations between the two empires were most friendly, and when Arcadius, the Emperor of the East, died he committed his son Theodosius to the protection of Yezdigird. The Persian monarch accepted the trust, selecting a learned eunuch to be the guardian of the youth, and throughout his reign there was no question of war with the Eastern Roman Empire.

His Policy towards the Christians.—The Christian community, which had been crushed and almost annihilated by the long and ferocious persecutions of Shapur the Great, gradually recovered after his death. We hear of the election of a Catholicus of Seleucia during the reign of Shapur III., but it was not until that of Yezdigird I. that the position of the Christians was officially ameliorated. Marutha, a Mesopotamian bishop, was sent with an embassy which announced the succession of Theodosius II. to his guardian. He won the Great King's favour by curing him of a malady, and gained considerable influence over him. The royal favour soon bore fruit, and, in A.D. 409, a *firman* was issued permitting Christians to worship openly and to rebuild their churches. This decree was as important to the Eastern Church as the more famous Edict of Milan was to the Church of the West. It formally conferred upon the community the status of what is known to-day in Turkey as a *millat*, or Christian subject people, organized as a Church and dealing with the Government through its religious head, who is appointed by that Government.

This edict was followed by the Council of Seleucia, held in A.D. 410, at which the decrees and the creed of the Council of Nicaea were agreed to and adopted. Wigram holds that no representative from Persia[1] had attended this famous Council, which was convened in A.D. 325 mainly in order to combat the doctrines of Arius. That ecclesiastic taught that there was a difference between the Father and the Son, inasmuch as the Father was from all time, whereas the Son had had a beginning. In other words, the Son was ομοιουσιος, of "like nature," rather than ὁμοούσιος, of "one nature" with the Father. These two words differ only by a single letter (iota) in the Greek language, but the immense difference represented by this letter divided and convulsed Christendom. At the Council of Nicaea, Athanasius, who was the moving spirit, secured the adoption of the formula that "the Son is of one Essence with the Father," and the Council anathematized every one who declined to accept this view. Wigram is of opinion that Persia was not only untroubled by the Arian controversy, but was even ignorant of it, which, in view of its precarious position, was most fortunate.

Yezdigird at this time possibly contemplated baptism, and even went so far as to persecute the Magians, who bestowed on him in consequence the opprobrious epithet by which he is known to history. After a time, he apparently realized that he had gone too far for prudence, and, returning to the old faith, he authorized the destruction of the Christian sect, with the result that a terrible persecution raged for five years in circumstances of special cruelty.

The Curious Legend of his Death.—Little else is known of this monarch, who is credited with having founded the city of Yezd.[2] His death at the otter-haunted Lake of Sovar or Su, now known as Chashma-i-Sabz, or "Green Fountain," romantically situated in the heart of the Nishapur mountains, is described by Firdausi. According to this story a white horse "with round thighs and short legs like a wild ass" came out of the lake. The monarch gave orders for its capture, but no one succeeded in the attempt. He himself then took a saddle and approached the horse, "which moved neither fore nor hind leg. When he placed the saddle on its back

---

[1] *The Assyrian Church*, p. 58.—James of Nisibis was present at the Council, but Nisibis, at that time, formed part of the Roman Empire. A John "of Persia" appears, but this is possibly a misreading for "Perrha."

[2] According to Persian legend, which was possibly inspired by the hopeless sterility of the place, Yezd originally served as a prison to which Alexander sent his enemies. It owes its prosperity entirely to its situation at the junction of several routes.

and tightened the girth, that rushing monster did not stir." When, however, he passed behind its quarters "that stony-hoofed one became enraged, thundered and kicked him with both hind legs so that his head and crown fell into the dust." The horse then disappeared into the waters of the lake and was no more seen.

The Contested Succession of Bahram Gur, A.D. 420.—Upon the death of Yezdigird I. the nobles attempted to pass over both his sons, Bahram and Shapur, the former because he had been brought up among the desert Arabs, and the other for the equally inadequate reason that he had left Armenia, which was under his rule, to push his claims to the throne. Bahram, however, was a virile personality, and being supported by a force of Arabs, prevailed on the nobles to submit to him without the horrors of a civil war. The Persian legend represents him as placing the crown between two raging lions, and when Khusru, or Chosroes, his cousin, who was the choice of the nobles, declined to make the attempt, Bahram, with the courage which was so conspicuous throughout his career, attempted to take possession of it and succeeded.

His Campaign against Rome, A.D. 420-421.—The persecution of the Christians which Yezdigird had initiated during the latter years of his reign was continued with zeal by the new monarch. So fierce was its character that a large body of refugees crossed the border and placed themselves under Roman protection. This incensed Bahram, who demanded the surrender of his subjects, and when this was refused declared war.

The Romans were the first to take the field, and crossing the Tigris, ravaged Arzanene, one of the five provinces won back by Shapur the Great. Their leader Ardaburius, an Alan by descent, then marched into Mesopotamia and besieged Nisibis. Bahram, however, came to the rescue with a large force and the Romans withdrew. Moses of Chorene[1] refers to the thirty days' siege, by Bahram in person, of Theodosiopolis (the modern Erzerum), in the Roman province of Armenia. According to his account the Persians were beaten back by the exertions of the bishop, who not

---

[1] Ammianus Marcellinus carries his valuable work no further than A.D. 378—the year of the battle of Adrianople; consequently inferior authorities have to be used in dealing with this period.

only encouraged the defenders, but personally worked the *balista* with signal success, and killed a Persian prince.

In the field, Bahram and the Roman general agreed to be represented by champions. The Romans chose Areobindus the Goth, who eluded the thrust of his adversary's spear and then entangled him in a net and killed him. Bahram accepted the result and withdrew. Meanwhile, in Mesopotamia Ardaburius annihilated a Persian force which he had lured into an ambush. The Arab allies of the Persians had also suffered disasters. Consequently Bahram was ready to make terms and received a Roman envoy. The proud "Immortals" begged to be allowed to make a final effort, hoping to find Roman precautions relaxed during the negotiations ; but, after they had secured a temporary advantage at the beginning of the battle, reinforcements arrived to support the legions, and the "Immortals" were cut off to a man.

The Peace with Rome, A.D. 422.—The terms of the peace which was made in A.D. 422 have not been preserved. It is, however, believed that not only were Christians to be permitted to take refuge in the Roman Empire, but Bahram agreed to abstain from further persecution. On the Roman side, Zoroastrians were also secured from all risk of persecution. In connexion with this campaign, Gibbon mentions the noble act of the bishop of Amida, who melted down and sold all the church plate in his diocese. With the proceeds he ransomed seven thousand Persian prisoners and sent them back to Bahram. Possibly this act of true Christian charity had its influence in inducing the King of Kings to cease his persecutions, which were in fact as impolitic as they were cruel.

The Declaration of the Independence of the Eastern Church, A.D. 424.—These persecutions had one important result in causing the leaders of the Eastern Church to realize that it was better for them to be independent of the Western Church, and thereby at any rate avoid the charge of disloyalty to their sovereign. Consequently, in A.D. 424 the so-called Council of Dad-Ishu was held, at which the Catholicus, Dad-Ishu, was begged to resume his throne as Patriarch, and it was decreed that in future absolute obedience should be rendered to him and that there should be no appeal to "Western Patriarchs." The results fully justified this policy ; for thereafter less is heard of persecution of the Christians.

Persian Armenia reduced to a Satrapy, A.D. 428.—In the same year that peace was concluded with Rome, Bahram, whose failure before Theodosiopolis had weakened his position in Persian Armenia and made him ready to meet the wishes of its inhabitants, appointed a son of Bahram-Shapur to be its king. Again, however, the turbulent nobles were dissatisfied, and, after six years' unrest, petitioned for the appointment of a Persian Satrap. Their wish was acceded to, and thus, by the act of its own leaders, even the limited independence of Persian Armenia was brought to a close. It is interesting to note how leading a part the Patriarch Isaac took in opposing this act of political suicide, which brought a Christian people under the yoke of a Zoroastrian power.

The Coming of the White Huns.—Reference has already been made to the Yue-Chi [1] as having in 163 B.C. dispossessed the Sakae from their habitat in the Tarim basin. In 120 B.C. the Yue-Chi drove the Sakae out of Bactria, which they occupied and which remained their centre for many generations. In 30 B.C. one of their tribes, the Kwei-Shang, subdued the others, and the nation became known to the Romans as the Kushan. Antony sent ambassadors to this people and Kushan chiefs appeared in Rome during the reign of Augustus. Their power gradually waned, and they were finally supplanted by a race known to the Chinese as the Yetha, to the classical writers as the Ephthalites or White Huns, and to the Persians as the Haytal, the name in all three instances being apparently derived from Ye-tai-li-to, the chief : the newcomers, though of a similar stock, were entirely distinct from the Yue-Chi whom they drove out. This powerful tribe crossed the Oxus about A.D. 425, and according to the Persian chroniclers the news of their invasion caused a widespread panic.

The Campaigns of Bahram Gur against the White Huns. —Bahram appeared to lose his senses upon hearing of the invasion ; for, instead of collecting all the forces of the empire, he started off on a hunting expedition to Azerbaijan, turning a deaf ear to the prayers and remonstrances of his councillors. But as soon as he was lost to sight in the Elburz range he travelled with the utmost rapidity, collecting forces as he made for the eastern frontier and concealing his movements with complete success. He decided upon a night surprise, and, adopting tactics somewhat similar to those of

[1] Chapter XXIX.

Gideon, who dismayed the Midianites by breaking pitchers, attached skins filled with pebbles to his horses' necks. He completely surprised his enemy, whose horses stampeded; he slew the Khan and many of his men, and captured the Khan's chief wife together with immense booty. To complete his victory he followed up the enemy across the Oxus, defeated them again, and compelled them to sue for peace. There is no doubt as to the substantial accuracy of the account of this campaign, for peace prevailed, so far as his eastern provinces are concerned, during the remainder of Bahram's long reign. At the same time the menace of invasion by these nomads overshadowed Persia and constituted the principal preoccupation of its monarchs for several generations.

The story of Bahram's expedition to India, where the Indian King, in return for his services against the common enemy, is believed to have presented to him the provinces of Sind and Makran, cannot be regarded as authentic; but I do not reject it as entirely devoid of historical basis. At any rate it is universally believed in Persia that, as narrated by Firdausi, Bahram introduced twelve thousand Luris or Gypsies into Persia from India to provide music and dancing for his people. These Luris are believed to have been the ancestors of the Persian gypsies, and the legend points to considerable intercourse between Persia and India at this period.

Bahram Gur, the Mighty Hunter.—The affection with which Bahram is still regarded by Persians is mainly due to the fact that he remains for all time the model of a mighty hunter. So much is this the case that he is invariably referred to by the sobriquet of *Gur*, or Wild Ass, that beast having been his favourite quarry. In pursuit of it, indeed, he ultimately lost his life in a quicksand near Asupas to the south-west of Abadeh. As FitzGerald's translation of *Omar Khayyam*[1] runs:

> And Bahram, that great Hunter—the Wild Ass
> Stamps o'er his Head, but cannot break his sleep.

His Achievements and Character.—The reign of this great monarch may be summarized by saying that he concluded

---

[1] The original runs:

> Bahram who, all his life, was capturing the wild ass (*Gur*):
> See how the grave (*Gur*) has captured Bahram.

In this instance the original is of fuller meaning than the translation.

SILVER DISH OF BAHRAM GUR

an unsuccessful war with Rome on honourable terms, he settled the affairs of Armenia, and he decisively defeated the invading White Huns. He administered justice without partiality, he encouraged agriculture, science, and letters, and did not allow his love of sport to interfere with his duties. When he died, in A.D. 440, Persia was at the zenith of her power and prestige.

Yezdigird II., his Campaigns against Rome and the White Huns.—Bahram Gur was succeeded by his son Yezdigird II., who came to the throne in A.D. 440. He declared war upon Rome immediately after his succession apparently on account of encroachments by the Roman frontier officials. The Emperor Theodosius was most anxious to avoid hostilities, and his representative succeeded in concluding a treaty according to which no fortifications were to be constructed by either power near the common frontier. There were also other terms, one of which was that Rome should annually pay to Persia a sum of money, in consideration of which the latter power agreed to maintain a powerful force at Darband or Derbent, the point where the spurs of the Caucasus run down to the Caspian Sea. Yezdigird afterwards turned his attention to his eastern frontiers and engaged in a series of campaigns from A.D. 443 to 451, in the course of which he apparently sustained more than one defeat.

His Persecutions in Armenia and Mesopotamia.—As was to be expected, the *Mobeds* were incessantly urging that Armenia should be won back to the old faith. Policy, too, undoubtedly suffered from the fact that the hill province invariably looked to Christian Rome. It was decided to attempt to win over the Armenians by kindness and conciliation, and, in order to effect this, Mihr-Narses, the Vizier, was despatched on a special mission, in which he totally failed. Force was then applied and the Armenians ultimately broke up into two hostile parties, with the result that after years of warfare the Christian party was defeated, in A.D. 455 or 456, the patriarch Joseph suffered martyrdom, and the remnant of the militant Christians fled from the country. This persecution spread apparently to Mesopotamia, and we read that at Karka, west of Holwan, John the Metropolitan was put to death with thousands of other Christians. Karka to-day is known as Karkuk or Kirkuk, and it is of no small historical interest to find that every year a solemn assembly is still convened to commemorate the death of these martyrs, at the little church on the hillock outside the town which was dyed with their blood.

The Usurpation of Hormisdas, A.D. 457, *and his Overthrow by Firuz*, A.D. 459.—Yezdigird II. died in A.D. 457, and Hormisdas, the younger son, seized the throne in the absence of his elder brother Firuz—the Perozes of the European writers—who was Governor of Sistan. Hearing of this usurpation the latter fled to the White Huns, who gave him sanctuary and furnished him with a force by the aid of which he defeated and captured Hormisdas. He subsequently regained possession of the province of Albania to the west of the Caspian Sea, which had taken advantage of the civil war to revolt. His administration was renowned for its high standard of efficiency, and it is recorded that, although at this period the Persian Empire from the Oxus to the Tigris suffered from a terrible famine lasting for several years, supplies were imported from every quarter by the capable monarch and there was no loss of life.

The First Campaigns of Firuz against the White Huns.— As in the case of his predecessors, the wars against the White Huns were the leading preoccupation of Firuz. His first campaigns were unsuccessful and he consequently made peace, one of the terms being that Khush-Newaz, or " The High-Minded "—the Persian title for the King of the White Huns—was to receive one of his daughters in marriage. He foolishly insulted his formidable enemy by sending a female slave to act the part of a royal princess, and when the imposture was discovered there was naturally intense indignation. By way of revenge, Khush-Newaz asked Firuz to lend him some officers to direct a campaign, and when they arrived, to the number of three hundred, they were seized and a few of them were put to death. The remainder were mutilated and sent back, with a message explaining that this was done to avenge the insult put upon the royal house of the White Huns.

War again broke out and Firuz fixed his headquarters at the city of Gurgan, close to which I examined the ruins of a wall running from the Caspian Sea, north of the River Gurgan, which Rawlinson believes was built by this monarch as a defence against the White Huns : it is now termed *Sadd-i-Iskandar*, " The Barrier of Alexander," [1] or *Kizil Alang*, the " Red Wall."

[1] *Journal R.G.S.* for January 1911.

From this base Firuz invaded the enemies' country and was lured by a feigned panic and flight into a steep wooded valley with no exit, the entrance to which was occupied after the passage of his army. When he realized that he was trapped he opened negotiations. Lenient terms were accorded by his humane foe and a treaty was made on the conditions of perpetual peace and of homage by prostration.[1] To this latter humiliation the Great King agreed under compulsion ; but, by performing the ceremony at sunrise in the direction of the East, he was advised by the *Mobeds* that he might be considered to have adored the Persian divinity and not a mortal.

The Revolt of Armenia, A.D. 481–483.—The policy of Zoroastrianizing Armenia had been continuously applied by renegade Armenians and Persian officials until the country was goaded into revolt. An opportunity occurred when Firuz was defeated by the Kushans, who at this period inhabited the maritime provinces of the Caspian Sea. The Armenians sprang to arms and captured Artaxata ; and Sahag, of the noble Bagratide family, was elected King. In the following year two Persian armies operated against both Armenia and Iberia, which had joined the revolt ; but through the detestable treachery of the King of Iberia the Armenians who had come to his aid were defeated and their King slain. Vahan, the Commander-in-Chief, however, escaped, and for a long time was hunted as a fugitive ; but the death of Firuz changed the whole situation and resulted in the restoration of Christianity.

The Defeat of Firuz by the White Huns and his Death, A.D. 483.—Firuz suffered intense mortification from the humiliation inflicted on him by Khush-Newaz, and burned to wipe out the stain. It had been laid down in the treaty that he should never pass a certain pillar with his army ; and in order to get round his engagement he resorted to the casuistical device of digging it up and drawing it in front of his troops. With a large force, including 500 war elephants, he marched eastward to Balkh, where the White Huns awaited him. When the Persian army drew near, an appeal was made to the soldiers not to perjure themselves, and this, according to Tabari, caused the desertion of half the force.

[1] According to Tabari, Firuz was lured across a desert in which he lost almost the whole of his army and was thus obliged to submit.

The remainder, advancing with Firuz at their head, were enticed over a trench masked by boughs of trees and were ignominiously defeated, Firuz himself being among the slain. Thus fell Firuz, known by his countrymen as "the brave," after a long reign marked by a series of failures and defeats.

Persia tributary to the White Huns, A.D. 483–485.—Firuz was succeeded by his brother Volagases, known to the Byzantines as Balas. The task of making terms with the White Huns was confided to the Governor of Sistan, who collected a large force to impress Khush-Newaz, whom he furthermore astonished by his own skill in archery. The negotiations were so far successful that the prisoners were released; but the White Hun monarch imposed a tribute on the Great King, which was apparently paid for two years.

The Agreement with Armenia.—Volagases, whose policy was eminently conciliatory, turned his attention to Armenia, where Vahan proposed terms which included the destruction of all fire altars, full liberty for Christian worship, and an edict of toleration. Before the negotiations were finally concluded, Volagases became involved in a civil war through the claims to the throne of Zaren, a son of Firuz. The astute Vahan came to his rescue with a strong force of Armenian cavalry, which won the day, and Volagases thereupon promptly ratified the terms of the agreement. Shortly afterwards Vahan was made ruler of Armenia; and then for the first time Armenia and Iberia became contented provinces of the Persian Empire.

Controversies on Doctrine among the Christians in Persia.— During the reign of Firuz the question of the nature of God was again convulsing the Christian world, and this time the church in Persia took sides in the controversy. I do not propose to treat of these conflicts on theological questions with any fulness, but it is necessary to describe them briefly because they were of considerable political importance.

The question dealt with at the Council of Nicaea finally passed with the dying out of Arianism, but in the fifth century Christendom was divided on the following points. Had Christ one nature or two natures? In other words, was there both a divine and a human nature? And, again, was Mary the Mother of God, or only of the Man-Christ?

Nestorius,[1] who had been appointed Patriarch of Constantinople in A.D. 428, taught that Mary was the Mother of Christ but not of God, and that there were two natures and two persons. Cyril of Alexandria dominated the Third Council of the Church, held at Ephesus in A.D. 431, which condemned this doctrine in twelve anathemas; and at a Second Council of Ephesus, held in A.D. 449, his monks assaulted their opponents and generally threw such discredit on the Council that it was named the Latrocinium or " Gathering of Brigands." At the Fourth Council of the Church, held at Chalcedon in A.D. 451, the doctrine of the " one person in two natures " and the primacy of the See of Rome were established. In the Eastern half of the Empire, the feeling upon the whole was in favour of the doctrine of the " one nature " ; and this Monophysite heresy, as it is termed, dominated the Church of the Empire of Byzantium for some time, and was the only doctrine with which the Church in Persia was brought into contact.

At Edessa there was a certain Bar-Soma, who was expelled when Ibas, the bishop, was sent into exile by orders of the Latrocinium. When the bishop was acquitted at the Council of Chalcedon, Bar-Soma came back with him, and after the bishop's death in A.D. 457 he returned to Persia, his native land, and became Archbishop of Nisibis. He was a capable, unscrupulous man ; and when the Patriarch, in corresponding with some " Roman bishops," used the expression " God has given us over to an accursed kingdom," Bar-Soma, into whose hands the letter had fallen, betrayed the writer into the hands of Firuz, by whom he was executed.

Bar-Soma was now all powerful in the Church, and marched through the land armed with the royal authority to establish the doctrine of the " two natures in God." Firuz probably felt that this act would produce a final separation from a Monophysitic Church, and aided Bar-Soma, who used force freely. On the other hand, it appears that his doctrines were generally approved, the mass of the people realizing that, if there were opposition and hostility to the Church of Constantinople, there would be no further persecutions in Persia. And so the event proved. Another

---

[1] The character of Nestorius may be judged by the first homily he preached before the Emperor Theodosius, which ran : " Exterminate heretics and with you I will exterminate the Persians."

important rule now introduced was that permitting the clergy to marry ; and this sweeping away of the unhealthy idea of celibacy was certainly influenced by the sane, if material, ideals of Zoroastrianism. To-day the illogical custom prevails in the Assyrian Church, by which term the Nestorians who live between Baghdad and Urumia are known, that the clergy may marry, but that bishops must be strictly celibate.

Yet another task, and one of much importance, was carried through by Bar-Soma. In A.D. 489, the Emperor Zeno broke up the college at Edessa on account of its Nestorianism, and Bar-Soma at once established it at Nisibis. As Wigram points out, this was a great deed, and, as the Nestorians taught the Arabs, through whom so much of mediaeval culture reached Europe, the debt we owe to Bar-Soma is not a small one.

To conclude this brief account, Armenia at the Council of Vagharshapat (the ancient capital, now termed Echmiadzin), held in A.D. 491, formally repudiated the Council of Chalcedon, and thereby apparently declared in favour of monophysitism, but in reality declined to acknowledge the primacy of the Patriarch of Constantinople. This declaration separated Armenia, and separate it still remains from every other church.

KOBAD.

CHAPTER XXXIX

THE CRUSHING OF THE WHITE HUNS

> After passing a desert and a morass, they (the Huns) penetrated through the mountains, and arrived, at the end of fifteen days' march, on the confines of Media. . . . They encountered the Persian army in the plains of Media ; and the air, according to their own expression, was darkened by a cloud of arrows. But the Huns were obliged to retire, before the numbers of the enemy.—GIBBON, *Decline and Fall*.

The Accession of Kobad, A.D. 487.—Kobad (the name is a later form of Kavad) was a son of Firuz who took refuge with the White Huns after making an abortive attempt to seize the throne. He was kindly received by Khush-Newaz, but it was not until three years after his arrival that a force was prepared to aid him in substantiating his claims. It would appear that this change of policy was connected with the refusal of Balas to continue to pay tribute ; but there was no civil war, as that monarch opportunely died in A.D. 487, or, according to another account, was blinded and thereby rendered unfit to reign. Kobad was then recognized as the Great King.

His Campaigns against the Khazars.—A campaign against the Khazars, a barbarous tribe which raided across the Caucasus into the valley of the Kur, was the earliest exploit of Kobad's long reign. This Turkish tribe, which has impressed itself so deeply on Persian history that the Caspian Sea is still known by Persians as the Khazar Sea,[1] was defeated with ease in the first encounter, a large number being killed and immense booty captured.

[1] *Vide* vol. i. p. 26.

The Rise of Mazdak.—Just about this period, Mazdak, an inhabitant of Persepolis, or, according to Tabari, of Nishapur, began to convert thousands to his doctrines, which were an early form of Communism. According to these, all men were born equal and had the right to maintain their equality through life. Consequently property and women should be held in common. On the more spiritual side he taught abstemiousness, devotion, and the sacredness of animal life. For the propagation of his tenets he resorted to imposture. A tube was constructed from a cavern beneath the fire-altar, and, with the help of a confederate, Mazdak professed to converse with the sacred element. He carried out the fraud with such complete success in the presence of the sovereign that Kobad enrolled himself among his disciples. So encouraged were the followers of the new religion by the royal support that even Christian Armenia was almost goaded into rebellion by their intolerant proselytism.

The Deposition of Kobad and his Imprisonment, A.D. 498–501.—As a result of the monarch's conversion to the tenets of Mazdak, his unpopularity became so great that a conspiracy was formed by the chief *Mobed*, the nobles, and the army ; Kobad was deposed and Zamasp, his brother, was placed on the throne. In spite of the general clamour for the death of Kobad, his kindly brother refused to order his execution, but confined him instead in the famous Castle of Oblivion.

His Second Reign, A.D. 501–531.—Kobad, however, by the aid of his wife, who, according to some accounts, carried him off concealed in her bedding, escaped to the White Huns, and they espoused his cause with vigour. Zamasp declined to fight for the throne, and Kobad in consequence received the submission of his refractory subjects. At the same time he prudently withdrew official support from Mazdak, although as an individual he still adhered to his doctrines.

His First War with Rome, A.D. 503–505.—Under Kobad the eighty years' peace with Rome came to an end and the almost continuous series of campaigns was begun which, by exhausting both powers, paved the way for the Arab conquest. Among the terms of the peace concluded in A.D. 422 between Yezdigird II. and Theodosius II., as mentioned in the previous chapter, was one by which Rome engaged to pay a certain sum annually towards the expenses of the Derbent garrison.

During the years of peace which had existed between the two powers, this subsidy had not been paid, and Kobad, being in urgent need of money with which to reward his Ephthalite allies, demanded the whole amount due. The Emperor Anastasius not unnaturally resisted the claim on the ground that it was obsolete, and war was the consequence.

The campaign opened with a sudden invasion of Roman Armenia which was entirely successful, Theodosiopolis, which was unprepared for a siege, surrendering almost at once. After laying waste the country, Kobad marched to Amida, famous for its siege by Shapur the Great. This great fortress was also taken, after eighty days, although at a heavy cost of 50,000 men, and these successes were followed up by the annihilation of a Roman army. Unfortunately for Persia, an invasion by the Ephthalites caused the Great King to hasten with most of his troops to Khorasan in A.D. 503. Hearing of his departure, the Romans took heart, crossed the Tigris, and besieged both Amida and Nisibis. At this juncture an embassy arrived from Kobad, and the Romans, unaware of the straits to which Amida was reduced, paid one thousand pounds' weight of gold in exchange for it. On the terms of the *status quo ante* a peace was concluded in A.D. 505 for a period of seven years.

The Final Campaign against the White Huns, A.D. 503–513. —The war with the White Huns lasted for ten years and was, so far as can be surmised, entirely successful ; but no details are known. From this period onwards, these formidable nomads ceased to be of primary importance in the policy of Persia, and when they are again mentioned, in the reign of Noshirwan, they are no longer the invaders, but are invaded by the ever-victorious Great King. In short, the White Hun peril, which had threatened Iran for so long, had passed away.

The Massacre of the Mazdakites, A.D. 523.—The Mazdakites since the restoration of Kobad had steadily increased in numbers. But they felt their position to be very insecure ; for, on the death of Kobad, his successor might, and indeed probably would, order them to be extirpated. They therefore engaged in a conspiracy to persuade Kobad, now an old man, to abdicate in favour of his son Phthasuarsas, who agreed to establish their religion as that of the State if he succeeded to the throne. Kobad, hearing of the plot, feigned willingness to abdicate, summoned the leading Mazdakites to assist at the solemnity, and then had them massacred.

The Rebellion in Iberia.—Freed from the war with the White Huns and from internal troubles, Kobad was able to turn his attention to his relations with Rome. He was, however, deterred from active hostilities, by a rebellion which broke out in Iberia owing to his folly in revoking his predecessor's policy of toleration and insisting on the renunciation of Christianity in favour of Zoroastrianism. Gurgenes, the Iberian monarch, applied to Rome for help. This was promised but was not effectually given, and in consequence Gurgenes fled to Lazica, the modern Imeretia and Mingrelia, a country which was destined shortly to be the theatre of a war between the two great powers.

The Second War with Rome, A.D. 524-531.—During the ten years of the war with the White Huns, Rome had steadily encroached on the frontier of the Persian Empire, more especially by building a great fortress at Dara or Daras, on the southern slopes of Mons Masius, within a day's march of Nisibis. Kobad despatched an embassy to complain of this violation of the treaty, but obtained little satisfaction from Anastasius. The latter died in A.D. 518, and was succeeded by Justin, the Captain of the Guard, who continued the Roman policy of aggression. He made an alliance against Persia with a king of the Huns who dwelt north of the Caucasus, and also accepted the allegiance of a prince of Lazica, a state which Kobad held to be a Persian dependency. War was not declared immediately, and we read that about A.D. 520 Kobad proposed that Justin should adopt his favourite son, Chosroes, who, although not the eldest, was destined to succeed him, and to reign as the illustrious Noshirwan. Kobad probably hoped that just as Theodosius had benefited by the guardianship of Yezdigird, so his own favourite son would benefit by the proposed arrangement and be accepted with greater readiness as Great King. Justin, however, declined.

Consequently when Iberia was invaded and a Persian force entered Lazica, Rome, in A.D. 526, invaded Persian Armenia, the renowned Belisarius holding a command in the expedition. This campaign ended in defeat for the Romans, who were also unsuccessful in Mesopotamia. Next year little was attempted on either side ; and in A.D. 528

the Romans, now under the command of Belisarius, were again defeated. The Emperor Justinian, realizing that the forces at the disposal of Belisarius had been too weak, appointed him " General of the East " and organized a powerful force of 25,000 men, including many Massagetae. The Persian General, Firuz the Mihran, advanced on Dara, and it is interesting to be able to read, after the lapse of many centuries, the correspondence which passed between the two commanders. Both appealed to heaven to aid the right, and Firuz with true Persian arrogance closed the final letter with the demand that a bath and breakfast should be prepared for him inside the walls of Dara.[1]

The Roman army, acting on the defensive, occupied a carefully prepared position, protected in front by a deep ditch. Firuz, whose numbers were double those of Belisarius, began the battle with storms of arrows, his army being superior in archery. But apparently there was no adequate reserve of arrows, and a hand-to-hand contest followed, in which the Roman left, hard pressed, was saved by a charge of Massagetae cavalry. Immediately afterwards the " Immortals " broke the ranks of the legionaries on the Roman right, where Firuz had delivered his main attack. The battle appeared to be won, but again the cavalry of the Massagetae charged, and cut the Persian pursuing column into two. This decided the hard-fought day. The Persian losses were severe, but there was no pursuit, Belisarius being content with the repulse of the enemy.

This battle is of considerable interest as showing how the Roman legions had deteriorated and how the Persian forces had improved. In no previous battle which is recorded do the Persians fight hand to hand with such discipline and organization ; and, but for the brilliant cavalry charges of the Massagetae, Rome, although fighting with every advantage of situation, and in the manner which best suited the legionaries, would have been defeated. It is, of course, possible that, had the battle been fought out on the lines of envelopment by mounted archers adopted at Carrhae, the Roman army would have been overwhelmed without a close encounter ; and it must be remembered that the Persian army was double that of Rome.

In Armenia, too, the Roman forces defeated the army

---

[1] *Vide The Seventh Monarchy*, p. 369, where the letters are given in full.

of Kobad in two battles, and thus the season closed disastrously for the Great King, who was now too old to direct his armies in person. The year 529 was important only for the raid of the savage Saracen Mundhir, of Hira,[1] who ravaged Syria up to Antioch, and whose bloody sacrifice of 400 nuns to the goddess Al-Uzza, the planet Venus, must have sent a thrill of horror throughout Christendom.

In A.D. 531, after negotiations which led to nothing, an attempt was made to invade Syria, in alliance with the Saracens under Mundhir. Information, however, reached the watchful Belisarius, who by dint of forced marches was able to interpose his army between the invaders and Antioch. Foiled in its main object, the Persian army retreated, and Belisarius, whose ranks were filled with Isaurians, Lycaonians, and Arabs, decided to permit their retreat unmolested. His men, however, clamoured to be allowed to pursue, with the result that a battle fought close to Callinicus nearly ended in a Roman disaster, the Isaurians and Lycaonians fleeing panic-stricken from the field, and leaving the Roman right wing exposed. By masterly tactics Belisarius changed his position and fought with his back to the Euphrates until evening, when the Persians drew off, and he was able to transport his army across the river. This was the last battle of the war, and the death of Kobad caused the withdrawal of the Persian army.

The Importance of the Reign of Kobad.—If we count the years of the usurpation of Zamasp as falling within the reign of Kobad, that monarch ruled for over forty years. Although perhaps he cannot compare with the greatest member of his dynasty, it is evident that his military capacity was high. It is surmised that his deposition was due to his determination to restore the power of the throne, and his ultimate success proves that his political acumen was as great as his military prowess. To his credit must be placed the final defeat of the White Huns, and, if details of the ten years spent in campaigns against these formidable nomads—who, it must be remembered, had defeated and killed Firuz and placed Persia under tribute—were forthcoming, it is probable that Kobad's record would be even more honourable than it is. According to Tabari, he founded more cities than any other

---

[1] The rise of this state is narrated in *A Literary History of the Arabs*, by R. A. Nicholson, p. 38 ff. *Vide* also Chapters XLII. and XLIV. of the present work.

monarch, the best known in Persia being Kazerun, situated between Bushire and Shiraz, not far from Shapur. He also founded Ganja in the Caucasus, now called Elizabetpol.

At his death, notwithstanding the failure of his last campaign, the prestige and power of Iran were very high, and he left behind him an army trained to fight both White Huns and Romans, a splendid body of seasoned veterans.

The Connexion between China and Persia under the Sasanian Dynasty.—The disappearance of the Arsacid [1] and birth of the Sasanian dynasty was not known in China. But for the first time we find mention in Chinese records of a state called Po-sz or Persia.

To take up the thread of Chinese history at the point where it was dropped in Chapter XXXIV., dynastic convulsions had caused all intercourse with Persia to cease for more than two hundred years, until in the middle of the fifth century the reigning member of the Toba Wei dynasty, which ruled Northern China from A.D. 386 to 584, despatched an envoy to Po-sz. The Persian monarch sent a return mission with gifts of tame elephants, which was detained by the people of Khotan, but was finally released. In all, some ten missions passed between Persia and the Northern China dynasty between A.D. 455 and 513. The description given by the Chinese is of considerable value and merits free quotation. It runs : " Po-sz state has its capital at Suh-li (Ctesiphon) . . . with over 100,000 households. The land is fairly level and produces gold, silver, coral, amber, very fine pearls, vitreous ware and glass ; crystals, diamonds, iron, copper, cinnabar, mercury ; damask, embroidery, cotton, carpeting and tapestry. . . . The climate is very hot, and families keep ice in their houses. The land is stony sand for the great part, and for irrigation purposes water has to be conducted. Their five cereals, birds, beasts, etc., are pretty much as in China. . . . The land produces famous horses, large asses, and camels. . . . Then they produce white elephants, lions, and great bird eggs ; there is a bird shaped like a camel,[2] having two wings which enable it to fly along but not to rise. It eats grass and flesh, and can also swallow fire."

---

[1] It is interesting to note that a group of petty states in the Lower Oxus region retained the name of An-Sih or Parthia late into the sixth century.

[2] It is interesting to know that in modern Persian the ostrich is termed the " camel-bird." Every Chinese ambassador was especially struck by the ostrich or its eggs.

An account of the King sitting on a gold lion throne with his splendid crown, and a description of the national dress and of the custom of succession are given. Even the titles of the Court are mentioned, the *Moh-u-tan* being evidently the *Mobeds*, and the *Sipahbud* or Commander-in-Chief being disguised under the form of *Sieh-po-puh*. Special reference is made to the marriage of brother and sister, which is reprobated, to the exposure of the dead, and even to the class which to the present day is kept apart and looked upon as unclean by the Zoroastrians on account of its bearing corpses to the *dakma* or tower of exposure.

Apart from this most valuable general description of Persia, as seen through Chinese eyes, we have the following account of various special embassies : " During the period Shen-Kwei (A.D. 518–520) [1] their state sent envoys to bring up a letter accompanying articles of tribute, which runs : ' The Great Country's Son of Heaven is born of Heaven. We hope that the place where the Sun comes out will always be of the Son of Heaven in Han (land). The Po-sz State King Ku-hwo-tu (Kobad) makes 1000 and 10,000 respectful obeisances.' The Court accepted this approvingly, and from this time onward they often sent to make offerings at Court. In the second year (A.D. 555) their King [2] again sent envoys to offer local articles."

These delightful chronicles hardly require comment, and the more they are examined the more their accuracy is evident, as the pages of this work show. There is nothing of greater interest in history than to find that the description of a country and of a people which has been collected from many various, yet in the main similar, sources is suddenly confirmed from a wholly different quarter.

---

[1] Kobad, as detailed above, sat on the throne of Persia from A.D. 487 to 531. He was also known as Kavad or Kavat, which closely resembles the Chinese form.
[2] The famous Noshirwan was reigning at this time.

NOSHIRWAN THE JUST.

CHAPTER XL

NOSHIRWAN THE JUST

The slave who can be bought and sold is freer than the miser : the former may become free, but the latter never.—From the *Maxims of Noshirwan.*

The Disputed Succession of Noshirwan, A.D. 531.—The story runs that when Kobad was fleeing to the White Huns, he married the daughter of a peasant at Nishapur, who bore him Anushirwan or Noshirwan, termed Chosroes by western writers, and Kisra by the Arabs, who is justly held to be the most illustrious member of the Sasanian dynasty. He was the favourite son of his father, who regarded him as a mascot because it was at Nishapur [1] that he heard of the death of Volagases, and thus he looked upon him as born under a lucky star.

Upon the death of Kobad, Kaoses, the eldest son, assumed the insignia of royalty. But Mebodes, the Grand Vizier, produced the will of Kobad in favour of Noshirwan, who was thereupon proclaimed Great King. There was, however, a strong party which supported Zames, the second son of Kobad, and, as he was blind in one eye and consequently ineligible for the throne, his adherents decided to crown his son and appoint the father to be regent. This conspiracy being discovered, Noshirwan took ruthless action and put to death all his brothers together with their entire male offspring, the son of Zames, by name Kobad, alone escaping.

The Execution of Mazdak and the Massacre of his Followers.—Equally ruthless was the action taken against

---

[1] The late Nasir-u-Din Shah possessed a similar mascot, a Kurdish boy who was not related to him. It is extraordinary to what lengths this superstition is still carried in Persia.

Mazdak, who had escaped the former massacre. He and one hundred thousand of his followers were put to death, and the sect was crushed for the time being by this awful severity. Some centuries later we have the authority of Nizam-ul-Mulk for the statement that the Ismailis were the descendants of the Mazdakites. Masudi states that the title of Noshirwan, or the " New King," was assumed after this massacre of the Mazdakites ; but it is more correctly derived from *Anushak-ruban*, signifying " of Immortal Spirit."

Peace concluded with Rome, A.D. 533.—It is a curious fact that Noshirwan, whose fame rests to a considerable extent on his remarkable military exploits, was eager upon his accession to the throne to make peace with Rome. Probably he did not yet feel secure enough at home to embark on foreign campaigns. Justinian, on his part, desired to be free to face more vital issues in Italy and Africa. Both sides being similarly disposed, terms were easy to arrange, and the war which had dragged on for thirty years was concluded on the following terms : (1) Rome agreed to pay eleven thousand pounds of gold [1] towards the upkeep of Derbent and other fortresses in the Caucasus, which continued to be garrisoned by Persian troops ; (2) Rome was allowed to keep Dara, but not as her headquarters in Mesopotamia ; (3) in Lazica there was to be a restoration on both sides of captured forts ; and (4) Rome and Persia were to be allies for ever.

Roman Successes in Africa and Italy, A.D. 533–539.—Rome gained immensely by the treaty as Justinian, served by the illustrious Belisarius, only required freedom from war in the East to reconquer North Africa and Italy. Indeed the victories that crowned his arms in the six years after the peace were so striking that Chosroes, who at first had contented himself with asking for a share of the spoils, became thoroughly alarmed by the prospect that as soon as the West was subdued, its united forces under Belisarius would overwhelm Persia. His fears were increased by ambassadors whom he received from the Ostrogoths in Italy and from Armenia in A.D. 539, who pointed out that, unless he declared war immediately, while Belisarius was still engaged in Italy, it would be too late. Urged by these weighty reasons, Noshirwan abruptly ended the so-called eternal peace.

---

[1] A sum equivalent to about half a million pounds sterling.

The Capture and Sack of Antioch by Noshirwan, A.D. 540.

Rome was totally unprepared for the invasion of Noshirwan, who, instead of wasting his strength in attacking the fortresses of Mesopotamia, crossed the Euphrates below Circesium, the frontier fortress already referred to in connexion with the expedition of Julian. He treated with pitiless cruelty the first town that he captured in order to strike terror throughout Syria, and marched towards rich Antioch, ravaging the open country and extorting ransoms as he proceeded. Antioch had suffered from a series of earthquakes little more than a decade previously, its fortifications were badly designed and in a broken-down condition, and there was no adequate garrison for its defence. Consequently the capital of Syria with its priceless treasures fell an easy prey to Noshirwan, who, in pursuance of his policy which aimed at inspiring terror, destroyed every house and building that was not ransomed. As was invariably the case under the Parthian and Sasanian Monarchs alike, there was no idea of annexation and administration, but only of raiding and destruction.

Having attained his chief object, the Great King was ready to make peace, and terms were finally agreed upon by which he was to receive (*a*) five thousand pounds of gold as a war indemnity ; and (*b*) five hundred pounds of gold to be paid annually towards the upkeep of the Derbent and other garrisons. Pending ratification of the treaty, Noshirwan visited Seleucia, the port of Antioch, where he bathed in the blue waters of the Mediterranean Sea, and in unconscious imitation of the old Assyrian conquerors erected altars and offered sacrifices. On his return march he extorted contributions from Apamea, Edessa, Dara, and other cities along the northern route, although it would appear that he received notice of the ratification of the treaty at Edessa. As a result of this flagrant breach of faith, Justinian, for whom the entire position of affairs had been changed by the victory of Belisarius in Italy, denounced the recently concluded treaty and threw the entire responsibility for the rupture upon Noshirwan. The Great King, who had certainly shown to little advantage in these proceedings, spent the following winter in building a Grecian city on the model of Antioch in the neighbourhood of Ctesiphon. According to Tabari, so exact was the copy of the original that the Antiochene captives found their way to their new houses without any difficulty !

The Campaigns in Lazica, A.D. 540-557.—Reference has already been made to Lazica, the ancient Colchis, which in A.D. 522 had received Roman protection. As time went by, an irksome commercial monopoly had been imposed by the Roman Governor, who had established himself at the port of Petra. At first there had been no tribute demanded and no question had been raised of admitting a Roman garrison. Consequently the Lazic King felt aggrieved, and in A.D. 540 appealed to the Court of Persia. Noshirwan, on this occasion, displayed considerable imagination, if not insight. He realized that to hold Lazica would impose a heavy drain on his resources ; but he dreamed of the day when he might launch a great fleet on the Black Sea and attack the Roman possessions, if not Constantinople itself, and on this account he agreed to grant his protection to the suppliant King. Giving out that he was summoned to repel an invasion of the Huns in Iberia, he rapidly marched through that country, and before it was possible for Roman reinforcements to arrive he had besieged and captured Petra, with the result that Lazica became for the time being a Persian province and the Persian Empire reached to the Black Sea. As may readily be understood, the yoke of the Great King was soon found to be heavier than that of Rome, more especially as the Lazic nation had been converted to Christianity.

Noshirwan, realizing the hopelessness of holding the country without effecting radical changes, determined to remove the entire population and to fill their place with subjects of his own. In pursuance of this stupendous scheme, he attempted to procure the assassination of the Lazic King Gubazes. The plot, however, failed, and the intended victim appealed to Justinian, who afforded him protection. Thus war again broke out in A.D. 549 and it raged for eight years. Petra was besieged by the Romans, and its garrison was so reduced in numbers that a mine which had been dug would, if used, have resulted in the capture of the place. But the Roman General delayed, hoping for the promise of a specific reward from Justinian, and in the meanwhile a Persian army thirty thousand strong suddenly appeared on the scene and drove off the besiegers. The country being unable to maintain a large force, only five thousand Persians were left to support the garrison, and this field army was completely dispersed with very heavy losses by an allied Roman and Lazic force.

In the following year a decisive action was fought in which Rome gained a complete victory owing to the death of the Persian general, who was shot by an arrow. Petra was then again besieged, and this time, after a memorable defence in which the utmost gallantry was displayed by the heroic Persian garrison, practically every member of which was killed or wounded, the great fortress fell. Yet once more the position changed; for a large Persian force, supported by elephants, appeared on the scene and reduced Lazica, except a few districts to which Rome clung. This was the state of affairs in A.D. 551, when peace was concluded. But inasmuch as both Lazica and the country of the Saracens were excluded from the operation of this peace, it afforded no relief to the sorely-tried Gubazes and his people.

In A.D. 552 the balance of success lay with the Persians, and but for their lack of capacity they would have driven the Romans out of the country. Gubazes had complained to Justinian against the Roman generals, and the latter, in self-defence, had accused the King of meditating treachery. In consequence they received permission to arrest him, and, as he offered resistance, he was killed. Thereupon the Lazi again changed sides; but, as Persia gave no effectual support, in A.D. 555 they made terms with Rome, stipulating that the murderers of their King should be punished and that his brother Tzathes should be appointed to succeed him.

The Persian general, when too late, appeared in the field with a large force and attacked the Roman post of Phasis at the mouth of the river of that name. Being superior in numbers the Persians would probably have stormed the weak wooden defences; but the Roman general with much astuteness spread a rumour of the impending arrival of an army from Byzantium, which caused the Persian Commander to divide his forces, so that he was ultimately defeated and driven out of the country. This disaster convinced Noshirwan that his dream of fighting Rome by sea was fantastic, and that Lazica was too distant for him to hold. Moreover, during this period he was engaged in other wars, for which he desired to keep his hands free.

The Second Peace with Rome, A.D. 562.—In A.D. 557 a truce was arranged for a period of five years, and this finally culminated in a peace which was concluded in A.D. 562. In return for withdrawing from Lazica and waiving all claims to it, Noshirwan was guaranteed 30,000 pieces of gold annually. The other articles provided that Christians were not to be persecuted, although forbidden to proselytise ; that Dara was not to be the headquarters of the Prefect of the East ; and that Persia was to undertake the charge of Derbent. Finally the peace was to last for fifty years.

Upon the whole this treaty was favourable to both contracting powers ; for Rome received Lazica though paying a sum of money in return. The other articles were equally fair and reasonable and indicate that both sides were weary of the war. It was, of course, certain that Persian vanity would represent the money as tribute paid by Rome, and Tabari informs us that this was the case : but the great Western Power does not appear to have felt any serious loss of prestige from a payment which secured the possession of a fertile and strategically valuable province.

The Coming of the Turks.—The Turks, the Tu-chueh of the Chinese, derived their descent from the Assena clan of the Huing-nu or Huns.[1] In A.D. 433, owing to the aggression of the third Toba Emperor, five hundred families migrated to the borders of the kingdom of the Jwen-Jwen, where they derived their name of Turk from a hill shaped like a helmet, which is still termed *Durko* in some of the many Turkish dialects. They served the Jwen-Jwen as iron-workers, and gradually became so strong that their chief, Tumen, demanded a princess of the paramount tribe in marriage. The demand was refused, and in the war that ensued the Jwen-Jwen were so utterly defeated that their name is never even heard again.

The Turks first appear in Persian history about the middle of the sixth century, at which period they were organized in two divisions. The Eastern Turks owned the northern districts, from Mongolia to the Ural Mountains, and the Western Turks held sway from the Altai Mountains to the Sir Daria. Tumen, the first *Khakan*, died in A.D. 533, and was succeeded by his son Kolo, whose reign was very short, and

---

[1] *Vide* E. H. Parker's *A Thousand Years of the Tartars*, Bk. IV. ; also *The Heart of Asia*, p. 29.

it was his brother, Mokan Khan, who entered into relations with Noshirwan, in A.D. 554.

The Subjugation of the White Huns.—To return to the White Huns, it would appear that Noshirwan, like Justinian after the first peace, was able to take advantage of the truce and the treaty of peace which followed it to wage the series of campaigns that have placed him on the pinnacle of fame. But, as there are no detailed chronicles to which reference can be made for dates, a general outline only can be given.

The Ephthalites, who had been crushed by Kobad, were again invaded in their own country by Noshirwan, aided by the *Khakan* of the Turks. The Persian arms were entirely successful, the White Hun monarch was slain, and his territories were divided between Noshirwan and his allies. So far as is known, the Oxus was made the boundary once again, and by this agreement Persia recovered historical Balkh. Noshirwan, to seal the treaty, married a daughter of Mokan Khan, and his heir was the offspring of this marriage.

The Campaign against the Khazars.—Of less importance than the campaign against the Ephthalites was the attack on the Khazars. This people, which had already been defeated by Kobad, was attacked by Noshirwan, who ravaged their territory and massacred the wild tribesmen by thousands.

The Arabian Campaign, circa A.D. 576.—About the beginning of the sixth century of our era, the Abyssinians, who were a Christian people, had invaded and taken possession of the Yemen, which became a province of Abyssinia. Under Abraha, a famous warrior, the hold of the conquerors was greatly strengthened and several churches were erected, among other places at Sana. The results of these campaigns were naturally pleasing to Rome, and just as naturally displeasing to Noshirwan, who thirsted for fresh conquests and decided to reduce Arabia and incidentally to drive out the Abyssinians. At his court there happened to be a refugee prince of the old Himyarite stock, who had escaped to Persia and repeatedly urged Noshirwan to add to his laurels by expelling the invader. An expedition was prepared which sailed down the Persian Gulf, doubled Ras-al-Hadd, and, coasting along the southern side of Arabia, reached Aden in safety. There the Himyarites rallied in large numbers to their Prince, the Abyssinians under Masruk, the last member of the Abraha dynasty, were attacked and defeated, and the Himyarite prince was placed on the throne as the Viceroy of Noshirwan. Truly a remarkable expedition when it is realized that the distance from Obolla to Aden was about 2000 miles.

According to Tabari, Noshirwan also despatched an expedition to India which resulted in the gain of some provinces. There does not seem to be any certainty as to such a campaign, but there may well have been an expedition in this direction.

The Campaign with the Turks.—Possibly the occupation of the Trans-Oxus provinces of the Ephthalites increased the power of the Turks so that they became a potential menace to Persia. At any rate we learn that Dizabul, or Silzibulos, in A.D. 567 sent an embassy to the Great King with proposals for an alliance. Noshirwan, in deep perplexity, adopted the foolish course of poisoning the ambassadors and stating that they had died from natural causes! Enraged at this outrage Dizabul despatched an embassy to the Court of Justin, who made a treaty and sent a return embassy in A.D. 569. Meanwhile the Turks invaded Persia, but apparently fled at the approach of a Persian army. Failing to succeed by force of arms, Dizabul sent a second embassy to the Court of Byzantium in A.D. 571, and begged Justin to denounce the peace with Persia, which had run only nine years.

The Third War with Rome, A.D. 572–579.—Curiously enough, Justin broke the peace with Persia for almost exactly similar reasons to those which impelled Noshirwan to invade Syria after his first treaty of peace with Rome. In other words, he was afraid that the rival power was becoming too strong. Furthermore, the Great King was already fully seventy years of age and it was hoped that his powers were failing. But the old lion was still a dangerous antagonist, and no sooner was his kingdom menaced than he took the field in person with a large army, drove off the Roman force which was besieging Nisibis and pursued it to Dara, which he invested. Meanwhile a flying column, six thousand strong, raided Syria, burned the suburbs of Antioch, destroyed Apamea, and after ravaging far and wide rejoined Noshirwan before Dara.

This great fortress was surrounded by lines of circumvallation, its water-supply was diverted, and towards the close of A.D. 573 it surrendered, with the result that the Emperor Justin, overwhelmed by the disaster, abdicated in favour of Count Tiberius. The new Emperor purchased a year's truce at the cost of 45,000 gold pieces, and the time was employed in the recruiting and organization of large forces from the Rhine, the Danube, and the frontier provinces. But the heart of Tiberius failed him, and he purchased an extension of the truce for three years, at the rate of 30,000 gold pieces per annum, with the condition that Armenia was not to benefit by it.

The mountain province was invaded immediately after the conclusion of the partial truce, and Noshirwan speedily subdued Persian Armenia. He then attacked Roman Armenia; but his progress was checked by a partial reverse and the capture of his baggage by a Scythian Chief, Kurs, who was in the service of Rome. Shortly afterwards, the Great King avenged this reverse by surprising a Roman camp by night. He then withdrew for the winter, and the Roman leader took advantage of his absence to plunder Persian Armenia. In A.D. 576 a Roman army suffered a crushing defeat. In the following year there was no important military event, and in A.D. 578 the rival armies devastated far and wide, unopposed by one another. On this occasion Maurice, destined to succeed to the purple, after ravaging Persian Armenia, entered Arzanene and Eastern Mesopotamia. He furthermore despatched a raiding band into Kurdistan, where the aged Noshirwan viewed their ravages from the high mountains of his summer retreat. He fled to Ctesiphon, and there shortly afterwards died.

The Christian Community under Noshirwan.—In Chapter XXXVIII. we saw how the declaration by the Church in Persia affirming the "two natures" in Christ had cut it off from the neighbouring empire, which was monophysitic so far as its Eastern half was concerned. Under Justin, however, there was a return to dyophysitism on the part of the Eastern Roman Empire and a reconciliation with Rome. This might have led to a revival of persecution in Persia, but, fortunately for the Church, Mar Aba the Great, a converted Zoroastrian, was Patriarch, and although Noshirwan, upon the rebellion of his Christian son, Nushishad, threatened to blind Mar Aba and to throw him into a sand pit, the fearless Patriarch was able to clear himself before the Great King, who though severe was just, and sincerely admired him.

The activity of the Persian, or Nestorian, church at this

period was indeed wonderful. By A.D. 540 bishoprics had been founded at Herat and Samarcand. In the following century the first effort for the conversion of China was made. This mission, which was destined to attain considerable success, was so Persian in character that the Nestorian churches it founded were known as "Persian temples." The same religious enterprise was also responsible for the legend of Prester John. India, too, was a scene of fruitful missionary labour, the results of which are still visible.[1]

During the sixth century a Persian bishop, Ivon by name, is said to have visited England. In 1001 his body was miraculously discovered by a ploughman in Huntingdonshire, and a church was dedicated to the saint, who has given its name to St. Ives.[2] This is, I believe, the earliest recorded connexion between Iran and England. About the same time a certain Hormisdas, or "The Gift of Hormuz," was elected Pope, and there is little doubt that this constitutes an early link between Persia and Europe.

The Character and Achievements of Noshirwan.—Noshirwan "the Just" is undoubtedly the most illustrious figure in the history of Iran, so far as it is known to the Persians, who, as already stated, are profoundly ignorant of the achievements of Cyrus the Great, of Darius, or indeed of any ruler of their country before the Sasanian dynasty. His character appears to have been a mixture of strength and justice; and this is what appeals to the Oriental, who despises kindliness in his ruler, if unaccompanied by strength and capacity. His achievements, which are referred to in detail in the following chapter, included the organization of a carefully graded land-tax in money, accompanied by a regular annual assessment of the crops. He also created a regular standing army with fixed pay, and he checked the abuse which stills prevails in Persia, albeit in a decreasing degree, of the drawing of pensions and salaries for non-existent men. His fostering care of agriculture, which included the reclamation of waste lands by grants of seeds, implements, and beasts, was constant throughout his reign, and, realizing that there was a need for a larger population, he insisted that every man and woman should marry and work. Both mendicancy and idleness were punishable offences under this strenuous monarch.

---

[1] *Dawn of Modern Geography*, vol. i. pp. 211-223.
[2] *Words and Places*, by Isaac Taylor, p. 231.

NOSHIRWAN THE JUST

He realized also the importance of communications, from neglect of which so many empires have decayed and perished. He maintained the safety of the roads, and encouraged travellers to visit Persia, showing his guests much hospitality and liberality. Among them were seven Greek Neo-Platonist philosophers whom Justinian expelled, and Browne believes that the importance of their visit, in its influence on the later mysticism of the Persians, was considerable.

The devotion to knowledge of this many-sided ruler was equally pronounced. Aristotle and Plato he read in a Persian translation, which was made by his orders. He instituted a university at Gundisapur, where medicine was specially studied, while philosophy and other branches of literature were not neglected. The edicts of Ardeshir were republished during this reign and declared to be the supreme law of the land. A *Khudhay-Namak*, or " Book of the Kings," giving all the known history and legend of Persia, was also written, and it was mainly on this work that the famous epic of Firdausi was based. Even from distant India were brought the works of Pilpay, the literary precursor of Aesop's fables, and from the same land the game of chess [1] was introduced, and indigo. It is also to be recollected that it was two enterprising Persian monks who brought silkworm " seed," as it is termed to-day, from still more distant Khotan. Indeed, at this period, Persia was the central mart for the exchange of ideas between the East and West.

Many are the stories of this monarch, and among them Masudi gives the following :

" The Ambassador of the Roman Emperor was shown and admired the magnificence of the palace of Noshirwan. But having observed that the square in front of it was irregular in shape, he inquired the reason and was informed that an old woman owned the adjacent land, which she refused to sell at any price, and that the King would not take it by force. The Ambassador exclaimed, ' This irregularity is more beautiful than the most perfect square.' " Many of Noshirwan's maxims have been preserved. One of them is to the effect that the most precious treasure and the most useful in time of need is a benefit conferred on a generous

---

[1] The Indian game was termed *chatranga*, or " four ranks." When adopted by the Persians it was misnamed *shatranj* and connected with the word " Shah " by the loyal sons of Iran. Our word " chess " is derived from the Persian form, through the French *échecs*.

man. Another runs, "The days of good fortune flee in the twinkling of an eye, but the days of ill fortune appear to last for months."

Mention has been made of the dazzling victories of this illustrious monarch, and when beside them we place his equally splendid achievements in other spheres of action, his justice, his capacity for organization, his wide-minded toleration and his sagacity, the impression produced is of a character of surpassing grandeur, which is rightly cherished by all true sons of Iran.

Buzurgmihr.—No account of Noshirwan would be complete without a reference to his celebrated Vizier, Buzurgmihr. This remarkable man first attracted the royal notice when acting as tutor to his son Hormuz, who at first resented the tutor's zeal, but finally showed him intense respect and affection. Buzurgmihr was soon made Vizier, and many of Noshirwan's reforms may be attributed to his signal capacity. The introduction of chess is also believed to have been due to his influence.

In the famous stories of the East, it is told how there was once a conference of philosophers in the presence of Noshirwan and the question of what constituted the greatest unhappiness was discussed. A Greek philosopher gave as his view an imbecile old age with poverty; and an Indian colleague disease of the body added to cares of the mind. Buzurgmihr said, "For my part I hold that extreme misery is for a man to see the end of his life approaching without having practised virtue." This reply won over the foreign philosophers to the views of the great Vizier, who exercised enormous influence during the reign of Noshirwan and of his successor. According to general belief he was put to death by Khusru Parviz on account of his belief in the doctrines of Christianity.

KING TRAMPLING A FALLEN FOEMAN.
(Sasanian Gem in British Museum.)

CHAPTER XLI

ORGANIZATION, LANGUAGE, AND ARCHITECTURE UNDER THE SASANIAN DYNASTY

There is a great ymage on horsbacke, seemyng to be of a boysterouse man : who they saie was SAMPSON ; about the which arr many other ymages apparailed of the frenche facon, with longe heares, and all those ymages arr of halfe relieuo —JOSAFA BARBARO, on the Sasanian Rock Sculptures.

The Administration of the Sasanian Empire.—Few pages are more interesting than those in which Tabari [1] describes the reorganization of the administration by Noshirwan ; and his exposition of the principles on which the Great King acted is corroborated by Masudi. As the system was adopted by succeeding monarchs, and indeed by the Caliphs, I propose to describe it in some detail.

Upon his succession to the throne, Noshirwan, finding that Persia was suffering from tyranny, injustice, corruption, insecurity, fanaticism, and crime, set himself with an iron will to the task of carrying out reforms which would combat these great evils. His first step was to form four great satrapies : (*a*) the East comprising Khorasan and Kerman ; (*b*) the West including Irak and Mesopotamia ; (*c*) the North including Armenia and Azerbaijan ; and (*d*) the South including Fars and Khuzistan. This somewhat dangerous innovation, which gave immense power to four governors, was safeguarded by

[1] Vol. ii. pp. 222-232. I have also consulted *L'Empire des Sassanides*, by A. Christensen.

the prestige and personal activity of the Great King and by a service of spies which was ubiquitous.

The Land Tax.—Of far greater importance than this division of the empire was his financial settlement. The custom, dating possibly from Achaemenian times, had been that the state received a proportion of the produce fixed according to the richness of the soil, and ranging from one-tenth to as much as one-half. This system of taxation, which was made more onerous by the exactions of the officials, not only discouraged the cultivator from increasing his output, but also caused much waste, since the crops could not be reaped or the fruit collected until the tax-collector was ready to take the share due to the state.[1]

Noshirwan, with keen insight, substituted a payment in money and in kind, each measure of ground being taxed at a *dirhem*[2] and one fixed measure of the produce. These payments, which applied only to the sown land, were never increased, and in consequence the cultivator was free to work for his own benefit, sure of reaping what he sowed. It is stated that an annual survey was made of all the land under cultivation. This is difficult to believe because of the enormous staff the work would have required ; but it is certain that there was a remarkable advance in efficiency. In addition to the land tax, there was an assessment on fruit trees, a tax on property, and a poll tax. Payment of these taxes was made in three instalments, at intervals of four months, and to prevent oppression the Magians were allowed to act as inspectors.

Improvements in Irrigation and Communications.—Apart from these special reforms, Noshirwan was constantly improving the water supply, on which then, as now, most of the crops depended, by the construction of dams and in other ways. He promoted the growth of population by dowering the poor and by importing bodies of captives. Of equal importance was his care for communications of every kind. The chief arteries of commerce were guarded, and ample provision was made for the repair of bridges and the upkeep of the roads. To the European traveller in Persia of to-day

---

[1] Tabari, ii. p. 152, tells an interesting story of how Kobad saw a child beaten by its mother for picking a bunch of grapes, which she took from it and tied on to the vine. The woman, in reply to the monarch's inquiry, explained that the King's share had not been collected, and that, consequently, they dared not touch their vir es. The peasants were *adscripti glebae* with obligation to perform labour.

[2] A *dirhem* was worth about 7d.

nothing is more striking than the utter neglect of roads and bridges, and it is sad to think that the inhabitants are content to have it so. In the administration of justice, although Noshirwan was pitiless when necessary, perhaps for the first time in the history of the country severity was tempered with mercy, more especially in the case of the young.

These reforms, it may be objected, depended on the prestige and incessant vigilance of one man ; and to a certain extent this is true. It is, however, equally true that a great man, especially if spared to rule for a long period, stamps an administration with his personality. Not only would the cultivators be less ready to tolerate extortion after enjoying the blessings of justice for more than a generation, but the tax-collectors themselves must have been more efficient and less rapacious than in the days which preceded these far-reaching reforms.

The Army.—In no respect is there a greater contrast between the Parthian and Sasanian dynasties than in the composition of their armed forces. Under the Parthians light horsemen carrying nothing but the bow constituted the principal arm, heavy cavalry being but few in number and rarely playing a decisive rôle ; the infantry, as in modern Persia, scarcely counted. Under the Sasanians victory or defeat depended on the splendid cavalry. It was heavily armed, like the knights of mediaeval Europe, the supply of light cavalry being left to somewhat despised allies such as the Saracens. The Persian cavalry soldier, as we see him on the bas-reliefs, wore a helmet and a coat of mail, and was further protected by a round shield. His weapons included a heavy lance, a sword, a mace, and a bow and arrows. The horse, too, was so much protected by armour that the dray-like chargers of the bas-reliefs were as necessary as was the similar horse of the mediaeval European knight, whose descendant draws the brewer's cart in modern England. The archers, like the English bowmen of the Middle Ages, formed the most important part of the infantry, being trained to shoot with great accuracy and rapidity from behind the wattled shields which the Achaemenians had adopted from the Assyrians, and which had remained ever since as an article of equipment in the Persian army. The rest of the infantry, whose function was to support the archers, was armed with spears and swords, but wore little defensive armour. As the accounts of the campaigns show, these armies were able to fight Roman legionaries on equal terms, whereas the Parthians almost invariably avoided a hand-to-hand contest.

As described in Chapter XXII., it was at Arbela that elephants first appeared in a recorded battle, but no mention is made of the part they played. From that time forward their importance was considerable, although they were neglected by the Parthians. They were taken even to remote Lazica by the Sasanian troops, and, as will appear later, the elephant corps rendered signal service against the Arabs.

The Sasanian empire furthermore showed its superiority to the earlier dynasty by studying the art of besieging cities and by developing siege trains. Against the Parthians a fortified city was practically impregnable, whereas the Sasanian monarchs, especially in the later period, captured almost every fortress of importance which they invested. The usual method was to advance by means of trenches and under the protection of wattled shields to the ditch, which was filled up with fascines and earth. Battering rams and other engines were then brought up, and when a breach was effected an assault was delivered. Or a mound was erected on which *balistae* were planted, and the enemy was driven from his defences. There is, of course, no reason to suppose that the Sasanians excelled the Romans, who were their teachers, in the art of besieging cities; but they were enormously in advance of the Parthians in everything that belonged to the scientific side of war.

In Noshirwan's army no money was paid except to efficient men who were completely armed, and, if members of a cavalry corps, properly mounted. There is a typical story that when the Great King appointed a Paymaster-General with full authority, that official would not exercise his functions until Noshirwan himself appeared on parade to draw his pay. The Great King duly rode on to the ground, was carefully inspected, and, being found to be short of the two extra bowstrings which formed part of a mounted officer's equipment, was directed to go to the palace and return fully equipped. To his credit, Noshirwan obeyed, and upon being finally passed was given his pay, fixed at four thousand and one *dirhems*, or £112, which was the highest salary permissible.

It appears that the great monarch reverted to Ardeshir's

policy of a regular standing army, as against the old system of feudal levies.

The Monarch and his Court.—The Sasanian monarch lived in a court whose splendour and luxury were unsurpassed by that of any dynasty in the world's history, in which connexion Diocletian wore robes copied from those of the Sasanian monarch and the rules of procedure at his court were taken from the same source. The bas-reliefs have preserved for us a faithful representation of the splendid armour, the rich embroideries, and the superb horse trappings affected by the Great King. His surroundings were gorgeous, and conspicuous among his treasures was the royal " Paradise " carpet, 70 cubits long and 60 broad. To quote Muir, " it represented a garden, the ground wrought in gold, and the walks in silver ; meadows of emeralds, and rivulets of pearls ; trees, flowers, and fruits of sparkling diamonds, rubies, and other precious stones." This unsurpassed carpet, the great golden throne with its ruby supports, and the priceless crown which had to be suspended owing to its great weight, have struck the imagination of mankind.

Stately too were the ceremonies, in which the king sat remote on his throne behind curtains, not even the highest of the nobles being allowed to approach his person unless specially summoned. Masudi tells us that there were three great divisions at Court. The Knights and Princes stood thirty feet from the curtain on the right of the throne. A similar distance farther back were marshalled the Governors and tributary kings who resided at Court ; and, finally, the buffoons, singers, and musicians formed a third division. Guards were probably stationed on the left of the throne. When the King gave permission for a subject to approach he tied a handkerchief over his mouth to prevent his breath polluting the " Sacred Presence " and, passing behind the curtain, fell prostrate until bidden to rise.

In some respects the position of women was good, for as a rule they were not secluded. Khusru Parviz, however, kept perhaps the largest harem ever recorded, Tabari giving the number of its occupants as 12,000 ! At the same time he was devotedly attached to Shirin. As was customary in the Achaemenian dynasty, there was one chief wife, who was generally of the blood royal, though this rule was by no means invariably observed. The number of his women must have ruined many of the weaker monarchs, and it was a terrible drain on the resources of the Empire.

The chief pastime of the Great King was the chase, in which the quarry was usually collected into "paradises," or else a large district was beaten and the game driven within a netted inclosure. Hawking also was a sport of great antiquity, and a Chief Falconer was among the great officers at the Sasanian Court.

The game of polo was played by the Sasanian monarchs, and we read in the Pahlavi history already mentioned, that the founder of the dynasty was sent for to the court of Ardawan, where he accompanied the King's sons both to the chase and to the polo ground. This is the earliest historical reference to polo, so far as I know. The recognition of Shapur I. when tested at this game has been already narrated.

Among the later monarchs, not only Khusru Parviz, but even Shirin and her ladies, played polo, as the following lines from Nizami prove :

> When he (Khusru) reached the polo ground,
> The fairy-faced ones curvetted on their steeds with joy.
> They started play, when every Moon
> Appeared a Sun, and every partridge a hawk.
> . . . .
> At times the Sun bore off the ball, at times the Moon.
> Now Shirin won and now the Shah.

Of indoor games chess has already been referred to. Music was evidently held in high esteem, as the bas-reliefs show ; and even while shooting the Great King kept his orchestra close at hand to celebrate his prowess. Probably the music which is still played in the chief cities of Persia to greet the rising and the setting sun dates back to this period.[1]

The Pahlavi Language.—The question of the languages in use during the Sasanian period is somewhat complicated and obscure. An extensive literature, estimated by West [2] to be equal in bulk to the Old Testament, has come down to us in Pahlavi.[3] This term applies rather to the script than to

---

[1] *The Glory of the Shia World*, pp. 86, 87.

[2] *Extent, Language, and Age of Pahlavi Literature*, p. 402. Browne also deals briefly with this question in *A Literary History of Persia*. I would here acknowledge my considerable indebtedness to Professor Browne's works.

[3] It is desirable to explain the exact signification of various terms. The word "Pahlavi" means "Parthian," from Parthava, the form in which that proper name appears on the Behistun inscriptions. By Persians it is vaguely used to denote archaic Persian, whereas in European writers it signifies the Persian of the Sasanian period. *Huzvarish* is the term which

the language, but it is generally employed to denote the official language of Persia under the Sasanian dynasty. Its earliest use has been traced back to the fourth century B.C., and the latest work written in it dates from the ninth century A.D. But during the latter half of its existence the use of Pahlavi was confined to the copying of works already written in that language. An amazing peculiarity of the language is that what was read was entirely different from what was written. For instance, for the title "King of Kings" the Aramaic *Malkan-Malka* was *written*, whereas *Shahan-Shah* was *read*. Other common examples are *lahma*, written for bread, whereas *nan* was read, and so forth. Such a procedure was not unnatural to people whose scripts were composed entirely of ideograms and symbols,[1] or rather, who always continued to treat these groups of letters as ideograms. Browne, moreover, aptly points out that in the *siyák*, or "numbers," used for accounts at the present day throughout Persia, abbreviated and mutilated forms of the Arabic names for the different numbers are employed.

In Chapter IX. I have dealt briefly with the Avesta, which was written in a special language termed Avestic, and had been neglected until the establishment of the Sasanian dynasty, when it was carefully collected and compiled by Ardeshir. Here, again, it was in a great measure owing to the explanations in Pahlavi that the study of the Zoroastrian scriptures became practicable. Until comparatively recently the Zoroastrian scriptures were termed the Zend-Avesta in Europe; but it is now understood that Zend is the "explanation" of the old text in Pahlavi: Pazend, a term which is also used, is a "re-explanation." It may be asked what is the relation between modern Persian and Pahlavi. The reply is that Pahlavi is archaic Persian as it was spoken before the introduction of Arabic, and, if read out to the educated inhabitant of modern Persia, by which means the *Huzvarish* element disappears, it would be found to be intelligible to some extent.

Pahlavi Rock Inscriptions. — The Pahlavi inscriptions chiselled on the rocks, many of which have been deciphered,

---

includes the Aramaic words appearing in Pahlavi texts. So numerous are these that "the verbal terminations, the suffixed pronouns, and the construction of the sentence" are frequently the only Persian part of the text.

[1] Persian servants who cannot write frequently keep their accounts by drawing a lamb, a fowl, a duck, or grains of rice in their account books.

possess considerable historical importance. That at the
Naksh-i-Rajab dates from the reign of Ardeshir.[1] It is written
in two forms of Pahlavi and accompanied by a Greek translation. At the end of the eighteenth century de Sacy made a
successful attempt to translate it with the aid of this ; but,
in spite of this brilliant success and the labours of devoted
workers in the field, much still remains to be accomplished for
the elucidation of these old-time records.

Pahlavi Literature.—West divides Pahlavi literature into
three divisions, as follows : .
(*a*) Pahlavi translations of Avesta texts ;
(*b*) Pahlavi texts on religious subjects ; and
(*c*) Pahlavi texts on non-religious subjects.

Division (*a*) includes twenty-seven works ; but, as West
points out, they cannot be regarded as specimens of Pahlavi
literature, " because the Parsi translators have been fettered
by the Avesta arrangement of the words."

Division (*b*) is represented by fifty-five works, containing
half a million words. Much literature of value is included
in this class, the *Dinkart*, or " Acts of Religion," and the
Bundahishn, or " Ground Giving," being especially important.
Other works are given by West, besides numerous sayings,
commentaries, and traditions.

In the last division there are only eleven works. Oldest
of these is the *Yatkar-i-Zariran*, a Pahlavi romance, written
about A.D. 500. This story, as Browne points out, " assumes
throughout a certain acquaintance with the whole epic cycle."
It treats of only one episode in the National Epic, but the
essential features of the legend are the same in the original,
in Tabari, and in the *Shahnama* ; and this fact is of great
importance. Of still greater value is the Pahlavi *Karnamak-i-
Artakhshatr-i-Papakan*, or " The Deeds of Ardeshir Papakan,"
which has been translated into German by Nöldeke. It was
written about A.D. 600, and a comparison with the *Shahnama*
again shows how carefully Firdausi followed his Sasanian
authorities. Other works include treatises on the wonders
of Sistan and on the game of chess. No poems have come
down to us from Sasanian times.

The Models of the Sasanian Architects.—Little remains
of the architecture and art of the preceding Parthian dynasty,
and it is impossible to praise what there is. The Sasanian

---

[1] It is given as a heading to Chapter XXXVI.

kings indeed inherited the glorious monuments of the Archaemenians in a very different condition from that in which we see them to-day, but it was to Ctesiphon and Hatra that they turned to find a model for their needs. In this connexion it is to be remembered that the seat of Persian power was not in Persia proper but rather in the Tigris and Euphrates valley, and that Ctesiphon, inherited from the Parthians, was the real capital.

The Main Features of Sasanian Architecture.—The older Sasanian palaces, some of the best known of which I propose to describe very briefly, are practically all built on one plan, which is extremely simple.

The buildings, which were oblong rectangles, generally lay East and West, with a superb Porch or Arch in the exact centre as its culminating feature, and this feature is still retained in Persian ecclesiastical and domestic architecture. A second feature was the number of square rooms, vaulted with domes and opening one into another. A court was an invariable feature, as in modern Persia, and nowhere was there a second storey. The decoration was carried out by means of arched recesses, cornices, and pilasters, much as at Hatra. Internally stucco and painting were employed.

The Firuzabad Palace.—To the south-east of Shiraz on one of the two routes leading to Bushire was situated Jur, now Firuzabad, the earliest existing Sasanian palace, which is believed to date from the middle of the third century A.D. The ground plan is an oblong measuring 320 feet by 170 feet with a single entrance consisting of a fine arch, opening into a vaulted hall 90 feet long by 43 feet wide. On either side of this noble feature are lesser halls similar in character. Beyond these principal chambers were three square rooms surmounted by elliptical brick domes, which are the earliest extant example of the dome [1] in Persia. These apartments, with their ornamented doorways and false windows, led into small rooms opening on to a large court some ninety feet square, round which were built rooms of various sizes. The external ornamentation consisted of high narrow arches and reed-like pilasters which gave a simple and decidedly severe character to the whole pile, not, however, out of keeping

---

[1] "The History and Evolution of the Dome in Persia," by K. A. C. Creswell (*Journal R.A.S.*, July 1914). It is now generally accepted that Firuzabad is older than Sarvistan, although at one time the contrary opinion prevailed.

with its fortified character. Not far from Firuzabad is Sarvistan, another palace of a somewhat later date, which, however, bears a close relationship to the older palace.

The Tak-i-Kisra.—The famous " Arch of Khusru "[1] which moved the wonder of the Arabs so deeply, as will be seen in Chapter XLII., is unfortunately now but a fragment of the superb vaulted hall spanning 25.80 metres, in which the Great King, seated on his golden throne, showed himself to his subjects. Even in its decay this vast Audience Hall has excited the admiration of generations of travellers journeying up the Tigris to Baghdad. Ornamentation was given to the façade by dividing it up by means of string-courses and pilasters, and, as may be seen from the illustration, the result was most effective. No sufficient indications are left to enable us to trace the ground plan of this magnificent palace, the supreme architectural effort of Noshirwan, but there is little doubt that it was arranged on the lines of the palaces already described. Its ruin is used by Khakani to serve as a warning, in the lines :

> Know, O heart ! Behold the warning !
> Look from thy eyes and see in the
> *Aywan* of Madain,[2] the mirror of warning.
> At once by way of the Dijla, take up thy abode at Madain :
> And from thy eyes start a second
> Dijla on the soil of Madain.

The Palace of Khusru at Kasr-i-Shirin.—Firuzabad and Sarvistan were comparatively small, and were not designed to accommodate large retinues, but we now turn to a palace of a different type. At Kasr-i-Shirin, on the western slopes of the Zagros, the *Imarat-i-Khusru*, or " Palace of Khusru," dating from early in the seventh century, is set in a park 6000 metres in circumference, of which the walls, rising in places to 6½ metres, can still be traced. Only the roots of date-palms and of pomegranates are now visible in this vast pleasaunce ; but the Arab writers have detailed the beauty of the gardens and the number of rare animals which wandered about the park in perfect freedom.

The magnificent palace, in front of which glittered an

---

[1] It is termed the *Aywan* or *Tak-i-Kisra*, the former being the older form. The meaning of both words is the same.

[2] Madain, or " The Cities," was the name by which the Arabs designed Ctesiphon. According to tradition it was founded by the fusion of seven towns. The Dijla is the Tigris.

artificial sheet of water, lay east and west; its length was 342 metres and its greatest width 187 metres. To the east there was a double ramp rising to a terrace 99 metres in width, supported by vaulted chambers, three of which formed an entrance to a long corridor on to which many rooms opened. The main entrance was by the ramp and across the terrace to a second incline adorned by twenty-four columns, which led to the apartments of the Great King. The first immense hall was divided into three aisles and led to a square chamber. Then other chambers were entered, and a colonnade looked on to a central court. The royal chambers (as at Persepolis) had wooden roofs, and the other rooms were generally vaulted. The material employed is much inferior to the dressed limestone of the Achaemenian architects and consisted of boulders embedded in plaster, materials which both abounded in the neighbourhood. The columns were composed of bricks cut to shape and plastered, and here again there is a marked contrast to the magnificence of the Achaemenians.

The Palace at Mashita.—The palace at Mashita was also built by Khusru Parviz early in the seventh century. Erected on a smaller scale than the *Imarat-i-Khusru*, it has ornamentation of surpassing richness, the hard stone being divided up into triangles in which are carved rosettes, surrounded by an artistic tracery of foliage and fruits, among which animals of many kinds may be recognized. Indeed it is believed that nowhere within the limits of the Persian Empire was there ever such sumptuous and elaborate decoration as that lavished by foolish Khusru Parviz on a palace situated far from Iran, which he was not destined to enjoy for more than a few years.

The Bas-Reliefs at Naksh-i-Rustam.—By far the most famous and typical examples of Sasanian art are the bas-reliefs at *Naksh-i-Rustam*, or "Figure of Rustam," as they are termed, other and similar interesting examples of which are to be found at Shapur and elsewhere. In Chapter XV. I have referred to the tombs of the mighty Achaemenian sovereigns which were cut in the face of a cliff, and it is below these that the Sasanian monarchs with considerable appropriateness have engraved the record of their triumphs. Before describing the figures which stand out so grandly as one approaches the artificially-scarped cliff, it is of some interest to note that, as in the case of the rock sculptures of Behistun, their true character has been proved only within the last hundred years. Persians for many centuries have refused to see in the great bearded warriors anything but a representation of Rustam, their matchless champion, and this error is still perpetuated in the term "Figure of Rustam" invariably used by all classes in referring to the bas-reliefs. European travellers have, of course, made mistakes in their accounts, none of which are so quaint as that of Josafa Barbaro, the Venetian traveller of the fifteenth century, whose delightful description forms the heading to this chapter. Even Niebuhr, at the end of the eighteenth century, accepted the Persian identification with Rustam, and it was not until the middle of the nineteenth that the error of attributing half the sculptures to the Parthian dynasty was finally given up.

The bas-reliefs at *Naksh-i-Rustam* are seven in number, of which the fourth or central group is the most important. It commemorates the capture of the Emperor Valerian, the crowning military exploit of the Sasanian dynasty. The description given by Curzon is so masterly that I cannot do better than quote it. He writes: "This panel is $35\frac{1}{2}$ feet long and 16 feet high, its level at the bottom being about 4 feet above the soil. The central figure, of more than human stature, is Shapur, seated on horseback and receiving the homage of the two Romans, the captive Caesar and Cyriadis or Miriades, the obscure fugitive of Antioch, who was elevated by the scorn of the conqueror to the imperial purple. The Sasanian King presents the handsome features so familiar from sculptures and coins, with thick outstanding clusters of curls, and wears the mural crown surmounted by the globe. His well-trained beard is tied in a knot below his chin ; a necklet of large stones or ornaments hangs about his throat ; and behind him in the air, as also from his sword hilt and plaited charger's tail, float the dynastic fillets or frilled ribands. His lower limbs are clad in the flowing *shulwars* of the period; while his left hand grasps his sword hilt, his right is outstretched to meet the uplifted hands of the standing Cyriadis, to whom he appears to be giving the *cydaris* or royal circlet. The Syrian wears the Roman dress, as also does the kneeling Caesar, whose hands are outstretched in mute supplication, and whose face wears an expression of piteous appeal. Valerian also has a chaplet round his head ; and both captives have shackles or fetters round their ankles."

Three of the other tablets represent a spirited equestrian combat. The seventh portrays the investiture of Ardeshir Papakan with the *cydaris* by the god Hormuzd. This bas-relief, which is believed to be the oldest, is somewhat crude, the god and the monarch bestriding horses, represented as standing with their heads touching one another, which are quite disproportionate to their riders. The figure on the right hand of the spectator is the god, who holds a sceptre in his left hand, while with his right he presents the *cydaris* to Ardeshir. The founder of the Sasanian dynasty tramples on a prostrate enemy, probably Ardawan, the last Parthian monarch.

The Hunting Scenes of Khusru Parviz.—We will now turn to the famous Tak-i-Bustan, or " Arch of the Garden," near Kermanshah, which commemorates the reign of Khusru Parviz. The monuments consist of two deep arches cut out in the face of the mountain, the largest measuring over 30 feet in height and 22 in depth. On the surface of the rock the keystone is a crescent, and in the spandrels are winged Victories, probably the work of Greek artists, as is also the carved ornamentation on each side of the grotto. The inner wall is divided into an upper and lower compartment. In the upper Khusru Parviz is represented receiving chaplets from two supporters ; in the lower there is an equestrian figure of the same monarch. The sides of the arch are covered with two bas-reliefs which represent in the one case a stag-hunt and in the other a boar-hunt. In the stag-hunt, the quarry is being driven by elephants into an enclosure formed by nets, where the monarch is apparently shown in various parts of the tablet as arriving, hunting, and returning home. The sport represented is probably that of one of the " Paradises," and its artificial character is emphasized by the presence of musicians. In the boar-hunt the driving is again done by elephants and the monarch shoots the wild boar from a boat. Here again the game has been collected into an enclosure, and musicians are still more apparent, seated in boats. In a corner the pigs are realistically shown in the process of being cleaned and packed on elephants. Altogether, these pieces repay prolonged study.

The Work of the Sasanian Silver-smiths.—This attractive art is represented by three dishes. In the first (p. 434) Bahram Gur is shown as killing a lion with his sword, and in the second (p. 442), Shapur II. is hunting stags. The monarchs can be identified by their head-dresses, which were changed with every reign. The third dish (p. 456) shows a grand hunt, lions, boars, and wild sheep all being graphically reproduced. Technically this art is of interest, owing to the fact that the figure subjects are not cast in one piece with the dish, but made separately by the repoussé process and soldered into their places in the design.

The Statue of Shapur I.—In a cave close to Shapur lies the only Persian statue known to exist, which unhappily has not been spared by the iconoclasts. Originally it was carved out of a single block of stone and was attached to the roof of the cave. Upon entering the huge opening the visitor sees a pedestal 4 feet high, cut out of the living rock, on which the sandalled feet still remain. The statue itself lies behind, in a terribly mutilated condition, but it is possible to recognize the effigy as that of Shapur I., who would with much appropriateness preside over the city which he had founded.

An Impression of Sasanian Architecture and Art.—This brief account, which is supplemented by the illustrations, records what is best in Sasanian art, and it remains to summarize the general impressions it conveys. It has to be remembered that these palaces were constructed with a view to safety and also to keeping the monarch invisible. Within these limitations the architect was called upon to construct a great hall in which the monarch could remain concealed by curtains, but which had to hold thousands of ministers, nobles, guards, and attendants. This great hall alone counted, and it will be conceded, when we take into consideration the climate which favoured a building open at the front, that the Sasanian architects deserve much credit. At any rate, a thousand years later the great mosque at Meshed was built on this model, which is still the only one used in Persia.

Just as in their palaces, so also in their bas-reliefs the Sasanian artists sought their models in the works of their predecessors. But their art showed a great improvement on their models. The figures, more especially that of Shapur I., are noble, dignified presentments, and although the horses may strike the observer as clumsy in the tablets where they are represented as standing still, yet when portrayed at the charge they are full of life and animation. In the hunting scenes life and movement appear in every detail of the pictures, and throughout the sculptures the armour and horse trappings are represented with great fidelity and much artistic taste. Perhaps, as at Persepolis, there is a certain monotony of theme ; yet, in view of the utter weakness of the Parthian models and the low state of art at that period throughout the Near East, it is creditable to the Sasanian dynasty that the awakening of the national spirit produced magnificent palaces and rock-sculptures, which have enriched the art of mankind.

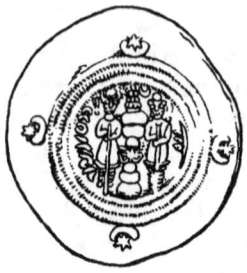

KHUSRU PARVIZ.

CHAPTER XLII

KHUSRU PARVIZ AND HERACLIUS

> At dawn the Lady of the Cycle bare
> A boy with golden head, with yellow hair ;
> That Moon was born at happy fortune's rise ;
> " God aid him," cried the angels from the skies.
> In two weeks Khusru grew to full moon fair ;
> A year, then as the *Night of Power* [1] his hair,
> His cypress on its foot began to stand
> And cooed the pheasant of his meadow land.
> Upon his rose-bud mouth there fell the dew
> And heart-sore for his cheek the tulip grew.
>
> " The Birth of Khusrú Parviz "
> (Trans. of Ahi by Gibbs, *Hist. Ottoman Poetry*, vol. ii. p. 311).

The Continuation of the Roman War by Hormisdas IV.—Hormazd, known as Hormisdas IV. to the Western writers, was the son of Noshirwan by the daughter of the Khan of the Turks, and he succeeded to the throne without opposition. At first he promised to rule in the spirit shown by his great father, but very soon he developed the characteristics of a tyrant. The war with Rome continued its weary and indecisive course, as the new monarch declined to make peace on the condition of exchanging Arzanene, with Aphumon its chief fortress, for Dara, which the Roman Emperors were naturally anxious to regain. Negotiations having fallen through, Maurice sent out raiding parties across the Tigris during the summer of A.D. 579, which met with no organized opposition and were able to destroy the crops and inflict much damage. In A.D. 580 he collected a fleet at Circesium

---

[1] The *Night of Power* is the night on which the koran was sent down from heaven—the evening of the 27th day of Ramazan.

with the apparent intention of following in the footsteps of Julian, especially as he thought that he had won over the Saracens to his side. However, these desert tribesmen proved treacherous, and their chief Adarman with a large force threatened Callinicus, thereby compelling the Byzantine general, whose line of communications was in danger, to forgo his ambitious project and to march against Adarman, whom he defeated. In A.D. 581 Maurice gained a signal victory over a Persian army which was attacking Constantia ; but instead of following up his success he hastened to Constantinople, where the dying Emperor Tiberius appointed him his successor to the purple.

After the departure of Maurice from the seat of war, the Persians upon the whole had the upper hand, although they were once defeated by Philippicus, the brother-in-law of Maurice. Heraclius, father of the future Emperor of the same name, appeared on the scene, but as only one portion of the troops was under his command, he was unable to effect anything of importance. In A.D. 588 there was a serious mutiny in the Roman Army, but a Persian force which drove the invaders out of Arzanene was ultimately beaten near Martyropolis. In the following year this important fortress fell through Roman treachery, and Philippicus, being defeated in his attempt to retake it, was recalled. Comentiolus succeeded to his post, with Heraclius as his second in command, and decided to invade Mesopotamia. In a battle near Nisibis he was worsted and fled ; but Heraclius restored the day, and in the end won a signal victory, killing the Persian general and seizing his camp.

The Invasion and Defeat of the Turks, circa A.D. 588.—While the war in Mesopotamia was being waged year after year in a wholly indecisive manner, Persia was threatened by an invasion of the Turks, who probably saw their opportunity in the unpopularity of Hormisdas and his entanglement in the war with Rome. But Hormisdas possessed a general of remarkable ability in Bahram Chubin, who, contenting himself with a small force of picked veterans, aged about forty, beat the Turks in a battle in which the Great Khan himself was slain. This was followed by a second desperate struggle, in which the Khan's son was made prisoner. The booty captured was enormous, and in the pages of Mirkhond[1] it

[1] Mirkhond, the historian of the fifteenth century, is referred to in Chapter LXI.

is stated that 250,000 camels were required to carry it ! Tabari, who tells in a delightful manner how the Great Khan's war elephants and war lions were compelled to turn tail by flights of arrows and were then covered with fire, which they carried raging into their own ranks, is more moderate and gives only 256 camel loads of gold and precious stones.[1]

The Campaign in Lazica, A.D. 589.—Immediately after the defeat of the Turks, Hormisdas ordered the victorious general to invade Lazica, which was found to be unguarded. A Roman army, however, speedily assembled and Bahram suffered defeat in a battle. The Great King, who was madly jealous of his general, in his folly took advantage of this reverse not only to supersede but to insult Bahram, to whom he sent a distaff, some cotton, and a woman's dress.

The Revolt of Bahram Chubin and the Assassination of Hormisdas.—Stung to the quick by the insult offered to it in the person of its general the army in Lazica revolted, and, being joined by the army of Mesopotamia, marched on Ctesiphon. A force sent by Hormisdas also threw off its allegiance to the tyrant ; and a palace revolution sealed his fate. Deserted by his subjects, he was blinded by his brothers-in-law Bostam and Bindoes and afterwards assassinated.

The Accession of Khusru Parviz, A.D. 590.—His eldest son Chosroes II., known in Persian history as Khusru Parviz or " The Victorious," and venerated as the last famous King of the Sasanian dynasty, was placed on the throne, which it seemed most unlikely that he would occupy for more than a few months.

His Defeat and Flight to Mesopotamia.—Upon his accession Khusru Parviz wrote a letter to Bahram Chubin, in which he pointed out that, as Hormisdas was dead, there was no longer any reason for refusing to return to his allegiance or to accept the second place in the empire. The rebel general sent a most insolent answer, bidding his Sovereign strip off his diadem and come to him to receive the governorship of a province. Khusru, in spite of this unpromising reply, again wrote to remonstrate, but in vain. He marched to meet the rebel army, and again attempted to negotiate, all to no purpose, and being surprised by a night attack he was forced to take refuge in flight. Unable to defend Ctesiphon, he made for the Euphrates, pursued by a force of 4000 men.

[1] Vol. ii. p. 262.

But his uncle Bindoes, by personating the Great King, deceived the pursuing force and drew it after him.[1] Time being gained by this ruse, Khusru, guided by an Arab chief named Iyas, reached Circesium in safety. There he was treated with the utmost kindness and respect by his Roman hosts, and was installed at Hieropolis until the Emperor's orders should be received.

His Restoration by a Roman Army, A.D. 591.—The Emperor Maurice debated for some time what line or policy he should pursue, but finally the illustrious refugee was informed that the Roman Emperor looked upon him as his son and would place an army at his disposal with which to defeat Bahram. In return it was stipulated that Persian Armenia should be ceded to Rome, as also the fortresses of Dara and Martyropolis.

Meanwhile Bahram had seized the throne; but when it was known that Khusru had been promised the support of Rome, his position was undermined by conspiracies and mutinies. In the spring of A.D. 591 Khusru marched to the Tigris, which he crossed after surprising and capturing Bryzacius, Bahram's general. The nose and ears of this unhappy captive were at once cut off, and he was afterwards brought in at a banquet to be mocked by the Great King and his guests. Then, Theophylactus tells us, he was killed as " the crown of all."

Marching down the Tigris, the army of Khusru succeeded in effecting a junction with a force raised in Azerbaijan by his uncles, although Bahram, it might be supposed, should have strained every nerve to prevent this. At the same time a detached force of Roman troops obtained possession of both Seleucia and Ctesiphon, which must have been a serious blow to the pretender.

The first battle between the two forces ended in the breaking of Bahram's centre by the Roman troops. He retreated to the hills, where he repulsed with loss the efforts made by the Great King to pursue him. That night, however, he confessed his weakness by withdrawing to the mountains of Kurdistan, and taking up a position near the famous fortress of Canzaca or Shiz, already mentioned as having been besieged by Antony. Khusru followed up the retreating enemy, and the second great battle was fought after Bahram had received a

---

[1] The story is well told by Tabari, vol. ii. p. 280.

detachment of war elephants and other reinforcements. The contest was stubborn, but in the end decisive. Bahram attempted to break the right wing of the Romans; but it was reinforced by Narses, their skilful general, who finally, as in the earlier battle, broke the centre of the rebel army. Bahram himself escaped [1] along the route followed by the fugitive Darius when fleeing from Alexander the Great, and took refuge with the Turks; while the victorious Khusru marched in triumph to Ctesiphon, where he dismissed his allies with splendid gifts and reascended the throne of his ancestors which was now his by right of conquest.

His position, however, was by no means secure, and conscious that he was disliked by his subjects, he retained a bodyguard of 1000 legionaries. He also attempted to strengthen himself in the estimation of his subjects by punishing all those who were in any way responsible for the death of his father, not sparing even his uncles to whom he owed so much. Furthermore, he was fortunate enough to be able to contrive the assassination of Bahram, whose return to Persia with an army of Turks was a contingency that was always possible and much to be dreaded.

The Outbreak of War with Rome, A.D. 603.—During the reign of Maurice, the relations between the courts of Constantinople and Ctesiphon were most amicable, and when, in A.D. 602, Maurice was murdered, Khusru determined to avenge his benefactor. His task was lightened by the fact that Narses, who had commanded the Roman troops to whom Khusru owed his throne, had refused to recognize Phocas, and held Edessa against him.[2] Everywhere the Persian armies were victorious, and in A.D. 605 the Great King took Dara after a siege lasting nine months. This signal success was followed by the capture of Amida and other fortresses in Eastern Mesopotamia. In A.D. 607 the Persian army captured Harran, Edessa, and other strongholds in Western Mesopotamia, and crossing the Euphrates took Hieropolis, Berhoea—the Aleppo of to-day—and other cities. Simultaneously a second Persian force, after invading Armenia, passed into neighbouring Cappadocia and even ravaged peaceful Phrygia, Galatia, and Bithynia. Indeed the invaders

[1] There is an interesting story of how Bahram during his flight discussed the situation with an old woman who, ignorant of his identity, described him as "a silly fool who claims the kingdom, not being a member of the Royal House."

[2] He was, however, eventually lured to Constantinople and burned alive in the market-place.

penetrated so far that the inhabitants of Constantinople for the first time saw villages burning on the opposite shore.

The Battle of Zu-Kar, circa A.D. 610.—About this period, between A.D. 604 and 610 according to Nöldeke, but in A.D. 611 according to Muir, there occurred a short campaign which passed almost unnoticed at the time, but was recognized in later years as fraught with consequences of grave importance. On the eastern edge of the desert which separates the valley of the Euphrates from Jerusalem, the Arab state of Hira at this period was ruled by a chief named Noman.

Owing to a subtle intrigue woven by a deadly enemy, who knew that the Arabs were unwilling to give their daughters to the Persians, Khusru Parviz heard of the beauty of Noman's daughter, and desire was kindled to add her to his extensive seraglio. The Arab prince declined the honour, and the Great King, incensed at the refusal, sent an army under Iyas of the Tayy tribe, who had aided him during his flight, with orders to seize Noman and his state. News of the expedition preceded it, and Noman escaped to the Shaybani, to whose chief, Hani, he confided his property. He then came to plead his cause in person before the Great King, by whom he was executed.

The Shaybani were called upon to surrender the property of Noman, but refused. An expedition forty thousand strong, composed of Arabs and Persians, was despatched to execute the commands of the Great King, and after a series of conflicts the Arab contingent deserted during the final battle of Zu-Kar and the Persian army was cut to pieces. As Tabari puts it, " This was the first occasion on which the Arabs took revenge on the Persians." This remark hardly conveys the momentous consequences of the battle, which was fought just as Mohamed began his career. Had it ended in a Persian victory, the difficulties of the Arab invaders would have been immeasurably greater, and the rise of Islam might have been cut short.

The Accession of Heraclius, A.D. 610.—Meanwhile the Byzantine empire was passing through a period of anarchy. Phocas, an officer of low rank, had been elected to lead the army of the Danube against Constantinople ; and when, in A.D. 602, a revolt within the city resulted in the abdication of Maurice, he was elected Emperor. He proved incapable of dealing with the difficult political situation. He paid an increased tribute to the Avars, and he made no effort to cope with the Persian problem. This state of affairs continued for eight years, until in A.D. 610 Heraclius, son of the Governor of Africa, who had maintained his position against Phocas, was invited to head a movement against the usurper. He reached Constantinople with a fleet unopposed and was there proclaimed Emperor. Upon his accession he at once faced the gloomy political situation and began to reorganize the administration.

The Sack of Antioch and the Capture of Jerusalem by the Persians.—In A.D. 611 Khusru Parviz, taking advantage of the confusion, again invaded Syria, and after defeating a feeble Roman force sacked Antioch and Apamea. In the following year he invaded Cappadocia for the second time, and in A.D. 614 he took Damascus. From this centre his general in the ensuing year preached a war of extermination against the Christians, and being joined by a body of 26,000 Jews, he besieged, captured, and sacked Jerusalem, carrying off the " True Cross," which was regarded throughout Christendom as the most sacred treasure in the world. The letter of the haughty conqueror to Heraclius re-echoes the famous summons of Sennacherib :

" Khusru, greatest of gods and master of the whole earth, to Heraclius his vile and insensate slave. You say that you trust in your god. Why, then, has he not delivered Jerusalem out of my hands ? . . . Do not deceive yourself with vain hope in that Christ, who was not even able to save himself from the Jews, who slew him by nailing him to a cross."

Nor was this the limit of conquest ; for in A.D. 616 the Persian general, Shahr-Baraz, crossed the desert, surprised Pelusium, and captured Alexandria, the great and wealthy emporium of Egypt. No resistance was offered, and Persian troops once again, after an interval of more than nine centuries, occupied the Nile valley. Persian prestige must have been greatly increased by this campaign.

The Fall of Chalcedon, A.D. 617.—Farther north a second army had passed through Cappadocia and invested Chalcedon, which lay on the Bithynian coast opposite Constantinople. Heraclius had an interview with the Persian general Shahin, on whose advice he despatched ambassadors to the Great

King. The mission was a failure. Khusru Parviz not only imprisoned the ambassadors, but threatened his general with death for not bringing Heraclius himself bound in chains to the foot of his throne. In A.D. 617 Chalcedon fell, and with this success Persia almost regained the empire held by the Achaemenian dynasty. But little appears to have been done in the way of organization, and probably the only matter deemed important was the levying of revenue. On the other hand, that the occupation was intended to be permanent is shown by the construction of the palace at Mashita in Moab.

The Desperate Condition of the Roman Empire.—The empire of Byzantium might well be supposed to have fallen before the might of the Great King, reduced as it was to Constantinople, some ports in Asia, and fragments of Italy, Greece, and Africa. As if the outlook were not gloomy enough, the Avars overran Thrace and threatened to invest the capital from the land side. The situation was indeed so desperate that Heraclius decided to flee as far as Carthage. His treasure had already been embarked when his project leaked out and the people rose. The Patriarch sided with them and Heraclius was forced to swear in St. Sophia that he would never desert the fortunes of his capital. The loss of the " True Cross " and the letter of Khusru rallied the people and caused a strong outburst of religious feeling, as it was realized that the fate of Christendom hung in the balance. The Church led the way by melting down its plate for money, and the free dole of corn at Constantinople was abolished without opposition.

The Famous Campaigns of Heraclius, A.D. 622–627.—Few if any campaigns in history are more dramatic than those which have conferred imperishable glory on Heraclius. Though all seemed well-nigh lost, he still retained one priceless advantage, the great possession of sea power. Few examples of the value of the command of the sea are more convincing than those given by the desperate Emperor, who in A.D. 622 left Constantinople absolutely safe, with the enemy less than a mile away, and sailed on an expedition which was to save Europe from Persian domination.

The Victory over Shahr-Baraz, A.D. 622.—In spite of bad weather, the Emperor passed the Hellespont, traversed the Aegean Sea and safely reached Issus, famous for the victory of Alexander the Great. As he expected, Shahr-Baraz was ordered to attack the Roman army, and in a battle fought near the Armenian frontier Heraclius won the first victory that had been obtained since the death of Maurice. This concluded the first campaign, and the Emperor, well satisfied with the results, returned to Constantinople for the winter.

The Flight of the Great King, A.D. 623.—In the following year, thanks again to sea power, Heraclius disembarked in Lazica and marched to invade Armenia, accompanied by large contingents of allies, among whom were the Khazars. Khusru, who was probably taken by surprise, proceeded with a force of 40,000 men to Canzaca or Shiz and gave orders to his two field armies to unite and attack the Emperor. But in face of the speed of Heraclius, who bore down rapidly on Khusru, the distances were too great for the Persian generals. The Great King evacuated his position, his army dispersed, and he himself escaped only by moving about in the mountains of the Zagros range until the approach of autumn drove the Emperor back to Albania in the valley of the Kur to winter. These successes must have restored the prestige of Rome to no small extent, for everywhere Heraclius destroyed cities and villages, including Urumia, the birthplace of Zoroaster, and put out the sacred fires.

The Surprise of the Army of Shahr-Baraz, A.D. 624.—In A.D. 624 Khusru attempted to take the offensive, and sent an army to detain the Emperor in Albania, but the force was inadequate and Heraclius once again marched south into Armenia. There he was threatened by three separate Persian armies, and to ensure an engagement before they united, he retreated, with the result that he beat off two of these forces and then attacked and completely defeated the third. He concluded this campaign by surprising Shahr-Baraz, whose army he almost annihilated and whose camp he captured. The winter was spent at Salban, identified with the modern town of Van.

The Defeat of Shahr-Baraz on the Saras, A.D. 625.—The fourth campaign was opened by a descent upon Arzanene and the recovery of Amida and Martyropolis, after which Heraclius marched westwards to the Euphrates, which he found his old opponent Shahr-Baraz holding in force. But the Emperor crossed by a ford and marched into Cilicia, where he was once again in touch with the sea. Shahr-Baraz followed, and a stubborn but indecisive battle was fought on the Saras. During the following night the Persian general retreated. The valour of the Emperor is said to have drawn from Shahr-Baraz the following remark : " Dost thou see the Emperor, how boldly he engages in the battle, against what a multitude he contends alone, and how, like an anvil, he cares not for the blows showered upon him ? "[1] Truly a notable eulogy to have extorted from a valiant foe ! The following winter was spent by Heraclius in Cappadocia.

The Siege of Constantinople and the Defeat of Shahin, A.D. 626.—The following year Khusru, seriously alarmed at the turn in the tide of war, made a supreme effort. He effected an alliance with the Khan of the Avars and then formed two great armies, one of which was destined to oppose Heraclius, while the other was to co-operate with the Avars and capture Constantinople. Heraclius, who was perhaps unable to meet the huge armies now set in motion, left a force to defend the capital, and a second, under his brother Theodore, to oppose the first Persian field army, while he himself marched to Lazica, where he made an unsuccessful attack on Tiflis.

In his absence Theodore, aided by a hailstorm which drove into the face of the Persians, defeated Shahin, the captor of Chalcedon, who shortly afterwards died broken-hearted under his master's displeasure. Meanwhile the Avars assaulted Constantinople, but failed signally and retired, sea power having prevented the Persian army from assisting at the siege, which they had the mortification of watching as impotent spectators.

The Sack of Dastagird and the Flight of Khusru Parviz, A.D. 627.—The situation was consequently all in favour of Heraclius, who, in the autumn of A.D. 627, made a dash on Dastagird, the residence of the Great King, seventy miles north of Ctesiphon. Upon reaching the neighbourhood of the Great Zab, he waited for a Persian army which was at Canzaca to appear, as he dared not risk the cutting of his communications. On the 12th of December a great battle was fought near Nineveh, and although the Persian general was slain his army did not break up, but retired to a fortified camp, where reinforcements were received. Heraclius now pressed on, and Khusru took up a position protected by a deep canal, known as the Baraz Rud, in the neighbourhood of Dastagird. But his heart failed him when his great adversary approached, and to his lasting discredit he abandoned

---

[1] Theophanes, p. 263 A.

his capital and fled. His army rallied on the Nahrwan canal, and Heraclius, who was informed of the depth of the water and of the great force, strengthened by two hundred elephants, which was holding it, decided not to besiege Ctesiphon, but to be content with his successes. He consequently marched northwards and reached Canzaca in March, a fact which proves that his army was now organized to fight and to march in the winter.

The Deposition and Death of Khusru Parviz, A.D. 628.—The craven conduct of Khusru Parviz and the sack of his capital had shattered his prestige. Moreover the loyalty of his nobles was undermined by his insulting the corpse of the dead Shahin, and still more by his attempt to execute Shahr-Baraz. He also imprisoned and probably put to death other unsuccessful generals.

In these circumstances everything was ripe for a rebellion. A strong party, headed by the commander of the Ctesiphon garrison and including many nobles, seized the unfortunate Khusru, and confined him in the " House of Darkness," where he was fed on bread and water and insulted in a most vindictive fashion. Many of his children, including his favourite son Merdasas, whom he had destined to succeed him, were killed before his eyes, and finally he was himself put to a lingering death.

His Character.—No monarch looms larger in Persian literature and art than Khusru Parviz, who was famous alike for his power, his magnificence, his treasures, his love for his Christian wife the beauteous Shirin, and his deep affection for his black horse Shabdiz. No monarch of his dynasty had such splendid successes, and, had he possessed any capacity for administration, his empire might have been as wide in extent as that of his Achaemenian predecessors. On the other hand, he was certainly unfortunate in that his contemporary on the throne of the Roman empire was a soldier so brilliant as Heraclius.

Tabari, dilating on his riches and magnificence, mentions the golden throne with its four legs composed of rubies ; also his fifty thousand camels, horses, and donkeys ; his thousand elephants ; his twelve thousand women, his lump of malleable gold which could be used like clay,[1] and his

---

[1] In the *Journal Royal Asiatic Society* for October 1910, p. 1136, a reference is made to this unique treasure.

napkin which had only to be thrown into the fire to be cleaned. His character was full of contradictions, and probably deteriorated owing to his wonderful early successes in war, which, however, he owed chiefly to his generals and not to his own leadership. In his youth he was no coward. He was at one period influenced by Christianity, and it seems certain that he was attached to Shirin throughout. In his old age he became tyrannical and vindictive, and when his prestige fell he fell with it.

The Progress of Christianity under the later Sasanian Monarchs.—When we examine the position of the Christian Church in Persia, we find Hormisdas, the successor of the illustrious Noshirwan, pursuing his father's liberal policy towards his Christian subjects. It is recounted that, upon being pressed by the Magi to order a persecution on the ground of Christian disloyalty, he replied, " My throne stands on four supports and not on two, on Jews and Christians as well as on Zoroastrians." Khusru Parviz, who had spent some time on the Roman side of the frontier, was more favourable to Christians than any of his predecessors. This was partly owing to the constant influence exercised by Shirin, who founded many churches and monasteries, and letters are extant which show how strongly the Great King believed in the prayers of a Christian saint ;[1] indeed, in one of the earliest campaigns, the aged Patriarch Sabr-Ishu was compelled to accompany the army, to bring it good luck. At the same time Shahr-Baraz was permitted to preach a war of extermination against Christians. Later on, when Heraclius was winning his brilliant victories, Khusru seized the treasures of all the churches in the empire and, as far as it was in his power to do so, compelled the acceptance of the Nestorian heresy.

Wigram[2] points out that although Bar-Soma was a Nestorian, yet the confession of the Patriarch Ishu-Yabh, who visited the Emperor Maurice, was accepted as orthodox. He believes that it was mainly the condemnation of Theodore of Mopsuestia which led to the separation of the Assyrian or Syrian Church from that of Rome.

---

[1] A specimen letter is given in *The Seventh Oriental Monarchy*, p. 497. *The Book of Governors*, by Thomas, Bishop of Marga (edited by Wallis Budge), contains much interesting information about the Nestorian Church from A.D. 595 to 850. In vol. ii. chap. xxxv. it is made out that Shamta, a Christian bishop, originated the plot against Khusru Parviz.

[2] *The Assyrian Church*, p. 220.

YEZDIGIRD III.

CHAPTER XLIII

THE OVERTHROW OF THE PERSIAN EMPIRE BY THE ARABS

> Whatever thou hast said regarding the former condition of the Arabs, is true. Their food was green lizards ; they buried their infant daughters alive ; nay, some of them feasted on dead carcasses, and drank blood. . . . Such was our state. But God, in his mercy, has sent us, by a holy prophet, a sacred volume, which teaches us the true faith.—*The Arab Ambassadors' Address to Yezdigird III.*

The Accession of Kobad II. and the Peace with Rome, A.D. 628.—Siroes, known as Kobad II., succeeded to the throne and was proclaimed king upon the deposition of his father. His first act was to make peace with Heraclius, and the letter he wrote has been preserved, together with the purport of the Emperor's reply. It was clear to both monarchs that the war was inflicting terrible harm on their respective states, and as Heraclius had only fought his brilliant campaigns in pursuance of a policy of active defence, he was quite ready to meet the views of Kobad. The terrible twenty-six years' war was concluded by a peace on the terms that all conquests and prisoners should be surrendered by both belligerents.

Among the conditions was included the surrender of the "True Cross," which Heraclius in person restored to its shrine in Jerusalem amid scenes of great rejoicing. This day of triumph was celebrated in September 629. At this very time a band of Arabs from the interior attacked the Arab levies of Heraclius stationed to the east of the River Jordan. Probably the incident was deemed one of little importance, but yet it was a sinister portent, being the first attack of Islam on victorious, but exhausted, Christendom.

The Massacre of his Brothers and his Death, A.D. 629.—Kobad II. had inaugurated his reign by a remission of taxes and by a release of prisoners. He also sought out the victims of his father's injustice and compensated them by every means in his power. Against these acts of clemency, which were probably more specious than genuine, must be set the fact that he massacred his brothers. A few months later he was himself carried off by a visitation of plague, which was raging at that time in the Near East.

The Usurpation of Shahr-Baraz and his Death, A.D. 629.—The Persian Empire, worn out by the long struggle with Rome and with only a minor as heir to the throne, was nearing its end. The proclamation of Artaxerxes, a boy of seven or even younger, as Great King gave Shahr-Baraz, who had not carried out the orders of Kobad to evacuate the conquered provinces, the opportunity he had been awaiting. He was supported by Heraclius, with whom he made an agreement to evacuate Egypt, Syria, and Asia Minor, and to pay a sum of money in addition. So strongly did Heraclius take his side that he even united the families by a double marriage, and so far as could be judged Shahr-Baraz seemed destined to found a new dynasty. But the words of the old woman to Bahram Chubin again proved true, and although the murder of the young sovereign was easily accomplished, Shahr-Baraz enjoyed the throne for less than two months. He was killed by his own soldiers, who dragged the corpse through the streets of the capital, crying out, " Whoever, not being of the blood-royal, seats himself upon the throne of Persia, will share the fate of Shahr-Baraz." During his short period of power, the provinces he had promised to evacuate were made over to Heraclius, and a Persian army was defeated by the Khazars, who invaded Armenia.

A Period of Anarchy, A.D. 629-634.—Two sisters, daughters of Khusru Parviz, were placed on the throne, but quickly disappeared, and, just as before the downfall of the Achaemenian dynasty, anarchy prevailed, pretender after pretender aspiring to the throne and perishing almost immediately. Their names I relegate to a footnote.[1]

The Accession of Yezdigird III., A.D. 634.—Yezdigird III.,

---

[1] They were as follows : Puran-Dukht, a daughter of Khusru Parviz, was succeeded by Gushnaspdeh. He in his turn was succeeded by Azarmi-Dukht, a sister of Puran-Dukht. Then came Khusru III., Khurrazad—Khusru, Firuz, Farrukhzad—Khusru and Hormuzd or Hormisdas V.

a scion of the house of Sasan, and according to Tabari a son of Shahriar by a negress and grandson of Khusru Parviz, who was living in obscurity at Istakhr, was ultimately seated on the throne of the convulsed and distracted empire. Like the unhappy Darius Codomannus, whom he resembled in many ways, he was doomed to see the overthrow of a mighty dynasty, of which he was the last monarch.

The Campaign of Khalid against the Western Provinces of the Persian Empire, A.H. 12–13 (633–634).—It was a new power that now suddenly appeared in Arabia and brought about the downfall of Persia. The rise of Islam and the steps which led to the invasion both of Irak and of Syria will be dealt with in the following chapters.[1] Here we are concerned with the Moslem campaigns which, directed in the first case against the outlying western provinces of the Persian Empire, culminated in its overthrow.

The Arab leader Khalid, already famous as a warrior, led an army composed almost entirely of Beduin Arabs, and marching north not far from the shore of the Persian Gulf invaded the frontier province of the Great King.

He first summoned Hormuz, the Governor of the province, in the following terms: "Accept the Faith and thou art safe; else pay tribute, thou and thy people; which, if thou refusest, thou shalt have thyself to blame. A people is already on thee, loving death even as thou lovest life."

The frontier stage of the Persian Empire was Hafir, situated some miles at the back of the modern Koweit (Kuwait), and there the first battle was fought. The Persians held the water supply, and Khalid, exclaiming, "The springs shall be for the braver of the two," prepared to attack. Challenged by Hormuz to single combat, the intrepid Arab, in spite of an attempt at an ambuscade, slew his adversary, and the Moslems charged their dispirited enemy and put them to flight. The spoil was great, and among other trophies an elephant was captured and sent to Medina. The victory which was easily won is known as the "Battle of the Chains," from the fact that some of the Persian soldiers were chained together to prevent flight.

The pursuit that followed nearly led to disaster, the victors being met by Persian reinforcements at the great

---

[1] In the case of dates relating to Islam, the year of the *Hijra* is given first, with the year of the Christian era in brackets.

Tigris canal. For some time the Moslems were in imminent danger and compelled to act on the defensive; but on the arrival of their main body a second victory was secured, and more spoils rewarded the splendid valour of Khalid, who ranks among the great generals and leaders of men. Yet a third victory was won at Walaja, near the junction of the Tigris and Euphrates, over a combined Persian and Arab force, but on this occasion after a desperate contest.

A month later Khalid fought the hardest battle of the entire campaign. Having marched northward up the Euphrates he was attacked by a large army composed of Arabs and Persians at Allis, which lies almost exactly half-way between Obolla and Hira. The fight began with a charge of the Arabs, who fought on behalf of Persia, in which their leader was slain by Khalid. The Persian army then attacked, and the issue hung long in the balance before it inclined to Khalid, who had vowed that his foes' blood should flow in a crimson stream. To redeem his savage oath he collected every prisoner for a general butchery, and the corn of the victorious host was ground by a crimson river. Khalid continued his march up the western channel of the Euphrates and surprised Amghisia. He then used water transport and besieged Hira, which capitulated in spite of its strength, and was granted easy terms. This part of the campaign was concluded by the capture of Anbar and Ain Tamar to the north.

But the victor was not destined to enjoy repose. An urgent summons for aid arrived from Iyas, who was attempting to co-operate with him by way of Duma in the middle of the desert, but who was unable to hold his own. The arrival of Khalid, fresh from his victories, changed the entire position, and the hostile tribes were attacked by the combined forces and defeated with heavy loss. The fort of Duma was stormed and its garrison put to the sword.

After returning in triumph to Hira, Khalid engaged in further operations from Ain Tamar, against both the Taghlib Arabs and the Persians, and success continued to crown his arms. Following up the Euphrates he reached Firaz on the Syrian border, and there rested his army during the fast of Ramazan. His arrival alarmed the Byzantine garrison, which in view of the common danger was joined by a Persian force; and the united army advanced across the Euphrates and attacked Khalid, who once more gained a decisive victory, slaughtering the enemy by thousands. The date of this battle was A.H. 12 (634). It was the last fought by Khalid in the Persian campaign, for shortly afterwards he was ordered to hand over the command to Mothanna and to march with half his army to the aid of the army on the Yermuk, which was in difficulties. The great soldier obeyed, though reluctant to leave to others the conquest of the Persian Empire; but encouraged by the promise that he should return when a victory in Syria had been won, he divided his army with Mothanna, and again marched across the Nafud or desert to Duma, after bidding farewell to the comrades whom he was never again to command.

The Campaigns of Mothanna, A.H. 13–14 (634–635).— The position of Mothanna with a force of only 9000 men to fight the huge armies of the Great King was extremely insecure, and brings out well the utter weakness of the Caliph's strategy. But, as Khalid had previously sent back the women, the children, and the sick, the Arab commander was free to take the field with his entire force. Hearing before long of the approach of a Persian army, he quitted Hira, crossed the Euphrates, and near the site of ancient Babylon boldly awaited the attack. An elephant that headed the Persian army and frightened the horses of the Arabs was surrounded and brought to the ground, and the Moslems, delivering an irresistible charge, broke the Persians and chased them to the gates of the capital. Then Mothanna, realizing that without reinforcements he could hardly expect even to hold his own, proceeded to Medina and explained the situation to Abu Bekr. The latter, from his deathbed, gave orders to Omar to raise without delay a further levy for the Persian campaign.

At first no one responded to the summons, but Abu Obayd of Tayif, encouraged by a stirring speech from Mothanna, agreed to go, and was given command of the thousand men who were first enlisted. Returning to his army, Mothanna learned that a powerful column of the enemy was advancing on Hira with a second column in support. He therefore evacuated the entire district and retreated into the desert towards Medina, where he awaited the arrival of Abu Obayd at the head of a force now considerably increased. After the junction of the forces the Arabs attacked the two

Persian armies in succession, and in neither case met with any obstinate resistance.

Rustam, the Persian Governor of Khorasan, who was now invested with full powers at Ctesiphon, speedily organized a fresh army, which he placed under Bahman, the " beetle browed." This force marched to a spot near Babylon where the Arabs succeeded in crossing the Euphrates by a bridge of boats. The elephants, of which Bahman had thirty, so frightened the Arab horses that they refused to charge, and the attack had to be made on foot. Abu Obayd was seized and trampled to death by a huge white elephant which he had wounded. Leader after leader was killed, and for the first time the Arabs wavered. A soldier, inspired by the heroic idea that the army should conquer or perish, cut the first boat adrift, and this act caused a panic. Mothanna, who mainly on account of his being a Beduin Arab and not of high birth had been superseded by Abu Obayd, now rushed to the front and strove to hold the Persians at bay while the bridge was being restored ; but his efforts—in the course of which he was wounded—were only partially successful, and the Moslem loss was 4000, while 2000 Arabs fled back to Medina. In short, after this battle, which is known as the " Battle of the Bridge," Mothanna could muster only 3000 men, and, had Bahman pursued, the whole army must have been annihilated. But, fortunately for the Arabs, news of a rising at Ctesiphon reached the victor, who hastened back to the capital, and Mothanna, who never despaired, fell back unmolested on Allis.

Omar met the disaster with the grand spirit which inspired the first Caliphs, and reinforcements soon began to pour in. Meanwhile Mothanna had been recruiting among the friendly tribes, and when fresh troops reached him from Medina he took the field once more. He met the enemy close to the site of Kufa, on the right bank of the western branch of the Euphrates, known then as Bowayb.

The Persian army, encouraged by its previous victory, crossed the bridge without hesitation and advanced on the Moslems in three great columns, headed by elephants. At first the advantage lay with the assailants, but Mothanna, among whose allies was a Christian chief, made a great charge which broke the Persian centre. This decided the fate of the day, and the defeated Persians were killed or drowned

almost to a man. The Moslem casualties were heavy ; but
the victory of Bowayb was deemed well worth the cost,
owing to the crushing losses suffered by the enemy, the vast
spoils captured, and the immunity thereby secured for the
great raiding expeditions which followed. Mothanna, whose
wounds at the " Battle of the Bridge " had been serious, died
a few months later. In him the Moslems lost one of the
greatest of their generals.

The Organization of a Great Army for the Persian War,
A.H. 14 (635).—The capture of Damascus in A.H. 14 (635)
and the defeat of the Byzantine army on the Yermuk, and
again in the valley of the Jordan, had transformed the entire
military and political situation. There was no longer any
need to keep the main Moslem army in Syria, and it was
possible to divert the victorious veterans for the conquest
of the Persian Empire. A summons to arms produced a
ready response, and levies hastened in from every corner of
Arabia.

Sad was chosen to be the leader of this great force. Noted
as " the first who drew blood in Islam " and as a famous
archer, the new Amir had considerable military qualifications,
and as a nephew of the Prophet's mother possessed much
influence. Supported by Omar, who drained the country
of its fighting men, he collected 30,000 warriors, in whose
ranks served no fewer than 1400 *Ashab*, or " Companions of
the Prophet."

Sad closely observed the advice of Mothanna, given in
a deathbed message, to keep the friendly desert in his rear,
and, leaving the women and children at Odzayb, marched
forward to historical Cadesia, a plain which was bounded on
the west by the Trench of Shapur—at that period a running
stream—and on the east by the western branch of the
Euphrates. Here the Arab camp was formed close to a
bridge of boats, and Sad waited until the enemy came to
attack him on a battle-field selected by himself.

The Embassy to Yezdigird, A.H. 14 (635).—It was at this
period that by the orders of Omar twenty leading Arabs were
despatched to summon Yezdigird to embrace Islam. The
rabble of Ctesiphon jeered at their homely garments, and
compared their bows to a woman's distaff ; but the lean,
hardy, and martial sons of the desert impressed the Great
King and his soft courtiers, who had certainly heard of the

fall of Damascus. Through an interpreter Yezdigird was called upon to embrace the new faith or to pay tribute. Like a true son of Iran, in his reply he referred with contempt to their misery, their eating of lizards, and their infanticide. With simple dignity the Arabs acknowledged that they had been as described ; but now all this was changed. " We are poor and hungry ; yet will the Lord enrich us and satisfy us. Hast thou chosen the sword ? then between us shall the sword decide." What a subject for a great painter ! Yezdigird was furious at the lack of respect shown to him and at the tenor of the message, and dismissed the Arabs with the intimation that, but for their being ambassadors, he would have put them to death.

The Battle of Cadesia, A.H. 14 (636).—In the following year an extraordinary effort was made by the ill-fated monarch. An army numbering 120,000 men was raised and placed under the command of Rustam, who advanced across the Euphrates to find the Arab forces. The battle of Cadesia (or more correctly Kadisiya), which ranks in importance with that of Issus among the decisive battles of the world, was fought on four successive days. On the first the Persians had the advantage, as the Arab horses fled from the elephants, though the position was partly restored by an attack made on the elephants by archers. On the second day the reinforcements from Syria began to stream into the Arab camp. At first there were skirmishes, but subsequently the Arabs defeated the Persian cavalry, and the day closed in favour of the Moslems, whose losses were but one-fifth of the Persian, which amounted to 10,000 men.

On the third day the elephants, which once more appeared in the fighting line, were attacked by Cacaa, the leader of the Syrian advance guard, who thrust his lance into the eye of the great white elephant. A second elephant had both its eyes put out, and the whole body then stampeded through the Persian ranks. The Arab army was further encouraged by the arrival of the main column from Syria, and when night fell their *moral* was much superior to that of their enemies. Indeed so confident were they that, disdaining repose, they attacked in isolated parties throughout the night, which is known as " The Night of Clangour." On the fourth and final day the Arabs had already shaken the Persian centre, when they were aided by a sandstorm, which drove into the faces of the enemy and completed his discomfiture. Rustam, the Persian general, heedless of the great name he bore and of the supreme importance of the trust confided to him, had taken refuge among his baggage mules to escape the violence of the storm, but the Arabs charged among them, and he was hurt by a sack. Seized with panic, he attempted to swim the canal, but was pursued and slain by Hillal, son of Alkama, who mounted his throne and shouted out, " By the Lord of the Kaaba, I have slain Rustam." The Persian army became panic-stricken, and was driven back into the canal, where thousands perished.

This battle was decisive, the Persian *moral* being affected not only by the losses in the battle but also by the fact that the famous *Dirafsh-i-Kawayan*, the historical standard of Persia, was among the spoils. It is related that the soldier who captured it sold it for the equivalent of £800, whereas the actual value of its jewels was £30,000.

The Capture of Madain, A.H. 16 (637).—In accordance with the instructions of Omar, Sad rested his army for two months after the crowning victory of Cadesia. He then re-entered Hira, and thereafter, crossing the Euphrates near the great mound of Babylon, gradually cleared the country of the enemy as far as the Tigris. After these operations he was at length in a position to advance upon Madain, and, sweeping aside an attack made by the Queen-mother, whose champion was slain in single combat, he stood with the Arab army on the edge of the Tigris, across which on their dazzled vision broke the famous Arch of Chosroes. In awe the rude sons of the desert gazed at the wondrous pile, of which they had doubtless all heard an account. " *Allah ho Akbar* " broke involuntarily from thousands of throats as the wild Arabs realized that this was their goal, and that " Now hath the Lord fulfilled the promise which he made unto his Prophet."

The western quarter of the city, the ancient Seleucia, on the right bank of the river, was too strong for the Arab engines, but during the siege the country far and wide was overrun and subdued. Negotiations were opened by Yezdigird, who proposed to surrender everything west of the Tigris if the remainder of his dominions were left to him. This offer was refused with contempt, and shortly afterwards the western quarter was evacuated by the Persians.

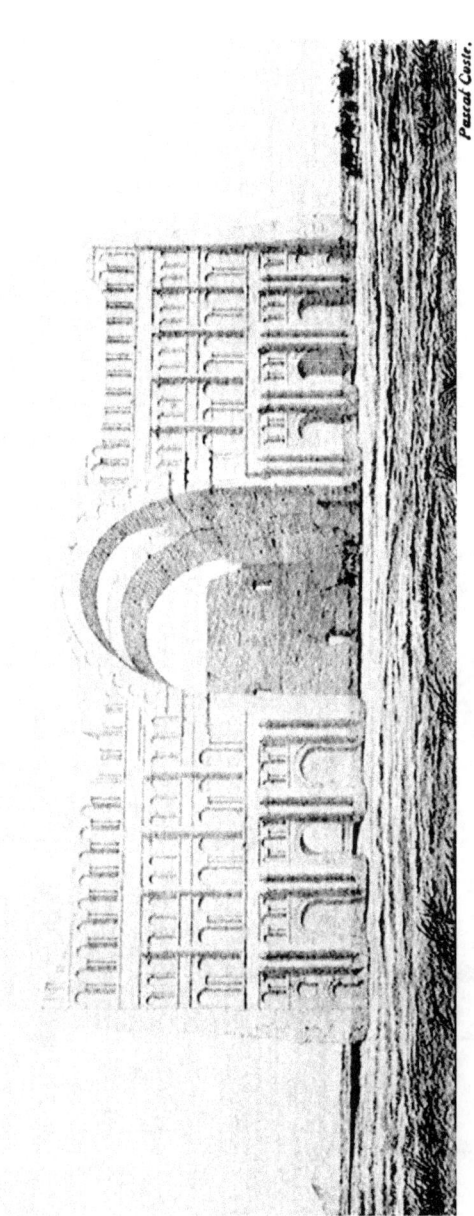

THE ARCH OF CHOSROES, CTESIPHON.

(To-day only the left section of the building and part of the arch remain standing.)

OVERTHROW OF PERSIAN EMPIRE

The position of the Great King was still by no means hopeless, as the swift current of the Tigris flowed between him and the Arabs, who showed no capacity for shipbuilding. But Yezdigird contemplated flight; and Sad, hearing of a point where the Tigris was less swift, boldly swam his horsemen across it. Practically no defence was made on the left bank, and the Persians, thinking only of escape, left their splendid capital to the erstwhile despised " eaters of lizards."

The service of victory held in the capital of the Great King, like that at Khartoum twelve centuries later, was the culmination of the marvellous campaign. To quote from Muir : " The lesson was a passage of the Koran which speaks of Pharaoh overwhelmed in the Red Sea ; and also this verse, thought peculiarly appropriate :

> ' How many Gardens and Fountains did they leave behind,
> And Fields of Corn, and Dwelling-places fair,
> And pleasant things which they enjoyed !
> Even thus We made another people to inherit the same.' "

The booty was rich, so rich indeed that the Arabs were in a dream and wandered about through the gorgeous palaces and gardens, scarcely understanding what the various treasures were. Gold was seen for the first time by the majority of the soldiers; camphor they mistook for salt; and when the booty was divided each of the 60,000 men received some £500, which to most of them must have been wealth. Indeed the golden throne and the wonderful objects in the treasury, among which was a horse made of pure gold, were a theme on which the Arab writers were never tired of dilating.

The Battle of Jalola, A.H. 16 (637).—Sad was anxious to follow up the broken Persian army to Holwan, a strong fortress in the defiles of the Zagros ; but Omar, with statesmanlike prudence, forbade any advance during the summer, and the victors, while consolidating their power, enjoyed to the full the many delights of Madain. In the autumn, however, news reached the Arabs that a large Persian force had been assembled and that its advance guard was stationed at Jalola, reputed to be an impregnable fortress. Thither Hashim and Cacaa were despatched at the head of 12,000 men, to find themselves constantly attacked by the Persian troops. Reinforcements were received on both sides, and in a battle outside the fort the Persians were again defeated in a storm after desperate fighting which recalled the "Night of Clangour." Yezdigird, who never appeared in the fighting line, fled to Rei, and Cacaa, seizing Holwan, garrisoned it for Islam. The spoil was again rich and included the almost incredible number of 100,000 horses drawn from the pastures of Media, descendants without doubt of the celebrated Nisaean horses of the Achaemenians.

The Annexation of Mesopotamia and the Capture of Obolla, A.H. 16 (637).—Omar, whose ambitions were certainly not world-wide, in reply to a letter asking for permission to pursue the Persians on to the Iranian plateau, replied as follows: " I desire that between Mesopotamia and countries beyond the hills shall be a barrier, so that the Persians shall not be able to get at us, nor we at them. The plain of Irak [1] sufficeth for our wants." Sad consequently turned his energies to subjugating Mesopotamia, and so successful was he that before very long Islam held sway over that fertile region. Southwards, too, towards the Persian Gulf a separate force under Otba captured the port of Obolla, the emporium of the trade with India, situated not far from Basra, which afterwards superseded it.

The Foundation of Basra and of Kufa, A.H. 17 (638).— After the capture of Obolla the Arabs constructed a cantonment on its ruins, and this had gradually grown into a town; but so damp was the climate and so intolerable were the insect pests that a new site was sought and Basra was chosen, some ten miles to the north-west of the present city, which occupies the site of Obolla. No city of the Moslems, except perhaps Baghdad, recalls more of the glamour of the East than the "Balsara's haven" of Milton, whence Sindbad the Sailor started on his memorable voyages. To-day its creeks are lovely and its commerce thriving; but its climate is both hot and unwholesome, and I never look back on the summer months which I spent at this, the chief and only port on the Shatt-al-Arab, with any pleasure. Kufa was also founded under instructions from Omar, who was struck by the sallow faces of the Arabs who had settled at Madain. It was chosen as being in touch with the desert to which the Arabs owed

---

[1] The Arabs called the valleys of the Tigris and Euphrates up to Mesopotamia by the name of Irak-i-Arabi. North-east of it the adjacent provinces of upland Persia were first termed Jibal or "Mountains." The later name Irak-i-Ajami or "Irak of the Persians," the word *ajam* literally signifying "barbarous," dates from the twelfth century A.D. At one time Kufa and Basra were known as the two Iraks.

so much of their virility, thus superseding Hira, from which it was distant but a few miles, and also Madain. Muir points out that these two new cantonments, with their purely Arab inhabitants, which rapidly grew to be cities with populations of 150,000, influenced the literature and theology of Islam more than the whole of the rest of the Moslem world.

Throughout these campaigns, which in one sense culminated in the foundation of these cities, it is extraordinary with what set purpose the Arab invaders not only conquered, but settled down with their families in the conquered provinces. In Persia I have met numerous Arab tribes who know the exact date of their arrival in Iran, and there seems to have been little if any regret for their deserted homeland in Arabia.

The Failure of the Expedition from Bahrein.—The one expedition of the Moslems which failed was an attempt by Ala, Governor of the Bahrein province, to invade Fars by sea. Leaving his ships unprotected, the adventurous Arab marched inland, and for some distance met with no opposition. At length an unsuccessful battle was fought and he found himself hemmed in. He was, however, able to despatch a messenger to Medina, and Otba was sent with a force of 12,000 men which effected a junction with the army of Ala, beat off the enemy, and retired on Basra.

The Conquest of Khuzistan and the Capture of Shuster, A.H. 19 (640).—Encouraged by this success against Ala, Hormuzan, the Satrap of Khuzistan, raided the Arabs from Ahwaz, and Otba consequently determined to make an advance. Hormuzan was driven across the Karun and Ahwaz was ceded to the Arabs. Hormuzan, however, remained to be finally dealt with, and in A.H. 19 (640) he was routed at Ram Hormuz, the site of the great victory of Ardeshir, and retired on Shuster, now the capital of the province, which held out for eighteen months but was ultimately captured. Hormuzan was sent to Omar to have his fate decided by the Caliph. The astute Persian, on being received, asked for a cup of water, but feigning fear of instant death hesitated to drink it. " Fear nothing, your life is safe until you have drunk the water," said the Caliph. In reply Hormuzan flung the cup to the ground. Omar, although outwitted, kept his word, and Hormuzan, who embraced Islam, was spared and granted a pension. Curiously enough, it was the defence he made for breaking faith with the Arabs, alleging orders from the Great King, which finally convinced Omar of the necessity of fighting the campaign to a finish.

The Battle of Nahavand, A.H. 21 (642).—In A.H. 20 (641) Yezdigird had again collected a large army, with contingents from every province of the empire which had not been subdued. The Caliph realized that an offensive policy was the best, and entrusted the supreme command to Noman, whom he had summoned from Khuzistan. The force under him numbered 30,000, and he was indirectly aided by an advance which the Khuzistan army made on Persepolis. The Moslems marched *via* Holwan, and learning that the Persian army, 150,000 strong under Firuzan, who had held a command at Cadesia, was encamped at Nahavand, some fifty miles south of Hamadan, the Arab general immediately marched to attack it.

The Persians, in spite of their enormous numerical superiority, acted on the defensive, and being protected by a strong line of fortifications, refused to do more than skirmish, hoping thereby to wear out the Arabs. Noman's supplies being exhausted, he resorted to a clever artifice, and marched off in feigned retreat, spreading a rumour of Omar's death. Firuzan pursued, and thanks to this ruse the decisive battle was fought on ground selected by Noman. The Arabs charged with irresistible courage and the Persians fled. Even the death of Noman in the hour of victory made no difference, and the Persians, including Firuzan, caught among the narrow defiles, were overtaken and massacred, their losses being computed at over 100,000 men. The result of this final battle, which may be compared with Arbela (just as the battles of the Chains and of Cadesia have their parallels in the battles of the Granicus and of Issus), was practically a foregone conclusion, but the Arabs term it the " Victory of Victories."

The Annexation of the Provinces of Persia.—Tabari describes at some length the rapid annexation of the various provinces of Persia, and incidentally shows that each province was left to organize its own resistance without any help from the fugitive Great King. By instructions received from Omar, the Arab army, after gaining its decisive victory at Nahavand, marched on Isfahan, and this important city capitulated after a battle in which the aged Persian general was killed. In the following year the Arab army advanced into Kerman and, gaining a victory on the frontier of the province, marched as far as the fertile valley of Jiruft to the south-east and as far north as the province of Kuhistan and the town of Tabas. Yet another column was directed on Sistan. Zaranj, the capital, was not captured, but when the Moslems occupied the province it was surrendered. Finally, the irresistible Moslem arms were turned against barren Makran, which Omar fixed as the eastern limit of conquest.

To the north-east, the Persian governor of Rei collected a force from the Gurgan, from Tabaristan and from Kumis, but, partly owing to treachery, he was defeated. The Moslem troops subsequently marched east by the great highway along which the last monarch of the Achaemenian dynasty had fled before Alexander, and, crossing the Elburz, received the submission of the governor of Gurgan. Two columns moved on Azerbaijan, which then stretched as far north as the famous fortress of Derbent, and all this rich, desirable country submitted. The conquest of Khorasan was apparently undertaken last of all. Tabaristan alone, thanks to its pathless forests, maintained an independent existence under hereditary princes termed *Sipahbud*, or Commanders-in-Chief, until about A.D. 760.[1]

The Semites had held sway in the Babylonian and Assyrian empires until they were succeded by the Aryans of Media and Persia. They in their turn for five centuries were dominated by a Turanian race until, in the third century A.D., the Aryans reasserted their supremacy. For a period of four centuries the splendid Aryan dynasty of the Sasanians was paramount and nearly overthrew the Roman Empire, but it grew weak and decrepit, partly owing to the strong feeling which forbade a successful general to aspire to the throne. Persia, torn by intestine troubles after a generation of weakening wars, fell, albeit not without a gallant struggle, at Cadesia. On that stricken field the power passed again to the Semites, some twelve centuries after the fall of Nineveh.

The Death of Yezdigird III., A.H. 31 (652).—Yezdigird, a craven member of a fighting family, fled from Rei to Isfahan, from Isfahan to Kerman, and thence to distant Balkh. The Emperor of China was appealed to but refused help, and the

---

[1] *Vide* Ibn Isfandiyar's *History of Tabaristan*, edited by Browne (Gibb Memorial); also Chapter XLIX.

Turks espoused his cause for a time and then withdrew. Finally he ended his inglorious career in a miller's hut near Merv, where he was murdered for his jewelry. Tradition has it that the Christian bishop summoned his flock to bury him, and that a shrine was erected over his tomb. Nor is his memory quite forgotten, as the Parsis with touching fidelity annually, on September 12, celebrate the day of his accession which inaugurated the Alam Shahi era, the last to be recognized by them.

Thus ignominiously, ten years after Nahavand, perished the last unworthy sovereign of the illustrious Sasanian line. There is laid to his charge no great crime, but since lack of virility and valour is in autocratic monarchs a worse defect than many crimes, Yezdigird III., like Darius Codomannus, whom he closely resembled, stands condemned, and rightly condemned, at the bar of history.

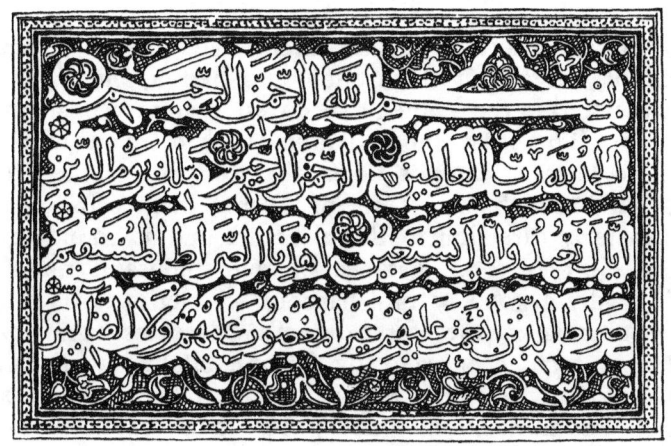

THE OPENING *SURA* OF THE KORAN.

CHAPTER XLIV

THE CAREER OF MOHAMED AT MECCA

> Praise be to God, the Lord of creation,
> The most merciful, the most compassionate !
> Ruler of the day of Reckoning !
> Thee we worship, and invoke for help.
> Lead us in the straight path ;
> The path of those towards whom Thou hast been gracious ;
> Not of those against whom Thy wrath is kindled, or that walk in error.
> *The Fatiha or Opening Sura of the Koran.*

A Description of Arabia.—The rise of Islam [1] was an event of such overwhelming importance to Persia that, although some of its results have been referred to in the previous chapter, it seems advisable to deal with it in a connected way from the beginning.[2]

The peninsula of Arabia, with an area four times as large as France, has a central tableland termed Najd, which covers one-half of the peninsula and averages some 3000 feet in altitude. Round this in every direction, and especially to

---

[1] Islam signifies " to resign oneself " (*sc.* to the will of God). A follower of the religion is termed a Mussulman, Muslim, or Moslem, the second form being the participle of Islam. The term " Mohamedan " is not usually applied by Moslems to themselves, except so far as it has been adopted owing to European influence.
[2] Among the authorities consulted are *The Caliphate* and also *The Life of Mahomet*, by Sir William Muir ; *Geschichte der Chalifen* (4 vols.), by Dr. Gustave Weil ; *A Literary History of the Arabs*, by R. A. Nicholson ; and *Arabia, the Cradle of Islam*, by Rev. S. M. Zwemer.

the south, lie deserts. Beyond these wastes stretch chains of mountains, for the most part low and barren, but in Oman to the east and in the Yemen to the west attaining considerable elevation. The coast line of Arabia, backed by an unbroken mountain barrier, extends down the Red Sea to the Straits of Bab-ul-Mandeb, or "Gate of Tears," thence in an east-north-easterly direction to Ras-al-Hadd, and so round to the Persian Gulf, a total distance of four thousand miles, in which hardly a good natural harbour or inlet is to be found. The peninsula is therefore difficult of access from every quarter, a fact recognized by its inhabitants, who call it *Jazirat-ul-Arab*, or "the Island of the Arabs." Nor are its internal communications good; for the great desert, the *Ruba-al-Khali*, or "Solitary Quarter," has, from time immemorial, divided the country, separating the north from the south. It is in consequence, perhaps, of this natural barrier that we find at an early period the rude nomads of the north speaking Arabic and the more civilized inhabitants of Yemen and the south Himyarite, a tongue which died out before the sixth century of our era, leaving Arabic supreme.

In the physical geography of Persia we noted the remarkable fact that between the Indus and the Shatt-al-Arab no river of any importance reaches the sea. Persia is a country of riverless desert, with a rainfall of less than ten inches in the north and perhaps five inches in the south; but Arabia is less favoured still. There also desert is the salient feature, and no rivers are to be found; but both in its deserts and in its lack of water Arabia is more "intense," to use the geographical term, than neighbouring Iran. At the same time, ruins of cities in the deserts and other evidence tend to show that Arabia was a less arid country some two thousand years ago than it is to-day.

The Importance of Mecca.—On the trade with the East, rather than upon any local products, depended the prosperity of Arabia. Even as far back as the tenth century B.C. the spices, peacocks, and apes of India were brought by ship to the coast of Oman. From Hadhramaut, the province lying opposite India, the caravan route ran to Marib, the capital of the Sabaean kingdom, and thence by way of Mecca and Petra to Gaza. A glance at the map will show how Mecca, which lay about half-way between Hadhramaut and Petra, must have benefited by this land commerce, and explain why it became a centre of population and a resort of merchants.

The importance of this trade is shown in the book of Ezekiel, in which the prophet refers as follows to the riches of Tyre : [1] " Arabia, and all the princes of Kedar, they occupied with thee in lambs, and rams, and goats : in these were they thy merchants. The merchants of Sheba and Raamah, they were thy merchants : they occupied in thy fairs with chief of all spices, and with all precious stones, and gold. Haran, and Canneh, and Eden, the merchants of Sheba, Asshur, and Chilmad, were thy merchants."

This quotation from a Jewish prophet, who is known to have been sent into captivity by the orders of Nebuchadnezzar in 599 B.C., sufficiently attests the ancient importance of this trade, and it is of special interest to find that Aden, the Eden of Ezekiel, was known by the same name more than two thousand years before it was annexed by Great Britain. It was probably in the first century of the Christian era that the Indian trade began to pass by water through the Bab-ul-Mandeb and up the Red Sea, with the result that the caravan routes were gradually deserted and the erstwhile thriving cities dwindled and waned.

The Ancient Religion of the Arabs.—Muir, our great authority,[2] believes that the religious rites practised at Mecca can be traced to the Yemen, of which district its earliest inhabitants were probably natives. They brought with them the system of Sabeanism, which implied belief in one God coupled with worship of the heavenly bodies. To-day the survivors of the sect, many of whom live in the neighbourhood of Basra and Mohamera, are misnamed " Christians of St. John the Baptist " by travellers, although they speak of themselves as Mandeans. They practise baptism and ceremonial ablutions, hold the book of Psalms to be sacred, and adore especially the north star.[3] Edwin Arnold has expressed the debt due to Sabeanism in the following words : " Islam was born in the desert, with Arab Sabeanism for its mother

---

[1] Chap. xxvii. 21-23.

[2] I have not gone into the sources of the biography of Mohamed, but would refer the student to chap. i. of Muir's work.

[3] *Vide* Zwemer's *Arabia, the Cradle of Islam*, chap. xxviii., for an interesting account of the modern Sabeans. The Arabs gave them the name of *Al-Maghtasila*, or "The Washers," from their ceremonial ablutions, and this, being misunderstood by the Portuguese, gave rise to the misnomer mentioned above.

and Judaism for its father; its foster-nurse was Eastern Christianity." There is much truth in this view.

The ancient Arabians had seven temples, dedicated to the seven planets. They also worshipped goddesses, three of whom are mentioned in the Koran under the names of Allat, the special idol of Mecca; Al-Uzza,[1] the planet Venus; and Mana, a sacred stone. There was also an idol for every day of the year in the temple at Mecca.

The Kaaba.—The centre of worship at Mecca was the Kaaba.[2] This sacred temple contained, embedded in the eastern corner, a reddish-black stone, which is believed to be a meteorite; it is semicircular in shape and very small, measuring only some six inches by eight. This was reverently kissed by pilgrims, who made seven circuits round the sacred building. In the case of the " Lesser Pilgrimage " it was also necessary to walk seven times between the hills of Safa and Marwa; and in the " Greater Pilgrimage " Arafat, a small hill to the east of Mecca, had to be visited, stones had to be cast against the Evil One in the Mina valley, and the pilgrimage concluded by the sacrifice of victims. The strength of Jewish influence accounts for the reputed connexion of this pre-Moslem ritual with Abraham; the deserted Ishmael is believed to have discovered the sacred well Zemzem by kicking the ground, and it was Abraham and Isaac who built the Kaaba and instituted the pilgrimage.

The Ancestors of the Prophet Mohamed.—Among the Arabs birth was of the first importance, and consequently a brief account must be given of Mohamed's ancestry and tribe. Towards the middle of the fifth century a certain Kussai, chief of the Kureish[3] tribe, was the ruler of Mecca, and he gathered into the city his fellow-tribesmen. Apart from the civil rights which conferred on him leadership in war and jurisdiction in peace, Kussai held the keys of the Kaaba, which gave him the prerogative of providing water for the pilgrims. After his death and that of his eldest son a feud broke out among his descendants. The elder branch refused to share any of their privileges with the younger, and for a

---

[1] It was in honour of this goddess that Mundhir, the Saracen Prince of Hira, sacrificed 400 nuns, as mentioned in Chapter XXXIX.

[2] The word signifies a cube.

[3] Kureish is believed to be derived from a word signifying a "highly-bred camel." If this be correct, it is a curious coincidence that Zoroaster's name is supposed to have an almost similar meaning. *Vide* Chapter IX.

while it seemed likely that the dispute would be settled by the sword. The supporters of the elder branch dipped their hands into a bowl of blood and invoked the aid of the gods, and Hashim, the leader of the younger, also swore an oath with much circumstance. Ultimately it was decided that the custody of the keys and the right of raising the war banner should be retained by the elder branch, but that the younger should provide the pilgrims with water and food.

As the years went by, Hashim, a striking personality, acquired a great reputation for generous hospitality, and in consequence he was envied by his nephew Omayya, who in vain attempted to rival him. At length Omayya challenged his uncle to a trial before a judge, who was to pronounce upon the question of personal merit. Hashim was forced by tribal opinion to take up the challenge, but on the condition, demanded by him, that the loser should pay fifty black-eyed camels and leave Mecca for ten years. The decision was given in his favour, and Omayya quitted Mecca for Syria, after handing over the fifty camels, which were slaughtered to make a feast. The incident is of importance, because from it dates the rivalry between the Omayyad and Hashimite factions, a rivalry destined to bear baleful fruit. About A.D. 500 Hashim in mature age married an heiress of Medina, and from this marriage a son, Shiba, was born. Hashim died in A.D. 510, and his prerogatives passed to his elder brother Al-Muttalib, who continued the family tradition of open-handed hospitality.

Shiba was allowed to live for some years at Medina, but at last his uncle brought him to Mecca, where he was at first mistaken for a slave and called Abdul Muttalib, or "The Slave of Muttalib," a sobriquet which stuck to him through life. A family quarrel concerning property was decided in his favour on the arrival of eighty of his maternal relatives from Medina, and when Al-Muttalib died he succeeded to his dignities. For some time his influence was slight, as he had only one son ; but one day he was so fortunate as to rediscover the site of the sacred well of Zemzem, which had existed, as we have seen, in ancient times. The possession of this well at once gave its owner immense power in thirsty Mecca, and with the birth of other sons his prestige became as great as that of his father. But he had made a rash vow that, if granted ten sons, he would sacrifice one of them to the Fates. When the number was reached lots were cast and fell on Abdulla, the youngest. As the father was preparing to fulfil his dreadful oath, he was persuaded to cast lots between the boy and ten camels, which represented the blood fine for a man's life. Nine times the lot fell upon the boy, but at the tenth throw it fell at last on the camels. They were slaughtered to the number of one hundred and given to the inhabitants of Mecca.

Abdulla, who was thus saved from death, upon reaching the age of twenty-four, was married by his father to a relative, Amina [1] by name. Directly after the marriage he started on a trading expedition to Syria. On his return he died at Medina, and on the 20th of August, A.D. 570, his widow gave birth to a son, who was Mohamed [1] the Prophet.

The Political Situation in Arabia before and after the Birth of the Prophet.—Among the earliest foreign relations of the Kureish tribe which have been recorded is a so-called treaty concluded by Hashim with the Ghassanide prince, a Christianized Arab Shaykh, whose capital, Bostra, lay to the east of the Jordan. Hashim is also said to have received a rescript from the Emperor allowing the Kureish to travel in Syria, but in all probability it was the local representative of the Emperor who signed the document.

In Chapter XL. reference has been made to the invasion and occupation of the Yemen by the Abyssinians, whose capital at that period was Aksum, near the Red Sea littoral. In A.D. 570, the year of the Prophet's birth, Abraha,[2] the capable Abyssinian Viceroy, marched on Mecca, ostensibly to avenge an insult offered to the church at Sana, but probably intending to destroy the Kaaba from political motives. Brushing aside all opposition, he reached Tayif, three stages east of the Sacred City. Thence he despatched raiding parties which captured, among other live stock, two hundred camels belonging to Abdul Muttalib. Following with his main body, which included that portentous monster an elephant, he halted outside Mecca and sent envoys to inform the panic-stricken Arabs that he had no desire to injure them but was determined to destroy the Kaaba. Abdul Muttalib proceeded to the camp of the enemy to treat with

---

[1] Amina is the feminine form of *Amin*, signifying "trustworthy." The name of the Prophet is more correctly written Muhammad. The word signifies "The Praised."
[2] Abraha is the Abyssinian form of Ibrahim or Abraham. An inscription cut by his orders has recently been found (*vide Encyclopaedia of Islam*).

Abraha, who restored his camels but would not be turned from his purpose.

The legend runs that Abdul Muttalib would only ask for his camels, and in reply to a contemptuous remark from Abraha retorted that the Kaaba needed no human defender. On the fateful day the elephant refused to advance, and the failure of the expedition is commemorated in the following verses from the Koran : " Hast thou not seen how thy Lord dealt with the army of the Elephant ? Did he not cause their stratagem to miscarry ? And he sent against them flocks of little birds which cast upon them small clay stones, and made them like unto the stubble of which the cattle have eaten." The passage is a glorified description of an epidemic of small-pox—also termed " small stones " in Arabic—which is historical. The Abyssinian army retreated, and Abraha died at Sana of the foul disease. The news that the Kaaba had been protected by divine intervention must have spread far and wide, and greatly enhanced both the sanctity of the Shrine and the prestige of the Kureish.

Upon the death of Abraha his son Yaksum held the viceroyalty for only four years, to be succeeded by Masruk. It was during Masruk's reign that the famous expedition was despatched by Noshirwan, which resulted in the expulsion of the Abyssinians and the reinstatement of the old Himyarite monarchs under the suzerainty of the Great King. Tabari,[1] who is the authority for this campaign, states that Saif, upon his accession to the throne, was visited by Abdul Muttalib, who is known to have died in A.D. 578. Consequently the date of this campaign must have been between A.D. 574 and A.D. 578.

The Childhood, Youth, and Early Manhood of Mohamed.—The prospects of the infant Mohamed were not bright. His father was dead and his entire property consisted of a slave girl, five camels, some goats, and a house. At the same time he possessed powerful relations. In accordance with custom, the infant was entrusted to a nomad woman, Halima of the Beni Sad, and among the free sons of the desert Mohamed remained until he was six years old. His constitution benefited by the open-air life, although apparently he was subject to epileptic fits. Moreover, the Beni Sad were held to speak the purest Arabic, and the Prophet in after years used to

[1] Vol. ii. pp. 203 ff.

boast, "Verily, I am the most perfect Arab amongst you; my descent is from the Kureish, and my tongue is the tongue of the Beni Sad." Among a people who counted eloquence as the highest of gifts, this upbringing was of great advantage. It is to the credit of Mohamed that he never forgot his foster-mother, and always treated her and her family with generosity and kindness. In his sixth year the lad was taken back to Medina, and when he returned there forty-seven years afterwards he was able to identify the house and to recall the details of the life he had led in it.

Amina shortly afterwards decided to take the child to Mecca, but died on the road. The orphan was most kindly treated by his grandfather until his own death, which occurred when Mohamed was eight years old. With this event the Hashimite branch of the family suffered a loss of prestige and influence which accrued to the Omayyad section instead, and remained with it until the conquest of Mecca by the Prophet.

Abu Talib, the uncle to whom the orphan had been entrusted, treated him with the utmost affection, a fact which seems to indicate that the boy possessed attractive qualities. When only twelve years old he was taken by his guardian on a caravan journey to Syria, which must have enlarged the horizon of his experience.

At the annual fair held at Ocatz, to the east of Mecca, his young mind was doubtless influenced by listening to the contests in poetry among bards of the various tribes. There he would also hear Jewish and Christian preachers. About this period, during the time of the fair, a blood feud arose through the murder of a chief of the Hawazin by a rival, who had a confederate among the Kureish. This occasioned several desperate skirmishes, at one of which the Prophet was present; but he did not distinguish himself. Indeed, at no time in his career did he display martial qualities.

Apart from these skirmishes, dignified by the name of the Sacrilegious War, the Prophet spent his youth as a shepherd, a mean occupation which usually fell to the lot of slaves. In after years he said, "Verily there hath been no prophet raised up, who performed not the work of a shepherd." He must have been held in esteem at Mecca, since it is recorded that he was termed Al-Amin or "The Faithful."

Had it not been for the poverty of Abu Talib, it is possible that Mohamed would have continued to lead a shepherd's life, which suited his reserved and meditative nature. But at the age of twenty-five necessity drove him to Syria in part charge of a caravan belonging to Khadija, a wealthy widow of the Kureish. At Bostra he bartered his goods successfully, and upon his return Khadija fell in love with the handsome youth, and married him after obtaining her father's consent by a ruse. The marriage was happy and Mohamed lived contentedly with Khadija, although his two sons both died. It appears that, while continuing to manage her own affairs as before, she admired her husband's qualities and realized that he was no ordinary man.

Time passed, and when Mohamed was about thirty-five years of age the Kaaba was rebuilt. Each of the four divisions of the Kureish took charge of a wall, and when the structure had risen four or five feet above the ground, the Black Stone had to be built once again into the east corner. The question who should have the honour of placing the stone into position led to heated debate until an aged citizen suggested that the first man to arrive on the spot should be asked to decide. By chance Mohamed came up, and, being informed of the case, placed the stone on his cloak and called on each chief to raise a corner of it. Thus the stone was borne into the new temple, where the hands of Mohamed set it in position. He may well have thought that his opportune arrival was divinely ordained. As mentioned in Chapter XLII., the battle of Zu-Kar was fought between A.D. 604 and 611. Mohamed, who followed such events with the keenest interest, upon hearing of the victory of the Arabs, is said to have exclaimed, " This is the first day whereon the Arabs have obtained satisfaction from the Persians ; through me have they obtained help ! " Little that is worthy of note has been recorded of this period. Mohamed, relieved of all worldly cares and surrounded by a few faithful friends and kinsmen, was able to devote himself to contemplation and prayer, and it is related that, like other Prophets, he frequently went into the desert to meditate.

The Divine Commission conveyed by Gabriel.—Muir's work is nowhere more masterly than in his analysis of the steps which led Mohamed to proclaim himself the Prophet of God. " He was seated or wandering amidst the peaks of Hira, buried no doubt in reveries, when suddenly an apparition rose before him. The heavenly Visitant stood clear and close beside him in a vision. It was no other than Gabriel,[1] the Messenger of God, who now appeared in the sky, and, approaching within 'two bows' length,' brought from his Master this memorable behest :

> Recite in the name of the Lord who created,—
> Created Man from nought but congealed blood ;—
> Recite ! for thy Lord is beneficent.
> It is He who hath taught (to write) with the pen ;—
> Hath taught man that which he knoweth not."[2] . . .

The Assumption of the Prophetical Office, A.D. 613-614.—In A.D. 613-614, the forty-fourth year of his life, we find Mohamed proclaiming himself a divinely inspired Prophet, sent by God to the people of Arabia. His followers, though very few, were both honest and devoted. Among them were Khadija, his wife, Zayd, his adopted son, and Ali, son of Abu Talib, his cousin. Of far greater weight was the adherence of Abdulla, Abu Bekr, a member of the Kureish, a man of substance, and of the highest personal character. Other converts included Sad, Othman, and Abdur Rahman, who himself brought four more converts. Thus slowly during the three or four years which followed the assumption of the prophetic office some forty followers, all of them loyal to the core, threw in their lot with Mohamed.

The behaviour of his fellow-citizens was such as might have been expected. At first, having known Mohamed from boyhood, they treated his claims with contempt, and regarded him as a harmless visionary ; but gradually, owing to their connexion with the Kaaba, these feelings changed into open hostility, which showed itself in persecution. This drew all the more attention to the doctrines expounded by the Prophet, who was himself protected by Abu Talib. Others, however, who had no protectors were imprisoned or exposed to the glare of the sun or ill-treated in other ways.

The Temporary Emigration to Abyssinia, A.D. 615.—So hot did the persecution become and so black was the outlook that Mohamed recommended his followers to seek a temporary asylum in Christian Abyssinia, and in A.D. 615 a party of eleven men fled to the port of Shuayba, near Jeddah, and thence reached Africa in safety.

---

[1] Muir considers that Mohamed confused Gabriel with the Holy Ghost.
[2] This, the ninety-sixth *sura* or chapter, was the starting-point of Islam, and Mohamed himself used to refer to it as his first inspired utterance.

THE ANGEL GABRIEL APPEARING TO MOHAMED
(From F. R. Martin's *Miniature Paintings of Persia, etc.*)

CAREER OF MOHAMED AT MECCA

The historical interview with the Negus is recorded by Ibn Hisham,[1] and the narrative presents a truly remarkable picture of early Islam. In reply to a question by the Negus as to why the refugees, although separated from their own people, entered not into the Christian religion, the Moslem leader said, " O King ! We were a barbarous folk, worshipping idols, eating carrion, committing shameful deeds, violating the ties of consanguinity, and evilly entreating our neighbours, the strong among us consuming the weak ; and thus we continued until God sent unto us an Apostle from our midst, whose pedigree and integrity and faithfulness and purity of life we knew, to summon us to God, that we should declare His unity, and worship Him, and put away the stones and idols which we and our fathers used to worship in His stead ; and he bade us be truthful in speech, and faithful in the fulfilment of our trusts, and observing of the ties of consanguinity and the duties of neighbours, and to refrain from forbidden things and from blood ; and he forbade immoral acts and deceitful words, and consuming the property of orphans, and slandering virtuous women ; and he commanded us to worship God, and to associate naught else with Him, and to pray and give alms and fast." Well might the Negus weep upon hearing this exposition of faith, and exclaim, " Verily, this and that which Moses brought emanate from one Lamp ! "

[1] Ibn Hisham wrote the earliest biography of the Prophet about A.D. 828.

QUOTATION FROM THE KORAN.
(From a MS. in the British Museum.)

CHAPTER XLV

THE FLIGHT TO MEDINA AND THE ESTABLISHMENT OF ISLAM

O true believers, take not my enemy and your enemy for your friends, showing kindness toward them ; since they believe not in the truth which hath come unto you, having expelled the apostle and yourselves from your native city, because ye believe in God, your Lord.—*The Koran.*

The Hijra, or " Emigration," to Medina, A.D. 622.—The claims of Mohamed made but slow progress as the years passed. The enmity of the Kureish was so intense that for two or three years they placed the Hashimite section of the tribe under a ban and refused to have any dealings with them ; and the Prophet had the misfortune to lose by death not only the faithful Khadija but also Abu Talib, whose unswerving support of his nephew, although he himself remained an idolater, affords a fine testimony to the nobility of both.

Shortly after the death of Khadija, Mohamed attempted to convert the men of neighbouring Tayif, but the mission was a complete failure. He left the city, pursued by the rabble, and returned to Mecca hopeless as to the future. But brighter days were in store, for his teaching had made so deep an impression on pilgrims from Medina that the majority of its Arab inhabitants became converted to his creed, and the Jews, who formed a large percentage of the population, observed in amazement that the idols were thrown down and that belief in one God was acknowledged.

An invitation to leave hostile Mecca for friendly Medina was given by a band of seventy leading citizens at a secret meeting held near Mecca, and shortly after this the Prophet's adherents began to migrate in small parties. Mohamed and the faithful Abu Bekr remained until the last. To put their enemies off the track they first hid in a cave to the south of Mecca for a few days, and then, in the fifty-third year of the Prophet's life, on June 20, A.D. 622, the famous journey was begun. From this date the Moslem era starts, the word *Hijra*, incorrectly written Hegira, signifying " Emigration." No saying is truer than that " a prophet is not without honour, but in his own country, and among his own kin, and in his own house," and, had not Mohamed been strong enough to face the odium of what the Arabs regarded as a deed of shame by quitting his own people and proceeding to Medina, Islam would in all probability have died with its Prophet, now already in middle age.

The Erection of the First Mosque at Medina.—At Medina he was received with honour and rejoicing, and was pressed by various leading men to become their guest. Unwilling to identify himself with any one tribe, he courteously replied that where the camel sat down there would he dwell. The beast stopped and sat down in a large open courtyard in the eastern quarter of the city. Mohamed purchased the land, and erected upon it the first mosque, a square building of stone, brick, and palm logs. The *Kibla*, towards which the faithful prayed, was Jerusalem. The *Azan*, or Call to Prayer, was now instituted, running as follows : " Great is the Lord ! Great is the Lord ! I bear witness that there is no God but the Lord : I bear witness that Mohamed is the Prophet of God. Come unto prayer : Come unto Salvation. God is Great ! God is Great ! There is no God but the Lord ! " The traveller from the West to this day finds nothing more solemn or more striking than to be awakened in the early dawn by the beautiful cadence of this call to prayer.

The Breach with the Jews.—In spite of the welcome given to the Prophet and the support of his kinsmen, he encountered not only local jealousies but the hostility of the three tribes of Jews towards the new religion. In token of his breach with these, he suddenly directed the faithful to follow his example and pray towards Mecca. This reversal of custom was upon the whole a politic stroke ; for, although it laid Mohamed open to a charge of inconsistency, it must have gratified the people of Arabia by preserving to Mecca its pre-eminence in the ceremonial of the new faith.

The Battle of Badr, A.H. 2 (623), *and the Expulsion of the Beni Kainucas*.—For some six months after their arrival at Medina the *Muhajarin*, or " Refugees," were busily occupied in settling down, and in sending for their families, whom the Kureish allowed to depart, although they might well have kept them as hostages. Attacks were then made on the Mecca caravans trading with Syria, but at first without result. In the second year of the *Hijra*, however, a small caravan was captured on the road between Mecca and Tayif, and a member of the Kureish tribe was killed. Such was Mohamed's first success.

He was soon to gain a greater victory, the results of which all Moslem historians have rightly regarded as marking a new era for the religion he taught. Hearing that a rich caravan belonging to Mecca was on its way back from Syria, the Prophet proceeded to Badr with 300 men, hoping to intercept it. News, however, reached Mecca, and the full force of the Kureish marched out to the rescue. The caravan meanwhile escaped by travelling off the main route, and the Prophet, upon reaching Badr, learned that an army of 900 Kureish was encamped in the neighbourhood. His enemies, upon learning that the caravan was safe, were not anxious to fight with their fellow-tribesmen ; but Mohamed, feeling that he must win or retreat in disgrace, decided to attack. The battle, as was customary, was preceded by single combats, in which the Moslems were invariably successful, and in the engagement which ensued they carried all before them, the Kureish fleeing, after sustaining a loss of forty-nine killed against fourteen on the other side. Among the slain were some of Mohamed's leading enemies, and those among the prisoners who were specially obnoxious to the Moslems were butchered in cold blood. The remainder were taken to Medina, where they were well treated until ransomed. Of the rich spoil taken the Prophet reserved one-fifth for himself, and divided the remainder equally. The victory of Badr was a turning-point in Islam ; for if the Prophet had returned to Medina a fugitive, his enemies would probably have prevailed against him. As it was, his success against a force of the Kureish three times as strong as his own justified him before his followers in ascribing the victory to divine aid. In the eighth *sura*, or "series," we read, "And ye slew them not, but God slew them."

The year after the battle of Badr, Mohamed felt himself strong enough to attack the Beni Kainucas, one of the three tribes of Jews resident in Medina. The other two made no attempt to come to the aid of their co-religionists, and the unfortunate Beni Kainucas were forced by lack of supplies to submit. The Prophet at first intended to massacre all the men, but in the end they were permitted to leave Medina after being stripped of their property. As they were goldsmiths and armourers by occupation their departure did not furnish landed property to the Moslems.

The Battle of Ohod, A.H. 3 (625), *and the Expulsion of the Beni Nazir.*—The career of the Prophet was not without vicissitudes. In A.H. 3 (625) a Kureish force 3000 strong, burning to avenge the defeat at Badr, attacked the Moslem army, which only mustered 1000 men, at Ohod, outside Medina. As at Badr, the Moslems had the advantage in the single combats, but in the general hand-to-hand contest which ensued, the superior numbers of the Kureish won the day. Mohamed was wounded, and but for his foresight in fighting with his back to some crags, there might well have been an irretrievable disaster. As it was, he lost seventy-four warriors, and his prestige was sensibly lowered. But his burning eloquence gradually persuaded his followers that these reverses were but to test them, and in the following year he strengthened his position by driving out the second of the Jewish tribes. The Beni Nazir were agriculturists, and when they yielded and quitted Medina, the Prophet was able to distribute rich lands and date-groves among his chief supporters.

The Siege of Medina and the Massacre of the Beni Koreitza, A.H. 5 (627).—Two years after the battle of Ohod a still larger army of the Kureish, 10,000 strong, marched on Medina. There could be no thought of meeting such an overwhelming force in the field ; so by the advice of Salman, a Persian captive, Medina was fortified. This unexpected artifice, held to be unworthy of Arabs, entirely baffled the Kureish, who after making some unsuccessful assaults broke up camp and marched off. Upon their retirement Mohamed massacred the Beni Koreitza, the third Jewish tribe residing in Medina, which had had dealings with the invaders, and his followers benefited by the rich booty thus acquired. By the repulse of the Kureish the disgrace of Ohod had been wiped out, and the position of Mohamed, whose enemies, the Jews, had disappeared from Medina, was now supreme in that city.

The Truce of Hodeibia, A.H. 6 (628).—The next important step taken by the Prophet was to attempt the pilgrimage to Mecca. This was in the sixth year after the *Hijra*, and although the Kureish refused to permit Mohamed and his followers to enter the Sacred City, a truce was made, known as the Truce of Hodeibia, and it was agreed that the pilgrims would be admitted in the following year. The chief importance of the pact was that, for the first time, he had negotiated with the Kureish on equal terms.

The Embassies sent by Mohamed, A.H. 7 (628).—Few events in the life of Mohamed are of greater interest than the letters sent by him to Heraclius, to the Great King, to the Governors of Yemen and of Egypt, and to the King of Abyssinia. That to the Great King is said to have run as follows : " In the name of God, the Merciful, the Compassionate. From Mohamed, the Apostle of God to Khusru son of Hormuzd. But to proceed. Verily I extol unto thee God, beside whom there is no other God. O Khusru ! Submit and thou shalt be safe, or else prepare to wage with God and with his Apostle a war which shall not find them helpless ! Farewell ! " According to the legend, the Great King tore up the epistle, and the Prophet on hearing of it prayed, " Even thus, O Lord ! rend Thou his kingdom from him ! "

The Conquest of Khaybar, A.H. 7 (628).—The conquest of Khaybar, a rich district inhabited by Jews and situated about one hundred miles north of Medina, was the next exploit of the conquering Prophet. The Jews were surprised and offered but little resistance after the death of their champion Merhab, who was cut in two by Ali, now the son-in-law of the Prophet, whose daughter Fatima he had married. The theme is a popular one in Persian art, as is proved by the illustration facing p. 534. The seizure of the land by Mohamed added considerably to his resources, and the booty was very rich. Moreover, he had now destroyed the last centre of Judaism in the vicinity of Medina, and henceforward there is little or no mention of the Jews.

THE ESTABLISHMENT OF ISLAM

The "Fulfilled Pilgrimage," A.H. 7 (629).—Perhaps there is no more extraordinary event in the history of the Prophet than the "Fulfilled Pilgrimage." In accordance with their agreement the Kureish vacated the city of Mecca for three days, and Mohamed at the head of 2000 men performed the rites by encircling the sacred spot seven times, riding seven times between Safa and Marwa, and sacrificing the victims brought from Medina. On the following day the *azan* was sounded, and Mohamed led the service in the same manner as at Medina, while the Kureish from the adjacent hills looked down with wonder at the extraordinary spectacle. The pilgrimage undoubtedly augmented the prestige of the Prophet, who was shortly afterwards joined by Khalid, the great general, and by other men of importance.

The Battle of Muta, A.H. 8 (629).—The raids from Medina now extended to the borders of Syria, and so great was the alarm inspired by Mohamed's activity that at Muta, near the Dead Sea, his main force of 3000 men was opposed by the imperial troops. Charged by a Roman phalanx supported by Arabs on either flank, Zayd, the commander, and his successors were killed one by one, and only the genius of Khalid saved the defeat from becoming a disaster. As it was, the losses were heavy.

The Capture of Mecca, A.H. 8 (630).—The defeat at Muta cannot have shaken the prestige of the Prophet very severely, since a few months later he crowned his successful career by suddenly marching on Mecca at the head of 10,000 men. No resistance was attempted, and as he treated his fellow-tribesmen with magnanimity, they became converts in large numbers. After superintending the destruction of the idols in the sacred enclosure, Mohamed gave orders for all private images to be broken. This was effected without difficulty, and thus without a single battle the sacred city of Mecca was won and with it the hegemony of Arabia. This achievement was completed by the crushing of the Hawazin tribe which occupied the country to the south-east of Mecca.

The Last Campaign of Mohamed, A.H. 9 (630).—The campaign of Tebuk was the last undertaken by the Prophet in person. He heard that the Emperor was organizing a large force, and with remarkable courage and energy prepared to meet it. He assembled a powerful army, said to have numbered 30,000, of which one-third was cavalry, and marched to Tebuk, to the east of the Gulf of Akaba. There he learned that there was no truth in the rumours of invasion, and consequently directed his efforts to extending and consolidating his power. The Christian prince of Ayla, at the head of the Gulf of Akaba, summoned to submit and pay tribute, immediately complied, and with him a treaty was concluded. Duma was captured by Khalid, and its Christian chief embraced Islam. After these successes the Prophet returned home with greatly increased prestige, and when Tayif, the last town to resist him, surrendered, his power reached its zenith.

The Final Orders of the Prophet.—At the end of A.H. 9 (631) Mohamed promulgated at Mecca by the mouth of Ali the famous " Release," allowing idolaters four months in which to embrace Islam, and giving notice that in case of refusal they would be crushed. To Jews and Christians, as possessing revealed scriptures, slightly better terms were announced. They were, however, to be reduced to tribute and humbled. This proclamation was followed up by the despatch of embassies to every part of Arabia, the whole of which, including even distant Oman, submitted to the now all-powerful Prophet, and embraced Islam.

The " Farewell Pilgrimage," A.H. 10 (630).—The venerable Prophet was sixty-three years of age and full of honour when he made what is known as the " Farewell Pilgrimage." This set the seal on his success, and it is impossible to follow him to it without sympathy and appreciation of his achievements. His farewell to the people of Mecca ends with the exclamation, " O Lord ! I have delivered my message and discharged my Ministry."

The Death of Mohamed, A.H. 11 (632).—Shortly after his return from Mecca, Mohamed was seized with fever, and for some days suffered severely. One morning, as Abu Bekr was leading the prayers, the congregation was delighted by the appearance of the Prophet, who spoke to the people after the service. But this was a last effort, and the exhaustion it occasioned brought on his death.

His Character.—No impartial student surveying the career and character of Mohamed can fail to acknowledge his loftiness of purpose, his moral courage, his sincerity, his simplicity, and his kindness. To these qualities must be added unsparing energy and a genius for diplomacy. Muir is well advised in distinguishing between the early period of adversity and the later years in which success and power were achieved; for it was almost inevitable that as the Prophet became the ruler of Arabia the worldly side of his character should develop at the expense of the spiritual. Instances of cruelty and treachery are undoubtedly proved against him; but it is always to be borne in mind that in judging this extraordinary man we must apply not the standard of our own time, but that of a period and of a world in which cruelty was rife. Like Solomon, whom he resembled in character, he became uxorious in his old age, and for this characteristic also the same allowance must be made. It is certain that he never lost the love and admiration of men of the highest character, such as Abu Bekr and Omar, and to the end he retained his simplicity, his kindliness, and his courtesy to rich and poor alike. Moreover, he continued throughout his career to proclaim himself "a simple prophet and a warner," though he might easily have made higher claims.

Exactly what the Arabs thought as to the meaning of Islam, may be realized from the following tradition: "Gabriel one day came in the form of an Arab and, sitting near the Prophet, exclaimed, ' O Messenger of Allah, what is Islam?' The Prophet replied: ' Islam is to believe in Allah and his Prophet, to recite the prescribed prayers, to give alms, to observe the fast of Ramazan, and to make the pilgrimage to Mecca.'"

The introduction of Islam brought many benefits to the Arabs. It taught the unity of God, enjoined brotherly love towards all fellow-believers, proscribed infanticide, secured rights for women and consideration for slaves. Alcohol was strictly forbidden. Impartial observers have told me that in India Islam has raised millions of men in self-respect and other virtues to a wonderful extent, and I have already shown how beneficent was its effect upon the Arabs. In the case of the Mongols the change was no less marked, as may be seen by contrasting the savagery of Chengiz with the kindness, the consideration, and the justice of Ghazan, whose many virtues were undoubtedly due to his genuine conversion to Islam. In Africa, too, when the negro adopts Islam he generally rises in the scale of humanity. While remaining an African, he is better dressed, better mannered, and altogether a better and cleaner man. On the other hand, a negro when Christianized is sometimes unable to assimilate our more complex civilization, and in such cases becomes a caricature of the European. These remarks apply to a certain extent to the Asiatic also, but in a lesser degree, because the Semite and the Aryan start from ancient civilizations of their own.

If, as I believe, religion is made for man and not man for religion, it is impossible to withhold approval and admiration from a man whose achievements have been so great. But against these undoubted benefits of Islam there are some things to be set on the other side. The list includes polygamy, the seclusion and veiling of women, slavery, narrowness of thought, and harsh treatment of non-Moslems. As for polygamy, it is slowly dying out owing to progress and economic circumstances, and the veil too, with all that it stands for, is beginning to disappear in Turkey. It must be recollected that even in Christian Spain the women are partially secluded, and perhaps wisely.

We come to slavery. This very ancient practice of mankind was accepted by Mohamed who, however, wrote: "Honour Allah and be kind even to your slaves." In Persia, at any rate, slaves are kept only as domestic servants, and are particularly well treated, being with reason trusted more than hired servants; in this connexion, the child borne by a slave to her master belongs to his class and is born free. Can we, with a recollection of Hawkins, who bought negroes in Africa to sell in America, throw stones at slavery among Moslems? I think not. Freedom of thought and private judgment are gradually asserting themselves among Moslems, just as among Roman Catholics, however much the *mullas* in the one case or the Pope in the other may deny these privileges. Moreover, until quite modern times it has been the general custom of man to persecute those from whom he differed on religious grounds, and the Moslems certainly have not treated Christians more harshly than the inquisitors did. Toleration is, in fact, a sentiment of recent growth.

If the lives of great men are studied, imperfections are invariably revealed, and in many cases the greater the man the more conspicuous the faults. Personally I hold that Mohamed was, with all his human frailties, one of the greatest of mankind; that he was impelled by the highest motives to beat down idolatry and fill its place with the much higher conception of Islam, and that by so doing he rendered an immense service to the human race, a service to which I pay homage.

The Koran.—The book known as the Koran[1] is the foundation of Islam. It is regarded by more than one hundred millions of mankind as the actual word of God. It consists exclusively of the revelations which Mohamed claimed to receive through Gabriel as messages direct from God. These messages were received throughout the twenty-three years of his prophetical life, and were recited by Mohamed before his followers and committed both to memory and to writing. In the stage of culture which prevailed at that period in Arabia writing was a rare accomplishment, and the general belief is that the Prophet himself could neither read nor write ; memory was therefore much stronger than among modern civilized races, and during the lifetime of Mohamed many of his followers had committed to memory the whole of the Koran. To-day the title of *Hafiz*, which implies this sacred accomplishment, is one of honour. But it must not be supposed that during Mohamed's life the order of the various chapters and verses was settled. Indeed we know that this was not the case, for Omar, after the overthrow of Moseilama, pointed out to Abu Bekr that the losses among the reciters of the Koran had been heavy, and suggested that its various portions should be collected. This pious task was entrusted to Zayd, the Chief Secretary of the Prophet, who sought out the fragments and gathered them together, "from date-leaves, from tablets of white stone and from the breasts of men." This was the official and authoritative edition ; but a generation later, under Othman, a second edition was prepared by a committee consisting of Zayd and three members of the Kureish tribe. The original copy of the first edition was produced for this purpose, and a final authoritative edition was prepared, all existing copies being burned after its issue. In consequence of this care, there is no question whatever that the Koran, as read to-day all over the Moslem world, is identical with that published during the Caliphate of Othman. In the sequence of some of the verses there is confusion, but throughout there is no question as to their genuineness and accuracy. When we consider the times in which they had their origin this is remarkable.

---

[1] Koran signifies "reading aloud." The syllable *Al* which is occasionally prefixed is the definite article.

The Koran is universally admitted to be written in the most perfect Arabic, the dialect of the Kureish tribe, and it is held to be as much a masterpiece of literature as we esteem our Bible to be. Moreover, the Koran is read to-day exactly as it was dictated by Mohamed, whereas we cannot deny that the Bible is a translation.

To enlarge upon the doctrine preached in the Koran would be beyond the scope of this work. The one aim and object of Mohamed in the Meccan *suras* was to convert his fellow-countrymen from idolatry to the worship of one God. To effect this, the Prophet, who deeply felt his responsibility, extolled the omnipotence of God and derided the impotence of the idols in passages of rhymed rhetoric. The penalties of hell and the sensual and material pleasures of Paradise are graphically described, and throughout, as Nicholson says, " his genius proclaims itself by grand lyrical outbursts." As an example I quote one of the early *suras*, which runs :

> When the Sky shall be severed,
> And when the Stars shall be shivered,
> And when the Seas to mingle shall be suffered,
> And when the graves shall be uncovered—
> A soul shall know that which it hath deferred or delivered.[1]
> O Man, what beguiled thee against thy gracious Master to rebel,
> Who created thee and fashioned thee right and thy frame did fairly build ?
> He composed thee in whatever form he willed.
> Nay, but you disbelieve in the Ordeal ! [2]
> Verily over you are Recorders honourable,
> Your deeds inscribing without fail.

To conclude, the revelations at Medina deal with what may be termed the business side of religion ; laws, ordinances, and manifestos all finding place side by side with occasional but rare outbursts of flaming genius. Yet behind it all were the call to monotheism and the denunciation of idolatry, on which the Koran can claim, and justly claim, to stand.

---

[1] *I.e.* what it has done or left undone.
[2] The Last Judgment.

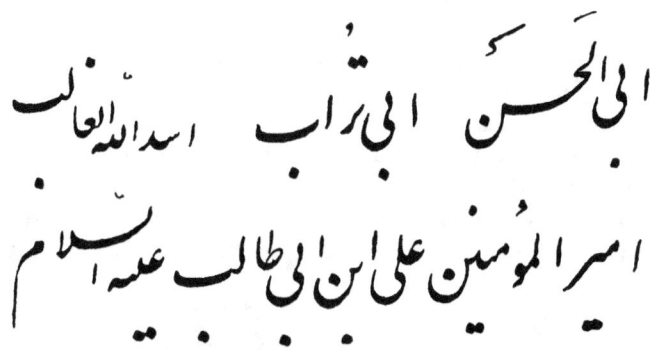

Father of Hasan, Father of Dust, The Victorious Lion of Allah, The Commander of the Faithful, Ali son of Abu Talib, on Him be Peace!

THE TITLES OF ALI.
(Through the courtesy of H.E. the Persian Minister.)

CHAPTER XLVI

ISLAM UNDER THE FIRST FOUR CALIPHS

Politically Persia ceased for a while to enjoy a separate national existence, being merged in that great Muhammadan Empire which stretched from Gibraltar to the Jaxartes, but in the intellectual domain she soon began to assert the supremacy to which the ability and subtlety of her people entitled her.—BROWNE.

The Period of the Caliphate, A.D. 632–1258.—The Caliphate began with the election of Abu Bekr in A.D. 632 and lasted until A.D. 1258, when Hulagu Khan sacked Baghdad and put Motasim Billah to death. For nearly three centuries after this catastrophe the title of Caliph was perpetuated in Egypt by descendants of the House of Abbas who lived under the protection of its Mameluke rulers, until in A.D. 1517 Sultan Selim, the Osmanli, having conquered the Mameluke dynasty, induced the helpless Caliph to transfer to him the title and insignia. It is on this transaction (recorded in Chapter LXII.) that the Sultans of Turkey base their claim to the sacred position of Caliph and to other high titles.

The Caliphate falls into three well-defined periods:

1. That of the First Four Caliphs, A.D. 632–661, the period of the Theocracy of Islam.[1]

2. The Omayyad Caliphs, A.D. 661–749, the period of Pagan Reaction.

[1] *Vide* Browne, *op. cit.* p. 210.

3. The Abbasid Caliphs, A.D. 749-1258, the period of Persian Ascendancy.

The Genealogical Table of the Kureish.—In order to show the descent of the various dynasties, and their claims of kinship with the Prophet, it is convenient to give the following genealogical table, which is taken from Lane-Poole's *Mohamedan Dynasties*, an invaluable guide to the student :

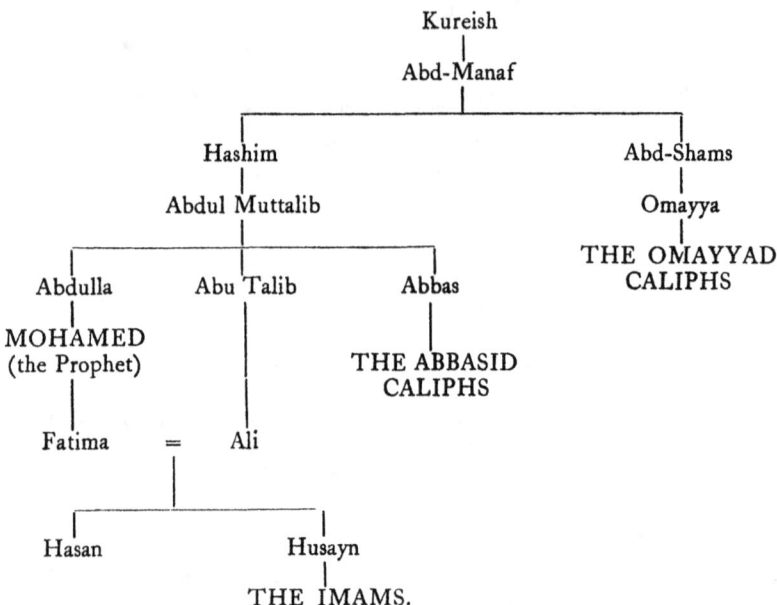

The Election of Abu Bekr.—Even before the Prophet was buried, there was very nearly bloodshed in Medina at the meeting at which Abu Bekr was chosen to be the Caliph,[1] or " Successor " of the Prophet. He was sixty years old at the time of his election, and was naturally of a mild character. But belief in the Prophet filled him with a moral courage unsurpassed in the records of history.

The Rebellions, A.H. 11 (632).—Before his illness the Prophet had given orders for an expedition to avenge the disaster of Muta ; but Osama, its commander, on hearing of the calamity which had befallen Islam, brought back the banner entrusted to him. Abu Bekr showed his fearlessness by immediately insisting that this expedition should be

---

[1] *Khalifa Rasul Illah*, or " Successor of the Prophet of Allah," is the full title.

carried through, although it left the city almost defenceless, and his decision was justified by the result. Yet the courage it showed was extraordinary ; for insurrections broke out all over Arabia, and only Medina, Mecca, and Tayif stood firm for Islam. Medina itself was besieged, or rather blockaded, by neighbouring tribes, but Abu Bekr called out every man capable of bearing arms, attacked the Beduins, and drove them off with slaughter. As Muir points out, defeat at this juncture might well have involved the disappearance of Islam, and to Abu Bekr must be given all credit for the victory. After two months of serious danger the return of Osama as a victor enabled the Caliph, whose prestige must have been enormously enhanced, to crush the insurrections.

With supreme confidence Abu Bekr summoned the leaders of Islam, and, dividing Arabia into eleven districts, despatched a column to each. The most important command was given to Khalid, whose first act was to march north to attack the Beni Tayy and Beni Asad, who had espoused the cause of Toleiha, a rival prophet. The Beni Tayy were won over by diplomacy, while the Beni Asad deserted their Prophet in the battle and then submitted.

In a second campaign the Beni Temim were massacred by Khalid. But his hardest fight was with Moseilama, a rival Prophet, who was supported by the Beni Hanifa of Yemama, at the back of Al-Katif, a tribe which numbered 40,000 fighting men. The struggle was desperate, and in the first charge the Moslems were beaten back to their camp. But they rallied and broke the Beni Hanifa, who took refuge in a walled garden. The Moslem heroes leapt down among them, and the " Garden of Death," as it was termed from the slaughter, was never forgotten. In the slaughter, which was terrible on both sides, the Moslems lost 1200 men, among whom were thirty-nine warriors bearing the honoured title of *Ashab* or " Companions " of the Prophet. This was the crowning victory, and a few months later, within a year of Mohamed's death, peace reigned once again in Arabia, every district of which had been visited by the irresistible columns of Abu Bekr.

The Battle on the Yermuk, A.H. 13 (634).—In Chapter XLIII. I have confined myself to the campaigns waged against Iran ; it will be appropriate here to give a brief account of the wonderful exploits of Islam in other fields.

It must be borne in mind that almost our sole authority for these is Arab tradition. But although in details this is naturally partial and one-sided, there is little or no doubt as to the main facts.

The victories of Abu Bekr left the Arab tribes defeated and sullen ; but the call to war and plunder welded them together and, as success followed success, tribe after tribe not only sent out its fighting men, but marched in its entirety to settle in more fertile lands.

The strategy of the Caliph in attacking the Roman and Persian Empires simultaneously must have seemed to be midsummer madness, and, judged by all ordinary canons, it was so. But in the end the madmen won, although they were compelled from time to time to neglect one field of operations in order to ensure success in another.

In A.H. 12 (633) Khalid started on his victorious career against the Persian Empire, and in the same year a second Khalid, son of Said, was despatched with instructions to organize the friendly tribes on the Syrian frontier, but to avoid fighting unless attacked. Having in A.H. 13 (634) incautiously pushed northwards towards Damascus, he found his communications cut near the Sea of Tiberias, and thereupon fled panic-stricken, leaving his camp to the enemy. The retreating Arabs were rallied by Ikrima, who had already distinguished himself in Hadhramaut, and Abu Bekr sent such large reinforcements that the army of Syria became the main army of Islam, as compared with the weak force entrusted to Khalid. We read that there were more than one thousand " Companions " in its ranks. Organized into four divisions, with a total strength of 30,000, apart from a reserve of 6000 men under Ikrima, it marched north, and working in independent columns eventually threatened Syria, from Hebron on the west to Damascus on the east.

Heraclius despatched four armies to overwhelm the scattered columns, which thereupon united on the left bank of the Yermuk, an eastern tributary of the Jordan. There the two hosts faced one another for months, without risking any decisive action. Abu Bekr in great anxiety ordered Khalid to leave Irak, and that general, with 9000 men, made one of the greatest desert marches on record and joined the Syrian army. In A.H. 13 (634) he gained a complete victory, known as the battle of Wakusa, over a vastly superior Byzantine army. Thousands of the enemy were driven over a chasm, and the victory, although purchased at heavy cost, won Syria for Islam.

The Death of Abu Bekr and the Accession of Omar, A.H. 13 (634).—After Abu Bekr had ruled Islam for two years he felt his end approaching, and appointed Omar his successor. He then continued to occupy himself with public business until his death, which removed from the stage one of the noblest, simplest, and bravest characters known in history. Among his favourite aphorisms was the following : " One of the best of men is he who rejoices over a penitent, prays for a sinner, and aids a charitable man in his good work."

The first act of Omar was to remove Khalid from his command, after which he raised reinforcements to aid the army in the field by every possible means. As long as he lived the forces of Islam were directed with consummate skill.

The Capture of Damascus, A.H. 14 (635).—Damascus, one of the oldest cities in the world, was the goal of the victorious Arabs. Being unversed in the art of besieging, they made no scientific approaches but merely invested the city, and for months little or no progress was effected. Finally Khalid, who although deposed from the command was still the real leader, crossed the moat by night on inflated skins, escaladed the battlements, and captured the city. A second victory on the plain of Esdraelon ended the campaign and riveted the Moslem yoke on Syria. Reinforcements were then despatched to Irak, where they arrived just in time to win the battle of Cadesia.

The Capture of Antioch and the Capitulation of Jerusalem, A.H. 15 (636).—After the battle of the Jordan the Moslems marched northwards and besieged Hims, the ancient Emessa, which capitulated. Antioch, too, surrendered after a battle fought outside its walls, and Heraclius, scarcely more than a decade after his splendid victories over Persia, withdrew from Syria, leaving Jerusalem to its fate. The Holy City of Christendom capitulated in A.H. 15 (636), and Omar arrived in person to receive its submission. He marked this historical event by acts of clemency and by the foundation of the mosque which bears his name to-day.

The Conquest of Egypt, A.H. 19–20 (640–641).—While the Arabs were making good their position in South-Western Persia before advancing on to the Iranian plateau, Amr started from Palestine to invade Egypt with a force of only 4000 men. Omar, alarmed at the risk that was being run, at first thought of recalling his daring general, but on realizing that this was impossible sent him considerable reinforcements. With an army now 15,000 strong he had the country at his mercy. He first annexed Upper Egypt, and then marched on Alexandria, the second city of the Byzantine Empire, to which he laid siege. The death of Heraclius, occurring at this juncture, prevented the despatch of a relieving squadron, and the city capitulated on terms. Not content with these conquests, the forces of Amr marched west along the southern coast of the Mediterranean as far as Tripoli.

The Assassination of Omar, A.H. 23 (644).—By this time the power of Islam had been firmly established. The empire of the Chosroes had been annexed and that of Byzantium defeated and deprived of its fairest and richest provinces. Omar, under whose master mind these wonderful campaigns had been conducted with entire success, had been Caliph for ten years and, although sixty years old, was still full of energy when an assassin's knife laid him low. A Persian slave, known as Abu Lulu, complained to the Caliph that he was assessed too heavily by his master at two *dirhems* a day. Omar, who knew the man, replied that for a clever artificer like him, who was believed to be able to construct a mill driven by wind,[1] the amount was not excessive. Abu Lulu made a threatening reply, and the following morning stabbed the Caliph while he was leading the prayers in the mosque.

Thus died the greatest Moslem after the founder of the religion himself, a man of courage, simplicity, sagacity, with a passion for justice and duty,[2] a combination of qualities which eminently fitted him to control the destinies of Islam during the critical decade of conquest. Nevertheless in Persia the name of Omar is execrated, and the anniversary of his death is celebrated as a day of rejoicing by Persians. Until recently they were accustomed to burn the effigy of the Caliph who conquered Iran.

The Accession of Othman, A.H. 24 (644).—Omar upon his death-bed expressed the wish that Abd-al-Rahman should be his successor, but he refused, and the matter was referred

---

[1] This is believed to be the earliest mention of a windmill. *Vide* also Chapter I.
[2] It was a favourite maxim of Omar's that "the most miserable Governor is he whose subjects are miserable."

to a body of electors. In the end, however, Abd-al-Rahman was permitted to make the choice. For long he wavered between Ali and Othman, but finally declared the latter to be the Caliph. Othman's reign lasted for twelve years, but from the outset it was clear that he did not possess the necessary qualities for dealing effectively with a difficult situation. Even under the iron rule of Omar it was impossible to curb the insubordinate spirit shown by the Arabs of Kufa and Basra. The best hope lay in maintaining the prestige of the Kureish tribe, but this powerful instrument was weakened through the impolicy of Othman, who favoured his own branch, the Omayyad, with the result that the influence of the Kureish was paralysed by divisions which were widened by lapse of time.

The Expansion of Islam to the West, A.H. 25–31 (646–652). —The limits of Moslem expansion had not yet been reached, and under Abu Sarh, a foster-brother of Othman, the Arabs pushed west of Barca and even threatened Carthage, whose Governor was defeated in a hard-fought battle. This period, too, saw the launching of the first Moslem fleet, in A.H. 28 (649). Its initial enterprise resulted in the capture of Cyprus, and three years later it won a naval victory off Alexandria, under the command of Abu Sarh.

The Campaigns in Persia, A.H. 31 (652).—The death of Omar had been the signal in Persia for a widespread but badly organized insurrection, and the Moslem leaders sought not only to reconquer what had been lost but to extend the sway of Islam eastwards. Ibn Aamir, the Governor of Basra, who was entrusted with the conduct of the campaign, first reduced the province of Fars, and then marched across the Lut and invaded the province of Kuhistan, of which he obtained possession. After these successes he sent a summons to submit to the Governor of Herat, who craftily replied that he would do so when Nishapur was taken. Ibn Aamir proceeded to invest Nishapur, while at the same time devastating the neighbouring valley of Tus. His troops suffered severely from the cold, but he reduced the city by blockade, and its Governor paid a sum of 700,000 dinars, together with many articles of value. Thereupon the Governors of Herat and of Merv both made terms. It was in this same year that, as already mentioned, Yezdigird was murdered, and his death must have been a great relief to the Caliph. Ibn Aamir, pressing constantly eastwards, won a great victory on the

Oxus, which led to the submission of Balkh and other outlying provinces of the Persian Empire. His generals crossed the Hindu Kush, subdued Kabul, and conquered the Sistan and Kerman provinces. The advance, however, was not unchequered by reverse, for the Arabs were defeated by the Khazars in Azerbaijan, and an entire army perished in the snows of Kerman.[1]

The Murder of Othman, A.H. 35 (656).—As the years went by dissatisfaction with Othman grew deeper. His favouritism towards his own kinsmen of the Omayyad branch was resented by the Hashimite branch at a time when the Beduins of Kufa and Basra were ready to rise against the supremacy of the Kureish. In A.H. 34 (655) Said, the Governor of Kufa, was expelled by its ever-turbulent inhabitants, and Othman, instead of inflicting any punishment, weakly yielded to the storm and appointed another Governor.

In the following year forces from Kufa, Basra, and Egypt converged on Medina, and after an initial failure besieged the palace. The octogenarian Caliph was deserted by the leading men of the city and murdered, meeting his end with dignity and courage.

The Election of Ali, A.H. 35 (656).—After this ghastly tragedy there was a reign of terror in Medina, during which Ali, the cousin and son-in-law of the Prophet, was elected Caliph. As a boy he had been one of the earliest converts to Islam, and during the Prophet's life he had shown great heroism and conspicuous ability on the battlefield. Of late years he had lived at Medina, where he enjoyed respect, but had taken no leading part in public affairs. In appearance he was short, stout, and bald.

Muavia, the Governor of Syria.—Among the ablest and most powerful of the Arab chiefs was Muavia, whose father, Abu Sofian, had commanded the Kureish at the battle of Ohod, but had afterwards been converted to Islam. Muavia, who was destined to found the Omayyad dynasty, had distinguished himself in the early campaigns, and had been appointed by Omar to the governorship of Syria, a post which he held for many years. He had visited Medina before the assassination of his kinsman Othman, and had begged to be allowed to lead a Syrian army to his defence, but the aged

---

[1] I would locate the scene of this disaster in Sardu, as the Arabs occupied Jiruft. *Vide* Yule's *Marco Polo* (Cordier's edition), vol. i. p. 313.

Caliph had refused his proffered aid. After the murder Muavia acquired possession of Othman's blood-stained shirt and hung it up in the mosque at Damascus, but he refrained from any definite action until he knew what course Ali would pursue.

The Proclamation of War against Muavia by Ali, A.H. 35 (656).—Upon his election to the Caliphate Ali was advised to pursue and punish the assassins, but declined on the ground that he lacked the power. At the same time he was unwise enough to dismiss Muavia, in spite of entreaties to leave him in his post until his own position was secure. Muavia thereupon encouraged the belief that Ali was in collusion with the murderers, and consequently no other course was open to the newly elected Caliph but to proclaim war against him.

The Battle of the Camel, A.H. 36 (656).—Ali was unfortunate in having Ayesha, the favourite wife of the Prophet, as his enemy. She was used as a tool by Talha [1] and Zobayr, who seized Basra after a struggle with the loyalists. Upon the receipt of reinforcements from Kufa, Ali advanced on Basra and attempted to avoid civil war, but failed owing to an attack brought on by the murderers of Othman. Consequently, the Battle of the Camel, so called from Ayesha's appearance in the fighting line in a camel litter, was fought with intense bitterness and with terrible losses on both sides. Talha and Zobayr were killed and Ayesha was captured. The vanquished were treated with magnanimity, but the battle was a heavy blow to the best interests of Islam, and might have been avoided had Ali from the first denounced the assassins of Othman and refused to have any dealings with them.

The Battle of Siffin, A.H. 37 (657).—After his victory at Basra, Ali proceeded to Kufa, which he made his capital. Organizing a large army, he marched up the Tigris and traversed the desert of Mesopotamia to the Euphrates, which he crossed. Muavia was ready with a powerful force, and after a fruitless attempt at reconciliation and much desultory skirmishing the battle of Siffin was fought in A.H. 37 (657). This desperate combat was distinguished by many feats of courage and raged for three days without decisive result. Muavia, becoming disheartened, agreed to a stratagem suggested by Amr, and caused his men to advance with scrolls

---

[1] Talha had saved Mohamed's life at Ohod.

of the Koran fixed to their lances, and crying out : " The law of the Lord ! Let that decide between us ! " Ali, realizing that it was only a ruse, would not stop the conflict, but his fanatical soldiers threatened to desert him unless he agreed to appoint an arbitrator. Even in this his hand was forced, since he was not allowed a free choice, but was compelled to place his interests in the hands of Abu Musa, a supporter who was at best but lukewarm.

The Arbitration, A.H. 37 (658).—Duma in the heart of the desert was the place appointed for the momentous decision, and thither Amr, the conqueror of Egypt, who represented Muavia, and Abu Musa both proceeded, followed by thousands of Arabs from both sides who assembled to hear the judgment. The two umpires agreed in private that both Ali and Muavia should be set aside and a fresh election held. Abu Musa gave this decision in public, but the astute Amr, who spoke after him, declared that he agreed to the deposition of Ali but confirmed Muavia as the heir of Othman, the avenger of his blood, and the best entitled to succeed as Caliph. This was an astonishing success for Muavia, who was proclaimed Caliph at Damascus, and a heavy blow for Ali, whose supporters, however, did not counsel him to resign the Caliphate.

The Kharijites.—Though destined after lapse of time to be revered as the equal of Mohamed by the Persian nation, Ali was most unfortunate during his life. No sooner had he been obliged, much against his own judgment, to accept arbitration than 12,000 of his soldiers separated themselves from the army on the ground that the cause of Islam had been abandoned to godless arbitrators, swearing that they would serve no Caliph, and insisting on " No rule but that of the Lord alone." Ali showed considerable patience, but before setting out after the arbitrament to attack Muavia, he was forced to deal with these fanatical sectaries, who were committing horrible excesses of every kind. The majority were allowed to disperse, but 1800 refused all terms and were killed to a man. The Kharijites or " Separatists " appeared again and again, not only in Irak but also in Persia, the remote Kerman province in particular being periodically troubled by the appearance of these visionaries in dangerously large bands.

The Last Years of Ali's Caliphate.—Ali had raised a large force for invading Syria once more, but after the diversion against the Kharijites it melted away so rapidly that the entire expedition had to be abandoned. The Arabs, indeed, were curiously indifferent to Ali. In the following year, A.H. 38 (658), he lost Egypt through an unwise change of Governors, and this misfortune preyed upon his mind; but he made no grand effort to retrieve his position. In the course of the same year rebellion was stirred up in Southern Persia by Khirrit, an Arab chief whose views resembled those of the Kharijites. Up to this point, it would seem, only Moslems had fought in these civil wars, but Khirrit raised Persians, Kurds, and Christians, and drove the Arab Governor out of Fars, and much blood was shed before he was slain and order re-established. Ziad, an illegitimate half-brother of Muavia, whom Ali now appointed to Fars, showed great capacity both in restoring peace and in the administration of the country; indeed he was compared to Noshirwan. In A.H. 40 (660) Ali made peace with Muavia, and it seemed as though at last his troubles were ended.

His Assassination, A.H. 40 (661).—The fanatical Kharijites, seeing that they could not force their doctrines on the empire, were in hopeless mood. Three of them discussed the gloomy situation, and resolved each to kill a leader of Islam, Ali, Muavia, and Amr being the selected victims. Amr escaped through being absent on the day they had fixed for the deed, Muavia was wounded and recovered, but Ali was mortally stabbed. With the magnanimity which characterized him, he gave orders that, if he died, the assassin should be executed but not tortured. After making his will, the unfortunate Caliph passed away and with him ended the period of theocracy in Islam.

His Character.—Ali stands out as the Caliph who was too noble and high-minded for his surroundings. He refused to be guided by the dictates of expediency and was, in consequence, no match for his adroit and intriguing rival Muavia, who would stoop to the lowest and most criminal means to gain his purpose. At the same time he was narrow, with a vein of indecision which at times gave place to obstinacy. His rigid insistence on honesty in accounts was much resented by the greedy Arabs who plundered the empire. But his perfect integrity and devotion to high ideals, combined with his simplicity and unassuming manners, make him a most attractive figure, and the people of Persia have chosen wisely in making him what we may term their Patron Saint, though, indeed, he is much more than that.

Some of his aphorisms were : " A liberal education is better than gold," to which was added, " No learning availeth if common sense goeth not with it " ; " The wealth of a wise man is in his wisdom, and the wealth of a fool is in his possessions " ; " No words are good unless good deeds go with them."

The Position of Persia.—" Hellenism," says Nöldeke, " never touched more than the surface of Persian life, but Iran was penetrated to the core by Arabian religion and Arabian ways." This weighty saying should be constantly borne in mind in considering the consequences of the conquest of Persia by the Arabs, for it is the key to the whole situation. After the battle of Nahavand Persian resistance to the Arabs was merely local and the country was subdued without any great difficulty, although a general insurrection broke out upon the death of Omar and there were occasional risings during the Caliphate of Ali. The Zoroastrians were not offered the choice between Islam and the sword, as is generally supposed, but were permitted to retain their religion on the payment of a poll-tax. Salman, who has already been mentioned as fortifying Medina against the Kureish, was the earliest Persian convert, and was numbered among the " Companions " of the Prophet. His example was followed later on by thousands, among whom was a body of Daylamite soldiers who embraced Islam and settled at Kufa. But even conversion brought no true equality, and in order to secure their lives and property the Persian nobles had to humble their pride and become clients of the Arabs. The contempt which the conquerors displayed towards the people they subdued, stronger than that of the Normans for the conquered Saxons, is exemplified in their bitter saying, " Three things only stop prayer : the passing of a client, an ass, or a dog." [1] On the other hand, the finances of the country were modelled on the Persian system and the administration was manned by Persians in spite of efforts to keep them out.

We read of Zoroastrians still forming the majority in Fars in the tenth century ; of others who flourished in remote Kuhistan, the central portion of modern Khorasan, and of some who emigrated by way of Hormuz to India. But the

[1] *Vide* Jurji Zaydan's *History of Islamic Civilization*, p. 70 (Gibb Memorial).

emigrants were few in number, and from references which abound in the Arab chroniclers it is clear that fire temples and Zoroastrian communities existed in many parts of Persia until comparatively recent times. To-day the only two important bodies of adherents to "the good religion" reside near Yezd and Kerman ; but I recollect being informed that the inhabitants of various villages to the north-west of Yezd had not been converted to Islam until early in the nineteenth century.[1]

Although Persia ceased for a time to exist as an independent state, she soon asserted her intellectual superiority over the Arabs, whom, as the centuries went by, lack of education and capacity drove back to the deserts from which they had originally issued. At the same time the contemptuous treatment of the Persians was persisted in for many generations.

[1] *Ten Thousand Miles*, etc., p. 156.

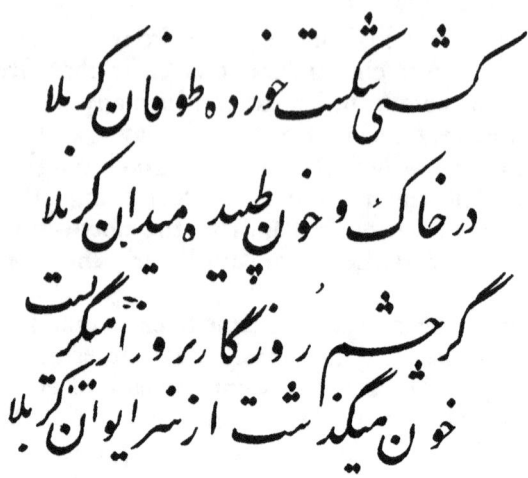

(Through the courtesy of H.E. the Persian Minister.)

CHAPTER XLVII

THE TRAGEDY OF KERBELA

>The ship is broken, shattered by the storm of Kerbela;
>Fallen in the dust and blood on the field of Kerbela.
>If the Eyes of the World openly wept
>The blood would have risen above the Arch of Kerbela.
>
>From the *Elegy of Muhtasham*.

The Accession of Hasan and his Abdication, A.H. 40 (661).—Upon the death of Ali, Hasan, his eldest son by Fatima, was elected Caliph. Muavia prepared to march against Kufa, where an army 40,000 strong rallied to support the claims of the house of Ali. But Hasan, unworthy son of a noble father, was more occupied with the pleasures of the harem than with the toils of administration or the dangers of war. He sent a vanguard of 12,000 men to the front and kept the main body behind at Madain, where he himself remained dallying among the gardens, afraid to try his fortune on the battlefield. On a false report that the vanguard had been cut to pieces, the fickle Kufans looted the camp of the Caliph and attempted to seize his person, hoping to make good terms for themselves with his rival. Panic-stricken, Hasan wrote hurriedly to Muavia announcing his submission. He offered to abdicate and make Medina his home if granted the contents of the treasury at Kufa and the revenues of a Persian province ; adding, however, the further stipulation that the imprecations against his dead father should cease to form a part of the public prayers. Muavia made no difficulty about these terms, except that he refused to stop the imprecations against Ali. He undertook, however, to arrange that they should never be heard by Ali's son.

Content with this, Hasan, accompanied by his enormous harem, quitted Kufa without regret and passed off the stage into seclusion at Medina, where he died some eight years later from consumption brought on by constant excesses. Persian tradition declares that he was poisoned by Muavia, but of this there is no proof ; on the contrary, it was to his interest that the family should continue to have a harmless voluptuary as its head.

The Death-bed Warning of Muavia to Yezid, A.H. 61 (680).—On his death-bed Muavia sent a message to Yezid, his son and destined successor, warning him of the troubles which lay before him. The message ran, " As for Husayn, the restless men of Irak will give him no peace till he attempt the empire ; when thou hast gotten the victory, deal gently with him, for truly the blood of the Prophet runneth in his veins. It is Abdulla son of Zobayr that I fear the most for thee. Fierce as the lion, crafty as the fox, destroy him root and branch." Had the dying Caliph's advice been followed, the course of history would have been affected.

The Invitation to Husayn from the Inhabitants of Kufa.—The news of Muavia's death produced, exactly as that astute ruler had predicted, a strong feeling at Kufa in favour of Hasan's younger brother Husayn, who was now the head of the house of Ali, and letters were written promising the support of the entire population of Irak, if he would proceed to Kufa. On a strict view of the case Husayn put himself entirely in the wrong by listening to these treasonable overtures ; but when all the circumstances are considered it is difficult to blame him for championing the rights of his house, which an unworthy brother had bartered for money and ignoble ease. Moreover, Husayn was probably in straitened circumstances, owing to his elder brother's action in appropriating to his own use the greater part of the family income, while, nevertheless, as head of the family, he had become responsible for maintaining not only his own wives and children but also those of his brothers and other relatives.

The true friends of the house of Ali at Mecca begged Husayn not to trust to the fickle Kufans, and perhaps their influence would have prevailed but for the interested advice of Abdulla ibn Zobayr, who clearly saw that his own ambition to attain the Caliphate could never be realized as long as Husayn lived.

The March on Kufa.—Husayn, desirous of testing public sentiment at Kufa, sent his cousin Muslim ahead to rally his adherents; but Obaydulla, who had been appointed to the governorship, seized and killed the envoy. The son of Ali may well have been dismayed on learning the terrible news, which made his expedition almost hopeless. But he doubtless realized that he had gone too far to retreat, while his relations clamoured to avenge the death of Muslim. Consequently a little party of thirty horse and forty foot—the numerical weakness was a sign of poverty—quitted Mecca and marched north to Kufa. As if to make the military conditions still more unfavourable, this tiny force was accompanied by women and children. The messages received on the way were more and more discouraging, and the situation was well summed up by a traveller coming from Kufa, who exclaimed, " The heart of the city is with thee, but its sword is against thee." The Beduins at first rallied to the standard of Husayn, but finding the position hopeless, gradually deserted the doomed band.

As they approached Kufa, a chief named Al Hurr barred their further progress, but courteously intimated that they might move either to the left or to the right. Accordingly, leaving Kufa to the right, they made a somewhat aimless detour round the city until their further progress was arrested by Amr, who, according to Persian legend, was bribed by the promise of the governorship of Rei to lead the troops against Husayn. In true Arab fashion many interviews took place, in the course of which Husayn offered to submit, on condition that he was either permitted to return home or sent to Damascus. Obaydulla, seeing the prey in his grasp, refused consent to any conditions and sent Shimr[1]

---

[1] I have seen the man who acted the part of Shimr at the Passion Play set on and beaten. Breaking away, he rushed to the Governor-General for protection, screaming with fear and exclaiming, " I am not Shimr, but Your Excellency's cook ! " Cases are known in which players acting the part of Shimr have been killed.

—whose name is perhaps the most execrated in Persia—to force Amr to seize the Pretender's party, or to supersede him if he declined to act.

The Tragedy.—On the tenth of the month of Moharram A.H. 61 (680), the closing scene was enacted on the plain where the city of Kerbela subsequently grew up round the tomb—known as *Mashhad*, or "Place of Martyrdom"—of Husayn ; it was built as a memorial of the tragedy. Cut off from the river, and with only a rough barricade to protect their rear composed of tents pegged together and some reeds and tamarisk, the little band prepared to fight to the death, with a heroism that challenges our admiration through all the centuries that have since passed. Tradition says that before the battle joined Al Hurr left the ranks of the Kufans and ranged himself on the side of Husayn, exclaiming, " Alas for you ! you invited him and he came, and you not only deceived him, but are now come out to fight against him. Nay, you have hindered him and his wives and his family from the water of the Euphrates, where Jews and Christians and Sabeans drink, and where pigs and dogs disport themselves ! "

The combat was hopelessly uneven from the beginning ; deadly arrows flew from thousands of bows and kinsman after kinsman fell. Husayn at first was intentionally spared, but, as he was plainly determined to die rather than submit, he too was attacked in the end, his tents were set on fire, and he retreated to the river, burning with thirst. Here Shimr and some of the cavalry closed in upon him ; he was mortally wounded by an arrow, and then in a calculated burst of savagery was ridden over by the horsemen. Not a fighting man was left alive, but like the defenders of Thermopylae they left deathless fame behind them. When the seventy heads were brought to Obaydulla, and he callously turned that of Husayn over with his staff, the voice of an aged Arab rose in protest. " Gently ! " he said ; " it is the grandson of the Prophet. By Allah ! I have seen these very lips kissed by the blessed mouth of Mohamed ! "

The Journey to Damascus and the Return to Medina.— The two little sons of Husayn, Ali Asghar and Husayn, his two daughters, and his sister were sent to Damascus. There the Caliph, having secured the destruction of the family, disowned responsibility for the acts of his officials and entertained the orphans with respect and consideration until arrangements were made for their return to Medina. In that city they lived, pouring out the stories of their woes to the pilgrims who visited the tomb of the Prophet, until dark clouds of indignation gathered against the Omayyad dynasty.

The Passion Plays.—This tragedy was the origin of the Passion Plays, which are acted annually not only in Persia, where Shiism is the official religion, but also throughout Asia wherever Shia Moslems gather together. I have been a spectator of these plays, and can testify that to listen to the shrill ululations of the women and the grief of the men is so moving that it is difficult not to execrate Shimr and Yezid as fervently as the rest of the audience. Indeed the Passion Plays represent a force of poignant grief which it would not be easy to estimate, and the scenes I have witnessed will remain unforgotten so long as I live.[1]

The Historical Basis of the Shia Sect.—It was as the result of this tragedy that the Shia or " Faction " of Persia came into existence. It is asserted by Arabic writers, among the earliest being Al-Yakubi [2] of the ninth century of our era, and it is universally believed by Persians, that Husayn married the daughter of Yezdigird, who is known throughout Persia as " Shahr-bánu " or the " Queen." She figures among the heroines in the Passion Plays, and Browne gives a translation of one of the parts in his felicitous verse :

> Born of the race of Yezdigird the King
> From Noshirwan my origin I trace.
> What time kind Fortune naught but joy did bring
> In Rei's proud city was my home and place.
> There in my father's palace once at night
> In sleep to me came Fatima " the Bright " ;
> " O Shahr-bánu "—thus the vision cried—
> " I give thee to Husayn to be his bride ! "

As the play proceeds, Shahr-bánu is brought to Medina as a prisoner of war by Hasan, who treats her chivalrously. Omar, however, orders her to be sold as a slave.

> But Ali then appeared upon the scene,
> And cried, " Be silent, fool and coward mean !

---

[1] In chap. xii. of *The Glory of the Shia World* I have attempted to give the tragedy from the Persian point of view.

[2] *Ed.* Houtsma, vol. ii. p. 293 (quoted from Browne's work). " Among the sons of Husayn were Ali Akbar, who was killed at Taff and left no offspring . . ., and Ali Asghar, whose mother was Harar, the daughter of Yezdigird, whom Husayn used to call Ghazala (' the Gazelle ')."

> These gentle women, traitor, void of grace,
> Shall not stand naked in the market-place!"
> Light of mine eyes! After such treatment dire,
> They gave me to Husayn, thy noble sire.

In other words, as Alexander the Great is believed to be of Achaemenian descent on his father's side, so the descendants of Husayn inherit the same royal blood through the illustrious Sasanian dynasty. Now the doctrine of the divine right of kings was fervently accepted by Persia under the Sasanian dynasty, as the previous chapters have shown, and there is no doubt that belief in the Sasanian origin of the descendants of Husayn has been the main cause for the faithful adherence of Persia to the house of Ali. This ideal is fundamentally opposed to the democratic conceptions of the Arabs.

Its Religious Basis and Doctrines.—But this important matter has a religious side. Ali was the first cousin and perhaps the first male convert of the Prophet. He was also his adopted son, and by marrying Fatima became his son-in-law. In other words, since the Prophet had no sons who grew up, the connexion of Ali with the founder of Islam was closer than that of any other man, and he was moreover much beloved by his father-in-law, whom he served with conspicuous loyalty and courage. The Shias firmly believe that the angel Gabriel visited the Prophet at Mecca during the course of the "Farewell Pilgrimage" and instructed him to proclaim Ali as his successor. The ceremony was performed during the course of the return journey at the Pool of Khumm, where a throne was constructed from camel-saddles. Ali was set thereon by the Prophet, who then enfolded the "Lion of Allah"[1] in such a close and long embrace that his virtues were transmitted to his illustrious son-in-law. This investiture is annually commemorated in Persia as "the Festival of the Pool of Khumm." In accepting it as authoritative, the Shias naturally reject as usurpers Abu Bekr, Omar, and Othman, and deem Ali and his descendants, the Imams,[2] to be the only true successors of the Prophet. So exalted is Ali, the "Hand of God," that the saying runs, "Mohamed is a city of learning, Ali is its gate."

The sacred Imams, whose nature knew no sin and whose bodies cast no shadow, are the intercessors between man and

---
[1] One of the many titles of Ali.
[2] Imam signifies a spiritual and temporal ruler and leader by divine right.

God. They are invested with supreme spiritual leadership and hold in consequence a far higher position than that of the prophets. It is believed that the twelfth Imam never died, but in A.H. 260 (873) disappeared into miraculous concealment in the mysterious city of Jabulka, from which he will reappear on the Day of Judgment in the mosque of Gauhar Shad at Meshed, to be hailed as the Mahdi or "Guide" and to fill the earth with justice.

It is needless to say that beliefs such as these render those who hold them bitterly hostile to the general body of Moslems, who rest their doctrine on the authority of the Prophet and the early Caliphs—including, of course, Ali. As will be seen later on, bloody wars have raged between the Sunnis or "Traditionists" and the Shias analogous to those between the Roman Catholics of Spain and our Protestant ancestors, and to-day union between these two great divisions of the Moslem world appears to be as unattainable as ever. It is important to note that Sunni *mujtahids*, or Doctors of the Sacred Law, follow the interpretation of that law, as laid down by the founders of the four orthodox sects, viz. Hanbali, Shafai, Hanafi, and Malaki, and this interpretation is immutable. Shia *mujtahids*, on the other hand, while following the laws of the Koran as interpreted by the Imams, may modify their meaning or interpret it anew. This is rarely done, but the fact that it may be done prevents the Shias from falling into the rigid narrowness of the Sunnis, which is hostile to all progress.

It remains to add that, in consequence of this doctrine of the Imams, the Shahs of Persia have no religious authority in their kingdom, whereas the Sultan of Turkey is the acknowledged Caliph among Sunnis. Indeed, the position of the Shahs since the downfall of the Safavi dynasty is theoretically that of usurpers, although in practice they were absolute monarchs until the mystic word "constitution" was heard in Persia. It may further be observed that Shias make pilgrimages to Kerbela, the scene of the martyrdom of Husayn, and "Kerbelai" is a title which ranks only second to that of "Haji." They also visit the tomb of Ali at Najaf. In Persia the Sacred City and the Glory of the Shia World is Meshed, where, as described in Chapter L., Riza, the eighth Imam, is buried, and "Meshedi" is the third and last title of honour affected by Shia pilgrims.

OMAYYAD DIRHEM.

CHAPTER XLVIII

PERSIA A PROVINCE OF THE OMAYYAD CALIPHATE

Men of Kufa, I see before me heads ripe for the harvest and the reaper, I am he. I seem to myself to see blood between turbans and shoulders. I am not one of those who can be frightened by an inflated bag of skin, nor need any one think to squeeze me like dried figs. . . . The Prince of the Believers has spread before him the arrows of his quiver, and has tried every one of them by biting its wood. It is my wood he has found the hardest and the bitterest, and I am the arrow which he shoots against you.—The Speech of HAJJAJ BIN YUSUF.

The Omayyad Dynasty.—In the preceding two chapters, and more especially in the last, events which have concerned Persia both from the religious and from the political aspect have been treated in some detail, and Muavia, the founder of the Omayyad dynasty, has been given a secondary position. But it would be impossible in a history of Persia to ignore the importance of the Omayyad dynasty, which ruled the vast Moslem empire for nearly a century, and I have therefore devoted to it a special chapter.

The Position of Muavia strengthened by the Adherence of Ziad.—Muavia began his reign in Syria in A.H. 35 (656), and he became Caliph of the entire Moslem world upon the abdication of Hasan in A.H. 40 (661), but it was not until two years later that he entered into possession of all the lands of the Caliphate. It was at this date that Ziad, Ali's Governor of Fars, became reconciled to him, and presented himself under a safe-conduct at Damascus, bringing all arrears of revenue, and in addition a million pieces as a gift. His remarkable capacity secured the Caliph's public acknowledgment of his relationship with himself, and he was appointed Governor of Basra, where he ruled the turbulent Arabs with a rod of iron. Later on Kufa was added to his administration, and there he introduced a reign of terror for the purpose of crushing conspiracies that boded ill for the future of the Omayyad dynasty. The Arab chroniclers state that no viceroy ever enjoyed such powers as Ziad, who ruled from the Euphrates to the Indus and Jaxartes, and maintained a court modelled on that of the Great King.

Moslem Progress in the East.—During the Caliphate of Muavia the yoke of the Arabs was fixed more securely on the East. Herat, which had rebelled in A.H. 41 (662), was stormed, and so was Kabul two years later. Ghazni, Balkh, and Kandahar were visited by Moslem armies. In A.H. 54 (674) the Oxus was crossed and Bokhara captured, and in A.H. 56 (676) Samarcand fell to the Moslems, who strengthened their position up to the Jaxartes on the north and to the Indus on the south. In short, they became successors of Alexander the Great.

From Basra and Kufa Ziad governed Persia through his sons. The province of Khorasan, which at this period comprised the Moslem empire east of the Lut as far as the confines of India, was divided into four great districts, with their centres at Nishapur, Merv, Herat, and Balkh respectively. Of these cities only the first-named lies within the limits of modern Iran. It was at this time, too, that Arab colonies were planted in Khorasan, traces of which still survive, although the Mongol invasions shattered their power. I have, indeed, myself frequently come across small bodies of Arab tribesmen, and a regiment termed the *Arab va Ajam* is still recruited in the Shahrud district.

The Achievements and Failures of Muavia.—Muavia certainly ranks as one of the great Caliphs. Owing to his sagacity, his hold on Damascus was never seriously threatened, and he converted it into the magnificent capital of the Caliphate. His successful campaigns to the confines of India have been referred to, but his great attempt to capture Constantinople failed, mainly owing to the invention of "Greek fire," which enabled the Greek navy to defeat that of the Moslems, while the latter were almost simultaneously beaten on land. Muavia sued for peace and agreed to surrender all his conquests and to pay an indemnity and tribute. Curiously enough, this heavy blow in the West does not appear to have shaken the power of the Caliph in the East.

Yezid declared Heir-Apparent, A.H. 56 (676), *and his*

THE OMAYYAD CALIPHATE

Succession in A.H. 61 (680).—While at the zenith of his power and prestige, Muavia decided to designate Yezid, his eldest son, as his successor. Syria and Irak acquiesced in the innovation, whereas at Mecca and Medina the outcry was loud and bitter. But Damascus was now the capital, and the protests even of sacred Mecca could be disregarded by the Caliph, who forced its inhabitants to take the oath of fealty at the point of the sword. The feeling that was excited found expression in an epigram which Masudi has preserved :

> We're filled full of wrath, and were we to drain
> The blood of Omayya, our thirst would still pain :
> While wasting your people, ye still without care,
> Ye sons of Omayya, go hunting the hare.[1]

Muavia died in A.H. 61 (680), and thanks to the effective arrangements he had made, Yezid, his son by the daughter of a Beduin chief, succeeded to the Caliphate as if it had been a hereditary throne, although his tenure of it did not by any means continue untroubled. He was specially addicted to the pleasure of the chase, as the epigram just quoted shows, and gave very little attention to affairs of State. But he does not appear to have been an incompetent ruler, and he hardly merits the invective with which his name has been loaded on account of the tragedy of Kerbela.

The Rebellion of Ibn Zobayr, A.H. 61 (680).—As Muavia had foretold, Abdulla ibn Zobayr proved a dangerous man. Having himself sent Husayn to his death on the field of Kerbela, he took advantage of the unpopularity this deed brought upon the Caliph to head a rising against him. For a time the crafty rebel pretended to be loyal, and Yezid was naturally loath to take extreme measures ; but at last, in A.H. 63 (682), he was obliged to send a force to Medina, which, after defeating the troops of Ibn Zobayr, plundered the city of the Prophet for three days. Mecca was next attacked, and in the course of a two months' siege the Kaaba was burned. At this critical juncture news was received of the death of Yezid, and the army in consequence withdrew, leaving Ibn Zobayr for the time being securely in possession of the Sacred City.

The Bokhara Campaign.—While the great events of which we have taken notice were occurring at the centre of the

---

[1] Masudi, ii. 50. The translation is quoted from *Omayyads and Abbasids* by Zaydan.

Moslem world, there was expansion, together with confusion, disturbance, and internal discord, farther east. On his succession to the Caliphate Yezid appointed Salm ibn Ziad to Khorasan. He found Bokhara in rebellion, its Queen having offered her hand to the Turkish King as the price of his assistance. Salm, aided by his general Muhallab, whose connexion with Khorasan was intimate and distinguished, defeated the combined armies, the Queen was forced to sue for peace, and Salm returned in triumph to Merv.

Faction Fighting of the Northern and Southern Beduin, A.H. 46–65 (666–685).—The East, and more especially Khorasan, had been convulsed for many years by feuds between the Arabs of the North and the Arabs of the South which broke out in civil war. The fighting had raged for a year without intermission when it culminated in a victory gained at Herat by the Modhar, or Arabs of the South, who inflicted a loss of 8000 killed on the enemy. Other battles were fought and much blood was shed, and all progress was necessarily brought to a standstill by these dangerous jealousies.

The Divisions in the Caliphate, A.H. 61–73 (680–692).— The Caliphate after the death of Yezid was filled by a weakling boy who died in a few months, and Yezid's kinsman Merwan, who was elected in his place, lived for only a year. Abdul Malik, Merwan's son, succeeded him and ruled for some years, with Ibn Zobayr holding the Sacred Cities, Irak, and the East as a rival Caliph. The situation was still further complicated by a certain Mukhtar, who gained possession of Kufa as the agent of Mohamed, son of the Caliph Ali, known from his mother as the Hanifite. Mukhtar was killed by Musab, brother of Ibn Zobayr, who in turn was defeated and killed by Abdul Malik in A.H. 71 (690). Ibn Zobayr, who probably would have been elected Caliph had he shown more enterprise after the death of Yezid, was attacked for the second time in A.H. 72 (691). It was on this occasion that Hajjaj bin Yusuf, the celebrated general and administrator who was the incarnation of the spirit of the Omayyad dynasty, first played a leading part. He showed no respect for the Sacred City, which he besieged, and Ibn Zobayr, deserted by many of his followers, met a soldier's death in A.H. 73 (692), after thirteen years of successful independence, during which he had been a constant rival of the Caliphs. The Caliphate of Abdul Malik was then acknowledged throughout the Moslem world.

The Massacre of the Enemies of Husayn, A.H. 66 (685).—
In A.H. 65 the Kharijites, whose sinister activity kept Persia perpetually convulsed, visited the tomb of Husayn at Kerbela and bewailed their desertion of his cause. They then invaded Syria, but were defeated and returned to Kufa. In the following year there were tribal fights in Kufa which ended in a massacre of all who had opposed Husayn. Persians exult over the just retribution which fell upon Shimr, Amr, and other citizens, many of whom were put to death with torture ; and owing to the vigilance of Mukhtar but few escaped. The heads of Amr and his son were sent to the Hanifite, who appears to have been merely a tool of a crafty intriguer.

The Azrakites.—In A.H. 74 (693) Irak was threatened by a branch of the Kharijites, termed Azrakites, and, as the Arabs were unwilling to fight in these campaigns, Hajjaj was appointed Governor. Arriving suddenly at Kufa, he sat in the mosque with his face veiled until asked his name, when he delivered the speech which is quoted at the head of this chapter. Frightened by such menacing language, the citizens streamed out to the camp and the peril was averted ; but time after time insurrections of these fanatics broke out, unhappy Kerman serving as their headquarters, until, weakened by divisions, the bands broke up, to be eventually crushed by the able general Muhailab, who as a reward was appointed Governor of Khorasan.

The Rebellion of Ibn-al-Ashath, A.H. 80 (699).—During the course of the campaigns beyond Sistan an Indian monarch named Rutbil had defeated a Moslem force by luring it into the defiles of what is now Afghanistan. To avenge this humiliation, a powerful army was despatched under Ibn-al-Ashath ; but he, conceiving himself unjustly treated by Hajjaj, rebelled. Supported by his entire army, he was welcomed everywhere, and Hajjaj fled from Basra, where the Pretender was received as Caliph. Hajjaj, however, collected an army in Syria, and Ibn-al-Ashath was defeated and escaped to Kerman. Ultimately he took refuge with Rutbil, who to please Hajjaj surrendered him to his emissary.

The Rebellion of Musa ibn Khazim.—The state of anarchy which prevailed in Khorasan and the loose nature of Arab authority make it almost impossible to give within reasonable compass a consecutive and intelligible narrative of events. They may be illustrated by the career of Musa, son of Khazim. Owing to tribal feuds he sought refuge at Samarcand, and he then obtained possession of the province of Termez, which he ruled for fifteen years. In the end he was attacked by a large force and slain.

Death and Character of Abdul Malik.—The reign of Abdul Malik, albeit a stormy one, marked the culminating point of the Omayyad dynasty. Westwards he extended the limits of the Caliphate in North Africa and he engaged in intermittent hostilities with the Byzantine Empire, but not as an aggressor. Successful on the whole, he was undoubtedly an able ruler, with a conciliatory policy, but he owed much to the brilliant abilities of Hajjaj. The Arab chroniclers mention that during his reign the Caliphate first minted a coinage, and also that the accounts of the exchequer were first conducted in Arabic instead of Persian, which must have involved a serious loss of influence to the subject race.

The Campaigns in Central Asia, A.H. 86-96 (705-714).— Under Welid, the son and successor of Abdul Malik, the Moslem arms penetrated farther and farther eastwards, substituting conquest for what had hitherto been little more than raids. Kutayba,[1] who ably conducted these operations in Central Asia, chose Merv for his headquarters, and every year made a successful campaign, generally crossing the Oxus and sometimes the Jaxartes. Balkh, Tokharistan, and Ferghana were his first objectives; then the fall of Baykand, a trading centre in Bokhara, secured for him booty of inestimable value. In A.H. 90 (709) the city of Bokhara itself was taken. A rising occupied Kutayba's energies in the following year, but he was soon free to attack Rutbil in Sistan. In A.H. 93 (712) he turned his arms towards Khiva, where after gaining a success he heard that Samarcand was in the hands of rebels. Leading his veterans by forced marches, he began the siege of that city, whose king on the arrival of battering-engines lost heart, and peace was made on the terms that a heavy tribute should be paid and a levy of horsemen supplied. The conqueror was allowed to enter Samarcand, where he destroyed the fire temples and built a mosque, but he broke his plighted word and retained the city as a Moslem possession. In the last two years of this eventful decade Kutayba reached Kashgar.

[1] The campaigns of Kutayba are detailed with some fulness in *The Heart of Asia*.

A curious legend of this campaign has been preserved, according to which the Arab general swore to take possession of the soil of China. The " King " (probably the frontier governor) released him from this oath by sending him a load of soil to trample on, a bag of Chinese money to symbolize tribute, and four royal youths on whom he imprinted his seal. The whole story has a delightful touch of reality.

The Advance to the Indus, A.H. 89–96 (707–714).—During the reign of Welid the Moslem hosts, under Mohamed ibn Kasim, the first Moslem to make his mark in India, marched into Sind from Makran and captured Multan, where the value of the spoil was estimated at 120,000,000 pieces. The death of Welid put an end to any further advance, but the Moslems remained in Sind permanently. There, so long as tribute was duly paid, they permitted the worship of idols in direct violation of the Prophet's order.

The Achievements of Welid, A.H. 86–96 (705–714).—The short reign of Welid was one of essential grandeur, marking as it does the zenith of Moslem power. If a comparison be desired, it may be said that Abdul Malik compares with Kobad and Welid with Noshirwan. His victorious armies marched to the frontiers of China and to the Indus; while in the West the conquest of Spain was an even more splendid and substantial achievement. Much of the credit for these great gains was due to the personality of the Caliph, whose authority was supreme and whose word was law from the frontiers of China to the Atlantic. We learn from Chinese sources that, between 713 and 755 A.D., ten embassies from Persia were received by the Celestials, the first having evidently been despatched by Welid. Special reference is made to embroideries of " fire-hair " as forming part of the offerings, asbestos being presumably meant.

The Campaigns of Yezid in Gurgan and Tabaristan, A.H. 98 (716).—Yezid, son of Muhallab, was appointed Governor of Khorasan to succeed Kutayba, who upon the succession of Sulayman to the Caliphate had rebelled and been killed. Yezid's arms were directed in the first instance against Gurgan,[1] the ancient Hyrcania, which with neighbouring Tabaristan had maintained its independence, although it lay across the direct route from Irak to Central Asia. Yezid

---

[1] For the campaign in Tabaristan, *vide* Ibn Isfandiyar's *History of Tabaristan*, by Prof. E. G. Browne (Gibb Memorial). The Arabic form of Gurgan is Jurjan.

captured Dihistan, and drove the inhabitants of Gurgan into the Elburz, where they were finally forced to submit. After butchering many prisoners and ravaging the country he invaded Tabaristan, the modern Mazanderan. In this campaign he at first successfully marched through the plain country and occupied Sari. A battle was fought in which the Moslems routed the enemy, but being lured into an ambush they suffered such severe losses that Yezid was glad to purchase his safe retreat for 300,000 dinars. Returning to Gurgan, which had revolted, he besieged its prince for seven months in a stronghold situated on a mountain top which was accessible by only one route. This was probably Kala Maran, to which I have already referred in connexion with the Parthian capital. In the end he made prisoners of the garrison, and was able to fulfil a dreadful vow similar to that of Khalid by grinding wheat into flour for his bread with the blood of his victims, thousands of whom also were impaled along the roads leading to the city.

The Second Attempt on Constantinople, A.H. 99 (717).—Less than forty years after the failure of the first attempt on the capital of the Byzantine Empire, Sulayman from every part of his dominions collected forces which he deemed sufficient for this task. He relied on blockade rather than on an assault, but, thanks to the huge stocks of corn which had been stored, to "Greek fire," and to an unusually severe winter, the Moslems were ultimately forced to abandon the siege, their fleet being subsequently wrecked in the Aegean. These two repulses from the walls of Constantinople served Christendom far better than the more famous victory of Charles Martel, the importance of which, in my opinion, has been somewhat exaggerated.

Khorasan under the Caliphate of Omar II., A.H. 99–101 (717–720).—Sulayman died after a short reign of less than three years, and was succeeded by the pious Omar, to whose credit lies the abolition of the curses against Ali, which must have given dire and continual offence to generations of devout Moslems. Omar improved the position of the inhabitants of Khorasan, many of whom, though converted to Islam, suffered none the less on that account from the exactions of the tax collector. Sending for representatives of the oppressed, the Caliph himself went into their case, dismissed the Governor, and laid down that all Moslems should be placed on terms of perfect equality. He enjoined justice towards the Persians who remained Zoroastrians, forbidding the destruction of their fire temples though not permitting the erection of new pyres.

The Reign of Yezid II., A.H. 101–105 (720–724).—Omar II. was succeeded by Yezid II.,[1] son of Abdul Malik. But the new Caliph had first to crush a rebellion raised by his namesake the son of Muhallab, who had seized Irak, and so far made good his position that governors ruled in his name in Fars, Kerman, and other centres in Persia. Maslama, the Caliph's brother, was selected to lead the Syrian army, which defeated the rebels, Yezid, their chief, being killed in the battle. His brothers, who fled by sea to the Kerman province, were put to death and their families were sold as slaves. As a reward for his great services Maslama was appointed Governor of both Irak and Khorasan. To the latter province he sent his son-in-law Said, an effeminate man quite out of place as Warden of the Marches. In spite of Moslem expeditions there was a general rising of the hordes in Khojand and Ferghana, and the Sogdians, who remained loyal, suffered considerably before help could be afforded them. When troops arrived on the scene they attacked the Sogdians, who had by that time broken away from their allegiance, and there was much indecisive fighting and raiding. Altogether during the reign of Yezid II. the decadence of the Omayyad dynasty becomes more marked.

The Abbasid Propaganda.—It was about this period that Mohamed, great-grandson of Abbas, the uncle of the Prophet, began to advance the pretensions of the Hashimite branch of the Kureish. To conciliate the Shia party, it was claimed that the rights of the house of Ali had been surrendered and merged in the Abbasid representatives. Mohamed, who lived in retreat in the wilds of Palestine, but yet close to the caravan route running from Mecca to Syria, created a centre from which he directed an ardent propaganda. Gradually his emissaries began to visit Khorasan, where they found a fruitful soil, more especially among newly converted Persians, who occupied the inferior position of "clients." The pioneers were put to death, but the cause prospered nevertheless, and gained many adherents throughout Persia and Irak.

---

[1] The examination by this Caliph of the first recorded English traveller to the East is related in Chapter LII.

The Rebellion of Zayd, A.H. 122 (740).—The Abbasid party was greatly strengthened by the attempt of Zayd, a grandson of Husayn, to raise a rebellion. The Kufans, true to their record, covenanted with him but failed him when he raised his standard. He died fighting bravely, and with him the cause of the Shias was lost for the time being, while the opposition to the Omayyad dynasty became more united in favour of the house of Abbas.

The Caliphate of Hisham, A.H. 105–125 (724–743), *and the Battle of Tours*, A.D. 732.—During the comparatively long reign of Hisham the decline of the Omayyad dynasty continued. I have mentioned briefly the only incidents which directly concern Persia. But the fact should not be overlooked that it was during the Caliphate of Hisham that the Moslems invaded France. For Europe the issue of the battle won by Charles Martel in A.D. 732, exactly a century after the death of the Founder of Islam, was of great importance, although the Moslem invasion was perhaps less an attempt at permanent conquest than a terrible raid.

Welid II. and Yezid III., A.H. 125–126 (743–744).— The last Caliphs of the Omayyad dynasty call for little mention. Welid, a profligate ruler, was killed by his cousin Yezid, who himself died a few months later. The whole of the Moslem world was in a state of anarchy, during which Ibrahim, the successor of Mohamed, worked strenuously to advance the Abbasid cause.

The Rebellion of Abdulla, Ibn Muavia, A.H. 126–129 (744– 747).—During the Caliphate of Merwan II., who succeeded Yezid III., there were various insurrections in Syria, which were crushed with the vindictive cruelty that was now usual. Of greater importance was the rebellion of Ibn Muavia, a descendant of Jafar, brother of Ali. Upon the accession of Merwan the Pretender was acknowledged at Kufa, but, being deserted by its ever fickle inhabitants, he retreated to Madain, where thousands rallied to his standard. With this force and the support of the Kharijites, Ibn Muavia established himself at Istakhr, and his Governors ruled in Isfahan, Rei, and Kumis. In A.H. 129 (747) the Pretender was defeated by the Syrian troops and, like other pretenders, fled to Khorasan. Abdur Rahman bin Muslim, destined to be famous as Abu Muslim, was at this time established at Merv, nominally in the interests of the Hashimite section of the Kureish, but actually as the agent of the house of Abbas. Ibn Muavia not unnaturally looked to him for support, but was put to death by the Governor of Herat, through Abu Muslim's influence.

The Raising of the Black Standard in Khorasan, A.H. 129 (747).—Everywhere the weakening control of the central power allowed the Arabs to waste their strength in internal feuds, and alike in Spain in the extreme west, in Africa, in Syria, and in Irak, the situation was most gloomy for the Caliph. In Khorasan, too, the able Governor Nasr, who had proved his military capacity by defeating and capturing Kursul the Khakan, was opposed by the Yemenite faction, and the ceaseless quarrel between Modhar and Yemen convulsed Khorasan as much as it was convulsing Spain.

At this juncture Abu Muslim raised the black standard of the house of Abbas, which bore the following inscription from the Koran : " Permission to fight is accorded to those who take up arms because they have been unjustly treated." This remarkable man, destined to overthrow the Omayyad dynasty and to set the house of Abbas in its stead, was purchased as a slave at Mecca by Mohamed, the head of the Abbasid family. Showing conspicuous ability, he was employed as a confidential agent, and constantly travelled between Southern Palestine and his native province Khorasan. As a part of this propaganda, he gave out that he was an incarnation of the Deity, a claim that was widely acknowledged.

It was in consequence of his reports that active steps were taken. Intrigues conducted with consummate skill resulted in the capture of both Herat and Merv. Nasr reported that 200,000 men had sworn allegiance to Abu Muslim, and concluded his appeal for help against the growing movement with the following celebrated verses :

> I see amidst the embers the glow of fire, and it
>   wants but little to burst into a blaze,
> And if the wise ones of the people quench it not,
>   its fuel will be corpses and skulls.
> Verily fire is kindled by two sticks, and verily
>   words are the beginning of warfare.
> And I cry in amazement, " Would that I knew
>   whether the House of Omayya were awake or asleep ! "

Merwan attempted to send reinforcements to his Viceroy, and he arrested Ibrahim, who henceforth disappears from the scene ; but Abul Abbas and Abu Jafar, Ibrahim's brothers, escaped to Kufa, where they were protected and remained in hiding.

Meanwhile Kahtaba, the able general of Abu Muslim, had twice defeated Nasr, at Nishapur and again at Gurgan. Worn out and a fugitive, Nasr fled through Rei and died before reaching Hamadan. Kahtaba, following close behind, entered Rei, defeated the Caliph's army, which had marched up from Kerman, and took Nahavand. He then avoided Ibn Hobaya at Jalola and descended into Irak. The Syrian General, however, forestalled him and fell back on Kerbela. An encounter followed near that city, when Kahtaba defeated the army of the Caliph but lost his own life. Under his son, Ibn Kahtaba, Kufa was taken, and Abul Abbas, emerging from hiding, was after a time proclaimed Caliph by the victorious army.

The Battle of the Great Zab, A.H. 132 (750).—While this struggle was going on, another force, detached by Kahtaba from Nahavand, defeated the troops of Merwan's son Abdulla and occupied Upper Mesopotamia. The Caliph, who lived at Harran, at last took the field in person, crossed the Tigris, and marched down its left bank with an army 120,000 strong. He crossed the Zab by a bridge, intending to fight a decisive battle with the Abbasid forces commanded by Abdulla, uncle of Abul Abbas. To stimulate the avaricious Arabs Merwan told them that he had brought treasures with which to reward them. This caused a movement towards the camp on the part of some of the tribesmen which was mistaken for flight. A panic ensued and the entire army fled, thousands being drowned in the Great Zab. From the field of battle the victors advanced on Mosul and the unfortunate Merwan was hunted down and killed. With him perished the Omayyad dynasty.

The Condition of Persia under the Omayyad Dynasty.—In this chapter I have given as far as possible the history of Persia as a province of the Moslem Empire. In a period of universal tyranny and oppression, when tyrants like Hajjaj represented the Caliph, it is certain that the Persian people were worse treated than under the first four Caliphs, who invariably attempted to secure justice and to repress tyranny and corruption. The inhabitants of Khorasan were largely instrumental in the overthrow of the Omayyad dynasty. It was among them that the Abbasid agents found their most devoted followers, and we have the remarkable spectacle of a people risking life and property to serve a man of an alien race whom they had never seen, and serving him with rare fidelity and devotion. It was this spirit inspiring the followers of the Black Standard which enabled them to overcome the Arabs of Syria, who were lukewarm so far as the Caliph was concerned, and thought merely of their personal, or at most their tribal interests. Consequently, in a sense the victory won by the men of Khorasan may be regarded as a sign of national awakening on the part of the oppressed Persians, who must have been conscious that in all that made for civilization they were superior to their Arab masters.

ABU MUSLIM.

CHAPTER XLIX

PERSIAN ASCENDANCY IN THE EARLY ABBASID PERIOD

> The ascendancy of the Persians over the Arabs, that is to say of the conquered over the victors, had already for a long while been in course of preparation; it became complete when the Abbasids, who owed their elevation to the Persians, ascended the throne. These princes made it a rule to be on their guard against the Arabs, and to put their trust only in foreigners, Persians, especially those of Khorasan, with whom, therefore, they had to make friends.—DOZY, *Histoire d'Islamisme.*

The End of Moslem Unity.—The Omayyad dynasty and the empire of Islam were interchangeable terms, but this is not true of the Abbasid dynasty, which was never acknowledged in Spain and from the first but intermittently in Africa. In Persia, as will be seen, independent dynasties arose as the Caliph grew weak, until the appalling cataclysm of the Mongol invasion, sweeping across Iran, ended the degenerate house of Abbas and with it the Caliphate as a great power.

A second fact of special importance, so far as Persia is concerned, is that the Abbasids owed their success to armies raised in Khorasan, on which they relied to maintain the dynasty against the Arabs. The martial vigour of the latter had naturally deteriorated, owing to the luxury which their extraordinary successes had induced and the system whereby they were maintained, without working, at the expense of the Moslem empire, just as in later days the Manchus were maintained in China. So hostile was the dynasty to the Arabs that Abu Muslim's orders from Ibrahim, the brother of Abul Abbas, were to "see that there be not one left in Khorasan whose tongue is the tongue of the Arabian, but he be slain." Strange orders these from a member of the Kureish tribe!

The Accession of Abul Abbas, A.H. 132 (749).—After the victory of Kahtaba in the neighbourhood of Kufa, Abu Salma, an agent of the Hashimite cause in Khorasan, took possession of Kufa and governed under the title of "Vizier of the house of Mohamed." The two brothers of Ibrahim who had been in hiding now emerged. Abdulla, Abul Abbas was the younger, but of a noble mother, and consequently his claims were held to be greater than those of Abu Jafar, whose mother was a slave-girl. It might have been expected that the proclamation of Abul Abbas as Caliph would immediately follow, but Abu Salma continually delayed until his hand was forced by members of the Abbasid party who brought Abul Abbas to the Great Mosque. There he ascended the pulpit and inveighed against the infamous Omayyads, who had usurped the rights of the Prophet. He is said to have ended his fierce denunciations by exclaiming, " I am the Great Avenger and my name is *Saffah*, 'the Shedder of Blood.' " By this title Abul Abbas is known in history, although it is not certain that he conferred it upon himself.

The Massacre of the Omayyads.—The title of the Caliph was made good by acts of ferocity directed against the many members of the fallen dynasty. Each scion of the house was hunted for his life. In Palestine the uncle of the Caliph added treachery to cruelty. He proclaimed an amnesty and confirmed it by a feast to ninety members of the family. When all were seated a poet declaimed against the evil deeds of the Omayyad house, and at this signal they were murdered to a man. A carpet was drawn over the ninety corpses and the banquet was resumed! One of the family, born under a lucky star, escaped the general slaughter, and after wandering as a refugee in Africa was invited to reign in Spain, where he founded a new Omayyad dynasty which attained considerable splendour.

The Reign of Abul Abbas and his Death, A.H. 136 (754).— The reign of Abul Abbas was stormy throughout, and it may have been due to his cruelty that a rebellion broke out in Syria and Mesopotamia, where large armies still supported the Omayyad cause. Basra, too, defied the Khorasan troops of the Hashimite general, and had there been a master-mind to give unity to these efforts it might have gone hard with the house of Abbas ; but none such was to be found. Ibn Hobayra clung to Wasit at a time when his army might have saved the Omayyad cause in Syria, and he was induced to capitulate. The Khorasan veterans at length captured Basra, and although in Khorasan and other outlying provinces risings occurred, the Abbasid dynasty was before long firmly established.

The treachery and ingratitude of Abul Abbas were displayed in the assassination of Abu Salma, who was waylaid when returning from a feast given in his honour by the Caliph. Shortly afterwards Abul Abbas himself died of smallpox. The five years of his reign had been marked by massacres, treachery, perjury, and ingratitude on a scale until then unprecedented in the annals of Islam.

Abu Jafar, Mansur, A.H. 136–158 (754–775).—Abu Jafar, who succeeded to the Caliphate and assumed the title of *Mansur* or Victorious, was faced with a serious rebellion headed by his uncle Abdulla, the Conqueror of Merwan. Abu Muslim was sent to oppose him, and the Pretender in desperation butchered 17,000 Khorasan troops whom he knew he could not trust. Abu Muslim in the end succeeded, and Abdulla was taken prisoner and placed in custody at Basra.

The Execution of Abu Muslim, A.H. 137 (754).—Just as Abul Abbas had planned the assassination of Abu Salma, so the ungrateful Mansur determined to kill the too-powerful Abu Muslim. The latter, suspecting treachery, asked one of his friends how he thought he stood with the Caliph. The friend replied in a parable. "A lion had its foot pierced by a thorn, so that it was unable to move; and a simple-minded, well-meaning man, seeing its weakness and hearing its moaning, took pity on it, approached it, and drew forth the thorn from its foot. Thereupon the lion slew the man; 'for,' it said, 'thou art a meddlesome fellow, and perhaps thou may'st assist some other lion, and it may drive me from my hunting ground.'" Abu Muslim replied that, if he ceased to care for the tender sapling he had planted, passers-by would pluck it up. He thereupon returned to Court, where, after listening to reproaches from the Caliph expressed in the most violent terms, he was cut to pieces. Thus perished, at the early age of thirty-five, the man to whose genius and devotion the house of Abbas mainly owed its success. Retribution may have been due for the blood of thousands of opponents slain by his orders, but he had served his masters with consistent loyalty and rare devotion, and his fate brands Abu Jafar as guilty of the blackest ingratitude.

The Rebellions in Persia, A.H. 138 (756), *and* A.H. 141–143 (758–760).—In A.H. 138 (756) a rebellion broke out in Persia,

THE EARLY ABBASID PERIOD

Sindbad, a follower of the old religion, having collected a force to avenge his master Abu Muslim, who, he stated, upon being threatened by Mansur, had pronounced the "Most Great Name" of God, and had flown away in the form of a white dove. For some three months Sindbad held the country from Rei to Nishapur, and the rebellion was not crushed until sixty thousand of his followers had been killed. Three years later the Governor of Khorasan rebelled, but was defeated by Ibn Khuzayma, with whom was associated Mehdi, the Caliph's son and eventual successor. It is an indication of the growing importance of Khorasan that Mehdi was afterwards appointed its Governor. The *Sipahbud*[1] of Tabaristan, with whom Sindbad had taken refuge after his defeat, and to whose care the treasure of Abu Muslim had been entrusted, also took the field, with the result that Tabaristan was now conquered by the Moslems and the *Sipahbud* in despair took poison.

The Ravandis, A.H. 141 (758).—It was about this time that a strange Persian sect which believed in the transmigration of souls and held that the Caliph was temporarily inhabited by the Deity, suddenly invaded the palace of Mansur, crying out, "It is the house of our Lord, he that giveth us food to eat and water to drink." The Caliph, relying on his own authority to quell the tumult, imprisoned their leaders, whereupon they stormed the prison and nearly killed him. These fanatics, who were called Ravandis from the town of Ravand near Isfahan, continued to exist until the beginning of the tenth century. They were, curiously enough, the cause of the institution of a "sentry horse," which thenceforward was always kept ready saddled at Court for an emergency.

The Rebellion of the Descendants of Hasan, A.H. 144 (761). —A much more serious danger than the rebellions in Persia threatened Mansur when Medina and Basra rose to support the claims of the house of Ali. The rebellious cities were dealt with one after the other, and at Medina the Pretender was deserted and fell fighting. His brother Ibrahim took possession of Basra and then marched on Kufa, but he too fell in battle, and his army broke up and dispersed.

The Foundation of Baghdad, A.H. 145 (762).—Mansur was the founder and builder of Baghdad, which under his grandson Harcun-al-Rashid was destined to enshrine the imperishable memories of the romantic East as recorded in

[1] *Vide* Chapter XLIII.

the glowing pages of the *Arabian Nights*. In forming the new city he had the statesmanlike design of removing the army from the neighbourhood of Kufa and Basra, which were hotbeds of intrigue ; and by reason of its position a few miles above the ancient Madain, and the permanent establishment of the Court within its walls, it soon became the capital of the Empire. Cantonments were built on the eastern bank of the river, with three separate camps, for the Khorasan levies on which Mansur depended and for the Yemen and Modhar tribes.

The Rising at Herat, A.H. 150 (767).—The latter years of the reign of Mansur were comparatively peaceful. There was a rising at Herat under *Ustad* or " Master Craftsman " Sis, who declared himself a prophet, and occupied Khorasan and Sistan until Ibn Khuzayma defeated him with heavy slaughter. Perhaps the chief importance of the event lies in the fact that the rebel's daughter Khayzran was taken by Mehdi into his harem, and became the mother of Hadi and of Haroun.

Persian Influence under Mansur.—During the long reign of Mansur Persian influence became more and more marked. The Court dress was Persian, and literature, medicine, and astronomy began to be studied under the patronage of the Caliph, who was the first to order Greek scientific works to be translated into Arabic and, in many other ways, sowed the seed of the Golden Age of Islam. Moreover, the Caliphate, which possessed no good traditions of administration on which to rely, adopted the same system as that by which the Sasanian monarchs had ruled. Chief of the great officers was the Vizier. The first holder of that title, as has been already mentioned, was Abu Salma. He was assassinated, and his immediate successor was poisoned. The office then passed to the famous Barmecides or descendants of Barmak, a title borne by the high-priest of the great fire-temple, or, more probably, Buddhist monastery, of Balkh, who was their ancestor. The Barmecides ruled for more than fifty years (A.D. 752–804), and by their splendid abilities and generous patronage of learning and science did much to create the splendour of the Abbasid dynasty.

Mehdi, A.H. 158–169 (775–785).—Mansur during his lifetime had appointed Mehdi his successor, and when he died the reaction from his capable yet harsh and gloomy rule found expression in praises of Mehdi, who is described as " the brilliant moon in beauty ; the spring-time from his perfumes and suavity; the lion by his courage; and the sea, with its resounding waves, is the emblem of his munificence and generosity." Nor were these praises wholly unmerited; for the new Caliph inaugurated his reign by deeds of mercy, and steadily developed the Empire, improving communications, fortifying important centres, founding towns and villages, and encouraging poetry, literature, and music. On the other hand, there must be laid to his charge instances of cruelty to his ministers and generals, and the fact that he organized a persecution of the Manichaeans, even establishing a special department to deal with these heretics.

The Veiled Prophet of Khorasan, A.H. 158–161 (774–777).—To the beginning of Mehdi's reign belong the incidents made familiar to English readers in Moore's well-known poem. Its hero, Mokanna, known as *Hakim Burkai*, or "the Physician with the face-veil," was born at Karez, which is now a squalid village on the road between Meshed and Herat. He taught the immanence of the Deity in Adam, in Abu Muslim, whose name was still intensely revered, and in himself.[1] For four years he held Central Asia, until, being besieged and seeing no hope, he cast himself into a tank of vitriol.

Hadi, A.H. 169–170 (785–786).—Mehdi's favourite son was Haroun, who had gained much glory in a campaign to the Bosphorus in A.H. 156, and he wished to pass over his elder son Musa, better known as Hadi; but the latter refused to renounce his rights, and on the sudden death of Mansur he was proclaimed Caliph without opposition. His reign, however, was short and unimportant, and when he died, after ruling for about a year, he was succeeded by his brother, who has achieved enduring fame as Haroun-al-Rashid, or "Aaron the Upright." Under him the golden age of Islam was ushered in.

[1] Browne points out the essential identity of all these sects, and gives details in vol. i. chap. ix. of his work.

END OF VOL. I

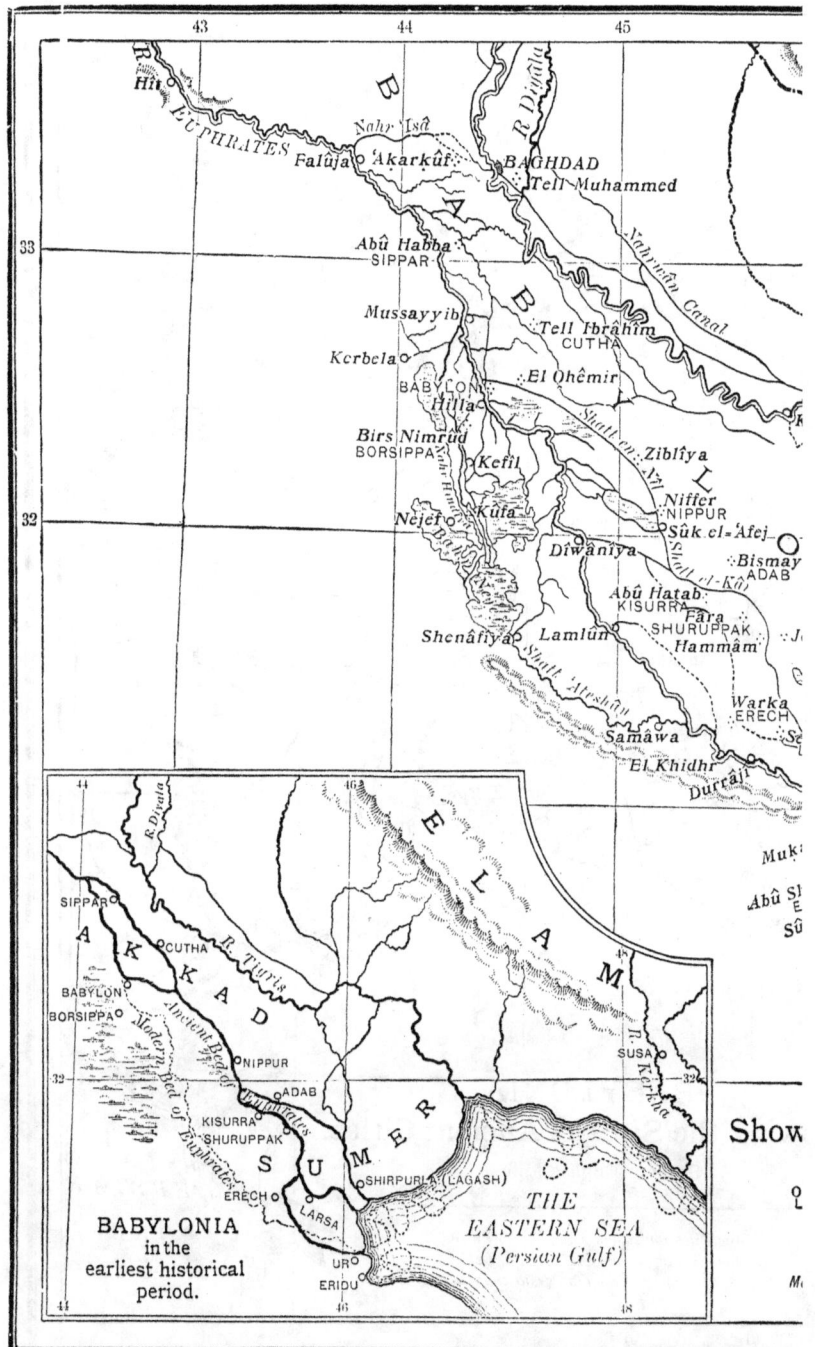

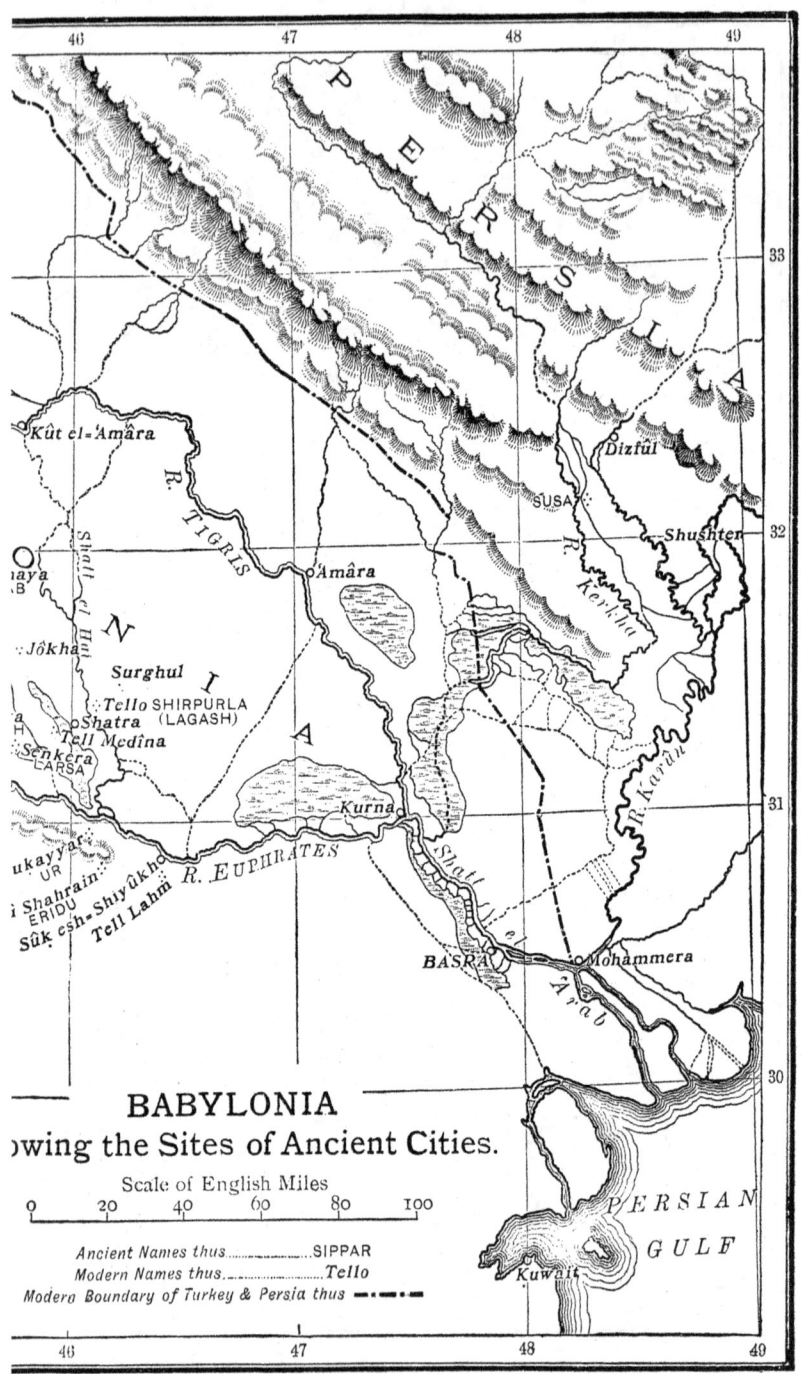

For Product Safety Concerns and Information please contact our EU representative GPSR@taylorandfrancis.com
Taylor & Francis Verlag GmbH, Kaufingerstraße 24, 80331 München, Germany

www.ingramcontent.com/pod-product-compliance
Lightning Source LLC
Chambersburg PA
CBHW071711300426
44115CB00010B/1382